INSIGHT○C...

CRUISING
& CRUISE SHIPS

2024

BY DOUGLAS WARD
THE WORLD'S FOREMOST AUTHORITY ON CRUISING

TABLE OF CONTENTS

FROM THE AUTHOR

Welcome to the 2024 edition of *Insight Guides Cruising & Cruise Ships* – the book's 39th year of continuous publication.

The cruise industry – still recovering from the effects of the Covid-19 pandemic – is fiercely competitive, with marketing opportunities hyped to the limit. Awards, often in the form of magazine or online readers' polls, provide a perfect opportunity and are extremely valuable to the cruise companies.

Yet these polls are only ever as good as the number of people who vote in them, the number and types of ships, the criteria, and experience for measuring quality. So, if a magazine initiates a readers' poll and no readers have cruised aboard a certain ship, it will not receive any votes. Votes go to the most-traveled ships, which are not necessarily the best. Magazines often don't state their criteria or methodology. The results are therefore unreliable and subjective.

At Insight Guides, we state our criteria, clearly and honestly. That's why *Insight Guides Cruising & Cruise Ships 2024* is the most authoritative and dependable guide on the market.

OVER 6,400 DAYS AT SEA

In welcoming new readers, I should mention my background for assessing cruise ships on your behalf. I first fell in love with ships when, in 1965, I sailed aboard Cunard Line's 83,673-ton ocean liner RMS *Queen Elizabeth* – at that time the world's largest passenger ship (one of the eight-strong Cunard fleet). It was also the year that The Beatles had a hit with (appropriately) *Ticket to Ride*. I was working on the final transatlantic sailing of RMS *Queen Elizabeth*, and three weeks later, joined *Queen Elizabeth 2* (the ship became known, affectionately, as *QE2*) in the John Brown shipyard on Scotland's Clydebank.

The first edition of this book, personally reviewing, testing, and evaluating 120 ships, was published in 1985 (as the *Berlitz Handbook to Cruising*), when cruising was viewed as expensive and uncommon. Today, this guide is the most highly regarded source of com-

parative information for cruise purchasers, cruise industry executives, cruise travel agents, and crew members alike.

To date, I have participated in more than 1,130 cruises, including 160 transatlantic crossings, plus countless Panama, Corinth, and Suez Canal transits, shipyard visits, numerous ship-naming ceremonies, overnights, and maiden voyages.

This book is a tribute to everyone who made my seafaring experiences possible, especially my mother and father, and I thank the cruise lines for their assistance during the complex scheduling, sailing, inspection, evaluation, and rating processes.

HOW TO USE THIS BOOK

This book is divided into two sections. The first helps you to define the cruise vacation, advises on how to find it, and provides a wealth of information. Special sections are included for expedition ships, sail-cruise ships, and around-the-world cruises.

The book's second section profiles ocean-going cruise ships. From large to small, from unabashed luxury and exclusivity to ships for the budget-minded, they are all here.

The ratings and evaluations are a painstaking documentation of my personal work. I travel throughout the world and I sail for many days each year. All evaluations are made objectively, without bias, partiality or prejudice.

My intention has always been to make this the most informative and useful guidebook possible, and to help you to make informed decisions about the ship(s) you choose for your next cruise(s).

Most of the statistical information contained in the ship profiles has been supplied by the cruise companies. You are welcome to send details of any errors or updates to hello@insightguides.com. Always check any prices given in this book with your respective cruise line, as some may have changed since this book went to press.

NEW TO CRUISING?

Are you all at sea about cruises, when it seems like everyone around you has taken one, but you haven't? Here's what you'll need to know before you first step aboard.

More than 60 companies operate around 350 ocean-going cruise ships (over 5,000 gross tons), and pre-Covid, provided cruise vacations to more than 30 million passengers annually. The Covid-19 pandemic changed everything in 2020, when the cruise industry went into lockdown. By mid-2022, however, the cruise industry was getting back on its feet, although with fewer older ships, many new ships, and unfortunately, many changes to itineraries due to the ever-changing scenario surrounding the pandemic and the effects of the conflict in Ukraine.

THE CHOICE IS HUGE

Selecting a cruise really is an obstacle course, like trying to choose between different models of car; you start with a base price, then choose all the optional extras before getting the model you want. It's *not* the inclusive vacation that you thought you were buying, but an 'unbundled' product that requires you to make decisions.

The good news is that an ocean cruise can be a memorable vacation, but after your first cruise, be prepared for the feeling of addiction that so often hits.

The trick is to find the right ship and cruise to suit your needs – whether you are a solo traveler, a couple, a family with children, or simply well-traveled.

WHAT EXACTLY IS A CRUISE?

A cruise is a change from everyday life – a (mostly) pre-paid, hassle-free vacation. You sleep in the same bed each night, the ship takes you from destination to destination, and you use a single currency on board. Everything's close at hand and there are always polite crew to help you. A cruise facilitates multi-generational togetherness, solo adventuring, and escapism. And, some of the world's most beautiful places are best seen by cruise ship.

WHY TAKE A CRUISE?

Value for money. A cruise represents excellent value for money, considering everything that is provided and available.

Convenience. You may be able to drive to your embarkation port (doorstep cruising). If not, the cruise line or your booking agent can make your travel arrangements. Once on board, you simply unpack – once!

Comfort. A cabin is your home away from home. It can be as small as a cubicle (at about 60 sq ft/6 sq m), as large as a villa (at over 4,000 sq ft/372 sq m), or anything in between.

Food. Dining is one of the pleasures of a cruise. All meals are included, and most ships can accommodate specific dietary needs. There may also be additional cost-extra specialty venues.

Family togetherness. A cruise offers a safe, family-friendly environment, and many ships have good children's facilities and supervised activities.

Learning experience. Some ships have guest speakers/lecturers, so you can learn while you cruise.

Adventure. A cruise can be an adventure. It can take you to places difficult to reach by almost any other means, such as the Antarctic, the Arctic, or remote islands.

Health. A cruise is therapeutic. You can pamper yourself in a spa (body-pampering treatments are at extra cost). Simply pace yourself to stay healthy.

The words say it all!

Celebrity Silhouette, Labadee Island.

Entertainment. Cruise ships provide a range of professional entertainment, from colorful large-cast productions and acrobatic shows to intimate classical instrumental recitals and jazz combos.

WILL I NEED A PASSPORT?

Yes, plus any appropriate authorizations and visas. If your passport is valid, ensure there is at least six months left on it after the cruise.

10 STEPS TO A GOOD FIRST CRUISE EXPERIENCE

1. FIND A CRUISE-BOOKING SPECIALIST

While the Internet may be a good research tool, it pays to find a specialist (note: some Internet-only 'agencies' with slick websites can disappear without trace – with your money).

Describe your preferences (relaxation, visiting destinations, adventure, activities, entertainment, etc.), so the agent can find a cruise and ship that is right for you.

They will guide you through the details, including cabin choice and dining arrangements. They may also have insider tips, knowledge about available discounts, upgrades, and pre- and post-cruise programs.

2. WHERE TO?

Choose your preferred area: Alaska (summer only), Australia/New Zealand, the Bahamas, the Baltic, Bermuda, the Caribbean (may be too hot in the summer months), Hawaii, Indian Ocean, the Mediterranean, the Middle East, Northern Europe, South Africa, South America, South Pacific, Southeast Asia, the US East Coast, etc. Special themes, such as Carnival in Rio or Formula One racing in Monte Carlo would determine your cruise dates.

3. HOW LONG?

Decide on the length you want, and allow traveling time to get to and from your ship if it is far from your home. A standard cruise length is seven days, although you could try a three- or four-day short-break cruise. In Northern Europe 12–14 days are more typical, while for an around-South America cruise, you'll need 30 days or so. For visiting the Antarctic, allow 14–21 days, while an around-the-world cruise takes 90–120 days.

4. CHOOSE THE RIGHT SHIP.

Size matters! Choose the right size ship for your needs. Do you want to be with 100, 500, 1,000, or 5,000-plus others on your vacation? (Generally speaking, the larger the ship, the greater the focus on it as the destination in its own right.) Or perhaps you would like to experience cruising under sail, with specialist lecturers, on an adventure/expedition cruise, or a coastal/an inland waterways cruise. If you don't want children around, there are child-free ships.

5. CHOOSE THE RIGHT ACCOMMODATION.

For a first cruise, choose an outside cabin with a balcony. In an interior ('no-view') cabin, you won't know how to dress when you wake up, because you can't see the weather outside. If you are prone to motion sickness (uncommon, but it can happen), choose a cabin in the ship's center.

The average cabin aboard a large resort ship is 180–215 sq ft (17–20 sq m); anything less and you will feel cramped. For more space, you'll pay more.

6. DINING.

There may be two dinner seatings (typically at 6pm and 8.30pm). Many ships have several dining venues (some cost extra), so you can go where and when, and with whom, you like.

7. HEALTH AND FITNESS.

Book spa treatments early for your ideal treatment time. Some companies allow online bookings, which means planning in advance.

8. FAMILIES.

Most large resort ships have very good facilities for youngsters; mid-size and small ships are more limited (some have none). Children usually love cruising, finding it educational, fun, sociable, and safe.

9. DRESS CODE.

Casual during the day; smarter in the evenings. No formal attire is needed, except on a transatlantic crossing aboard Cunard's *Queen Mary 2*, where formality is part of the tradition. Remember that ships move, so flat or low-heeled shoes are recommended for women.

10. EXTRA EXPENSES.

Unless included, budget extra for items like shore excursions, drinks or drink 'packages,' meals in extra-cost dining venues, spa treatments, casino gaming, gratuities, souvenirs, and gifts.

DIGITAL DETAILS

Today, we expect 'always on' cell phones (mobiles). But leave port, and your phone automatically locks into a ship's digital marine network (which is chargeable). At sea, your phone will be out of range of land-based carriers and slower than normal. Some ships have notices outside their restaurants prohibiting the use of cell phones (out of respect for other passengers).

WHAT TO EXPECT

So, you've arrived at the airport closest to your ship's embarkation point, with your luggage. A cruise company representative will be holding a sign with the cruise line's name. Your luggage – make sure it has your cabin number displayed – is placed together with that of other passengers. The next time you see your bags should be in your cabin.

Check-in desks are in the passenger terminal. If you have suite-grade accommodation, there will be a separate check-in desk.

GETTING ABOARD

After health protocols and security screening, head to the gangway. You will probably be greeted by snap-happy photographers, ready to take your portrait, bedraggled as you may be after having traveled for hours. Say no (firmly) if you don't want your photograph taken. At the ship end of the gangway, staff will welcome you aboard.

Sunrise in the southern Atlantic Ocean.

Relaxing on a day at sea aboard a large resort ship.

THINGS TO CHECK

Check that your cabin is clean and tidy, beds are properly made, and the bathroom has towels and soap. For any problems, tell your cabin steward.

Memorize the telephone number for medical emergencies, so you know how to call for help.

Your luggage may not have arrived yet – particularly if it is a large resort ship – but don't wait in the cabin...

take a walk. If you are hungry, head to the buffet (some may be crew-served, not self-serve, post Covid).

Familiarize yourself with the ship's layout. Learn which way is forward and aft, and how to reach your deck and cabin from the stairways. It is also a good time to learn how to get from your cabin to the outside decks in an emergency.

CONTROL THAT THIRST

Picture this: you're thirsty when you arrive in your cabin. You see a bottle of water with a tab around its neck. Read the notice on the tab: 'This bottle is provided for your convenience. If you open it, your account will be charged $4.50.'

On deck, you are greeted by a smiling waiter offering colorful drinks. But, put your fingers on the glass as he hands it to you and he'll also ask for your cruise card. There, you've just paid $8.95 for a drink full of ice worth 5¢.

The cost of drinks soon adds up. Note that aboard some ships mixers such as tonic for gin may be charged separately.

THE SAFETY DRILL

A Passenger Safety Drill must take place before a ship leaves from the port of embarkation (this was introduced following the *Costa Concordia* tragedy in 2012.) It is mandatory that you attend the drill, and pay attention – it could save your life. Directions to your assembly station are posted on the back of the cabin door. Many ships today have a safety video playing on the cabin infotainment system.

THE BRIDGE

A ship's navigation bridge is manned at all times, at sea and in port. Besides the captain, who is master of the vessel, other senior officers take 'watch' turns for four- or eight-hour periods. In addition, junior officers are continually honing their skills as experienced navigators, waiting for the day when they will be promoted to master.

The captain is always in command at times of high risk, such as when the ship is entering or leaving a port, when the density of traffic is particularly high, or when visibility is severely restricted by poor weather.

Navigation has come a long way since the days of the ancient mariners, who used only the sun and the stars to calculate their course across the oceans. The space-age development of sophisticated navigation devices (using satellites) has enabled us to eliminate the guesswork of early navigation (the first global mobile satellite system was introduced in 1979).

A ship's navigator today uses a variety of sophisticated instruments to pinpoint the ship's position at any time and establish its course.

CRUISING UNCOVERED

Many cruise line websites and brochures are hype over reality. We answer the questions most frequently asked by those new to this type of vacation, and by experienced passengers.

Cruises are packaged vacations, offering overall good value for money, with accommodation, meals, and entertainment included. But watch for the little hidden extras that are not made clear in brochures. For example, some companies sell 'drinks-inclusive' fares, while others let you choose from one of several 'beverage package' add-ons.

Here are some of the most commonly asked questions, covering items the online or printed brochures often gloss over.

IS CRUISING GOOD VALUE?

Yes, thanks in part to the economic downturn in 2020 as a result of the Covid-19 pandemic, which forced cruise lines to offer more incentives such as onboard credit, upgrades, flexible cancellation policies, and other perks.

The cruise price is protected by advance pricing, so you know before you go that the major outgoings have been set. A fuel surcharge is probably the only additional cost that may change at the last minute.

ISN'T CRUISING EXPENSIVE?

Compare what it would cost on land to have accommodation, all meals, entertainment, fitness, sports, other leisure activities, educational talks, cocktail parties and other social events provided, plus transportation to different destinations, and you'll see the good value of a cruise.

6 QUESTIONS TO ASK A TRAVEL AGENT

1. Is air transportation included in the cabin rate quoted? If not, how much will it be? What other costs will be added – these can include port charges, insurance, gratuities, shore excursions, laundry, and drinks?
2. What is the cruise line's cancellation policy?
3. If I want to make changes to my flight, routing, dates, and so on, are there any extra charges?
4. Do you have preferred suppliers, or do you book any cruise on any cruise ship?
5. Is your agency bonded and insured? If so, by whom?
6. Have you sailed aboard the ship I want to book or that you are recommending?

What you pay determines your accommodation size, location, and style. Choices range from basic to luxury, so give yourself a budget, and ask your professional travel supplier how to make the best use of it.

IS THE BROCHURE PRICE FIRM?

Cruise prices are set by cruise company sales and marketing departments as the price they would like to achieve to cover themselves against currency fluctuations, international bonding schemes, and the like. But discounts and incentives attract business, and so there is always leeway. Booking agents receive a commission, so, as a consumer, always ask for the 'best price,' watch for special offers in newspapers and magazines, and talk to your preferred agent.

HOW DO I GET THE BEST DISCOUNT?

Book ahead for the best discounts and accommodation choice, as they normally decrease closer to the cruise

Allure of the Seas in Haiti.

Cunard's three Queens dance in the river Mersey on May 26, 2015 in Liverpool.

date. The first cabins to sell out are usually those at minimum and maximum prices (the most expensive suites). Premium rates usually apply to Christmas/New Year cruises. Make sure that all port charges and government fees are included in the quote.

Although bargains do exist, always check the cabin location and what's included. Highly discounted fares may apply only to certain dates and itineraries; for example, the eastern Caribbean instead of the more popular western Caribbean.

Bargain prices may be subject to a booking deadline or may be 'cruise only,' so you must arrange your own transportation. If air transportation *is* included, changes or deviations may be difficult.

You could be limited to an early seating for dinner aboard a two-seating ship (less convenient if you are busy with activities or excursions during the day). Highly discounted fares may not apply to children, and port charges, 'handling' fees, fuel surcharges, or other taxes may be extra.

SHOULD I BOOK ONLINE OR THROUGH A TRAVEL AGENT?

You've found an ideal cruise online – fine. But, if a cruise line suddenly offers special discounts for your sailing, or cabin upgrades, or if things go wrong with your booking, your Internet booking service may prove difficult to access for post-purchase questions. Your travel agent, however, can probably make special discounts work for you and perhaps even provide upgrades.

The Internet may be a useful resource tool, but I would not recommend it as the place to book your cruise, unless you know exactly what you want, and can plan ahead (also note that it doesn't work for group bookings). You can't ask questions, and much of the information provided is simply marketing hype. Most websites providing cruise ship reviews have paid advertising, or something to sell, and the sound-bite information can be misleading and outdated. Be aware that many Internet booking agents are unlicensed and unregulated, and some add a 'booking fee.'

If you do book with an Internet-based cruise agency, you should confirm with the cruise line that the booking is confirmed and that any payments have been received. Large travel agency groups and consortiums often reserve blocks of cabins; even smaller independent agencies may be able to access discounts unavailable online. Cruise lines consider travel agents as their preferred distribution system and provide special discounts and value-added items not available online.

DO TRAVEL AGENTS CHARGE FOR THEIR SERVICES?

Travel agents do not charge for their services, but they earn a commission from cruise lines. Consider them your business advisor, not just a ticket agent. They will handle all matters relevant to your booking with updated information on itinerary changes, fuel surcharges, discounts, and travel and cancellation insurance.

Your travel agent should find exactly the right ship for your needs and lifestyle. Some sell only a limited number of cruise lines (known as 'preferred suppliers'), because they receive 'overrides' on top of their normal commission. (They may know their limited number of ships well, however.)

WHAT'S THE DIFFERENCE BETWEEN A 'GUEST' AND A 'PASSENGER'?

Many cruise lines call their passengers 'guests.' As a hotel guest you would pay to stay, whereas airlines carry passengers, under the legal term used in the Warsaw Convention. Passenger and Carrier are terms used in cruise/cruise-tour ticket contracts issued by cruise lines. Therefore, you are a passenger, not a guest.

HOW DO I GET MY CRUISE DOCUMENTS?

Most cruise lines have changed to online documentation and check-in. You will need to print your boarding passes, travel documents, and luggage tags, or ask your cruise-travel agent if they can do this for you.

Your documents will allow you to pass through a port's security to get to your ship. Only a few of the more upscale cruise lines, expedition companies, and sail-cruise ship lines might still have wallets and paper documents, cruise tickets, luggage tags, and colorful destination booklets – cruise lines operating large resort ships have all abandoned such niceties.

SHOULD I PURCHASE CANCELLATION INSURANCE?

Yes, if it is not included, as cruises (and air transportation to/from them) must be paid in full before your documents are issued. Cancel at the last minute – even for medical reasons – and you could lose the whole amount. Pay by credit card, if you use one – you are more likely to get your money back if your booking agency goes bust. Note that many lines do not return port taxes, which are not part of the cruise fare. All cruise lines normally charge full fare if you don't turn up on embarkation day.

TRAVEL INSURANCE

Cruise lines and travel agents routinely sell travel cover policies that, on close inspection, appear to wriggle out of payment due to a litany of exclusion clauses. Examples include pre-existing medical conditions (ignoring this little gem could cost you dearly) and valuables left unattended on a tour bus, even if the guide says it is safe and that the driver will lock the door.

WHICH ARE THE MAJOR CRUISE LINES?

There are nine major cruise lines (defined as those with 10 mid-size or large ships or more): AIDA Cruises, Carnival Cruise Line, Celebrity Cruises, Costa Cruises, Holland America Line, MSC Cruises, Norwegian Cruise Line, Princess Cruises, and Royal Caribbean International.

ARE THERE ANY BAD SHIPS IN A CRUISE LINE?

No, because each ship offers a different cruise experience, depending on the size, facilities, and operating area. Having said that, it's likely that the newest ships will offer the latest facilities, propulsion systems, environmentally friendly design, and equipment.

WON'T I GET BORED?

No chance! Whether you want to lie back and be pampered or be active nonstop, you can do it on a cruise. And, in case you think you may feel cut off without contact, almost all large resort ships (those carrying over 2,501 passengers) have ship-wide Wi-Fi, Internet access, movies, and digital music libraries.

WHY IS IT SO EXPENSIVE FOR SOLO TRAVELERS?

Almost all cruise lines base their rates on double occupancy, so when you travel alone the cabin portion of your fare reflects an additional supplement. Although most new, large resort ships are built with cabins for double occupancy, there are exceptions, such as Norwegian Cruise Line, with some ships providing 'Studio Cabins' specifically designed for one person, and Saga Cruises, with two ships that have 81 solo-occupancy cabins. Some companies also sell two-bed cabins at a special single rate, sometimes for selected cruises.

HOW ABOUT HOLIDAY SEASON CRUISES?

Celebrating the festive lifestyle is even more special aboard ship, where decorations add to the sense of

---

7 TIPS TO GET THE BEST TRAVEL INSURANCE

1. Shop around. Don't accept the first travel insurance policy you are offered.
2. If you purchase travel cover online, check the credentials of the company underwriting the scheme. Deal with well-established names instead of looking for the cheapest deal.
3. Read the policy details carefully and make sure you know exactly what you are covered for.
4. Beware the 'box ticking' approach to travel cover, which is often done quickly in lieu of providing proper advice. Insurers should not apply exclusions that have not been clearly pointed out to you.
5. Ask for a detailed explanation of all exclusions (including those for 'hazardous' sports like horseback riding, cycling, kayaking, jet-skiing, or ziplining), excesses, and limitations.
6. If you purchase your own air transportation, check whether your insurance policy covers you if the airline fails, or if bad weather prevents you from joining your ship on time.
7. Check the procedure you need to follow if you are the victim of a crime, such as your wallet or camera being stolen while on a shore excursion.

5 RIP-OFFS TO WATCH OUT FOR

1. Internet charges. Cruise lines often overcharge for use of the Internet; connections are by satellite and continuous connection cannot be guaranteed.

2. Currency conversion. Using a credit card to pay your onboard account may incur unseen currency conversion charges, known in the trade as dynamic currency conversion (DCC), depending on what currency the ship operates in. When you pay your bill, the price quoted is recalculated into a 'guaranteed' price, often higher than the rate quoted by banks or credit card companies.

3. Double gratuities. Some cruise lines typically imprint an additional gratuity line on signable receipts for such things as spa treatments, extra-cost coffees, and other bar charges, despite a 15 percent gratuity having already been added. Example: for an espresso coffee costing $3.00, a 15 percent tip of 45 cents is added, thus making the total cost $3.45. If the gratuity is 18 per cent this would be $3.54. You sign the receipt, but one line above the signature line says 'Additional Gratuity' – thus inviting you to pay a double gratuity.

4. Transfer buses. The cost of airport transfer buses in some ports, such as Athens and Civitavecchia (the port for Rome). A cheaper option is to take the train instead.

5. Mineral water. The cost of bottled mineral water for shore excursions. Example: one cruise line charges $4.50, but then adds another 15 percent service charge or gratuity 'for your convenience', even though you open it yourself!

---

occasion. However, the large resort ships are usually full during the main holiday periods. (Don't travel at these busy times if you want to have the facilities of a large resort ship, but want to be able to relax.)

WHAT ABOUT 'SPRING BREAK' CRUISES?

If you take a cruise aboard one of the large resort ships, such as those of Carnival Cruise Line, Norwegian Cruise Line, and Royal Caribbean International,

Outdoor breakfast aboard *Seven Seas Voyager*.

during the annual Spring Break (usually in March) expect to find hordes of students causing mayhem.

CAN I CRUISE TO ANTARCTICA ABOARD A LARGE RESORT SHIP?

A few large resort ships claim to include Antarctica on their itineraries, but you'll be very disappointed. Ships carrying over 500 participants are not allowed to land passengers and are restricted to 'scenic' cruising, so the likelihood of a large resort ship zooming in on penguin colonies is extremely slim. Choose one of the specialist expedition companies with ships that carry a maximum 200 passengers to experience this vast frozen continent properly (they use marine gas oil as propulsion fuel, instead of heavy fuel oil). Some companies claim to have hybrid ships with battery power, but batteries do not perform well in cold environments. In other words, it's marketing hype in overdrive!

WHAT ARE SHORE EXCURSIONS?

At each port of call you can go ashore and explore the surrounding areas on a guided tour (a good way to see the main sights and highlights), or independently. In most cases, shore excursions cost extra, although some cruise lines (the more upscale ones) may include one shore excursion in each port.

DO SHIPS HAVE BATHTUBS?

Bathtubs are on their way out, except for in higher-priced suites on large resort ships, or the smaller, more luxe ships. They have now largely been replaced by spacious glass-enclosed showers.

DO CRUISE LINES HAVE LOYALTY PROGRAMS?

Many companies have loyalty clubs or programs which offer discounts, credits, and onboard benefits unavailable to non-members. Programs are based either on the number of cruises taken, or, more fairly, on the number of nights sailed. There's no charge to join, but many benefits to gain if you keep cruising with the same line.

Some companies allow you to transfer point levels to a sister brand. There are usually several levels (a maximum of six at present), such as Silver, Gold, Platinum, Diamond, Titanium, etc., depending on the cruise line. Reaching the higher levels requires more effort because the cruise companies are overwhelmed by the sheer number of passengers in their respective clubs/programs.

WHAT DO THE LETTERS IN FRONT OF A SHIP NAME MEAN?

There are three key ship prefixes: MS = Motor Ship; MV = Motor Vessel; RMS = Royal Mail Ship (there's only one – *Queen Mary 2*).

WHY IS A SHIP CALLED 'SHE'?

Ships are traditionally referred to as 'she' because the sailors (who were male) considered the ship as a protective mother.

HOW DO I BOOK MULTIPLE CABINS CLOSE TO EACH OTHER?

Cruise lines (and cruise travel agents) like to book multiple cabins at the same time and are usually accommodating. Book early for the best chance of getting adjacent cabins, and do avoid guaranteed cabins.

IS THERE ENOUGH TO KEEP KIDS BUSY?

Many cruises provide families with more quality time than any other type of vacation, and family cruising is the industry's largest growth segment, with activities tailored to various age groups (see the Cruising for Families and Ship as a Destination chapters).

DO WE NEED TO TAKE TOWELS AND SOAP?

No. Both are provided by the cruise ship. Some ships have individual soaps, and some fit liquid soap and shampoo in wall-mounted dispensers. Towels for the pool deck are provided either in your cabin or by the pool.

DO CRUISE SHIP POOLS HAVE LIFEGUARDS?

In general, no (exceptions include Disney Cruise Line, Norwegian Cruise Line and Royal Caribbean International).

DO YOUTH PROGRAMS OPERATE ON PORT DAYS?

Most cruise lines also operate programs on port days, although they will not be as extensive as on days at sea.

ARE THERE ADULTS-ONLY SHIPS?

Companies that operate small and mid-size adults-only ships include P&O Cruises (*Arcadia, Aurora*), Saga Cruises (*Spirit of Adventure, Spirit of Discovery*) and Virgin Voyages (*Resilient Lady, Scarlet Lady, Valiant Lady*). The minimum age may be different depending on the company, so check for the latest information.

A birthday aboard a Carnival Cruise Line ship.

DO SHIPS PROVIDE A DAILY PROGRAM FOR EACH DAY AT THE BEGINNING OF THE CRUISE, SO I CAN PLAN MY DAYS AHEAD?

No, but except for minor changes that may need to be made each day (due to weather conditions or itinerary changes, for example), there's nothing to stop you planning your own daily program.

HOW CAN I CELEBRATE A BIRTHDAY OR ANNIVERSARY?

If you have a birthday or anniversary or other special occasion to celebrate during your cruise, let the cruise line know in advance. They should be able to arrange a cake for you, or a special 'Champagne breakfast' in bed. Some cruise lines offer anniversary packages – for a fee – or a meal in an alternative restaurant, where available.

DO CRUISES SUIT HONEYMOONERS?

Absolutely. A cruise is the ideal setting for romance, for shipboard weddings aboard ships with the right registry (they can also be arranged in some ports, depending on local regulations), receptions, and honeymoons. And for those on a second honeymoon, many ships can perform a 'renewal of vows' ceremony; some will make a charge for this service.

IS A REPOSITIONING CRUISE CHEAPER?

When ships move from one cruise region to another, it is termed 'repositioning.' For instance, when ships move between the Caribbean and Europe, typically in April/ May, or between Europe and the Caribbean (typically in October/November), cruise fares are often discounted. The ships rarely sail full, so the value for money is excellent. Some cruise lines use this time to do essential maintenance work, so always check before you book to make sure that all facilities will be available.

DO SHIPS HAVE ATM MACHINES?

Very few have ATM machines, and using one usually means there will be a charge for it. Celebrity Cruises, for example, charges $6 every time you withdraw cash from the machine, even if you want only a small amount. If a Celebrity ship is in Europe, the ATM machine will still only dispense US dollars.

HOW INCLUSIVE IS ALL-INCLUSIVE?

All cruise lines have different interpretations of the word 'inclusive.' It usually means that transportation, accommodation, food, and entertainment are wrapped up in one neat package. If drinks are included, it is mostly a limited range of low-quality brands (standard spirits) chosen by the cruise line, with bartenders overgenerous with ice for cocktails. 'Mostly inclusive' might be a better term to use.

TELL ME MORE ABOUT EXTRA COSTS

While cruise lines offer appealingly low fares, most try hard to maintain revenues by increasing the cost of onboard choices and extras (particularly for restaurants not included in the cruise fare), including beverages. Expect to spend at least $25 a day per person on extras, plus gratuities (unless they are included). The approximate price per person for a typical seven-day cruise aboard a well-rated mid-size or large resort ship, based on an outside-view, two-bed cabin is $1,000.

This is less than $150 per person per day, which seems reasonable when you consider all it covers. However, your costs can increase when you start adding on extras such as excursions, drinks (unless they are included), mineral water, Internet access, and

7 MONEY-SAVING TIPS

1. Research online, but book through a specialist cruise-travel agency.
2. Cut through the sales hype and get to the bottom line, and make sure that all taxes and fees are included.
3. Book early – the most desirable itineraries and cabins go first. If air travel is involved, remember that air fares rise in peak seasons.
4. Book a cabin on a lower deck – the higher the deck, the more expensive it will be.
5. An interior (no view) cabin is cheaper, if you can live without natural light.
6. Be flexible with dates – go off-season when fares are lower.
7. Purchase travel cancellation insurance – your cruise is an investment, after all.

other items. Many cruise lines automatically add gratuities of varying amounts (typically $15–23 per person, per day).

WHAT ARE PORT CHARGES?

These are levied by various ports visited, rather like city taxes imposed on hotel guests. They help pay for the infrastructure required for facilities including docks, linesmen, security and operations personnel, and porters at embarkation and disembarkation ports.

A spot of social dancing aboard *Queen Elizabeth*.

SHOULD I TAKE A BACK-TO-BACK CRUISE?

If you are considering two seven-day back-to-back cruises, for example eastern Caribbean and western Caribbean, bear in mind that many aspects of the cruise – menus, one or more ports, entertainment, even the cruise director's jokes and spiel – may be duplicated.

DO SHIPS HAVE DIFFERENT CLASSES?

Gone are official class distinctions. Differences are now found mainly in the type and size of accommodation chosen, its location, and whether you have butler service or drinks included.

Hotels have presidential suites, executive floors, and so forth, while airlines have First Class, Business Class, and Economy Class (some airlines now have different levels and prices in economy, such as premium economy, 'no-frills' and hand-luggage-only economy). In other words: Pay More, Get More.

Some cruise lines have a 'concierge lounge' for use only by occupants of accommodation designated as suites, thus reviving the two-class system.

'Private Enclaves' (exclusive 'ship within a ship' areas) have been created by Carnival Cruise Lines (*Carnival Mardi Gras*), Celebrity Cruises (some ships), MSC Cruises (Yacht Club, with drinks included, aboard the larger ships), Norwegian Cruise Line (The Haven), Resorts World Cruises (Dream Palace), and TUI Cruises (*Mein Schiff 1–6*, with access to an exclusive 'X' Lounge indoor-outdoor facilities) for occupants of the most expensive suites, in an effort to insulate them from the masses. The result is a 'ship within a ship' (private enclave with key-card access).

Most companies have, in essence, created two classes: (1) Suite-grade accommodation; (2) Standard cabins (either exterior view or interior – no view).

Cunard has always had several classes for transatlantic travel (just like scheduled airlines), but this is designated by restaurant (Queens Grill, Princess Grill, or Britannia Restaurant), assigned according to the accommodation grade chosen.

DO SHIP'S DECKS HAVE NAMES OR NUMBERS?

Ships can have both names and/or numbers. Historically, ships used to have only deck names (example: Promenade Deck, 'A' Deck, 'B' Deck, 'C' Deck, Restaurant Deck, and so on). As ships became larger, numbers started appearing (copying ferry deck markings).

However, some ships do not have a Deck 13; examples include the ships of AIDA Cruises, Carnival Cruise Line, Celebrity Cruises, Costa Cruises, MSC Cruises (*MSC World Europa* only), P&O Cruises Australia (*Pacific Encounter* and *Pacific Explorer* only), Princess Cruises, or Royal Caribbean International, or any cabin with the number ending in 13 in it.

Resorts World Cruises ship Genting Dream doesn't have a Deck 14 (as it is considered unlucky for Chinese passengers, their main clientele), while the ships of MSC Cruises don't have a Deck 17 – considered unlucky by Italians. (When it is written in Roman numerals – XVII is an anagram of VIXI which in Latin translates as 'I have lived' – which implies death).

CAN I EAT WHEN I WANT TO?

Most major cruise lines offer 'flexible dining', so you can choose (with some limitations) when you want to eat, and with whom you dine, during your cruise – or a choice of several restaurants. As with places to eat ashore, reservations may be required, you may also have to wait in line at busy periods, and occupants of the top suites get priority.

Aboard large resort ships (2,501-plus passengers) the big entertainment shows are typically staged twice each evening, so you end up with the equivalent of two-seating dining anyway.

WHAT IS SPECIALTY DINING?

Mass dining isn't to everyone's taste, so many ships have dining venues other than a main restaurant. These usually cost extra, but the food quality, preparation, and presentation are decidedly better. You may need to make a reservation.

WHAT IS THE MINIMUM AGE FOR DRINKING ALCOHOL?

Aboard most ships based in the US and Canada the minimum drinking age is 21. However, for ships based throughout the rest of the world, it is generally 18. But you should always check with your chosen cruise line.

ARE DRINKS PACKAGES GOOD VALUE?

Not unless you intend to drink a lot. They can vary hugely between cruise ships. Packages are per day, for each day of the cruise, per person, whether or not you use it (you probably won't use it as much when you go ashore for the day, for example). Some have a maximum number of drinks per day, while some also add a mandatory gratuity. Also, the choice may not include your favorite brands ('premium' brands come at an extra cost). On port-intensive itineraries when you are off the ship almost every day, think about the number of drinks you need; it may better to 'drink as you go.'

10 THINGS NOT INCLUDED IN 'ALL-INCLUSIVE'

1. Dining in extra-cost restaurants
2. Premium (vintage) wines
3. Specialty teas and coffees
4. Wine/spirit tastings/seminars
5. Spa treatments
6. Some fitness classes
7. Personal training instruction
8. Use of steam room/saunas
9. Casino gaming
10. Medical services

Poolside movie screens adorn large resort ships, including *Carnival Destiny*.

WHAT DOES A TYPICAL DRINKS PACKAGE COST?

Typically, about $50–60 per day, per person, plus gratuity, if you book ahead of your cruise; all persons in the same cabin must purchase the package. Note that on some European cruises, you may also be charged VAT (Value Added Tax).

CAN I BRING MY OWN BOOZE ON BOARD?

No, at least not aboard most cruise lines, as it will be confiscated. Some smaller lines might, however, turn a blind eye if you bring your favorite wine or spirit on board for in-cabin consumption.

HOW ABOUT SERVICE STANDARDS?

To estimate the standard of service, look at the crew-to-passenger ratio – provided in each ship profile in this book. The best service levels are aboard ships with a ratio of one crew member to every two passengers, or higher.

DO SHIPS HAVE ROOM SERVICE?

While most cruise ships provide free 24-hour room service, some ships charge a delivery fee for food and beverage items, (particularly late at night). A room service menu will be in your cabin. Aboard sail-cruise ships such as those of Sea Cloud Cruises or Star Clippers, there is no room service. Anyone in suite-grade accommodation may get additional services like afternoon tea-trolley service and evening canapés. Some ships may offer room service specials like a champagne breakfast (at an extra cost).

SHOULD I TIP FOR ROOM SERVICE?

No. It's part of the normal onboard duties the hotel staff are paid for. Watch out for staff aboard the large resort ships saying that they do not always get the tips that are 'automatically added' to onboard accounts – it's a ploy to get you to tip them more in cash.

DO ANY SPECIAL FOOD EVENTS TAKE PLACE?

In addition to birthdays, anniversaries and other celebrations, special events, special celebration dinners, or 'foodertainment' event may be featured once each cruise. Examples include a Champagne Waterfall (Princess Cruises) and Rijsttafel (pronounced 'rice-taffle'), rice-based Indonesian meal to which small items of meat, seafood, and vegetables are added (Holland America Line).

Some cruise lines feature a British Pub Lunch (featuring fish and chips, or sausages and mash) or late-morning 'Frühschoppen' (German sausages, pretzels, and beer). Others still offer an old standby, the Baked Alaska Parade, also known as 'Flaming Bombé Alaska.' This usually happens on the night before the last night of a typical cruise (also known as 'Comment Form Night'), although some companies have replaced this with a Chef's Parade. Traditionally, February 1 is the official Baked Alaska Day.

DO SHIPS STILL USE PLASTIC STRAWS FOR DRINKS?

Most cruise companies have totally replaced plastic straws with paper or bamboo straws.

DO SHIPS STILL SERVE BOUILLON ON SEA DAYS?

Some ships carry on the tradition of serving or making late-morning bouillon on sea days. Examples include the ships of Cunard, Fred. Olsen Cruise Lines, Hapag-Lloyd Cruises, Hebridean Island Cruises, P&O Cruises, Phoenix Reisen, and Saga Cruises.

DO ALL SHIPS HAVE USB SOCKETS IN THE CABINS?

Most new ships (those under five years old) do, but many older ships do not. The best advice is to take a USB charger plug with you, according to the type of electrical socket provided.

DO ALL SHIPS HAVE SELF-SERVICE LAUNDERETTES?

Some cruise lines have ships that have them (AIDA Cruises, Carnival Cruise Line, Cunard, Holland America Line, Princess Cruises, for example), and some don't (Celebrity Cruises, Costa Cruises, MSC Cruises, Norwegian Cruise Line, Royal Caribbean International). Companies that don't have them may offer special price 'family bundles.' Many ships have a retractable clothesline in the bathroom however, which is good for small items.

DO SHIPS HAVE PROPER DANCE FLOORS?

No. For social dancing, a properly 'sprung' wood floor is the best for social (ballroom) dancing. Ships with good, large wooden dance floors include *Asuka II, Aurora, Britannia, Queen Anne, Queen Elizabeth, Queen Mary 2*, and *Queen Victoria*.

DO ALL SHIPS HAVE SWIMMING POOLS?

Most do, but some do not. The largest are the half Olympic size (82ft/25m in length) pools aboard *Celebrity Apex, Celebrity Beyond, Celebrity Edge*, and *Mein Schiff 1–6*. Most, however, are a maximum of just over 56ft (17m) long.

Some ships have 'infinity' pools on an aft deck, so, when you are in the pool it looks like you are at one with the sea (examples include *MSC Preziosa* and *Viking Sun*).

Some ships have separate adult-only, family pools, and toddler pools, such as *Disney Dream, Disney Fantasy, Disney Magic, Disney Wish*, and *Disney Wonder*. The family-friendly large resort ships usually have separate pools and tubs for children in different age groups located within children-only zones, or aqua parks. Some ships have pools that can be covered by retractable glass domes – useful in inclement weather; others only have open-air pools, yet cruise in cold weather areas in winter. A few ships have heated pools – examples include *Independence of the Seas, Spirit of Adventure*, and *Spirit of Discovery*.

While most pools are outside, some ships also have indoor pools located low down, so that the water doesn't move about when sea conditions are unkind. Examples include *Spirit of Adventure* and *Spirit of Discovery*.

Some ships have only a 'dip' pool – just big enough to cool off in on hot days, while others may have hot tubs only (no pool).

Note that when there is inclement weather, the pools are emptied to avoid the water sloshing around.

DO ALL SHIPS HAVE FRESHWATER POOLS?

All the ships of Disney Cruise Line and most of the large resort ships (such as *Symphony of the Seas*) have freshwater pools. Some ships, however, have saltwater pools, with the water for the pools being drawn from the sea, and filtered.

HOW ARE SWIMMING POOLS KEPT CLEAN?

All pools have chlorine added (a minimum of 1.0–3.0 ppm in recirculated swimming pools), while some have chemically treated saltwater pools. Pools are regularly checked for water-flow rates, pH balance, alkalinity, and clarity – all entered in a daily log.

DO ANY SHIPS HAVE WALK-IN POOLS (INSTEAD OF STEPS)?

Not many, because of space considerations, although they can often be useful for older passengers. Some ships do, however (examples include *Aurora*).

WHAT'S THE DIFFERENCE BETWEEN AN OUTSIDE AND AN INTERIOR CABIN?

An 'outside' (or 'exterior') cabin has a window (or porthole) with a view of the outside, or there is a private balcony for you to step on to be outside. An 'interior'

Europa provides free bicycles for passengers.

(or 'inside') cabin means that it doesn't have a view of the outside, although it may have a 'virtual' window or balcony.

SOME BALCONY CABINS APPEAR RATHER CHEAP. IS THERE A CATCH?

It may be cheaper because it has an obstructed view – often because it is in front of a lifeboat. Always check the deck plan because it may be that it's only partially obstructed.

IS LNG OR DIESEL THE BETTER FUEL?

LNG (Liquified Natural Gas) is being touted as the fuel of the future, and results in lower emissions. This is only partially true, and doesn't make it harmless, because LNG still produces carbon dioxide, plus storage tanks are extremely large.

ARE ANY SHIPS POWERED BY LIQUEFIED NATURAL GAS (LNG)?

Yes, the following companies have LNG ships in service or on order: AIDA Cruises, Carnival Cruise Lines, Costa Cruises, MSC Cruises, and P&O Cruises. Some ships have dual fuel capability, including LNG. One challenge is assigning enough space to store the fuel.

CAN I VISIT THE BRIDGE?

Usually not – for insurance and security reasons – and never when the ship is manoeuvring into and out of port. However, some companies run extra-cost 'Behind the Scenes' tours. The cost varies, but it can be as much as $150 per person.

ARE THERE ANY FEMALE CAPTAINS?

Yes, there are. Some examples (in the year order they became captain):
2007: Karin Stahre-Jansen, Sweden (Royal Caribbean International)
2010: Inger Klein Olsen, Faroe Islands (Cunard)
2010: Sarah Breton, UK (P&O Cruises)
2011: Lis Lauritzen, Denmark (Royal Caribbean International)
2013: Margrith Ettlin, Sweden (Silversea Cruises)
2016: Belinda Bennet, UK (Windstar Cruises)
2016: Kate McCue, USA (Celebrity Cruises)
2016: Serena Melani, Italy (Regent Seven Seas Cruises)
2018: Nicole Lagosch, Switzerland (AIDA Cruises)
2019: Kathryn Whittaker (Sea Cloud Cruises)
2020: Wendy Williams (Virgin Voyages)
2022: Caz Palmer (Hebridean Island Cruises)
Serena Melani became the first female captain to launch a new ship, the *Seven Seas Splendor*, in 2020. There will be many more in future, as the role of women in the once male-dominated cruise industry increases, setting an example in the world of hospitality.

CAN I BRING GOLF CLUBS?

Yes, you can. Although cruise lines do not charge for carrying them, some airlines (especially the budget ones) do. Some ships cater for golfers with mini-golf courses on deck and electronically monitored practice areas.

Golf-themed cruises are popular, with 'all-in' packages allowing participants to play on some of the world's most desirable courses. Hapag-Lloyd Cruises

Passing through the Pedro Miguel Locks on the Panama Canal.

RULES OF THE ROAD

Ships, the largest moving objects made by man, are subject to stringent international regulations. They must keep to the right in shipping lanes, and pass on the right (with certain exceptions). When circumstances raise some doubt, or shipping lanes are crowded, ships use their whistles in the same way that an automobile driver uses directional signals to show which way he will turn. When one ship passes another and gives a single blast on its whistle, this means it is turning to starboard (right). Two blasts mean a turn to port (left).

The other ship acknowledges by repeating the same signal. Ships switch on navigational running lights at night – green for starboard, red for port, plus two white lights on the masts, with the forward one lower than the aft one.

A ship's funnel (smokestack) is one other means of identification, each line having its own design and color scheme. The size, height, and number of funnels were all points worth advertising at the start of the 20th century. Most ocean liners of the time had four funnels and were called 'four-stackers.'

and Silversea Cruises, for example, operate several golf-themed sailings each year.

DO CELL (MOBILE) PHONES WORK ON BOARD?

Most cruise lines have contracts with maritime phone service companies. Cell (mobile) phone signals piggyback off systems that transmit Internet data via satellite, but they can be pricey. When your ship is in port, the ship's network may be switched off, and you will pay the going local (country-specific) rate for mobile calls if you can manage to access a local network.

ARE THERE ANY SHIPS WITHOUT IN-CABIN WLAN WIRING? I AM ALLERGIC TO IT.

The 94-passenger *Sea Cloud II* comes to mind, as well as some of the older ships that have not been retrofitted with WLAN cabling.

WHERE CAN I WATCH MOVIES?

Some ships have real movie theaters, but most don't. Many large resort ships have large show lounges that are also equipped for screening movies (mainly in the afternoons), or have huge open-air movie screens on the pool deck.

Some ships have small-capacity screening rooms, typically for 100–200 passengers, where movies may be shown several times daily, and special rooms for showing 3D and 4D movies (these often include fast-paced adventure movies, surround sound, and moving seats). Carnival's 4,000-passenger *Carnival Vista* was fitted with the first IMAX theater at sea.

Movies are provided by a licensed film distribution or leasing service. Many newer ships have replaced or supplemented movie theaters with in-cabin infotainment systems (with pay-on-demand movies).

ARE THERE ANY SHIPS WITHOUT TELEVISIONS?

Yes – the 64-passenger sail-cruise ship *Sea Cloud*.

CAN I TAKE AN IRON TO USE IN MY CABIN?

No. However, some ships have self-service launderettes (see page 19), which include an ironing area. Check with your cruise line.

WHAT IS EXPEDITION CRUISING?

Expedition cruises are operated by specialists such as Hapag-Lloyd Expedition Cruises and Quark Expeditions, using small ships that have ice-strengthened hulls or specially constructed ice-breakers that enable them to reach areas totally inaccessible to standard cruise ships. These vessels have a relaxed, casual atmosphere, with multiple expert lecturers and expedition leaders accompanying every voyage. (See page 94.)

WHAT IS A PANAMAX SHIP?

This is one that conforms to the maximum dimensions possible for passage through the Panama Canal – useful particularly for around-the-world voyages. The 50-mile (80-km) canal transit takes from eight to nine hours.

IS THERE A CRUISE WITHOUT PORTS?

Yes, but it isn't really a cruise. The transatlantic crossing – around 3,000 miles from New York to Southampton, England (or vice versa) – aboard *Queen Mary 2*, normally takes about seven days. (When RMS *Queen Elizabeth* and RMS *Queen Mary* were in service, the transatlantic crossing took five days.)

CAN I SHOP IN PORTS OF CALL?

Many passengers embrace retail therapy when visiting destinations such as Dubai, St. Maarten, St. Thomas, and Singapore, among many others. However, it is prudent to exercise self-control. Remember that you'll have to carry those purchases home at the end of your cruise.

DO I HAVE TO GO ASHORE IN EACH PORT?

Absolutely not! In fact, many passengers enjoy being aboard 'their' ship when there are virtually no other passengers aboard – the ship becoming the destination. Also, if you book a spa treatment, it could be less expensive during this period than when the ship is at sea. Many ships have price differentials for sea days and port days.

CAN I BRING MY PET?

No, with one exception: on the transatlantic crossings aboard the Cunard ocean liner *Queen Mary 2*, which has carried more than 500 pet animals since its debut in 2004 (the one-way cost is $800–1,000 for

Looking at the horizon helps with seasickness.

a single kennel; cats are required to have two kennels – one as a litter tray – at a cost of $1,600. It has 22 air-conditioned kennels for dogs and cats (no birds) and dedicated kennel attendants. Pets must have the required certification and vaccination against rabies.

CAN I FLY IN THE DAY BEFORE OR STAY AN EXTRA DAY AFTER THE CRUISE?

Cruise lines often offer pre- and post-cruise stay packages – either included or at additional cost. The advantage is that you don't have to do anything else – all will be taken care of. If you book a hotel on your own, however, you may have to pay an 'air deviation' fee if you don't take the cruise line's air arrangements, or you want to change them.

WHAT ARE THE DOWNSIDES TO CRUISING?

Much-anticipated ports of call can be aborted or changed due to poor weather or other conditions. Some popular ports (particularly in the Caribbean) can become extremely crowded – there can be up to 12 ships at the same time in Barcelona or St. Thomas, disgorging 20,000-plus people.

Many common irritations could be fixed if the cruise lines really tried. Entertainment, for instance, whether production shows or cabaret acts, is typically linked to dinner times, which can be inconvenient.

WHAT LEGAL RIGHTS DO I HAVE?

It would seem almost none! After reading the Passenger Ticket Contract, you'll see why. A 189-word sentence in one contract begins 'The Carrier shall not be liable for …' and goes on to cover the legal waterfront. Check all your documentation very carefully before you travel.

WHERE DID ALL THE MONEY GO?

Apart from the cruise fare itself, incidentals could include government taxes, port charges, air ticket tax, and fuel surcharges. On board, extra costs may include drinks, mini-bar items, specialty coffees, shore excursions (especially those involving flightseeing tours), Internet access, beauty treatments, casino gaming, photographs, laundry and dry-cleaning, babysitting services, wine tasting, bottled water placed in your cabin, and medical services.

A cruise aboard a ship belonging to a major cruise line could be compared to buying a car, whereby motor manufacturers offer a basic model and price, and then tempt you with optional extras to inflate the cost. Cruise lines say income generated on board helps to keep the basic cost of a cruise reasonable. In the end, it's up to you to exercise self-restraint to keep those little extras from mounting up to a very large sum.

DOES A SHIP'S REGISTRY (FLAG STATE) MATTER?

Not really. Some years ago, cruise ships used to be registered in their country of operation, so Italian Line ships (with all-Italian crews) would be registered in Italy, and Greek ships (with all-Greek crews) would be registered only in Greece, etc. Many years ago, to avoid prohibition, some American-owned ships were re-registered to Panama. Thus was born the flag of convenience, now called the 'Flag State.'

Today's ships no longer have single-nationality crews, however, so where a ship is registered is not of such great importance. The ships of Cunard and P&O Cruises, for example, are registered in Bermuda, so that weddings can be performed on board.

Today, the most popular flag registries are (in alphabetical order): the Bahamas, Bermuda, Italy, Japan, Malta, the Marshall Islands, Panama, Portugal, and the Netherlands. This fragmented authority means that all cruise ships come under the IMO (International Maritime Organization, within the United Nations) when operating in international waters – 12 nautical miles from shore. A country only has authority over the ship when it is either in one of its own ports or within 12 nautical miles offshore.

Some companies may want to change their registry and flag because of high crew pension costs, but most, once registered, tend to be loyal.

HOW ARE SHIPS WEIGHED?

They aren't. They are measured. Gross tonnage is a measurement of the enclosed space within a ship's hull and superstructure (1 gross ton = 100 cubic ft).

WHY IS A COIN LAID UNDER THE MAST OF SHIPS AS THEY ARE BUILT?

According to a 2,000-year-old shipbuilding tradition, the coin brings good luck and also protects the ship's keel.

HOW LONG DO CRUISE SHIPS LAST?

In general, a very long time. For example, during the *QE2*'s almost-40-year service for Cunard, the ship sailed more than 5.5 million nautical miles, carried 2.5 million passengers, completed 25 full world cruises, and crossed the Atlantic more than 800 times. But the *QE2* was built with a very thick hull, whereas today's thin-hulled cruise ships probably won't last as long. Even so, the life expectancy is typically a healthy 30 years.

WHERE DO OLD CRUISE SHIPS GO WHEN THEY'RE SCRAPPED?

They go to the beach. They are driven at speed onto a not very nice beach at Alang, India, or to Chittagong in Bangladesh, or to Pan Yo in China – the main shipbreaking places. Greenpeace has claimed that workers, including children, at some sites have to work under primitive conditions without adequate equipment to protect them against the toxic materials that can be released into the environment. In 2009, a new IMO guideline – the International Convention for the Safe and Environmentally Sound Recycling of Ships – was adopted.

WILL I GET SEASICK?

Today's ships have stabilizers – large underwater 'fins' on each side of the hull – to counteract any rolling motion, and most cruises are in warm, calm waters. As a result, fewer than three percent of passengers become seasick. Yet it's possible to develop some symptoms – anything from slight nausea to vomiting.

Both old-time sailors and modern physicians have their own remedies, and you can take your choice or try them all, as follows:

When you notice the first movement of a ship, walk back and forth on the deck. You will find that your knees will start to get their feel of balance and counteraction.

Find a place where the sea breeze will blow into your face (fresh air is arguably the best antidote to seasickness), and, if you are nauseous, suck an orange or a lemon.

Eat lightly. Don't make the mistake of thinking a heavy meal will keep your stomach anchored. It won't.

When on deck, focus on a steady point, such as the horizon.

Dramamine (dimenhydrinate, an antihistamine and sedative introduced just after World War II) will be available aboard in tablet (chewable) form. A stronger version (Meclizine) is available on prescription (brand names for this include Antivert, Antizine, Bonine, and Meni-D). Ciba-Geigy's Scopoderm (or Transderm Scop), known as 'The Patch,' contains scopolamine and has proven effective, but possible side effects include dry mouth, blurred vision, drowsiness, and problems with urinating.

If you are really distressed, the ship's doctor can give you, at extra cost, an injection to alleviate discomfort. Note that this may make you drowsy.

A natural preventive for seasickness, said to settle any stomach for up to eight hours, is ginger in powder form. Mix half a teaspoon in a glass of warm water or milk, and drink it before sailing.

'Sea Bands' are a drug-free method of controlling motion sickness. Usually elasticated and available in different colors, they are slim bands that slip onto the wrist. They have a circular 'button' that presses against the acupressure point Pericardium 6, or P6 (Nei Guan) on the mid-forearm. Attach them a few minutes before you step aboard and wear on both wrists during the cruise.

Another drug-free remedy is Reletex, a watch-like device worn on the wrist. First used for patients undergoing chemotherapy, it emits a small neuro-

Carnival Splendor's striking funnel.

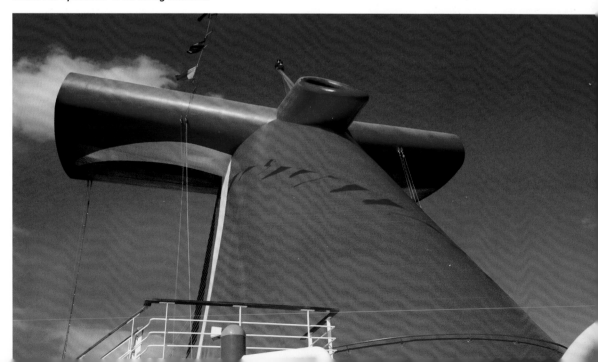

modulating current that stops peristaltic waves in the stomach causing nausea and vomiting.

IS HAVING HAY FEVER A PROBLEM?

People who suffer from hay fever and pollen allergies may benefit greatly from a cruise. Almost all sufferers I have met say that their symptoms simply disappear on a ship – particularly when it is at sea.

ARE HYGIENE STANDARDS HIGH ENOUGH?

News reports often focus on hygiene and sanitation aboard cruise ships. In the 1980s, the North American cruise industry agreed with the Centers for Disease Control and Prevention (CDC) that hygiene and sanitation inspections should be carried out once or twice yearly aboard all cruise ships carrying American passengers, and the Vessel Sanitation Program (VSP) was born. The original intention of the VSP was to achieve and maintain a level of sanitation that would lower the risk of gastro-intestinal disease outbreaks and assist the cruise industry to provide a healthy environment for passengers and crew.

It is a voluntary inspection, and cruise lines pay handsomely for each one. For a ship the size of *Queen Mary 2*, for example, the cost would be around $18,000; for a ship the size of *Azamara Journey*, it would be about $9,000. The inspection points are well accepted by the international cruise industry. Inspections cover two main areas: 1) water sanitation, including free

Helping to stop norovirus.

chlorine residuals in the potable water system, swimming pool, and hot tub filters; and 2) food sanitation: food storage, preparation, and serving areas, including bars and passenger service pantries.

The ships score extremely well – those that undergo inspections, that is. Some ships that don't regularly call on US ports would possibly not pass the inspections every time. Older ships with outdated galley equipment and poor food-storage facilities would have a harder time complying with the United States Public Health (USPH) inspection standards. Some other countries also have strict health inspection standards. However, if the same USPH inspection standards were applied to restaurants and hotels ashore in the US, it is estimated that at least 95 percent or more would fail.

WHAT ABOUT HYGIENE ON BOARD?

Several cruise lines have a three-step (green, yellow, and red) alert level in place should any passenger be ill. Crew members dealing with passengers are alert to any signs of illness, which are then reported to supervisors and the ship's medical department. When ships are at sea, standard sanitizing procedures include constant wiping down and spraying surfaces in cabins and public areas with broad-spectrum nano-emulsion or phenol-based disinfectants.

WHAT ABOUT THE NOROVIRUS?

This temporary but highly contagious condition occurs worldwide. Humans are the only known hosts, and only the common cold is reported more frequently than viral gastroenteritis as a cause of illness in many countries. For example, about 23 million Americans each year are diagnosed with the effects of the Norwalk-like virus (NLV gastroenteritis, also known as winter vomiting virus or norovirus). It is more prevalent in adults and older children than in the very young.

Norovirus is part of the 'calicivirus' family. The condition itself is self-limiting and characterized by nausea, vomiting, diarrhea, and abdominal pain. Although it can be transmitted by person-to-person contact, it is more likely to arrive via contaminated surfaces, food, and water.

A mild and brief illness typically occurs 24 to 48 hours after consuming contaminated food or water, and lasts for 24 to 72 hours. If you board a ship after norovirus has struck, bread and bread rolls, butter, and salt and pepper dispensers may not be placed on tables, but available on request during meals.

When an outbreak occurs, the ship will immediately be sanitized, and affected passengers may be confined to their cabins to stop the condition spreading. Crew members and their livelihoods can also be affected, so they will want any outbreak contained as quickly as possible.

In my experience, almost all outbreaks have occurred because someone has brought the condition with them from ashore.

How can you avoid the bug? Don't drink from aircraft water dispensers on the way to join your cruise – they are seldom cleaned thoroughly (request or buy bottled water instead). Always wash your hands thoroughly before eating (particularly when going to the buffet), and after using the toilet, both on an aircraft and a ship. Ships constructed after October 2011 must provide washbasins in buffets (one per 100 seats) under the United States Public Health's Vessel Sanitation Program regulations. Several cruise lines show a 'Wash Your Hands' video at muster stations (or on infotainment systems) following the passenger emergency drill.

Ships provide liquid gel dispensers as a preventative – at the gangway and outside or in food venues (especially at buffets).

Collins cigar smokers' lounge aboard *Europa 2*.

HOW ABOUT CORONAVIRUS?

Following the worldwide outbreak of Covid-19 in 2020, the cruise industry implemented even stricter hygiene and sanitation controls aboard its ships. The advice being to wash your hands thoroughly and consistently (you may want to take extra moisturiser/hand cream to counteract the effects of constant hand washing), practise social distancing, and wear a face mask (if required).

WHAT IF I AM CONFINED TO MY CABIN?

If your cabin is small, to avoid 'cabin fever' you can always exercise somewhat by stepping in place, do some yoga or other stretching exercises to stay in shape. (One positive is that you will probably eat less, so it may be a good way to lose weight!) Above all, think positive. What may be of concern is the fact that aboard some ships, the cabin air-conditioning cannot be turned off.

WHAT ABOUT THE CARBON FOOTPRINT OF CRUISE SHIPS?

Some companies, such as Virgin Voyages, offset direct climate change emissions by purchasing carbon offsets. In 2018, Royal Caribbean Cruises Ltd. acquired a wind farm to offset up to 12 percent of its ships' CO_2 output. In 2019, Lindblad Expeditions began offsetting 100 percent of its emissions, and in January 2020, MSC Cruises became the first major line to achieve carbon neutral operations. Cruise lines such as Hapag-Lloyd Cruises use catalytic converters to reduce emissions, while others (Carnival Cruise Line and Norwegian Cruise Line, for example) use 'scrubber' technology to recover exhaust gases for re-use. (See Cruising and the Environment, page 179.)

WHAT DO SHIPS DO ABOUT GARBAGE?

The newest ships are models of recycling and efficient waste handling. Cooking oil, for example, is turned into biodiesel. Garbage is sorted into dry and wet bins, and the dry garbage is burned on board or compacted for offloading in selected ports. Aluminum cans are offloaded for recycling. As for sewage, ships must be three nautical miles from land before they can dump treated sewage and 12 miles for sewage and food waste.

WHERE IS SMOKING ALLOWED?

Smoking is allowed only in designated areas on open decks. Almost no cruise companies allow smoking in cabins or on balconies. Some lines place a notice in each cabin advising you that a hefty cleaning fee will be added to your onboard account if evidence of smoking in your cabin is found. Almost all cruise lines prohibit smoking in restaurants and food service areas.

WHAT ABOUT CIGARS?

These cruise lines have cigar smoking lounges: Asuka Cruise, Hapag-Lloyd Cruises, MSC Cruises, Regent Seven Seas Cruises, Silversea Cruises, and TUI Cruises. Hapag-Lloyd Cruises' *Europa* and *Europa 2* have the largest selection of cigars.

Note that the air purification system in a ship's cigar lounge will not be effective enough if someone comes in to smoke a cigarette, and you may suffer the consequences of inhaling second-hand cigarette smoke.

WHAT ABOUT VAPING?

In general, vaping is generally only permitted in the same areas as cigarette smoking. For most cruise ships, that means not in your cabin or on a cabin balcony. Cruise lines do not allow weed vapes or marijuana in any shape or form, whether it is for medical use or not. For the latest information, you should check with the cruise line.

HOW ABOUT FREIGHTER TRAVEL?

Slow freighter voyages appeal to independent travelers (about 3,000 passengers annually travel aboard them) who don't require constant entertainment, but want comfortable accommodation and the joy of days at sea. However, freighters do not have a doctor on board. For more information, contact the specialists:
www.cruisepeople.co.uk
www.freightertravel.co.nz

THE CHRONOLOGY OF CRUISING

From adventurous but humble beginnings to the floating resorts of today, here is a comprehensive history of the fascinating world of cruising and cruise ships.

In 1835, a curious advertisement appeared in the first issue of Scotland's *Shetland Journal*. Headed 'To Tourists', it proposed an imaginary cruise from Stromness in Scotland, round Iceland and the Faroe Islands, and hinted at the pleasures of cruising under the Spanish sun in winter. Thus, it is said, the journal's founder, Arthur Anderson, created the concept of cruising. Just two years later, Anderson, along with his partner Brodie Wilcox, founded the great Peninsular Steam Navigation Company (later to become P&O).

Soon after, Samuel Cunard started transatlantic sailings, from Liverpool to Halifax, across the most dangerous ocean in the world, the North Atlantic, with a steam-powered sailing vessel, *Britannia*, on July 4, 1840. Every year since then, a Cunard ship has operated scheduled transatlantic liner service between the old and new worlds.

Cunard linked up with BOAC in the early 1960s.

Sailing for leisure soon caught on. Even writers such as William Makepeace Thackeray and Charles Dickens boarded ships for the excitement of the voyage, not just to reach a destination. The Victorians, having discovered tourism, promoted the idea widely. Indeed, Thackeray's account of his legendary voyage in 1844, from Cornhill to Grand Cairo by means of the P&O ships of the day, makes fascinating reading, as does the account by Dickens of his transatlantic crossing aboard a Cunard ship in 1842. P&O's *Tagus*, which journeyed from London to the Black Sea in 1843, was the subject of Mark Twain's *The Innocents Abroad*, published in 1869.

In 1900, the first ship purpose-built for cruising (*Prinzessin Victoria Louise*) was constructed for Germany's Hamburg America Line. In the 1920s, following World War 1, taking a cruise became the thing to do for the world's well-to-do. Being pampered in grand style became fashionable – and is still the underlying concept of cruising. The ship took you and your belongings anywhere, fed you, accommodated you, relaxed you, and even entertained you. At the same time, it even catered for your servants – who, of course, accompanied you.

A trio of ocean liners, built for the White Star Line (*Britannic*, *Olympic*, and *Titanic*). The *Olympic* had a swimming pool, and really created the model by which ships for leisure holidays would become in the future.

THE FIRST BOOZE CRUISES

Cruising for Americans was helped greatly by Prohibition in the 1930s. After all, just a few miles out at sea, you were free to consume as much liquor as you wished. Inexpensive three- and four-day weekend 'booze cruises' from New York were preferable to 'bathtub gin'. Shortly thereafter, cruises added destinations as well as alcohol. In time, the short cruise was to become one of the principal sources of profit for the steamship companies of the day.

DID YOU KNOW...
...that the ocean liner *Amerika* in 1938 was the first ship to have an alternative restaurant open separately from the dining salons? It was named the Ritz Carlton.

INTERNATIONAL RIVALRIES

During the 1930s a battle raged between the then largest cruising companies of the world, as Britain, France, Germany, and the United States built ships of unprecedented luxury, elegance, glamor, and comfort at the time. Each country competed to produce the biggest and best. For a time, quality was somehow related to funnels (smokestacks): the more a ship had the better. Although speed had always been a factor, particularly on the transatlantic crossings, it became a matter of national ambition and pride to have the fastest and the best.

The first ship designed specifically for cruising from the USA after World War II was *Ocean Monarch* (Furness Withy & Company Ltd). The ship was awarded a gold medal by the U.S. Academy of Designing for 'outstanding beauty and unusual design features of a cruise ship'. Its maiden voyage, in 1951, was from New York to Bermuda. I worked aboard this ship for a short time, as an entertainer.

One of the most renowned cruise ships of all time was Cunard's *Caronia* (34,183 tons), conceived in 1948. It was designed and built to offer a transatlantic service in the peak summer months, and then spend the rest of the year operating long, expensive cruises. Outstanding features were its single giant mast and large funnel, which, at the time, was the largest. The hull was painted four shades of green, supposedly for the purposes of heat resistance and easy identification. Lovingly known as the 'Green Goddess' and 'the millionaires ship', it was one of the first to provide a private adjoining bathroom for every cabin – a true luxury.

In 1950, an all-American star cruise took place aboard Cunard Line's RMS *Queen Elizabeth*, with some very special guests from the world of stage, screen, and sport – Noel Coward, Walt Disney, Judy Garland, Rita Hayworth, Fred Perry, Frank Sinatra, and Elizabeth Taylor.

THE BIRTH OF MODERN-DAY CRUISING

In June 1958, Pan American World Airlines (aka: PanAm) flew the first commercial jet aircraft (a Boeing 707) across the Atlantic and forever altered the economics of transatlantic travel, because the airline introduced economy airfares. It was the last year in which more passengers crossed the North Atlantic by sea than by air.

In the early 1960s, passenger-shipping directories listed over 100 passenger lines. Until the mid-1960s, it was cheaper to cross the Atlantic by ship than by plane, but the appearance of the jet aircraft changed that rapidly, particularly with the introduction of the Boeing 747 in the early 1970s. In 1962, more than one million people crossed the North Atlantic by ship; in 1970, that number was down to about 250,000.

The success of the jumbo jets created a fleet of unprofitable and out-of-work passenger liners that appeared doomed for the scrap heap. Even the famous

The USS *Rijndam* in 1900.

big 'Queens', noted for their regular weekly transatlantic service, were at risk. Cunard White Star Line's RMS *Queen Mary* (80,774 tons) was withdrawn in September 1967. Cunard Line's sister ship RMS *Queen Elizabeth*, at 83,673 tons the largest passenger liner ever built (until 1996), made its final transatlantic crossing in October 1968.

Ships were sold for a fraction of their value. Many shipping lines went out of business and ships were sold for scrap. Those that survived attempted to mix transatlantic crossings with voyages south to the sun, even though they lacked proper air-conditioning. The Caribbean (including the Bahamas) became appealing. Cruising became an alternative to land-based vacations, and thus, a new industry was born, with new companies being formed exclusively for cruising.

Then smaller, more specialized ships arrived. They were capable of getting into the tiny ports of developing Caribbean islands (there were no commercial airlines taking vacationers to the Caribbean then, and few hotels). Instead of cruising long distances south from more northerly ports such as New York, companies established their headquarters in Florida. This not only avoided the cold weather, choppy seas, and expense of the northern ports but also saved fuel costs because of the shorter runs to the Caribbean. Cruising was reborn. California became the base for cruises to the Mexican Riviera, and Vancouver on Canada's west coast became the focus for summer cruises to Alaska.

Flying passengers to embarkation ports was the next logical step, and soon a working relationship emerged between the cruise lines and the airlines. Air/sea and 'sail and stay' packages thrived – joint air, cruise and hotel vacations with inclusive pricing. Some old liners came out of mothballs, purchased by emerging cruise lines and were refurbished for warm-weather cruising operations, often with their interiors redesigned and refitted. During the late 1970s, the modern cruise industry grew at a rapid rate.

MSC Seaside **under construction at the Fincantieri shipyard in northern Italy.**

CRUISING TODAY

Today's cruise concept has changed little from that of earlier days, although it has been improved, modified, refined, expanded, and well packaged for ease of consumption. No longer the domain of affluent, retired people, the cruise industry today is vibrant and alive with passengers of every age and socio-economic background. Cruising is no longer the shipping business, but the hospitality industry (although some cruise ship personnel may appear to be in the hostility industry).

New ships are larger than their counterparts of yesteryear, yet cabin size has become 'standardized' to provide more space for entertainment and other public facilities. Today's ships boast air conditioning to keep out heat and humidity; stabilizers to keep the ship on an even keel; a high level of maintenance, safety, and hygiene; and greatly enhanced emphasis on health and fitness facilities.

Cruise ship design has moved from the traditional, classic, rounded profiles of the past (example: the now retired *Queen Elizabeth 2*) to the extremely boxy shapes with squared-off sterns and towering super-structures today. Although ship lovers lament these design changes, they have resulted from the desire to squeeze as much as possible in the space provided (you can fit more in a square box than you can in a round one, though it may be less aesthetically appealing). Form follows function, and ships have changed from ocean transportation to floating vacation resorts.

Although ships have long been devoted to eating and relaxation in comfort (promulgating the maxim 'Traveling slowly unwinds you faster'), ships today offer more activities, and more learning and life-enriching experiences than before. And there are many more places you can visit on a cruise: from the continent of Antarctica to the city of Acapulco, Bermuda to Bergen, Dakar to Dominica, Shanghai to St. Thomas, or if you prefer, perhaps nowhere at all.

The cruise industry is a $75 billion business worldwide. It provides employment to a growing number, both directly (there are, for example, over 200,000 shipboard officers, staff, and crew, plus about 30,000 employees in cruise company offices), and indirectly (suppliers of food components and catering, beverage suppliers, mechanical and electrical parts, port agents, transport companies, destinations, airlines, railways, hotels, and car rental companies, for example). In 2019 (pre-Covid shutdown), more than 30 million people worldwide took a cruise, packaged and sold by cruise lines themselves, and through tour operators and travel agents. That number then dropped dramatically, the result of national lockdowns and problems with supply chains, airlines, and transportation.

BUILDING A MODERN CRUISE SHIP

More than any other type of vessel, a cruise ship has to fulfil fantasies and satisfy exotic imaginations. It is the job of the shipyard to take those fantasies and turn them into a ship without unduly straining the laws of naval architecture and safety regulations, not to mention budgets.

Although no perfect cruise ship exists, turning owners' and company dreams and concepts into ships that embody those ideals is the job of specialized marine architects and shipyards, of consultants, interior designers, and a mass of specialist suppliers. Computers have simplified this complex process, although shipboard management and operations personnel often become frustrated with designers who are more idealistic than they are practical. Ships represent a compromise between ideals, safety regulations, and restrictions of space and finance. The solution is to design ships for specific areas and service conditions.

Ships used to be constructed from the keel (backbone) up. Today, they are built in huge sections, then joined together in an assembly area (typically over 100 sections for a resort ship such as Royal Caribbean International's *Wonder of the Seas*, each section weighing over 450 tons, most of which are extensively pre-outfitted). The sections may not even be constructed in the shipyard – simply assembled there. The design of today's ships is completely computer-based.

Formerly, passenger spaces were slotted in wherever there was space within a given hull. Today, computers provide highly targeted ship design, enabling a new ship to be built within two years instead of within the four or five years it took in the 1950s.

The maximum noise and vibration levels allowable in the accommodation spaces and recreational areas are stipulated in any owner's contract with the shipyard. Vibration tests are carried out once a ship is built and launched, using a finite method element of evaluation; this embraces analyses of prime sources of noise and excitation, namely the ship's propellers and main engines.

Prefabricated cabin modules, including *in situ* bathrooms complete with toilets and all plumbing fixtures, are standard today. When the steel structure of the relevant deck is ready, with main lines and insulation already installed, cabin modules are then affixed to the deck, and power lines and sanitary plumbing are swiftly connected. All waste and power connections, together with hot/cold water mixing valves, are arranged in the service area of the bathroom, and can be reached from the passageway outside the cabin for maintenance.

CRUISING TOMORROW

Current thinking in ship design is increasingly follows two distinct paths: large resort ships or very small-sized ships (including expedition-style ships with ice-hardened hulls).

The large 'resort' ships use 'economy of scale' to help operators keep the cost per passengers down. Several companies now have ships measuring over 150,000 tons, accommodating over 5,000 passengers, with the 'bigger is better' principle being pursued for all it's worth. Some were too wide to transit the Panama Canal, until new locks were built and introduced in 2018.

Small ships, where the 'small is beautiful' concept has taken hold, are particularly found in the exclusive top-of-the-range area. Cruise lines offer high-quality ships of low capacity, which can provide a highly personalized range of quality services. This means better trained, more experienced staff (and more of them to serve fewer passengers), higher-quality food and more meals cooked to order. Small ships can also visit more uncrowded ports.

Other cruise lines have expanded by 'stretching' their ships. This is accomplished literally by cutting a ship in half, and inserting a newly constructed mid-section, thus instantly increasing capacity, adding more accommodation and public rooms, while maintaining the same draft.

Whatever direction the design of cruise vessels takes in the future, ships are becoming increasingly environmentally friendly.

MODERN CRUISE CHRONOLOGY

1960

- Passenger shipping directories listed more than 30 companies operating transatlantic voyages, from the 'Old World' (Europe) to the 'New World' (USA/Canada). Many ships were laid up between 1960 and 1970, and most are sold for a fraction of their value.
- *Britannic* (26,943 gross tons, when built), the last passenger ship to wear the White Star Line colors, was taken out of service (the White Star Line itself merged with Cunard Line in 1934).
- The British hairdressing concession Steiner (started by Herman and Abigail Steiner) was awarded its first sea-going concession to operate the salon aboard the Royal Mail Lines ship *Andes*, followed by Cunard Line's RMS *Queen Elizabeth* and RMS *Queen Mary*. Steiner expanded rapidly, with contracts aboard the ships of P&O.
- P&O and Orient Lines merged, and the combined company became P&O Orient Lines, later just P&O.
- The Intergovernmental Maritime Consultative Organisation (IMCO) met in London. The occasion was the Convention for the Safety of Life at Sea (SOLAS

1960) and update several improvements made since the adoption of the previous convention of 1948, which required ships to carry life rafts, as a partial substitute for lifeboats.

1961

- Epirotiki Lines introduced fly-cruise vacations, which became standard in the cruise industry for millions of cruisegoers.
- Charalambos A. Keusseouglou, who began his career at Home Lines (the immigrant passenger carrier), founded Sun Line.
- The United States Maritime Commission (FMC) is founded as an independent government agency to regulate ocean transport and commerce.

1962

- Compagnie Générale Transatlantique's ocean liner SS France (a steamship, hence the designation SS), at 1,035ft (315m) became the longest passenger ship ever built (until then). It entered regular transatlantic service, between Le Havre and New York, in February.

1963

- Cunard Line's RMS Queen Elizabeth (RMS stands for Royal Mail Ship, due to the contract that Cunard Line had with the British Government, to carry the Royal Mail from the UK to the USA), made an experimental cruise from New York to the West Indies. As a result, full air conditioning was fitted in 1965–66 to facilitate more extensive cruise activity during the winter season, when transatlantic crossings proved challenging to operate.

1964

- The Italian company Flotta Lauro (Lauro Lines) purchased two ex-Holland America Line ships, and renamed them Achille Lauro (original name: MS Willem Ruys) and Angelina Lauro (original name: MS Oranje). Note that MS stands for motor ship.

1965

- Canadian-born entrepreneur Stanley B. McDonald founded Princess Cruises, which went on to become one of the best-known cruise brands. He started by chartering Princess Patricia from Canadian Pacific Limited.

1966

- The UK's National Union of Seamen (NUS) went on strike, which affected the crew of ships such as RMS

DID YOU KNOW...

...that the first solo-occupancy cabins built as such were aboard the Cunard Line's Campania, whose maiden voyage was in 1893?

DID YOU KNOW...

...that the first ship to be fitted with interior plumbing was the 6,283-ton Normandie of 1883?

Queen Elizabeth and RMS Queen Mary. The author was then working aboard RMS Queen Elizabeth, left the ship in Cherbourg and flew back to the UK (it was my first flight). I rejoined the ship when it returned to Southampton prior to re-commencing the transatlantic service some months later.

- Blount Small Ship Adventures was founded by Luther H. Blount, an engineer and inventor of the American steam trawler. He built his small cruise vessels in his own shipyard in Warren, Rhode Island.
- Commodore Cruise Line was founded in Miami. Its first ship, Discovery, was acquired as a result of a canceled order for ferry company Wallenius Lines and was modified into a format for cruise operations.
- Holland America Line introduced the casual buffet eating concept.
- Soviet transatlantic service re-started, with the Black Sea Shipping Company's Aleksandr Pushkin inaugurating service between Montreal and Leningrad (it was renamed St. Petersburg in 1991) for the first time since 1949.
- The Norwegian company Klosters Reederei joined Miami businessman Ted Arison to market Caribbean cruises from Miami.
- Florida hotelier Sanford Chobol and Edwin Stephan together founded Commodore Cruise Line.
- As a result of a fire one year earlier aboard the American ship Yarmouth Castle, with the loss of almost 90 passengers, amendments were made to the Safety of Life at Sea (SOLAS) safety regulations. New maritime regulations were enacted. These required safety inspections, fire drills, and structural design changes to all newly-built ships.

1967

- Cunard Line withdrew the transatlantic liner RMS Queen Mary from service. The ship was sold and sailed to Long Beach, California, for operation as a floating hotel, museum, and convention center.

1968

- Commodore Cruise Line's first ship (the newbuild MS Boheme) was chartered from Wallenius Lines). Commodore Cruise Line was founded two years previously.
- Cunard's RMS Queen Elizabeth was withdrawn from its regular transatlantic service in November (the author was on board for the final crossing from New York to Southampton).
- Cunard refused delivery of Queen Elizabeth 2 from the ship's world-famous builder, John Brown (Scotland), in December, because of unacceptable turbine vibration. Repairs led to a five-month delay to

An Epirotiki Lines ship.

its maiden transatlantic crossing.
- Royal Caribbean Cruise Line (RCCL) was founded in Norway by a consortium of three Norwegian shipping companies (Anders Wilhelmson, I.M. Skaugen & Company, and Gotaas Larsen.
- The USA's Boise Cascade purchased Princess Cruises from its founder, Stanley B. McDonald, who repurchased it two years later.

1969
- Lars-Eric Lindblad's *Lindblad Explorer* (designed for close-in expedition cruising) was launched. The ship became known as 'the little red boat'.
- United States Lines' loss-making transatlantic steamship *United States* was laid up in Philadelphia, USA.

1970
- Royal Viking Line was founded in Norway by three corporate partners, who each contributed one ship: Bergen Line (*Royal Viking Star*); A.F. Klaveness (*Royal Viking Sea*), and Nordenfjeldske (*Royal Viking Sky*). All three ships measured approximately 21,500 gross tons and were built by Wartsila Helsinki New Shipyard. They were specifically designed for long-distance cruising and particularly for leisurely single seating dining. *Royal Viking Star* was slightly shorter (by approximately two feet) than the other two ships, and the interior layout was slightly different in that it included a small chapel, the only one of the three ships to do so.

- Germany's Norddeutscher Lloyd and Hapag (Hamburg American Line) merged to become Hapag-Lloyd.
- Princess Cruises was founded by Seattle-based entrepreneur Stanley McDonald. He first became involved with cruise ships when, during planning for the 1962 World's Fair in Seattle, he chartered *Princess Patricia*, then owned by the Canadian Pacific Railroad, because Seattle did not have enough hotel rooms. It was very successful. He got permission to use the name Princess, and thus was born name Princess Cruises.

1971
- Cunard Line was sold to the UK's Trafalgar House Investments (Trafalgar House plc). The new management sold *Carmania* and *Franconia* in order to purchase two smaller ships then under construction (*Cunard Ambassador* and *Cunard Adventurer*) in Italy.
- Holland America Line purchased one million shares of Westours, which provided a controlling interest in the Alaska tour company.
- Royal Cruise Line was founded by Greek shipping magnate Pericles Panagopoulos.

1972
- Ted Arison (co-founder of Norwegian Cruise Line) started his own cruise line – Carnival Cruise Lines. It began with just one second-hand ship, *Mardi Gras* (ex-*Empress of Canada*). Sadly, the ship ran aground on its first voyage. A drink was created (by person-

nel working for a different cruise line) which became known as *Mardi Gras* on the rocks.
- Holland America Line changed its passenger ships to the Dutch registry.
- Sitmar Cruises began operations with one ship, TSS *Fairsea*.
- The Arab Oil Embargo caused the price of oil to jump from $3 per barrel to $12 per barrel. It was also the start of a worldwide recession, and was probably responsible for the demise of several companies.
- The International Regulations for the Prevention of Collisions at Sea (COLREGS) were adopted in October as a convention of the International Maritime Organisation (IMO). The new regulations entered into force in 1977 and were designed to update and replace the Collision Regulations of 1960, particularly with regards to the Traffic Separation Schemes (TSS). Federal authorities from member countries were designated to implement and enforce the updated regulations via the Coast Guard.

1974

- Ted Arison purchased full ownership of the troubled Carnival Cruise Line from its parent company, the Boston-based American International Travel Services (AITS). He assumed the company's debt of $5 million by paying just $1, and renamed it Carnival Corporation.
- The UK's P&O purchased the USA-based Princess Cruises.
- Compagnie Générale Transatlantique sent the loss-making *France* into lay-up.

The cast of *The Love Boat*.

- The Port Authority of New York and New Jersey opened its rebuilt Passenger Ship Terminal in Manhattan, at piers 88, 90, and 92.
- Royal Cruise Lines' first ship, *Golden Odyssey*, built to accommodate the equivalent load of a Boeing 747 jumbo aircraft (425 passengers), was introduced.

1975

- Cruise Lines International Association (CLIA) was formed, to promote the benefits of cruising and cruise vacations.
- Cunard Line's *Queen Elizabeth 2* (*QE2*) became the largest ocean liner to pass through the Panama Canal.
- The USA's Centers for Disease Control and Prevention (CDC) established its Vessel Sanitation Program, designed to help the growing leisure cruise industry in preventing and controlling the spread of gastrointestinal diseases aboard cruise ships.

1976

- *Island Princess* and *Pacific Princess* (Princess Cruises) became 'stars' in the American television show *The Love Boat*. The show was broadcast from 1976 to 1990, and some 25 episodes were made. The pilot episode was filmed aboard the 730-passenger *Sun Princess*, with subsequent filming aboard the *Pacific Princess* and *Island Princess*.
- Cunard Line introduced *Cunard Countess* and *Cunard Princess*, for informal Caribbean cruises. The ships were originally ordered by the supplemental airline ONG Airways for the low-cost fly-cruise market, but Cunard obtained them when the airline fell into financial difficulties. The two ships were completed at the Cantieri Navali La Spezia shipyard in La Spezia, Italy.
- The Italian Line and Lloyd Triestino ceased transatlantic passenger operations.

1977

- Holland America Line purchased and absorbed Monarch Cruise Lines.
- The new international regulations for preventing collisions at sea (COLREGS) are entered into force.
- Norwegian Caribbean Lines purchased an island in The Bahamas. It was developed and became Great Stirrup Cay, for the sole use of its passengers on day visits.
- P&O demerged the company's Australian operations, and acquired Sitmar Cruises. This resulted in the renamed P&O Cruises Australia.
- World Explorer Cruises was founded with one chartered ship, *Universe*.

DID YOU KNOW...

...that the first à la carte restaurant aboard a passenger ship was in the German ship *Amerika* of 1905?

DID YOU KNOW...

...that the first vessel built exclusively for cruising was Hamburg-Amerika Line's two-funnel yacht, the 4,409-tonne *Princessin Victoria Luise*? This luxury ship even included a private suite reserved for the German kaiser.

1978

- Richard Hadley founded United States Cruises, with a view to converting and updating the SS *United States* from an ocean liner into a cruise ship.

1979

- American Hawaii Cruises was formed to operate cruises in Hawaii, with its base in Honolulu.
- The transatlantic ocean liner SS *France* was purchased by Lauritz Kloster, of Norway. It was rebuilt for cruises to the Caribbean, renamed *Norway* and transferred to Norwegian Caribbean Lines in Miami.

1980

- Sea Goddess Cruises was founded by Helge Naarstad, of Norway.
- Denmark's United Steamship Company (DFDS) founded Scandinavian World Cruises to operate one-day cruises from Miami (the company subsequently became SeaEscape).
- Peter Deilmann Cruises (based in Neustadt, Germany), started ocean-going operations with the newbuild *Berlin* (the company had previous chartered older ships). The company was established in 1968 to operate river cruises.
- Two Royal Caribbean ships – *Nordic Prince* and *Song of Norway* – were 'stretched' with the addition of a mid-section. It was the first time this technique had been applied in the cruise industry. The work was undertaken at the Wartsila shipyard in Finland, the ship original builder of the ships. The new mid-section increased the length of each ship from 550ft to 635ft, and the passenger capacity increased by 328.
- All three Royal Viking Line ships (*Royal Viking Sea*, *Royal Viking Star*, and *Royal Viking Sun*) were 'stretched' with the addition of a mid-section.

1981

- The transatlantic service provided by Soviet-registered ships was discontinued due to a US embargo.
- Astor Cruises was formed in the UK.
- *Das Traumschiff* (*The Dream Ship*) was Germany's answer to the USA's *The Love Boat*, with a storyline based on a German cruise ship. Several actors played the part of the ship's captain throughout the series.

1982

- The British Government requisitioned Cunard's *Queen Elizabeth 2* (*QE2*) for use as a troop carrier during the Falklands conflict between Argentina and

The *QE2* leaves for the Falkland Islands, 1982.

Britain. The *QE2* sailed with 3,000 troops on board. Cunard's Captain Peter Jackson was in command of the 650 crew members who volunteered, including John Butt, the ship's cruise director.
- P&O Cruises' *Canberra* was also requisitioned for use as a troop carrier, and the ship carried 2,200 troops.

1983

- P&O appointed Jeffrey Sterling as chairman in order to fend off an unwanted takeover bid for Cunard Line's owners, Trafalgar House, which also purchased Norwegian America Cruises (NAC), and its two long-distance cruise ships – *Sagafjord* and *Vistafjord*.
- P&O acquired Swan Hellenic from the Swan family.
- Premier Cruise Lines, a subsidiary of Premier Cruises, was founded, with headquarters in Miami.
- Salen-Lindblad Cruising's *Lindblad Explorer* (known as the 'Little Red Boat' because the ship's hull was painted red) became the first passenger ship to successfully navigate the Northwest Passage, sailing 4,790 miles (7,700km) from Saint John's, Newfoundland, to Point Barrow, Alaska. Unfortunately, the ship sank in Antarctica (the first passenger ship to do so) in November 2007 after striking an iceberg. Thankfully, all passengers and crew were rescued.

1984

- Crown Cruise Lines was founded in Boca Raton, Florida.

- Dolphin Cruise Line was founded in Miami.
- Regency Cruises was founded in New York.
- Sundance Cruises was founded in Los Angeles.
- Windstar Sail Cruises re-launched commercial sail-cruise vessels with three ships, ordered from French shipyard Société Nouvelle des Ateliers et Chantiers du Havre. The company was created by Karl Gosta Andren.
- Network TV advertising was used in the United States for the first time by Carnival Cruise Lines.

1985

- The Chandris Group of Companies acquired Fantasy Cruises from GoGo Tours of New York. The company was renamed Chandris Fantasy Cruises in the USA, and Chandris Cruises in the UK. New York-based Fred Kassner co-owned GoGo Tours (and co-founded Liberty Travel).
- The first international satellite system is put into operation by Cospas-Sarsat, a joint effort between the United States, Canada, the Soviet Union, and France. The system was designed to aid in distress tracking, for search and rescue operations.

1986

- Direct-dial satellite telephone calls were introduced to cruise ships.
- Signet Cruise Line was founded in Norway. Owing to a lawsuit brought by an American who claimed the right to the name Signet, the company changed its name in 1988 to Seabourn Cruise Line.
- Eastern Cruise Lines, Western Cruise Lines, and Sundance Cruises (each with one ship) merged to become Admiral Cruises, with headquarters in Miami.
- Cunard acquired Sea Goddess Cruises and its two small upscale ships Sea Goddess I and Sea Goddess II.
- Labadee, on Haiti's northern coast, is leased to Royal Caribbean Cruise Line for use as a private island venue.

1987

- Carnival Cruise Lines made its first public stock offering, on the New York Stock Exchange, with a total of 20 percent of its common stock offered.
- Cunard's Queen Elizabeth 2 was converted at Lloyd Werft's shipyard in Bremerhaven, Germany, from steam turbine to diesel-electric power, the largest conversion of its kind in maritime history, at a cost of $100 million. The conversion provided nine medium speed turbo-charged MAN L58/64 diesel engines, with a maximum output of 44 Megawatts, to provide a maximum service speed of 32 knots. However, the required service speed of 28.5 knots could be achieved using only 7 engines (each weighed over 400 tons), which provided ample spare capacity. The original steam turbines were of the Parmetrada design, and the boilers were the largest ever built for marine use.
- Ocean Cruise Lines merged with Pearl Seas Cruises.

- Princess Cruises replaced almost 500 unionized British hotel and catering staff aboard its five ships, with non-union employees.

1988

- Carnival Cruise Lines purchased Holland America Line, including its land-based hotel/transport operations (Westours), plus Windstar Cruises.
- Commodore Cruise Lines sold its 1968-built Bohème to San Donato Properties – affiliated with the Church of Scientology. The ship was renamed Freewinds and used for cruises from the Dutch island of Aruba in the Caribbean.
- Compagnie du Ponant was founded by Jean Emmanuel Sauvé, Philippe Videau and other former officers of the French Merchant Navy, specifically to cater to the growing number of French cruise passengers.
- Crystal Cruises was formed as a wholly-owned division of Japan's Nippon Yusen Kaisha (NYK).
- Royal Caribbean Cruise Line merged with Admiral Cruises to form Royal Admiral Cruises (the company later became Royal Caribbean Cruises).
- Seabourn Cruise Line's first ship, Seabourn Pride, entered service.

1989

- American Cruise Lines, which operated small vessels for intracoastal cruising in the USA, went into bankruptcy.
- The Chandris Group of Companies created Celebrity Cruises, destined to become a more upscale cruise line. Its first ship was Meridian, which was converted from the former SS Galileo Galilei, built originally in 1963 for Lloyd-Triestino's liner service from Italy to Australia. The first ship built specifically for Celebrity Cruises was Horizon.
- Pericles Panagopoulos sold Royal Cruise Line to Norway's Kloster Group.
- Japan's Showa Line debuts the small Oceanic Grace – its first purpose-built cruise ship.
- Lindblad Travel was declared bankrupt.
- Renaissance Cruises was formed by Fearnley & Eger (a 120-year-old Oslo-based shipping concern) with a view to building eight small identical 'premium' ships.
- The Panama Canal celebrated its 75th birthday.

DID YOU KNOW...

...that the word POSH is said to come from ocean liner voyages? When ships (of the Peninsular and Oriental Steam Navigation Company) on voyages between the UK and India sailed outbound (eastward) through the Suez Canal and the Red Sea, cabins on the port side were much in demand, while on the way back (westward), it was preferable to book a cabin on the starboard side. This was to avoid the hot sun (there was no such thing as air-conditioning). Thus – Port Out, Starboard Home was shortened to the acronym POSH.

1990

- Starlite Cruises (part of the Piraeus-based Lelakis Group) was formed.
- Ocean Cruise Lines, with two ships (*Ocean Islander* and the large *Ocean Princess*) was purchased by Croisières Paquet, itself owned by the French giant Accor leisure company, and operator of *Mermoz*.
- Japan Cruise Line entered the Japanese cruise market with the 21,884-ton, 390-passenger *Orient Venus*, built by Japan's Ishikawajima Heavy Industries The ship was originally designed and built for charters and incentive cruises.
- At the start of the Gulf War, the US government chartered Cunard's *Cunard Princess* for a period of six months for use as a rest and relaxation center in Europe for US service personnel engaged in the Persian Gulf.

1991

- Carnival Cruise Lines acquired a 25 percent stake in Seabourn Cruise Line.
- Renaissance Cruises was sold to an international group of investors.
- Finland's Effjohn International purchased Crown Cruise Line.
- Seawind Cruise Line commenced cruise operations.
- Royal Caribbean Cruise Lines ended the Admiral Cruises brand. The company's two remaining ships (*Azure Seas* and *Emerald Seas*) were sold.
- Japan's NYK purchased the USA-based expedition cruise company, Salen Lindblad Cruising.

1992

- Costa Cruise Lines introduced its Euro-Luxe cruise concept when *CostaClassica* debuted.
- Admiral Cruises, with two ships, ceased operations.
- Carnival Cruise Lines deployed its *Mardi Gras* to accommodate 600 staff members made homeless by Hurricane Andrew (the author's apartment and office in Miami were also destroyed in the hurricane).
- The Chandris Group and Overseas Shipholding Group (OSG) agreed to form a joint venture company – to be called Celebrity Cruise Lines, Inc.
- Chargeurs and Accor, the French property and leisure industries group that own Paquet Cruises and Ocean Cruise Lines, purchased a 23 percent stake in Costa Crociere, parent company of Costa Cruises.
- Festival Cruises was founded in Miami by George Poulides. The company acquired *The Azur* from Chandris Cruises, and *Starward* from Norwegian Cruise Line the following year, and renamed it *Bolero*.
- Majesty Cruise Line started operations.

The eye-catching funnel on Dolphin Cruise Line's SS *SeaBreeze*.

1993

- American Classic Voyages (incorporated in 1985 as the Delta Queen Steamboat Company) owner of American Hawaii Cruises, was formed to operate ocean-going ships under the US flag.
- Carnival Cruise Lines created Fiesta Marina Cruises for the Spanish-speaking Latin American market; it was phenomenally unsuccessful.
- Portugal-based entrepreneur George Poulides founded Festival Cruises, in Greece. The company was known as First European Cruises in the USA.
- SeaQuest Cruises – with one ship – ceased operations.
- Expedition ship *Frontier Spirit* was returned to its Japanese owners. It was then chartered to Germany's Hanseatic Tours and renamed *Bremen*.
- Star Cruises was founded in November, in Asia, as part of Malaysia's Genting Group, with the company's corporate headquarters based in in Hong Kong.

1994

- The USA's Delta Queen Steamboat Company changed its corporate name to American Classic Voyages Company. It owned American Hawaii Cruises and the Delta Queen Steamboat Company.
- The UK's Trafalgar House, Cunard's parent company, signed an agreement to purchase the rights to

the name Royal Viking Line, together with *Royal Viking Sun*. The smaller *Royal Viking Queen*, which entered service in 1992, was not included in the sale, and went to Royal Cruise Line, becoming *Queen Odyssey* and later *Seabourn Legend*.

- In the USA, Radisson Diamond Cruises and Seven Seas Cruise Line merged to become Radisson Seven Seas Cruises (RSSC).
- American Family Cruises closed its doors due to lack of business.
- Norway-based Kloster Cruise was declared bankrupt. This resulted in the discontinuation of its two cruise brands, Royal Cruise Line, and Royal Viking Line, both with headquarters in San Francisco.

1995

- British company Airtours purchased *Southward* from Norwegian Cruise Line and *Nordic Prince* from Royal Caribbean Cruises, and started a new division, named Sun Cruises.
- Regency Cruises filed for bankruptcy; its ships are placed under arrest.

1996

- Kloster Cruise (parent of Norwegian Cruise Line and Royal Cruise Line) announced the closure of its Royal Cruise Line division. *Crown Odyssey* and *Royal Odyssey* were transferred to Norwegian Cruise Line as *Norwegian Crown* and *Norwegian Star*, respectively. *Queen Odyssey* went to Seabourn Cruise Line as *Seabourn Legend*. *Star Odyssey* was sold to UK-based Fred. Olsen Cruise Lines and renamed *Black Watch*.
- The Carnival Corporation purchased a 30 percent interest in UK operator Airtours.
- Cunard (and its parent company Trafalgar House) were purchased by Norwegian shipping company Kvaerner. The legendary *Queen Elizabeth 2* was included in the sale.

1997

- Dolphin Cruise Line was purchased by Premier Cruise Line, and its three ships were painted in Premier Cruise Line colors, with a bright red hull and a white upper structure.
- Carnival Corporation, jointly with the UK's Airtours, purchased all the shares of Italy-based Costa Cruises.
- Hapag-Lloyd acquired Hanseatic Tours, together with its single expedition ship, *Hanseatic*.
- Premier Cruises purchased Holland America Line's *Rotterdam*, and renamed it *Rembrandt*.
- Miami-based Majesty Cruise Line, with two ships, ceased operations.
- P&O Cruises' much-loved long distance ship *Canberra* was withdrawn from service and sent to Pakistan for scrapping.
- Royal Caribbean International purchased Celebrity Cruises (from the UK's Chandris Group of companies) for $1.3 billion. The company decided to keep both brands as separate entities.
- Windstar Cruises purchased the sail-cruise ship *Club Med 1* and renamed it *Wind Surf*.

P&O Cruises' *Canberra* was requisitioned for use as a troop carrier during the Falklands conflict.

1998

- Australia repealed its cabotage laws, allowing international cruise ships to dock and operate from Australian ports without restrictions.
- Kvaerner sold Cunard for $500 million to a consortium that included the USA-based Carnival Corporation, which owned Airtours, Costa Cruises, Holland America Line, Seabourn Cruise Line, and Windstar Cruises.

1999

- Crown Cruise Line was reintroduced as an 'upscale' division of Commodore Cruise Line. The company chartered *Crown Dynasty*, and later purchased the ship.
- Imperial Majesty Cruise Line, headquartered in Plantation, Florida, was founded, and started operations by chartering *OceanBreeze* from Premier Cruise Line.

2000

- Star Cruises took full control of Norwegian Cruise Line, after purchasing the outstanding shares held by the Carnival Corporation.
- P&O Group separated its cruising activities from the rest of the group, by placing emphasis on its core business; it had five cruise divisions – Aida Cruises, P&O Cruises, P&O Cruises Australia, Princess Cruises, and Swan Hellenic.
- Costa Cruises became 100 percent owned by the Carnival Corporation.
- Canaveral Cruise Lines (1 ship), Commodore Cruise Lines (2 ships), Crown Cruise Line (1 ship), Delfin Cruises (2 ships), and Norwegian Capricorn Line (1 ship), Premier Cruise Line (7 ships) and Sun Cruises (3 ships), all ceased operations.

2001

- Commodore Cruise Line became defunct.
- Spain's Pullmantur purchased *Oceanic* (formerly Premier Cruise Lines' *Big Red Boat I*) and *Seawind Crown* (formerly operated by Premier Cruise Line) for the Spanish-speaking market.
- The Carnival Corporation sold its 25 percent shareholding in the UK's Airtours.
- Renaissance Cruises (10 ships) ceased operations following the 9/11 terrorist attacks on the US. So did American Hawaii Cruises, United States Lines, Delta Queen Coastal Cruises, Hyundai Asan, and Leisure Cruises.

2002

- Empress Cruise Lines (1 ship) and Valtur Tourism (1 ship) ceased operations.
- SeaDream Yacht Club began with two ships, *SeaDream I* and *SeaDream II*.
- Golden Sun Cruises became Golden Star Cruises with one ship – *Aegean I*.

2003

- The Carnival Corporation and P&O Princess Cruises merged to become the world's largest cruise company, with over 60 ships and 13 brands (A'Rosa Cruises, Aida Cruises, Carnival Cruise Lines, Costa Cruises, Cunard Line, Holland America Line, Ocean Village, P&O Cruises, P&O Cruises Australia, Princess Cruises, Seabourn Cruise Line, Swan Hellenic Cruises, and Windstar Cruises).
- Ibero Cruises (Iberocruceros in Spanish) was founded as a cruise division of Viajes Iberojet in Madrid, Spain, to market cruises to the Spanish- and Portuguese-speaking market.
- Oceania Cruises was founded by Frank del Rio and Joe Watters, with two ships, *Insignia* and *Regatta* (the former Renaissance Cruises' *R1* and *R2*).
- Regal Cruises, with one ship, ceased operations.
- Sun Bay Cruises, with two ships, ceased operations.
- Mauritius Island Cruises was founded, with two ships, *Island Sky* and *Island Sun* (formerly Renaissance Cruises' *R7* and *R8*).
- Voyages of Discovery started operations, with one ship.

2004

- The Port Authority of New York and New Jersey underwent a further renovation to accommodate new and larger cruise ships. The renovation included the decommissioning of Pier 92. The remaining piers (88, 90, and 94) were renovated and adapted to handle the newer, larger cruise ships.
- Festival Cruises ceased operations; its six ships were impounded and sold at auction.
- Royal Olympia Cruises – a victim of high ship and operating costs against the backdrop of a highly discount marketplace – ceased operations, but recovered somewhat, albeit with a smaller fleet.
- Australian tour operator Around the World Cruises (one ship) and Mare Nostrum Cruises (one ship) ceased operations.
- Norwegian shipbuilding and engineering company Kvaerner was amalgamated to the newly formed subsidiary of Aker ASA – Aker-Kvaerner, and renamed Aker Solutions in April 2008.

2005

- Orion Expedition Cruises, established in Australia in 2004, started operations with one small ship, *Orion*.
- Cruise North Expeditions was founded by the Inuit to operate no-frills expedition-style cruises to the

Canadian Arctic.

- Mauritius Island Cruises ceased operations; its two ships were sold to a Bahamian company. These were then chartered to Noble Caledonia (UK) and Travel Dynamics International (USA).
- Radisson Seven Seas Cruises changed its name to Regent Seven Seas Cruises.
- Spanish Cruise Line, with one ship, ceased operations.
- UK-based Sun Cruises (My Travel) ceased operations.
- NCL America, a division of Norwegian Cruise Line launched *Pride of America* after purchasing the unfinished ship from the USA's Ingalls Shipbuilding. The ship was towed to Germany, where it was lengthened by the insertion of a new mid-section. This was completed at the Lloyd Werft shipyard.

2006

- Royal Caribbean International purchased the Spanish tour operator Pullmantur.
- Abou Merhi Cruises ceased operations; its only ship, *Orient Queen* (ex-NCL's *Starward*), was acquired by Cyprus-based Louis Cruise Lines.
- Holiday Kreutzfarhten (Holiday Cruises) with two ships (*Lili Marleen* and *Mona Lisa*) ceased operations.
- Pearl Seas Cruises was founded by American Cruise Lines for international cruises. The company ordered two ships.
- CLIA (Cruise Lines International Organization) and ICCL (International Council of Cruise Lines) merged to become CLIA, and moved to Miami.
- Luther H. Blount (aged 90), founder of American Canadian Caribbean Line, donated *Niagara Prince* (value $6.5 million) to Rhode Island College, Roger Williams University, and the Wentworth Institute of Technology.
- *Radisson Diamond* was sold by the Finnish banks that owned the ship, to Chinese gambling interests, headed by Stanley Ho, for use in Hong Kong as a floating casino.
- Voyages of Discovery went public, and was listed on the UK stock market.

2007

- Carnival Corporation sold Swan Hellenic Cruises to the UK's Lord Jeffrey Sterling.
- Carnival Corporation signed a Letter of Intent with Orizonia Corporation, Spain's largest travel company (owners of Iberojet's cruise division). Later during the same year, Carnival Corporation acquired 75 percent of Iberostar Cruises – which became Ibero-

Cruceros – and sold Windstar Cruises to Ambassadors International.
- Royal Caribbean Cruises entered into a joint venture with Germany's tour operator TUI.
- Louis Hellenic Cruises 1986-built *Sea Diamond* (originally *Birka Princess*) struck an underwater rock and sank off Santorini. Some 1,600 passengers and crew were evacuated. It is understood that the nautical chart of the Hellenic Hydrographic Office was inaccurate.
- Oceania Cruises was bought for $850 million by the equity finance group Apollo Management.
- Celebrity Cruises created a sub-brand, and named it Azamara Cruises.
- *Queen Elizabeth 2* (affectionately known as *QE2*) was sold for £50 million ($100 million) to the state investment company in Dubai, to become a floating hotel and museum.
- Royal Caribbean International and Pullmantur Cruises jointly created CDF Croisières de France with one ship, *Bleu de France*.
- Quark Expeditions and its fleet of ships (both owned and chartered), was acquired by First Choice, co-owners (together with Royal Caribbean) of Island Cruises.
- Regent Seven Seas Cruises was acquired by Apollo Management for around $1 billion.
- In August, 50 percent of Norwegian Cruise Line (NCL) was sold to Apollo Management.
- Windjammer Barefoot Cruises ceased operations in October; its four tall ships (*Legacy, Mandalay, Polynesia*, and *Yankee Clipper*) left passengers and crew stranded in the Caribbean and South America. A recently acquired fifth ship, *La Mer* (for which 646 timeshares had been sold) was never put into service. Of these ships, only *Legacy* would be SOLAS 2010 compliant.
- Clipper Cruise Line (USA), Travelscope Cruises (UK), and Globalia's Travelplan Cruceros (Spain) ceased operations.
- Glacier Bay Cruise Line, with two ships (*Wilderness Discoverer, Wilderness Explorer*) ceased operations.
- Holiday Kreutzfarhten (Holiday Cruises; *Mona Lisa*) ceased operations.
- Pearl Seas Cruises was created by Charles Robertson, owner of American Cruise Lines, for international cruises.

2008

- CDF Croisières de France (part of Royal Caribbean Cruises) commenced operations with one ship (*Bleu de France*).

- The Bahamian/Danish ship owning company Clipper Group acquired 50 percent of Miami-based ship management company ISP (International Shipping Partners)
- Fred. Olsen Cruise Lines 'stretched' its *Braemar* by 102ft (31m).
- Carnival Cruise Lines' *Celebration* became *Grand Celebration* for Spain's Iberocruceros.
- Almost all cruise lines added or increased their fuel surcharges to future cruises in the face of rising oil prices.
- Spain's Quail Cruises, part of Quail Travel, entered the budget market with one chartered ship.
- African Safari Cruises/Star Line Cruises (one ship, *Royal Star*) ceased cruise operations.
- American Safari Cruises was purchased by Dan Blanchard, the company's former CEO.
- SeaEscape (one ship, *Island Escape*) ceased operations.
- Van Gogh Cruises (Club Cruise) was formed to take over the former Travelscope Cruises, but soon ceased operations after becoming insolvent.
- Golden Sun Cruises ceased operations.
- Orient Lines effectively ceased operations under NCL/Star Cruises ownership.

2009

- Island Cruises was acquired by TUI Travel's Thomson Cruises division.
- Celebration Cruise Line, based in Palm Beach, Florida, started operations, with one ship.
- Cruise & Maritime Voyages (CMV) was founded in the UK following the bankruptcy filing of Germany-based Transocean Tours.

- TUI Cruises started operations with one ship (*Mein Schiff*).
- Thomson Cruises acquired *Costa Europa* on a 10-year charter (with an option to purchase), and renamed it *Thomson Dream*.
- Miami-based Imperial Majesty Cruise Line, which operated short cruises to Nassau, ceased operations, but was replaced by Celebration Cruise Line.
- Royal Caribbean International introduced the world's largest cruise ship – *Oasis of the Seas*. It was the first cruise ship to include a 'zipline' experience for passengers.
- Transocean Tours was declared insolvent. The company was restructured, with the guarantee of backing from Premicon, owners of Transocean's single ship, *Astor*.
- Adriatic Cruises ceased operations. Its single ship, *Dalmacija*, was laid-up in Rijeka, Croatia.
- Elegant Cruises, with one ship, *Andrea*, ceased operations and was declared bankrupt.
- The Panama Canal celebrated its 10-year milestone since its handover to the Panamanian people from the United States.

2010

- New SOLAS regulations prohibit the use of combustible materials in all new cruise ships.
- Cunard appointed its first female captain, Inger Klein Thorhauge.
- The Ocean Village brand disappeared; its two ships (*Ocean Village* and *Ocean Village Two*) were sent to join the P&O Cruises Australia fleet, to become *Pacific Dream* and *Pacific Jewel*.
- UK-based Cruise & Maritime Voyages chartered

Oasis of the Seas, the ship that revolutionized the cruise industry.

Captain Inger Klein Thorhauge in 2023.

Marco Polo and *Ocean Countess* for UK passengers, for child-free cruising from UK ports.
- The UK-based Island Cruises (one ship) almost disappeared, but was rescued by Thomson Cruises.
- NCL America was merged into Norwegian Cruise Line (NCL).
- New Company Ola Cruises started operations from La Guaira (the port for Caracas, Venezuela), with one ship, *Ola Esmerelda* (formerly Fred. Olsen Cruise Lines' *Black Prince*), for domestic cruises only.
- Ocean Star Cruises, a start-up based in Mexico, commenced operation with one ship, *Ocean Star Pacific*. The ship's engines failed on the first day of the first cruise. The ship (ex-*Nordic Prince*) was scrapped in 2014.
- NCL introduced the first abseiling wall at sea aboard *Norwegian Epic*.
- Spain's Quail Cruises (part of the Quail Travel Group) changed its name to Happy Cruises.
- Greece's cabotage law was repealed in September.
- Blue Ocean Cruises was founded in Mumbai, India.
- easyCruise ceased operations (*easyCruise Life* was sold to Blue Ocean Cruises).
- Cruise West (based in Seattle) filed for insolvency in October, after 64 years in business. The company had a fleet of nine small ships.
- Delfin Cruises filed for bankruptcy, after Restis Shipping arrested *Delphin Voyager* for non-payment of the charter/lease agreement. Victor Restis stayed

on the ship in Piraeus for three days. The crew was not paid, and office personnel lost their jobs.
- Alaskan Dream Cruises was founded by David C. Allen, president of Allen Marine Tours, of Sitka, Alaska, and the company purchased two ex-Cruise West ships.
- InnerSea Discoveries (American Safari Cruises) purchased the website and data lists of defunct small-ship cruise company Cruise West.
- The Yachts of Seabourn changed its name to Seabourn.
- Pearl Seas Cruises rejected the newbuild Pearl Mist from its Canadian shipyard.

2011

- Windstar Cruises' parent company Ambassadors International, filed for bankruptcy in April. In May, Windstar Cruises was purchased by the private equity company Whippoorwill Associates and Anschutz Corporation, for its Xanterra Parks & Resorts division.
- Polar Star Expeditions (owned by Karlsen Shipping Company, of Halifax, Nova Scotia) ceased operations after its single expedition ship *Polar Star* (a Swedish icebreaker converted for passenger cruises) grounded in Alaska.
- Caspi Cruises, Israel (two ships) ceased operations in July. One ship, *Mirage 1* (ex-*Southward*) was sold at auction, and *Rio* (ex-*Aegean Pearl*) became notorious because the crew refused to leave because they were collectively owed $600,000 in back pay.
- Conflicts and civil unrest in the Middle East forced Egypt, Libya, and Tunisia port call cancellations.
- Several cruise lines changed their around-the-world cruise itineraries due to pirate action off the coast of Somalia.
- Disney Cruise Line introduced the first ever water coaster at sea. It goes between and through the ship's two red funnels, and is called the AquaDuck.
- Discovery Cruise Line – based in Fort Lauderdale, Florida, ceased operations (one ship, *Discovery Sun*).
- Happy Cruises (part of Spain-based Quail Travel) ceased operations.
- Passat Cruises was founded in Hamburg, Germany.
- *American Eagle* (American Cruise Lines) was withdrawn from service, awaiting sale.
- *Atlantic Star* (Kyma Shipping Management) was withdrawn from service, and laid up in Marseille, France. The ship had steam turbine propulsion.
- *Le Levant* was sold to Paul Gauguin Cruises. *Le Diamant* was sold to International Shipping Partners (ISP/Quark).

- G.A.P. Adventures changed its name to G Adventures, after the U.S. District Court told GAP Adventures it must do so to ensure no confusion with GAP Inc. clothing retailer.
- Sea Voyager Expeditions commenced service with a single ship, *Sea Voyager*.

2012

- Seoul-based Harmony Cruises started operations with one (bareboat) chartered ship – *Harmony Princess* (ex-*Costa Marina*).
- Ambience Cruises started operations with one ship – *Princess Daphne* – on a three-year charter from Classic International Cruises.
- Passat Cruises, with one ship (*Delfin*) started operations, with some of the same management as the insolvent Hamburg-based Delfin Cruises.
- Berlin-based FTI Cruises (established by Dietmar Gunz as Frosch Touristik in 1983) started operations with one ship – *FTI Berlin* (ex-*Spirit of Adventure*, formerly operated by Saga Cruises). From 2014, the ship sailed as *Berlin*.
- *Costa Concordia* sustained severe damage along its port side and capsized close to the island of Giglio in Tuscany, Italy, with the unfortunate loss of 32 lives. As a result, regulatory bodies urgently reviewed safety and evacuation procedures. New procedures were introduced by Costa Cruises in September the same year.
- SeaDream Yacht Cruises introduced a 'Raw Food' menu aboard its two boutique ships. The menus are in conjunction with the Hippocrates Institute in Florida.
- Premier Cruises was founded (by the owners of Volga Cruises) to purchase the boutique-sized *Andrea* (later renamed *Serenissima*), and market the ship in the international marketplace.
- Ponant Cruises was sold to the popular French sandwich-making company Pret a Manger (owned by British company Bridgepoint – formerly NatWest Equity Partners, which also owned Leeds-Bradford Airport, Virgin Active health clubs, and Fat Face clothing).
- Rio Cruises' only ship (MV *Rio* – owned by Eagles Shipholding, and managed by Core Marine, Athens) was arrested in Israel. The ship was sold at auction to Venus Hlfgot, Israel, and renamed *Venus*.
- Three of the five ships belonging to Classic International Cruises were arrested in September (*Arion*, *Athena*, and *Princess Danae*). A fourth ship (*Princess Daphne*) was placed under arrest in October.
- Ola Cruises (one ship) ceased its operations. The ship was not SOLAS 2010 compliant and was sold for scrap.

2013

- Costa Cruises established sub-brand Costa neoCollection for 'longer itineraries and 'slow cruising.'
- Disney Cruise Line introduced trained lifeguards aboard its four ships (the only company to do so).

- *Saga Ruby* was retired. *Quest for Adventure* becomes *Saga Pearl II* in November.
- Lindblad Expeditions acquired Orion Expedition Cruises (one ship, *Orion*).
- Portuscale Cruises purchased four ships formerly belonging to Lisbon-based Classic International Cruises, following the death of its founder, George Potamianos, in 2012.
- InnerSea Discoveries changed its name to UnCruise Adventures in 2013.

2014

- Celebration Cruise Line (one ship) ceased operations.
- Kristina Cruises sold its single ship (*Kristina Katarina*) and was restructured to become a tour operator.
- Coral Princess Cruises was purchased by Kalland Capital Holdings and renamed Coral Expeditions. The company specializes in close-up visits to Australia's The Kimberley region and Papua New Guinea.
- Madrid-based Ibero Cruceros ships *Grand Celebration* and *Grand Holiday* were absorbed into the Costa Cruises fleet. *Grand Celebration* became *Costa Celebration*, while *Grand Holiday* became *Magellan* for UK-based Cruise & Maritime Voyages.
- Costa Crociere (Costa Cruises) signed the notarial deed establishing the transfer of ownership of *Costa Concordia* to the Saipern/San Giorgio del Porta consortium, for demolishing and recycling the wreck.
- Norwegian Cruise Line Holdings entered into a definitive agreement to acquire Prestige Cruises In-

Disney Dream's AquaDuck, the first-ever shipboard water coaster.

ternational, owners of Oceania Cruises and Regent Seven Seas Cruises, including the assumption of debt.

- Orion Expedition Cruises (with one ship, *Orion*) was acquired by Lindblad Expeditions. The ship was renamed *National Geographic Orion*.
- Germany-based Ambiente Cruises ceased operations.
- Germany-based Passat Cruises ceased operations.
- *Deutschland*'s operating company MS Deutschland Beteiligungsgesellschaft (MSDB) filed for insolvency.
- Ponant Cruises was rebranded to Ponant.
- Premicon (PHMSA), the fund that owns the 590-berth *Astor*, operated by UK-based Cruise & Maritime Voyages (CMV), filed for insolvency.

2015

- Carnival Corporation & plc signed a memorandum of understanding with state-owned enterprise China Merchants Group to explore the possibility of two joint ventures – a domestic cruise line for China and turnaround and transit port development.
- Attempts to sell MS *Deutschland* failed, resulting in the cancellation of the ship's itineraries and the dismissal of shoreside staff at Reederei Peter Deilmann's offices, which confirmed Reinhold Schmid-Sperber as administrator of both MS *Deutschland* Beteiligungsgesellschaft mbH and Reederei Peter Deilmann.
- Crystal Cruises was acquired from Japan's Nippon Yusen Kaisha (NYK) by Genting Hong Kong.
- Genting Hong Kong announced a new brand – Dream Cruises.
- Carnival Corporation created 'Fathom' as a venture to attract 'people-to-people' socially-connected cruises from Miami, with a single ship *Adonia* (acquired from the P&O Cruises fleet).
- Harmony Cruises ceased operations (one ship, *Club Harmony*, ex-*Costa Marina*).
- Haimark Line files for bankruptcy. The line's single ship, *Saint Laurent* (ex-*Cape May Light*) was laid-up (Clipper Cruises owns the ship).
- Iberocruceros ceased operations. *Grand Celebration* became *Costa Celebration* for Costa Cruises. *Grand Holiday* became *Magellan* for the UK's Cruise and Maritime Voyages (CMV). *Grand Voyager* was sold to China's Bohai Ferry to become *Taishan*.
- China's HNV ceased operations. The company's only ship, *Henna*, was withdrawn, awaiting sale.
- Portuscale Cruises filed for bankruptcy.

DID YOU KNOW...

...that when sailing from England to the Caribbean in "the old days" a rule of thumb was to sail south until the butter melts, then proceed west?

- TUI Group sold Quark Expeditions to hedge fund Travelopia.
- Viking Cruises' first newbuild ocean ship, *Viking Star*, debuted.
- Voyages of Discovery was delisted from the UK stock market.

2016

- Island Cruises ceased operations. Its single ship, *Island Escape*, was sold.
- Haimark Line declared bankruptcy, and began undoing its Cuba cruise bookings.
- Norwegian Cruise Line (NCL) celebrated 50th anniversary.

2017

- All Leisure Group's cruise division (with two ships, *Minerva* and *Voyager*) ceased operations. Hebridean Island Cruises (part of All Leisure Group) was sold to HP Shipping, and the ship was chartered back to HIC for eight years.
- Ambiente Cruises, with one ship, ceased operations.
- CDF Croisieres de France (a subsidiary of Pullamtur Cruises) ceased operations.
- Fred. Olsen Cruise Line celebrated 170 years of history.
- Fathom, the 'social-conscience' cruise line (part of the Carnival Corporation) ceased operations. Its single ship, *Adonia*, was returned to P&O Cruises.
- Royal Caribbean International and Norwegian Cruise Line introduced trained swimming pool lifeguards aboard their ships.
- Thomson Cruises changed its name to Marella Cruises.
- Voyages of Discovery ceased operations.

2018

- In a ceremony aboard *Celebrity Equinox*, Francisco Vargas and Benjamin Gray became the first same-sex couple ever to be legally married at sea on a major cruise line, according to Celebrity Cruises.
- AIDA Cruises appointed its first female captain, Nicole Langosch.
- SkySea Golden Era Cruises (one ship) folded.
- *AIDAnova* (Aida Cruises), the first LNG-powered cruise ship, debuted.
- American Queen announced it would purchase Victory Cruise Lines and its two ships, *Victory I* and *Victory II*.
- Royal Caribbean completed purchase a 66.7 percent share of Silversea Cruises. Manfredi Lefebvre retained a 33.3 percent stake.

2019

- Mystic Cruises changed its name to Atlas Ocean Cruises.
- CSSC (China State Shipbuilding Corporation), in a joint venture with Carnival Corporation, introduced its first ship, the former *Costa Atlantica*, but Covid-

Cruise ships moored in the UK's Weymouth Bay during the pandemic.

19 intervened and the ship was laid-up.
- *Oriana* was withdrawn by P&O Cruises.
- Saga Cruises debuted its first newbuild, the 987-passenger *Spirit of Discovery*.
- Scenic introduced its first ocean-going ship, the 228-passenger *Scenic Eclipse*.
- India's Zen Cruises (Essen Group, headed by Subhash Chandra) commenced operation with one ship (*Karnika*, ex-*Pacific Jewel*), under the brand Jalesh Cruises.

2020
- *Costa Mediterranea* was transferred to the China State Shipbuilding Corporation (CSSC) as part of a joint venture with the Carnival Corporation. However, Covid-19 interfered with its start-up, and the ship was laid-up.
- The Covid-19 pandemic grounded almost all cruise ships. The first ship affected was the 2,670-passenger *Diamond Princess* (Princess Cruises), built in Japan.
- One by one, the major cruise lines announced suspension of operations, and the temporary mothballing of their ships. The smaller operators followed suit a little later, forced to do so because of the loss of flight availability.
- Aurora Expeditions, however, did not stop, and in April, the company officially announced that 81 (of 126) passengers onboard *Greg Mortimer* had tested positive for Covid-19. One passenger and two crew members were 'medevaced' (by tender) from the ship anchored off Montevideo, Uruguay, and hospitalized in Montevideo. The passenger later died in the clinic. A few days later, 35 crew members tested positive.
- Ports around the world became silent, not wanting to accept cruise ships. Workers were laid off or placed on temporary suspension.
- The stock market value of the major cruise lines was sent in a downward spiral.
- Cruise line presidents who lost their jobs due to the Covid-19 pandemic included Larry Pimentel (Azamara), Rick Meadows (Cunard/Seabourn), and Orlando Ashford (Holland America Line).
- Royal Caribbean Group completed the 100 percent buyout of Silversea Cruises.
- Cruise Saudi (owned by Saudi Arabia's Public Investment Fund) acquired an 8 percent ($430 million) stake in the Carnival Cruise Corporation, essentially as a means to acquire its Seabourn brand.

2021
- Ports around the world turned their noses up at the cruise industry. Any ships trying to continue operations found conditions extremely frustrating, and any passengers testing positive for Covid-19 were turned away from any ports that were still operational.

2022
- Several governments around the world announced the relaxation of restrictions for cruising. Many cruise lines eagerly restarted operations, anxious to kick-start revenue generation and reduce the mountain of debt. Unfortunately, several airlines

canceled flights due to staff shortages (due to Covid-19 and lack of staff), making it challenging for cruise lines to transport passengers to their ships.

- The itineraries of several ships were rejigged due to the ongoing, and worsening, crisis in Ukraine.
- Genting Hong Kong collapsed, mainly as a result of the Covid-19 epidemic. Its Genting Cruise Lines division went into liquidation, as did Crystal Cruises and Star Cruises. Genting Cruise Line's only ship, *Genting Dream*, which debuted in 2016, was owned by a group of Chinese banks under a leaseback arrangement to Genting.
- The former Genting Cruise Lines re-emerged as Resorts World Cruises, with a single ship, *Genting*

20 NOTABLE CRUISE SHIP FIRSTS

1966
- Cunard first marketed the idea of one-class cruising aboard the dual-purpose ocean liner/cruise ship *Queen Elizabeth 2*. The concept was for the ship to undertake transatlantic liner service during the summer months, and sun-seeking cruises during the winter. Passengers shared the same public room facilities.
- Cunard's *Queen Elizabeth 2* (*QE2*) became the first passenger ship to be equipped to navigate by space satellites orbiting 600 miles above the earth.
- The *QE2* also became the first passenger ship to have a theater (seating 531) equipped with the latest simultaneous translation equipment in booths for up to three languages.

1977
- Norwegian Cruise Line passengers became the first to experience a 'private island' visit. It was to Great Stirrup Cay, part of the Berry Islands chain in The Bahamas, approximately 62 miles from Nassau. The island, measuring 268 acres, was purchased from the Belcher Oil Company by the cruise line, and developed for visits by its cruise ships.

1978
- Carnival Cruise Lines introduced the very first waterslide at sea aboard its *Festivale* (built in 1862 for Union Castle Line as *Transvaal Castle*). The small slide was adjacent to the swimming pool, and they've been getting larger, longer, and crazier ever since.

1984
- Princess Cruises' *Royal Princess* was the first all-balcony cruise ship. The ship was named in Southampton by Diana, Princess of Wales, who smashed a bottle of Krug champagne against the ship. The ship was transferred to P&O Cruises and renamed *Artemis* in 2005.

1998
- Disney Cruise Line introduced 'Rotation Dining' aboard *Disney Magic*, with three main restaurants, all with identical seating layouts, and dining times, but different themed decor: Lumierés, Rapunzel's Restaurant, and Animator's Palette (the signature of this book's author is behind one of its walls – inscribed during a visit to the shipyard.
- Disney Cruise Line introduced 'magical portholes' aboard *Disney Dream* for its viewless interior passenger cabins. High-definition cameras were installed on the exterior of the ship, which fed live video to wall-mounted framed 'porthole' monitors.

1999
- Royal Caribbean International introduced the first ice-skating rink at sea – Studio B - aboard *Voyager of the Seas*, with helmets supplied by the ship.

2003
- Royal Caribbean International was the first cruise line to introduce a rock-climbing wall aboard a cruise ship. *Voyager of the Seas* was the first ship to have one.

2004
- Cunard introduced the first Planetarium at Sea, aboard its ocean liner *Queen Mary 2*, with soundtracks narrated by Hollywood stars, including Harrison Ford, Sigourney Weaver, and Tom Hanks.
- Princess Cruises became the first cruise line to install permanent movie screens and projection facilities on the open pool deck of *Caribbean Princess* (although Cunard used to show movies sometimes on deck in warm weather regions aboard *Cunard Countess* in the 1980s, using a portable projector).

2006
- Norwegian Cruise Line was the first cruise line to install a bowling alley, aboard its mid-size ship *Norwegian Pearl*.

2008
- Celebrity Cruises was the first to install real grass, in the 15,000-sq-ft (1,394-sq-m) Lawn Club aboard *Celebrity Solstice*.
- Cunard's *Queen Mary 2* became the first ocean liner to have a joystick on its navigation bridge that can move the ship sideways, or at an angle, or keep station over a fixed spot on the earth, via the use of satellite and wind gauge. The system involves the pods at the ship's aft, and the bow thrusters at the front.

2009
- Royal Caribbean International's large resort ship *Oasis of the Seas* was the first cruise ship to include a 'zipline' experience for passengers, as well as the first surf simulator ('Flow Rider') and first Coney Island-inspired 'boardwalk', also aboard the same ship.

2017
- Norwegian Cruise Line introduced the first open-air go-cart racetrack at sea (just forward of the ship's low-height funnels) aboard its large resort ship *Norwegian Joy*.

2023
- Resorts World Cruises and Tao One, a Singapore-based Taoist non-profit organisation, presented the world's first lion dance competition at sea in March, aboard *Genting Dream*.

Dream. The ship started operations with Singapore as its home port.

- Abercrombie and Kent (A&K), now headed by Manfredi LeFebvre (former owner of Silversea Cruises), purchased Crystal Cruises and its two ocean-going ships (*Crystal Harmony* and *Crystal Serenity*).
- The Royal Caribbean Group purchased Silversea Cruises, following an intense bidding war, adding it to their collection of major brands of Azamara, Celebrity Cruises, and Royal Caribbean International.
- In July, the USA's Centers for Disease Control (CDC) ended the Covid-19 program for cruise ships. Around the same time, aboard Holland America Line's *Zaandam,* over 20 percent of its passengers tested Covid-19 positive!
- Silversea Cruises purchased the 2022-built *Crystal Endeavor* and renamed it *Silver Endeavor.*
- *AIDAprima* (Aida Cruises) became the first cruise ship to successfully use biofuel to provide power to the ship during a port stay. The test took place in the port of Rotterdam, home of the biofuel company.
- In August, most of the large USA-based cruise lines announced the relaxation of Covid-19 rules, allowing passengers from certain ports to sail, with testing requirements eased.
- Also in August, a new French low-budget start-up cruise company appeared. Companie Francaise de Croisieres (CFC) planned to start operations following the refurbishment in February 2023 of the 1993-built *Maasdam*, renamed *Renaissance.*
- New French company Exploris was launched as an expedition cruise line with one ship (the former *Silver Explorer*).
- In September, requirements for Covid-19 testing were discontinued in most countries. However, in the following month, a resurgence in some countries created uncertainty again, and the use of masks increased.
- New start-up company Four Seasons Yachts and hotel group Aman Resorts announced plans to start cruise divisions.
- For the FIFA World Cup soccer (football) tournament in Doha, Qatar, the organisers chartered three ships from MSC Cruises: *MSC World Europa, MSC Opera,* and *MSC Poesia.* It was the first time the World Cup has been held in the Arab world.
- In October, Carnival Cruise Line announced that crew members were no longer required to wear face masks.
- Health and safety measures relating to the Covid-19 pandemic were slowly but surely pushed back during the last few months of the year. Cruise lines removed the vaccine mandate pre-cruise testing for vaccinated passengers, and mask mandates following the CDC's decision to discontinue the voluntary program for cruise ships earlier this year.
- In October, MSC Cruises took delivery of *MSC World Europa*, the world's largest LNG-powered cruise ship, which also incorporated fuel cell technology.

The LNG-powered MSC *World Europa*

- In November, some 800 passengers aboard *Majestic Princess,* were reported as Covid-19 positive after a 12-day cruise from Sydney to New Zealand. The ship was carrying 3,300 passengers, with a crew of 1,300.
- Carnival Cruise Shipping announced the formation of Adora Cruises to serve the Chinese source market.
- Celebrity Cruises unveiled its Virtual Cruise Experience in the Metaverse. Dubbed the 'Wonderverse', it allowed computer users to have a 'see before you sail' experience aboard *Celebrity Beyond*.

2023

- Several major cruise lines increased the amount of their automatic pre-paid and onboard gratuity charges, and some increased their Wi-Fi access charges.
- At the end of a successful Christmas and New Year cruise, passengers aboard Cunard's *Queen Victoria* experienced a two-day dry-docking in Cadiz, Spain, while they were still on board! This was for emergency propeller repairs to the Azipod azimuth propeller system.
- The 184,541-ton *MSC Euribia* made maritime history in June, when it sailed between the shipyard in Saint-Nazaire (France), with guests joining in Amsterdam and Copenhagen (Denmark), prior to a spectacular naming ceremony with film actress Sophia Loren. The ship achieved net zero greenhouse gas emissions – the first cruise ship to do so.

WHAT'S AHEAD

Cruise companies battle it out to provide attention-getting facilities to woo newcomers to cruising.

Over 70 brand-new ships of various size and type are presently scheduled to debut up until December 2027, with some stunning facilities for comfort, smart technology, the latest in propulsion and hybrid propulsion (including LNG – liquified natural gas) and emissions controls, and the elimination of as much plastic material as possible. The creative juices have also been flowing from the interior designers, particularly with social distancing and passenger flow in mind.

In 2022, 18 new ocean-going cruise ships were delivered. These varied from the 106-passenger *Emerald Azzurra* (Emerald Waterways) to the 5,734 passenger *Wonder of the Seas* (Royal Caribbean International).

A Royal Caribbean International *Oasis*-class ship.

Demand for innovation and the latest facilities continues to propel new ship orders, with companies investing billions of dollars in order to compete and update their existing ships' hardware. Experienced passengers expect better-quality food and dining experiences, and simplified cruise pricing. Today, you pay only for what you want – I call it the 'pay-more, get-more' principle.

Ship design constantly evolves, with more streamlining of the shape and the bows (the front). The large resort ships are now assigning more space for outdoor promenades, alfresco indoor-outdoor eateries, and beach-style facilities for warm-weather itineraries.

INTERIOR DESIGN

Progressive spaces is the buzzword to describe multi-use public rooms; many incorporate mood-lighting to create day-to-night venues. With more fire-retardant materials (fabrics and soft furnishings) now certified for marine use, designers have a greater variety from which to choose.

TECH: THE FUTURE IS HAPPENING NOW

Smart tech allows for faster embarkation/disembarkation – a welcome development. Aboard some of the newest ships, you can use your smartphone (or wristband or coin-sized medallion) to open your cabin door, access your account, provide interactive directions, have beverages delivered to your cabin (or wherever you are), make reservations for dinner or shore excursions, buy drinks, buy casino tokens, participate in trivia challenges, and more.

Other tech-rich features have already been introduced, such as facial recognition for embarkation/disembarkation, personal digital assistants, plus voice activation and recognition technology. Looking ahead, cabins may become self-cleaning and robots could handle your laundry, serve your meals, and maybe even wash your hair!

WHAT CHALLENGES LIE AHEAD?

The main challenges ahead for cruise companies include sourcing qualified operations crew and hotel service staff (particularly waiters with a passion for service, not just gratuities) with the right language

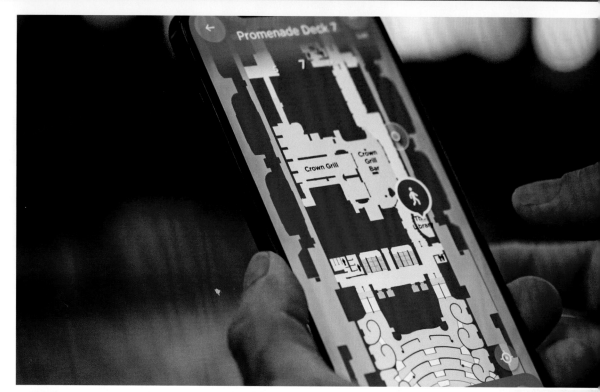

The Ocean Compass App on a Princess Cruise.

skills, improving infrastructure in ports of call, and scheduling destination calls, not to mention the constantly increasing regulatory measures.

WHAT IS THE COST OF A NEW CRUISE SHIP?

The cost of building a cruise ship today varies not only according to size, but also whether it is a one-off design, or one of a series of ships. The first ship in a series of identical or similar ships always costs more, because of the cost of design and development. However, it is not simply a question of the cost to construct the ship, but also the added costs incurred to outfit it with all the required details and special features needed to attract passengers (such as waterslides, race-car tracks, interactive entertainment features).

For example, a small ship such as the 604-passenger *Seabourn Ovation* would cost $250 million; the 928-passenger *Viking Venus* (Viking Cruises) cost $400 million; the 4,004-passenger *Norwegian Bliss* (Norwegian Cruise Line) cost $700 million; the 5,400-passenger *World Europa* (MSC Cruises) cost $1.25 billion; and the 5,734-passenger *Wonder of the Seas* (Royal Caribbean International) cost approximately $1.3 billion.

NONSTOP REFURBISHMENT

Ships no longer in the first flush of youth need cosmetic surgery and regular makeovers in order to keep up their appearance and attract cruisegoers. Items such as balcony doorframes need replacing, suites/cabins need updating, and navigational, safety, and technical machinery needs updating. For example, in 2019 Royal Caribbean International started a three-year program of revitalizing its ships, adding more commonality in practical features and eateries, as well as focussing on its 'private' island day attractions.

Cruise companies often add more cabins during refurbishment, increasing occupancy levels and more revenue possibilities, but reducing the amount of space per passenger (passenger space ratio). Usually, there is no corresponding increase in the number of crew so the crew to passenger ratio decreases. Also, because no new elevators are added, there is greater congestion and increased waiting time.

Companies with older ships tend to sell them off to smaller or new operators.

STRETCH MARKS

'Stretching' older ships may also make sense due to the cost of a new ship and the typical two-year time frame needed for completion and delivery. Even so, refits are expensive, at around $2 million a day, with that figure being pushed up by material, equipment, and labor costs. Silversea Cruises, for example, 'stretched' its *Silver Spirit* in 2018 by adding a new 49ft (15m) mid-section in a 'cut-and-insert' operation at Fincantieri's shipyard in Palermo, Italy. While a 'chop-and-stretch' operation adds more cabins, frustratingly, additional elevators are rarely installed to help with the increased number of passengers.

A Princess Cruises ship in Mahogany Bay, Roatan, an island in Honduras.

CHOOSE WHERE TO CRUISE

Cruise lines visit around 2,000 destinations, from the Caribbean to Antarctica, from the Mediterranean to the Baltic, and from Northern Europe to the South Pacific.

Where can I go on a cruise? As the saying goes: the world is your oyster. On a cruise, destinations come to you effortlessly.

There are more than 30,000 different cruises to choose from each year, and about 2,000 cruise destinations. A cruise can also take you to places inaccessible by almost any other means, such as Antarctica, the North Cape, or the South Sea islands.

Itineraries vary widely, so different companies may offer the same or similar ones simply because they are tried and tested. Narrow the choice by noting the time spent at each destination call (some ships may stay overnight in port) and whether the ship docks in port or lies at anchor – it can take time to get ashore by tender.

CARIBBEAN

There are more than 7,000 islands in the Caribbean Sea, although many are uninhabited. Caribbean cruises are usually destination-intensive, with three, four or more ports in one week, depending on whether you sail from a Florida port or from a Caribbean port such as Barbados or San Juan. This means you could be visiting at least one port a day, with little time at sea for relaxation, so by the end of the cruise you might need another week to unwind. Saying that, you'd otherwise need a private jet to accomplish a destination a day, so a cruise is far better value.

June 10 to November 30 is the official Caribbean Atlantic hurricane season (this includes Bermuda, the Bahamas, and Florida). Cruise ships can change course quickly to avoid weather problems, which can also mean a change of itinerary. When that happens, cruise lines will generally not offer compensation, nor will travel insurance providers.

Geographically, the Caribbean region is large enough to be split into sections: eastern, western, and southern.

Eastern Caribbean. Cruises sail to the Leeward and Windward islands, and might include calls at Antigua, Barbados, Dominica, Martinique, Puerto Rico, St. Croix, St. Kitts, St. Maarten, St. Lucia, and St. Thomas.

Western Caribbean. Cruises sail to the Cayman Islands, Mexico, and Jamaica, and might call at Calica, Cozumel, Grand Cayman, Grand Turk, Playa del Carmen, Ocho Rios, and the island of Roatán.

Southern Caribbean. Cruises might call at Antigua, the Netherlands Antilles (Aruba, Bonaire, Curaçao), Barbados, La Guaira (Venezuela), Tortola, and San Juan.

Cuba, the Caribbean's largest island, which has nine World Heritage sites, holds a fascination for many. Several cruise lines have called there in the past with no US passengers on board.

'PRIVATE' ISLAND BEACH DAYS

Several cruise lines with Bahamas/Caribbean itineraries feature a 'private island' day. NCL pioneered the trend when it bought a former military outpost in 1977. So far, it has spent millions upgrading and adapting its facilities (Silver Cove – a cost-extra section only for adults, was added in 2019).

These islands, or secure protected beaches, usually leased from the owning governments, have all that's needed for an all-day beach party. There are no reservations to make, no tickets to buy, no hassles with

Perfect Day at CocoCay, Royal Caribbean's private island in the Bahamas.

taxis. But you may be sharing your 'private' island with more than 5,000 others from a single large resort ship.

Such beach days are not all-inclusive, however, and command premium prices for some items, such as snorkel gear and mandatory swim vests, rental pleasure craft, 'banana' boat fun rides, floating beach mats, private waterfront cabanas for the day, sunfish sailboat rental, floating foam mattresses, and hammock rental.

Renting an air-conditioned cabana with private deck and sunbeds for the day (or half day) will set you back around $500 (there are just 11 at Harvest Caye, an island base for exploring Belize).

A bonus is that such an island will not be cluttered with hawkers and hustlers, as are so many Caribbean beaches. And, because they are 'private,' there is security, and no fear of being mugged.

The new Thrill waterpark at Royal Caribbean International's CocoCay includes an over-the-water zipline, 13 waterslides, and a wave pool, at extra cost. The most dramatic island experience, however, has much more to do with nature than the beaches. It's MSC Cruises' newly introduced Ocean Cay marine reserve island (on a 100-year lease), developed jointly with the Bahamas government and designed by ecologists at a cost of $200 million, which opened in 2019. One highlight is that the cruise ships stay late in Ocean Cay, so evening events can take place. Another smaller (even more) private island nearby is available to rent for up to 40 persons.

Another 'private beach stop' (it's not really a private island) opened in 2021 at Bimini Beach Club. Virgin Voyages beach club is on the north island of Bimini (Bahamas), created jointly with Resorts World Bimini.

Crown Princess in Glacier Bay, Alaska.

Disney Cruise Line is developing around 20 percent of a property known as Lighthouse Point, in Eleuthera (Bahamas), scheduled to open in 2024. It includes an open-trestle pier that eliminates the need to dredge a ship channel.

Royal Caribbean International has signed an agreement with the government of Antigua and Barbuda for the exclusive use of a half-mile long strip of beach for its Royal Beach Club days; facilities will include private cabanas, swimming pool, and food outlets. It is scheduled to open in 2025.

ALASKA

Alaska is popular (well over one million people traveled by cruise ship in 2018) because it is still a vast, relatively unexplored region, and cruise ships offer the best way to see the state's magnificent shoreline and glaciers. The wide range of shore excursions includes floatplane and helicopter tours, mostly to glaciers and salmon fisheries. Other excursions include 'dome car' rail journeys to Denali National Park to see North America's highest peak, Mt. McKinley.

Pre- and post-cruise journeys to Banff and Jasper National Parks can be made from Vancouver.

There are two popular cruise routes: **The Inside Passage Route**, a 1,000-mile (1,600-km) stretch of protected waterways carved by Ice Age glaciers. This usually includes visits to tidewater glaciers, such as those in Glacier Bay's Hubbard Glacier or Tracy Arm – just two of the 15 active glaciers along the bay's 60-mile (100-km) coastline. Glacier Bay was established in 1986 as a biosphere reserve, and in 1992 the 3.3-million-acre (1.3-million-hectare) park became a World Heritage Site. Typical ports might include Juneau, Ketchikan, Skagway, and Haines. **The Glacier Route** usually includes the Gulf of Alaska during a one-way cruise between Vancouver and Anchorage. Typical ports might include Seward, Sitka, and Valdez.

Holland America Line and Princess Cruises own many facilities in Alaska (hotels, tour buses, even trains), and between them have invested hundreds of millions of dollars; in fact, Holland America Line is Alaska's largest private employer. Both companies take in excess of 250,000 passengers to Alaska each year. Other lines depend on what's left of the local transportation for their land tours. In ports with limited docking space, some ships anchor rather than dock.

With so many cruise passengers visiting Alaska, and several large resort ships likely to be in port on any given day, there's so much congestion in port that avoiding crowded streets can be difficult. Even nature is retreating; with more people around, wildlife is harder to spot. And many of the same shops found in the Caribbean are now found in Alaska.

The more adventurous might consider one of the more unusual Alaska cruises to the far north, around the Pribilof Islands (superb for bird-watching) and into the Bering Sea.

Alaska can be wet and windy, and excursions may be canceled or changed. Even if it is sunny in port, glaciers have their own weather systems and helicopter flightseeing excursions are vulnerable. Take an Alaska cruise in May or August, when it gets darker earlier, for the best chance of seeing the Northern Lights.

GREENLAND

The world's largest island, the inappropriately named Greenland (Kalaallit Nunaat), in the Arctic Circle, is around 82 percent covered with ice – actually compressed snow – up to 11,000ft (3,350m) thick. Its rocks are among the world's oldest, yet its ecosystem is one of the newest.

The glacier at Jacobshavn, also known as Ilulissat, is the world's fastest moving, creating a new iceberg every five minutes. Gunnbjorn Fjeld, the island's highest mountain at 12,000ft (3,700m), is also the highest mountain north of the Arctic Circle. Greenland, which was granted home rule by Denmark in 1978, makes a living from fishing. The island is said to have more dogs than people – its human population is around 58,000 – and dogs are an important means of transport. If your expedition voyage begins in Greenland, you'll probably fly to Kangerlussuaq to join the ship.

ICELAND

Cruising around Iceland, just south of the Arctic Circle, and her fjords is akin to tracing Viking legends across the land of fire and ice. Geysers, lava fields, ice sheets, hot springs, fjords, inlets, remote coastal stretches, waterfalls, snow-clad peaks, and the towering icebergs of Jökulsárlón can all be part of an Icelandic adventure cruise, as can seeking out the elusive Northern Lights (Aurea Borealis) at night. Cruises typically visit the capital, Reykjavík, and Akureyri, the largest town in the north.

CANADA/NEW ENGLAND

These 10- to 14-day cruises travel between New York or Boston and Montreal (northbound and southbound). Ports may include Boston; Québec City, Québec; Charlottetown, Prince Edward Island; Sydney and Halifax, Nova Scotia; Bar Harbor, Maine; and Saguenay, Québec.

The ideal time to sail is during the fall, when the leaves dramatically change color. Shorter five-to-seven-day cruises – usually from New York or Boston – go north to take in the fall foliage.

EUROPE AND THE MEDITERRANEAN

Traveling within Europe (including the Aegean, Baltic, Black Sea, Mediterranean, and Norwegian fjord areas) by cruise ship makes economic sense. Although no single cruise covers every port, cruise ships do offer a comfortable way of exploring a rich mix of destinations, cultures, history, architecture, lifestyles, and cuisines – without you having to pack and unpack each day.

European cruises have become increasingly popu-

A Viking Ocean Cruises ship in Venice.

lar because so many of Europe's major cities – Amsterdam, Athens, Barcelona, Copenhagen, Dubrovnik, Genoa, Helsinki, Lisbon, London, Monte Carlo, Nice, Oslo, St. Petersburg, Stockholm, and Venice – are on the water. It is far less expensive to take a cruise than to fly and stay in decent hotels, paying extra for food and transport. You will not have to try to speak or understand different languages when you are aboard, as you would ashore (unless you prefer to) – if you choose the right ship. Aboard ship you use a single currency – typically US dollars, British pounds, or euros. A wide variety of shore excursions are offered. Lecture programs provide insights into a culture before you step ashore.

Small ships are arguably better than large resort ships, as they can obtain berthing space – the large resort ships may have to anchor in more of the smaller ports, so it can take time to get to and from shore, and you'll probably have to wait for shore-tender tickets. Many Greek islands are accessible only by shore tender. Some companies allow more time ashore than others, so compare itineraries in the brochures; it's probably best to choose a regional cruise line (such as Celestyal Cruises) for these destination-intensive cruises, for example.

THE BALTIC AND NORTHERN CAPITALS

A Baltic and Northern capitals cruise is an excellent way to see several countries in a week or so, and enjoy different architecture, cultures, cuisines, history, and stunning scenery. The season for most cruises to this region runs from May to September, when the weather really is at its best. These cruises typically start from Bergen or Copenhagen, and usually include Stockholm (the gateway to the archipelago is awash with islands and country cottages), Helsinki, and Tallinn.

NORWEGIAN FJORDS

These cruises usually include a visit to Bergen and a tram ride to the peak of Mt. Floyen, with stunning views over the city and harbor on a good-weather day. A highlight could be a visit to Troldhaugen in Bergen – the stunning home (and now a museum) of Edvard Grieg, Norway's most famous composer.

However, it is the sheer scenic beauty of cruising in fjords such as Eidfjord, Geirangerfjord, Hardangerfjord, and Sognefjord that inspires travelers. Typical visits will include Bergen, Flåm, Olden, Ålesund, and Oslo.

AROUND THE BRITISH ISLES

Traveling around the British Isles' more than 7,455 miles (12,000km) of coastline by cruise ship provides a unique perspective. The major sights – and some unexpected gems – of England, Scotland, Wales, the Republic of Ireland, and Northern Ireland can be covered in a single cruise that typically lasts 10–14 days. Although Great Britain consists of thousands of islands, it is compact, and the actual sea time is short. But the range of experiences is vast: the turquoise waters off the Scilly Isles and the coast of Cornwall in England's southwest; the northern highlights in Scotland's more remote, naturerich islands; the laid-back lifestyle of Ireland; the charm and distinctive voices of Wales; and then there are towering castles, incredible gardens, the England of Shakespeare, and, of course, the coastline itself.

CANARY ISLANDS

The sun-kissed Islas Canarias, a Spanish archipelago, and the outermost region of the European Union, are

Pride of America sails past the Na Pali coast, Kauai.

located just off the northwest coast of mainland Africa – they are actually closer to Africa than Europe. With a year-round average temperature of 70°F (21°C), the islands provide a fine setting for a winter escape.

The islands of Gran Canaria, Tenerife, La Gomera, Lanzarote, Fuerteventura, La Palma, and Hierro make up the itinerary of some cruises to the region.

A Canary Islands cruise usually includes a call at Funchal on the Portuguese island of Madeira. Another attraction here is Ponta de São Lourenço, which offers some of the island's most stunning views.

GREEK ISLANDS

Cruises that start or end in Athens (Piraeus is its port) may include visits to some of the most popular Greek islands and destinations such as Hydra, Poros, Mykonos, Santorini, Patmos, Katakolon, Delos, Itea, and Zakynthos.

Small ships sometimes sail through the slender Corinth Canal (you can almost touch the high walls of the waterway), which connects the Gulf of Corinth with the Saronic Gulf in the Aegean Sea. The canal, which is 4 miles (6.4km) in length and just 70ft (21.4m) wide at its base, separates the Peloponnese from the Greek mainland, thus making the peninsula an island.

MIDDLE EAST

The Middle East cruise region includes the Arab countries bordering the Arabian and Red seas, and the southeastern Mediterranean. Countries with cruise facilities and places of historic interest are: Bahrain, Egypt, Iran (one of the author's favorite shore excursions was to the ancient site of Persepolis, near Shiraz), Jordan, Oman, Qatar, and the United Arab Emirates (UAE). You will need to carry your passport with you in almost all these countries.

Travel warnings by government bodies can have an impact on your insurance coverage, so do check for the latest information. Also, check current government advice on how safe it is to travel to specific countries on sites like https://travel.state.gov and www.gov.uk/foreign-travel-advice. Cruise companies, however, always adjust their itineraries as needed to avoid problems.

Abu Dhabi, Dubai, and Jeddah are the main cruise bases, although cruise terminal and handling facilities are still limited. For most Middle Eastern destinations, note that public displays of affection such as hand-holding or kissing are not permitted, and you cannot drink alcohol in a public place. Also, if you fly in with prescription medicines, make sure you have an appropriate, signed prescription, and check current government advice as to what medicines are permitted. The best time to go is November to April.

SOUTH AFRICA AND INDIAN OCEAN

Attractions include cosmopolitan cities, wine tours, wildlife safaris, unspoiled landscapes, and uninhab-

CRUISE LINES: PRIVATE ISLANDS

Cruise line	Name of island	Location	Opened
Carnival Cruise Line	Amber Cove	Dominican Republic	2015
Celebrity Cruises	Catalina Island	Dominican Republic	1995
Costa Cruises	Serena Cay	Dominican Republic	1996
Disney Cruise Line	Castaway Cay	Bahamas	1998
Disney Cruise Line	Lighthouse Point	Bahamas	2024
Holland America Line	Half Moon Cay	Bahamas	1997
MSC Cruises	Ocean Cay Marine Reserve	Bahamas	2019
Norwegian Cruise Line	Great Stirrup Cay	Bahamas	1977
Norwegian Cruise Line	Harvest Caye	Belize	2015
Princess Cruises	Princess Cays	Eleuthera, Bahamas	1992
Royal Caribbean International	Coco Cay	Bahamas	1990
Royal Caribbean International	Labadee	Haiti	1986
Virgin Voyages	Bimini	Bahamas	2021

ited beaches. Itineraries include sailings starting or finishing in Cape Town, along the western side of Africa, with possible calls at Walvis Bay, the Cape Verde archipelago, and the Canary Islands, or cruising to East African ports such as Port Elizabeth, Richards Bay, Durban, Zanzibar, and Mombasa (Kenya). Some cruise lines focus on sailings from Cape Town to eastern islands in the Indian Ocean, such as Madagascar, Mauritius, Reunion, the Seychelles, and the Maldives.

THE MEXICAN RIVIERA

These cruises typically sail from Los Angeles or San Diego, along Mexico's west coast, calling at ports such as Cabo San Lucas, Mazatlán, Puerto Vallarta, Ixtapa/Zihuatanejo, Manzanillo, and Acapulco. They may include a call in the Baja Peninsula, Mexico's northernmost state. Be aware that there has been a considerable amount of crime even in the most visited ports (Puerto Vallarta and Manzanillo) in the past few years. Also, a number of cruise tourists have been caught out by rip tides and rogue waves when swimming in Cabo San Lucas.

PANAMA CANAL

Some cruises take you through the Panama Canal, constructed by the US after the failure of a French effort begun in 1882 with a labor force of over 10,000 but plagued by disease and financial problems – more than 22,000 people died. The US took over the building effort in 1904, and the waterway opened on August 15, 1914, shaving more than 7,900 nautical miles off the distance between New York and San Francisco. The canal runs from *northwest* to *southeast* (not west to east), covering 51 miles (82km) of locks and gates and dams. Control of the canal passed from the US to Panama in 2000.

Between the Caribbean and the Pacific, a ship is lifted 85ft (26m) in a continuous flight of three steps at Gatun Locks to Gatun Lake, through which it travels to Gaillard Cut, where the canal slices through the Continental Divide. It is lowered at Pedro Miguel Locks 31ft (9.4m) in one step to Miraflores Lake, then the remaining two steps to sea level at Miraflores Locks before passing into the Pacific.

Ships move through the locks under their own power, guided by towing locomotives. The 50-mile (80-km) trip takes eight to nine hours. All this effort isn't cheap; cruise ships over 30,000 tons pay a fee of $134 per occupied bed. So, a ship with 3,000 passengers would pay a one-way transit fee of $402,000!

Most Panama Canal cruises depart from Fort Lauderdale or San Juan, calling at islands such as Aruba or Curaçao before entering the canal and ending in Acapulco, Los Angeles, or San Francisco. In 2008, the Inter-American Development Bank approved a $400 million loan to help finance the historic Panama Canal Expansion Program. The new three-step locks feature 16 rolling instead of miter gates, each weighing around 3,300 tons. The visitor center may be included in tours from the port of Colon.

HAWAII AND ITS ISLANDS

The islands of Hawaii, America's 50th state, are a tropical feast. Although relatively close together, they have many differences. For example, the lush, Garden-of-

PANAMA CANAL LOCKS

While the existing Panama Canal locks measure 963x106ft (293.5x32m), with 39.5ft (12m) maximum draft, the new ones are 1,200x160ft (366x49m), with 49.9ft (15m) maximum draft. They allow almost all cruise ships, including Royal Caribbean International's *Oasis of the Seas*-class and Cunard's *Queen Mary 2*, to pass – *Disney Wonder* was the first cruise ship to go through the new locks, in April 2017 – although there is still the problem of a bridge at Panama City not being high enough for some ships to pass underneath. These ships need more than 200ft (61m) of air draft – the height from the waterline to the topmost part of the ship – but the present limit of the Panama Canal is 190ft (58m).

Eden-like Kauai is a world away from Oahu, with its urban metropolis of ever-busy Honolulu. The two parts of the Big Island, Kona and Hilo, are really opposites.

Several cruise lines feature Hawaii once or twice a year, usually on Circle Pacific or special sailings, but only one ship is allowed to cruise in the state year-round: Norwegian Cruise Line's US-flagged *Pride of America*. Note that anything purchased aboard, including drinks, is subject to Hawaii sales tax, although this doesn't apply to ships registered outside the US.

SOUTH AMERICA

Cruises around Cape Horn between Santiago or Valparaíso in Chile and Buenos Aires in Argentina (with Patagonia and the magnificent Chilean fjords in between) are increasingly popular. The optimum season is November to March, and most cruises last 14 days. However, operating costs are high, because several countries are involved. Pilotage charges, for example, are among the highest in the world. Chile and Peru require compulsory tugs (extra cost). Steep charges for provisioning and supplies, visa complexities, and infrastructure issues also push up the cost.

Sailing southbound, ports might include Puerto Montt (Chile), Punta Arenas (Chile), and Ushuaia (Argentina), the world's southernmost city and the starting point for many expedition cruises to the Antarctic.

Coming up the continent's east coast, ports may include Puerto Madryn (Argentina) and Montevideo (Uruguay). Slightly longer itineraries might include a call at Port Stanley in the Falkland Islands.

A few cruise lines also operate seven-day cruises from Rio de Janeiro, Brazil – mainly for Brazilians, who typically love to dance the night away and don't rise until nearly afternoon. Called 'eat late, sleep late' cruises, these are generally aboard large resort ships chartered to local companies.

AMAZON RIVER

The Amazon River is long – around 4,080 miles (6,566km) from close to its source in the Peruvian Andes, to Belém on South America's Atlantic coast – and contains one-fifth of the earth's water supply. Home to a tenth of the planet's animal species and plant life, it has approximately 1,100 tributaries, and is often so wide you can't see the riverbank on the opposite side. Between 400 and 500 indigenous communities live among the Amazon rainforest – the world's largest tropical rainforest, at 5.5 million sq km.

Cruises usually start in the Caribbean from ports such as Barbados and end up in Manaus (or vice versa), although starting in Manaus, with its muddy red-brown water, and ending up in the clear blue waters of the Caribbean may be the more appealing option. Calls along the way may be made in Parintins, Alter do Chão, Santarém, and Belém. Only the real expedition ships, such as Hapag-Lloyd Cruises' *HANSEATIC nature*, *HANSEATIC inspiration* or *HANSEATC spirit* can venture farther upriver from Manaus (Brazil) to as far as Iquitos, Peru, close to the source.

Manaus, located around 1,000 miles (1,600km) from the ocean, was built by barons of the rubber industry. Today, it is a gaudy metropolis (home to over 1.7 million); its opera house, built in 1896, remains a much-visited icon and still stages concerts.

One must-do shore excursion is a rainforest walk with a knowledgeable Brazilian guide to give you an insight into the richest variety of life on the planet. But make sure you have plenty of insect repellent – more than 200 varieties of mosquito inhabit the Amazon Basin.

THE OCEANS ON WHICH WE SAIL...

Oceans – large bodies of saline water – form 71 percent of the surface of the earth and are a major component of its hydrosphere. Some 86 percent of the water we drink comes from oceans, and they absorb up to half the carbon that we humans launch into the atmosphere. The world's oceans form an incredible natural recycling organ.

In addition, there are many seas (smaller branches of an ocean). These are often partly enclosed by land, the largest being the South China Sea, the Caribbean Sea, and the Mediterranean Sea.

In size order, the world's five oceans are:

Pacific Ocean. The planet's largest ocean, the Pacific measures a colossal 60,060,700 sq miles (155,557,000 sq km). That equates to some 28 percent of the earth and means it is equal in size to all of the land area of the earth. It is located between the Southern Ocean, Asia, Australia, and the Western Hemisphere.

Atlantic Ocean. The world's second-largest ocean measures 29,637,900 sq miles (76,762,000 sq km) – a relative puddle compared with the Pacific. Located between Africa, Europe, the Southern Ocean, and the Western Hemisphere, it includes the Baltic Sea, Black Sea, Caribbean Sea, the Gulf of Mexico, the Mediterranean Sea, and the North Sea.

Indian Ocean. Next is the Indian Ocean, which is just slightly smaller than the Atlantic, at 26,469,900 sq miles (68,566,000 sq km). It is located between Africa, the Southern Ocean, Asia, and Australia.

Southern Ocean. Quite a drop down in size is the world's fourth-largest, and also its newest ocean, measuring 7,848,000 sq miles (20,320 000 sq km). The Southern Ocean extends from the coast of Antarctica to 60 degrees south latitude.

Arctic Ocean. Finally, there's the Arctic Ocean, which measures some 5,427,000 sq miles (14,056,000 sq km) – a mere baby compared with its big brothers. What it lacks in size (in ocean terms, that is), it makes up for in terms of outreach, extending between Europe, Asia, and North America. Most of its waters are north of the Arctic Circle.

GALÁPAGOS ISLANDS

These volcanic islands, an archipelago 600 miles (966km) west of Ecuador in the Pacific Ocean, are a microcosm of our planet. Some 13 major and 7 minor islands plus scores of islets make up the Galápagos, which are fed by the nutrient-rich Cromwell and Humboldt currents. The fertile waters can be cold, even on the equator.

The Ecuadorians jealously guard their islands and prohibit the movement of almost all non-Ecuador-registered cruise vessels within its boundaries. The best way to follow in the footsteps of Charles Darwin, who visited the islands in 1835 aboard the *Beagle*, is to fly to Quito and cruise aboard an Ecuadorian-registered vessel.

The government of Ecuador set aside most of the islands as a wildlife sanctuary in 1934, while uninhabited areas were declared national parks in 1959. The national park includes approximately 97 percent of the islands' landmass, together with 20,000 sq miles (52,000 sq km) of ocean. The Charles Darwin Research Station was established in 1964, and the government created the Galápagos Marine Resources Reserve in 1986.

The Galápagos National Park tax is $100 (children aged 2–12 pay $50), plus $10 for an Immigration Control Card, which must be obtained before you travel. Smoking is prohibited on the islands, and no more than 50,000 visitors a year are admitted. Part of the tax is used to finance conservation. No ships can visit most islands more than once in a 14-day period. Some cruise lines require vaccinations for cruises that include Ecuador, although the World Health Organization does not. In 2019, the 100-passenger Celebrity Cruises' *Celebrity Flora* – a new ship specially designed and built for the Galápagos experience debuted, and in 2021, Silversea Cruises' *Silver Origin* followed.

AUSTRALIA AND NEW ZEALAND

Australia and New Zealand offer a wealth of cruising possibilities, with a growing number of port cities attracting cruise ships. Apart from the major destinations, such as Sydney, Melbourne, Brisbane, and Perth (Australia), and Auckland, Christchurch, and Wellington (New Zealand), there are numerous smaller destinations, such as Adelaide, Cairns, and the Great Barrier Reef.

Then there's Tasmania's Hobart and the stunning former penal colony of Port Arthur – Tasmania's official top tourist attraction, renowned for its beautiful grounds. Scenic cruising along Tasmania's coastline is glorious, particularly in the area such as Wineglass Bay and Great Oyster Bay. The best time to go is November to March, ie summer in Australasia.

The extraordinarily beautiful Kimberley region, in Australia's Northwest Territories, essentially in the area between Broome and Darwin, is a must for chasing waterfalls (particularly the King Cascades Waterfall on the Prince Regent River), and coral reefs. The best

Passengers encounter a giant tortoise in the Galápagos Islands.

time to go is in April or May, after the rainy season, for the best waterfall action (as well as fishing and mud crabbing). Landings are by Zodiac inflatable rubber craft or by helicopter for a visit to the sandstone formation of the 350-million years old Bungle Bungle Range.

ASIA

With such a rich tapestry of different countries, cultures, traditions, food, and sights to see, Asia should be high on the list of places to visit for the inquisitive traveler, and what better way to do this than by cruise ship. China, Japan, Indonesia, Malaysia, Singapore, Thailand, and Vietnam can all be visited by cruise ship. Indeed, 'marquee' ports such as Singapore, Yokohama, and Bangkok are all good points from which to join your cruise. The region has so much to offer that it is worth taking a cruise of 14 days or longer to discover some of the most fascinating destinations. Avoid September and October, however, because this is typhoon (hurricane) season. During the winter season, most ships move south to the Australia and New Zealand.

SOUTH PACIFIC

The region is large, and so are the distances between island groups. Still, the area has inspired many people to travel to them to discover the unique lifestyle of its indigenous peoples. The region encompasses Tahiti and her islands in French Polynesia, the Marquesas, Trobriand, Pitcairn, and Cook Island groups, among others – like string of pearls. Some magical names come to mind – Bora Bora, Moorea, Easter Island, Fiji, and Tonga.

SHIP AS A DESTINATION

While a cruise takes people to incredible places, large resort ships entice people to stay on board by creating floating mini-cities packed with entertainment and dining venues.

Wonder of the Seas debuted in 2022 to become the world's largest cruise ship – surpassing *Symphony of the Seas* by being one meter longer, with a greater tonnage measurement, and even more passengers! Large Resort Ships (LRS) are simply mini-cities packed with entertainment, multiple activity and sports centers for families with children, stunning water parks with towering waterslides and thrilling rides, multi-level atriums, many dining choices, spas and fitness facilities, and a huge range of accommodation – priced according to size, grade and location. In fact, there is so much choice, there's hardly any time left to even think about going ashore.

Your onboard time is increasingly reliant on your smartphone, sensor-enabled or wearable device to guide you and 'personalize' (control) your vacation experience, so there could be less contact with the service crew than in years gone by.

Suggestion: skip a port and stay on board, and you can avoid long lines and irritating tender ticket operations when going ashore independently or for shore excursions, and security and health screening when coming back on board. And, voilà, a more relaxing (this is a relative term aboard a large resort ship) experience – and finally time to sit and read a good book or two. Naturally, this option may be best for regular passengers who have 'been there, done that'.

Large resort ships can also be a good choice for anyone with impaired mobility who wants to travel in comfortable surroundings, with multiple dining choices, entertainment options, and medical facilities close at hand. However, some large resort ships have somewhat disjointed layouts, so it's wise to check the deck plan carefully, or speak to your specialist booking agent or the cruise line directly, to make sure it is suitable for you.

Large resort ships have many restaurants, eateries, and casual food venues. These provide a chance to try a range of cuisines, although some may incur extra charges. The ships will typically have a steakhouse or *churrascaria* (for steaks and grilled seafood), an Italian restaurant, and an Asian venue. Other restaurants may specialize in Indian, or Japanese-style (sushi bar and teppanyaki grill) food; some ships feature delis and fast-food outlets, including burger bars, pizzerias, cake and ice cream shops. One popular trend is for extra-cost fish and seafood venues, with fishmonger-style displays of fish and seafood on crushed ice. There may also be supper clubs, usually with entertainment such as dinner and a show.

It was Royal Caribbean International who, in 2009, introduced the then-revolutionary *Oasis of the Seas*, the largest cruise ship in the world at the time and the first to measure over 200,000 tons, carrying around 5,408 vacationers at double occupancy. Why revolutionary? Well, because the ship's beam (width) was increased to 65m (213ft), which allowed for a split, V-shaped aft superstructure. It also meant that the ship could be taller, increasing the amount of usable space. Designers then created seven different 'neighborhoods,' including a large indoor Royal Promenade as the central focal point – like a high street. In effect, the ship became a 'mobile resort vacation' for families. And so, the large resort ship became the destination.

Symphony of the Seas' **Central Park.**

Pride of America's **Washington Library.**

THE BOAST

Companies with large resort ships constantly try to generate media interest through boasts of ships with the 'largest day bed at sea,' 'the longest waterslide at sea,' 'the only ice rink at sea,' or 'the longest indoor promenade.' This may be true (at least for a few months), but it merely invites competition to see who can add more gizmos, develop more tech, and create more media hype in the tabloid newspapers and weekend sections, as well as online.

A recent trend is to include an open promenade deck; many cruise ships built before 2010 considered them an unnecessary waste of space and a throwback to the ocean liner era and transatlantic crossings. However, the whole wraparound deck is not always dedicated solely to walking, because it often also acts as an extension of indoor-outdoor dining venues. While this is good in fine weather conditions – and a welcome relief to the busyness and noise of the pool deck – it is not so practical when cruising in cooler climates such as Alaska. A few sunloungers may also be strewn around the promenade deck.

FLOATING CITIES

A typical 5,000-passenger ship might include the following facilities:

POOL AND ACTIVITY DECKS

Most large resort ships have them: huge waterparks on an upper outer deck (often called a lido or pool deck) that are gallons of fun in the sun, with oodles of fairground bling. For children, special play areas include wave pools and water play areas with huge drench-a-minute water buckets, unexpected water sprays, water pistols, water cannons and other watery elements. For toddlers, a splash pool typically includes some well-known children's characters.

Teens, older children, and adults can enjoy active pursuits such as jungle-style rope-walking courses high above the deck (some ships include narrow 'planks' that take you stepping gingerly over the water – with a safety harness, of course), surf-riding, rock-climbing and abseiling walls, and flying weightless simulators.

Some ships have neat rides such as a SkyRide – aboard one of two bicycle capsules you pedal while suspended on a track above the deck (Carnival Cruise Line's *Carnival Horizon*, *Carnival Panorama*, *Carnival Vista*). Other ships have cost-extra activities such as real go-karts for racing on the largest racetrack at sea (Norwegian Cruise Line's *Norwegian Bliss* and *Norwegian Encore*), or roller-coasters for thrill-seekers (Carnival Cruise Line's *Mardi Gras* has two-seater speed machines hurtling at up to 40mph/60kph). Disney Cruise Line's new ship, currently under construction, will have the longest roller-coaster at sea, at 984ft (300m), with 93 pillars anchored to the deck to support it.

Also, there are (no charge) cliff-hanging ziplines (aboard Royal Caribbean International's *Allure of the Seas*, *Harmony of the Seas*, *Oasis of the Seas*, *Symphony of the Seas*, and *Wonder of the Seas*) that have you scream-zooming (zip-lining) over The Boardwalk and its inward-facing balcony cabins. Aboard *MSC Seaside*, *MSC Seashore*, and *MSC Seaview*, the zipline goes from mast to funnel – some 150 meters – taking you through a series of large hoops as you whizz along. A night-time ride is a real blast!

SIMPLE PLEASURES

In the days of the ocean liners (from the 1920s to 1960s), there were few facilities outdoors other than a promenade deck for strolling, with shuffleboard and ring toss about the extent of it. Indoor promenades were often provided, simply because of the amount of wind experienced on the North Atlantic crossing from the Old World to the New World.

Ships built specifically for cruising in warm-weather areas in the 1970s began adding more outdoor facilities to cater to the growing number of families with children. Considered the most eye-catching, innovating item at the time was the introduction of a rock-climbing wall aboard a *Voyager of the Seas*-class ship in 1999.

The most popular attractions for many (whether child, teen, or adult), however, are the waterslides. These are either a body slide (where you slide down a tube with the power of the water swooshing you along), a tube slide (where you sit in an innertube and are carried away by the water), a drop slide (where you feel like you have the floor swept out from under you), or a bowl slide (where you are whizzed around a huge bowl before being emptied out onto a long open tube).

Aboard *Norwegian Epic*, for example, you sit on an inflatable inner tube and plummet down a short tube slide before emerging into a large, highly colorful open-to-the-skies bowl, which speeds you round and round, getting closer to the center of the bowl, from where you are sucked down an enclosed tube only to splash out at the end of the slide. It's a 200-ft (60-m) ride and a great experience... screaming is optional)!

Carnival Cruise Line, Norwegian Cruise Line also have vertical drop waterslides (some ships) where the floor drops out from under you and you power down and around, with see-through panels that let you catch a glimpse until you are flushed out at the end. Meanwhile, aboard many Royal Caribbean International ships, you'll find The Ultimate Abyss – a 100-ft (30-m) vertical drop waterslide as you plummet downwards through 10 decks in a heart-stopping 13 seconds. But aboard *MSC World Europa*, a similar 'dry slide' drops you down an amazing 11 decks, constantly twisting and turning.

Arguably, the most extensive waterpark/pool deck innovations can be found aboard the ships of Carnival Cruise Line, MSC Cruises, Norwegian Cruise Line, and Royal Caribbean International – and, almost all the attractions are free. Note that aboard some large resort ships, various facilities may not be available on port days. Therefore, it's important to choose the right ship and itinerary that balances port days with sea days.

The end result, however, has been an invasion of what used to be simple sunbathing and pool areas – although swimming pools and hot tubs often take up lots of space, with little left for lounging – and sun-loungers get crammed together in long rows. This is particularly true aboard ships that feature a pay-extra 'retreat' (or 'sanctuary') for adults, usually positioned at the front of the ship, with its own pool(s), hot tubs, bar, eatery, and open and shaded lounging areas.

LIBRARIES

One common feature of destination ships is a library – in fact, this is the most popular room for passengers aboard the Cunard ocean liner *Queen Mary 2*, whose superb library contains over 8,000 books, in several languages. Some large resort ships have libraries and comfortable chairs for reading, but others don't be-cause, for many cruise companies, a library is a non-revenue area. The companies with libraries (or 'lifestyle lounges' that usually include a coffee shop) are: Holland America Line, MSC Cruises, Norwegian Cruise Line (but not *Norwegian Bliss*, *Norwegian Breakaway*, *Norwegian Encore*, *Norwegian Getaway*, or *Norwegian Joy*), Princess Cruises, and Royal Caribbean International.

ARTWORK UNCOVERED

Large resort ships often have whimsical, eclectic piec-es of art as decorative elements, features, photo op-portunities, and talking points, created specifically for each ship. Some sculptures have beautifully rounded shapes and graceful lines, while moving kinetic sculp-tures or decorative lighting can transform an other-wise sterile atrium (lobby) space. A striking artwork installation often becomes the central focal point, par-ticularly aboard the ships with multi-deck atriums.

One fine example would be the classic car. Indeed, there appears to be a constant connection between Roy-al Caribbean International and cars. It started with the race-red 1964 Morgan convertible sportster (formerly owned by the chairman of Royal Caribbean Cruise Ltd) that appeared on the Royal Promenade of Royal Carib-bean International's *Voyager of the Seas*. The trend took off, and replicas of similar Morgan cars from the 1960s (each in a different color) were also installed aboard *Voyager*-class ships – *Freedom of the Seas* (black), *In-dependence of the Seas* (iridescent blue), and *Liberty of the Seas* (orange). Replicas then appeared on the Royal Promenade of the Oasis-class ships: a red 1936 Mer-cedes-Benz 540K on *Allure of the Seas*; a black Jaguar XK 120 Roadster on *Harmony of the Seas*; a black 1936 Auburn Bobtail Speedster on *Oasis of the Seas*; a rolled-up red VW Beetle aboard *Symphony of the Seas*.

Ships may also house artwork collections from es-tablished or up-and-coming artists. You can even take a step-by-step tour of the artwork and decorative in-stallations in some ships, like you would in a gallery. *MSC Grandiosa*, for example, features the first profes-sionally curated fine-art museum at sea.

Some ships have self-guided art tours – ideal when in port and most passengers are off discovering. This is one of the cultural benefits of cruising aboard a large resort ship.

Note that there are also invasive art auctions (nor-mally not on port days), but these are not items from the interior decor of the ship. Also, the 'art' sold is an eclectic mix of items, usually by a specialist concession, and is of questionable value.

ENTERTAINMENT

Entire 'book' shows feature Broadway/West End musicals such as *Cats*, *Grease*, *Hairspray*, *Mamma Mia*, *Priscilla Queen of the Desert*, and *Saturday Night Fever* aboard Royal Caribbean International ships. Aboard the ships of Disney Cruise Line you could see *Beauty and the Beast*, and *Toy Story*, among others.

Large-scale original production shows featuring 16–20 singers and dancers (including male and female lead vocalists) and stunning backdrops are often better than the shows you might see on New York's Broadway or in London's West End. Some ships also have stunning aerobatic and acrobatic performances to take your breath away.

Aboard most Royal Caribbean International ships, a large ice rink hosts superb ice-skating shows, and the ice rink itself can often be used by passengers for daytime skating experiences and lessons.

Some ships also have comedy clubs, typically for late-night, adult-only comedy. Casinos are also considered entertainment, but aboard most ships, the casino will be closed when docked, as will the shops, depending on the region and port (although it is a requirement in most ports, there is no actual global regulation).

EXCLUSIVITY

Exclusive communities aboard large resort ships are proliferating. These 'gated' areas are for those paying extra to live in a larger suite, with access to 'private' facilities, lounges, and sunbathing areas. Ships that have them include *Carnival Mardi Gras*, *Celebrity Apex*, *Celebrity Beyond*, *Celebrity Edge*, *Genting Dream*, *MSC Divina*, *MSC Fantasia*, *MSC Grandiosa*, *MSC Meraviglia*, *MSC Preziosa*, *MSC Seaside*, *MSC Seashore*, *MSC Seaview*, *MSC Splendida*, *MSC Virtuosa*, *MSC World Europa*, *Norwegian Bliss*, *Norwegian Breakaway*, *Norwegian Epic*, *Norwegian Escape*, *Norwegian Gem*, *Norwegian Getaway*, *Norwegian Jade*, *Norwegian Jewel*, *Norwegian Pearl*, and *Resorts World One*. Two-class cruising – in some cases, multi-class cruising – certainly is back in vogue. However, these gated areas do not include the main lounges, main restaurants, showlounges, and other main public areas.

SPAS

An increasing amount of space is dedicated to spa and fitness centers, with a wide range of facilities and services, including saunas and steam rooms, hairdresser's and barber's, facials, massages, and other body-pampering treatments (including couples' rooms), acupuncture, salt baths, etc. Many ships have whole accommodation sections with private spa access, and spa-themed amenities and decor.

SPORTS FACILITIES

Although it depends on which large resort ship you choose, you may be able to try sky-diving on an iFly simulator, go ice-skating, or take a spin in go-karts. There may be the chance to try your hand on the climbing walls, rope walks, surf-riders, or virtual reality sports (F1 driving in a simulator, for instance).

You may be able to play basketball, go bowling, tee off on the mini-golf courses, or try one of the three

The London-inspired Royal Promenade on *Voyager of the Seas*.

SEVEN REASONS TO STAY ON BOARD

1. Experience the ship and all it has to offer – without the crowds.
2. Enjoy a leisurely start to the day and indulge in a late breakfast (perhaps in bed), because it's your vacation. Try something different: one of the areas, facilities, or activities that you have not been able to experience yet.
3. Make the most of a quieter spa experience – have a body-pampering treatment, often at a discount.
4. Go to the library (assuming your ship has one) and read a book, and relax without even looking at a digital device.
5. Try one of the sports-related activities at a more relaxed pace.
6. Take an uninterrupted self-guided tour of all the artwork that you can't see well when the ship is busy.
7. Take the opportunity to snap photos of the public rooms and other spaces without others getting in the shot.

activities always found aboard the ocean liners of yesteryear – shuffleboard, ring toss, and table tennis. For something gentler there's walking on an open promenade deck that encircles the ship. Afterwards, you could head to a sports bar to watch a good game.

SHOPS

Shopping at sea is a favorite sport for many; the attraction being the marketing gimmick 'duty free,' which is cruise-ship speak for goods sold in a foreign country that have entered that country without the imposition of local import taxes. The idea is that anything purchased would be at a lower price than in your home country.

You'll usually find shops clustered in a group, typically in a boulevard-like setting, or arranged around the atrium lobby decks. Brand names are always popular with shoppers looking for something special or a 'bargain' in jewelry and wristwatch stores. During each cruise, 'special' sales are held – ideal for finding that inexpensive gift for someone, in relative comfort. The shops are not open when the ship is in port, however, due to international regulations.

FAMILIES WITH CHILDREN

Kids have a whale of a time aboard the large resort ships, and some companies have tie-ins with well-known brand names, including characters from the Walt Disney stable aboard the Disney Cruise Line ships; Dr. Seuss aboard Carnival Cruise Line ships; and Lego (think bricks and play walls) and Chicco aboard the ships of MSC Cruises. On a port day, there may be fewer activities, but there will still be plenty for the young ones, and that leaves parents with more me-time.

PORT DAYS

If you decide not to go ashore on a port day (the 'great escape' for most passengers), you'll find you have much of the ship to yourself. Waiting times for popular sports activities will vanish. Selected spa treatments will often be offered at a discount. Lines will disappear from the reception desk, the spa, at the buffet or burger bar (both with crew-served food). Intrusive revenue announcements will be silenced. The casino and shops will be closed, but you're unlikely to miss them for a day.

For a little peace and quiet on the pool deck, however, it might be possible to ask a pool deck supervisor to turn down the volume of the music. Another benefit is you'll get better, faster service should you need anything, and if you want to book another cruise, the sales desk will be easier to get to.

The colorful pool on board *Navigator of the Seas*.

CHOOSE THE RIGHT SHIP

What's the difference between large and small ships? Are new ships better than older ones? Here is the low-down to make sure you select the right ship on which to sail away.

There's something for virtually all tastes when it comes to which ship to choose. Ships are measured (not weighed) in gross tonnage (GT) and come in four principal sizes (based on lower bed capacity):

Large resort ships: 2,501–6,500 passengers (measure 101,001–230,000 gross tonnage). *Think:* double-decker bus (with some seats better than others).

Mid-size ships: 751–2,500 passengers (50,001–101,000 gross tonnage). *Think:* long-distance coach (comfortable seats).

Small ships: 251–750 passengers (5,001–50,000 gross tonnage). *Think:* mini-van (some are executive types; some are more mainstream).

Boutique ships: 50–250 passengers (1,000–5,000 gross tonnage). *Think:* private car (luxury, mid-range, or compact).

LARGE RESORT SHIPS (2,501–6,500 PASSENGERS)

These ships provide a well-packaged vacation (I call it 'Crowd Cruising'), usually in a seven-day cruise.

However, if you meet someone on the first day and want to meet them again, make it a specific place and time; remember that your new acquaintance may always be at a different meal seating.

It is the standard of service, entertainment, lecture programs, level of communication, and finesse in dining services that can move these ships a few points into higher rating categories. Choose a higher-priced suite and the service improves. In other words: Pay More, Get More (PMGM).

Large resort ships are like supermarket sausages – incredibly homogenous. They are also highly programmed. It is difficult, for example, to go for a swim at night – pools are usually netted over by 6pm and sunloungers are stacked and secured, so having champagne delivered to outdoor hot tubs for a romantic late-night celebration is impossible. The flexibility for which cruise ships were once known has gone – victims of company 'policy,' centralised control, and reliance on interactive digital devices. Welcome to 'conveyor-belt' cruising, with few cultural offerings. Also, because there's 'music' everywhere, take some noise-canceling headphones if you want to read a book in a 'quiet' place. If you are in search of seclusion, you can, however, hide out in a private section (at an extra-cost 'retreat'), and only venture out in public when you want or need to.

One notable result of the 2020 Covid-19 outbreak was the fact that the virus easily spread throughout ships (as with any land-based resort), due partly to poor air-circulation (particularly to interior no-view cabins), and partly because large resort ships carry passengers of senior years, many with underlying health conditions.

MID-SIZE SHIPS (751–2,500 PASSENGERS)

These ships suit the smaller ports and are more maneuverable than the large resort ships. Several operate around-the-world cruises and other long-distance itineraries to destinations not really feasible aboard many small ships or large resort ships. It's much eas-

Good signage aboard *Celebrity Reflection*.

ADVANTAGES AND DISADVANTAGES OF LARGE RESORT SHIPS

Advantages	Disadvantages
They have the widest range of public rooms facilities and features, often a walk-around promenade deck outdoors, and more space.	Finding your way around the ship can be frustrating at first, and there are more passengers.
They generally have more dining options.	The itineraries are limited by ship size, and there may be tender ports where you need to take a number, sit in a lounge, and wait... and wait.
The newest ships have state-of-the-art electronic interactive entertainment facilities.	They are floating hotels – with many announcements – and cost-extra items. They are like retail parks surrounded by cabins.
You can expect abundant entertainment, including lavish Broadway musicals and Las Vegas-style production shows.	Finding quiet spaces to read a book is challenging, except in a pay-extra retreat.
There are more facilities and activities for people of all ages, particularly for families with children.	There may be a lack of available elevators at peak times.
Children of all ages will have a whale of a time.	Room-service breakfast is not generally available on the day of disembarkation.
They generally sail well in open seas in bad weather.	You may have to use a sign-up sheet for fitness equipment like treadmills or exercise bikes.
Announcements could be in several languages.	The restaurant staff is trained to provide fast service, so it's almost impossible to dine at leisure.
The large choice of cabins means a wide range of prices.	Food is prepared on a large scale – cooking for 5,000 is not quite the same as cooking for a dinner party of eight.
There will be a variety of passengers on board – good for socializing.	Telephoning room service can be frustrating due to automatic telephone-answering systems.
Floating malls offer shopping opportunities for clothing, watches, and jewelry.	Expect lines for embarkation, reception, buffets, shore excursions, security checkpoints, and disembarkation.
The ships have large spas and extensive body-pampering facilities.	Each evening, deckchairs are taken away, or strapped up, and can't be used.
They have numerous outdoor aqua park facilities, and thrilling rides and slides.	In-cabin music is typically supplied through the cabin infotainment system; it may be impossible to turn off the picture while listening.
There are casino gaming facilities.	Some large resort ships have only two main passenger stairways (three is better in case of an emergency evacuation).

Royal Caribbean's mega-ship *Wonder of the Seas*.

National Geographic Endeavour II in the Galápagos National Park.

ier to find your way around, so less walking is involved, and lines seldom form.

There is a big difference in the amount of space available. Accommodation varies from large 'penthouse suites' with butler service to small interior cabins with no view. These ships will generally be more stable at sea than 'small ships,' due to their increased size and draft. They provide more facilities, more entertainment, and more dining options than smaller ships, although they are principally geared to couples. There is some entertainment but the showlounges are smaller – better for cabaret and small group performances.

THE 20 LARGEST SHIPS

Ship name	Cruise line	Gross tonnage	Passengers	Debut
Wonder of the Seas	Royal Caribbean	236,857	5,734	2022
Symphony of the Seas	Royal Caribbean International	228,081	5,503	2018
Harmony of the Seas	Royal Caribbean International	226,963	5,479	2016
Allure of the Seas	Royal Caribbean International	225,282	5,408	2010
Oasis of the Seas	Royal Caribbean International	225,282	5,400	2009
MSC World Europa	MSC Cruises	215,863	5,400	2022
Costa Smeralda	Costa Cruises	185,010	5,224	2019
Costa Toscana	Costa Cruises	185,010	5,322	2022
Arvia	P&O Cruises	184,700	5,200	2022
MSC Euribia	MSC Cruises	184,541	3,502	2023
AIDAcosma	Aida Cruises	183,900	5,200	2022
AIDAnova	Aida Cruises	183,900	5,000	2018
Iona	P&O Cruises	183,900	5,200	2020
Carnival Celebration	Carnival Cruise Line	183,521	5,374	2022
Carnival Jubilee	MSC Cruises	181,808	5,282	2023
Carnival Mardi Gras	Carnival Cruise Line	181,808	5,282	2021
MSC Virtuosa	MSC Cruises	181,549	4,842	2021
MSC Grandiosa	MSC Cruises	181,000	4,842	2019
MSC Bellissima	MSC Cruises	171,598	4,488	2019
MSC Seashore	MSC Cruises	170,412	3,502	2021

ADVANTAGES AND DISADVANTAGES OF MID-SIZE SHIPS

Advantages	Disadvantages
They are neither too large, nor too small; their size and facilities often strike a happy balance.	Few mid-size ships have large showlounges for large-scale production shows, so entertainment tends to be more of the cabaret variety.
It is easy to find one's way around.	They don't offer as wide a range of public rooms and facilities as the large resort ships.
They generally sail well in bad weather, being neither high-sided like the large resort ships, nor of too shallow draft like some of the small ships.	Most activities will be geared to couples, and solo travelers might feel left out.
Lines seldom form, except on ships approaching 1,600 passengers.	Aboard some ships, bathrooms may be small and cramped.
They appear more like traditional ships than most of the larger vessels, which tend to be more 'boxy' in shape and profile.	There are fewer opportunities for social gatherings.

There are more structured activities than aboard small ships, but less than aboard large resort ships.

SMALL SHIPS (251–750 PASSENGERS) AND BOUTIQUE SHIPS (50–250 PASSENGERS)

Choose a small or boutique ship for an intimate cruise experience and fewer fellow passengers. These are more like small inns than mega-resorts.

Some of the world's most exclusive cruise ships belong in this group – but so do most of the coastal vessels with basic, unpretentious amenities, sail-cruise ships, and the expedition-style cruise vessels that take passengers to see natural wonders and off-the-beaten-track places.

Select this size of ship if you don't need much in the way of entertainment gambling casinos, several restaurants, fitness classes and sports facilities, or waiting in lines for anything. If you want to swim early morning or late evening, or have champagne in the hot tub at midnight, it's easier aboard boutique or small ships than aboard larger ships, where more rigid programs lead to inflexible, passenger-unfriendly thinking.

Most have 'open seating' for dining, so you can sit with whoever you wish, whenever you wish, for meals. Small ships are capable of offering true culinary excellence, with fresh foods cooked to order.

Of course, the smaller the ship, the fewer the facilities and public rooms, and they may not sail as well in open sea conditions; except for the specialist expedition ships, they are best in warm-weather areas. Pools will be small, but some ships carry watersports equipment, launched from an aft platform.

WHAT ABOUT AGE?

A ship's condition depends on the level of maintenance it has received, and whether it has operated on short or longer cruises – short cruises cause more wear and tear. Many passengers like older ships, as they tend to have fewer synthetic materials in their interior decor. It's inevitable that most older ships won't match the latest high-tech hardware, but today's ships simply aren't built with the same loving care as in the past.

ADVANTAGES AND DISADVANTAGES OF SMALL SHIPS/BOUTIQUE SHIPS

Advantages	Disadvantages
Most provide 'open seating' in the dining room; this means that you can sit with whoever you wish, whenever you wish, for all meals.	They don't have the bulk, length, or beam to sail well in open seas in inclement weather conditions.
They provide a totally unstructured lifestyle, offering a level of service not found aboard most of the larger ships, and no – or almost no – announcements.	They don't have the range of public rooms or open spaces that the large resort ships can provide.
They are at their best in warm-weather areas.	Options for entertainment are more limited than on larger ships.
They are capable of offering true culinary excellence, with fresh foods cooked to order.	The cost – this is the upper end of the market, and doesn't come cheap.
They're more like small inns than mega-resorts.	The size of cabin bathrooms (particularly the shower enclosures) is often disappointing.
It's easy to find your way around, and signage is usually clear and concise.	The choice of shore excursion opportunities is more limited.
They provide an 'open bridge' policy, allowing passengers to visit the navigation bridge when it is safe to do so.	Swimming pools will be very small; in fact, they are more like 'dip' pools.
Some small ships have a hydraulic marina water-sports platform at the stern and carry equipment such as jet skis and scuba/snorkeling gear.	Many of the smaller ships do not have balcony cabins because the accommodation decks are too close to the waterline.
They can visit the more off-beat ports of call that larger ships can't.	
When the ship is at anchor, going ashore is easy and speedy, with a continuous tender service and no lines. Access to these less-crowded ports means more exclusivity.	

CHOOSE YOUR ACCOMMODATION

From interior cupboard-size cabins to lavish suites you can get lost in, there are shipboard living spaces for all wallets, but there's more to it than price tag.

Ideally, you should feel at home when at sea, so it is important to choose the right accommodation, even if most of your time in it is spent with your eyes shut. Choose carefully (dependent on your budget, of course), for if you find that your cabin (incorrectly called a 'stateroom' by some companies) is too small when you arrive on board, it will be almost impossible to change it.

Cruise lines designate cabins only when deposits have been received, although they may guarantee the grade and rate you request.

There are four main types of accommodation (with variations on each type, such as those designed for mobility-limited passengers): interior (no-view or virtual-view) cabins, outside-view cabins with a window, outside-view cabins with a balcony (or virtual balcony), and suites (the largest type of accommodation).

CABIN SIZES

Your cabin provides similar facilities to a hotel room, except space. Most cruise companies favor providing large public rooms over large cabins.

Today's ships have more standardized cabin sizes, because they are made in modular form. I consider 193 sq ft (18 sq m) to be the absolute *minimum* acceptable size for a cabin today.

CABIN LOCATION

I recommend an 'outside-view' cabin for your first cruise; an 'interior' (no view) cabin has no portholes or windows, so it's more difficult to get oriented or to gauge the weather, although it's good for anyone who likes a darkened room to sleep in.

Cabins in the ship's center are more stable and tend to be quieter and vibration-free. Ships powered by diesel engines can transmit vibration to aft cabins.

Generally, the higher the deck, the higher the cabin price, and the better the service (a leftover from transoceanic times, when upper-deck cabins and suites were superior).

THE SUITE LIFE

Suites are the most luxurious and spacious of all shipboard accommodation, and typically come with butler service. A suite (in the sense of a 'suite of rooms') should comprise a lounge separated from a bedroom by a solid door (not just a curtain or half-height room divider), a bedroom with a large bed, one or more bathrooms, and abundant walk-in closet and drawer space. The best suites are in the most desirable position and are private, have good views, and the highest-quality bed linen and pillow choice. Some cruise lines inaccurately describe their accommodation as suites (or 'junior' suites), but beware, many are nothing more than large cabins with curtains dividing lounge and sleeping areas.

'Private Enclaves' (exclusive areas) have been created by Celebrity Cruises (*Celebrity Apex, Celebrity Beyond, Celebrity Edge, Celebrity Reflection, Celebrity Silhouette,* and *Celebrity Solstice*), Dream Cruises (Dream Palace), MSC Cruises (Yacht Club), Norwegian Cruise Line (The Haven), and TUI Cruises (*Mein Schiff 1–6,* 'X' Lounge) for occupants of the most expensive suites, in

Premium cabin aboard *Marella Discovery*.

10 CABIN LOCATIONS TO AVOID

Avoid booking a cabin in one of the following spots:

1. Cabins under the pool deck (noise is created by people dragging deck chairs, pool party games, and loud music).
2. Cabins under the exterior promenade deck (noise and thumping from people jogging and walking, or moving sun loungers).
3. Cabins under or above late-night venues such as discos and lounges or bars with music.
4. Cabins adjacent to a self-service launderette (due to noise from machines and people).
5. Cabins looking into a central atrium (they won't be very private) and will be subject to noise from parades, entertainment, and loud music.
6. Cabins with 'obstructed views' (these are often heavily discounted or offered at the last minute and can be noisy).
7. Cabins on a lower deck aft, due to noise from the engines and generators.
8. Cabins forward on a lower deck, due to noise from bow thrusters, or arrival in tender ports when anchors are lowered.
9. Cabins with interconnecting doors, due to noise from your neighbors, and thin walls.
10. Cabins adjacent to crew or service doorways as these often slam shut.

9 THINGS A BUTLER CAN DO

1. Assist with unpacking your suitcase
2. Bring you board games or a pack of cards
3. Supply menus for dining venues and serve course-by-course meals in your suite
4. Arrange a private cocktail party
5. Arrange for laundry/cleaning items
6. Make dining reservations
7. Provide afternoon tea or canapés
8. Shine your shoes
9. Make your spa reservations

'SPA SUITE' ACCOMMODATION

Spa suites – not to be confused with 'thermal spa suites' (comprising sauna, steam room, and herbal showers) found in the spa – are usually located adjacent to it. They often have 'spa-added' features such as a bathroom with window into the sleeping area, bathtub, and mood lighting, and perhaps health teas or herbal infusions. Some cruise lines may include a spa treatment such as a massage or facial, in the 'spa suite' package, and unlimited spa access. Some ships also have a spa-food-menu-only restaurant.

ARE BALCONIES WORTH IT?

Romeo and Juliet thought so. And they're addictive, too. A private balcony (or veranda, terrace, or lanai), for which you pay a premium, is just that. It is a mini-terrace adjoining your cabin, where you can sit, enjoy the private view, smell the sea, dine, or have a massage.

Some private balconies aren't so private, though. Balconies not separated by full floor-to-ceiling partitions don't quite cut it (examples include *Carnival Sunshine*, *Queen Mary 2*, *Seven Seas Voyager*, or *Volendam*), so you could be disturbed by noise from your neighbor.

Many large resort ships have balconies that are too small to accommodate even two reclining chairs; they may have plastic matting or plain painted-steel decking instead of traditional (expensive) hardwood. The average size of a cabin balcony aboard a large resort ship is about 9 by 6ft (2.7x1.8m) or about 55 sq ft (5.1 sq m), but they can measure as much as 30 times that.

Suites with forward-facing private balconies may not be so good, as the wind speed can make them all but unusable when the ship in underway. Examples include *Silver Cloud*, *Silver Dawn*, *Silver Muse*, *Silver Shadow*, *Silver Spirit*, *Silver Whisper*, *Silver Wind*, *Star Legend*, and *Star Pride*. And when the ship drops anchor in ports of call, the noise pollution can be extremely irritating.

For the best in privacy, an aft balcony suite is hard to beat, and some of the largest afloat can be found there – sheltered from the wind, such as aboard *Marina* and *Riviera* (Oceania Cruises).

Note that having a balcony means that space is often taken away from either the cabin or the bathroom,

an effort to insulate their occupants from the masses. The result is a 'ship within a ship' (private enclave with key-card or digital access).

Suite occupants share the rest of the ship with those in lower-priced accommodation. However, all the extras that are included (particularly in Dream Palace accommodation aboard the ships of Dream Cruises, which are far more generous and inclusive than the others) add up to an extremely good deal, and highly recommended. Staying in a suite gets you more (or larger) personal amenities, including well-known brand names such as Aqua di Palma, Bulgari, Canyon Ranch, Clarins, Etro, Ferragamo, Guerlain, L'Occitane, and Therapies (by Molton Brown).

WHAT'S THE DIFFERENCE BETWEEN A BUTLER AND A CONCIERGE?

A butler is a personal attendant who will try to make your stay as comfortable and pleasing as possible. They will attend to packing, unpacking, personal service requests inside your suite (food and beverage items, shoe shine, for example). A real butler will have different clothing for day and evening, including proper 'tails.'

A concierge is helpful for making reservations and bookings outside your ship, such as for restaurant reservations ashore, private excursions, other transportation, car rental, etc. A real concierge wears a special two crossed golden keys lapel pin, noting that they are members of a society called Led Clefs d'Or, founded in Paris in 1929.

which is why bathrooms are smaller and almost none have bathtubs.

One of the most novel balcony additions is found aboard the expedition cruise ships *HANSEATIC inspiration*, *HANSEATIC nature*, and *HANSEATIC spirit*, where two suites have hydraulically extendable balconies with a solid glass floor – so you get the sensation of sitting on or just above the water, and space is not taken away from the interior.

All private balconies have railings to lean on, but some have solid steel plates between the railing and deck, so you can't look out to sea when seated (*Dawn Princess*, and *Sea Princess* are examples). Ships with clear-glass balconies are better (*Aurora*, *Brilliance of the Seas*, *Mein Schiff 1–6*, and *Radiance of the Seas*, for example), or ones with horizontal bars.

Lower deck 'cove balcony' cabins are closer to the waterline, and less expensive; they are private because the balcony is created by cutting a hole directly into the hull instead of being built as part of the cabin module itself. However, the lower section of the balcony is of solid steel instead of glass, as in a regular balcony.

Balcony doors can be heavy and difficult to open. Many ships have doors that slide open (examples include *Norwegian Gem*); a few have doors that open inward (these include *Silver Cloud*, *Silver Wind*, *Star Breeze*, *Star Legend*, and *Star Pride*); some have doors that open outward (such as *Nieuw Statendam*, *Marella Discovery 2*, and *Queen Elizabeth*).

BALCONY-LESS BALCONIES

A 'new' type of balcony emerged in 2018, aboard *Celebrity Edge* (but lacking a mosquito screen, so those pesky insects can come and visit you whenever they want!). Copied from riverships in Europe, it consists of floor-to-ceiling windows in two parts, with the upper section lowered by electric touch button. This creates a 'balcony' like space, but is just a large opening window. The advantage is that it doesn't take space away from the cabin and allows the fresh air in. However, it doesn't work for sunbathers, or for anyone wanting to sit on a (real) balcony and have food, or drinks. In other words, they are 'pretend balconies' that just don't work well for ocean-going cruise ships.

'FRENCH' BALCONIES

A 'French' balcony (also called a 'Juliet' or 'Juliette' balcony) is neither French, nor a balcony as such. It is a full floor-to-ceiling sliding door with a tiny ledge that allows you to stick out your toes and engage with the fresh air, and with railings for safety.

INTERIOR-VIEW BALCONIES

Inwards-facing balcony cabins can be found aboard Royal Caribbean International's *Allure of the Seas*, *Harmony of the Seas*, *Oasis of the Seas*, *Symphony of the Seas*, and *Wonder of the Seas*. These 'interior' balcony cabins overlook one of two 'neighborhoods': Central Park, with its trees and plants, or The Boardwalk, aft (these are simply outside balcony cabins, so if it rains, your balcony *can* get wet). Also, people scream as they career along the Zipline above Boardwalk balconies, so they can be noisy in the daytime. However, when no one is zipping, you may have a view of the sea (and perhaps the acrobatic AquaShow) aft.

BALCONIES THAT LACK PRIVACY

If you choose a Riviera Deck (Deck 14) balcony cabin aboard *Azura* or *Ventura*, for example, you can oversee many balconies on the decks below yours – particularly those on C Deck and D Deck – because they are built out to the ship's sides. It would be unwise to sunbathe or sit naked on your balcony. Not only that, but almost *all* balcony cabins can be seen from the navigation bridge, where the staff members are equipped with binoculars (for lookout purposes).

INTERIOR 'VIRTUAL' BALCONIES

For the latest in interior design, there's the 'virtual' balcony. Royal Caribbean International's *Anthem of the Seas*, *Ovation of the Seas*, *Quantum of the Seas*, *Spectrum of the Seas*, and *Wonder of the Seas* have them, as do many interior cabins retrofitted on *Navigator of the Seas*. They provide an 'outside' feel, featuring 6ft 7in (2m) 'screens' with live video feed from cameras mounted on the front and back of the ship fed through fibre-optic cables. With curtains on either side of the (almost) floor-to-ceiling wall 'screen' (which you can turn off), the 'balcony' is positioned on a forward- or

Seven Seas Explorer suite balcony.

Spa suite bathroom aboard *Europa*.

aft-facing cabin wall. Naturally, these cabins command a premium price.

UPSTAIRS AND DOWNSTAIRS

Some ships have 'loft'-style or 'duplex' accommodation, with a living room downstairs and bedroom upstairs. Examples include *Allure of the Seas*, *Anthem of the Seas*, *Celebrity Apex*, *Celebrity Beyond*, *Celebrity Edge*, *Celebrity Reflection*, *Celebrity Solstice*, *Harmony of the Seas*, *Oasis of the Seas*, *Ovation of the Seas*, *Quantum of the Seas*, *Queen Mary 2*, *Spectrum of the Seas*, *Symphony of the Seas*, and *Wonder of the Seas*.

FAMILY CABINS

Some large resort ships have suites/cabins that can sleep up to 14, but most 'Family' cabins sleep 3 or 4 (typically with twin- or queen-sized beds for adults, and a pull-out sofa bed for the youngsters). In busy school vacation periods these tend to sell quickly, so planning ahead is important.

An alternative is to look for cabins with interconnecting doors – good for parents with teenagers, for example; the door can be locked from both sides.

SOLO TRAVELER CABINS

Solo travelers have long been considered an afterthought by most cruise lines, although some firms are now beginning to appreciate how useful cabins specifically designed for solo travelers can be. Instead of turning away business, companies such as Cunard have retrofitted their ships with several cabins for solos. Interestingly, the now-retired *Queen Elizabeth 2* (or *QE2*, as she was known) had 132 cabins for solo travelers.

Norwegian Cruise Line has approximately 100 well-designed, very small 'studio' cabins for solo travelers aboard *Norwegian Bliss*, *Norwegian Breakaway*, *Norwegian Epic*, *Norwegian Escape*, *Norwegian Getaway*, and *Norwegian Joy*. Saga Cruises is another company with numerous (larger) solo traveler cabins. Some cruise lines offer their double-occupancy cabins for solo travelers, at a special price.

If you are traveling with friends and in a party of three or more and don't mind sharing a cabin, you'll save money, so can choose a higher-grade cabin.

HOW MUCH?

Accommodation cost is related to size, location, facilities, and services. It may be better to book a low-grade cabin on a good ship than a high-grade cabin on a poor ship, depending on your budget.

CABIN NUMBERS

Nautical tradition aboard ships dictates that even-numbered cabins should be on the port side (left when looking forward; the same as the lifeboats), and most companies follow this rule. Some companies however – including Celebrity Cruises, MSC Cruises, Saga Cruises, and TUI Cruises – have odd-numbered cabins on the port side.

Meanwhile, aboard Royal Caribbean International's *Freedom of the Seas*, *Independence of the Seas*, and *Liberty of the Seas*, outside cabins have even numbers, and interior (no-view) cabins have odd numbers. But AIDA Cruises places both even- and odd-numbered cabins on the same side, whether port or starboard side. The admiralty would never approve!

FACILITIES

The standard is a small private bathroom with shower, washbasin, and toilet. Higher-grade cabins and suites may have full-size bathtubs and more space. Some have a whirlpool bath and/or bidet, a hairdryer, and more space. Most cabins come with the following: flat-screen television 'infotainment' system or television (regular satellite channels or closed circuit); two beds (possibly, another one or two upper berths), or a double, queen- or king-size bed (some twin beds can convert to form a double/queen). Depending on cabin size, they should also have: a chair, or chair and table, or sofa and table, or in higher grades, even a separate lounge/sitting area; telephone (for inter-cabin or ship-to-shore calls); refrigerator/mini-bar (higher grades); electrical outlets (110 and/or 220 volts) and USB data sockets; vanity/desk unit with chair or stool; personal safe; closet and drawer space, plus under-bed storage for suitcases; bedside night stand/table unit.

Some older ships may have upper and lower berths only. A 'berth' is a nautical term for a bed held in a wooden or metal frame. A 'Pullman berth' tucks away out of sight during the day, usually into the bulkhead or ceiling. You climb up a short ladder at night to get into an upper berth.

AND, SO TO BED

Bed frames are usually made of steel or tubular aluminum for fire-protection purposes, although some older ships may have (flame-retardant) wood frames. Some have rounded edges, while others have square (sharp) edges (watch your legs on these), particularly when the mattress is contained within the bed frame.

Some beds have space underneath for luggage, while others have drawers fitted for additional storage space, so your luggage has to be stored elsewhere in the cabin.

MATTRESSES

These can be hard, semi-hard, or soft. If your mattress is not to your liking, ask your cabin steward if it can be changed – most ships have spares. Bed boards are also usually available to make the bed firmer.

Some cruise lines provide simple foam mattresses, while others place more emphasis on providing extra support and comfort. Regent Seven Seas Cruises, for example, provides a custom-designed 'Suite Slumber Bed' – a plush euro-top mattress capped with a dou-ble layer of memory foam and dressed in the finest linens to assure a refreshing sleep.

There are differences between mattress sizes in the UK, US, and Europe, depending on which supplier is used when a ship is outfitted or when bed frames and mattresses are replaced.

DUVETS

Down duvets, fine bed linens, and plush mattresses are what superior sleeping environments are all about. Duvets are usually goose down or cotton filled, and range from 3.5 togs (thin) to 13.5 togs (thick), the tog rating being the warmth measurement. Anyone with allergies should try a spun down duvet, which is filled with non-allergenic polyester microfiber.

Duvet covers can be for single, double, queen-, or king-size mattresses. If you request a queen-size bed configuration, request an overlay, otherwise there may be a crack between the separate beds (not all ships have these).

Duvet covers and sheets of 100 percent cotton (up to 400 thread count) are best, but may be more difficult for a ship's laundry to handle.

PILLOWS

Many ships have a 'pillow menu' in suite-grade accommodation, with a choice of several different pillow types, including hop-filled or hypoallergenic, goose down, Hungarian goose down (considered the best), silk-filled, body pillow (as long as an adult body, providing full support at to the head and neck at the top and, lower down, to legs and knees), Tempur-Pedic, isotonic or copycat memory foam.

BEDSIDE READING LIGHTS

Some cruise lines say they have bedside reading lights, but these may be LED or halogen lights embedded in the ceiling, which are not as good as reading lights, and neither are table lamps beside the bed (often fitted with low wattage bulbs). The best reading lights are those fitted on a flexible arm beside the bed.

STATEROOM VS CABIN EXPLAINED

In the 1830s, the steamer *George Washington* had 26 cabins, and, since there were then 26 states in the United States union, each room was given the name of a state. Since that time, US-based companies have called their cabins 'staterooms.' In most other countries, 'stateroom' means 'rooms of state.'

10 REASONS WHY BALCONIES ARE POPULAR

1. You can access fresh air.
2. You can see the sea.
3. You get the maximum amount of natural light.
4. You can have tea/coffee or breakfast outside.
5. You can see what the weather is like, to decide how to dress.
6. You may see the stars (and shooting stars) at night.
7. You can sunbathe in private – assuming that the ship is in the right position and your balcony isn't overlooked.
8. You can escape from the noise of entertainment areas.
9. You can take pictures of the sea from within your cabin.
10. You can boast about it to your friends.

Lego Experience on an MSC cruise.

CRUISING FOR FAMILIES

Cruising can be a great vacation for families, but be sure to choose the right cruise line and ship for your needs.

A cruise really does suit families with children, and can be the easiest and most convenient way to enjoy some time away from the stresses and strains that having a young family can bring. Cruising with a multi-generational family can also be organised seamlessly.

Ships provide a safe, virtually crime-free, contained environment, and for younger kids, there are so many fun things to entertain them (particularly aboard the newest ships); for older children and teens, there is plenty to do, giving them a certain level of independence, which always goes down well. Planning family vacations can be complicated at the best of times, with so many details to take care of. But getting your kids – particularly tweens and teenagers – involved in the planning process can work wonders when choosing the right ship, facilities, and activities together. Establish safety guidelines, and rules, before you go. Here's what you need to know.

FAMILY-FRIENDLY SHIPS

The newest and largest resort ships, such as *MSC World Europa* (MSC Cruises) and *Wonder of the Seas* (Royal Caribbean International) have outstanding facilities for children of all ages, including extensive water parks with slides, adrenaline-pumping dry-slides, rope-climbing courses, mini-golf, and other neat things. With dining, entertainment, sporting and active outdoor areas, wellness facilities, and more included, it making a cruise an idea family vacation.

AIDA Cruises, Carnival Cruise Line, Disney Cruise Line, Dream Cruises, MSC Cruises, Norwegian Cruise Line, Princess Cruises, Royal Caribbean International, and TUI Cruises employ teams of trained counsellors, with special programs off-limits to adults. Other cruise lines may have simple token programs during the major school holidays, with limited activities and few general staff allocated to look after children. Check whether the cruise line offers the right facilities for your needs. Many ships have full programs for children during days at sea, but these may be limited when the ship is in port. If the ship has a playroom, ask if it is open and supervised on every day of the cruise. All programs are included in the cost of your cruise.

Carnival Cruise Line, Disney Cruise Line, MSC Cruises, Norwegian Cruise Line, Princess Cruises, and Royal Caribbean International provide pagers (or wrist bands) for parents; others provide them only for special-needs children. In-cabin telephones aboard some ships can be set to 'in-cabin listening,' allowing parents to call their cabin from any of the ships' telephones and eavesdrop.

Children get colored bracelets to wear at all times. These identify which muster station they belong to in the event of an emergency, and show which activity programs they are enrolled in.

Some youth programs allow older children to sign themselves out of youth centers, if authorized to do so by a parent. This makes it easy for children to meet family members somewhere – by the pool or restaurant, for example – or the cabin. If authorization isn't granted, only designated adults can sign them out of programs, typically by showing some ID or by providing a password created at the beginning of the cruise.

The pool on board Royal Caribbean's *Navigator of the Seas*.

Disney Cruise Line, Norwegian Cruise Line and Royal Caribbean International have trained lifeguards during pool open hours. Other cruise lines expect parents to watch their children when using a ship's swimming pools. For example, in 2015, an eight-year-old boy drowned in the pool aboard *Liberty of the Seas* because of a lack of parental supervision.

Note that a ship's medical department is not set up for pediatric services, as cruise ship doctors are generalists, not specialists.

Aboard one of the ships catering to more international passengers – such as Costa Cruises, Dream Cruises, or MSC Cruises – your youngsters may find themselves with children speaking other languages. This may be a little confusing for them at first, but in most cases, it will prove to be an adventure in learning and communication that adds immensely to their vacation.

AGE GROUPS

Cruise lines generally divide young cruisers into distinct age groups. As an example: infants (3 months up to 3 years); children (3–10); pre-teens (11–12); and teens (13–17).

CRUISING WITH BABIES AND INFANTS

Many new or recent parents want to take their babies with them when they cruise. Check the minimum age requirements for your chosen cruise line; they vary according to the cruise, length, and region. By choosing the right ship, a cruise with baby should be much more enjoyable than most package holidays on land. The biggest attractions include only having to pack and unpack the baby things once, plus the convenience of having everything (food, entertainment, activities, etc.) absolutely on hand. There may also be a crèche/nursery, plus there's always room service, if you prefer to dine in your cabin.

Bottle warmers are available for babies, as are bottle sterilizers – upon request – so there is no need to bring your own. Highchairs are also available upon request for meal times. For babies already on solids, menu items can be pureed and blended for them.

Check the ship's itinerary to see whether the vessel docks alongside in each port. This is easier than being at anchor, when shore tenders must be used; these may require you to go down a rigged ladder to a small boat waiting to take you ashore, which is not easy with an infant in tow.

Check with the cruise line or your booking agent before you book as to what equipment is available, and whether any of it needs to be pre-booked (a refrigerator for milk, for example). Some cruise ships will lend you cribs, strollers (some charge a rental fee), bouncy seats, books, toys, cots, bed guards, and other items.

An inexpensive umbrella-type stroller is invaluable in airports, aboard ship (Carnival Cruise Line offers them for rent aboard ship), and ashore. Small is better because it takes up less space in cabins, elevators, and buffet areas. It will be easier to manoeuvre at the cruise terminal, and for negotiating open deck areas.

Consider taking a car seat for flights, buses, and taxis, and a sling-style or papoose baby carrier, or a backpack, for hands-free carrying when negotiating stairways, and shore outings.

Request a crib as soon as possible and book early (ships carry only a limited number). However, while it is fine to order cribs and camp beds, you'll soon find there's little room to move about, so book as large a

---

SUGGESTED PACKING LISTS FOR INFANTS

Traveling by plane? Suggested items for your carry-on bag:
Diapers (nappies) or pull-ups and changing pad.
Antibacterial wipes (take plenty).
Snacks.
Drinks (small).
Small toys and books to keep your infant happy.
Pacifiers (dummies) and bibs (if your child needs them).
A camera (or smartphone).

Suggested items for your checked luggage:
Diapers (nappies) or pull-ups, deodorized disposal bags, and wipes, if your child is not potty-trained.
Any toiletries your infant may need, including special baby soap and shampoo (these are not provided by cruise lines), lotions, sunscreen, toothbrush, and toothpaste.
Outlet plugs for childproofing.
Clothes.
Bibs.
Pacifiers (dummies).
First-aid kit and any medication such as pain relievers, fever reducers, and the name and contact details of your infant's pediatrician (for comfort).
Plastic bags for any snacks for shore excursions.
Ziplock bags – useful for soiled clothing.
Portable potty seat (if your infant is potty-trained).
Swim diapers.
Swim vest: make sure it's of an approved type.
Sunglasses and sun hat (if your cruise is in or to a warm weather area).
Bottles and sip cups: cruise lines don't provide these. They can be washed in your cabin, so a little dish detergent and bottle brush could be useful.
Formula: ready-to-feed variety is convenient but bulky.
Alternatively, bring powder and buy bottled mineral water from the ship's bar (a more expensive option).
Utensils.
Inflatable toys such as beach balls and zoo animals are inexpensive and easy to pack (you won't be able to borrow toys from the ship's playroom).
Picture books to keep them amused.

In the It's A Small World Nursery aboard *Disney Dream*.

cabin as your budget allows. If you have a non-walker, consider a balcony cabin to give you more breathing space – you can relax on the balcony, while your infant naps in the cabin.

Disposable diapers (nappies), wipes, and sterilizing fluid can be purchased aboard most family-friendly ships, but they are expensive, so it may be wise to bring your own supplies. If you book a Disney Cruise Line ship, you may be able to order diapers and other products online for delivery to your cabin.

As for laundry, it's best to use the launderette, if your ship has one – not all do, so check before booking. Pack all-detergent sheets (they are easier to transport than liquid detergent). Many ships offer laundry 'bundles' (either a set number of items, or all-you-can-bundle into a provided laundry sack), depending on the cruise line, for a set price.

You will need to look after your child the whole time unless you choose a ship with a proper nursery with qualified staff. Ships with a nursery for ages 6–36 months include *Allure of the Seas, Anthem of the Seas, Disney Dream, Disney Fantasy, Disney Magic, Disney Wish, Disney Wonder, Harmony of the Seas, Oasis of the Seas, Odyssey of the Seas, Quantum of the Seas, Spectrum of the Seas, Symphony of the Seas,* and *Wonder of the Seas*. Ships with a free night nursery include *Arvia, Azura, Britannia, Iona, Queen Anne, Queen Elizabeth, Queen Mary 2, Queen Victoria,* and *Ventura*.

Children under three need to be potty-trained to take part in any group activities. Check with the cruise line whether babies and infants are allowed in paddling and swimming pools, and whether they must wear swim diapers.

Note that you may have to bathe infants/small children in a cabin with a small shower enclosure, possibly with a fixed-head shower. Choosing a cabin with a bathtub makes it easier to do bath time. Some ships (those of Costa Cruises, for example) have baby baths available; Disney Cruise Line has bathtubs in all cabins. Make sure you have adequate medical insurance, and take your infant's medical information in case of an emergency.

MINIMUM AGE ACCEPTED

It is important to check the minimum age requirements for your chosen cruise line and itinerary, because they can vary according to the cruise, length, and region. Here is our list of 12 principal cruise lines and the minimum age allowed for sailing, which was correct at time of going to press.

Carnival Cruise Line
Minimum sailing age: 6 months (12 months on transatlantic, Hawaii, and South America cruises).

Celebrity Cruises
Minimum sailing age: 6 months (12 months for transatlantic and transpacific and some South American cruises).

Costa Cruises
Minimum sailing age: 6 months.

Cunard
Minimum sailing age: 6 months (some sailings); 12 months for transatlantic and transpacific crossings, world cruise segments, and Hawaii cruises.

Disney Cruise Line
Minimum sailing age: 3 months.

Dream Cruises
Minimum sailing age: 6 months (note: any child whose

travel document is attached to the parent's passport must travel with the accompanying parent).

Holland America Line
Minimum sailing age: 12 months.

MSC Cruises
Minimum sailing age: 3 months.

Norwegian Cruise Line
Minimum sailing age: 6 months.

P&O Cruises
Minimum sailing age: 6 months (12 months for transatlantic cruises) aboard the family-friendly ships *Azura*, *Britannia*, *Oceania*, and *Ventura*.

Princess Cruises
Minimum sailing age: 6 months.

Royal Caribbean International
Minimum sailing age: 6 months for many itineraries; 12 months for any cruises with three or more sea days, and for all transatlantic, transpacific, Hawaii, and South Pacific cruises.

BABYSITTING

If you take baby (or babies) along, and you want some time to yourself, you'll need the services of a babysitter. Some, but not all, ships have babysitting services; some have restricted hours (meaning you'll need to be back by midnight like a grown-up Cinderella); and some have group babysitting, not in-cabin care. In some ships, stewards, stewardesses, and other staff may be available as private babysitters for an hourly charge. For example, *Queen Mary 2* has children's nurses and English nannies. *Azura*, and *Ventura* have a 'night nursery' for two- to five-year-olds.

FEEDING INFANTS UNDER THREE

Selected baby foods are stocked by ships catering to infants, but ask your booking agent to get confirmation in writing that they will be provided. Some cruise lines may even mash food up for your child, if you ask. If you need a special brand of baby food, advise your booking agent well in advance, or bring your own. Parents providing organic baby foods, such as those obtained from health-food stores, should be aware that cruise lines buy their supplies from general food suppliers and not from the smaller specialized food houses. You may need to check in advance whether the ship has whole or soy milk available, for example.

CRUISING WITH CHILDREN AGES 3–10

Assuming, that they don't get seasick, children of this age should love cruising. They love to get involved right from the planning stages, learning how big the ship is, what facilities it has on board, etc. All very exciting!

One thing to note – if your budget allows, and you think your young children will be happy at sea for this long – is that it's best to avoid cruises of fewer than seven days, because they tend to attract the party-going types out for a good time.

Once on board, go to the children's clubs and sign in your youngsters – you need to give their name, cabin number, and details of allergies to any foods or materials (this typically applies up to an age according to cruise line). You'll probably be given a pager in case you need instant contact. Children's activities are mostly about team participation events, so they may

Rock-climbing is a popular on-board activity for teenage travelers.

seem highly programmed to some youngsters used to getting their own way.

In addition to the clubs, there are plenty of other facilities on deck that will appeal to children of this age, from aqua parks to chill-out rooms and sports activities such as rope courses. Most large resort ships close their pools at 6pm, although those of MSC Cruises are exceptions to this – aboard *MSC Grandiosa*, for example, one large, covered family pool is open until 9pm.

DISNEY GOES CRUISING

In 1998, Disney Cruise Line introduced the first of two large resort ships for families with children, with cruises of three, four, and seven days. *Disney Magic* and *Disney Wonder* were joined by *Disney Dream* in 2011 and by *Disney Fantasy* in 2012. The casino-free ships have ambitious entertainment programs, all centered around Disney and its stable of famous characters. Disney has its own Art Deco passenger terminal at Port Canaveral, Florida, plus a fleet of special motorcoaches.

Each ship carries over 40 children's and youth counsellors, plus lifeguards at the family pool. Families preparing to sail with toddlers under three can access an online service to order baby supplies in advance of their cruise and have them delivered to their cabin. The service, exclusive to Disney Cruise Line, is provided by Babies Travel Lite (www.babiestravellite.com), an online retailer with more than 1,000 brand-name baby products including diapers, baby food, infant formula, and specialty travel items. The ships sail in the Caribbean, the Bahamas, Alaska, the Mediterranean, and the Baltic. Disney calls at its own 1,000-acre (405-hectare) private island on Bahamas and Caribbean cruises – about 50 miles (80km) north of Nassau in the Bahamas, Castaway Cay has its own ship-docking pier. Locals say it had been a military landing strip that was once used by drug runners. Beaches are divided into family-friendly and adults-only 'quiet' sections.

BARBIE IS ABOARD

Royal Caribbean International and Mattel have free Barbie-related activities in the Adventure Ocean youth club, plus an additional cost 'Barbie Premium Experience,' with pink cabin decorations, a Barbie doll blanket, tote bag and toothbrush, special tea with pink cupcakes and dainty dishes, and a mermaid dance class featuring dances from the movie *Barbie in a Mermaid Tale 2*, among other perks.

DR. SEUSS IS ABOARD TOO

Not to be outdone, Carnival Cruise Line's 'Seuss at Sea' program has an array of immersive youth, family, dining, and entertainment experiences featuring the amazing world and words of Dr Seuss. Main dining rooms aboard each ship feature 'The Green Eggs and Ham Breakfast' with the Cat in the Hat and Friends. Children (parents can go too) can eat playful foods from Dr. Seuss's imagination, notably green

eggs and ham, moose juice, goose juice, fruit and pancake stacks, funky French toast, and more. (Note that traditional breakfast favorites are also available.) Dining room staff members wear Dr Seuss-inspired uniforms, and characters such as the Cat in the Hat, Thing One and Thing Two, and Sam join families at their tables for interaction and photo opportunities. This takes place on the first sea day of each cruise (as an extra-cost activity).

There are Dr Seuss-themed toys, games, and arts and crafts activities. Some ships have a Dr Seuss Bookville Seuss-themed play space with iconic decor, colors, shapes, and funky furniture, where families can relax. And movies such as *The Cat in the Hat* and Dr Seuss's *How the Grinch Stole Christmas* are shown outdoors on Lido Deck Seaside Theater screens.

Carnival also introduced 'Seuss-a-Palooza Story Time,' an interactive reading event that brings the characters of Dr Seuss to life. It usually takes place inside a tent on the main showlounge stage on a sea day.

There may also be a Character Parade, with Dr Seuss characters, along the Promenade, and Dr Seuss-themed retail items are also for sale.

CRUISING WITH OLDER CHILDREN (PRE-TEENS 11–12)

Some cruise lines provide extra attention for the 'tweens.' Supervised group activities and activity/play centers mean that parents won't have to be concerned, and will be able to enjoy themselves, knowing that their children are in good hands, enrolled in special programs. Activities may include make-up and cookery classes, arts and crafts projects, group games, interactive computer programs, character parades and

Junior chefs of Princess Cruises.

scavenger hunts, and watching movies and video wall programming. Then there are the outdoor activities such as waterslides, miniature golf, and swimming and other sports events for the pre-teens.

CRUISING WITH TEENAGERS (13–17)

Teens love cruising, too, and many large resort ships have dedicated 'no adults allowed' zones and chill-out rooms (with the latest in movies, gaming, and music). Teens-only activities include deck parties, pool parties, sports tournaments, poolside games, karaoke, discos, dances, computer games, video arcades, activity clubs, and talent shows. Some ships provide musical instruments for jam sessions (Royal Caribbean International, for example). Sports-style activities include rock-climbing, rollerblading, basketball, and riding a wave surfer, dodgem cars, or go-karts.

With some cruise lines the fun can extend ashore, with beach barbecues, 'chill out' and sports events. There's usually almost unlimited food, too, although some of it may not be very nutritious.

CHOOSING THE RIGHT CABIN

Cruise lines know that 'families who play together want to stay together.' Although connecting cabins and Pullman beds are nothing new on family-friendly ships, brands such as Disney Cruise Line, Dream Cruises, Norwegian Cruise Lines, and Royal Caribbean International have taken group-friendly accommodations more seriously than some others.

Families cruising together often find that sharing a confined space causes distress. It's best to choose the largest accommodation option you can afford. Before booking, check the size of the cabin and pace it out at home, remembering that the size quoted on ship deck plans includes the bathroom. If you have a large or extended family, cabins with interconnecting doors may be the most practical option.

Certain ships may work best for certain age groups. For example, multigenerational groups might consider large resort ships such as Royal Caribbean International's *Allure of the Seas, Harmony of the Seas, Oasis of the Seas, Symphony of the Seas,* or *Wonder of the Seas,* or Disney Cruise Line ships thanks to their wide range of facilities and eateries.

If you are a large or extended family, some ships (such as those of Norwegian Cruise Line) have family cabins and suites that can sleep up to 14. Larger cabins or suites simply have more space than standard cabins and may include sofa beds.

If you are traveling with teens, consider booking them an adjoining cabin or one across the hallway from yours. You get your own space, your teens will have their own bathroom and privacy, and you give them freedom, but at arm's length. If your children are younger, a cabin with an interconnecting door is a good option, if the budget allows. Many ships have cabins with two lower beds and one or two upper berths. In some cabins, the two lower beds cannot be pushed together to form a queen-size bed for parents. This means mom and dad and one or two children all have separate beds. Some ships, such as *Disney Dream, Disney Fantasy, Disney Magic, Disney Wish, Disney Wonder, Europa 2, Norwegian Bliss, Norwegian Breakaway, Norwegian Epic, Norwegian Escape, Norwegian Getaway,* and *Norwegian Joy* have cabins with two bathrooms, and a privacy curtain to screen off your youngsters.

Dependent on how young your children are (and how safe you feel this would be), you might like to opt for a cabin with a balcony. An interior (no-view) cabin may be fine for a short cruise, but could be claustrophobic on a longer one. To get access to fresh air without a balcony, you would have to keep trudging up to the open deck, carrying towels and other paraphernalia. However, if you don't anticipate spending much time in your cabin, an interior (no-view) cabin is cheaper, although the storage space limitations may prove frustrating.

CHILD FARES

Children under two travel free with many cruise lines and airlines. Most cruise lines offer special rates for children sharing their parents' cabin. The cost is often lower than third and fourth person share rates.

Although many adult cruise rates include airfare, most children's rates don't. Also, although some lines say children sail 'free,' they must pay port taxes as well as airfare.

EATING WITH CHILDREN

Flexibility is the key. Coaxing children out of a pool and getting them dressed and ready to sit quietly for a four-course dinner every night can be tough. Work out a compromise by eating dinner together occasionally at the buffet. Most ships offer a tempting menu of children's favorites as well as special mealtimes for children.

CHILDREN WITH SPECIAL NEEDS

If a child has special needs, advise the cruise line before you book. Children needing one-to-one care or assistance must be accompanied by a parent or guardian when in the children's play center.

PRACTICAL MATTERS: PASSPORTS

Note that separate passports are required for all children traveling internationally. If you have an *adopted* child, you may also need Adoption Placement Papers, as well as the child's Birth Certificate.

CONFIRMING A GUARDIAN'S IDENTITY

A Parent and Guardian Consent Form (PGCSA) will be needed at or before embarkation, if you are a parent, grandparent, or guardian with a passport surname different from that of any child traveling with you. Without this form, which includes passport information of the child's legal parent, you will be denied boarding. Check with your cruise provider if you are unclear.

SINGLE PARENTS

Some cruise lines, such as Disney Cruise Line and P&O Cruises, have introduced their versions of the 'Single Parent Plan'. This offers an economical way for single parents to take their children on a cruise, with a parent and one child sharing a two-berth cabin, or a parent with more children sharing a three- or four-berth cabin.

As a single parent with just one child, you may have to pay for two adults (double occupancy), so it is important to check the pricing policy of each cruise line you're interested in. It may also be better to take an adult friend and share the cost (in some cases, your child could travel free).

FAMILY REUNIONS AND BIRTHDAYS

A cruise can provide the ideal place for a family get-together, with or without children, and, because it's an almost all-inclusive vacation, you won't have to haggle about who pays for the extras.

With pricing that includes accommodation, meals, entertainment, use of most of the ship's recreational facilities, and travel to various destinations, a cruise represents very good value for money. Cruise lines also make special offers for groups. Let your travel agent make the arrangements, and ask for a group discount if there are more than 15 of you.

Family groups may have the option to ensure even greater value by purchasing everything in advance, from cruise fares to shore excursions, drinks packages, spa packages, and pre-paid gratuities. Additional savings can be realized through reduced fares for third and fourth passengers in each cabin, and some cruise lines offer 'kids sail free' programs.

FORMAL NIGHTS

Some ships have nights when traditional 'formal attire' is the suggested dress code. If you don't want your children to dress formally (although some children really enjoy getting dressed up – it's a bit like going to a birthday party or prom night), you can opt out of the festivities, and simply head for one of the casual dining options instead. Or your kids may prefer to opt

---

SHIPS THAT CATER BEST TO INFANTS

Disney Cruise Line: *Disney Dream, Disney Fantasy, Disney Magic, Disney Wish, Disney Wonder*
MSC Cruises: *MSC Bellissima, MSC Divina, MSC Fantasia, MSC Grandiosa, MSC Meraviglia, MSC Preziosa, MSC Seaside, MSC Seashore, MSC Seaview, MSC Splendida, MSC Virtuosa, MSC World Europa*
P&O Cruises: *Arvia, Azura, Britannia, Iona, Ventura*
Royal Caribbean International: *Allure of the Seas, Harmony of the Seas, Oasis of the Seas, Odyssey of the Seas, Ovation of the Seas, Quantum of the Seas, Spectrum of the Seas, Symphony of the Seas, Wonder of the Seas*

out and go to the children's clubs or teen rooms and hang out while you go to the captain's cocktail party.

TIPS FOR CRUISING WITH CHILDREN

Take wet wipes for those inevitable clothes stains, and anti-bacterial hand wipes and face wipes to keep you cool when it's hot outside.

Take a highlighter pen – good for marking the daily program and shore excursion literature, so you can focus on what's important to you and the children.

Take an extension cord or power strip (although note that not all cruise lines allow them), because there will be plenty of things to plug in (chargers for games consoles, cell (mobile) phones, iPads, etc.). Most cabins provide only one electrical outlet.

A pop-up laundry basket could prove useful for keeping everyone's dirty laundry separate from clean items (useful in small cabins).

Refillable water bottles (empty until you are on board ship) are useful for shore excursions, beach days, and other outings.

Take lots of high-factor sunscreen (SPF50 or above).

A set of walkie-talkie radios can prove useful for keeping track of everyone's whereabouts – if everyone remembers to turn them on!

Glow sticks – kids love them – for use as night lights (they are cheap and come in different colors – one for each night.)

SHORE EXCURSIONS

Note that shore excursions in the Caribbean and Alaska are expensive for children – in fact, almost the same prices as for adults. Many cruise ships in the Caribbean visit a 'private' island for a day. Lifeguards will be on duty at assigned swimming locations. Operators take advantage of the captive market, so rental of beach and watersports items can be expensive.

It is advisable not to book a long shore excursion if you have an infant, unless you know that they (and you!) can handle it. Diaper-changing facilities are likely to be limited (and non-existent on buses).

CAN YOU CRUISE WHEN PREGNANT?

In 2010, a 30-year-old woman on a four-night Baja cruise aboard *Carnival Paradise* gave birth on board to a premature baby. While in 2016, a woman who gave birth three weeks early, one day before the ship berthed in Brooklyn, called her baby Benjamin Brooklyn. So it can happen.

If your pregnancy is routine and healthy, there is no reason not to go on a cruise. Indeed, a cruise could be a great getaway before you deal with the things associated with an upcoming childbirth. First, ask about any restrictions imposed by your chosen cruise line. Some cruise lines may let you sail even in your 27th week of pregnancy (as in the second case above), but most will not accept you from your 24th week onwards. You may

The children's area aboard *MSC Fantasia*.

be required to produce a doctor's note. (It is advisable to check with your doctor or midwife that you are safe to travel, prior to sailing, anyway.)

Be sure to purchase travel insurance that will cover you for last-minute cancellation and medical treatment due to pregnancy complications, both on board and in ports of call.

HOW GRANDPARENTS CAN BRIDGE THE GENERATION GAP

Many children love to go cruising with grandparents, perhaps because they anticipate fewer restrictions than they have at home. And busy parents like the idea, too, particularly if the grandparents contribute to the cost and offer the possibility of a rest.

Having enrolled their grandchildren in age-related groups for daytime activities aboard ship (note the limitations on activities for children under three, as mentioned above), grandparents will be able to enjoy the adults-only facilities, such as the wellness and spa treatments. Not surprisingly, it's the large resort ships that provide the widest choice of facilities for both age groups. For those not averse to ubiquitous cartoon characters, Disney Cruise Line provides some facilities for adults and children in separate areas, but also allows them to mix in others.

BEFORE YOU LEAVE HOME

Grandparents should remember that, in addition to their grandchildren's passports, they should also bring along a letter signed by the parent authorizing any necessary medical attention. A Parent and Guardian Consent Form (PGCSA) will be needed at or before embarkation, if you are a grandparent (or parent or guardian) with a passport surname different from that

The Epic Plunge waterslide on *Norwegian Epic*.

---

5 GREAT SPLASH-TASTIC WATERSLIDES

Waterslides are always a highlight for youngsters, who can't wait to go for a ride once they are on board.

Aquaduck (Disney Cruise Line)
This waterslide is four decks high and extends over the edge of the ship – scary. You'll find it on *Disney Dream* and *Disney Fantasy*.

Epic Plunge (Norwegian Cruise Line)
This waterslide will have your youngsters doing the loop-de-loop down a long slide that ends in – surprise, surprise – a nice big splash.

Kaleid-O-Slide (Carnival Cruise Line)
This waterslide, which you'll find on *Carnival Vista*, ends in a giant funnel that swirls you around and spits you out with a splash!

Caesar's Slide (Dream Cruises)
The half-million-dollar stainless steel waterslide aboard *Explorer Dream* starts 34.5ft (10.5m) above the deck and swirls and swoops over 328ft (100m) before emptying out into a water break.

---

of any child traveling with you. Check with your cruise provider about this.

Ground rules should be established with a child's parent(s) present to avoid potential problems. An important issue is whether a child will be allowed to roam the ship unsupervised, given that some cruise lines allow children as young as eight to sign themselves out of supervised programs. Walkie-talkies are a good solution to this issue. They work well aboard ships, and allow adults and children to stay in constant touch.

ON BOARD

Most cruise lines offer scheduled activities from 9am to noon, 2–5pm, and 7–10pm. This means you can drop your grandchild off after breakfast, relax by the pool, go to a lecture, or take part in other activities, and pick them up for lunch. After a couple of hours together, they can rejoin their friends, while you enjoy an afternoon movie or siesta.

SHORE EXCURSIONS

Consider your grandchild's interests before booking expensive shore excursions (example: flightseeing in Alaska). It's also best to avoid long bus rides, shopping trips, and scenic tours, and better to choose excursions that feature water and/or animals. Examples include snorkelling, aquariums, or nature walks. Remember to pack snacks. In some ports, it may be better to explore on your own. If your grandchildren are very young, full-day shore excursions are a probably bad idea.

CRUISING FOR SOLO TRAVELERS

Cruise prices are geared toward couples. Yet about one in four cruise passengers travels alone or as a single parent. How do they fare?

Cruising, in general, is designed for couples. Many solo passengers feel that cruising penalizes them, because most lines charge them a solo-occupancy supplement. The reason is that the most precious commodity aboard any ship is space. Since a solo-occupancy cabin is often as large as a double and is just as expensive to build, cruise lines feel the premium price is justified. What's more, because solo-occupancy cabins are at a premium, they are less likely to be discounted.

SOLO SUPPLEMENTS

If you are not sharing a cabin, you'll be asked to pay either a flat rate or a solo 'supplement' to occupy a double-occupancy cabin by yourself. Some lines charge a fixed amount as a supplement, regardless of the cabin category, ship, itinerary, or length of cruise. Since there are so few solo-occupancy cabins, it's best to book as far ahead as you can. One notable exception is Norwegian Cruise Line, whose *Norwegian Bliss*, *Norwegian Breakaway*, *Norwegian Epic*, *Norwegian Es-*

cape, *Norwegian Getaway*, and *Norwegian Joy* all have a whole section with 'Studio' cabins – small, but much in demand for solo travelers.

Some cruise lines charge low solo supplements on selected voyages. Saga Cruises has no additional supplements for solo travelers on any cruise (*Saga Adventure* and *Saga Discovery* each has 81 designated solo-occupancy cabins – the highest percentage of any company's ships). Look out for sneaky cruise lines that may try to charge you *twice* for port charges and government taxes by including a phantom second person in the cabin you occupy as a solo traveler – check your final invoice carefully.

GUARANTEED SOLO TRAVELER RATES

Some lines offer solo travelers a set price for a double cabin but reserve the right to choose the cabin. This means that you could end up with a rotten cabin in a poor location or a wonderful cabin that happened to be unallocated.

Cunard provides social dance hosts.

SOLO DINING

A common irritation concerns dining arrangements. Before your cruise, make sure that you request a table assignment based on your personal preferences; table sizes are typically for two, four, six, or eight. Do you want to sit with other solo travelers, with couples, or a mixture of both? And are you happy to sit with passengers who might not speak your language?

Once on board, make sure you are comfortable with the dining arrangements, particularly in ships with fixed table assignments, or request a move to a different table. Aboard ships with open seating or other dining venues, you can choose which venue to eat in, and when.

CRUISING FOR WOMEN TRAVELING SOLO

A cruise ship is as safe for women as any major vacation destination. It may not, of course, be entirely hassle-free, but it should not be a 'meat market' that keeps you under constant observation.

If you enjoy meeting other solo travelers the easiest way is to participate in scheduled activities. However, beware of embarking on an affair with a ship's officer or crew member (strictly not allowed), as you may not be the only one to have done so.

GENTLEMEN CRUISE HOSTS

The female-to-male passenger ratio is typically high, especially among older people, so some cruise lines provide male social hosts. They may host a table in the dining room, appear as dance partners at cocktail parties and dance classes, join bridge games, and accompany women on shore excursions.

A DJ keeps youthful late-night clubbers dancing.

These men, usually over 55 and retired, are outgoing, mingle easily, and are well groomed. First introduced aboard Cunard's *Queen Elizabeth 2* in the mid-1970s, gentlemen dance hosts are now employed by a number of cruise lines, including Cunard, Holland America Line, Regent Seven Seas Cruises, and Silversea Cruises.

If you think you'd like such a job, do remember that you'll have to dance for several hours most nights, and be proficient in just about every kind of dance.

OPTIONS FOR LGBTQ+ TRAVELERS

Several US companies specialize in ship charters or large group bookings for gay and lesbian passengers. These include the California-based Atlantis (www.atlantisevents.com), San Francisco's lesbian specialist Olivia (www.olivia.com), or New York's Pied Piper Travel (www.piedpipertravel.com).

In 2018, an LGBTQ+ Getaways Cruise took place aboard *Celebrity Silhouette*, organized by Cruises Inc., CruiseOne, and Dream Vacations (US companies). One drawback of LGBTQ+ whole-ship charters is that up to 20 percent more expensive than the equivalent general cruise. Another is that they have been greeted with hostility by religious objectors on some Caribbean islands such as Grand Cayman, Jamaica, and Bermuda. One Atlantis cruise was even denied the right to dock. But their advantage is that they provide an accepting environment and LGBTQ+-oriented entertainment, with some big-name comedians and singers.

Another idea is to join a LGBTQ+ affinity group on a regular cruise at normal prices; these groups may be offered amenities such as private dining rooms and separate shore excursions.

If you are concerned that on a mainstream cruise you might be seated for dinner with unsympathetic companions, opt for a cruise line offering 'open-choice seating' (where you sit where you want, when you want at dinner, and you can change the time you dine), for example Carnival Cruise Line, Celebrity Cruises, Holland America Line, Norwegian Cruise Line, Princess Cruises, and Royal Caribbean International (request this option when you book). That doesn't mean that any of the major cruise companies are not LGBTQ+-friendly – many have regular 'Friends of Dorothy' gatherings, sometimes scheduled and sometimes on request – though it would be prudent to realize that Disney Cruise Line, for example, will not really offer the ideal entertainment and ambience. Among the smaller companies, Windstar's ships have a reputation for being LGBTQ+ friendly.

Gay families are catered to by R Family Vacations (www.rfamilyvacations.com), although it's not essential to bring children. Events may include seminars on adoption and discussion groups for teenagers in gay families.

Transgender passengers may encounter some problems, such as the passport name being of one gender, while appearance and dress reflect another. Ships sometimes encounter problems in some ports when passenger ID cards do not match the gender on the ship's manifest.

CRUISING FOR ROMANTICS

No need to worry about getting to the church on time – you can be married at sea, get engaged, renew your vows, or enjoy a honeymoon.

Two classic TV shows, *The Love Boat* (US) and *Traumschiff* (Germany), boosted the concept of cruising as a romantic vacation, the natural culmination of which would be getting married at sea – the ultimate 'mobile wedding.' Such ceremonies have become such big money-earners that, after 171 years, Cunard changed the registry of its three ships in 2011 from its traditional home port of Southampton to Hamilton, Bermuda, partly because its British registry didn't allow for weddings at sea. As a result, couples can now say 'I do' aboard *Queen Mary 2* in the middle of the North Atlantic; the first such wedding was in May 2012.

SAYING 'I DO' ABOARD SHIP

This popular option includes a honeymoon conveniently in the same location and a 'wedding planner,' who can sort out all the nitty-gritty details such as arranging flights, hotels, transportation, and inclusive packages. For the bride, spa and beauty services are immediately on hand, and you literally can sail into the sunset after the reception.

Check first in your country of domicile whether such a marriage is legal, and ascertain what paperwork and blood tests are needed. It is up to you to prove the validity of such a marriage. The captain could be held legally responsible if he has married a couple not entitled to wed.

It is relatively easy to get married aboard almost any cruise ship when it's alongside in port, and several cruise lines offer special wedding packages. These include the services of a minister to marry you, wedding cake, champagne, bridal bouquet and matching boutonnière for the bridal party, a band or musician to perform at the ceremony, and an album of wedding pictures. Note that US citizens and 'green card' residents may need to pay sales tax on wedding packages.

Asuka Cruise, Celebrity Cruises, Cunard, Dream Cruises, P&O Cruises, Princess Cruises, Royal Caribbean International, and Sea Cloud Cruises – among others – offer weddings aboard their ships. The ceremonies can be performed by the captain, who is certified as a notary, when the ships' registry – Bermuda, Japan, or Malta, for example – recognizes such unions. Japanese citizens can also be married at sea aboard one of the Japan-registered cruise ships such as *Asuka II* or *Nippon Maru*.

Sunset aboard Cunard's *Queen Mary 2*.

PRACTICAL TIPS FOR HONEYMOONERS

Remember to take a copy of your marriage license or certificate, for immigration (or marriage) purposes, as your passports will not yet have been amended. Since you may well wish to share a large bed with your partner, check with your travel agent and cruise line to make sure the cabin you have booked has such a bed. Better still, book a suite. It's important to check and double-check to avoid disappointment.

If you plan to combine your honeymoon with getting married along the way – in Hawaii or Bermuda, for example – and need to take your wedding gown aboard, there's usually space to hang it in the showlounge dressing room, especially aboard the large resort ships.

A honeymoon couple enjoy being pampered aboard an MSC Cruises ship.

Expect to pay about $3,000 plus about $500 for licensing fees. Harbor-side or shore-side packages vary according to each potential port.

Even if you don't get married aboard ship, you could have your wedding reception on one. Contact the director of hotel services at the cruise line. The cruise line will go out of its way to help, especially if you follow the reception with a honeymoon cruise – and a cruise, of course, also makes a fine, worry-free honeymoon.

UK-based passengers should know that P&O Cruises hosts a series of cruises called the 'Red-Letter Anniversary Collection' for celebrating 10, 15, 20, 25, 30, 35, 40, 45, 50, 55, or 60 years of marriage.

GETTING MARRIED ASHORE

Another option is to have a marriage ceremony in an exotic destination with your reception and honeymoon aboard ship afterwards. For example, you could get married on the beach in Barbados or Hawaii; on a glacier in Juneau, Alaska; in a villa in Venice; in an authentic Tahitian village; in Central Park, New York; or on Disney's Castaway Cay in the Bahamas, with Mickey and Minnie at hand. Note that your marriage license must be from the jurisdiction in which you will be married. If you set your heart on a Bermuda beach wedding, for example, the license to marry must be obtained in Bermuda, no matter what your nationality is.

GETTING ENGAGED ABOARD SHIP

For those not quite ready to tie the knot, Princess Cruises has a special 'Engagement Under the Stars' package that allows you to propose to your loved one in a personal video that is screened just before an evening movie at a large poolside screen aboard some of the company's ships.

RENEWAL OF VOWS

Many cruise lines perform 'renewal of vows' ceremonies. A cruise is a wonderful setting for reaffirming to one's partner the strength of commitment. A handful of ships have a small chapel where this ceremony can take place; otherwise, it can be conducted anywhere on board. A most romantic time is at sunrise or sunset on an open deck. The ceremony is conducted by the ship's captain, using a non-denominational text.

Some companies have complete packages which include music, champagne, hors d'oeuvres, certificate, corsages for the women, and so on.

CRUISING FOR HONEYMOONERS

There are many advantages in honeymooning at sea: it is a hassle-free and safe environment; and you get special attention if you want it. It is easy to budget in advance, as one price often includes airfare, cruise, food, entertainment, several destinations, shore excursions, and pre- and post-cruise hotel stays. Also, some cruise lines offer discounts if you book a future cruise to celebrate an anniversary.

Although no ship provides real bridal suites, many have suites with king-size beds. Some also provide tables for two in the dining room, should you wish to dine together without having to make friends with others. A variety of honeymoon packages are available; these might include champagne and caviar for breakfast, flowers in your suite/cabin, complimentary cake, and a private cocktail party.

Some cruise ships have Sunday departures, so couples can plan a Saturday wedding and reception before traveling. Pre- and post-cruise hotel accommodation can also be arranged.

Most large resort ships accommodate honeymoon couples well. However, couples averse to crowds might try one of the smaller cruise ships such as those of Hapag-Lloyd Cruises, Regent Seven Seas Cruises, Sea Cloud Cruises, Seabourn, Silversea Cruises, or Windstar Cruises.

And for quiet moments? The deck to the forward part of a ship, near the bridge, is the most dimly lit part and the quietest – except perhaps for some wind noise.

CRUISING FOR SENIORS

People everywhere are living longer and healthier lives, and cruise lines are keen to cater to their particular needs.

Although cruise lines have been striving, with some success, to embrace all age groups, the over-60s remain an important segment of the market for cruise lines. Nowhere is this more evident than in Japan's 'Golden Week,' a collection of four national holidays within seven days in late April/early May, when seniors clamor for available cabins.

Making new friends aboard *Oasis of the Seas*.

One trend for seniors is toward longer cruises – even round-the-world cruises. Some opt for an adults-only ship such as *Arcadia*, (P&O Cruises), or *Spirit of Adventure* and *Spirit of Discovery* (Saga Cruises).

There are bargains to be had, too. Organizations for seniors such as AARP (American Association of Retired Persons) in the US and Saga in the UK often offer special discounts or upgrades.

If you have had major surgery or have mobility problems and cannot (or don't wish to) fly, think of 'no-fly' cruise, with embarkation and disembarkation in your home country. In the US, the number of 'homeland' ports increased dramatically following the terrorist attacks of September 2001. In the UK, cruise ships sail from ports in both the north and south of the country. The same is true elsewhere, as language-specific cruise lines and ships proliferate.

But all is far from perfect. Some cruise lines have yet to recognize that, with seniors as with other groups, one size does *not* fit all. Only a few, for example, take the trouble to provide the kind of items that millions of seniors need, such as large-print editions of daily programs, menus, and other printed matter.

SPECIAL DIETS

While the wide range of cuisine aboard many ships is a big attraction, cruise lines understand that many passengers are on special diets. Lighter menu options are available aboard most ships, as well as vegetarian and vegan choices. Options include low-sodium, low-fat, low-cholesterol, and sugar-free entrées (main courses) and desserts. A booking agent will ensure that special dietary needs are recorded.

HEALTHIER EATING

You really don't have to put on weight during a cruise. Many health-conscious seniors prefer smaller portions of food with good taste and nutritional value rather than overflowing plates.

Heart-healthy diets are in demand, as are low-fat, low-carbohydrate, salt-free, or low-salt foods. Denture wearers often request food that includes softer items.

Those seeking lighter fare should be aware that most cruise lines have an 'always available' section of heart-healthy items that can be cooked plainly,

WHY SENIORS LIKE CRUISING – BUT CAN OFTEN FIND IT FRUSTRATING

Thumbs up

- A cruise is an excellent choice for those who like to be independent while having the chance to meet other like-minded people.
- Cruising is mostly stress-free and relaxing. You don't have to keep packing and unpacking as you do on a land-based tour.
- It's safe. You travel and dine in comfort and safety, while your floating hotel takes you to a choice of around 2,000 destinations all over the world.
- Lecturers and lessons in everything from golf to computing provide a chance to learn something new.
- There's plenty of entertainment – shows, cinema, casinos, games, and dances.
- All main and buffet meals are included in the fare, and those passengers on special diets can be easily accommodated.
- Senior solo travelers, in particular, find it easy to meet others in a non-threatening environment. Some ships provide male dance hosts, screened and subject to a strict code of ethics, who can also act as escorts on shore excursions.
- Most ships have 24-hour room service and a 24-hour reception desk.
- Passengers with disabilities can find ships that cater to their needs.
- Ships carry a medical doctor and one or more trained nurses. In an emergency, treatment can be arranged.

Thumbs down

- Complicated online check-in procedures, and hard-to-read Passenger Ticket Conditions and Contracts are the cause of many complaints. Indeed, many passengers of senior years have poor or deteriorating eyesight, and find it challenging to read items with small print.
- Credit card-size electronic key cards to cabins – it is often unclear which end of these to insert, and difficult for those with poor eyesight.
- Booking events and meals via the in-cabin 'interactive' television/keypad system is user-unfriendly for many seniors. All services should be readily accessible via the telephone.
- Poor, difficult-to-read signage such as 'You are here' deck plans unreadable from farther away than an inch (2.5cm).
- Onboard literature often includes pages with white type on a colored background. However, many people with poor eyesight cannot focus well on white print. This is why newspapers and books are always printed using black ink on a lighter paper or background!
- Menus with small, hard-to-read typefaces (and non-black ink), and daily programs that require a magnifying glass to be legible.
- Buffets with plates only, requiring several visits, and cutlery too heavy to hold comfortably.
- Anything that requires a signature – for example: bar, shore excursions, spa bills with small print.
- Libraries with few books, if any, in large-print format – notably recent novels.
- The absence of a 'concierge' for seniors.
- Public toilets not clearly marked.
- The lack of music-free lounges and bars for conversation and drinks.

such as grilled or steamed salmon, skinless chicken breast, lean sirloin steak, or baked potatoes.

GENTLEMEN HOSTS

Because more female than male seniors cruise, cruise lines have developed 'gentlemen host' programs. These are gentlemen, typically over 55 years of age, selected for their social skills and competence as dance partners, for dining table conversation, and for accompanying passengers on shore excursions.

Cruise lines with gentlemen hosts include: Cunard, Holland America Line, P&O Cruises, Princess Cruises, Regent Seven Seas Cruises, Seabourn, Silversea Cruises.

ENRICHMENT PROGRAMS

Many seniors want to learn about a destination's history and culture rather than be told which shops to visit ashore. Lecturers of academic quality are found aboard some smaller ships such as *Spirit of Discovery* (Saga Cruises). Some lines have special-interest lecturers on topics such as archeology, food and wine, ornithology, and military history.

TIPS FOR SENIORS

If you are traveling solo, it's important to check the price of any single supplements.

If you take medication, make sure you have enough with you. Some ships have a dress-up code, while most are casual. Choose a ship according to your own lifestyle and tastes.

If you have mobility difficulties, choose one of the newer ships that have public rooms with an 'open-flow' style of interior design. Examples include *Arcadia, Balmoral, Eurodam, Nieuw Statendam, Queen Anne, Queen Elizabeth, Queen Mary 2,* and *Queen Victoria.* Older ships may have 'lips' or doors between public rooms.

BEST FACILITIES

Among the cruise lines that provide the facilities and onboard environment that seniors tend to enjoy most are: American Cruise Lines, Azamara, Fred. Olsen Cruise Lines, Hebridean Island Cruises, Holland America Line, Noble Caledonia, Oceania Cruises, P&O Cruises, Pearl Seas Cruises, Regent Seven Seas Cruises, Saga Cruises, Sea Cloud Cruises, Seabourn, and Silversea Cruises.

CRUISING TO SUIT SPECIAL NEEDS

For anyone with physical limitations, cruising offers one of the most hassle-free vacations possible, and almost all cruise ships have a medical center. But it's important to choose the right ship and to prepare in advance.

If you have a mobility issue or any other kind of physical disability (including visual or hearing impairments), a large resort ship really is a destination in itself, and provides a very comfortable way to travel in style, with accommodation, meals, entertainment, public rooms and open-air facilities in a hotel-style environment, plus abundant staff to help you have an enjoyable time. On-site medical facilities also add to the comfort factor, although they are mostly run by specially con-tracted staff who charge extra for their services. It's a very therapeutic environment. However, do tell the cruise line (or your travel agent) at the time you book about your physical disability; otherwise, you may le-gally be denied boarding by the cruise line.

Ships built in the past five to 10 years have the most up-to-date suites, cabins, and accessible shipboard fa-cilities for those with disabilities. Many new ships also have text telephones and listening device kits for the hearing-impaired (including in showlounges aboard some ships). Special dietary needs can often be met, and many cabins have refrigerators – useful for those with diabetes who need to keep insulin supplies cool.

DIALYSIS

If you have the need for hemodialysis, careful plan-ning should ensure that you have a successful vaca-tion away from home aboard a cruise ship. Your renal care unit will work with companies that specialize in providing cruises for hemodialysis patients.

Companies specializing in dialysis cruises also han-dle all booking, travel arrangements, and shipboard care. A renal care specialist team consisting of a nephrologist, dialysis nurse, and a certified technician will be provided as part of the booking. Only a limited

Many cruise ships offer an ideal environment for people with disabilities.

DOORS CAN PRESENT A CHALLENGE FOR WHEELCHAIR-USERS

The design of cruise ships has traditionally worked against people with limited mobility. To keep water out or to prevent water escaping from a flooded area, raised edges (lips) are often placed in doorways and across exit pathways, which are unfriendly to wheelchairs. Also, cabin doorways, at a standard 24in (60cm) wide, are not big enough for wheelchairs, for which about 30in (76cm) is needed.

Bathroom doors, whether they open outward or inward, similarly hinder maneuverability (an electrically operated sliding door would be better). Bathrooms in some older ships are small and full of plumbing fixtures, often at odd angles – awkward for wheelchair movement. Those aboard new ships are much better, but plumbing may be located beneath the complete prefabricated module, making the floor higher than that in the cabin, so a ramp is needed. Some cruise lines will, if given advance notice, remove a bathroom door and hang a fabric curtain in its place, and provide a ramp for the doorway if needed.

Access to outside decks may be through doors that need to be opened manually rather than via automatic electric-eye doors.

number of places are available on any ship with organized dialysis treatment and the right equipment. Several companies advertise dialysis cruises, but the following are the most experienced.

In Europe, contact: **DiaCare AG** (since 1981): www.diacare.ch.

In the UK (for UK residents): The UK's National Health Service (NHS) has an arrangement with the British company **Cruise Dialysis Limited** (since 2000), whereby it can make a partial payment of your dialysis treatment aboard ship. Contact: www.cruisedialysis.co.uk.

In the USA (for USA residents): **Dialysis at Sea** (since 1977). Contact: www.dialysisatsea.com.

Some ships (*Europa* and *Europa 2*, for example) have first-class dialysis equipment (such as the Fresenius 4008 B machine) permanently installed in a special dialysis room in the medical center.

WHEELCHAIR USERS

If you use a wheelchair, take it with you, because ships carry a limited number for emergency hospital use only. An alternative is to rent an electric wheelchair, which can be delivered to the ship on your sailing date.

Arguably the weakest point of cruising for people with limited mobility is any ship-to-shore tender operation. Ships' tenders simply aren't designed for wheelchair-users – and neither are landing platforms (exceptions include *Celebrity Apex*, *Celebrity Beyond*, *Celebrity Eclipse*, *Celebrity Edge*, and *Celebrity Silhouette*).

LITTLE PROBLEMS TO CONSIDER

Unless cabins and bathrooms are specifically designed, problem areas include the entrance, furniture configuration, closet hanging rails, beds, grab bars, the height of toiletries cabinet, and the wheel-in shower stall. The elevators may present a biggest obstacle, and you may get frustrated at the wait time involved. On older ships, controls often can't be reached from a wheelchair. Narrow hallways can be a problem when trying to pass housekeeping carts.

Some ships have access-help hoists installed at swimming pools. Examples include *Celebrity Apex*, *Celebrity Beyond*, *Celebrity Eclipse*, *Celebrity Equinox*, *Celebrity Reflection*, and *Celebrity Silhouette*, the pool in 'The Haven' aboard *Norwegian Breakaway*, *Norwegian Epic*, *Norwegian Escape*, *Norwegian Getaway*, *Norwegian Gem*, and P&O Cruises' *Arcadia*, *Arvia*, *Aurora*, *Britannia*, and *Iona*.

It can be difficult to access areas including the buffets, and many large resort ships provide only oval plates (no trays) in their casual eateries. So, do ask for help.

Some insurance companies may prohibit smaller ships from accepting passengers with severe disabilities. Some cruise lines will send you a form requesting the dimensions and weight of your wheelchair, stating that it has to fold to be taken inside the cabin.

Note that wheelchairs, mobility scooters, and walking aids must be stored in your cabin – they *cannot* be left in the hallway outside your cabin.

Only three cruise ships presently have direct wheelchair-access ramps to lifeboats: *Amadea*, *Asuka II*, and *Europa*.

AVOID PITFALLS

Start by planning an itinerary and date (as far in advance as possible), and find a cruise specialist agency suited to your needs. You should also follow up on all aspects of a booking yourself to avoid slip-ups; many cruise lines have a department or person to handle requests from disabled passengers.

Choose a cruise line that lets you select a specific cabin, not just a price category.

If the ship doesn't have any specially equipped cabins, book the best outside cabin in your price range, or choose another ship.

Check whether your wheelchair will fit in through your cabin's bathroom door or into the shower area and whether there is a 'lip' at the door. Don't accept 'I think so' as an answer. Get specific measurements.

Choose a cabin close to an elevator. Not all elevators go to all decks, so check the deck plan. Aboard *Costa Magica* and *Costa Fortuna*, for example, outside-view wheelchair-accessible cabins are located a long way from the elevators – a serious design error.

Smaller and older vessels may not even have elevators, making access to even the dining room difficult.

Douglas Ward tests accessibility around a ship.

Avoid, at all costs, a cabin down a little alleyway shared by several other cabins, even if the price is attractive. It's hard to access a cabin in a wheelchair from such an alleyway. Midships cabins are less affected by vessel motion – good if you are concerned about possible rough seas. The larger the cabin – and therefore more expensive – the more room you will have for maneuvering. Most importantly, don't even think about booking an interior (no-view) cabin, even if the price is attractive, because, in the event of an emergency, lighting (and backup systems) may fail. If this happens in the middle of the night, confusion can cause panic.

Hanging rails in the closets on most ships are positioned too high for wheelchair-users to reach – even the latest ships seem to repeat this basic error. Many cruise ships, however, have cabins to suit people with limited mobility. They are typically fitted with roll-in closets and have a pull-down facility to bring your clothes down to any height you want.

Meals in some ships may be served in your cabin, on special request, but few ships have enough space in the cabin for dining tables. If you opt for a dining room with two, fixed-time seatings for meals, the second is more leisurely. Alert the restaurant manager in advance that you would like a table that leaves plenty of room for your wheelchair.

Make sure that the contract specifically states that if, for any reason, the cabin is not available, that you will get a full refund and transportation back home as well as a refund on any hotel bills incurred.

Advise the cruise line of the need for proper transfer facilities such as buses or vans with wheelchair ramps or hydraulic lifts.

If you live near the port of embarkation, arrange to visit the ship to check its suitability – most cruise lines will be accommodating.

Hand-carry your medical information. Once on board, tell the reception desk help may be needed in an emergency.

COPING WITH EMBARKATION

The boarding process can pose problems. If you embark at ground level, the gangway may be level or inclined. It will depend on the embarkation deck of the ship, availability of a terminal-to-ship flybridge, and/or the tide in the port.

You may need to embark from an upper terminal level, so the gangway could be of the floating loading-bridge type, like those used at major airports. Some have flat floors; others may have raised lips at regular intervals.

SHIP-TO-SHORE TENDERS

Cruise lines should – but don't always – provide an anchor emblem in brochures for ports of call where a ship will be at anchor instead of alongside. If the ship is at anchor, the crew will lower you and your wheelchair into a waiting tender and then, after a short boat ride, lift you out again onto a rigged gangway or integral platform. If the sea is calm, this maneuver proceeds uneventfully; if the sea is choppy, it could vary from exciting to somewhat harrowing.

Holland America Line is one of the few companies to make shore tenders accessible to people with limited mobility, with a special boarding ramp and scissor lift so that wheelchair passengers can see out of the shore tender's windows. Celebrity Cruises' *Celebrity Apex, Celebrity Beyond, Celebrity Edge, Celebrity Silhouette, and Celebrity Solstice, for example,* provide the best solution, with a large platform called the Rising Edge for direct tender loading via an adjacent elevator.

HELP FOR THE HEARING-IMPAIRED

Difficulties for such passengers include hearing announcements on the public address system, using the telephone, and poor acoustics in key areas such as where shore tenders are boarded.

Some cruise lines have special 'alert kits.' These include 'visual-tactile' devices for those unable to hear a knock on the door, a telephone ringing, or the sound of an alarm clock. TUI Cruises' *Mein Schiff 1–6* all have movie theaters fitted with special headsets for those with hearing difficulties.

Finally, when going ashore, particularly on organized excursions, be aware that some destinations are simply not equipped to handle people with hearing impairment.

CRUISING FOR THE BLIND AND SIGHT-IMPAIRED

Any blind or partially sighted persons must be accompanied by a non-disabled person, occupying the same cabin. A few cruise lines will allow seeing-eye dogs (guide dogs).

All elevators and cabins have Braille text. Some large resort ships (examples include *Celebrity Reflection, Celebrity Silhouette, MSC Divina, MSC Fantasia, MSC Meraviglia, MSC Preziosa, MSC Seaside, and MSC Splendida*) have Braille pads subtly hidden under each lower section of handrail in the main foyers, which is user-friendly, and welcome.

RECENT IMPROVEMENTS

Many new ships now provide mobility-limited cabin bathrooms with collapsible shower stools mounted on shower walls, and bathroom toilets have collapsible arm guards and lower washbasins. Other cabin equipment may include a vibrating alarm clock, door beacon (with a light that flashes when someone knocks on the door), television with closed-caption decoders, and a flashing light as fire alarm. Other features to look out for include:
- Kits for the hearing-impaired, available on request.
- Induction systems for the hearing-impaired.
- Dedicated wheelchair positions in the showlounge or cinema.
- Electrical hoists to access pools and hot tubs.

Although public rooms do not have special seating areas, most showlounges do – almost always at the back, adjacent to the elevators – for wheelchair-users.

WHEELCHAIR ACCESSIBILITY

Wheelchair-users considering a cruise may be nervous at the thought of getting around. However, you will find that crew members aboard most ships are extremely helpful. However, before you book, check with your travel agent or the cruise company to make sure that any batteries used to power your wheelchair comply with the regulations of your chosen cruise line or operator. Also, most cruise lines will only accept mobility scooters with gel, dry cell, sealed lead acid, or lithium-ion batteries, due to fire and safety regulations. Further, if you take an electric scooter, you will need to store it inside your cabin (it cannot be left outside in the hallway due to safety regulations), so do check to make sure it will fit through the cabin doorway.

A cabin number in Braille aboard *Costa Serena*.

QUESTIONS TO ASK BEFORE YOU BOOK

Are any public rooms or public decks inaccessible to wheelchairs?

Will special transportation be provided for the transfer from airport to ship?

Will you need to sign a medical release?

If you need a collapsible wheelchair, can this be provided by the cruise line?

Can the ship supply a raised toilet seat?

Will crew members be on hand to help?

Will you be guaranteed a good viewing place in the showlounge if seated in a wheelchair?

How do you get from your cabin to lifeboats in an emergency, if the elevators are out of action?

Does the cruise line's travel insurance (with a cancellation or trip interruption) cover you for any injuries while you are aboard?

Most disabled cabins have twin beds or one queen-size bed. Anyone with a child with disabilities should ask whether a suitable portable bed can be installed.

CRUISING TO A THEME

A whole world of special-interest, hobby, and lifestyle-theme cruises awaits your participation.

What's your interest? Think of it and you'll probably find a cruise dedicated to it. These are the special cruises that don't really fit into the normal range of offerings, although they usually follow the same itinerary.

Theme cruises are primarily 'regular' cruises, but with additional programs, linked to personalities and subject specialists. With seminars and hands-on learning sessions, music, dances or concerts, sports, activities, and leisure on the menu, the possibilities are endless. Also, you travel with people who have the same interests, or passions, or to increase your knowledge of a particular subject. You could also be close to your favorite celebrity and get to talk to them in person.

If you are cruising as a regular passenger and not part of the theme cruise group (assuming that the ship is not a full theme cruise charter), be aware that some public rooms may be blocked off for one or more

Néstor Torres performs as part of The Grammy Experience aboard Norwegian Getaway.

days for special activities and functions – or even the whole cruise. Whole dining rooms may also be part of the theme charter and may be out of commission for regular passengers.

MUSIC ON THE HIGH SEAS

Music has always been a popular feature of shipboard entertainment, and special-interest music festivals, celebrations, and even competitions at sea have been part of the modern-day cruise scene since the 1960s. It's like having a special backstage pass to be up-close-and-personal with world-class musical talent.

Solo instruments are an unusual item for a theme cruise, but in 1986 the first Accordion Festival at Sea – with over 600 accordionists on board competing for financial and other prizes – took place aboard Chandris Fantasy Cruises' Galileo. It was not a full ship charter, so the other passengers were fascinated by the richness of performances of this versatile instrument.

Even before that, however, starting in 1976, a Classical Music Festival At Sea took place annually aboard the Paquet French Cruises' 650-passenger Mermoz (now long defunct) until the early 1990s (and wine, all other drinks, and shore excursions were included in the fare). The artistic director André Borocz organized the whole event, including booking about 70 musicians who sailed on each of these special cruises (either in the Mediterranean or Caribbean). World-class artists such as James Galway, Barbara Hendricks, Jean-Pierre Rampal, Maurice André, Mstislav Rostropovich, Yo-Yo Ma, Emmanuel Ax, Schlomo Mintz, Bobby McFerrin, and the English Chamber Orchestra sailed aboard the ship, with music concerts performed ashore – usually in the evening – in Caribbean venues such as Papa Doc's Citadelle in Haiti, La Popa Monastery in Cartagena, or, in Europe, the ancient Greek theater at Epidaurus, the Teatro Mercadante in Naples, or the ancient open-air theater at Xanthos, Turkey.

What was unusual, and fun, was to watch these world-famous artistes rehearsing in the daytime – often in their bathrobes – with passengers (also in bathrobes or casual clothing) attending; then, at around 6pm, everyone donned tuxedos for the evening. The close contact, and the interaction between performers and the music-loving passengers, was wonderful.

Suffice it to say that this was indeed a very special theme cruise.

In 1993 Paquet French Cruises was purchased by Costa Cruises, which was itself purchased by the Carnival Corporation in 1996. Then in 1999 Paquet Cruises was dismantled, and *Mermoz* was scrapped in 2008.

Today, several cruise lines have taken up the Classical Music Festival at Sea theme, with Hapag-Lloyd's annual Ocean Sun Festival the most prestigious and sought-after event.

The company also hosts the Stella Maris International Vocal Competition (opera, song, and oratorio) in cooperation with renowned opera houses throughout the world. Up-and-coming opera singers from around the world compete aboard *Europa* to win €15,000 and a recording contract with the German classical music record label, Deutsche Grammophon.

CELEBRITY SINGERS

In the early 1990s, Celebrity Cruises had Connie Francis, Liza Minnelli, and Gladys Knight and the Pips (among others) as headline acts in a special series of high-profile names to perform aboard the company's (then new) *Horizon* on the ship's popular New York to Bermuda cruises.

COOL JAZZ

Staying on the music theme, Big Band theme cruises have also always been popular, with bands such as the Glenn Miller Orchestra, Tommy Dorsey Orchestra, Count Basie Orchestra, and the Duke Ellington Orchestra all having been part of the music on the high seas theme. In October 2015, Cunard hosted the first-ever Blue Note-themed crossing aboard *Queen Mary 2* showcasing Blue Note's 75th anniversary All Star Band. It featured keyboardist Robert Glasper, trumpeter Keyon Harrold, tenor saxophonist Marcus Strickland, guitarist Lionel Loueke, bassist Derrick Hodge, and drummer Kendrick Scott. Herbie Hancock was the headline act on one of two more special Blue Note-themed crossings in 2016, as was jazz vocalist Gregory Porter.

Jazz greats such as Dizzy Gillespie and Clark Terry (trumpet), Woody Herman (clarinet), Benny Carter, Buddy Tate, Gerry Mulligan (saxophone), Junior Mance, Mel Powell, and Paul Broadnax (piano), Howard Alden (guitar), Keter Betts, Major Holley, Milt Hinton, and Kiyoshi Kitagawa (double bass), Chuck Riggs and Louis Bellson (drums), Mel Tormé (voice), the Harlem Blues and Jazz Band, and Joe Williams and the Festival Jazzers have all sailed and played on Norwegian Cruise Line's 'Floating Jazz Festival' cruises aboard the now-scrapped *Norway* and other ships in the fleet (organized by Hank O'Neal).

Today, the Smooth Jazz Cruise (also known as 'The Greatest Party At Sea') has been attracting well-known names such as the jazz violinist Ken Ford, guitarist-vocalist George Benson, bassist Marcus Miller, guitarist Earl Klugh, saxophonists David Sanborn,

ShipRocked cruise aboard the *Norwegian Pearl*.

Mindi Abair, Paul Taylor, and Richard Elliott, and jazz fans – principally aboard Holland America Line ships.

OFF YOUR ROCKER

Today, rock 'n' roll stars and fans have also taken to cruising, with music-themed charters of ships. The Moody Blues with Peter Dalton, Roger Daltrey, The Zombies, Carl Palmer and The Orchestra with ELO, Starship, Little River Band, and Yes have all featured on cruises. Not to be left out, grown-up 'boy bands,' including the Backstreet Boys and New Kids on the Block, have also been cruising.

Although the ShipRocked (www.shiprocked.com) cruise was canceled in 2021, it had a five-night sailing in 2022 from Galveston, Texas, aboard *Carnival Breeze* (including an onboard auction for the charity Cancer Sucks!) with around 20 bands and artists. In 2023 and in its 23rd year, the festival was extended to seven days and took place aboard *Carnival Magic*, sailing from Port Canaveral.

Expect more of the same, as rock 'n' roll and blues bands go cruising to replace the loss of land-based venues and revenue (merchandising aboard a cruise ship with a captive audience is a massive incentive).

Malt Shop Memories, which started in 2010 with its one-week music-theme specialist cruise, combines live performances by superstars with interactive events that bring artistes and fans together for its celebration of music, fashion, and fun of the '50s and '60s.

Classical music and jazz cruises tend to last 7–14 days, but most other music themes, such as rock 'n' roll or heavy metal, tend to be shorter (and less expensive).

SOUL TRAIN

Usually a full-ship charter, a re-creation of the popular music show *Soul Train* includes artists such as Gladys Knight and Earth, Wind and Fire, together with numerous artists that have been part of the television show, created and hosted by Don Cornelius. The artists, dancers, and fans have a blast, and enjoy close interaction

Darth Vadar on board a Disney Cruise Line's *Star Wars* Day at Sea.

with each other (www.soultraincruise.com). In 2016, Smokey Robinson performed aboard *Celebrity Constellation*.

GOING UP COUNTRY

Country and Western and Gospel music theme cruises also pop up occasionally. Stars who have sailed in the past few years include the band Alabama, Trace Adkins, Montgomery Gentry, Wynonna, Neal McCoy, Love and Theft, Craig Morgan, Lonestar, Kenny Rogers, Vince Gill, Larry Gatlin and the Gatlin Brothers, The Oak Ridge Boys, Mel Tillis, and Kathy Mattea. There are also songwriter workshops and karaoke (judged by the professionals), late-night dance parties, and a little unscheduled jammin' along the way.

FAMILY THEMES

Aboard the ships of Disney Cruise Line, *everything* is Disney – every song heard, every game played, every participation event, race, or party – it's the complete Disney at sea package.

Royal Caribbean International has its own star themes at sea, including characters from the DreamWorks Experience such as Alex from *Madagascar*, Fiona and Puss in Boots from *Shrek*, and Po from *Kung Fu Panda*.

CULINARY THEME CRUISES

Food and wine cruises have always attracted interest, although some are better than others. Most have tended to be more like presentation lectures at cooking stations set on a large stage, and always seem to leave audiences wanting to ask questions one-on-one rather than as part of a general audience.

Wine-themed cruises are especially popular with oenophiles (wine lovers), who get to meet owners and specialists from various world-famous vineyards with wine talks and tasting sessions as part of the pleasure of these special voyages.

STAR WARS

In 2016, Disney Cruise Line designated eight sailings aboard *Disney Fantasy* as *Star Wars* cruises, and *Star Wars* films were shown. A shipboard version of the Jedi Training Academy invited young Jedi hopefuls to learn light saber moves from a Jedi master. Families participated in *Star Wars* trivia games, while themed arts and crafts, games, and activities were featured daily.

Star Wars sailings showcase characters like Darth Vader, the Stormtroopers, Chewbacca, R2-D2, C-3PO, Boba Fett, and other characters from across the *Star Wars* galaxy, who will typically be aboard for meet-and-greet sessions.

The special cruises usually take place between January and March. May the Force be with you!

NOT YOUR REGULAR THEME CRUISE

Other unusual theme cruises include naturist vacations – clothing-free vacations. Bare Necessities has been doing it since 1990, although participants do dress to go to the dining room. The Big Nude Boat Cruise 2016 took place aboard *Celebrity Constellation*. Then there's Dream Pleasure Tours (http://dreampleasuretours.com), founded in 2007 for sensual indulgence. This company charters ships for hedonistic lifestyle cruises, including for the LGBTQ+ and swinger communities. A swingers' (adventurous couples) cruise took place in 2016 aboard *MSC Divina*, with a Bliss Cruise (for couples) aboard *Celebrity Silhouette*.

The Harley-Davidson Motorcycle Rally at Sea has been happening for around 10 years aboard the ships of Celebrity Cruises, with biker attire as the dress code. There's usually a contest for the best tattoo, among other things.

Then there's the 'High Seas Rally Cruise' – the 'World's Only Motorcycle rally on a Cruise Ship' aboard Royal Caribbean International's *Radiance of the Seas* from Port Canaveral.

Some cruises are just magical adventures in themselves. In 2013, everyone's favorite wizard, the venerable Harry Potter, took to the seas with his own theme cruise.

Other themed cruises include Wellness, Fitness, 'Mind, Body and Spirit,' and 'Life Modification' cruises (the first Holistic Health Cruise at sea was aboard *Cunard Countess* in 1976 and included Ida Rolf – the esteemed creator of the extreme massage technique known as Rolfing – on board). Then there's the 'Quilters of the Caribbean' cruise (https://stitchinheaven.com); castles and gardens cruises (www.hebridean.co.uk); and scrapbooking cruises (www.cruiseandcrop.com).

Several cruise lines also have golf-themed cruises, but perhaps the best packages are put together by companies including Hapag-Lloyd Cruises, Regent Seven Seas Cruises, and SeaDream Yacht Club, all of which operate smaller-size ships for a more personal experience.

CORPORATE CRUISING

Corporate incentive organizations and seagoing conferences need to have such elements as accommodation, food, or entertainment for delegates organized as one contract. Cruise companies have specialized departments to deal with all the details. Helpfully, many larger ships have almost identical cabin sizes and configurations.

Once a corporate contract is signed, no refund is possible, so insurance is essential. Although you may need only 70 percent of a ship's capacity for your purposes, you will have to pay for the whole ship if you want an *exclusive* charter.

Although you can contact cruise lines directly, I strongly recommend contacting the Miami-based ship charter specialists Landry & Kling (http://landrykling.com), who can arrange whole-ship charters for theme cruises.

MAIDEN AND INAUGURAL VOYAGES

It can be fun to take part in the maiden voyage of a new cruise ship. Or you could join an inaugural voyage aboard a refurbished, reconstructed, or stretched ship after a refit or drydock. However, you will certainly need a degree of tolerance – and be prepared for some inconveniences, such as slow or non-existent service in dining venues. Indeed, new restaurants – or reconfigured ones following a refit – may not even be operable.

Regular cruisers know that any maiden voyage is a collector's item, but Murphy's Law – 'If anything can go wrong, it will' – can prevail. If it is a new ship, for in-

stance, the crew may not be familiar with the layout, and some equipment may not be working properly, or may even be missing completely. Service aboard new or significantly refurbished ships (or a new cruise line) is likely to be uncertain and can easily end up a disaster. An existing cruise line may use experienced crew from its other vessels to help 'bring out' a new ship, but they may have problems training new staff. One example of things not going quite right was aboard P&O Cruises' brand new 5,200 passenger *Arvia*, when on its maiden voyage in December 2023, passengers had to wait a long time for dinner, and many restaurant bookings were botched.

Plumbing and electrical items tend to cause the most problems, particularly aboard reconstructed and refurbished vessels. Examples: toilets that don't flush or don't stop flushing; faucets (taps) incorrectly marked, where 'hot' really means 'cold'; and 'automatic' telephones that refuse to function.

In the entertainment department, items such as spare spotlight bulbs may not be in stock. Or what if the pianos arrive damaged, or audio-visual materials for the lecturers haven't been delivered? Or the manuals for high-tech sound and lighting equipment may be in a foreign language.

Items such as menus, postcards, writing paper, infotainment system remote control units, door keys, towels, pillowcases, glassware, and even toilet paper may be lost in the bowels of the ship (no pun intended), or simply not ordered.

If you feel any of these mishaps might spoil your cruise, I would advise you to wait until the ship has been in service for at least three months, by which time a ship will have 'bedded down.'

The author taking part in a culinary class aboard *Britannia*.

EXPEDITION CRUISING UNCOVERED

Since the Covid-19 pandemic there has been an explosion in the interest in 'going wild' and discovering nature, which has resulted in an upsurge in expedition cruising to learn more about planet Earth and its remotest places.

Like sport-utility vehicles, the newest expedition ships offer a comfortable lifestyle as a base to experience nature safely – no more being squeezed into telephone-box-sized cabins.

Expedition voyages today (they are not really cruises, per se) are poles apart from other types of cruising. Some confusion remains between expedition cruises and discovery/exploration cruises, which are more about nature and off-the-map destinations, with a sense of pioneering and adventure thrown in. Participants joining real (polar) expedition voyages need to be self-reliant and more interested in doing or learning than in being entertained, as they'll find themselves an active participant in almost every aspect of a voyage.

Naturalists, historians, plus academic and scientific lecturers are aboard each ship to provide background information and observations about wildlife (this is an excellent way to learn a lot while on your voy-

age). Aboard some ships, specialised crew members, skilled in maintenance and repairs, such as electricians, engineers, and plumbers, are vital because the ships cover remote areas, and can be far away from ports where spare parts can be obtained, all adding to the cost of operations.

Note that itineraries are *not* set in stone, and may be subject to change at a moment's notice, due sometimes to the fast-changing weather conditions.

COLLECTIBLE EXPEDITION/ EXPLORATION EXPERIENCES

Get some northern exposure by venturing all the way to the North Pole, by walking on pack ice in the Arctic Circle, or watching orcas and visiting penguin rookeries in Antarctica, the Falkland Islands, and South Georgia (the only place to see king penguins). Alternatively, you could go 'birding' in the Aleutian Pribilof Islands,

A Polar-Code compliant expedition ship nudging through ice.

search for 'lost' peoples in Papua New Guinea, explore the Amazon basin, view the Bradshaw rock art in the Kimberley, or watch real dragons on Komodo island.

COOL WEDDINGS IN ANTARCTICA

On February 22, 2021, the first official wedding took place in Antarctica. The bride, Courtnie Dodson, and groom, Brody Vermillion, were legally married. The ceremony was officiated by British Antarctic Territory registered Marriage Officer Bryan Clark. The ceremony, which took place on Danko Island, was witnessed by eight additional guests. Naturally, the bride wore white!

EXPLORING IN COMFORT

Expedition cruises used to mean utilitarian living conditions, but no longer does it mean a lack of creature comforts. Briefings and lectures bring cultural and intellectual elements to expedition voyages, which are all about being immersed in nature. An expedition leader has a team and works closely with the ship's captain and marine operations department. The ships are designed and equipped to sail in ice-laden waters, yet they have a shallow-enough draft to glide over coral reefs without damage. They must also adhere to the provisions of the International Code for Ships Operating in Polar Waters (Polar Code, PC), now in force.

Without traditional cruise ports, the ships must be totally self-sufficient, capable of long-range cruising, and totally environmentally friendly. There's no professional entertainment. Instead, recaps of the day's experiences take place each evening, and board games and library books are always available. Note: the 'library' is typically a few bookshelves filled with polar and nature-related reference books, usually part of the multimedia/observation lounge. Some ships have a separate lecture and multimedia room, while aboard the smallest ships, the observation lounge usually doubles up as the lecture room.

The expedition experience itself really comes alive by the use 'Zodiacs' – rigid (open) inflatable landing craft that can seat up to a dozen participants. Note that landings on icy terrain can be demanding and very challenging when there are no landing stages. The feel of sea spray and wind on your face gives you a thrill, and the sense of exhilaration that this really is something different from any cruising you may have done previously.

The construction and introduction of a wide range of new specialist expedition ships (built to PC6 classification) has been driven by the demand for exploration in highly comfortable, even luxurious surroundings. A PC6 classification allows for 'summer/autumn operation in medium first-year ice, which may include old ice inclusions.' Some ships are being built to PC2 classification, which allows for their operation in 'year-round operation in moderate multi-year ice conditions.' This allows these vessels to operate in the high Arctic summer (thus enabling them to navigate all the way to the North Pole – at least in theory).

Zodiacs on a 'soft' expedition in Papua New Guinea.

WHAT'S INCLUDED

- Experienced expedition leaders
- Specialist lectures
- All meals (breakfast, lunch, dinner)
- Coffee, tea, hot chocolate, around the clock
- All shore landings (as per the daily program)
- All Zodiac cruising (as per the daily program)

An expedition parka (for you to take home – so remember to allow extra space when you are packing)

Waterproof boots (on loan) for shore landings

HOW EXPEDITION CRUISING DEVELOPED

Lars-Eric Lindblad pioneered expedition cruising in 1966. The Swedish-American turned travel into adventure by going to parts of the world tourists had not visited. After chartering several vessels for voyages to Antarctica, he organized the construction of a small ship capable of going almost anywhere in comfort and safety. In 1969, *Lindblad Explorer* was launched; it soon earned an enviable reputation in adventure travel. Others followed.

To put together expedition voyages, companies turn to specialist advisers. Scientific institutions are consulted; experienced world explorers and naturalists provide up-to-date reports on wildlife sightings, migrations, and other natural phenomena. Sea days are spent preparing, and participants are kept physically and mentally active. Avoid such an adventure voyage if you are not completely mobile, because getting into and out of Zodiacs can be tricky, even in good weather conditions. In fact, two Quark Expedition passengers died when their Zodiac overturned on an excursion near Elephant Island in Antarctica in November 2022.

Expedition companies provide parkas and waterproof boots, but you will need to take waterproof trou-

PROTECTING SENSITIVE ENVIRONMENTS

Only ships capable of meeting new 'zero discharge' standards will be allowed to cross environmentally sensitive areas. Expedition cruise companies are concerned about the environment, and they spend a great deal of time and money in educating their crews and participants about safe procedures.

They observe the 'Antarctic Traveler's Code,' based on the 1978 Antarctic Conservation Act, designed to protect the region's ecosystem, flora, and fauna.

The Antarctic Treaty Meeting in Kyoto in 1994 made it unlawful, unless authorized by permit, to enter certain special protected areas (SPAs), or discharge or dispose of pollutants. The original Antarctic Treaty, signed in 1959 by 12 nations active in the region, defined Antarctica as all of the land and ice shelves south of 60 degrees south latitude (66 degrees, 33 minutes of latitude marks the Antarctic Circle). The signatories: Argentina, Australia, Belgium, Chile, France, Japan, New Zealand, Norway, South Africa, the Soviet Union, the UK, and the US.

Ships carrying over 500 participants are not allowed to land passengers and are restricted to 'scenic' cruising, so the likelihood of a large resort ship zooming in on penguins is low. It would not be possible to rescue so many passengers (plus crew) in the event of an emergency. Also, large resort ships burn heavy oil (now banned in the Antarctic region) rather than the lighter oil used by the specialist expedition ships, which also have ice-strengthened hulls.

sers (and plenty of warm clothing) for Antarctica and the Arctic, plus a good pair of sunglasses.

POLAR CODE

Many 'expedition' ships over 10 years old have already passed their sell-by date and don't comply with the IMO Polar Code requirements, which came into force in January 2017. These cover the construction, operational and technical equipment, crew training, search and rescue, environmental protection and procedural requirements for expedition cruise vessels operating in the polar regions of the world. Polar Code categories are PC1 to PC7, with PC1 being the highest ice class.

The safety section of the code applies to all passenger ships (ships constructed before 2017 must comply with the code by the first immediate or renewal survey). Ships must carry a Polar Ship Certificate (Category A: ships designed to operate in polar waters in at least medium first year ice and old ice; Category B: ships designed to operate in at least thin first-year ice; Category C: ships designed to operate in open water or in ice conditions less severe than those in Categories A or B).

WHAT'S AHEAD

If you see advertisements for cruises to Antarctica with ships carrying more than 500 passengers, showing pictures of penguins and seals, look the other way. Don't be taken in if you expect to step ashore and get close to the best locations for seeing penguins and seals up close. The International Association of Antarctica Tour Operators (IAATO) and the Antarctic Treaty parties prohibit ships carrying over 500 passengers from landing passengers in Antarctic waters. In other words, if you want to get up-close-and-personal to the wildlife, choose a small, specialized expedition ship.

In 2019, several new highly specialized expedition ships debuted, for the first time for many years. *Scenic Eclipse*, followed by *Crystal Endeavor* in 2021 (renamed *Silver Endeavour* in 2022) both carry submersible mini-vessels, including SEABOB underwater scooters. However, the per-person cost to participate is fairly prohibitive (plus you'll need to be covered by highly specialized insurance – for personal injury, medical expenses, evacuation and repatriation costs, and any pre-existing medical conditions), due to the use of one or two helicopters and other specialist equipment. Perhaps more useful are some of the landing craft aboard Hapag-Lloyd's specialist ships *HANSEATIC nature*, *HANSEATIC inspiration*, *and HANSEATIC spirit*. These include environmentally friendly, electric-powered Zodiacs, but no helicopters or submersibles, which are considered to be high-maintenance, with operational and logistics liabilities. The newest expedition ships also incorporate a dynamic positioning system – vital in polar ice conditions – where anchors cannot be used.

EXPEDITION LEADERS

The best expedition voyages are not only about the latest ships and technical equipment, but about the expedition leaders themselves, and their experience and professionalism. Also, perhaps the most experienced (and environmentally conscientious) company, Hapag-Lloyd Expedition Cruises does not add extra charges for such things as kayaking (in single or tandem kayaks), snow-shoeing, or paddle-boarding in ice-laden waters, or for other side excursions, whereas companies like Hurtigruten, Oceanwide, Poseidon, Quark, and several others – some of whom, such as Albatros Expeditions, Aurora Expeditions (AE Expeditions), and Oceanwide Expeditions, among others, don't own but charter their ships – do.

A DAY IN THE LIFE

Be prepared to be busy. On the first day, get used to your new surroundings, collect your appropriately-sized parka and boots and attend the safety and Zodiac landing briefings. Expedition voyages always include several early morning calls, nature sightings, and sheer physical endurance. But the result is worth all the effort, because the memories you will collect, and the experiences you will have, cannot be learned from books or television or by armchair travel – this is total immersion, and you need to be a participant, not simply a passive passenger!

Above all, to get the most out of any polar expedition cruise, be prepared to be flexible. Expedition ships can't always run to a time schedule, because there are so many variables when dealing with weather, ice conditions, landing areas, and other operational issues.

ANTARCTICA

Think of the 1983 theme from 'Antarctica' by Vangelis. Better still, see the 'Frozen Planet' for yourself. While Arctic ice is only a few feet thick, the ice of Antarctica is thousands of feet thick, and of many, many different colors. The continent – the world's largest desert – was first sighted in 1820 by the American sealer Nathaniel Palmer, British naval officer Edward Bransfield, and Russian captain Fabian Bellingshausen (the second man to cross the Antarctic Circle).

For most, it is just a windswept frozen wasteland – the ice mass contains almost 90 percent of the world's snow and ice (and 70 percent of the world's fresh water), while its treeless land mass is nearly twice the size of Australia. For others, it represents the last pristine place on earth, with an abundance of marine and bird life.

Around 45,000 people a year visit Antarctica, mostly by expedition cruise ships. The British research station Port Lockroy, located on Goudier Island in the Palmer Archipelago and established in 1944, is the most visited site in the Antarctic Peninsula, with about 20,000 expedition cruise visitors annually during the five-month austral summer. It is also the site for nesting Gentoo penguins. There is 24-hour sunshine during the austral summer, but not a single native inhabitant (volunteer staff at the station have a six-month contract). Its ice is as much as 2 miles (3km) thick, and its total land mass equals more than all the rivers and lakes on earth and exceeds the land mass of China and India combined. Icebergs can easily be the size of Belgium. The region has a raw beauty, vivid colors, and can overload the senses. Research stations set up by various nations are dotted about the Antarctic Peninsula, and because they are staffed mainly by scientists, they welcome expedition cruise visitors – particularly after being holed up for the harsh Antarctic winters, when going outside is next to impossible.

There are two ways to reach the cold continent by sea. The most popular route is from Ushuaia in Argentina (with connections from Puerto Williams in Chile), across the notorious, deep waters of the Drake Passage (fed by the powerful Antarctic Circumpolar Current) to the Antarctic Peninsula. The peninsula is visited (sometimes together with South Georgia) by the 'soft' expedition cruise ships and even normal-size cruise ships with ice-hardened hulls. From Ushuaia, it takes two days to reach the Antarctic Peninsula (about 560 nautical miles from Cape Horn), to see the pristine Antarctic ice and observe the wildlife. The best time is mid-November, when penguins come ashore for courtship and nesting. South Georgia is famous, because the explorer Ernest Shackleton is buried in Grytviken – a former Norwegian whaling station.

Photographing penguins in Antarctica.

The second route from Hobart (Australia) or Auckland (New Zealand) to the Ross Ice Shelf takes about seven days to reach the eastern side of the continent in the Ross Sea (hence it is more expensive than leaving from Argentina or Chile). On the way from Australia, Tasmania or New Zealand, adventure voyages might call at Balleny Islands, just below 70 degrees south latitude (the islands are named after English whaling captain John Balleny, who discovered the archipelago during an expedition to the high southern latitudes in search of sealskins and whale oil in 1837). Onwards to the more remote 'far side' – the Oates and Scott coasts, McMurdo Sound, and the famous Ross Ice Shelf – which can be visited only by genuine icebreakers, as the katabatic winds can easily reach more than 100mph (160kph). However, a highlight is a visit to Robert Falcon Scott's well-preserved Discovery Hut (built between 1902 and 1904) at Cape Evans on Ross Island – surrounded by McMurdo Station and its ice wharf. It has been frozen in time since 1912 (with over 8,000 items – including many tins of food). You can also visit Shackleton's hut from the Nimrod Expedition (1907–09) at Cape Royds on Ross Island (it contains over 5,000 items), and Mawson's huts at Cape Denison in the eastern sector (a replica of one of Mawson's

National Geographic Explorer, Lemaire Channel, Antarctica.

huts (built by the Mawson's Huts Foundation) opened in December 2013; it sits on the dockside in Hobart, Australia. Approximately halfway between Australia and Antarctica is Macquarie Island, home to virtually the entire world's population of royal penguins.

The first ship carrying participants on a complete circumnavigation of Antarctica was the 114-passenger *Kapitan Khlebnikov*, a Russian icebreaker chartered and operated by Quark Expeditions, in 1996–97. The powerful ship, with its 45-millimeter-thick ice-crushing hull, sailed from Stanley (Malvinas/Falkland Islands) and back.

Only 100 participants *per ship* are allowed ashore at any given time (so aboard the smaller ships, two landings per day are normal). If you cruise aboard one of the larger ships that claim to include Antarctica on their itineraries, it will only be to view the scenery from the ship. Moreover, the chances of rescue in the event of dangerous pack ice crushing a normal cruise ship hull are virtually nil.

Make no mistake, going to Antarctica can be treacherous, and rescue nowhere close at hand. For example, in 2013 *Akademik Shokalskiy*, with 74 people on board, became totally trapped in pack ice (which can surround any ship quickly in poor weather conditions) off east Antarctica, in the vicinity of Mertz glacier, approximately 1,500 nautical miles south of Hobart, Tasmania.

Most large ship operators thankfully exited Antarctica due to a ban on carrying or burning heavy fuel oil below 60 degrees south latitude (and marketing people haven't got a clue about the dangers of ice and erratic weather conditions), leaving travel to the region mainly in the hands of the specialist expedition ship operators. 'Antarctic' fuel (lighter-grade distillate fuel) is the world's highest cost fuel for ship use. How-

THE PRINCIPAL EXPEDITION COMPANIES

- AE Expeditions (Aurora Expeditions)
- Albatros Expeditions
- Antarctica21
- Antarpply Expeditions
- Atlas Ocean Voyages
- Aurora Expeditions
- Coral Expeditions
- G Adventures
- Hapag-Lloyd Expedition Cruises
- Heritage Expeditions
- Hurtigruten Expedition Cruises
- Lindblad Expeditions
- Ponant
- Poseidon Expeditions
- Quark Expeditions
- Silversea Expedition Cruises
- Viva Expedition Cruises

For more information on expedition cruise companies, see page 160.

ever, some large and mid-size ships also carry the special fuel, which allows them to continue traveling to Antarctica – although these are for cruising only, not passenger landings.

For real expedition cruising, choose a ship that includes a flotilla of Zodiacs, proper boot-washing and disinfection stations, expedition equipment, experienced expedition leaders, ice captains, and no extra charges for items like kayaking or hiking. Companies with the most experience that stand out from the crowd are Hapag-Lloyd Expedition Cruises, Quark Expeditions, and Poseidon Expeditions.

As I was completing this latest edition of the book, I saw a video on the website of an adventure travel company marketing expedition cruises to 'Falklands, South Georgia and Antarctica'. However, along with footage of icebergs, penguins, and seals, there was footage of polar bears – but there are no polar bears in Antarctica – they are found only in the northern (Arctic) hemisphere! This shows how amateurish some companies are in trying to attract customers to their discount offers.

Wildlife you may see or encounter includes orcas, dolphins, six species of Antarctic seals, penguins, and various species of lichen and flora, depending on the area visited.

BIOSCIENTIFIC CONCERNS

There is a growing concern among the bioscientific community that humans are introducing pathogens to the continent (reverse zoonosis). Although the established research stations appear to be the biggest part of the problem, it is likely that the number of expedition cruise visitors will be controlled and restricted further in the future to protect the wildlife – particularly birds (including penguins, of course).

Note: It is *absolutely forbidden* to take any food (not even nuts or seeds) with you on the icy shore landings in Antarctica (only water is permitted), and nothing should be left behind.

Expedition cruise operators are bound by IAATO regulations. When you return from a Zodiac 'wet' landing in icy waters, you'll go through a decontamination process, whereby everything (boots, walking poles, bags, etc.) is washed thoroughly.

TIMING

The Antarctic summer is from November to March, and the peak season of December and January provides the best chance for a calm Drake Passage crossing, when penguin chicks hatch, while in November and December, female seals nurture their pups. In November, abundant sea ice may mean it's not possible to land – particularly on the eastern side of the peninsula. February and March are late in the season, but it's the best time to see whales and fur seals in the peninsula, and when penguin chicks are moulting.

Tip: Ushuaia is the preferred starting point – ships that start in Buenos Aires or Montevideo take longer

The author and his wife at the true North Pole.

to get to the Antarctic Peninsula so you actually spend very little time there).

Tip: Choose a ship that carries less than 250 passengers for the best Antarctica expedition experience.

Tip: If you have a special diet, advise the cruise operator as early as possible, so that any necessary or unusual food items can be obtained.

Tip: Above all, be flexible – the weather can be extremely unpredictable, and proposed itineraries may have to be changed at short notice.

Typical temperatures in the region range from -10°C to +10°C. Expedition cruises to Antarctica go only in the Antarctic summer when the average is about 0°C (taking into account any wind chill factor).

PACKING FOR ANTARCTICA

Head: A woollen hat that covers your ears; a neck gaiter that can cover your face; polarized sunglasses to protect your eyes from the intensity of the sun's glare (and the intensified reflection of the sun on the ice and icebergs).
Body: Wear layers. Start with thermal underwear (tops and long johns made from hydrophobic fabrics rather than cotton), then fleece sweaters (parkas will be provided on board).
Hands: Waterproof gloves (one size larger than normal so that you can wear a thinner pair of lined gloves next to your skin).
Legs: Waterproof trousers (essential for Zodiac landings and exploration rides).
Feet: Waterproof boots will be supplied on board, but

CRACKING THE NORTHWEST PASSAGE

In 1984, Salen Lindblad Cruising (today known as Quark Expeditions) made maritime history with the pocket-sized *Lindblad Explorer* by negotiating a westbound voyage through the Northwest Passage, a 41-day epic that started from St. John's, in Newfoundland, Canada, and ended at Yokohama, Japan. The search for a Northwest Passage to the Orient – finding a sea route connecting the Pacific and Atlantic oceans through the treacherous Canadian Arctic Archipelago – had attracted brave explorers for more than four centuries, and, despite numerous attempts and loss of life including the English explorer Henry Hudson in 1610, a 'white passage' to the East remained an elusive dream. The Norwegian explorer Roald Amundsen's 47-ton ship *Gjoa* eventually navigated the route in 1906, taking three years to do so. It was not until 1943 that a Canadian ship, St. Roch, became the first vessel in history to make the passage in a single season. *Lindblad Explorer* became the 34th vessel, and the first cruise passenger ship to complete it.

remember to take plenty of warm socks.

Onboard: Everyday clothes (a welcome change from all the layers and waterproof clothing needed for venturing ashore).

Camera: Take clear waterproof bags (find a plastic alternative) to cover your camera, so that condensation forms inside the bag and not on your camera when returning from the cold to the warmth of your ship. Make sure you know how to operate your camera with gloves on – frostbite is a real danger. Pack extra batteries (the cold air quickly reduces battery life) and a battery charger.

THE HIGH ARCTIC

This is an ocean surrounded by continents, whereas Antarctica is an ice-covered continent surrounded by ocean. The Arctic Ocean itself is an immense, deep basin of polar water. The Arctic Circle itself is located at 66 degrees, 33 minutes, 3 seconds north, although this really designates where 24-hour days and nights begin, but crossing it can be a thrilling moment and personal experience (you may be able to go kayaking at this 'top of the world' location, for example). The Polar Zone includes the waters around the eastern coast of Greenland and the Canadian Arctic Islands, and the Arctic Basin. The High Arctic is best defined as that region north of which no trees grow, and where water is the primary feature of the landscape.

The High Arctic is under the strict guidelines of the Association of Arctic Expedition Cruise Operators (AECO), the body committed to minimizing the impact of visit to the Far North. These highly specialized expeditions to the 'Top of the World' (the North Pole, at 90 degrees north) are undertaken only at the height of the Arctic summer, in June and July, usually aboard the world's most powerful icebreaker – the Russian nucle-

ar-powered *50 Years of Victory* – which can crush ice up to 10ft (3m) thick (the ship can only operate in cold water conditions so that the water can cool the pressurized nuclear reactors). An onboard helicopter can whisk you between the ship and the North Pole, if the ship is unable to reach the exact geographic center (this would be verified by GPS and Inmarsat satellite coordinates) because of dense fog or other prevailing conditions.

THE NORTHWEST PASSAGE

Long sought after for its fascinating landscapes, and as a shortcut across the roof of the world, it was only in the 20th century that the very dangerous Northwest Passage linking the Atlantic and Pacific oceans was first navigated successfully. On the Canadian side, it is the Inuit people that have inhabited some of the islands and land masses, although life is getting harder for these hunter gatherers.

Passenger ships that have navigated it include *Lindblad Explorer* (1984), *World Discoverer* (1985), *Society Explorer* (1988), *Frontier Spirit* (1992), *Kapitan Khlebnikov* (1994, 1995, 1998, 2006, 2007, 2008), *Hanseatic* (1995, 1996, 1997, 1999, 2007, 2010, 2012), and *Bremen* (2009, 2010). In 2013, 2015, and 2017 unusual double crossings took place; *Hanseatic* went east to west, while *Bremen* went west to east. (Note: these ships have now either been scrapped, or changed names, or have been assigned to other duties). In 2016 and 2017, the much larger *Crystal Serenity* made a crossing escorted by a Canadian icebreaker when the ice cover was very thin, but in 2018, Ponant's *Le Boréal* and *Le Soléal* were forced to abandon their scheduled crossing because of heavy ice, under the advice of the Canadian Coast Guard. The only time to go is August to September, when the ice is at its thinnest.

OTHER 'EXPEDITION' AREAS

While this chapter covers the most sought-after expedition cruise areas, there are other 'soft' expedition cruises that take you to some of the less visited or accessible areas of the world, such as the Amazon River, the Galápagos islands, Greenland, the Kimberleys (Australia) and Papua New Guinea, among others. These are more about discovering places and areas seldom seen and not part of large resort ship cruising, but where the use of Zodiacs is an essential part of the experience; these small ships don't need an ice-hardened hull and all the equipment associated with ice-laden regions. These regions are covered in the 'Choose Your Destination' chapter.

All existing ships certified to SOLAS (Safety of Life at Sea) and sailing in polar waters, are expected to carry the Polar Code ship certificate. In the Antarctic, the Polar Code is in force in all waters further than 60 degrees north latitude; in the Arctic in all waters past 60 degrees north latitude (with deviations to include southern Greenland and Svalbaard, excluding Iceland and Norway).

COASTAL CRUISES

Being all at sea doesn't appeal? You can stay close to dry land by journeying round the coasts of Australia, Europe, Scotland, and North and South America.

GERMANY

As a result of the Covid-19 pandemic, a new, small cruise company, called Polar Quest, appeared featuring five-night cruises along the coast of northern Germany and including the nature islands of Sylt and Amrum. Cruises operate only during the summer, and the pocket-sized ship chartered is the 54-passenger *Quest*.

NORWAY

An alternative to traditional cruise ships can be found in the year-round coastal cruising along the shores of Norway to the Land of the Midnight Sun aboard the ships of Hurtigruten Norway, and newcomer Havila (the company started with the first of four new 15,519 gross ton, 640-passenger ships in 2022). These are small, modestly comfortable, working express coastal/cruise vessels that deliver mail, cars, small packaged goods, and foodstuffs, and take passengers to the communities spread along the country's shoreline.

Invariably marketed as 'the world's most beautiful voyage,' this is a 1,250-mile (2,012-km) journey from Bergen in Norway to Kirkenes, close to the Russian border (half of which is north of the Arctic Circle) and takes 12 days. The service started in 1893 to provide connection to communities when there were no roads, and the name Hurtigruten – meaning 'fast route' – reflects the fact that this coastal express was once the most reliable communication link between southern Norway and its remote north. It's a good way to meet Norwegians, who treat the service like a bus.

You can join at any of the 34 ports of call, and stay as long as you wish because the vessels sail every day of the year (some port calls are of only one hour or so – enough to get off and on and unload freight). Most ports are repeated on the return journey, but stop at different times, so you may get a different feeling for a place, even if you visited it previously.

Havila Krystruten: Double beds are available only in 'suite'-grade accommodation. Other cabins are either lower beds, or lower bed/upper berth configuration. The decor is minimal. Some cabins are wheelchair-accessible, and some are pet-friendly (with linoleum floor). Vessels are powered by LNG.

Hurtigruten Norway: Double beds are available only in 'suite'-grade accommodation (other cabins are severely dimensionally challenged, with sparse decor, furnishings, and minimal luggage storage space); many beds are fixed in an L-shape, or in a bed/sofa bed combination. Most of the ships do not have stabilizers, and there is no doctor on board, nor indeed any medical facilities, but gratuities are included.

At the height of summer, north of the Arctic Circle, there are almost 24 hours of daylight (there is no sunset between April 19 and August 23). Between November and February, the northern lights – if the atmospheric conditions are right – create spectacular arcs across the sky. Some specialist voyages are aimed at wildlife, birdwatchers, astronomy, and others, while onboard concerts and lectures celebrate the work of Norwegian composer Edvard Grieg.

The ships accommodate between 144 and 652 passengers. The newest ships have a wheelchair-friendly elevator, but, otherwise, they are plain, basic, simple, practical vessels, with canteen-style food that suits

A Hurtigruten ship on Norway's Arctic coast.

USA COASTAL SHIPS					
Company	Ship name	Entered service	Passengers (lower beds)	Crew	Passengers/ Crew Ratio
Alaska Dream Cruises	Admiralty Dream	1979	54	21	2.5/1
	Alaskan Dream	1986	40	18	2.2/1
	Baranof Dream	1980	50	19	2.6/1
	Chichagof Dream	1984	74	30	2.4/1
American Cruise Lines	American Star	2007	94	27	3.4/1
	American Constellation	2017	161	41	3.9/1
	American Constitution	2018	161	41	3.9/1
	Independence	2010	97	27	3.5/1
Lindblad Expeditions/ National Geographic Cruises	National Geographic Endeavour II	2005	96	63	1.5/1
	National Geographic Endurance	2020	126	112	1.1/1
	National Geographic Explorer	1982	152	70	2.1/1
	National Geographic Quest	2017	100	35	2.8/1
	National Geographic Sea Bird	1981	70	22	3.1/1
	National Geographic Sea Lion	1982	62	25	3.1/1
	National Geographic Venture	2018	100	35	2.8/1
UnCruise Adventures	Wilderness Adventurer	1983	60	25	2.4/1
	Wilderness Discoverer	1992	76	26	2.9/1
	Wilderness Explorer	1976	76	26	2.9/1
Victory Cruise Lines	Victory I	2001	220	77	2.8
	Victory II	2001	220	77	2.8

the operating area. A 24-hour restaurant has items at extra cost. Alcoholic drinks prices are extremely high (you can take your own on board); as it is in Norway; the currency is the Norwegian krone.

Archipelago-hopping can be done along Sweden's eastern coast too, by sailing in the daytime and staying overnight in one of the many small hotels en route. One vessel sails from Norrtalje, north of Stockholm, to Oskarshamn, near the Baltic island of Öland, right through the spectacular Swedish archipelago.

The Hurtigruten Group operates a separate fleet of ships for expedition-style voyages to the Arctic, Antarctica, and Greenland, while Havila's ships can operate into the Arctic Circle when not on the Norwegian coastal route, and can sail for up to four hours on battery power alone.

SCOTLAND

The fishing town of Oban, two hours west of Glasgow by road, is the base for one of the world's finest cruise experiences. *Hebridean Princess* is a real gem, with Laura Ashley-style interiors – posh enough to have been chartered by Queen Elizabeth II for a family-only celebration of her 80th birthday in 2006. The food is extremely good, and includes locally sourced Scottish beef, local seafood, and seasonal vegetables. There's fine personal service.

This ship, owned by Hebridean Island Cruises, carries up to 50 passengers around some of Scotland's most magnificent coastline and islands. If you cruise from Oban, you can be met at Glasgow airport or railway station and taken to the ship by coach. A second ship, *Lord of the Glens*, is also owned and operated by Hebridean Island Cruises, and carries 54 passengers. Take lots of warm clothing, however (layers are best), as the weather can be changeable and often inclement.

Also providing pleasant cruise experiences to some of Scotland's hidden gems are two pocket-sized ships *Glen Massan* and *Glen Tarsan* of The Majestic Line. Both vessels sail from Oban and carry up to 12 passengers. It's about as far removed from cruising aboard the large resort ships as possible!

NORTH AMERICA

Coastal cruise ships flying the American flag offer a complete change of style from the large resort cruise ships. They are American-owned and American-crewed, and very informal. Being US-registered, they can start from and return to a US port without being

COASTAL CRUISE LINES IN NORTH AMERICA

The cruise companies are: Alaskan Dream Cruises, American Cruise Lines, Lindblad Expeditions/National Geographic, Pearl Seas Cruises, UnCruise Adventures, and Victory Cruise Lines (owned by American Queen Steamboat Company).

What differentiates them? American Cruise Lines, Pearl Seas Cruises, and UnCruise Adventures provide better food and service than the others. American Cruise Lines and Pearl Seas Cruises have (ocean-going) ships with larger cabins, and more public rooms. Drinks are included aboard the ships of American Cruise Lines and Victory Cruise Lines.

required to call at a foreign port along the way – which a foreign-flagged cruise ship must do.

Accommodating up to 200 passengers, the ships are rarely out of sight of land. These cruises are low-key, low-pace, and not really for active types. Their operators seek out lesser-known areas, offering in-depth visits to destinations inaccessible to larger ships, along both the eastern and western seaboards of the US, including Alaska.

Most passengers are seniors. Many prefer not to fly, and wherever possible drive or take a train to join their ship. During the summer, you might see a couple of children on board, but in general small kids are not allowed. There are no facilities for them, and no staff to look after them.

Hebridean Princess in the Scottish islands.

Destinations. Eastern US and Canadian seaboard cruises include the St. Lawrence River, Atlantic Coastal Waterways, New England (good for fall cruises), Cape Cod and the Islands – and Cape Cod Canal, the Deep South, and Florida waterways. Western seaboard cruises cover Alaska, the Pacific Northwest, California Wine Country, and Baja California/Sea of Cortez.

Inland, cruises can be found in the Great Lakes – typically sailing from Toronto or Windsor, Ontario (including a transit of the Welland Canal, which connects Lake Ontario and Lake Erie and forms a section of the Great Lakes Waterway and the St. Lawrence Seaway), and including calls at Windsor/Detroit, Cleveland, Sault Ste. Marie, Thunder Bay, Duluth, and Mackinac Island. Cruises focus on historically relevant destinations, nature and wildlife spotting, and coastal viewing. On some cruises, these boutique-size ships can dock adjacent to a town, allowing easy access on foot.

The ships. These pocket-sized 'D-class' vessels (USA classification) ships are under 2,500 gross tonnage and are subject neither to bureaucratic regulations nor to union rules. They are restricted to cruising no more than 20 miles (32km) offshore. Public room facilities are limited. Because the vessels are US-registered, there is no casino. They really are casual, no-frills ships with basic facilities, no swimming pools, little artwork, no glitz in terms of the interior decor, and their diesel engines and generators are noisy. They usually have three or four decks and,

Coral Discoverer at the Great Barrier Reef.

except for the ships of American Cruise Lines, sister company Pearl Seas Cruises, Lindblad Expeditions/ National Geographic, and Victory Cruise Lines, there is no elevator. Stairs can be steep and are not recommended for anyone with walking difficulties. Because of this, some have an electric chair-lift.

Accommodation is in small outside-view cabins, some opening directly onto a walking deck, which is inconvenient when it rains. Each has a picture window and tiny bathroom. They are basic, with little closet space – often just a curtain across a space with a hanging rod for clothes. Many don't have a television set or telephone. There's no room service, and you may have to turn your own bed down. Cabins are closer to the engines and generators than aboard larger ships, so the noise of the generator humming can be disturbing. The quietest cabins are at the front (bows) – although there could be noise from the bow thruster when arriving into and leaving ports. Most cruising is, however, done in the early morning, so that passengers can sleep better at night.

HAVILA SHIPS			
Ship name	Tonnage	Built	Berths
Havila Capella	16,776	2021	640
Havila Castor	16,776	2021	640
Havila Polaris	16,776	2021	640
Havila Pollux	16,776	2021	640

Tall passengers should note that the bed length rarely exceeds 6ft (1.8m). Although soap is provided, it is perhaps best to bring your own shampoo, conditioner, and other toiletries. Hot and cold-water lines may run close to each other in your bathroom, delivering neither hot nor really cold water, and sound insulation is quite poor.

Activities. The main evening event is dinner in the dining room, with one seating. This can be a family-style affair, with passengers at long tables, and the food passed around.

The food is decidedly American, with fresh local specialties such as crayfish, shrimp, and lobster. Menus aboard the ships of Alaskan Dream Cruises are very limited; those aboard the ships of American Cruise Lines and Lindblad Expeditions/National Geographic offer slightly more variety. You'll probably be asked in the morning to choose which of two main courses you'd like for dinner.

Evening entertainment is after-dinner conversation. Most vessels are in port during the time, so you can easily go ashore for any local nightlife, although most passengers simply go to bed early.

The cost. These cruises are expensive, with an average daily rate of $400–800 a person, plus gratuities of about $125 per person, per seven-day cruise (shared by all personnel).

SOUTH AMERICA

Cruises through misty, snow-capped Chilean fjords and Patagonia's narrow fjords and channels are operated by Australis aboard two 210-passenger ships (debuted 2018 and 2019). The ships carry six Zodiac rigid inflatables for close-in excursions and nature trails. The compact cabins (think rustic but practical) measure 177–220 sq ft/16.4–20.4 sq m; they have windows (no balconies) and twin or double beds, but almost no electrical sockets or USB outlets. There are two public rooms (Patagonia Dining Room and the Darwin Lounge), and naturalist guides accompany each cruise.

AUSTRALIA

The marine wonderland of the Great Barrier Reef, a World Heritage Site off the northeast coast of Australia, is the earth's largest living coral reef – it actually consists of more than 2,800 individual coral reefs. It is visited by around 70 local Australian boutique-size ship operators, who mostly offer short cruises to the reefs and Whitsunday Islands. The area is excellent for scuba diving and snorkeling.

June through September is humpback whale-watching season; the reef shelters the young whales, while the adults nurture them in the shallow waters. Note that the Australian government levies an environmental charge of A$6.50 per day (A$3.25 for those spending less than three hours in the Marine Park) on everyone over four years of age visiting the Great Barrier Reef and its environs.

CRUISING UNDER SAIL

Want to be free as the wind? Think about cruising under sail, with towering masts, the creak of the deck, and gleaming white sails to power the ship along.

There's simply nothing that beats the thrill of being aboard a multi-mast tall ship, sailing under thousands of square feet of canvas through waters that mariners have sailed for centuries. This is cruising in the traditional manner of seafaring, aboard authentic sailing ships, contemporary copies of clipper ships, or high-tech cruise-sail ships, which provides a genuine sailing experience, while keeping creature comforts.

Mealtimes apart, there are no rigid schedules, so life aboard can be liberatingly unstructured. Weather conditions sometimes dictate whether a scheduled port visit will be made or not, but passengers sailing on these vessels are usually unconcerned. They would rather savor the feeling of being at one with nature, albeit in a comfortable, civilized setting, and without having to do the work themselves.

REAL SAIL-CRUISE SHIPS

While we have all been dreaming of adventure, a pocketful of designers and yachtsmen committed pen to paper, hand in pocket and rigging to mast, and came up with a potpourri of stunning vessels to delight the eye and refresh the spirit. Examples include *Golden Horizon* (built as *Flying Clipper*), *Royal Clipper*, *Sea Cloud*, *Sea Cloud II*, *Sea Cloud Spirit*, *Star Clipper*, and *Star Flyer* – all of which have beautiful retro decor to convey the feeling of yesteryear and a slower pace of life.

Of these, *Sea Cloud*, built in 1931, superbly restored in 1979, and adapted to comply with the latest safety regulations of the International Convention for the Safety of Life at Sea (SOLAS), is the world's most exhilarating and romantic sailing ship. It sails in both the Caribbean and the Mediterranean.

Activities are few, so relaxation is the key, in a stylish but unpretentious setting. The food and service are extremely good, as is the interaction between the 69 passengers and 60 crew members, many of whom have worked aboard the ship for many years. One bonus is the fact that a doctor is available on board at no charge for emergencies or seasickness medication.

A modern interpretation of the original *Sea Cloud*, a second ship, named *Sea Cloud II,* was built and introduced in 2001, with a third, *Sea Cloud Spirit*, introduced in 2020.

In 2021, the UK-based Tradewind Voyages chartered the newly built five-masted *Golden Horizon,* the world's largest square-rigged sailing vessel. It was ordered by Star Cruises and originally named *Flying Clipper*, but not delivered to the company due to a dispute with the shipyard.

CONTEMPORARY SAIL-CRUISE SHIPS

To combine sailing with push-button automation, try *Club Med 2* (Club Méditerranée) or *Wind Surf* (Windstar Cruises) – with five tall aluminum masts, they are the world's largest sail-cruise ships – and *Wind Spirit* and *Wind Star* (Windstar Cruises), with four masts. Not a hand touches the sails; they are computer-controlled from the navigation bridge.

The traditional sense of sailing is almost absent in these ocean-going robots, because a computer keeps the ship on an even keel. Also, some find it hard to get used to the whine of the vessels' generators, which run the lighting and air-conditioning systems 24 hours a day.

The *Sea Cloud* crew goes up the rigging.

HOW TO MEASURE WIND SPEEDS

Understanding wind patterns is important to sailing ships, but the numbering system for wind velocity can confuse. There are 12 velocities, known as 'force' on the Beaufort scale, devised in 1805 by Sir Francis Beaufort, an Irish-born hydrographer and officer in Britain's Royal Navy. It was adopted internationally in 1874 as the official means of recording wind velocity. They are as follows, with descriptions of the ocean surface:

Force 0 (0–1mph): Calm; glassy (like a mirror).

Force 1 (1–3mph): Light wind; rippled surface.

Force 2 (4–7mph): Light breeze; small wavelets.

Force 3 (8–12mph): Gentle breeze; large wavelets, scattered whitecaps.

Force 4 (13–18mph): Moderate breeze; small waves, frequent whitecaps.

Force 5 (19–24mph): Fresh breeze; moderate waves, numerous whitecaps.

Force 6 (25–31mph): Strong breeze; large waves, white foam crests.

Force 7 (32–38mph): Moderate gale; streaky white foam.

Force 8 (39–46mph): Fresh gale; moderate waves.

Force 9 (47–54mph): Strong gale; high waves.

Force 10 (55–63mph): Whole gale; very high waves, curling crests.

Force 11 (64–72mph): Violent storm; extremely high waves, froth and foam, poor visibility.

Force 12 (73+mph): Hurricane; huge waves, thundering white spray, visibility nil.

From a yachtsman's viewpoint, the sail-to-power ratio is poor, so these sail-cruise ships have engine power to get them into and out of port. *Sea Cloud, Sea Cloud II, Sea Cloud Spirit*, and *Star Clipper* ships do it by sail alone, except when there is no wind, which seldom happens.

On some itineraries, if there's little wind, you could be motor-powered for most of the cruise, with only a few hours under sail. The three Windstar Cruises vessels and one Club Med ship are typically under sail for about 40 percent of the time.

The Windstar ships carry mainly North American passengers, while the Club Med vessel caters mainly to French speakers.

Another slightly smaller vessel is the chic *Le Ponant*. This three-mast ship caters to just 64 French-speaking passengers in elegant, yet casual, contemporary surroundings, advancing the technology of the original Windstar concept. The ship made news in 2008, when its crew was held to ransom by pirates off the Somali coast; no passengers were on board at the time.

WHEN THE ENGINE CUTS IN

Aboard the ships of Sea Cloud Cruises and Star Clippers, because they are real sailing ships, you could be under sail for most of the night when the ships are under way, as long as there is wind, of course, and on the days or part days at sea.

The ship's small engine is used for maneuvering in and out of port. In the Caribbean, for example, the trade winds are good for most of the year, but in the Mediterranean the winds are not so potent.

Aboard the ships of Windstar Cruises, however, the itineraries are so port-intensive that the computer-controlled sails are hardly ever used.

The beautiful *Sea Cloud* under full sail.

TRANSATLANTIC CROSSINGS

You may face some unpredictable weather but there's something romantic and adventurous about this classic ocean voyage.

This should be one of life's essential travel experiences. Crossing the 3,000 miles (4,830km) of the North Atlantic by a real ocean liner is a great way to avoid the hassles of airports. I have done it myself some 160 times and always enjoy it immensely – and unlike flying, there is no jet lag. Yet the days when ships were built specifically for crossings are almost gone. The only one offering a regularly scheduled service is Cunard's iconic *Queen Mary 2 (QM2)*, built with an extra-thick hull designed to survive the worst weather the North Atlantic has to offer.

Stepping aboard is like stepping back in time. It's a leisurely seven-day voyage, and just being at sea provides an intoxicating sense of freedom that few destinations can offer. Typically, on five of the seven days, the clocks will be advanced (eastbound) or put back (westbound) by one hour (there is a 5-hour difference between the UK and the east coast of the USA. You can take as many bags as you want, and even your pets – *QM2*'s kennels (12 on each of two levels) are overseen by a full-time kennel master, who can take your dog out for a walk along a special pathway (closed to passengers), adorned with a real British lamppost and a red New York fire hydrant. Special blankets are provided for cold weather crossings. Cats can also be carried, but you'll need two spaces (one for sleeping, and an adjacent one for litter). Pets can be visited (and walked) by their owners each day. Book well in advance if you want to travel with your pet, however, because the number of pets that can be carried is strictly limited. You will also need to carry the correct paperwork for your pet, including vaccination verification.

The 2,705-passenger *QM2* is the largest real ocean liner – it is not a cruise ship! – ever built, and a des-

tination on its own. New in 2004, it measures 148,528 gross tons. It has a wide walk-around promenade deck outdoors, the forward section of which is under cover from the weather or wind (three times around is 6,102ft/1,860m, or 1.1 miles/1.8km).

By comparison, *QM2*'s smaller half-sisters, the popular *Queen Elizabeth* and *Queen Victoria* both measure about 90,000 gross tons, and half-sister *Queen Anne* (new in 2023) measures about 114,000 gross tons (note: these were built as cruise ships and are not ocean liners). The venerable *QE2* (retired in 2008), measured 70,327 gross tons, while the ill-fated *Titanic* measured a much smaller mere 46,328 gross tons. The difference is that *QM2* has a specially strengthened hull designed to withstand the pressures of the North Atlantic and its unpredictable weather.

The North Atlantic Ocean can really be as smooth as glass or as rough as old boots, although in my ex-

Queen Mary 2 leaving New York City.

DID YOU KNOW...

That the first regular steamship service across the North Atlantic was inaugurated on 28 March 1838, when the 703-ton steamer *Sirius* left London for New York via Cork, Ireland?

That the winter of 1970–71 was the first time since 1838 that there was no regular passenger service on the North Atlantic?

Part of *Queen Mary 2*'s Illuminations auditorium converts into a planetarium.

perience it is rare for the weather to be bad for an entire crossing. But when it *is* a bit choppy, its heaving beauty really is mesmerizing – and never, ever boring. However, make sure you always use the handrails when you move around, and use the elevators rather than the stairs.

When the ship is under way at speed (above 25 knots – about 30 land miles per hour) on a windy day, a cabin balcony is pretty useless, and the promenade deck is a challenging place to be – if you can even get outside, that is! It can be bitterly cold on deck in winter in the open seas of the Atlantic, so you may never open your balcony door. If you do book a balcony cabin, choose the port side on westbound crossings and the starboard side on eastbound crossings – if the weather is kind and the sun is shining, you'll get the sun. Sometimes, visibility is low (think pea-soup fog), and you'll hear the ship's horn – a powerful, haunting sound – bellowing every two minutes.

Tip: If you have any dental concerns, take a dental repair kit (there is no dentist on board).

DURING THE CROSSING

Once *Queen Mary 2* has left port, and settled down at sea on the second day, the natural rhythm of life slows down, and you begin to understand that time spent at sea, with few distractions, is truly special, and completely different from any 'normal' cruise ship. It allows you some well-earned 'me' time – to pamper yourself in the spa, to attend a lecture by a well-known author or other personality, or simply to

relax and read a book from the wonderful library. Cunard has a list of '101 Things To Do On A *Queen Mary 2* Transatlantic Crossing' – just in case you really do want to be active. But, best of all, you can turn off your cell (mobile) phone – and have a complete digital detox. In fact, you will need to put your phone in Airline Mode in order to avoid excessive charges. If you don't, it will log into the Marine Communications Network, which is an expensive system linking land and sea beacons and satellites.

Apart from distinguished guest speakers, *QM2* has a wide variety of leisure facilities, including a superb planetarium (with several different shows, each narrated by a famous film star or TV personality, for which you will need to make a reservation), and a 1,000-seat theater for evening shows. There may also be acting classes, bridge (the card-playing kind) groups, big-band-style dance sessions, line dances, movies, keep-fit exercises, cooking, and computer classes, so you'll never be bored mid-ocean.

There are typically three 'formal' (tuxedo, dinner jacket) nights (one of which could be a 'Black & White' night) and four informal nights during a seven-night crossing, when an outbreak of elegance prevails, and gentlemen dance hosts (when carried) are kept busy by solo female passengers who love to dance.

One of the ship's most pleasurable and used facilities is its outstanding library and bookshop – the largest at sea. Located forward on Deck 8, it houses around 10,000 books (of which over 8,000 are in English and 800 in German, with others in Japanese, Spanish,

Italian, and French), housed in more than 100 glass-fronted cabinets that need to be locked by hand – a procedure that takes over 20 minutes (central locking was never part of an ocean liner setup). The lighting is good, making it easy to read the book titles, and the bookshelves have 'lips' so that the books won't fall out in heavy weather. Each person can take out two books, which are signed out by the duty librarian. However, the library is no longer run by Ocean Books, which always provided professional librarians who knew their books, but is now run by regular ship staff (the UK-based Ocean Books still provides the books, however, and cover each one in a protective skin. There are, however, a few cosy chairs to curl up on to read, or just admire the views out to sea.

If the weather's decent, you can even swim outside, although this tends to be rare – except in the height of summer – because of the ship's speed and wind speed.

Taking some 'me' time in the spa is another benefit of an ocean crossing. The facilities include a decent-sized indoor pool and relaxation area, sauna, steam room, and hammam (with its ergonomically curved benches and mosaic tiles), although they are only available in two-hour time slots (to control usage and enable cleaning of the facilities). You can also book a body-pampering treatment such as a massage.

Another classic thing to do is to enjoy the typically British afternoon tea, complete with cakes, scones, pastries, and finger sandwiches – all served by a rather hurried white-gloved staff – together with tea, and accompanied by live, light music.

The real challenge is that you'll find there simply isn't enough time to do everything, and there's no way you'll ever get bored aboard this ship.

You can even get married mid-Atlantic during a crossing. Cunard started its popular 'Weddings at Sea' program in 2012. The first couple to be married by the ship's captain was Dr. William DeLuca (from the US) and Kelly Lewis (from the UK). They couldn't decide whether to marry in the UK or the US, so they chose halfway between the two (it was their first crossing, and, indeed, their first-ever vacation at sea). The couple chose Cunard because of the company's 'distinguished history of transatlantic crossings.' Note that only one wedding per day can be arranged, with a time of 11am or 3.30pm. Ceremonies take place only on days at sea, and every detail is planned by an onboard wedding coordinator. The cost starts at $2,500.

A MEMORABLE ARRIVAL

The day before you arrive in New York, Southampton, or (occasionally) in Hamburg, Germany, the disembarkation procedures will arrive in your suite or cabin. If you are in a hurry to disembark, you can opt to carry your own bags by registering for 'Express Disembarkation.'

Arriving in New York is one of cruising's iconic experiences, but you'll need to be up early. You'll see the lights of Long Island on your starboard side at about

4.30am, while the Verrazzano–Narrows suspension bridge, at the entrance to New York harbor, will be dead ahead. QM2 usually passes the State of Liberty at about 6am – when a cabin with a balcony on the port side will give you the best views. The ship then makes a right turn opposite the statue towards the Brooklyn Cruise Terminal. On the occasions when the ship berths at Pier 90 in Manhattan at the Passenger Terminal, it will turn left towards the Hudson River – you'll get the best views of the Manhattan skyline at this point from a cabin with a balcony on the starboard side. Arrival always creates a sense of anticipation of what lies ahead, and the feeling that, after a week of being cosseted, you will be thrust back into the fast lane with full force – and then some.

LEAVING NEW YORK/ARRIVING IN SOUTHAMPTON

If you sail from Red Hook Point in Brooklyn, the last thing you'll notice before entering the ship is the overhead banner that declares: 'Leaving Brooklyn? Fuhgeddaboudit!' And that, dear reader, is *precisely* what a transatlantic crossing will have you do.

For arrival in Southampton, QM2 will usually round the Isle of Wight at about 4.30am, and be berthed alongside in Southampton by around 6.30am. Immigration is upon arrival in either New York or Southampton (or, possibly, Hamburg).

For arrival in Hamburg, the ship will sail along the Elbe River to arrive at the Cruise Center in HafenCity. If you carry your own luggage, you can take the sub-

The library on board *Queen Mary 2*.

Queen Mary 2 **arriving in New York.**

way from Uberseequartier to Jungfernstieg (it's just two stops from where the town hall is located.

REPOSITIONING CROSSINGS

Other cruise ships crossing the Atlantic Ocean are really little more than repositioning cruises – a way of moving ships that cruise the Mediterranean in summer to the Caribbean in winter, and vice versa, usually in spring and fall. Most of these ships cross the Atlantic using the sunny southern route, departing from southern ports such as Fort Lauderdale, San Juan, or Barbados, and ending the journey in Lisbon, Genoa, or Copenhagen via the Azores or the Canary Islands, off the coast of northern Africa.

These repositioning trips take longer – between eight and 12 days – but they do offer an alternative way of experiencing the romance and adventure of a crossing – with a number of sea days for total relaxation. Note that when the weather is not so good, the outdoor swimming pools will probably be out of use on repositioning crossings.

QUEEN MARY 2 FACTS

- The ship was built by ALSTOM Chantiers de l'Atlantique, in St. Nazaire, France.
- The hull is made up of 94 steel blocks, some weighing more than 600 tons.
- The keel was laid on 4 July 2002, and its float out was 16 March 2003.
- The ship is four football fields in length, and longer than 36 London buses (31.5ft each).
- The ship's four Mermaid pods were built by Rolls-Royce-owned Kamewa and Alstom Powers Motors. The forward two are fixed in place, while the aft two can turn through 360 degrees to steer and manoeuvre the ship.
- Her engines produce 157,000 horsepower, and her power plant produces enough electricity to light a city the size of Southampton (England).
- There are three thrusters of 3.2 Megawatts each - allowing the ship to turn in her own length without the use of tugs. These are operated with a fingertip touch by the captain.
- *QM2*, at 1,132ft long, is five times longer than Cunard's first ship, *Britannia* (230ft), which entered service on 4 July 1840.
- The ship is equal to the height of a 23-storey building (it has 17 decks that tower 200ft above the waterline). Its overall height was limited by the need for it to pass under New York's Verrazzano Narrows Bridge.
- The ships' whistles include an original whistle from RMS *Queen Mary*, so that her famous predecessor's voice would once again be heard on North Atlantic Ocean crossings. The sound is audible for ten miles.
- During construction, some 250 tons of paint were used on the ship's exterior.
- The ship has 1,100 fire doors, 5,000 fire detectors, and 8,350 automatic fire extinguishers.

- Each cabin grade is paired with a sea-view restaurant, including grill rooms for the higher categories.
- Maritime Quest, a pictorial history of the Cunard Line, its ships, and famous people who sailed aboard them, is installed during the fitting out process.
- The Royal Court Theatre (it's the main show lounge for 'production' shows and cabaret) has seating for 1,094.
- Illuminations has seating for 493. It is a cinema and auditorium, part of which converts into the only planetarium at sea (seating 150), for highly specialised presentations about the solar system, and other lectures.
- The dance floor in the Queens Room, which spans the whole beam (width) of the ship, is the largest at sea.
- The G32 Nightclub is named after the hull number given to the ship by the shipyard and is strategically located overlooking the stern (aft) of the ship, away from passenger cabins.
- The Promenade Deck is approximately 645yds/m, with one lap being just over one third of a mile.
- When *QMS* was built, it housed a $5 million art collection, which included a huge tapestry in the Britannia Restaurant.
- Four luxurious forward-view suites can be combined to create a single large suite of 5,016 sq ft (466 sq m).
- Children have their own deck area and swimming pool. Named Minnows, it is located aft of The Play Zone and The Zone.
- The special outdoor exercise area for dogs carried on transatlantic crossings includes a British lamppost and a New York fire hydrant.
- When built, the ship included 30 cabins specially designed for disabled passengers, and 36 cabins designed to accommodate deaf or hearing-impaired passengers.

WORLD CRUISES

Taking an around-the-world cruise is a great way to travel without having to pack and unpack constantly. But choose carefully: some ships spend very little time in ports.

Since Cunard operated its first world cruise aboard the *Laconia* in 1922 (an American Express Company charter), this has become the ultimate classic journey – more a voyage of discovery than a cruise. It is defined as the complete circumnavigation of the earth in a continuous one-way voyage, typically including both the Panama and Suez canals. Ports of call are carefully planned for their interest and diversity, and the entire voyage can last six months or longer.

It is about exchanging familiar environments with new ones: galas, glamorous evening soirées, themed balls (for example, Cunard's Black & White Ball and Royal Ascot Ball), well-known lecturers and entertainment that ranges from intimate recitals to large-scale shows and headline cabaret specialty acts. Best of all, you need pack and unpack just once during this long voyage.

An around-the-world cruise means letting time stand still, enjoying stabilized, air-conditioned comfort in luxury cabins, combined with extraordinary sightseeing and excursion opportunities on shore and overland.

It is also an excellent way of exchanging the northern winter for the southern sun in a grand voyage that is over 32,000 nautical miles long, following in the wake of Ferdinand Magellan, who led his round-the-world voyage in 1519–22.

Around-the-world cruises generally pursue the sun in a westbound direction, which provides the additional bonus of gaining an hour each time a ship goes into the next time zone. Travel in an eastbound direction –

between, for example, Europe and Australia – and you lose an hour each time. Each time zone is 15 degrees when measuring east or west from the Prime Meridian at Greenwich, England. A few ships that include an around-South America voyage will generally travel in a southbound, then westbound, direction.

There are four aspects to a good world cruise: itinerary, ship, price, and the cruise line's experience. Some of the most ambitious itineraries are those operated by Hapag-Lloyd Cruises and Phoenix Reisen. Hapag-Lloyd's world cruise aboard *Europa* for 2021/22 was a stunning 251 days long. Staying overnight in several ports of call means that you can plan to meet friends, go out for dinner, and enjoy nights out on the town. But check cruise line websites and brochures and itineraries carefully, because some ships spend surprisingly little time in port. There'll be lots of sea days, during which your suite or cabin can be a private refuge, so it really is worth choosing the best (largest) you can afford.

Around-the-world cruises appeal to anyone who delights in roaming the world in search of new expe-

Aurora **transiting the scenic Panama Canal.**

Queen Mary 2 in Sydney during a world cruise.

riences, sights, sounds, cultures, and aromas, and those wanting to escape a harsh winter.

In 2023, for example, the 128-day around-the-world cruise aboard *Costa Deliziosa* (Costa Cruises) left Trieste on January 6, to return on May 13. The ship sailed from the Mediterranean to the Arabian Peninsula, then east to India and the Maldives before heading south to Madagascar and South Africa. It then crossed the Atlantic Ocean to Brazil. The ship then headed south to Ushuaia at the tip of Argentina, sailed through the Beagle Channel and then headed north, from Chile to Panama, visited Central America and New York. After then heading east, it returned to Europe after taking in 52 scheduled destinations on four continents, and crossing three oceans.

Passengers came from about 40 different countries, with a predominance of French (about 500), Italians (about 360), and Germans (about 340), Swiss (about 160), Spanish (about 140), and Austrians (about 100). The oldest traveler was French (94 years old), and the youngest was Austrian (6 years old).

In practical terms, this mid-size ship (named in Dubai in 2010 and the first new cruise ship to be named in an Arab city – with a bottle of fig juice instead of the traditional bottle of champagne) was not built for long voyages, and has mostly small cabins with very limited storage space. Thankfully, of the 1,130 cabins, just under 70 percent have an outside view and 772 have a (narrow) balcony.

Dining was in the 1,264-seat Albatros Restaurant. Located aft, it has good ocean views, in one of two seating times. This, however, rather limited flexibility, particularly when the ship visited a port of call. Also, there were no wine sommeliers (wine was served by waiters and supervisors).

Aboard any ship featuring a round-the-world cruise comes the question of meals, in order not to be repetitious. The galleys of most of today's ships are simply not equipped to provide the kind of variety needed (including for passengers with special dietary requirements), not to mention the food storage space of any ship designed mainly for cruises of up to two weeks.

WORLD CRUISE SEGMENTS

If you want to experience some of the extra things that a full around-the-world cruise provides, but cannot spare the three months needed, most cruise lines offer part-world, or 'segment' cruises. This way you can try the ship and service levels before investing the time and money for a full circumnavigation. The most popular length is 20–30 days.

'Segmenters,' as they are known, typically add on a pre- or post-cruise stay in a destination, combining a cruise 'n' stay vacation. In this way, they can visit exotic, new, or favorite regions and destinations while enjoying the elegance, comfort, food, and good company of their cruise ship.

Remember that you get what you pay for. Ships we have rated at four stars or more will probably include shuttle buses from your ship to town centers; ships rated three stars or less will not.

Ships that roam worldwide during the year offer the most experienced world cruises or segments. In August 2016, for example, *Europa 2* operated a world voyage lasting 337 days; it was divided into three distinct routes and had over 20 segments.

WHAT DOES IT COST?

Prices for a full world cruise vary depending on the cruise line, the number of days, and the type of accommodation you choose. Substantial discounts and special incentives are offered if you book early. The lowest-grade cabins sell out fastest, so book early to secure a place. Cruise lines typically advertise only a 'from' price as a lead-in rate and provide the price for the largest suites upon application.

Passengers booking a full world cruise may enjoy a pre-cruise five-star hotel stay and an extravagant dinner with the cruise line's top executives, plus other special events during the cruise (not available to 'segmenters'), and onboard credits. Generally, excursions are not included (exception: Regent Seven Seas Cruises).

Some ships include alcoholic drinks and wine in their cruise fares (aboard the ships of Regent Seven Seas Cruises, Silversea Cruises, for example), but many do not. There will inevitably be the question of gratuities to staff, if not included in the fare, factor in about $20 per person, per day to your budget.

SHORE EXCURSIONS

Part of the excitement of an around-the-world voyage is the anticipation of seeing new destinations and planning how best to use your time, not just aboard, but in the destinations to be visited. This is where the expertise of a cruise line's shore-excursion department and concierge can prove worthwhile.

Aboard some ships, tailor-made excursions are available, as are extras such as arranging private cars with a driver and guide for a few hours or a whole day.

Overland tours lasting from one to five days are sometimes available. Here, you leave the ship in one port and rejoin in another a few days later – for example, leave the ship in Mumbai, fly to Agra to experience the Taj Mahal, and perhaps ride aboard the Maharajas' Express train, then fly to another port to meet back up with the ship. Depending on the 'overland' country, you may need to apply for a visa before your voyage.

One frustration for independent passengers not wishing to join organized excursions is the lack of port information. The answer is to do the research yourself. Books in the ship's library should help if you haven't done your homework before embarking, as will the Internet.

CELEBRATIONS AT SEA

On around-the-world cruises, special dates for English-speaking passengers are usually observed with decorations, dinners, dances, teas, and menus that reflect the occasion. Examples include:

Jan 25: Robert Burns Night (Burns Dinner).
Jan 26: Australia's National Constitution Day.
Feb 6: New Zealand (Waitangi) Day.
Feb 14: St. Valentine's Day.
Mar 1: St. David's Day (patron saint of Wales).
Feb/Mar (Tue before Lent): Shrove Tuesday (pancakes galore).
Mar 17: St. Patrick's Day (patron saint of Ireland – think green beer).

Apr 1: April Fool's Day (a morning of jokes and tricks).
Apr 23: St. George's Day (patron saint of England).
May 1: May Day (traditional Morris dancing).

Two very special ceremonies form part of the passenger participation events on a traditional around-the-world cruise:

Crossing the Equator, when, in Greek mythology, King Neptune (Neptunus Rex, the old man of the sea), his wife Amphitrite (goddess of the sea, wife of the god Poseidon), and the Royal Court initiate those crossing the line for the first time (called pollywogs). An old naval tradition, it is usually conducted at the poolside – with inevitable results. If it's done well, it can be a real hoot!

Crossing the International Date Line, where you gain or lose a day, depending on whether you're traveling eastbound or westbound. The imaginary line, at approximately 180 degrees longitude, isn't straight but zigzags to avoid splitting countries apart. Although it was established with international agreement, it has confused explorers, navigators, and travelers ever since. In Jules Verne's *Around the World in 80 Days* Phileas Fogg and his crew return to London one day late (or so they think), but it is the extra day gained by crossing the International Date Line that enables them to win their wager.

PLANNING

For world cruisegoers, one of the most important decisions to make will be about what clothes to pack for the different climates, geographical locations, weather, and other conditions. What is good is that once you are aboard, you will only need to unpack once, and you can take as much luggage as you wish. However, note that many ships have very limited storage space for luggage, and space for clothes may also be minimal. If you need to fly to join the cruise, you can send your luggage on ahead with a courier service.

The downside of cruising around the world aboard many ships is the size of the cabins, the lack of storage space, not just for clothes to wear, and shoes you might need for different climates, port visits, and shipboard activities, but also for personal toiletry items and all the other things you might need on a journey lasting three months or so.

Although all ships have laundries (located in behind-the-scenes crew areas not available to passengers), some also have launderettes for passengers (the place to go for 'inside' gossip), so you can clean items that you need to reuse quickly.

Tip: take a dental repair kit, because there is no dentist on board.

For an operator, planning a world cruise involves a daunting amount of organization. For example, more than 700,000 main meals are prepared during a typical world cruise aboard *Queen Mary 2*. A ship of this size needs two major crew changes during a three-month-long voyage. Hundreds of professional entertainers, lecturers, bands, and musicians must be booked and contracted, some more than a year in advance.

A Hurtigruten ship beneath the Northern Lights, Norway.

39 WONDERFUL CRUISE EXPERIENCES

During the 39-year lifespan of this book (originally published as the *Berlitz Handbook to Cruising*), I have been privileged to enjoy some wonderful experiences aboard the world's cruise ships. Here, in no particular order, are 39 wonderful cruise experiences.

FINGAL'S CAVE

Passing within an arm's distance of Fingal's Cave on the uninhabited island of Staffa (one of Scotland's Inner Hebridean Islands), as Felix Mendelssohn's *Hebrides Overture* (inspired by the real molten lava rock cavern) was played on the open back deck of the pocket-sized *Hebridean Princess*. At the time – late one chilly morning in spring – I was sitting wrapped in a tartan blanket under a grey, foreboding sky, enjoying a single malt whisky.

SLICE OF ICE

Watching from the observation deck above the bridge of *Hanseatic*, as the ship sliced slowly through the pack ice in the incredibly scenic, steep-sided Lemaire Channel in the Antarctic Peninsula.

'EUROPA'S BEST'

Tasting some beautiful artisan cuisine prepared by chefs whose restaurants had three Michelin stars aboard *Europa* for the annual Europa's Best event in Antwerp. Some of the finest cheese and wine producers from Austria, France, Germany, and Switzerland displayed their wares, too. This culinary heaven can be enjoyed by anyone with a ticket.

BITE OF APPLE

Gliding past the Statue of Liberty in the early-morning mist and then approaching the New York skyline, from the outside deck aboard *Queen Mary 2*. Anyone can experience this, whether aboard *Queen Mary 2* or any cruise ship sailing into New York.

THE ROYAL BOX

Having breakfast in a 'Royal Box' on deck aboard the boutique ships *SeaDream I* or *SeaDream II* while at sea in a warm weather area.

CULINARY TOUR DE FORCE

Enjoying freshly sliced tuna and yellowtail sashimi at Nobu Matsuhisa's Silk Road Sushi Bar aboard the former *Crystal Serenity*. Not only was this a culinary tour de force, but watching the Japanese chefs was entertaining too.

AMALFI MAGIC

Sitting on the corner balcony of a Club Suite aboard *Azamara Quest*, admiring the beautiful scenery of Sorrento, Italy, with the ship at anchor off the famed coastline and a Limoncello to hand.

CANDLES IN THE WIND

Dining by candlelight at the aft terrace café of *Aegean Odyssey* while watching the mesmerizing patterns created on the water by a full, seemingly orange moon in Southeast Asia.

NOODLES IN ALASKA

Sitting on my balcony, breathing in the fresh air, and enjoying room-service steaming hot udon (thick white) noodles made from wheat flour, while transiting Alaska's Inside Passage aboard *Nippon Maru*.

Douglas Ward at Shackleton's grave, South Georgia.

The Blue Lagoon thermal hot spring, Iceland.

SYDNEY SIGHTS

Being outside on deck watching as *Queen Mary 2* turned majestically in Sydney Harbour and sidled up to Circular Quay, close to the Sydney Harbour Bridge and Opera House. All this with hundreds of spectators.

BLUE LAGOON NIGHTS

Lying down in the padded 'Blue Lagoon' seating area at the stern of the *Sea Cloud,* watching the sails directing this wonderful tall ship and seeing a shooting star pass quickly overhead – an incredibly serene, and magical experience.

TRIBUTE TO SHACKLETON

One Christmas Day, paying homage in Grytviken – the former Norwegian whaling station in South Georgia – with passengers from the expedition ships *Hanseatic* and the former *Bremen*. We toasted the explorer Sir Ernest Shackleton with Aquavit poured on his grave.

THE GREEN FLASH

Cruising aboard a *Hurtigruten* ship, near Hammerfest or Honningsvag on the northern coast of Norway in October, and seeing the 'green flash' of the northern lights appear on the horizon, as the sun dipped and disappeared.

UNDER THE STARS

Standing on deck at the front of the ship, just before bedtime, in one of the wonderfully comfortable cotton sleep suits provided aboard the intimate, boutique-sized *SeaDream I* and *SeaDream II*. The rhythm of the ship was lulling me to sleep as it sailed to its next destination.

SPIDERMAN

Sitting in the netting hanging at the bowsprit (front) of the sail-cruise ship (tall ship) *Star Flyer* – an exhilarating experience. On this occasion, the ship was gliding gracefully through the water on a perfect, sun-filled day in the azure blue Caribbean Sea.

MISTY MORNING

Standing on the foredeck of a cruise ship entering Ha Long Bay, a Unesco World Heritage site in the Gulf of Tonkin, Quang Ninh Province, in northeastern Vietnam. Go in the early morning, when the mist is heavy, for an ethereal feeling of calmness. The dramatic limestone karsts (stone islands) surrounding the ship loom up from the sea-level cloud of heavy air.

QUEEN AND COUNTRY

Taking a bath in Cabin 1066 of the *Queen Elizabeth 2* one evening during a transatlantic crossing, listening to Elgar's *Pomp and Circumstance* on the in-cabin broadcast system and thinking: how incredibly British.

CANAL MOVE

Watching as steel-wired electric mules (each costing over $2 million) pull your cruise ship into position in one of the lock chambers at Miraflores Locks, in the Panama Canal.

BIRD'S-EYE VIEW

Being aboard a cruise ship sailing into or out of Venice, gliding past St Mark's Square. It's a view of Venice you only get from the deck (or balcony – if yours is on the correct side) of a waterborne vessel.

STEPS AWAY

Being aboard a small cruise ship moored alongside the State Hermitage Museum in St. Petersburg, Russia. This takes you literally just a few steps away from the iconic building – one of the largest and oldest museums in the world, with over three million items in its collection, including some stunning Fabergé eggs.

TITANIC POSE

Standing with outstretched arms, just like Kate Winslet in the movie *Titanic*, at the front of *Braemar*, as the ship glided slowly through the Swedish archipelago towards Stockholm.

ON TOP OF THE WORLD

Standing at 90 degrees north – the geographic North Pole (it's actually an ice flow, where the first human set foot in 1948) – literally looking down the world. I reached the North Pole in 2016 aboard the stunning Russian nuclear-powered icebreaker *50 Years of Victory*.

BATHTUB CRUISING

Staring at the horizon while lying in the bathtub in the 'wet room' (with heated floor) in one of the two Deck 10 Crystal Penthouse suites aboard the former *Crystal Symphony*, as the ship glided through the open water.

GRAND SPA

Sitting in the hot bath of the grand spa aboard *Asuka II* late at night – looking out over the city lights in Naha, the port for Okinawa, Japan.

PAW POWER

Being pulled by a team of huskies in Juneau, Alaska, as we sped past glaciers and ice peaks (taken in combination with a flight to Mendenhall Glacier).

SLIPPING AWAY

Sitting on the deck of a pocket-sized cruise ship in Glacier Bay, Alaska, watching the blue glacial ice calving, making you rock and roll as it slipped, slid, and crashed into the water within inches of your body.

MELTING AWAY

Sitting in a pool of silica- and sulfur-rich geo-thermal water in Iceland's man-made Blue Lagoon, close to the Svartsengi Power Station, and part of the lava field located on the Reykjanes Peninsula. This is offered as part of a tour from your cruise ship.

SURPRISE, SURPRISE

Meeting someone you never expected to, or thought possible to meet. On cruises over the years, I have been fortunate enough to meet, talk to, and have a

39 WAYS TO UPGRADE YOUR CRUISE EXPERIENCE

There are many ways to enhance your cruise and vacation – some of which will add little or no cost, some may cost more, but all add value and comfort. Your cruise booking agent may be able to help obtain some of these additional 'perks' at no additional cost to you. Here are 36 suggestions for you to consider.

1. Take a digital detox cruise – turn off your cell (mobile) phone for a whole cruise, or at least a few days.
2. Go farther afield – take a cruise to an area of the world you haven't yet been to.
3. If you need to fly to get to your ship, consider upgrading from Economy (Coach) Class to Business or First Class.
4. Upgrade your accommodation (if the ship is not full) by paying extra when on board.
5. Be the first to sleep in a brand-new bed by booking a maiden voyage aboard a brand-new ship.
6. Upgrade your accommodation, if the budget allows. Consider upgrading from an interior (no-view) cabin to one with a window, or a 'virtual' balcony.
7. Consider upgrading from a 'standard' cabin with a window to one with a balcony.
8. If possible, upgrade from a balcony cabin to a suite, as you'll get more 'perks', and better service.
9. Consider upgrading from a 'suite' with just a shower enclosure to a suite, with both a bathtub and a separate shower enclosure.
10. And think about upgrading from standard suite to a grand suite, a penthouse suite, or an 'owner's suite' for even more recognition and more 'perks.'
11. For a more intimate dining experience, reserve a table in one of the extra-cost (à la carte) restaurants.
12. Upgrade your fitness level – have a 'no elevator' day (or two, or more).
13. Try some food items you would not normally eat at home, such as Escargots de Bourgignon, Salmon Coulibiak, or Spanakopita, to upgrade your dining experience.
14. Upgrade your health by eating lighter, 'heart-healthy' options.
15. If you are a meat eater, have a meat-free day (numerous non-meat choices are available aboard any cruise ship).
16. For a special day, have breakfast in bed – with champagne.
17. Try a higher-quality wine or champagne on a special day (birthday, anniversary, or other celebration).
18. Book a culinary lesson aboard a ship with built-in cooking stations, so you can experience 'hands-on' with a professional.
19. Upgrade your drinks package from 'standard' to 'premium' and taste better brands, drinks, and wines.
20. Take a look at your ship at arm's length, from a 'glass capsule' on *Anthem of the Seas*, *Odyssey of the Seas*, *Ovation of the Seas*, *Quantum of the Seas*, or *Spectrum of the Seas*.
21. Try a new activity – sign-up for something you'd never considered doing before.
22. Learn something new: for example, how to play a keyboard instrument. You can take part in free hands-on classes aboard *Crystal Serenity* or *Crystal Symphony*.
23. Book a session or two with a personal trainer.
24. Join a Yoga and Pilates class. These are good for any age, because the movements are slow (unlike frenetic keep fit classes), and an inexpensive way to upgrade your personal fitness level.
25. If you've never had one, try a body-pampering treatment (suggestions: a full body massage, a facial, or, if you are traveling with a partner, a couples massage).
26. Have some relaxing 'me' time by booking a Day Spa, at extra cost. These are often offered at a reduced price on a port day, when most passengers are off the ship.
27. Book a private (extra-cost) deck night aboard *Azamara Journey*, *Azamara Pursuit*, or *Azamara Quest*. The experience involves drinks, a hot tub, and sleeping on deck.
28. If you're married, why not think about renewing your commitment in a Renewal of Vows ceremony?
29. Take a social dance lesson – learn how to do the waltz, foxtrot, quickstep, samba, or tango.
30. Reserve a 'Royal Box' (champagne and chocolates included) in the Royal Court Theatre for the show aboard Cunard's *Queen Elizabeth* or *Queen Victoria*.
31. Take a transatlantic crossing aboard a real ocean liner. *Queen Mary 2* is the only ship built for all weather conditions in the North Atlantic, and it's one of the best ways to arrive in a different continent without jet lag.
32. If you are traveling with a baby, take advantage of a night nursery (free aboard Cunard and P&O Cruises ships, but at an extra cost aboard most others), so you can have some 'me-time' in the evening – and some decent sleep.
33. When you come back from a morning excursion, instead of heading to the buffet, have a calm room-service lunch.
34. Get real insight into a place you want to visit by booking a private tour with a local guide.
35. Book a post-cruise stay, so disembarkation day becomes less frenetic and gives you time to adjust to 'normality.'
36. Take a cooking class aboard a ship that has a dedicated built-in culinary center.
37. With the increased interest in turmeric and its health benefits, having a curry at lunchtime aboard any P&O Cruises ship could prove beneficial.
38. Leave the kids at home (with grandparents) and choose an adults-only ship.
39. Close up the house and take an around-the-world cruise.

drink with some well-known film stars and other famous personalities including Elizabeth Taylor and Richard Burton, Tippi Hedren, Dame Margot Fonteyn, and the great conductor Leopold Stokowski.

PHOTO OPPORTUNITY

Being aboard a photo tender arranged by the cruise line (in my case, this was aboard a tall ship) and taking photographs as the tall ship was under full sail and not slowing down. An exhilarating experience that you can still enjoy.

PASSING THE LAVA

Being aboard a cruise ship off the north coast of Sicily, where you pass close to Stromboli in action. The almost-constantly erupting volcano bursts into life and emits incandescent lava.

NATURAL WONDERS

I was on deck aboard an expedition cruise ship in Antarctic waters when a number of killer whales (orcas) began splashing in the water just off the starboard side aft, making the ship roll. They were so close that I could have touched one of their dorsal fins. A spectacular show of nature.

NEW YEAR'S EVE PYROTECHNICS

Being aboard ship supping champagne while enjoying the magnificently colorful New Year's Eve fireworks display in Funchal, Madeira (Portugal). A cruise ship offers the very best vantage point for this fantastic display.

ZIP-A-DEE-DOO-DAH

Careening along the zipline strung between rows of cabins high above the deck of *Allure of the Seas*, *Harmony of the Seas*, or *Oasis of the Seas*. Quite a surprise to the occupants of some of the interior promenade balcony cabins!

MAIDEN CRUISE

Enjoying the anticipation and excitement of a maiden voyage aboard a brand new ship – an experience highly prized among cruise collectors. Just be prepared for the fact that it might not all be smooth sailing, and there might be teething troubles.

BIRDSEYE SHIP VIEW

Experiencing a new perspective from one of the 'glass capsules', aboard *Anthem of the Seas*, *Ovation of the Seas*, *Odyssey of the Seas*, *Quantum of the Seas*, or *Spectrum of the Seas*.

HAPPY EVER AFTER

Looking for a partner? I met my wife aboard a Japanese cruise ship many years ago. You too, could meet the person of your dreams aboard a cruise ship – it happens all the time.

New Year's fireworks in Madeira, Portugal.

ONE AND ONLY

While cruising between Cherbourg and Reykjavik aboard Le Commandant Charcot, my wife and I enjoyed a special tasting of ship-shaped chocolate, by the famed French celebrity master chef Alain Ducasse. It contains different percentages of chocolate, each from a different country. Afterwards, of course, I went to the Detox Bar, naturally!

GIN, GIN, GIN

I tasted a special tri-pack of miniature gins, made by the Summerhill Distillery in Scotland, for each of the three present Cunard ships. One, with an Oriental hint, for *Queen Elizabeth*; one, with an American twist, for *Queen Mary 2*, and one with a hint of Mediterranean flavours aboard *Queen Victoria*.

OVER THE SIDE

Sitting enjoying a cocktail or two and a light snack at sunset while on an 90-seat lounge/bar outside on the starboard side of the ship that moves vertically between decks 2 and 16, named Magic Carpet. The novelty and experience is quite special (it also acts as a platform for shore tenders), which I experienced aboard the contemporary *Celebrity Edge*.

LIFE ABOARD

This A to Z covers the astonishing range of facilities that modern cruise ships offer and tells you how to make the most of them.

AIR CONDITIONING

Cabin temperature is regulated by an individually controlled thermostat, so you can adjust it to suit yourself. However, aboard some ships, the cabin air conditioning can't be turned off.

ART AUCTIONS

Aboard many large resort ships, art auctions provide cruise line revenue. They are participation events – though 'free champagne' given to entice customers is usually sparkling wine and not authentic champagne, while most of the art is rubbish.

Art 'appraisal prices' are done by the art provider, a company that pays a cruise line to be on board. Watch out for 'retail replacement value,' a misleading term

'Me' time beauty treatment.

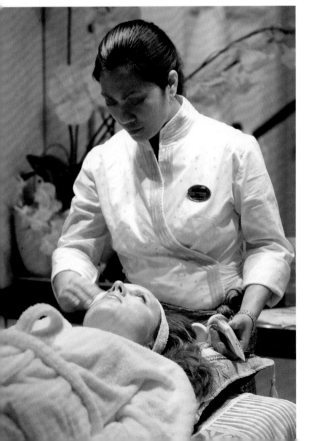

used by the art salespeople. Listen for phrases such as 'signed in the stone' – it means that the artists did not sign the work – or 'pochoire' (a stencil print less valuable than an original etching or lithograph). If the auctioneer tries to sell a piece of art (particularly a 'block' print or woodcut/engraving) with an 'authenticated signature,' don't buy it – when it's delivered to your home and you have it appraised, you'll probably find it's not genuine.

CASHLESS CRUISING

Your credit card imprint is taken at embarkation or when you register online, permitting you to sign for everything not automatically charged to your cabin. Before the end of the cruise, a detailed statement is delivered to your cabin, or available to view on your cabin TV or smart phone. You simply settle your account with one payment (by cash or credit card) before final disembarkation.

However, it's easy to overspend, so budget wisely and watch your spending. Some companies add a 'currency conversion service charge' to your credit card account if it is not in the cruise line's currency.

COMMENT CARDS

On the last (or penultimate) day of the cruise you will be asked to fill out a 'comment card.' Some lines offer 'incentives' such as a bottle of champagne. Be truthful, as the form serves as a means of communication between you and the cruise line (as in many chain hotels). Pressure from staff to write 'excellent' for everything is rampant, but, unless you highlight problems you have encountered, things will not improve.

DISEMBARKATION

This can be the most trying end to any cruise. The cruise director gives an informal briefing on customs, immigration, and disembarkation procedures. Before the ship reaches its disembarkation destination, you may receive a customs form to complete. Save any receipts from any 'duty-free' items you may have purchased in case a customs officer asks for them.

The night before arrival at your final destination, place your main baggage outside your cabin on retiring (the ship will give a time deadline). It will be col-

Disembarking from large resort ships can be tedious.

lected and offloaded on arrival. Leave out fragile items and the clothes you intend to wear for disembarkation (important) and onward travel – it is amazing just how many people pack absolutely everything. Anything left in your cabin will be considered hand luggage.

Remember to empty your personal safe. You cannot go ashore until all baggage has been offloaded and customs and/or immigration inspections or pre-inspections have been carried out. In most ports, this takes two to three hours after arrival.

On disembarkation day, breakfast may be early. You may be required to leave your cabin early, only to wait in crowded public rooms until your disembarkation grouping is called.

Once off the ship, you identify your baggage on the pier before going through customs inspection. Porters may be there to assist you.

DUTY-FREE LIQUOR

If you buy any 'duty-free' liquor along the way, it will be taken from you at the gangway as you re-board and given back to you before disembarkation. This is because cruise lines want you to buy your alcohol on board.

ENGINE ROOM

For insurance and security reasons, visits to the engine room are seldom allowed. Some ships have a technical information leaflet or a behind-the-scenes video on the cabin infotainment system. Some ships offer extra-cost 'Behind-the-Scenes' tours, which include the Engine Control Room (but not the engine room).

ETIQUETTE

Two points that are sometimes overlooked:
1) International copyright laws prohibit you from recording the professional entertainment shows.

2) It is fine to dress in a casual manner onboard ship, but disrespectful to staff if you enter a ship's dining room in just a bathing suit, or with bare feet.

GRATUITIES/TIPS

Aboard the large resort ships, tipping is mandatory rather than voluntary. Gratuities, typically of around $15 per person ($20 or so for occupants of suite-grade or butler-service accommodation), per day, are added automatically to your shipboard account. These may need to be converted to your credit card currency at the prevailing rate.

Be aware that cabin stewards have been known to scroll through passengers' accounts on the in-cabin infotainment system, and can tell if you have opted out of the automatic gratuity charge!

Gratuities are included in the cruise fare aboard some ships, but even so, extra gratuities are often expected by the staff. Aboard some ships, forceful suggestions are made regarding tips by tacky cruise directors.

Tips are normally given on the last evening of a cruise of up to 14 days' duration. For longer cruises, give half the tip halfway through, and the rest on your last evening.

Aboard many ships, a gratuity (typically 15 percent) is automatically added to your bar check, whether you get good service or not, and typically 15–20 percent may be added for spa treatments.

INTERNET ACCESS AND CELL (MOBILE) PHONES

Smartphone/cell phone use aboard ships is common, and most have ship-wide Wi-Fi (at a price, if it is not included in the cruise fare). Before you cruise, check with your phone operator for the international roaming rates applicable to your tariff for ports you're heading to.

Calls (at sea) are handled by a marine telecommunications network, which passes on international roaming charges to your phone operator. Signal strength can vary substantially from hour to hour. The farther north you get, the closer the telecommunications satellite is to the horizon, so signals tend to fade in and out, and waiting for web pages to load can be frustrating.

Turn off Data Roaming to save charges and Location Services to prevent apps from constantly trying to update your location. Turn off the 'Push' option relating to your email, because some accounts, including Gmail, push the data to your smartphone, incurring charges even if you don't open any emails. Turn off the option to synchronize data between devices, because it consumes bandwidth trying to keep your accounts up to date. Better still – have a digital detox and turn your mobile devices off completely.

LAUNCH (SHORE TENDER) SERVICES

Enclosed or open motor launches ('tenders') are used when your cruise ship is unable to berth at a port or island. In such cases, a regular launch service is operated between ship and shore for the port call. Aboard the large resort ships, you'll need to obtain a tender ticket, usually given out in one of the lounges, unless you are on an organized excursion, which take priority. The procedure can be lengthy.

When stepping on or off a tender, extend 'forearm to forearm' to the person who is assisting you. Do not grip their hands because this has the unintentional effect of destabilizing the helper.

LAUNDRY AND DRY CLEANING

Most ships offer a full laundry and pressing (ironing) service. Some ships may also offer dry-cleaning facilities. A detailed list of services, and prices, will be in your cabin. Your steward will collect and deliver your clothes. Some ships also have launderettes, well equipped with washers, dryers, and ironing facilities. There may be a charge for washing powder and for the use of the machines.

LIBRARY

Some ships have a library offering a selection of books, reference material, and periodicals. Aboard the smaller ships, the library is open 24/7. Aboard the large resort ships, the library may be open only for a few hours a day and lack a real librarian with whom passengers can discuss books and authors. *Queen Mary 2, Queen Anne, Queen Elizabeth,* and *Queen Victoria* have the largest libraries. Unfortunately, many ships state that they have a library, but this may be nothing more than a few shelves, with paperback books in no particular order. These ships often lack reference books such as a world atlas, Scrabble and crossword dictionaries, rules for board games, or a thesaurus.

Aboard specialist expedition ships, the library is one of the most important – and most used – facilities, and

Tenders transport passengers when a ship can't dock, as seen here aboard *Regatta*.

DID YOU KNOW...?

...*Splendour of the Seas* (now *Marella Discovery*) was the first ship to include an iPad in every cabin? This was in 2011.

...bingo game numbers aboard most ships only use numbers up to 75? On some UK-based cruise lines, bingo numbers go to 99.

...there is no Deck 13 aboard any ships of Princess Cruises? Good for the superstitious.

...Royal Caribbean International's *Legend of the Seas* (presently Marella Cruises' *Marella Discovery 2*) was named with the world's largest bottle of champagne? It had to be specially made and was a 'Sovereign-size' bottle (the equivalent of 34 bottles) of Moët & Chandon champagne.

...the first vessel built exclusively for cruising was Hamburg-America Line's two-funnel *Princessin Victoria Luise*? This luxury yacht even included a private suite for the German Kaiser.

...the United States Line's *Manhattan*, of 1931, was the first ship to have a cocktail named after it?

...when sailing from England to the Caribbean in 'the old days' a rule of thumb was to sail south until the butter melted, then proceed west?

...the longest bar aboard any cruise ship can be found aboard the ships of AIDA Cruises? It is 195ft (59.5m) long.

...someone forgot to score the champagne bottle when Dame Judi Dench named *Carnival Legend* in Harwich, England, on August 21, 2002? On the first two tries, the bottle didn't break. Then Dame Judi took the bottle in her hands and smashed it against the side of the ship. When it broke, the champagne went all over her, and she was dubbed Dame Judi Drench.

...from January 2000 until the ship was retired in 2008, octogenarian American Beatrice Muller made Cunard Line's *Queen Elizabeth 2* her permanent home at sea? She preferred life aboard to the daily drudgery of household chores and bills back home and paid a set amount to reside in Cabin 4068.

high-quality reference books on all aspects of nature, marine life, and polar exploration are provided.

LOST PROPERTY

Contact the reception desk immediately if you lose or find something.

MEDICAL CARE

Doctors aboard most cruise ships work as a concession. They are required to have current medical licensing, three years of post-medical school clinical practice, certification in emergency medicine, family practice, or internal medicine or experience as a GP or Emergency Ward doctor. So, if you have a serious health issue that predates your cruise, or a permanent disability, you need to be upfront about it (and any treatment) with your travel agent or the cruise line's reservationist before you book. They may be able to advise you on a ship that best meets your needs.

Anyone with long-term health issues should get prescriptions made up for the whole period of the cruise, because many places will not process prescriptions from other countries. Aboard some ships, you may be charged for filling a prescription as well as for the cost of any prescribed drugs. Take out a travel insurance policy that reimburses you for visits to the medical department, but check the small print. Insurance companies often refuse to pay out if you had any condition you didn't mention when you purchased the policy. Most medical care on cruise ships is perfectly adequate. In case it isn't, the cruise lines have a clause that says they are not responsible for the malpractice of their doctors.

PHOTOGRAPHS

Professional photographers on board take digital pictures of you at embarkation and during the cruise. They cover all the main events and social functions. Photographs can be viewed without any obligation to buy.

PRE-PAID DRINKS

Most large resort ships offer drinks packages to 'add value.' However, these booze-cruise packages really are a temptation to drink more. Some packages include wine, but it's the cruise line's choice – not yours.

RECEPTION DESK

Also known as the purser's office, guest relations, or information desk, it is centrally located, and is the nerve center for information and problems.

RELIGIOUS SERVICES

Interdenominational services are conducted aboard many ships – usually by the captain or staff captain. All Costa Cruises' ships have a small private chapel. Denominational services may also be held by clergy traveling as passengers.

ROOM SERVICE

Beverages and snacks are available at most times. Liquor is normally limited to the opening hours of the ship's bars. Some ships now charge extra for room service deliveries.

SAILING TIME

In each port, sailing and all-aboard times are posted at the gangway. The all-aboard time is usually half an hour before sailing. If you miss the ship, it's entirely your responsibility to get to the next port of call to rejoin the vessel.

SWIMMING POOLS

Most ships have swimming pools outdoors; some can be covered by glass domes in case of inclement weather, while a handful of ships have indoor pools located on a low deck. Pools may be closed in port owing to local health regulations. Diving is not allowed (pools are shallow).

Note that some ships use excessive chlorine or water-treatment agents, which might cause bathing suits to fade.

TELEPHONE CALLS

Most ships have direct-dial satellite telephones, so you can call anywhere in the world. Ships have an internationally recognized radio call sign, a combination of letters and digits, for example: C6SE7.

To reach a ship from land, dial the International Direct Dial (IDD) code for the country you are calling from, followed by the ship's telephone number.

Anyone without a direct-dial telephone should call the High Seas Operator. You will need to provide the name of the ship, and the ocean code: Atlantic East is 871; Pacific is 872; Indian Ocean is 873; Atlantic West/Caribbean/US is 874.

TELEVISION

Programming is obtained from a mixture of paid satellite feeds and onboard videos. Some ships lock on to live international news programs such as CNN or BBC World, or to text-only news services. Satellite television reception can sometimes be poor because ships constantly move out of the satellite's narrow beam.

VALUABLES

Most cabins have a small personal safe, but items of high value should be kept in a safety deposit box at the reception desk.

WATER SPORTS

Some small ships have a watersports platform aft. These ships usually carry windsurfers, water-ski boats, jet skis, water skis, and scuba and snorkel equipment, usually at no extra charge – except for scuba equipment. Make sure you are covered by your travel insurance before you use the equipment.

WINE AND LIQUOR

The cost of drinks on board may be lower than on land since ships have access to duty-free liquor. Drinks may be ordered in the dining room, at the ship's bars, or from room service.

Some ships sell duty-free wine and liquor to drink in your cabin. You can't normally take these into the dining room or public rooms, nor any duty-free wine or liquor bought in port. These rules protect bar sales, a substantial source of onboard revenue for many cruise lines.

Splashaway Bay aboard *Liberty of the Seas*.

CUISINE

Food is a multi-sensory experience. Taking time to enjoy the food and dining is a big part of the cruise experience.

Restaurants aboard any cruise ship are the collective lifeblood of the entire ship and hospitality experience. Apart from the facilities and destinations, it is the food that most people remember and talk about.

Cruise lines love to boast about their food – and often with their celebrity TV chefs – who only sail occasionally for a bit of show and marketing value. The reality is that most meals aboard most ships are not gourmet affairs. How could they be, when a kitchen has to turn out hundreds of meals at the same time? Most ships simply can't deliver the 'Wow' factor the brochure or website promises.

From morning until night, food is offered to the point of overkill, even aboard the most modest cruise ship. Aboard large resort ships, pizzas, burgers, hot dogs, ice cream, and frozen yogurt are almost always available. If you're still hungry, there's 24-hour room service, which, aboard some large resort ships, may cost extra. Some ships have extra-charge bistros, cafés, and patisseries.

As in most restaurants on land, you get what you pay for. High-quality ingredients cost money, so it is really unrealistic to expect low-cost cruises to offer anything other than low-cost, pre-cooked food (with an overabundance of carbohydrate-rich components such as potato, rice, pasta, and bread).

Most cruise ship cuisine compares favorably with hotel 'banquet' food. You can expect a selection of palatable and complete meals served properly in comfortable surroundings. Menus are typically displayed outside the dining room each day, or available on digital devices. Depending on the ship and dining venue, some menus (and wine lists) are larger than newspapers, while others are dinky, with little choice.

Major cruise lines bulk-purchase food items, which means low-quality ingredients and cheaper cuts of meat, often 'enhanced' with preservatives. That said, cruise lines do sometimes upgrade food items – Carnival Cruise Line and Royal Caribbean International, for example, introduced free-range eggs aboard their ships back in 2011. The current trend is for several 'alternative' (extra-cost) restaurants.

Food Tip: If you order an omelet, ask for it to be made (in front of you, if from a buffet) with real eggs – many companies use the more convenient, 'liquid egg' mix.

WHAT'S NEW?

Lighter meals are more sought after by passengers concerned about their health and weight, so 'bistro'-style cuisine is being introduced by more cruise lines (particularly the smaller companies, such as Oceania Cruises.

Chef Cornelius Gallagher puts the finishing touches to a Celebrity dessert.

BARBECUES AND HOT ROCK GRILLS

Some ships feature hot rocks cooking. This is for steaks, grilled meats, and seafood, presented on a platter with a sizzling hot rock base – so you can cook however little or well you want it done yourself. It makes for a pleasant change, in a casual pool deck environment. Seabourn and Silversea Cruises pioneered this option.

WHERE'S THE (USDA) BEEF?

Menus, particularly in extra-cost venues, often state that their steaks are made with prime USDA (United States Department of Agriculture) beef. It's wise to ask which grade (there are three main ones): USDA Prime (produced from young, well-fed beef cattle; this provides the best-quality meat, with more marbling, meaning more moisture and better flavor); USDA Choice (some marbling – good for decent-quality steak); and USDA Select (leaner, with a rougher texture, and no marbling – adequate for BBQ). Other grades are: Standard, Commercial, Utility, Cutter, and Canner. Several cruise ships have introduced cabinets (or maturation cellars), for drying meat. While the term 'dry-aged' beef confuses many, it comes from the British tradition of conserving beef by 'natural drying.' Some cuts are particularly good for grilling, with some breeds preferred over others, due to their individual specificity. Meat specialists talk about the depth of quality, mostly depending on the length of maturation (dry-ageing generally takes between 30 and 45 days).

FRESH VERSUS FROZEN

Aboard low-priced cruises, you will typically be served portion-controlled frozen food that has been reheated. Fresh fish and the best cuts of meats cost more, and this is reflected in the cruise price. Aboard some ships, the 'fresh' fish – often described as 'catch of the day' – has clearly had no contact with the sea for some time.

Also, note that many items of 'fresh' fruit may have been treated with 1-MCP (methylcyclopropene) to make them last longer – apples, for example, may be up to a year old.

Sushi bars are fashionable today. However, as the galley (kitchen) facilities on ships are generally inad-

equate to turn out food something as super-fresh as sushi, the only ships with authentic sushi bars and authentic sushi/sashimi are: *Asuka II*, *MSC Musica*, *MSC Poesia*, and *Nippon Maru*.

BREAD AND PASTRY ITEMS

While there are exceptions, much of the bread baked aboard cruise ships is unappealing, because, with little time for fermentation of natural yeast, it is made instead with instant dough that contains dried yeast from packets. Many baked goods and pastry items are made mostly from refined flours and sugars.

BUFFETS

Cruise ship buffets experienced some major trauma due to the global pandemic. In no way can buffets be considered luxurious, yet most ships have them (with food items served by crew) for breakfast, lunch, and even 'dinner.' Many are called Marketplace (or Market Place), trying to get you to believe that the food is 'farm-to-table' fresh, although they are as repetitive as canned laughter on television. The displays may look fine at first, but they don't after a few minutes of attack by passengers. Some newer ships include more 'active cooking' stations and food islands, which help to break up lines created by typical straight-line buffet counters (think: school lunches).

Dare to ask for something that's not on the display and any form of human communication ceases and supervisors become invisible. For example: trying to get a freshly cooked four-minute soft-boiled egg at a breakfast buffet presents a major challenge. I am always met with: 'We've only got the ones in the bowl (or dish)'. But the 'eight-minute' eggs in the bowl have been sitting there since they were boiled at 4.30am before the buffet opened, and they're still under the infrared heat lamp at 9.30am! Plus, there are typically no eggcups – or small spoons to eat them with!

Nor can you expect to find the following at most buffets: warm plates (for 'hot' food items), fish knives, a smoked salmon omelet, soya milk, brown rice, fresh herbs, loose tea, or freshly grated nutmeg for oatmeal. If you have food allergies, buffets will present a challenge, but, always, always, ask for help.

A prime example of luxury *not* being delivered can be seen aboard the ships of SeaDream Yacht Club, Seabourn, and Silversea Cruises where, on buffets, cheese is pre-diced or sliced – not exactly gourmet dining – where diners want to choose the amount themselves.

HOW BUFFETS EVOLVED

Lido deck buffets became popular because passengers relaxing at the poolside didn't want to dress to go to the dining room for lunch. So, buffets evolved from sunshine and the casual clothing concept.

Cruise ship buffets really started in 1969 with the introduction of Norwegian Caribbean Line's *Sunward* – an ex-Baltic cruise ferry – operating Miami to Baha-

CELEBRITY CHEFS

Several cruise lines have partnered with well-known chefs to devise menus for their cost-extra dining venues. Celebrity Cruises, for example, worked with three-star Michelin chef Michel Roux from 1989 until 2007. Even before that, the long-defunct Royal Viking Line worked with Paul Bocuse, with his own restaurant aboard *Royal Viking Sun*, now renamed Armera). It's worth paying extra because the price is far lower than in the celebrity chef's land-based restaurants.

Most celebrity chefs sail only one or two cruises a year, but Germany's three-star Michelin chef Dieter Müller set a new benchmark when he sailed for up to half a year to run his eponymous restaurant aboard Hapag-Lloyd Cruises' highly-rated *Europa*. In 2019 he retired and was replaced by Hamburg's energetic young three-star Michelin chef Kevin Fehling, whose land-based restaurant 'The Table' has just 20 seats.

Other celebrity chefs with seagoing connections include Daniel Bolud, Marco Pierre White, James Martin, Jamie Oliver, and Jacques Pepin.

Sushi may be one of the healthier casual eatery options available.

mas 'sunshine' cruises.

Sadly, almost all cruise ships today have buffets. They are popular because they are casual, simplistic, and you can take as much or as little as you want (or need). Thankfully, the 'all you can eat' type is going out of style. Now, more discerning passengers (including real 'foodies') look for healthier choices.

The 'Line System' consists of trays moved along rails in front of the buffet counters. The 'Island System' usually features 'active' stations (manned by cooks), with items (omelets, or pasta, for example) cooked individually to order.

Trays are usually used for the Line System. The plates are often oval-shaped and made from melamine, as they withstand high dishwasher temperatures.

Cold food displays are usually in white ceramic dishes, while hot food is usually displayed in stainless steel 'bain-marie' units.

DELI-STYLE (TAKE-AWAY) FOOD

Take-away deli-style food can be found in outlets aboard some ships, for times when you may want to sit somewhere quietly, but still have a little pre-wrapped casual snack (think: small ready-made sandwiches, wraps, burritos, salad 'pots' with quinoa or bulgur wheat, for example). This started with the so-called 'café culture' found in coffee and sandwich shops ashore.

POOLSIDE GRILLS

Poolside grills are popular, but usually attract long lines. Burgers and hot dogs may sound attractive, but are mostly disappointing. Aboard most large resort ships, it is rarely possible to grill burgers individually. Aboard small ships, however, they can be individually cooked to order.

Burgers are typically presented in a display tray for you to collect and then install your favorite toppings (typically tomato slices, onions, and an iceberg lettuce leaf), with mustard and tomato ketchup in packets or pump bottles. However, the burgers may have been steamed, not grilled, before being placed in the display tray, because steaming them keeps them moist. If you like yours grilled, say so.

As for hot dogs, these may be either grilled or steamed. Commercially supplied dogs will be pre-cooked and only need warming and serving in a white bread roll. In case you are unable to eat certain types of meat, you may need to ask whether they are made of beef, pork, chicken, or a combination of these or other meat.

If you are on a special diet, alternatives may be available, including vegetarian and vegan, fish, lobster burgers, or shrimp burgers.

SPECIALTY RESTAURANTS

Most new cruise ships have several restaurants and dining venues as alternatives to large main dining rooms. Extra-cost specialty restaurants were pioneered in 1936 in RMS *Queen Mary's* Verandah Grill, for first-class passengers only (who paid just over £1), and introduced in modern times by Norwegian Cruise Line in 1988 in The Bistro – an à la carte, extra-cost French dining spot. But it was Asia-based Star Cruises that introduced *multiple* venues – seven of them – aboard *Star Aquarius* in 1993; some were included in the cruise price, others cost extra. Thus, was born 'Freestyle Cruising' – or dine where you want, when you want, and with whom you wish.

Specialty restaurants are more intimate, reservations-required venues. The most popular are steakhouses, and Italian eateries. Celebrity chefs may add to the mix and establish their own 'at sea' dining venues, or collaborate on menus for shipboard eateries, although they seldom appear on board. Usually, the menu remains the same throughout each cruise (hence the chefs can concentrate on getting it right), and give as many passengers as possible the chance to book and enjoy the venue.

Some specialty restaurants can also be entertaining, such as in the Teppanyaki Grill aboard the ships of Dream Cruises, MSC Cruises, and Norwegian Cruise Line, for example. Watch the chefs chop, slice, and flip the food as they cook on an iron griddle next to the seating area. Twiddling and spinning utensils is part of the show!

CHEF'S TABLE

Pay-extra Chef's Tables, typically limited to a maximum 12 participants, are now found aboard many ships; they feature multiple fine-dining courses, with wine pairings for each course. The food is presented by the executive chef – hence the name Chef's Table.

COOKING CLASSES

Speaking of chefs, culinary (cooking) classes and food-preparation demonstrations are hot today (no pun intended) aboard a handful of ships, sometimes given by visiting celebrity chefs and pâtissiers. Some ships have built-in cooking equipment – whole kitchens with induction cooktops workstations and stainless-steel washbasins within self-contained fire zones – stuffed with the latest equipment for hands-on participants.

Some ships have a fully equipped studio kitchen for hands-on cooking classes (examples include *AIDAnova*, *Europa 2*, *Marina*, *Riviera*, and *Seven Seas Explorer*), each work station has an induction hob, washbasin, and preparation counter. P&O Cruises' *Arvia*, *Britannia* and *Iona* also have one called the 'Cooking Club' – created in conjunction with TV chef James Martin. *Europa 2* has state-of-the-art Miele equipment in its Miele Culinary Arts School, with the same heat level controls as found in the company's domestic kitchen equipment, while most built-in cruise ship cooking studios have industrial equipment, with different heat levels to those you would find on equipment for home use. There are between 12 and 24 cooking stations (for example, *Europa 2* has 12; *Seven Seas Explorer* has 18; *Britannia* has 24), so classes are limited in size accordingly.

The classes, typically on sea days, are part of the entertainment program and are fun and educational. Most incur a charge, with pre-weighed and portioned ingredients. You'll also be provided with an apron and a hat, given tips about food preparation, and you'll probably eat what you have learned to make (it may include a glass of wine or champagne – or two), which makes it a well-rounded, enjoyable experience. Typically, you will be asked to wear enclosed flat shoes, long trousers, and a long-sleeve top (for safety reasons).

Classes usually start with some background information, some food history, followed by a description of

the ingredients you will use and what you will learn to cook, as well as kitchen and equipment safety information. They typically last about 45 minutes to one hour.

Some cruise lines have associations with various cooking schools or food magazines. Examples include Holland America Line and America's *Food & Wine* magazine; Oceania Cruises and *bon appétit* magazine; Regent Seven Seas Cruises and Le Cordon Bleu culinary arts school (founded in Paris, France in 1895; today the educational organization has schools in most major cities around the world); Silversea Cruises and Relais & Chateau.

POP-UP TASTES

Pop-up kitchens can appear in showlounges or theaters aboard ships that lack a separate purpose-built culinary studio (Holland America Line started this trend). They can also be used when themed food and wine cruises are featured.

Culinary demonstrations are part of onboard programming, and often themed according to the region and itinerary.

Some cruise lines feature shore excursions that include culinary demonstrations (or even a little hands-on experience, such as pretzel making), but don't have built-in cooking facilities for passengers. Other ships have excursions to the local food market with the executive chef, followed by a meal later the same day using the chosen ingredients.

Cooking classes for children, in various age groups, are also popular, entertaining, and educational. Kids learn how to make cookies and pizza dough, among other things.

MSC Cruises, in conjunction with Endemol Shine Group, hosts a MasterChef Juniors at Sea cooking competition aboard all its ships for kids aged 5–12 years. Specifically designed to encourage an interest in cooking and healthy eating, the recipes were devised by Rukmini Iyer – 2013 MasterChef winner and author of two cookbooks, including *The Green Roasting Tin: Vegan and Vegetarian One Dish Dinners*.

SPECIAL DIETS

Cruise lines cater most to general tastes, and cruise ship food tends to be liberally sprinkled with salt, with vegetables often cooked with sauces containing dairy products, salt, and sugar. If you are allergic to ingredients such as nuts or shellfish, want lactose-free, salt-free, low-cholesterol, low-fat or fat-free, gluten-free, or semi-fluid food, or have any other dietary restrictions, let the cruise line know in writing well ahead of time and ask them to confirm that the ship can meet your needs. Once on board, check again with the restaurant manager.

Not all cruise ships cope well with those on vegan or macrobiotic diets who regularly need freshly squeezed juices; many large resort ships use commercially canned or bottled juices containing preservatives and may not be able to provide really fresh juices.

FEEL-GOOD FOOD

You can gain weight when cruising, but it's not inevitable. In fact, taking a cruise could be a good reason to get serious about your wellbeing. Weight- and health-conscious passengers should exercise self-restraint, particularly at buffets.

Many ships' menus include 'heart-healthy' or 'lean and light' options, with calorie-filled sauces replaced by so-called 'spa' cuisine. It may also be wise to choose

grilled or poached fish – salmon or sea bass, for example – rather than heavy meat dishes or fried food items.

Quality and variety are directly linked to the per-passenger budget set by each cruise line and are dictated by suppliers, regions, and seasons. Companies operating large resort ships buy fruit at the lowest price, which can translate to unripe bananas, tasteless grapes, and hard-as-nails plums. The smaller, more upscale ships usually carry better-quality ripe fruits as well as the more expensive varieties such as dragon fruit, carambola (starfruit), cherimoya, cactus pear, guava, kumquat, loquat, passion fruit, physalis (Cape gooseberry), rambutan, and persimmon.

Even some of the world's largest resort ships have 'calorie-control' eats, where nothing is more than 500 calories. Carnival Cruise Line has a Mongolian barbecue section on its buffets, and tofu is a regular feature, and you'll find Ayervedic breakfast items in *Europa 2*'s Yacht Club.

PLANT-BASED CUISINE

With the increase in wellness awareness, the interest in and demand for plant-based cuisine has skyrocketed. Although vegetarian, vegan, and Ayervedic options have been available aboard some ocean-going ships (and riverships) for many years, it is relatively recently that more effort has been put into the creative presentation of plant-based cuisine. For example, Michael Hoffman, a former Michelin-starred chef from Berlin, created a series of vegetarian meals and menus for Hapag-Lloyd Cruises (first introduced aboard *Europa* in 2018, and shortly after, aboard *Europa 2*, followed by the company's smaller, specialist expedition ships). Hoffman's restaurant in Berlin, Margaux, used 80 per-

Mouth-watering premium-quality Wagyu beef.

cent of the ingredients from his own garden, with the other 20 percent coming from personally known producers with an ethical codex (certification). His dedication to ethically sustainable vegetables includes a most caring attitude to cooking.

A separate plant-based cuisine selection was introduced aboard the two boutique ships of SeaDream Yacht Club in 2012. Originally called 'Raw Food,' the menus were created in conjunction with Florida's Hippocrates Institute. Today it is termed 'Living Food. Ingredients are raw, organic, enzyme-rich, and vegan: no meat, fish, eggs, or dairy items, with nothing heated above 118 degrees Fahrenheit (48 degrees Celsius), to retain as many micronutrients as possible.

Aboard most ocean-going ships, one of the challenges of such foods is its selection, supply, and storage, as well as having chefs trained in the art of care and creativity.

THE OATMEAL FACTOR

One factor that I have found to be quite consistent across most ships is what I call the 'oatmeal factor': how various cruise ships provide a basic item such as a bowl of oatmeal.

Standard. Hot oatmeal (supermarket brand oats) mixed with water, with little or no chance of obtaining tahini (sesame seed paste) to add taste to the oatmeal. It is served from a soup tureen at the buffet, and put it into a plastic or inexpensive bowl yourself (or it may be served in the dining room); it is eaten with plastic or basic canteen cutlery.

Premium. Hot oatmeal, water, salt, and a little olive oil; served in a higher-quality bowl, by a waiter or waitress, with hotel-quality (or better) cutlery. It's possible that the ship will have tahini, to add taste and creaminess. It's also possible that the waiter/waitress

FEEL-GOOD EATING TIPS

While a ship's buffet allows you to choose what and how much, there is a tendency for many passengers to overdo it. It's easy to consume more calories than you actually need, so pace yourself. Here are some tips on how to cut down on calories:

- Remember that you don't have to order – or eat – every course.
- Ask for half-size portions, or children's portions.
- Eat some items from the 'heart-healthy,' lighter options, or 'spa' menu, if available.
- Eat more fruits and vegetables – some ships have juicers, for freshly squeezed or fresh-pressed items (possibly as part of the spa menu); depending on the ship, there may be an extra cost for this.
- It's best not to go to the restaurant when you are 'starving.' Instead, try eating a healthy snack before any heavy meal.
- Try not to eat too late in the evening.
- Limit your alcohol intake.

will ask if you'd like hot or cold milk with your oatmeal. There may even be a doily between the oatmeal bowl and base plate.

Luxury. Hot oatmeal (medium or large flakes), water, salt, tahini, a little (extra virgin) olive oil, and nutmeg, with a dash of blended Scotch (whisky); served in a high-quality brand-name bowl (Versace), with base plate and doily, and Hepp- or Robbe & Berking-quality silverware. The waiter/waitress will ask if you'd like hot or cold milk with your oatmeal.

Incomparable. Hot Scottish (large flakes, hand-ground) oatmeal, water, sea salt, tahini, and nutmeg (grated at the table), high-quality cold-pressed olive oil, and a layer of rare single-malt Scotch; served in small-production hand-made chinaware, with base plate and doily, and sterling silver cutlery. The waiter/waitress will ask if you'd like hot or cold milk (or anything else) with your oatmeal.

SERVICE

Aboard many ships, passengers are often in a hurry (to get to a show or shore excursion) and want service to be fast. They also don't like seeing empty plates in front of them, and so service speeds up because waiters need to clear the empty plates away as soon as someone has finished eating a particular course ('American Service'). In what is termed 'European Service', however, there should *always* be a pause between courses, not only for conversation, but to let the appetite and digestive tract recover, and to anticipate the arrival of the next course.

PLATE SERVICE VERSUS SILVER SERVICE

Plate service. When the food is presented as a complete dish (now the normal presentation), as the chef wants it to look. It works well and means that people seated at a table will be served at the same time and can eat together.

Silver service. When the component parts are brought to the table separately, so that the diner, not the chef, can choose what goes on the plate and in what proportion (best when there is plenty of time, but this is rare aboard today's ships). What some cruise lines class as silver service is actually only silver service of vegetables, with the main item, whether it is fish, fowl, or other meat, already plated.

Note that few large resort ships provide proper fish knives or the correct soup spoons – oval for thin bouillon-style soups and round for creamy soups.

NATIONAL DIFFERENCES

Different nationalities tend to eat at different times. North Americans and Japanese, for example, tend to dine early (6–7pm), while many Europeans and South Americans prefer to eat much later (at least 8–11pm). Brazilians traditionally like dinner at midnight. During Ramadan, Muslims cannot eat during the daytime, but typically order room-service meals during the night.

Beef, lamb, and pork cuts are different on both sides of the Atlantic, so what you ordered may not be the cut, shape, or size you expected. For example, there are 15 British cuts of beef, 17 American cuts, and 24 French cuts. There are six American cuts of lamb, eight British cuts, and nine French cuts. There are eight American cuts of pork, 10 British cuts, and 17 French cuts.

SEATING

Depending on the size of the ship, it may have single, two, or open seatings:

Open seating. You can sit with whoever you wish at any available table, at any time the restaurant is open.

Single seating. This doesn't mean seating for single passengers. It means you can choose when you wish to eat (within dining room hours), but you will have the same table assigned for the whole cruise.

Two seatings. You are assigned (or choose) one of two seating times: early or late.

Some ships operate two seatings for all meals, and some do so only for dinner. Some ships operate a mix of open seating or fixed dining times, for greater flexibility. Dinner hours may vary when the ship is in port to allow for the timing of shore excursions. Ships that operate in Europe and the Mediterranean or in South America may have later meal times to suit their clientele.

THE CAPTAIN'S AND SENIOR OFFICERS' TABLES

The captain usually occupies a large table in or near the center of the dining room on 'formal' nights, with senior officers such as the chief engineer and hotel manager hosting adjacent tables. However, this tradition is disappearing, as ship dress codes are now ultra-casual. The table usually seats eight to 12 people picked from the passenger or 'commend' list by the hotel manager. If you are invited to the captain's table (or any senior officer's table), it is gracious to accept.

DINING ROOM AND GALLEY STAFF

Although celebrity chefs make the headlines, it's the ship's executive chef who plans the menus, orders the food, organizes and supervises staff, and arranges all the meals.

The restaurant manager, also known as the maître d'hôtel (not to be confused with the ship's hotel manager), is an experienced host, with shrewd percep-

Remy, a more upscale, top-deck restaurant aboard *Disney Dream*.

tions about compatibility. It is his or her responsibility to seat you with suitable companions.

The best waiters are those trained in hotels or catering schools. They provide fine service and quickly learn your likes and dislikes. They normally work aboard the best ships, where dignified professionalism is expected, and living conditions, salary and benefits are good.

Some lines contract the running and staffing of dining rooms to a specialist maritime catering organization. Ships that cruise far from their home country find that professional caterers, such as the Miami-based Apollo Group or Hamburg-based Sea Chefs, do an outstanding job.

HYGIENE STANDARDS

Galley equipment is in almost constant use, and regular inspections and maintenance help detect potential problems. There is continual cleaning of equipment, utensils, bulkheads, floors, and hands.

Cruise ships sailing from or visiting US ports are subject to in-port sanitation inspections. These are voluntary, not mandatory inspections, carried out by the United States Public Health (USPH) Department of Health and Human Services, under the auspices of the Centers for Disease Control (CDC). Cruise lines pay thousands of dollars for each inspection.

A tour of the galley proves to be a highlight for some passengers, when a ship's insurance company permits.

In accordance with international standards, all potable water brought on board, or produced by distillation aboard the ship, should contain a free chlorine or bromine residual equal to or greater than 0.2ppm (parts per million). This is why drinking water served in dining rooms may taste of chlorine.

ENTERTAINMENT

The bigger the ship, the bigger the show, with tired old song-and-dance routines now replaced by full-scale Broadway hits and Disney musicals.

Cruise lines with large resort ships compete to attract attention by staging super-lavish, high-tech, and expensive shows that are licensed versions of Broadway shows, with cruise lines signing partnership deals with musical producers, composers, and songwriters.

LAVISH PRODUCTIONS: WHAT'S PLAYING

Cats, Grease, Hairspray, Mamma Mia, Priscilla Queen of the Desert, and *Saturday Night Fever* are some of the shows performed on cruises. These big theater shows (aboard several Norwegian Cruise Line and Royal Caribbean International ships), with impressively large casts, are versions adapted to fit a large resort ship's showlounge stage, and typically last about 90 minutes. They are modified in order to fit in with the ship's operational schedule – and dinner. The performance standards, energy, and enthusiasm of these big musicals are outstanding – definitely giving the land versions a run for their money.

OTHER BIG SHOWS

Disney Cruise Line also produces some excellent stage shows, adapted for its ships, including *Aladdin: A Musical Spectacular*, plus *Believe*, developed specifically for *Disney Dream*. A proven family favorite is *Toy Story – The Musical*. Disney has many other entertainment shows for adults too.

The good news is you don't pay extra to see the show, except if it's part of a supper club venue and includes dinner. There are also few bad seats in the

A performance of *Grease* aboard *Harmony of the Seas*.

Priscilla Queen of the Desert aboard *Norwegian Epic*.

house, you don't have to find a parking place, or find a restaurant to eat in before or after the show – and there's always a handy bar nearby.

Royal Caribbean International's *Allure of the Seas*, *Harmony of the Seas*, *Oasis of the Seas*, *Symphony of the Seas*, and *Wonder of the Seas* each has an outdoor 'AquaTheater' (with a part-watery stage), for not-to-be-missed high-dive 'aquabatic' spectaculars. Also, on many Royal Caribbean International ships, stunning ice shows are featured in a special ice rink with arena bench seats. These are not only entertaining, but beautifully performed by award-winning professionals.

SHOWLOUNGES AND SHOWS

Large resort ship showlounges are high-tech auditoriums that would blow many theaters on land away. They house million-dollar arrays of light and sound technology, huge LED screens for backdrops and special effects, hydraulic stages that move in multiple directions, and complex fittings for aerial acts – first introduced aboard Celebrity Cruises first newbuild *Horizon* (now owned by another company), which debuted in 1990.

Colorful 'one-size-fits-all' Las Vegas-style production shows have evolved enormously aboard the large resort ships, as have stages, technical equipment, and facilities. Although they still can't match the budgets of the Las Vegas casino hotels, they certainly beat many land-based venues. Most production shows have two things in common: little or no audience contact, and intense volume. With few exceptions, the equation 'volume = ambience' is thoroughly entrenched in the minds of many young audio-visual staff.

Overall, there's little elegance in most production shows, and all are too long. The after-dinner attention span of most cruise passengers seems to be about 35 minutes, but most production shows run for about 35 to 45 minutes.

The majority of show 'dancing' today, consists of stepping in place, while pre-recorded backing tracks are often synthetic and grossly imbalanced.

Some cruise lines have a live showband to back the large-scale shows. The band plays along with a pre-recorded backing track to create an 'enhanced' or larger sound. Some companies, such as Disney Cruise Line, use only a pre-recorded track. This has little 'feel' to it, unlike a live showband that can generate empathy

and variation – and provide work for real musicians. Although live music may contain minor imperfections, which some might regard as 'characterful', most passengers would prefer it to canned music.

GREAT EXPECTATIONS

Many people, despite having paid comparatively little for their cruise, expect top-notch entertainment and the most dazzling shows with slick special effects, just as one would find in the best venues in Las Vegas, London, or Paris (at a price). There are many reasons why the reality is different. Cruise brochures tend to over-hype entertainment. International star acts invariably have an entourage that accompanies them to any venue: their personal manager, their musical director (often a pianist or conductor), a rhythm section with bass player and drummer, and a hairdresser. On land, one-night shows are possible, but aboard ship, an artist can seldom disembark after just one night, especially when it involves moving equipment, costumes, stage props, and baggage. This makes the deal logistically and financially unattractive for all but the largest ships on fixed itineraries, where a marquee-name act would be a draw.

Most entertainers don't enjoy being away from their 'home base' for long periods, as they rely on reliable phone and Internet access for managing their careers. Nor do they like the long contracts that most ships must offer in order to amortize the high costs.

ENTERTAINING BUT PREDICTABLE

So many acts from one cruise ship to the next are interchangeable with each other. Ever wonder why? It relates to the limited appeal of a cruise ship gig. Entertainers aboard ships must live with their audiences for several days and perhaps weeks – something unheard of on land – as well as work on stages aboard older

BEHIND THE SCENES

Staging a lavish production show can easily cost $1 million, plus performers' pay, costume design, cleaning and repair, music, and book royalty fees, and so on. To justify that cost, shows must remain aboard for 18 to 24 months.

Some smaller operators see entertainment as an area for cost-cutting, so you could find yourself entertained by low-budget singers and bands.

ships that were not designed for live performances.

Entertainment aboard large resort ships is directed toward family cruising. This is predominantly a family audience, so entertainment must appeal to a broad age range. That partly accounts for the frequency of formulaic Cirque du Soleil-style acrobatic routines and rope climbing.

A cruise line with several ships has an entertainment director and several assistants, and at their disposal are specialist agencies that specialize in cruise ships.

Mistakes do happen, however. It is no use, for example, booking a juggler who needs a floor-to-ceiling height of 12ft (3.7m) but finds that the ship has a showlounge with a height of just 7ft (2m) – although I did overhear one cruise director ask if the act 'could juggle sideways'; or a concert pianist when the ship only has an upright honky-tonk piano.

TRYING TO PLEASE EVERYONE

The toughest audience is one of mixed nationalities, each of which will expect entertainers to cater exclusively to their particular linguistic group. Given that cruise lines are now marketing to more international audiences in order to fill ever-larger ships, the problem of finding the right entertainment is far more acute – which is why *Queen Mary 2* is to be envied for the visual appeal of its 20-minute-long *Illuminations* planetarium shows.

Cruise lines operating small ships offer more classical music, guest lecturers, and top authors than seven-day package cruises heading for the sun.

Performers – and ship entertainers generally – need to enjoy socializing. Successful shipboard acts tend to be good mixers, are presentable when in public, do not take drugs or drink excess alcohol, are not late for rehearsals, and must cooperate with the cruise director.

Part of the entertainment experience aboard large resort ships is the glamorous 'production show,' the kind of show you would expect to see in a Las Vegas show palace – think flesh and feathers – with male and female lead singers and Madonna or Marilyn Monroe look-alike dancers, a production manager, lavish backdrops, extravagant sets, grand lighting, special effects, and stunning custom-designed costumes. Many cruise company executives know little about en-

Movie night on *SeaDream I.*

FAMOUS CRUISING MOVIES (IN DATE ORDER)

One Way Passage (1932). Bittersweet story about a shipboard romance between a man (William Powell) condemned to be executed and a terminally ill woman (Kay Francis).

The French Line (1954). Life aboard the French Line's *Liberté*, depicted as being frivolous, promiscuous and romantic. Stars Jane Russell, Gilbert Roland, and Arthur Hunnicutt.

An Affair to Remember (1957). Two movie greats (Cary Grant and Deborah Kerr) meet aboard a passenger ship, although most of the movie is actually about the Empire State Building in New York.

A Night to Remember (1958). Another movie about the last night aboard *Titanic*, this movie is dramatically realistic and quite terrifying in parts, and it makes you realize that oceans and seas can be treacherous. The cast includes Kenneth More, Anthony Bushell, Robert Ayres, and Honor Blackman.

The Last Voyage (1960). A movie about (what else) a sinking ship. Instead of effects, a real ship (*Ile de France*) was used in this gripping movie. Robert Stack and Dorothy Malone star.

Carry on Cruising (1962). A classic British comedy about a group of individuals (played by *Carry on* icons Kenneth Williams, Sidney James, and Kenneth Connor), who go cruising, with a heavy emphasis on innuendo and slapstick.

Ship of Fools (1965). A fine cast, including Vivian Leigh, Simone Signoret, and Lee Marvin, find themselves aboard the same pre-war passenger ship. A splendid example of character study.

The Poseidon Adventure (1972). There are some fine scenes of life upside down aboard a ship on this adventure movie starring Gene Hackman, Ernest Borgnine, Shelley Winters, and Roddy McDowell.

Titanic (1996). Although you already know the ending, the story and dramatic effects of this movie starring Leonardo DiCaprio and Kate Winslet make it compelling to watch, especially considering its length.

Out to Sea (1997). Starring Jack Lemmon and Walter Matthau this is a playful movie about two 'gentlemen hosts,' who join the cruise staff of a cruise ship in the Caribbean (it's not *quite* like this in real life). The ships used in the movie were Holland America Line's *Westerdam* and *Queen Mary* (the original, now a museum ship and hotel, located in Long Beach, California).

Speed 2: Cruise Control (1997). A madman hijacker takes control of a cruise ship (based on *Seabourn Legend*, whose real captain, Erik Anderssen, and other onboard staff, appeared in the film). The ending is dramatic (shot on the Caribbean island of St. Martin), but the plot is not. The engine room must be enormous, if the film is to be taken seriously! Sandra Bullock, Jason Patric, and Willem Dafoe star.

---

tertainment, and still favor plumes and huge feather boas paraded by showgirls who *step*, but don't *dance*.

Book back-to-back seven-day cruises (on alternating eastern and western Caribbean itineraries, for example), and you will probably find the same two or three production shows and the same acts on the second week of your cruise. The way to avoid seeing everything twice is to pace yourself.

OTHER ENTERTAINMENT

Most ships organize acts that, while not nationally known 'names,' can provide two or three different shows during a seven-day cruise. These will be singers, illusionists, puppeteers, reality TV show wannabes, hypnotists, and even circus acts, with wide age-range appeal. Also, comedians who perform 'clean' material can find employment year-round on the cruise ship circuit. These popular comics enjoy good accommodation, are mini-stars while on board, and may go from ship to ship on a standard rotation every few days. There are raunchy, late-night 'adults only' comedy acts in some of the ships with younger audiences, but few have enough material for several shows. In general, the larger a ship, the broader the entertainment program will be.

MOVIES ON DECK

Showing movies on the open deck has been part of the cruise scene since the 1970s, when they were often classic black-and-white films shown at midnight. In those days, the screens were small, roll-down affairs, and the projectors were set up on makeshift pedestals. The result was often images that vibrated, and sound that quivered.

Speed forward into the 21st century. Most large resort ships now have huge outdoor poolside LED movie screens that cost around $1 million each. The screens are complemented by 50,000- to 80,000-watt sound systems for a complete 'surround the deck' experience.

Princess Cruises started the trend (at this author's suggestion, no less, to Brian Langston-Carter) in 2004 aboard *Grand Princess* with its 'Movies Under the Stars' program, but now all companies with large resort ships have them. The experience is reminiscent of the old drive-in movies, the difference being that cruise lines often supply blankets and even popcorn free of charge.

Movies and other presentations are shown day and night, and may include special films for junior cruisers, as well as major sporting events such as the Super Bowl or World Cup soccer are also presented.

Smaller cruise ships, expedition cruise ships, and sail-cruise ships typically have little or no entertainment. Aboard those ships, after-dinner conversation, reading, and relaxation become the entertainment of choice.

WHAT'S ON

Entertainment is listed in the 'daily program' – a mini-newspaper for the day ahead that is delivered to your suite/cabin each night when your bed is turned down.

CASINOS

Place your bets. Glitzy onboard casinos flash their lights to attract your patronage, and bring Las Vegas-style gaming to open waters. But, watch out, Lady Luck can also bite your wallet.

SHIPBOARD CASINOS

The word casino comes from the Italian for 'little house,' which referred to a small part of a larger villa used for music, dancing, and socializing. Water-borne gambling started in the mid-1800s aboard Mark Twain-era steamboats on the USA's Mississippi River – when it quickly became a profession – with an estimated 600 to 800 of them plying their trade on the river during the Gold Rush days. Today's ocean-going cruise ships have really taken over (the first recorded casino was aboard the 1906 French ocean liner *La Provence*). So, whether you are a serious gamer or simply want to try your luck on the slot machines, shipboard casinos are now considered a major part of the entertainment, particularly aboard the large resort ships.

GAMES AND RULES

The most popular table games include a variety of poker (or video poker) games (Caribbean Stud, Let it Ride, Texas Hold'em, Three Card, etc.). Other table games include blackjack, single-deck blackjack, craps, and roulette. A few ships also have baccarat (including baccarat banque, chemin de fer, and punto

Norwegian Breakaway casino.

banco – the most widely played).

Ships must follow the gaming rules established by the Nevada Gaming Control Board, or other licensed jurisdiction – usually the flag state of the ship. House rules typically include the following provisions:

Only adults are allowed to play the slots or the tables.

Cruise lines must post at every gaming table the minimum and maximum betting limits for each game.

Nothing personal is permitted on the tables.

OPENING HOURS

Unlike casinos on land, most shipboard casinos are not open 24/7. They are always closed in port, although there are exceptions, such as in Bermuda, where they can open 9pm–5am, and Nassau, in the Bahamas, where they stay open 7pm–3am. Shipboard casinos are usually open once a ship leaves port, but not until it leaves territorial waters – 12 nautical miles away from the coastline (in Alaska it's 3 nautical miles). When a ship passes 24 miles, it is, according to international maritime law, in international waters.

OPEN ALL HOURS

Mobile gaming and wagering was introduced in 2013 by Celebrity Cruises (and in 2015 aboard some of the Carnival Corporation brands), enabling you to play almost anywhere on board – for example when lounging by the pool. You simply download the app prior to cruising (from the App Store for iOS devices, or from Google Play for Android devices).

PAYMENT

Payment for casino credit and chips/tokens can be made in several ways, including by credit card or a pre-loaded 'virtual wallet.' A few ships have cash-only machines, but most operate by touch cards (your cabin card) or tokens. Note that some cruise lines impose a 'service fee' if you charge cash or casino tokens to your cabin charge card (Carnival Cruise Line, for example). You may not be allowed to use any onboard credit to purchase casino play currency.

Some cruise lines have an app that can be downloaded to your smartphone and then used for playing at the casino once you have loaded and validated your 'virtual wallet' with the casino cashier.

WINNINGS

Any winnings (and left-over casino chips) must be cashed in on board.

VIP PLAYERS CLUBS

Some cruise lines reach out to (try to attract) 'high rollers' – those who might play in private clubs or VIP rooms on land, for high stakes. Cruise lines have their own versions of VIP clubs and attract players by giving perks (onboard credit, discounts on future cruises, etc.) and loyalty cards (these are different to a cruise line's loyalty club), just like casinos on land. Examples include Carnival Cruise Line (Ocean Players Club); Celebrity Cruises (Blue Chip Club); Norwegian Cruise Line (Casinos at Sea Players Club); and Royal Caribbean International (Club Royale). Typically, a minimum of $5,000 casino credit is required, with a maximum of $100,000. There may also be a separate check-in line for VIP club players. High rollers may be invited by a cruise line to travel free or at reduced cost, provided they participate in various (high-priced) tournaments.

SLOTS

Slot machines (invented in the 1890s by Charles Fey) bring in more than half of a casino's profits. If you like to play the slots, it may be better to sign up to a cruise line card club. This brings rewards, depending on how much you play. More play equals bigger rewards (including invitations to special events, discounted drinks, etc.). Sometimes, cruise lines offer double or even treble points after midnight. Winnings can be transferred to your card, so you can change machines.

The most popular slot machines are those of the 'reel' type, consisting of a number of spinning wheels that display fixed symbols, but video-display machines are increasing in popularity. Some are of the hybrid type – a mix of reel and video.

Many ships have penny slot machines, but these could turn out to be much more expensive than the 'lead-in' price (note that penny slot machines typically pay out based on the amount of money that is being bet, and not on the number of times the machine is used).

TOURNAMENTS

Shipboard casino and slot tournaments are programmed regularly, with blackjack and slots the most common. You participate by paying a certain amount, and then no more is spent during the tournament. Some ships provide free (or reduced cost) drinks as an added incentive.

SMOKING

Smoking is allowed in some shipboard casinos, depending on the cruise line. There is no smoking in casinos aboard the ships of Celebrity Cruises, Cunard, Oceania Cruises, Regent Seven Seas Cruises, Seabourn, Silversea Cruises, and Windstar Cruises. Some companies, such as Carnival Cruise Line and

Slot machines ready aboard *Genting Dream*.

Royal Caribbean International, have no-smoking sections within the casino, but in health terms this is as effective as having smokers at one end of an aircraft and non-smokers at the other.

DESIGN

Cruise ship casinos have evolved dramatically in terms of design, flow, and noise control. Most ships are designed so that passengers (including children) need to walk through them to reach either the restaurant or showlounge (although they won't be allowed to play the slots). However, aboard ships with multiple passenger room decks, this may not be the case – which means it's easier to keep children away from the slot machines.

Norwegian Spirit (Norwegian Cruise lines) has its casino facilities at one end of a main public room deck, behind closed doors, so children cannot walk through them.

WHICH CRUISE LINES DON'T HAVE CASINOS?

Examples include Disney Cruise Line, Hapag-Lloyd Cruises, Phoenix Reisen, Saga Cruises, Sea Cloud Cruises, Swan Hellenic, and Viking Ocean Cruises, plus many of the small-ship and expedition cruise lines. Also, Japanese cruise ships cannot pay in cash if you win, so soft toys ('gifts') are awarded instead, as prizes.

A LITTLE WARNING

Casinos are a major source of revenue for many cruise lines. So, if you plan to play, only do so with what you can afford to lose.

THE ODDS

Unlike land-based casinos, shipboard casinos don't need to compete with the casino next door, so don't expect the odds to be good. Note that some ships have blackjack tables with a card-shuffle machine to mix the cards, but this increases the odds in favor of the house.

EXCURSIONS ASHORE

Escorted tours in ports of call cost extra, but are often the best way to get a nutshell view of a destination and make efficient use of your limited time ashore.

Shore excursions used to be limited to cheesy city tours, but today they are extraordinarily varied, from crocodile-spotting in the Amazon to kayaking in Alaska, from elephant riding in Thailand to dogsledding in Greenland, and from helicopter trips over Hawaii's volcanos to semi-submersible ocean dives. Most offer good value, but it is very easy to spend more on excursions than on the actual cruise.

Unfortunately, in the post-Covid-19 era, shore excursions have become extremely difficult to offer and control, with conditions varying from country to country, and often totally inconsistent with the freedom offered as a vacation experience previously. The price of many excursions has risen due to increased operational expenses.

Playing with the stingrays in Nassau.

Shore excursions can enhance a destination visit and experience. Booking with a cruise line avoids the hassle of arranging your own excursions, and you'll be covered by the cruise line's insurance in case things go wrong. General city tours give you an overview and show you the highlights in a limited time period – typically about three hours. Other excursions provide a mind-boggling array of possibilities, including some that may be exclusive to a particular cruise line – even overland tours are available on longer cruises.

Not all tours are by bus. Some may be by bicycle, boat, car, or mini-van. Some cruise lines also offer private, tailor-made excursions to suit you, a family, or small group. A private car, with a tour guide who speaks your language, for example, may be a good way for a family to get to know a foreign destination.

To get the most out of your shore visits, doing a little research – particularly if you are visiting foreign countries – will pay dividends. Once on board, attend any shore-excursion lectures, or watch destination and shore-excursion videos on the cabin infotainment system.

Once your ship reaches a destination, it must be cleared by local officials before you can go ashore. In most ports, this is accomplished speedily. Meanwhile, you may be asked to assemble for your organized tours in one of the ship's public rooms. You'll need to carry the ship's identification card with you (for gangway check), and for re-boarding. Remember to take the ship's telephone number with you, in case of emergencies.

HOW TIRING ARE EXCURSIONS?

Most tours will involve some walking; some require extensive walking. Most cruise lines grade their excursions with visual symbols to indicate the level of difficulty.

A TICKET TO RIDE

Many companies with large resort ships charge extra for shuttle buses to take you from the port or other docking area to a local city or town center. The port with the highest charge is Venice, Italy, where the transport is by motorboat between the cruise terminals and St. Mark's Square.

Shopping on a shore excursion with Norwegian Cruise Line.

HOW EXPENSIVE ARE THEY?

For an average three-hour city sightseeing tour, expect to pay $40–100, and for whole-day excursions with lunch, $100–250. Flightseeing or seaplane sightseeing tours will cost $250–400, depending on the location, what is included, and the time involved – the flightseeing itself typically lasts about 30–45 minutes.

WHAT SHOULD I TAKE WITH ME?

Only what's necessary; leave any valuables aboard ship, and any money and credit cards you do not plan to use. Groups of people are often a target for pickpockets in some destinations. Also, beware of excursion guides who give you a colored disk to wear for 'identification' – they may be marking you as a 'rich' tourist for local shopkeepers. It's always prudent to wear comfortable rubber-soled shoes, particularly in older ports, where there may be cobblestones or other uneven surfaces.

HOW CAN I MAKE A BOOKING?

Some cruise lines allow you to book shore excursions online before your cruise, so some popular excursions may sell out before you even get to your ship.

If you need to cancel a shore excursion, you usually need to do so at least 24 hours before its advertised departure time. Refunds are at the discretion of the cruise line. Refunds for pre-paid tickets booked online can take a long time to make and can incur currency-exchange losses.

HOW TO TELL WHICH EXCURSIONS ARE GOOD?

If it's your first cruise, try to attend the shore-excursion briefing (or watch the in-cabin infotainment system). Read the excursion literature before you book.

Most excursions are designed for general interest. If you want to see something that isn't described in the excursion literature, skip it. Go on your own or with family/friends.

Brochure descriptions of shore excursions – often written by personnel who haven't visited the ports of call – can be imprecise. All cruise lines should adopt the following definitions in their descriptive literature, lectures, and presentations: the term 'visit' should mean actually entering the place or building concerned; the term 'see' should mean viewing from the outside – as from a bus, for example.

In the Caribbean, many sightseeing tours cover the same ground, regardless of the cruise line you sail with. Choose one and then do something different in the next port. The same is true of the history and archeology excursions in the Greek islands, where the same ancient gods put in frequent appearances.

WHAT IF I LOSE MY TICKET?

Report lost or misplaced tickets to the shore excursion manager. Aboard most ships, excursion tickets, once sold, become the sole responsibility of the buyer, and the cruise line isn't generally able to issue replacements.

White-water rafting in Costa Rica.

ARE THERE PRIVATE EXCURSIONS?

Most cruise line-organized excursions work on the 'one-size-fits-all' principle. More personalized alternatives exist for anyone seeking privately guided tours and land experiences. Tailor-made 'build-your-own' excursions, arranged by a 'travel concierge,' provide private tours. These could include lunch or dinner in a hard-to-book top-class restaurant, a visit to a private museum, or other bespoke requirements for small groups.

The right transportation and private guide will be arranged, and all arrangements taken care of – at a cost, of course. A cruise line destination 'expert' will plan an excursion, arrange the right transportation, and attend to all the other details that make the experience more personal. It's all about exclusivity – at a price.

GOING ASHORE INDEPENDENTLY – AND SAFELY

The main advantage of going independently is that you do so at your own pace and see what you want to see. If you hire a taxi for sightseeing, negotiate the price in advance, and don't pay until you get back to the ship or your destination. If you are with friends, hiring a taxi for a full- or half-day sightseeing trip can often work out cheaper than renting a car – and it's probably safer and more relaxing. Try to find a driver who speaks your language.

Exploring independently is straightforward in most destinations. If you don't speak the local language, carry some identification (but not your actual passport, unless required – take a photocopy instead), the name of your ship (and its telephone number, for emergencies), and the area in which it is docked. If the ship is anchored, and you take a launch to go ashore, observe landmarks near the landing place, and write down the location – or take a photo. This will help if you get lost and need to get back to the launch.

Remember that ships have schedules – and often tides – to meet, and won't wait for you if you return late. If you are in a launch port and severe weather approaches, the ship's captain could make a decision to depart early to avoid being hemmed in by a storm. Although this is rare, it has happened, especially in the Caribbean. If it does, in the port, locate the ship's agent, who will try to get you back on board.

Planning on going to a quiet, secluded beach to swim? First check with the shore excursion manager – some beaches may be considered off-limits because of a dangerous undertow, drug pushers, or persistent hawkers. And don't even think of going diving alone – even if you know the area well.

If you explore independently and need medical help, you could risk missing the ship when it sails. Unless the destination is a familiar one, first-time cruisers are probably safer booking excursions organized by the ship and vetted by the cruise line. Also, if you have a problem during a tour, the cruise line should be able to sort it out on the spot.

The main downside of going it alone is the possibility of delay or transportation breakdown, and you could miss the ship as a result. However, you are responsible for getting back to the ship. This may not be easy if the next port of call is in another country, and you don't have your passport. Also, be aware that cruise lines do change itineraries occasionally, due to weather, political, or other factors. If you book your own tours, and it's a tender port where the ship has to remain at anchor offshore, you may need to wait until passengers on the organized tours have been off-floaded. This can take two or more hours aboard some of the large resort ships. Above all, make sure your chosen travel insurance covers you fully.

SHOPPING ABOARD

Many ships have designer brands (clothing items, cosmetics, perfume, watches) on board at duty-free prices, so you don't need to spend time shopping ashore. Some ships have private rooms where you can view expensive jewelry or watches. Onboard shops are closed while the ship is in port, however, due to international customs regulations. Good discounts are often offered on the last day of the cruise.

SHOPPING ASHORE

Aboard ship, a 'shopping lecturer' will give a presentation about shopping in the various ports of call. Many cruise lines operating in Alaska, the Bahamas, the Caribbean, and the Mexican Riviera engage an outside company that provides the services of a shopping lecturer. Most talks are about designer jewelry and watches – high-ticket items that boost commis-

sions to cruise lines. The shopping lecturers heavily promote selected shops, goods, and services, authorized by the cruise line, which receives a commission. Shopping maps, with selected stores highlighted, are usually placed in your cabin, and sometimes include a guarantee of satisfaction valid for 30 days.

Some of the world's shopping havens put serious temptation in the way of visitors. Top of the list are Singapore and Dubai (especially in the Mall of the Emirates – a shopping resort rather than a mall – and the Dubai Mall, with over 1,200 shops, including the only Bloomingdale's outside the US).

SHOPPING TIPS

Know in advance just what you are looking for, especially if your time is limited; when time is no problem, browsing can be fun.

When shopping time is included in an excursion, be wary of stores repeatedly recommended by tour guides, as they may be receiving commissions from the merchants. Shop around before you purchase.

When shopping for local handicrafts, make sure they have indeed been made locally. It can happen that a so-called local product has in fact been made in a Far Eastern country. It pays to check. Be wary of 'bargain-priced' name brands such as Gucci bags and Rolex or Omega watches – they may be counterfeit. Check the serial numbers to see whether they are genuine or not. For watches, always check the guarantee.

Shopping in the center of Fort de France, Martinique.

SPAS AND WELLNESS FACILITIES

The 'feel-good factor' is alive and well aboard many cruise ships, which offer a wide array of hair, face- and body-pampering treatments.

Land-based health spas have long provided an array of body-pampering treatments to counter the stressful effects of everyday life. Responding to the rise in 'wellness' and 'mindfulness,' ships today have elaborate spas to rival those on land, where whole days of almost-continuous treatments are on offer, at a price. Once the domain of women, spas now cater almost as much for men.

Anyone unaccustomed to spas may find some of the terminology daunting: aromatherapy, hydrotherapy, ionithermie, rasul, thalassotherapy. Spa staff will help you choose the treatment that best suits you and your needs. Do visit the spa on embarkation day, when staff will be on hand to show you around and answer questions. Some cruise lines let you pre-book spa treatments online before your cruise.

Avoid booking massage treatments when the ship is about to leave port (usually in the late afternoon/ early evening), because there may be interruptive announcements, plus noise and vibration from propulsion machinery.

FACILITIES

Large resort ships may have facilities that include saunas, steam rooms, rasul chamber, several body-treatment rooms (including rooms for couples), thalassotherapy (saltwater) pool, relaxation area, changing/locker rooms, and a beauty salon. Some ships have acupuncture treatment clinics, and some have a built-in juice bar.

THERMAL 'SUITES'

Thermal suites provide a combination of various warm scented rain showers, saunas, steam rooms, and thalassotherapy pools, and the promise of ultimate relaxation. Most ships don't charge for use of the sauna or steam room, but some do. Some ships also add a gratuity to a spa day pass, while some ships limit the number of passes available – aboard Cunard's *Queen Elizabeth*, *Queen Anne* and *Queen Victoria*, for example, the limit is 40 people per day.

PERSONAL SPA SUITES

A 'personal' spa suite will typically consist of a large room with floor-to-ceiling windows, a heated floor, abundant relaxation space, towels, and bathrobes. They may also include a sauna, steam room, shower enclosure, tiled and heated relaxation loungers, hydraulic massage tables, and a choice of massage oils. Suites may also have herbal tea-making facilities and are usually bookable for a couple of hours, a half-day, or a full day.

Some ships feature a couples' experience, with private spa suites for rent by the day or half-day. Note that saunas and steam rooms may be mixed gender, or separate, depending on the cruise line.

Taking a salt bath aboard
Norwegian Breakaway.

A gym with a view on a Celebrity cruise.

PAMPERING TREATMENTS

Stress-reducing and relaxation treatments are offered, combined with the use of seawater, which contains minerals, micronutrients, and vitamins. Massages might include Swedish remedial massage, shiatsu, and aromatherapy oils. You can even get a massage on your private balcony aboard some ships.

Having a body-pampering treatment can be a delightful experience, because a ship can provide a serene environment. When it is enhanced with a massage or facial, the benefits can feel even more therapeutic. Before you book your relaxing massage, find out whether the treatment rooms are quiet enough, and whether announcements of any kind (except mandatory safety announcements) can be turned off.

Treatments aboard many ships are usually available only until about 8pm – the challenge being that most shipboard spas are run by concessions, with wellbeing treated as a daytime-only activity.

Tip: Check the daily program for any 'port day special' packages that may make the prices more palatable.

FITNESS CENTERS

Virtual-reality exercise machines are found in the techno-gyms aboard many ships, with state-of-the-art muscle-pumping and body-strengthening equipment, universal stations, treadmills, bicycles, rowing machines, free weights, and trampoline balancing.

Most fitness centers are open only until early evening. Typical exercise classes include high-intensity/low-impact aerobics, aquacise (pool-based) classes, interval training, stretch and relax, super body sculpting, fabdominals, sit and be fit, and walk-a-mile.

Group exer-cycling, kick-boxing, Pilates and yoga classes, body-composition analysis, and personal trainer sessions cost extra.

MASSAGE

Having a massage aboard ship can be a good stress-busting experience, although if it's not right it can prove frustrating, and expensive. A whole range of treatments and styles has evolved from the original, standard Swedish Remedial Massage.

Here are some of my own favorite massage moments (always taken in the late afternoon or early evening, and preferably just before sundown):

- Aboard *Celebrity Constellation, Celebrity Infinity, Celebrity Millennium,* or *Celebrity Summit,* on the balcony of a Sky Suite.
- Aboard *Royal Clipper,* in a private massage hut on an outside deck.
- Aboard *Genting Dream,* on the floor of a junior suite bedroom.
- Inside a beach cabana ashore on Castaway Cay or Half Moon Cay in the Bahamas, or as part of a private beach day (*SeaDream I* and *II*) in the British Virgin Islands.

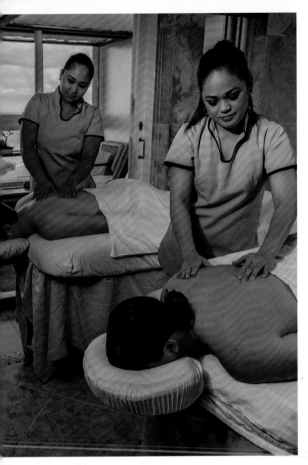

A romantic couples' massage in the Senses Spa & Salon aboard *Disney Magic*.

Make appointments for a massage as soon as possible to get the time and day of your choice. On some ships, massage may be available in your cabin (or on your private balcony), if it's large enough to accommodate a portable massage table.

A gratuity is often added automatically to spa treatments. Elixirs of youth, lotions and potions, creams, and scrubs – are all sold by therapists, typically at the end of your treatment, for you to use when you get home. But beware, these are expensive items, so don't fall for the sales talk.

OTHER BODY-PAMPERING TREATMENTS

Although massage is the most popular shipboard spa treatment, most ships also offer facials, manicures, pedicures, and possibly, teeth whitening, and acupuncture. Most are based on holistic Asian therapies. Some examples include: *mandi lulur,* a scrub made from herbs, essential oils, and rice to soften the skin; and *boreh,* a warm Balinese herb, rice, spice, galangal water, and oil body wrap for detoxification.

The spa will provide towels, robes, and slippers, but it's best to store valuables safely in your cabin prior to your appointment. Some spas offer disposable underwear for body treatments such as a Body Salt Glow or Seaweed Wrap.

Acupuncture. Used to prevent and remedy many maladies, this works by inserting super-fine needles into special points on the skin.

Halotherapy. This detox treatment uses a Himalayan crystal salt bed for deep relaxation and body detoxing. It involves lying on a bed of 290lbs (131.5kg) of Himalayan salt crystals heated from 90 to 104 degrees Fahrenheit (32–40 degrees Celsius), and breathing in the salt-infused air. The salt contains 84 essential minerals as fine particles.

Moxibustion. This is a treatment that involves the insertion of hair-thin needles, dipped into mugwort, into one of the body's many acupuncture points.

BODY SCRUB

This treatment cleanses and softens the skin, and draws out impurities using aromatic oils, creams, lotions, and perhaps sea salt, together with exfoliation (removal of dead skin cells).

BODY WRAP

Often called a body mask, this treatment typically includes the use of algae and seaweeds applied to the whole body. The body is then covered in aluminum foil and blankets. There are many variations on this theme, using mud from the Dead Sea or the Mediterranean, or sea salt and ginger, or cooling cucumber and aloe, or combinations of herbs and oils that leave you with a warm glow. The aim is to detoxify, firm, and tone the skin, and reduce cellulite.

FACIALS

Aromatherapy facial. This treatment typically uses aromatic oils such as lavender, sandalwood, and geranium, plus a rejuvenating mask and accompanying creams and essences to 'lift' the skin and facial muscles.

Rejuvenation facial. This is typically a classic French facial, which utilizes the latest skin care products enriched with essential plant and vitamin-rich oils. This facial aims to reduce lines and wrinkles.

Other popular treatments include eye lifting, volcanic mud masks, and manicures.

HAMMAM (RASUL CHAMBER)

This is a steam chamber (hammam) that is typically fully tiled, with a domed roof and Moorish decor. You paste yourself or your partner, if you are enjoying this as a couple, with three types of mud and sit down while gentle steam surrounds you. The various types of mud become heated, and then you're in a mud bath, after which you rub yourself (or perhaps each other) with large crystals of rock salt.

REFLEXOLOGY

The body's energy meridians exist as reflex points on the soles of the feet. The therapist uses thumb pressure to stimulate these points to improve circulation and restore energy flow throughout the body.

TEETH WHITENING

This treatment uses one of several methods, including bleaching strips, pen, gel, and laser bleaching. Carbamide peroxide, when mixed with water, forms hydrogen peroxide – the substance most used in teeth-whitening procedures. Power bleaching uses light energy to accelerate the process.

THALASSOTHERAPY

The use of seawater to promote wellbeing and healing dates back to ancient Greece. Today, shipboard spas have whole bath rituals involving water and flower petals, herbs, or mineral salts.

SPA CUISINE

Originally designed as low-fat, low-calorie meals for weight loss using grains, greens, and sprouts, spa cuisine now includes whole grains, seasonal fruits and vegetables, and lean proteins – ingredients low in saturated fats and cholesterol, low-fat dairy products, and reduced salt. These foods provide the basis for balanced nutrition and portion sizes, while maintaining some flavor, texture, and taste; foods are typically grilled rather than baked or fried.

About Face – 'me-time' for your face.

WHO RUNS THE SPAS?

Aboard many ships, the spa and fitness areas are operated by a specialist concession. Each cruise line may have a separate name for the spa, such as Greenhouse Spa (Holland America Line), Lotus Spa (Princess Cruises), OneSpaWorld (Virgin Voyages), etc.

Aboard the large resort ships, spa staff tends to be young, enthusiastic 'therapists,' who will try hard to sell you own-brand beauty products, for a commission.

Steiner Leisure is the largest concession, operating spas aboard more than 150 ships. Founded in London in 1901 by Henry Steiner, the company began its ambitious growth in 1926, when Herman Steiner got involved in the family beauty salon on his father's death. He opened salons throughout England, became official cosmetician to the late Queen Elizabeth the Queen Mother, and won his first cruise ship contract in 1956. The company closed its land-based salons in the 1990s, as its cruise ship business burgeoned.

Steiner Leisure (sold in 2015 to Catterton) brands include Elemis (a range of plant-based beauty products), Mandara Spa, Elemis Spa, The Onboard Spa Company, and OneSpaWorld.

Non-Steiner spa operators include: Canyon Ranch at Sea (Celebrity Cruises, Cunard, Oceania Cruises, Regent Seven Seas Cruises); Carita (Ponant); LivNordic (Viking Ocean Cruises); and Ocean Spa (Hapag-Lloyd, TUI Cruises).

TOP OF THE RANGE

Only a handful of the 70-plus ocean-going cruise lines operating internationally provides the kind of stylish ships aboard which the word 'no' is virtually unheard.

One person's luxury is another person's standard. Or, put another way: one person's standard is another person's luxury. Luxury (elegant, sumptuous) should be a flawless combination of ship, facilities, understated decor, culinary excellence, and impeccable service. Unfortunately, the words luxury (or luxe), and premium – have been degraded through constant overuse by marketeers and advertisers.

BROCHURES VS REALITY

Brochure photo (or video): A glass of champagne being enjoyed at embarkation.
Reality: it's sparkling wine.

Butler service aboard Silversea Cruises.

Brochure photo (or video): A couple having a romantic white tablecloth-dressed dinner for two outdoors on deck (with not a hint of a breeze).
Reality: Very few ships can deliver this.
Brochure photo (or video): A large resort ship, free from crowds or lines.
Reality: Nearly impossible, particularly at embarkation and disembarkation.

LITTLE AND LARGE

Size is important. Boutique and Small Ships (characterized by having 50–250 and 251–750 passengers, respectively) can get into ports that larger ships can't. They can also get closer to the center of large cities. For example, only the boutique-size ships (such as *SeaDream I* and *Sea Dream II*), can go through London's Tower Bridge and dock alongside HMS *Belfast*) in the heart of the city.

One area where 'luxury' ships differ least from large resort ships is in shore excursions, particularly in the Caribbean and Alaska, where almost all cruise operators are obliged to use the same local tour operators, and local tour operators treat all cruise passengers the same – as if they are children visiting for the first time.

Large resort ships that carry 2,501–7,000 passengers have some ultra-large penthouse suites or 'villas' with massive amounts of space, but, once you leave your accommodation, you really face the same food as everyone else on board. Also, these ships simply cannot provide the kind of personal service and attention to detail that the boutique/small ships can. There are, of course, exceptions – to some degree. For example, in the exclusive Dream Palace (Resorts World Cruises) ships, the Yacht Club of MSC Cruises and The Haven aboard Norwegian Cruise Line ships are examples of the good levels of better personal service that can be provided. However, once you leave your 'private living space,' you mix with everyone else, particularly if you want to see a show, have a coffee in the café, disembark at ports of call, or go on organized shore excursions. That's when you appreciate the fact that smaller is better: the boutique- and small-size ships cater to fewer passengers and are more relaxed.

These are ships suited to anyone not seeking the active, family-friendly, and entertainment-driven cruise experiences that large resort ships offer. They provide facilities and service levels hard to find else-where. While they boast about being the best, or boast the awards they receive annually from various bodies (often invited or coerced responses), few provide a fine luxury experience.

WHAT ARE THE DIFFERENCES?

Luxury varies by degrees. Although the differences are immediately noticeable when you sail aboard and compare them all, some of the variations in style, service, and – especially – staff training are far more subtle. One thing is certain: the word 'no' should be virtually unheard.

Some ships have more public space per passenger. Some have more highly trained service personnel rather than technical staff per passenger. Some have better food and service. Some have entertainment; some don't. Some have more fresh flowers in public areas than others – very evident aboard the ships of Hapag-Lloyd Cruises (plus its high ceilings) but not aboard Silversea Cruises' ships, for instance (where Prosecco – not champagne – is provided on embarkation).

Hapag-Lloyd has excellent lecturers, and a PGA golf professional aboard every cruise.

Suite occupants get more (or larger) personal amenities, including some of the more well-known brand names such as Aqua di Palma, Bulgari, Canyon Ranch, Clarins, Etro, Ferragamo, Guerlain, L'Occitane, and Therapies (by Molton Brown), or private label amenities. Many ships have bathrooms with two washbasins, as cruise lines think twin basins look good in a brochure, and for marketing purposes.

The following facilities, services, and approaches are found aboard the ships of Hapag-Lloyd Cruises, Seabourn, and SeaDream Yacht Club, but not aboard the ships of Regent Seven Seas Cruises, or Silversea Cruises:

- Anticipation – more widely practiced by better-trained staff, who are also more adept at passenger recognition (remembering your name and preferences).
- Waiters/waitresses escort guests to the dining table and to the dining room exit after meals.
- Relaxed embarkation/disembarkation at your leisure.
- Cabin stewardesses leave handwritten notes.
- No announcements, and no background music playing in public rooms, accommodation hallways, or elevators.
- The chef invites small groups of passengers to accompany him/her on visits to local food markets.

MORE SPACE, BETTER SERVICE

These ships have an excellent amount of open deck and lounging space, and a high passenger space ratio when compared to large resort ships (which are typically under 35 gross tons per passenger); the two SeaDream ships being the exception, due to their small size.

In warm-weather areas, the ships of Seabourn and SeaDream Yacht Club have fold-down aft platforms,

15 THINGS TO EXPECT

1. Flawless (well, close to) personal service and attention to detail.
2. Genuine champagne at embarkation (not sparkling wine).
3. Personalized stationery.
4. A crew that anticipates your needs, responds quickly to your requests, and doesn't say 'no' or 'impossible.'
5. No announcements (except for emergencies).
6. No background music in public rooms, hallways, and elevators.
7. High passenger space ratio (35 to 83 gross tons per passenger).
8. High crew to passenger ratio (1.5 to 1.0 or better).
9. The finest-quality bed linens, duvets, towels, and bathrobes.
10. A pillow menu.
11. High-quality toiletries.
12. No charge for on-demand movies or music.
13. More overnight or extended port stays.
14. Separate gangway for passengers and crew (where possible).
15. Shoeshine service.

with jet skis, kayaks, snorkeling gear, windsurfers, etc. at no extra cost, typically for one day each cruise (the others do not).

Hapag-Lloyd's *Europa 2* (space ratio: 83.0) and *Europa* (space ratio: 70.4) both *carry* a fleet of rigid inflatable craft for in-depth exploration and shore adventures, plus an ice-hardened hull and crew members who understand the *culture* of their passengers. They also have mattresses that are 7ft (2.1m) long.

A GOOD NIGHT'S SLEEP

These ships feature premium-quality mattresses and bed linen (all of 100 percent cotton, with a thread count of 300 or more). There is always a little brand-consciousness going on, and some may be better than others.

Silversea Cruises, for example, features Egyptian cotton sheets, pillowcases, and duvet covers by Pratesi, whose custom-made linens come from Tuscany, Italy – the company is known for supplying the Italian and other European aristocracy.

Good pillows are also important for a good night's sleep. You may be able to choose one of several different shapes and fillings, and depending on the cruise line, other choices might include hypoallergenic, hop-filled, or lavender-scented pillows.

A GOOD NIGHT'S SLEEP – OUTSIDE

For something quite different, SeaDream Yacht Club has indulgent 'Balinese Dream Beds' for sleeping under the stars (in a secluded area at the front of the ship on the uppermost open deck), a delightful idea

Penthouse suite aboard *Seven Seas Mariner*.

for honeymooners or anyone celebrating a special occasion. Custom-made pyjamas are supplied, and you can take them home with you.

CREATIVE CUISINE

Fine dining is the highlight of ships in this category and is more of an entertainment feature than these ships' entertainment shows – if there are any. Good company and conversation are crucial. You can expect to find plenty of tables for two, a calm and refined

TOP OF THE RANGE

These ships (listed alphabetically, by company) belong to seven cruise lines and are the cream of the cruise industry in terms of style, finesse, staff training, cuisine, service, hospitality, and finesse. The ships are fully reviewed in the ratings section of this book, with scores awarded for accommodation, food, service, entertainment, and the overall cruise experience.

Hapag-Lloyd Cruises: *Europa, Europa 2*
Regent Seven Seas Cruises: *Seven Seas Explorer, Seven Seas Grandeur, Seven Seas Mariner, Seven Seas Navigator, Seven Seas Splendor, Seven Seas Voyager*
Scenic Cruises: *Scenic Eclipse, Scenic Eclipse II*
Seabourn: *Seabourn Encore, Seabourn Odyssey, Seabourn Ovation, Seabourn Quest, Seabourn Sojourn*
SeaDream Yacht Club: *SeaDream I, SeaDream II*
Silversea Cruises: *Silver Muse, Silver Shadow, Silver Spirit, Silver Whisper, Silver Wind*
Windstar Cruises: *Star Breeze, Star Legend, Star Pride*.

dining atmosphere, open or one-seating dining, by candlelight (when permitted), with high-quality chinaware and silverware, large wine glasses, fresh flowers, a fine wine list, and sommeliers who can discuss fine wines. Service should be unhurried (not like the two-seating ships, where meals tend to be served as speed trials by waiters), well-paced, and unobtrusive.

It really is about non-repetitive, creative cuisine, high-quality ingredients, moderate portions, and attractive presentation, with fresh local fish and other items provided (when available) and cooked to order (not in batches), and meat of the highest grade. Caviar, foie gras, black/white truffles. and other exotic foods, and fresh vegetables (instead of frozen or canned vegetables) are among the products that feature. Caviar aboard *Europa* and *Europa 2*, from farmed sturgeon, is excellent, while aboard several other ships in this category it is from the American farmed hackleback variety of sturgeon, or paddlefish 'caviar' (calling it 'caviar' is really stretching it). The caviar from Uruguay aboard the Seabourn ships, however, is decent.

Some ships provide silver covers for entrées (main courses), creating extra 'wow' effect. Passengers may also be invited to visit local markets with the chef aboard the ships of Hapag-Lloyd Cruises, Seabourn, and SeaDream Yacht Club.

Some 'luxury' ships provide even more special touches. *Europa* and *Europa 2*, for example, make their own breakfast preserves and ice cream, as well as fresh-pressed or freshly squeezed or pressed juices (most others provide pasteurized juices from concentrate) on board. Mint tea is made with fresh mint leaves and not from a teabag, for example, and it i[...]n, and Silversea include all drinks, but only the properly served in a teapot. All (except Hapag-Lloy[...]dard brands and a limited choice of wines that Cruises) provide 'free' bottled mineral water. [...]e to your taste. Hapag-Lloyd Cruises doesn't

Lunch and dinner menus may be provided in your suite/cabin in advance, and special orders are often possible. Room-service menus are extensive, and meals can be served in your suite/cabin (either on the balcony or inside on portable or fixed tables). It is also possible to have a private dinner setup on deck – wonderful in the right location.

DRINKS: INCLUDED OR NOT?

Regent Seven Seas Cruises, Seabourn, SeaDream Yacht Club, and Silversea Cruises provide wine with dinner (Seabourn and Silversea also include wine with lunch), although the wines are typically young, and not from first-class houses. Real premium brands and classic vintage wines cost extra.

Hapag-Lloyd Cruises and Windstar Cruises include soft drinks and bottled water only (alcoholic beverages cost extra).

Regent Seven Seas Cruise Line provides an all-inclusive product, including gratuities (although passengers always seem to add more). Ponant, Regent, Seabourn,

[...]lcoholic drinks, as those favored by its discerning passengers tend to be of a superior standard to the brands carried by the other companies mentioned here (as an example, Hapag-Lloyd Cruises carries over 45 types of premium gin aboard both *Europa* and *Europa 2*, whereas Ponant's 'explorer' ships stock only the most basic brand of gin). In addition, this gets around the problem of passengers who can't or don't drink alcohol not wishing to subsidize those that do.

OTHER DIFFERENCES

Europa, Europa 2, Seven Seas Explorer, Seven Seas Mariner, Seven Seas Splendor, and *Seven Seas Voyager* include entertainment featuring multi-cast shows and cabaret acts; Hapag-Lloyd, Seabourn, and Silversea Cruises ships also do this, but to a lesser extent. The others have little or no entertainment as such, but instead rely on their intimacy and friendliness, and promote after-dinner conversation, or, aboard the ships of Ponant, Seabourn, and Silversea Cruises, individual specialist cabaret acts.

COMPARING LUXURY SHIPS

Ship name	Company (in alphabetical order)	Size	Passengers	Passenger space ratio	Crew to passenger ratio	Water sports toys	Hand-held showers
Europa	Hapag-Lloyd Cruises	Small	408	70.4	1.4	No	Yes
Europa 2	Hapag-Lloyd Cruises	Small	516	83.0	1.3	No	Yes
Seven Seas Explorer	Regent Seven Seas Cruises	Small	750	74.6	1.3	No	Yes
Seven Seas Mariner	Regent Seven Seas Cruises	Small	708	67.9	1.6	No	Yes
Seven Seas Voyager	Regent Seven Seas Cruises	Small	708	59.8	1.6	No	Yes
Scenic Eclipse	Scenic	Small	228	72.3	1.2	Yes	Yes
Scenic Eclipse II	Scenic	Small	228	NYR	NYR	NYR	NYR
Seabourn Encore	Seabourn	Small	604	67.2	1.3	Yes	Yes
Seabourn Odyssey	Seabourn	Small	450	71.1	1.3	Yes	Yes
Seabourn Ovation	Seabourn	Small	604	67.2	1.3	Yes	Yes
Seabourn Quest	Seabourn	Small	450	71.8	1.3	Yes	Yes
Seabourn Sojourn	Seabourn	Small	450	71.8	1.3	Yes	Yes
SeaDream I	SeaDream Yacht Club	Boutique	112	37.9	1.1	Yes	Yes
SeaDream II	SeaDream Yacht Club	Boutique	112	37.9	1.1	Yes	Yes
Silver Muse	Silversea Cruises	Small	596	78.8	1.4	Yes	Yes
Silver Shadow	Silversea Cruises	Small	388	72.8	1.4	No	No
Silver Spirit	Silversea Cruises	Small	608	64.9	1.5	No	No
Silver Whisper	Silversea Cruises	Small	388	72.8	1.4	No	No
Silver Wind	Silversea Cruises	Small	302	57.6	1.3	No	No
Star Breeze	Windstar Cruises	Small	312	47.0	1.7	Yes	Yes
Star Legend	Windstar Cruises	Small	312	46.9	1.7	Yes	Yes
Star Pride	Windstar Cruises	Small	312	47.0	1.7	Yes	Yes

MSC *World Europa*,
The Lanai.

THE LANAI

THE MAJOR CRUISE LINES

We compare what the major cruise companies have to offer when it comes to facilities, service, and ambience.

THE MAJOR CRUISE LINES

There are nine major cruise lines with 10 or more family-oriented large resort ships, equipped with attractions and play areas for passengers of all ages. They are AIDA Cruises, Carnival Cruise Line, Celebrity Cruises, Costa Cruises, Holland America Line, MSC Cruises, Norwegian Cruise Line, Princess Cruises, and Royal Caribbean International.

Except for family-owned MSC Cruises, all others listed here answer to investors, who seek potential profits from the investments. Consequently, they need to provide dividends (return on investment).

WHAT THEY ALL HAVE IN COMMON

All offer a well-packaged cruise vacation, generally of seven days, and typically with a mix of days at sea and days in ports of call; an abundance of food and several dining venues to choose from (some at extra cost); friendly service; colorful, large-scale production shows and cabaret entertainment; casinos; shopping malls; as well as extensive spa and fitness facilities.

The ships have a lot in common, too. All have art auctions, bingo, horse racing, shopping talks, sports facilities, programs for children and teens. Almost all are dedicated to generating onboard revenue.

Waiting for timed embarkation, disembarkation, tenders to take you ashore in ports where the ship has to anchor, shore excursions, and for buffets is inevitable.

WHAT MAKES THEM DIFFERENT

The ships may look similar, but many differ not only in their layout, decor, character, space, facilities, crew-to-passenger ratio, food and service, crew training and hospitality, but also in small details. Even towel sizes and the number of days between bed-linen changes can vary.

AIDA CRUISES

SHIPS

AIDAbella (2008), *AIDAblu* (2010), *AIDAcosma* (2022), *AIDAdiva* (2007), *AIDAluna* (2009), *AIDAmar* (2012), *AIDAnova* (2018), *AIDAperla* (2017), *AIDAprima* (2016), *AIDAsol* (2011), *AIDAstella* (2013)

ABOUT THE COMPANY

The former East German shipping company Deutsche Seereederei (DSR) and its marketing arm Seetours (Deutsche Seetouristik) were assigned the traditional cruise ship *Arkona* as part of the 1985 East–West integration. This included a contract with the Treuhandanstalt (the agency that privatized former East German enterprises) to build a new ship. It did this in 1996 with *Aida*, which was designed to appeal to young, German-speaking families, and created a seagoing version of the popular Robinson Clubs – a sort of holiday camp. When *Aida* first debuted, the company struggled.

In 1998 the company was purchased by Norwegian Cruise Line (NCL), which re-sold it to its original Rostock-based owners. The British company P&O ac-

Germany-based AIDA Cruises is one of the Carnival brands.

quired it one year later in 1999. It is now a successful multi-ship sub-brand of Carnival Corporation, under the control of its Costa Cruises division. AIDA Cruises became known for its large, buffet eateries, rather than traditional waiter service restaurants, due to the low crew numbers the ships were designed for.

WHAT IS IT REALLY LIKE?

The ships are family entertainment venues, with Club Teams (entertainment staff) that interact with youngsters and keep them occupied. The company also has its own recognized training academy in Rostock, Germany.

It is impossible to escape high decibel levels of loud music, with 'background' music played throughout the ships, including the cabin hallways and elevators around the clock.

There are three pricing levels – AIDA Premium, AIDA Vario, and Just AIDA – depending on what you want included.

CARNIVAL CRUISE LINE

SHIPS

Carnival Breeze (2012), *Carnival Celebration* (2022), *Carnival Conquest* (2002), *Carnival Dream* (2009), *Carnival Elation* (1998), *Carnival Freedom* (2007), *Carnival Glory* (2003), *Carnival Horizon* (2018), *Carnival Inspiration* (1996), *Carnival Jubilee* (2023), *Carnival Legend* (2002), *Carnival Liberty* (2005), *Carnival Luminosa* (2009), *Carnival Magic* (2011), *Carnival Mardi Gras* (2021), *Carnival Miracle* (2004), *Carnival Panorama* (2019), *Carnival Paradise* (1998), *Carnival Pride* (2002), *Carnival Radiance* (2000),

WHICH CRUISE LINE DOES WHAT BEST

 AIDA Cruises is for youthful German-speaking families who like lively surroundings and bright colors. The ships have edgy entertainment and take care of kids and teens well. The dress code is ultra-casual, and food is more about quantity than quality – unless you pay extra to eat in a 'specialty' restaurant.

 Carnival Cruise Line is for all-round fun, activities, and casinos for the lively, no-sleep-needed youth and young-at-heart market. Carnival doesn't sell itself as a 'luxury' or 'premium' cruise line, which it certainly isn't. It delivers exactly the well-packaged cruise vacation it promises. Its ships have good entertainment facilities and features, and some include extra-cost venues for the more discerning. The company calls its passengers 'The Fun Ones.'

 Celebrity Cruises is a 'premium' line offering 'modern luxury.' However, some aspects are not premium – for example, recorded music blaring over pool decks 24 hours a day is simply not relaxing. Celebrity Cruises is more akin to Royal Caribbean International in a more upmarket wrapper, with larger cabins and contemporary design features.

 Costa Cruises is all about quasi-Italian style and lively ambience for families. Swimming pools are full of children in peak holiday periods. Costa provides first-time cruise passengers with a packaged holiday that is a mix of contemporary surroundings and basic fare, accompanied by loud everything. Most passengers are Italian.

 Holland America Line has good touches for seniors and retirees, including some yesteryear traditions, cooking demonstrations, and specialty grill venues. The ships are best suited to those seeking an unhurried environment in good-quality surroundings. There's plenty of eclectic antique Dutch artwork, fairly decent food, and service from a smiling crew (though many lack the finesse expected from a so-called 'premium' product).

 MSC Cruises – a family-owned, Swiss-based company with an Italian heritage (its name is Mediterranean Shipping Company). The company displays fine pan-European flair, with a high level of service and hospitality training from a friendly, multilingual crew. It has evolved quickly as the 'new kid on the block.' Of the major cruise lines, it's also very clean. Bed linen and towels are changed frequently, unlike most brands.

 Norwegian Cruise Line is a really good choice for a first cruise for families with children, with a wide choice of eateries, great entertainment, and friendly service staff. Its ships are best suited to first-time, youthful solo passengers, couples, families with children, and teenagers who want upbeat, color-rich surroundings, plenty of entertainment lounges and bars, and high-tech sophistication, in a programmed, well-packaged vacation.

Princess Cruises offers a consistent product and somewhat restrained but chintzy decor. The company provides unpretentious middle-of-the-road cuisine, a good range of entertainment, and a good shore excursion program. On the down side, several of its ships are now quite dated.

Royal Caribbean International is known for its Caribbean itineraries for first-time cruisers and families with children of all ages. Its big ships are stunning, filled with high-tech gismos, gadgetry, and attractions, as well as colorful, large-scale entertainment, including slightly scaled-down versions of well-known Broadway shows. The food is more about quantity than quality.

Carnival Spirit (2001), *Carnival Splendor* (2008), *Carnival Sunrise* (1999), *Carnival Sunshine* (1996), *Carnival Valor* (2004), *Carnival Venezia (2023), Carnival Vista* (2016)

ABOUT THE COMPANY

Israel-born Ted Arison (born Theodore Arisohn), whose ambition was to be a concert pianist, founded Carnival Cruise Line, the world's largest and most successful single cruise line, in 1972, with one ship, *Mardi Gras* (formerly *Empress of Canada*). Carnival wanted to be different, and developed its 'fun ship' concept. It worked, appealing to people of all ages and backgrounds.

Its first new ship, *Tropicale,* built at the Aalborg Verft shipyard in Denmark, debuted in 1982. In 1984 Carnival started advertising on television, introducing a wider public to the idea of cruising fun. The company introduced the first cruise ship measuring over 100,000 gross tons – *Carnival Destiny* (now renamed *Carnival Sunshine*) – in 1996.

Today, the Carnival Corporation, parent company of Carnival Cruise Line, is run by Micky Arison (son of Ted Arison), who also owns the NBA's Miami Heat basketball team. More than 30 new cruise ships have been introduced since the line was founded in 1972, several of which have now been scrapped or sold.

WHAT IS IT REALLY LIKE?

Carnival's ships are well suited to multi-generational family groups. The dress code is ultra-casual – indeed, the waiters are better dressed than most passengers. Carnival is all about 'happy' and 'fun', with cruise directors telling participants to 'make some noise,' towels on the bed shaped like animals by cabin stewards, and high-volume scheduled participation activities. Overall, it's a rather impersonal cruise experience, and solo travelers can feel lost in the crowds of couples.

The open deck space may look adequate when you first embark, but on sea days you can expect your plastic sunlounger chair (if you find one that's free) to be kissing its neighbor (it may be tied to it). There are no cushioned pads, so the sunloungers are uncomfortable.

It is impossible to escape the loud music, and 'background' music is played in hallways, elevators, and pool decks 24/7.

Passenger niggles: Intrusive photographers, and the ship's daily program is mostly devoted to persuading you to spend money.

FOR CHILDREN

Carnival is family-friendly and carries over 700,000 children a year. 'Camp Carnival,' the line's child/youth program, is well organized. There are five age groups: Toddlers (ages two to five), Juniors (six to eight), Intermediate (nine to 11), Tweens (12–14, Circle C), and Late Teens (15–17, with Club 02).

Enjoying the splash park aboard a Carnival Cruise Line ship.

CELEBRITY CRUISES

SHIPS

Celebrity Apex (2021), *Celebrity Ascent* (2023), *Celebrity Beyond (2022), Celebrity Constellation* (2002), *Celebrity Eclipse* (2010), *Celebrity Edge* (2018), *Celebrity Equinox* (2009), *Celebrity Flora* (2019), *Celebrity Infinity* (2001), *Celebrity Millennium* (2000), *Celebrity Reflection* (2012), *Celebrity Silhouette* (2011), *Celebrity Solstice* (2008), *Celebrity Summit* (2001), *Celebrity Xpedition* (2022)

ABOUT THE COMPANY

Celebrity Cruises was the brainchild of Harry H. Haralambopoulos, and brothers John and Michael Chandris, London-based Greek cargo ship owners and operators of the long-defunct Chandris Lines and Chandris Cruises. In 1989, just as the cruise industry was gaining momentum, they wanted to create a newer, better cruise line, with new ships, larger cabins, and greater focus on food and service in the European tradition.

Its image as a 'premium' line is justified because the product delivery on board is superior to (and higher priced than) that of parent company Royal Caribbean Cruises Ltd (renamed Royal Caribbean Group), which bought it in 1997 for $1.3 billion. Celebrity Cruises is now more akin to Royal Caribbean International, but with a more upmarket wrapper, and a higher price point.

The ships are recognizable by a large 'X' on the funnel, denoting the third letter from the end of the Greek alphabet, the Greek 'chi' or 'Ch' in English, for Chandris, the founding family.

In 2007 Celebrity Cruises created sub-brand Azamara Cruises (now simply known as Azamara), with three ships (of around 700 passengers), but sold the brand in 2021 to investment group Sycamore Partners, who added a fourth ship of the same series.

WHAT IS IT REALLY LIKE?

The ships are clean and well maintained, and typically have good flower displays. The company delivers a well-defined cruise experience at a modest price. If the budget allows, book a suite-category cabin for extra benefits. Strong points include a good standard of service and a 'zero announcement policy.' Ships also showcase some eclectic sculptures and original artwork, from Picasso to Warhol.

The ships have more staff than other ships of comparable size and capacity, mainly in the housekeeping and food and beverage departments. However, the company has removed items such as personalized stationery from some accommodation grades, substituted cloth napkins with paper ones, and reduced the amount and quality of fresh flower displays (although there are still some).

Intrusive music is played almost everywhere, and it's hard to find a quiet corner to sit and read). Note that there is no deck 13 aboard the ships of Celebrity Cruises.

FOR CHILDREN

Junior passengers are divided into Shipmates (three to five years), Celebrity Cadets (six to eight years), Ensigns (nine to 11 years), Admiral T's (12–14 years), and Teens (13–17).

COSTA CRUISES

SHIPS

Costa Atlantica (2000), *Costa Deliziosa* (2010), *Costa Diadema* (2014), *Costa Fascinosa* (2012), *Costa Favolosa* (2011), *Costa Firenze* (2021), *Costa Fortuna* (2003), *Costa Mediterranea* (2003), *Costa Pacifica* (2009), *Costa Serena* (2007), *Costa Smeralda* (2019), *Costa Toscana* (2022)

ABOUT THE COMPANY

Costa Cruises traces its history back to 1860, when Giacomo Costa started an olive oil business. After he died in 1924, his sons, Federico, Eugenio, and Enrico, inherited the business, and bought *Ravenna*, a cargo ship, to cut transport costs for the family's olive oil empire. In 1948, Costa's first passenger ship, the *Anna 'C'*, carried passengers from Genoa to South America. In 1997, Costa Cruises was bought by the USA's Carnival Corporation and UK's Airtours plc. Three years later Carnival took full control.

Costa specializes in cruises for Europeans or passengers with European tastes – particularly Italians – during the summer.

Most of the ships are well maintained, although there are inconsistencies. The same is true of cleanliness – some ships are very clean, while others are a little dusty around the edges, as are its shore tenders. The company's safety procedures came under scrutiny when *Costa Concordia* struck rocks and capsized off the Italian island of Giglio in January 2012.

WHAT IS IT REALLY LIKE?

Costa is known for its loud, lively 'Italian' ambience, but there are few Italian crew members, although many of the officers are Italian. The dress code is strictly casual. Costa is for those who like to party; if you want quiet, take earplugs – good ones. Costa is the only major cruise line to include a chapel aboard its ships.

On European and Mediterranean cruises, most passengers speak Italian, Spanish, French, and German. On Caribbean itineraries, a high percentage of passengers speak Spanish.

Costa is best suited to young couples, singles, and families with children who enjoy big-city life, a multicultural social mix, outdoor cafés, constant activity,

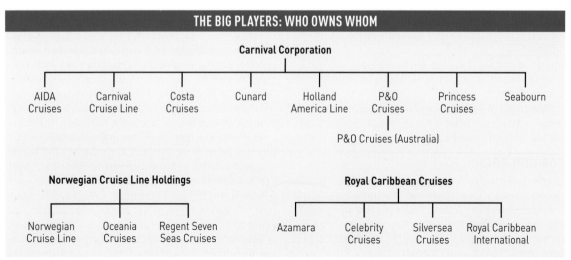

THE BIG PLAYERS: WHO OWNS WHOM

Carnival Corporation
- AIDA Cruises
- Carnival Cruise Line
- Costa Cruises
- Cunard
- Holland America Line
- P&O Cruises
  - P&O Cruises (Australia)
- Princess Cruises
- Seabourn

Norwegian Cruise Line Holdings
- Norwegian Cruise Line
- Oceania Cruises
- Regent Seven Seas Cruises

Royal Caribbean Cruises
- Azamara
- Celebrity Cruises
- Silversea Cruises
- Royal Caribbean International

Celebrity Equinox leaves Istanbul.

eating late, loud entertainment, and are happy with food more noted for quantity than quality.

Expect many children of all ages, especially during peak holiday periods; note that in Europe at certain times (such as Easter) schoolchildren have long vacations. On many European itineraries, passengers embark and disembark in almost every port, which makes for a disjointed cruise experience, with almost no start or end to a cruise. There is little information for those who want to be independent in ports of call. Note that there is no deck 13 aboard the ships of Costa Cruises.

FOR CHILDREN

Junior passengers are in three groups: Kids Club (ages three to six); Junior Club (seven to 12); and Teen Club (13–17). Programs vary by ship, itinerary, and season.

HOLLAND AMERICA LINE

SHIPS

Eurodam (2008), *Koningsdam* (2016), *Nieuw Amsterdam* (2010), *Nieuw Statendam* (2018), *Noordam* (2006), *Oosterdam* (2003), *Rotterdam* (2021), *Volendam* (1999), *Westerdam* (2004), *Zaandam* (2000)

ABOUT THE COMPANY

Holland America Line (HAL) was founded in 1873 as the Netherlands-America Steamship Company, taking immigrants to the New World from Rotterdam. It moved its headquarters to New York in 1971. It bought into Alaskan hotels and transportation when it acquired Westours in 1983 (when it moved its headquarters to Seattle) and is one of the state's biggest employers. In 1989, it was acquired by Carnival Corporation.

HAL carries both traditional cruise passengers (senior citizens, alumni groups) and multi-generational families. It tries hard to keep its Dutch connections, with antique artefacts and traditional decor, plus its well-liked service by Indonesian stewards. It rents a private island, Half Moon Cay, in the Bahamas, for use by its passengers.

WHAT IS IT REALLY LIKE?

All ships have teakwood outdoor promenade decks, while most rivals have artificial grass or some other form of indoor-outdoor covering, and lifestyle lounge-like Explorations Cafés have been built into each ship.

The company has a crew training school in Jakarta, Indonesia. Many crew members have been promoted to supervisory positions, but few have formal training, communication, or management skills.

Holland America Line operates many theme-related cruises, with life-enrichment lecturers, and its 'Culinary Arts' program includes celebrity guest chefs and interactive cooking demos. Lighter-option meals are available for the nutrition- and weight-conscious, as are Kosher (pre-prepared) meals.

FOR CHILDREN

Club HAL: Junior passengers are divided into three age groups: three to eight, nine to 12, and teens. Programming is based on the number of children booked

The Ocean Place complex aboard *Norwegian Getaway*.

on any given sailing, with children's counselors provided as needed.

MSC CRUISES

SHIPS

MSC Armonia (2004), *MSC Bellissima* (2019), *MSC Divina* (2012), *MSC Euribia* (2023), *MSC Fantasia* (2008), *MSC Grandiosa* (2019), *MSC Lirica* (2003), *MSC Magnifica* (2010), *MSC Meraviglia* (2017), *MSC Musica* (2006), *MSC Opera* (2004), *MSC Orchestra* (2007), *MSC Poesia* (2008), *MSC Preziosa* (2013), *MSC Seascape (2022)*, *MSC Seashore (2021)*, *MSC Seaside* (2017), *MSC Seaview (2018)*, *MSC Sinfonia* (2005), *MSC Splendida* (2009), *MSC Virtuosa* (2021), *MSC World Europa* (2022)

ABOUT THE COMPANY

The headquarters of the world's largest privately owned cruise line is in Geneva, Switzerland (it is also the home of parent company Mediterranean Shipping Company, the world's largest container shipping company), but was actually founded in Belgium in 1970. It started in the cruise business by acquiring Italian company Star Lauro in 1995, together with its two older ships, *Monterey* and *Rhapsody*. It then purchased *Melody*, and two almost-new ships from bankrupt Festival Cruises.

MSC Cruises has grown incredibly fast and is, unusually, owned by a shipping-based family, not a faceless corporation. In 2014, the company 'chopped and stretched' four ships to update them and accommodate more passengers (*MSC Armonia*, *MSC Lirica*, *MSC Opera*, and *MSC Sinfonia*). Then, 2017 saw the addition of *MSC Meraviglia* and *MSC Seaside* – stunning, very different ships with an array of facilities and family-friendly attractions. With the new ships came partnerships with leading brands such as Chicco, Cirque du Soleil, Lego, TechnoGym, Harmon, and Samsung. Starting in 2023, a new division (Explora Journeys), consisting of four ships, debuted for its growing number of premium passengers.

WHAT IS IT REALLY LIKE?

MSC Cruises' ships are suited to families with children, and good for those who enjoy big-city life, a multinational and multicultural atmosphere, outdoor cafés, and constant activity accompanied by plenty of live music and late nights.

MSC Cruises has different price categories, each including different things, so it's important to choose the right package for your needs. They are Bella (for a basic, price-driven experience), Fantastica (for greater comfort and flexibility), Wellness (aimed at health and fitness), and Aurea (for more inclusions).

MSC Bellissima, *MSC Grandiosa*, *MSC Meraviglia*, *MSC Seascape*, *MSC Seashore*, *MSC Seaside*, *MSC Seaview*, and *MSC Virtuosa* have large lounges, and restaurant and outdoor facilities exclusively for Yacht Club-grade occupants.

Why is the company so successful? It's the software (well-trained crew), its multi-national abilities, and attention to the finer details.

There are few announcements during a cruise. Given its multilingual emphasis, production shows and other major entertainment displays are more visual than verbal. For the same reason, the ships don't generally carry lecturers. Cigar lovers will find a selection of real Cuban smokes in the cigar lounges.

The decor is decidedly European/Mediterranean, with understated elegance and very high-quality soft furnishings and other materials, such as Italian marble, and Swarovski crystal glass stairways. Note: there is no Deck 17 on any MSC Cruises ship because it is considered unlucky. When it is written in Roman numerals – XVII is an anagram of VIXI which in Latin translates as 'I have lived' – which implies death.

FOR CHILDREN

Children are divided into three age groups, with facilities to match: Mini Club (ages three to nine); Junior Club (10–13); and Teenagers Club (over 14, with a pre-paid Teen Card available). MSC Cruises' mascot is Do-Re-Mi – the von Trapp family of *The Sound of Music* fame would no doubt be delighted.

NORWEGIAN CRUISE LINE

SHIPS

Norwegian Bliss (2018), *Norwegian Breakaway* (2013), *Norwegian Dawn* (2002), *Norwegian Encore (2019)*, *Norwegian Epic* (2010), *Norwegian Escape* (2015), *Norwegian Gem* (2007), *Norwegian Getaway* (2014), *Norwegian Jade* (2006), *Norwegian Jewel* (2005), *Norwegian Joy* (2017), *Norwegian Pearl* (2006), *Norwegian Prima* (2022), *Norwegian Sky* (1999), *Norwegian Spirit* (1998), *Norwegian Star* (2001), *Norwegian Sun* (2001), *Norwegian Viva* (2023), *Pride of America* (2005)

ABOUT THE COMPANY

Norwegian Cruise Line, the originator of contemporary cruising, was founded in 1966 by three Norwegian shipping companies as Klosters Sunward Ferries and was renamed Norwegian Caribbean Line in 1967. NCL also operates one ship with a mostly American crew and a base in Hawaii. Freestyle Cruising is how NCL describes its American bistro-style product. Its fleet is diverse, so the cruise experience can vary, but this makes for interesting character variation between the different ships. The senior officers are the only things that are Norwegian.

WHAT IS IT REALLY LIKE?

You should enjoy a good overall vacation in a lively, upbeat setting. The lifestyle is contemporary, fresh, creative, and sporty, with a casualness typical of youthful city dwellers, and with its 'eat when you want' philosophy, the shipboard ambience is ultra-casual. There is a high percentage of women in cabin and restaurant service departments.

There's plenty of lively music, constant activity, excellent entertainment, and food that's mainstream and acceptable, unless you pay extra to eat in a specialty venue. All this is delivered by a smiling, friendly service staff, who may lack polish, but are obliging.

FOR CHILDREN

Splash Academy and Entourage programs divide children into several age groups: Guppies (ages six months to three years); Junior sailors (three to five); First Mates (six to eight); Navigators (nine to 12); and two Teens groups (13–14 and 15–17). The clubs were developed in conjunction with UK-based King's Foundation and Camps, a charity that provides sports and activity programs.

A two-deck dining room is typical aboard Holland America Line ships.

PRINCESS CRUISES

SHIPS

Caribbean Princess (2004), *Coral Princess* (2002), *Crown Princess* (2006), *Diamond Princess* (2004), *Discovery Princess* (2022), *Emerald Princess* (2007), *Enchanted Princess* (2021), *Grand Princess* (1998), *Island Princess* (2003), *Majestic Princess* (2017), *Regal Princess* (2014), *Royal Princess* (2013), *Ruby Princess* (2008), *Sapphire Princess* (2004), *Sky Princess* (2019), *Sun Princess* (2024)

ABOUT THE COMPANY

Princess Cruises was founded by Stanley McDonald in 1965, with a chartered former passenger ferry *Princess Patricia* for cruises along the Mexican Riviera. In 1974, the company was bought by the UK's Peninsular and Oriental Steam Navigation Company (P&O), and in 1988 P&O/Princess Cruises merged with Italian line Sitmar Cruises. In 2000, Carnival Corporation and Royal Caribbean Cruises fought a protracted battle to buy Princess Cruises (Carnival won).

The company provides comfortable mainstream cruising aboard large resort ships, with global itineraries and colorful production shows. The ships have a higher-than-average passenger/space ratio, and service is friendly, not showy. In 2010 the company converted to digital travel documents.

WHAT IS IT REALLY LIKE?

The ships are clean and well maintained, and the open promenade decks of some ships have teak deck lounge chairs (others are plastic). Only *Coral Princess* and *Island Princess* have full walk-around open promenade decks; aboard the other ships you can't walk completely around the deck outside without negotiating steps. There is a good balance of officers, staff, and crew members.

HOW TO GET HITCHED AT SEA

Princess Cruises has the most extensive wedding program of any of the major lines, with its 'Tie the Knot' wedding packages. The captain can legally marry American couples at sea aboard its Bermuda-registered ships. This is by special dispensation and should be verified when in the planning stage, as it may vary according to where you reside.

Wedding at sea packages include a personal wedding coordinator, live music, a candlelit celebration officiated by the captain, champagne, fresh floral arrangements, a bridal bouquet, boutonnière, a photographer, and a wedding cake can all be laid on, depending on the inclusions chosen.

Tuxedo rental is available. Harborside or shoreside packages vary according to the port. For the latest rates, see Princess Cruises' website or your travel agent.

Each ship has poolside mega-screens for 'movies under the skies.' All cabins get turndown service and a pillow chocolate each night. Since 2012, smoking has been prohibited in cabins and on balconies.

Each ship has an extra-cost adults-only retreat ('The Sanctuary,'), with padded sunloungers, a swim-against-the-current pool, and outdoor cabanas for massages.

Princess's food and entertainment is geared to North American tastes, but passengers of all nationalities should feel at ease because this is highly organized, packaged cruising. The company is known for its large resort ship setting with good quality surroundings, high quality entertainment, and love of Hollywood.

Princess Cays is the company's own 'private island' in the Bahamas. It's all yours (along with a couple of thousand other passengers) for a day, although it's a short tender ride from the ship.

If Carnival's ships have the brightest decor imaginable, the decor aboard Princess Cruises' ships is the opposite – bland in places, with much use of neutral tones, calm colors, and pastels. Note that there is no deck 13 aboard the ships of Princess Cruises.

FOR CHILDREN

Children are divided into three age groups: The Treehouse (ages three to seven); The Lodge (eight to 12); and The Beach House (13–17).

ROYAL CARIBBEAN INTERNATIONAL

SHIPS

Adventure of the Seas (2001), *Allure of the Seas* (2010), *Anthem of the Seas* (2015), *Brilliance of the Seas* (2002), *Enchantment of the Seas* (1997), *Explorer of the Seas* (2000), *Freedom of the Seas* (2006), *Grandeur of the Seas* (1996), *Harmony of the Seas* (2016), *Independence of the Seas* (2008), *Jewel of the Seas* (2004), *Liberty of the Seas* (2007), *Mariner of the Seas* (2004), *Navigator of the Seas* (2002), *Oasis of the Seas* (2009), *Odyssey of the Seas* (2021), *Ovation of the Seas* (2016), *Quantum of the Seas* (2014), *Radiance of the Seas* (2001), *Rhapsody of the Seas* (1997), *Serenade of the Seas* (2003), *Spectrum of the Seas* (2019), *Symphony of the Seas* (2018), *Vision of the Seas* (1998), *Voyager of the Seas* (1999), *Wonder of the Seas* (2022)

ABOUT THE COMPANY

Royal Caribbean Cruise Line was founded by three Norwegian shipping company dynasties in 1969: Arne Wilhelmsen, I.M. Skaugen, and Gotaas-Larsen (more of a sleeping partner). Its first ship, *Song of Norway,* debuted in 1970, followed by *Nordic Prince* and *Sun Viking.* Royal Caribbean was different from Carnival and Norwegian Caribbean Line (as it was called then) in that it had brand new ships; the others had only older tonnage. In 1978, *Song of Norway* was transformed in the cruise industry's first 'chop-and-stretch' operation, while 1988 saw the debut of the first 'extra-large'

Oasis of the Seas' **Central Park.**

cruise ship, *Sovereign of the Seas* (since scrapped).

In 1997, Royal Caribbean International (RCI) bought Celebrity Cruises for $1.3 billion. Ten years later, the company created sister company Azamara Club Cruises (now, simply Azamara) with three ships (in essence operated by Celebrity Cruises). In 2018, the company purchased 67 percent of Silversea Cruises, and in 2020, purchased the remaining shares. In 2020, the parent company changed its name to Royal Caribbean Group, then in 2021, the group sold Azamara to Sycamore Partners.

WHAT IS IT REALLY LIKE?

RCI has carried well over 50 million passengers since its founding in 1970, and provides a well-integrated, fine-tuned, homogenous, but comfortable cruise experience. There's nothing royal about it except the name, because this is mainstream cruising. The ships are innovative, and all have some have public rooms, lounges, bars, and attention-grabbing gimmicks.

Its largest ships (*Oasis*-class, *Freedom*-class, *Quantum*-class, and *Voyager*-class) have a large mall-like indoor promenade – with eateries, bars, and shops, just like a high street – and they're rather like malls with ships built around them. Also, in placing emphasis on 'active' outdoors areas, relaxation space is greatly reduced.

The ships in the next group (*Brilliance of the Seas, Jewel of the Seas, Radiance of the Seas,* and *Serenade*

of the Seas) have many balcony cabins. *Enchantment of the Seas, Rhapsody of the Seas,* and *Vision of the Seas* also have abundant glass in public areas, but fewer balcony cabins. *Freedom of the Seas* introduced a concierge lounge for suite-grade occupants. All ships have a multi-track rock-climbing wall.

There is intrusive background music everywhere (including elevators and passenger hallways), and announcements for revenue-based activities, such as art auctions and bingo.

It is hard to escape the ship's photographers, as they're everywhere, but service personnel are friendly. The elevators talk to you, though 'going up/going down' is informative but monotonous. The 'Wayfarer' signage and illuminated picture display of decks are good, particularly aboard Oasis-class ships. However, there are no cushioned pads for deck lounge chairs.

Interior decor has strong Scandinavian design influences, and eclectic sculptures and artwork. In 2017, the company reduced the number of cabin categories, and standardized them across its ships. Note that there is no deck 13.

FOR CHILDREN

Children and teens are divided into seven age-appropriate groups: Royal Babies (six to 18 months); Royal Tots (18–36 months); Aquanauts (three to five years); Explorers (six to eight years); Voyagers (nine to 12 years); Navigators (12–14 years); and Teens (15–17 years).

THE SMALLER CRUISE LINES

The major cruise lines dominate the mass market, but dozens of smaller companies cater for more specialist tastes and small port experiences.

The international cruise industry comprises over 70 companies. While most major cruise lines are owned and operated by large corporations (except family-owned MSC Cruises), there are many smaller cruise lines. Some don't own their own ships, but charter them from ship-owning and ship-management companies for year-round or seasonal operation (Marella Cruises, for example).

These companies are listed in alphabetical order. For more information on expedition cruises, see page 94.

AE EXPEDITIONS

Part of the Aurora Expeditions group in certain markets. For more information, see the listing for Aurora Expeditions.

Ambassador Cruise Line's *Ambience.*

ABERCROMBIE & KENT

In 2022, the holding company chaired by Manfredi LeFebvre d'Ovidio acquired 85 percent of Abercrombie & Kent. The company purchased two ships (*Crystal Serenity* and *Crystal Symphony*), continuing to operate them under the Crystal Cruises brand.

ALASKAN DREAM CRUISES

Allen Marine Tours, owned by members of the Kaagwaantaan Clans of the Tlingit people, operates only in Alaska. It formed a new micro-cruise company, Alaskan Dream Cruises, in 2010, after buying two 78-passenger vessels when Cruise West declared insolvency and ceased operations. *Spirit of Columbia* and *Spirit of Alaska* became *Admiralty Dream* and *Baranhof Dream* in 2011. Another ship, *Chichagof Dream* (ex-*Nantucket Clipper*), was added in 2016.

ALBATROS EXPEDITIONS

A relative newcomer, the Denmark-based company founded by Soren Rasmussen, started as a tour operator in the 1980s, but year-round expedition-style cruising only became a reality in 2018 (with ships operated under charter). The company's expedition employees are enthusiastic, but whether they have the necessary experience when in challenging operating conditions in Antarctica remains to be seen. Albatros Expeditions has chartered two small expedition ships with an 'X' bow design from SunStone. The first (*Ocean Victory*) debuted in 2021; the second (*Ocean Albatros*) debuted in 2022.

AMBASSADOR CRUISE LINE

This company came into being as a result of the Covid-19 pandemic, and the collapse of Cruise & Maritime Voyages (CMV) in 2020. The new company, aimed primarily at British passengers, acquired the 1991-built ship *Regal Princess* (now renamed *Ambience*), and the 1989-built *AIDAmira* (now renamed *Ambition*).

AMERICAN CRUISE LINES

ACL was originally formed in 1974, at the beginning of American coastal passenger shipping, but went bankrupt in 1989, the ships were sold off, and the company lay dormant. The original owner, the late Charles A. Robertson, a renowned yachtsman who used to race 39-

Azamara Journey cruising the Norwegian fjords.

ft (12-m) America's Cup yachts, resurrected it in 2000, and built its own ships in its fully-owned small shipyard in Salisbury, Maryland, on the Chesapeake Bay.

ACL's ships (*American Constellation, American Constitution, American Spirit, American Star,* and *Independence*) ply the inter-coastal waterways and rivers of North America's coastal regions. They provide an up-close, intimate experience for passengers who don't need luxury, or much in the way of entertainment or pampering, but enjoy American history, culture, and service from an all-American college-age staff, who go through the company's in-house training programs. The 'D'-class vessels measure less than 2,500 gross tons, and are subject to neither bureaucratic regulations nor union rules.

In 2011, the company also started operating diesel-powered stern paddle-wheelers (replica steamboats) on the Mississippi River, and the Columbia and Snake rivers in the US Pacific Northwest. Port charges typically cost extra. The company's sister brand is Pearl Seas Cruises.

ANTARPPLY EXPEDITIONS

Based in Ushuaia, Argentina, this company specializes in (comparatively) inexpensive Antarctic expedition cruises including the Falkland Isles, the Weddell Sea and South Shetland Isles, plus South Georgia, during the austral summer. It has one 'soft' expedition ship, the basic and very dated *Ushuaia*, which was originally built for the United States agency NOAA (National Oceanic & Atmospheric Administration). The quality of its voyages and operation is nowhere near as good as the more experienced specialist international companies. Gratuities are not included.

ANTARCTICA21

This small company, based in Punta Arenas, is chartering a brand new 100-passenger small expedition ship (*Magellan Explorer*) for use on its Antarctica fly-cruise program, starting in 2019. The ship was built by ASENAV, in Chile. The company also operates a 71-seat aircraft for (two-hour) flights from Punta Arenas to King George Island, where the ship is based for the whole season. It provides a way to experience an Antarctic expedition cruise without having to sail across the Drake Passage (which takes about 36 hours).

ARANUI CRUISES

Founded in Polynesia in 1956 by the Wong Family (the company's original name was Wing Man Hing), this family-owned company has operated cargo and cargo/passenger ships in the Polynesia/Micronesia region, including the Austral and Gambier islands. The newest ship, the 280-passenger *AraMana* (set to debut in 2023 following a long delay due to the Covid-19 pandemic), is designed for passengers only, with Bora Bora as its home port.

ASUKA CRUISE

Nippon Yusen Kaisha, the world's largest shipping company, owned the well-known, US-based upscale brand Crystal Cruises before it became bankrupt un-

Crystal Serenity alongside in Malta.

der different ownership. It created its own NYK Cruise division – today branded as Asuka Cruise – in 1989 with one Mitsubishi-built ship, *Asuka*, for Japanese-speaking passengers. In 2006, *Asuka* was sold to Germany's Phoenix Reisen, and the former *Crystal Harmony* was transferred from the original Crystal Cruises (the present company is under new ownership) to become *Asuka II*. The ship, known for its excellent mix of Japanese and western food, operates an annual around-the-world or long Grand Pacific cruise, plus a wide array of both short and long cruises in the Asia-Pacific region. Coffee- and tea-making facilities are provided in each cabin, as is a large selection of personal toiletries. Gratuities are included. When this book was being completed, *Asuka III* was under construction at the Meyer Werft shipyard, and due to enter service in 2025.

ATLAS OCEAN VOYAGES

Atlas Ocean Voyages (changed from the former Mystic Cruises in 2019) is a Portugal-based cruise company (owned by Mário Ferreira and investors Certares) that owns and operates riverships on Portugal's Douro river. Two more identical ships *World Voyager* and *World Navigator* debuted in 2021 (the first delayed due to the pandemic), followed by *World Traveler* in 2022. *World Adventurer* and *World Discoverer* are due to debut in 2023. Two more ships, *World Seeker* and *World Explorer* are scheduled for 2024.

AURORA EXPEDITIONS

This specialist company was founded in 1991 by Australian Mount Everest veteran and geologist Greg Mortimer (he was the first Australian to climb Mount Everest), together with adventure travel specialist Margaret Werner. Until recently the company chartered various small, rugged but basic ships for its expedition-style cruises. In the latter half of 2019, new expedition vessel, *Greg Mortimer* debuted, followed by the slightly modified sister ship *Sylvia Earle*, in 2021 (both newbuilds are operated under charter from Sun-Stone Ships). Gratuities are not included, and some excursions and activities cost extra. The company is also known as AE Expeditions in certain markets.

AUSTRALIS

This company, based in Santiago, Chile, operates cruises to the Chilean fjords, Patagonia, and Tierra del Fuego – some of the world's most fascinating but hostile environments. It caters increasingly to an international clientele, with Spanish as the official onboard language (English is also spoken). Don't expect high standards on board, but the service is friendly, and the organization and operations are good. The cruises are 'all-inclusive,' with an open bar for beverages, including wine and gratuities. In 2013 the company shortened its name from Cruceros Australis to Australis.

AZAMARA

Founded in 2007 this company (formerly Azamara Cruises) is an offshoot of Celebrity Cruises. Having started with little direction, the company was revitalized in 2009–10 by Larry Pimentel. It operates three 700-passenger ships, taking passengers to smaller and less visited ports that the large resort ships can't get into.

Azamara prides itself on providing high-quality dining, and the ships offer a floating 'country club' experience. Its strengths are the food and European-style service; each ship has two extra-charge restaurants in addition to the main dining venues. Complimentary standard spirits, wines, and international beers during bar opening hours were introduced in March 2013. This line is in direct competition with the ships of Oceania Cruises – except that Oceania doesn't charge extra to dine in its specialty restaurants. However, Azamara tries to differentiate itself by providing more overnight port stays and longer stays, and more cultural excursions.

In 2019, the three-ship company changed its name from Azamara Club Cruises to simply Azamara. The company was purchased in 2021 by private equity firm Sycamore Partners, who immediately added a fourth ship.

CELESTYAL CRUISES

Established in 2014, Celestyal Cruises is a sub-brand of Cyprus-based Louis Cruises. Its two ships are dedicated to cruises in the Greek isles, Croatia, and Turkey – destinations with which the company's Cyprus-based parent company (Louis Cruises) has many years of experience, particularly with group travel.

CLUB MED CRUISES

Club Med became renowned for providing hassle-free family vacations. The first Club Med village was started in 1950 on the Spanish island of Mallorca, but the concept became so popular it grew to more than 100 vacation villages throughout the world.

Club Med Cruises, an offshoot, introduced its first oceangoing cruise vessel in 1990, the computer-controlled sail-cruise ship *Club Med II* (extensively refurbished in 2008). Aboard the all-inclusive ship, the so-called *gentils organisateurs* serve as cruise staff and 'rah-rah' cheerleaders, with entertainment and activity programs, for the mainly French-speaking passengers. *Club Med II* has a sister ship, Windstar Cruises' *Wind Surf*, which, by contrast, provides a relaxed onboard experience.

CORAL EXPEDITIONS

This small company, based in Queensland in northern Australia, was founded by fisherman-entrepreneur Captain Tony Briggs, but is now owned by Kallang Capital Holdings. The company (formerly Coral Princess Cruises) specializes in cruises of the Kimberleys in north-western Australia, the Great Barrier Reef, and other off-the-beaten track tropical areas in the Asia-Pacific region with boutique-size ships. The company's newest ships, the 120-passenger *Coral Adventurer* debuted in 2019, and sister ship *Coral Geographer* in 2021. Note that because that the ships operate only in warm weather conditions, this is not a 'real' expedition cruise company, but more of a coastal cruising company offering exploration voyages.

CORDELIA CRUISES

The company is based in Mumbai, India, and is owned by Waterways Leisure Tourism, which is owned by the Dream Hotel Group. The hotel group is controlled by the Indian-American hotelier Sant Singh Chatwal. The ship is tailored to passengers from the Indian subcontinent, with visits to Lakshadweep and other islands close to India. The company's only ship, *Cordelia Empress* was formerly *Empress of the Seas*.

CRYSTAL CRUISES

This company, which formerly belonged to another owner (Genting Hong Kong, who purchased the company and its ships from the original owner – Japan's NYK Group – for approximately $550 million in 2015), is now chaired by long-time cruise ship enthusiast Manfredi Lefebvre d'Ovidio (in conjunction with travel company Abercrombie and Kent), who purchased two of its ships: *Crystal Serenity* and *Crystal Symphony*. After updating and maintenance work, the two ships were returned to service for this well-known brand in 2023.

CUNARD

Cunard was established in 1839, as the British and North American Royal Mail Steam Packet Company,

Queen Elizabeth and *Queen Mary 2* rendezvous in Sydney.

to carry the Royal Mail and passengers from the Old World to the New. Its first ship, *Britannia*, sailed on its maiden voyage on American Independence Day in 1840. The author Charles Dickens crossed the Atlantic aboard the ship in 1842 together with 62 other passengers, 93 crew members, one cow, and, most important, Her Majesty's mails and dispatches. Since 1840, Cunard has always had ships built to sail across the North Atlantic. From 1850 until the arrival of *QE2* in 1969, all of the line's ships and those of White Star Line (with which Cunard merged in 1934) had several classes. Your luggage label, therefore, declared not only your name, but also what you could afford. Today, there's no class distinction, other than by accommodation grade.

Cunard celebrated its 175th anniversary in 2015. One is still reminded of the company's illustrious history. For example, Cunard was the first company to take passengers on regularly scheduled transatlantic crossings. It introduced the first passenger ship to be lit by electricity (*Servia*, 1881) and the first steam turbine engines in an ocean liner (*Carmania*, 1905. The line was the first to have an indoor swimming pool aboard a ship (*Aquitania*, 1914), and it pioneered the around-the-world cruise (*Laconia*, 1922). Cunard long held the record for the largest passenger ship ever built (*Queen Elizabeth*, between 1940 and 1996).

The ships incorporate a lot of maritime history and the grand traditions of ocean liners – as opposed to the other ships, with their tendency toward tacky high-street trappings. Cunard is also the *only* cruise line that lets you take your dog or cat with you (*Queen Mary 2* transatlantic crossings only).

While Samuel Cunard was from Halifax, Nova Scotia, he established the company in Liverpool. Today, the company is owned by the American Carnival Corporation. The four *Queens* were built in France and Italy, registered in Hamilton, Bermuda, with a home port of Southampton, England, but the onboard currency is the US dollar!

Cunard has four accommodation types, each linked to a specific restaurant: Queens Grill, Princess Grill, Britannia Club, and Britannia.

Cunard has one real ocean liner (*Queen Mary 2*), *which* provides a regular transatlantic crossing service between April and December, while the company's three other ships are more for regular cruise service, albeit with ocean-liner decor and style. The ships are best suited to a wide range of seasoned and well-traveled couples and solo travelers who enjoy the cosmopolitan setting of an ocean liner. Dressing more formally for dinner is encouraged, although with the exception of the grill rooms, the cuisine is largely of mass-market quality, but focuses on many traditional British and French dishes.

DISNEY CRUISE LINE

Disney Cruise Line is the most family-centric of all cruise lines. It was Lawrence (Larry) P. Murphy, executive vice-president of the Walt Disney Company, who was the guiding light in the early 1990s behind the expansion of the company into the cruise business. Previously, Disney had flirted with cruising by participating in a licensing agreement with a Florida-based cruise line, the now-defunct Premier Cruise Lines, with three vintage ships based in Port Canaveral. Murphy and other Disney executives explored the possibility of creating their own ships when the licensing agreement ran out. They concluded that pairing

Disney takes its brand to Alaska.

with an established cruise line wouldn't work because of Disney's policy of generous spending on the guest experience.

The solution: create a new cruise line, wholly owned and controlled by Disney, to be known as Disney Cruise Line. The company committed an astonishing $1 billion to the project.

Two mid-size ships, *Disney Magic* (1998) and *Disney Wonder* (1999) were the first cruise ships since the 1950s built with two funnels. Everything aboard the ships is Disney – every song, every piece of artwork, every movie and production show – and Mickey's ears adorn the ships' funnels. There is no casino and no library. However, its 'rotation dining' concept proved to be completely Disneylogical; you move, together with your waiter, to each of three identically sized restaurants – each with different decor – in turn.

A larger ship, *Disney Dream,* joined the fleet in 2011, and sister ship *Disney Fantasy* arrived in 2012. The first of two new (slightly larger, LNG-powered) ships, *Disney Wish*, arrived in 2022, with *Disney Treasure* set to arrive in 2024.

The next ship for Disney Cruise Line is due to arrive in 2025. *Global Dream* was originally ordered by the now defunct Genting Cruise Lines and was acquired by Disney Cruise Line in 2022. The huge ship will be completed by the Meyer Werft shipyard in Germany and is expected to carry over 6,000 passengers and be staffed by 2,300 crew members. The super-large ship, measuring 204,000 gross tons, measures 1,122ft (342m) long and 151ft (46m) wide. It will have 20 decks, be powered by green methanol, one of the lowest emission fuels, and is expected to showcase three funnels.

You can buy a package combining a short stay at a Disney resort and a cruise. Gratuities are not included in the cruise fare. Disney has its own cruise terminal at Port Canaveral, Florida, its design being an imaginative but close copy of the Ocean Terminal in Southampton, UK, frequented by yesteryear's ocean liners, although little used today. The terminal and pier were extended in 2010 and connected to a new parking garage.

EMERALD YACHT CRUISES

Emerald Yacht Cruises was created to provide small-ship experiences. Its sister company is Emerald Waterways, which debuted in 2014 and operates a fleet of river cruise ships in Europe, and charters others for cruises on the Mekong, Nile, and Volga rivers. The companies are ultimately owned by Australia's Scenic Group. The company's two ships are *Emerald Azzurra*, which debuted in 2022 as an all-inclusive product, followed by *Emerald Sakara* in 2023.

EXPLORA JOURNEYS

This new company (owned and operated by family-owned MSC Cruises) was announced in 2021. It was created to deliver a cruise experience that is the epitome of finesse, with 'transformation ocean journeys',

Fred. Olsen's *Braemar* on the Río Guadalquivir.

in marketing speak. The company started the project to cater to the growing number of MSC Cruises' Yacht Club passengers seeking a smaller ship environment and a more upscale travel experience. A series of four ships is on order, with a passenger count of 922 each, and the first ship was delivered in 2023.

FRED. OLSEN CRUISE LINES

This Norwegian family-owned/family-run company was founded in Hvitsten, a town on Oslofjord, Norway, in 1848. Today, a fifth-generation Olsen, Anette, owns and runs the company from its headquarters in Suffolk, England. The group also has interests in hotels, aviation, shipbuilding, ferries, and offshore industries. The company specializes in cruises for adults, who are usually retired and of senior years – typically over the age of 65.

Aboard the ships, interior design reflects many traditional design features, and dressing for dinner is expected on four nights during a two-week cruise. Many themed cruises, such as gardening and horticulture, and Scottish country dancing, hosted by recognized television celebrities, are regular features. The company welcomes solo passengers as well as couples and delivers a quintessentially 'British' cruise experience, albeit by a mainly Filipino hotel service staff.

The first ship dedicated exclusively to cruising debuted in 1987, and ships cruise year-round mainly from UK ports – good for UK-based no-fly passengers. Some ships operate fly-cruises from Canary Island ports, or Caribbean ports such as Barbados in winter.

HANSEATIC nature **in the Arctic.**

The company operates a fleet of pre-owned small- and mid-sized ships which are comfortable and well-maintained. However, the company's strengths are in its extremely friendly and helpful crew, the homely ship environment, and food geared to British tastes, including coffee-/tea-making facilities in all cabins. Also, drink prices are very reasonable.

The company has long supported the efforts of the UK's Royal National Lifeboat Institution (RNLI), and organizes fund-raising events to purchase new lifeboats for the charity.

HAPAG-LLOYD CRUISES

Germany's two most famous ocean-liner companies, the Bremen-based Norddeutscher Lloyd (founded in 1847) and the Hamburg-based Hamburg America Line (founded in the same year), merged in 1970 to become Hapag-Lloyd. The company no longer operates regularly scheduled transatlantic crossings but promotes instead ships in two different market segments (*Bremen* is operated by Hapag-Lloyd Expedition Cruises); the 408-passenger *Europa* and the informal 516-passenger *Europa 2* (for international travelers and families with children) are in the luxury market, for destination-intensive cruises. The staff on board makes all its own breads, soups, pâtés, jams, and preserves from scratch.

Hapag-Lloyd Cruises hosts the annual Stella Maris International Vocal Competition, which attracts top-notch up-and-coming operatic singers from around the world. A top prize of €15,000 is offered, as well as a Deutsche Grammophon recording contract. The company also sponsors an annual Ocean Sun Festival – for classical/chamber music devotees (concerts are often held ashore as part of the program). Gratuities are included.

HAPAG-LLOYD EXPEDITION CRUISES

The company started expedition cruises in 1990 with the 164-passenger *Bremen*, for its German-speaking passengers. As expedition cruising grew in popularity, the company took over *Hanseatic* from Hanseatic Tours. Both ships have now been replaced by three new ships.

The company is known for operating its ships in the most environmentally friendly manner, accompanied by the very best expedition leaders in the business.

The company publishes its own excellent handbooks (in both English and German) on expedition regions such as the Arctic, Antarctica, Amazonia, and the South Sea Islands, as well as exclusive maps. Gratuities are not included.

Two new expedition cruise ships (*HANSEATIC inspiration* and *HANSEATIC nature*) entered service in 2019, and *HANSEATIC spirit* in 2021. All three ships are equipped for shore power.

HEBRIDEAN ISLAND CRUISES

The company (formerly Hebridean International Cruises) was set up in 1989 under the Thatcher government's British Enterprise Scheme, and has its headquarters in Skipton, Yorkshire. It is independently owned and operates one all-inclusive boutique ship, *Hebridean Princess*, which conveys the atmosphere of English country-house life – and specializes in cruises for mature adults. All port taxes and gratuities are included, as are most excursions. The ship offers cruises around the Scottish islands, with occasional sailings to English ports, the Channel Islands, and Norway. Each cabin has coffee- and tea-making facilities. In 2020, the company added the 27-passenger *Lord of the Glens*. The late Queen Elizabeth II granted Hebridean Island Cruises a royal warrant in her jubilee year.

HERITAGE EXPEDITIONS

This youth-minded adventure travel company, formed in 1984, is based in Christchurch, New Zealand, and focuses on expedition-style cruising, specifically to Antarctica. The company was founded in 1985 by biologist Rodney Russ who worked for the New Zealand Wildlife Service for many years. Its principal ship is the chartered *Heritage Adventurer* (formerly the much-loved *Hanseatic,* previously operated by Hapag-Lloyd Cruises).

HURTIGRUTEN

The company, formerly known as the Norwegian Coastal Voyage, is an amalgamation of two shipping companies (OVDS and TVDS), and provides a year-round service along the Norwegian coast, calling at 34 ports in 11 days. The decor is best described as rustic – utilitarian and modest – and practical rather than beautiful. The ships provide a way to see the ports along the coast of Norway in a very modestly comfortable, laid-back manner.

HURTIGRUTEN EXPEDITIONS

This company has also dabbled in 'soft' expedition-style cruises, albeit aboard the *Fram* (think utilitarian, with very modest decor), built for polar and Greenland cruising. The high passenger capacity, dual-fuel, hybrid coastal and expedition-style ship, the much-delayed *Roald Amundsen* was delivered in 2019, with *Fridtjof Nansen* following in 2020. However, the vessels are rather large for true expedition cruising in Antarctica. They are moderately comfortable, but cabins aboard the converted ships are quite sparse, with little storage space – especially for outdoor wear. Some activities (such as sea kayaking and stand-up paddle-boarding excursions) are at extra cost. Gratuities are not included.

LINDBLAD EXPEDITIONS

Lars-Eric Lindblad started the concept of expedition cruising with a small single ship, *Lindblad Explorer* (known as the *Little Red Boat*), in 1969, taking adventurous travelers to remote regions of the world. Today, his son, Sven-Olof Lindblad, runs the company (he formerly ran Special Expeditions – a subsidiary of Lindblad Travel), but with an array of very small ships. It's all about nature, wilderness, wildlife, off-the-beaten-path adventures, and learning, with ships that provide basic levels of comfort, food, and service.

In partnership with the National Geographic Society, the company operates small, really, basic vessels for coastal cruises in the USA. National Geographic photographers take part in all cruises. The National Geographic Society celebrated its 125th anniversary in 2013, the year that Lindblad Expeditions merged with Capitol Acquisition Corporation and formed Lindblad Expedition Holdings Inc. The company purchased Australia-based Orion Expedition Cruises. Its only ship, also called *Orion,* was renamed *National Geographic Orion,* and transferred to the Lindblad fleet in March 2014. In 2020, a better expedition-style ship *(National Geographic Endurance)* debuted, followed by *National Geographic Resolution* in 2021. Gratuities are not included.

MARELLA CRUISES

In 1973, Thomson Cruises (the former name of Marella Cruises) ventured into the cruise industry when it chartered two ships, *Calypso* and *Ithaca,* from Greek-owned Ulysses Line. It was a disaster, and the company withdrew from cruising two years later (Ulysses Line became known as Useless Line). However, the company started again in 2002 (as Thomson Cruises) after seeing rival tour operator Airtours operate ships successfully. In 2017 the company changed its name to Marella Cruises (Celtic for 'Shining Sea'), which charters its ships, preferring to leave operations, management, and catering to specialist companies. Cruises are offered for the whole family aboard *Marella Discovery, Marella Discovery 2, Marella Explorer,* and *Marella Voyager* – catering principally to the British market. In 2022, the company

Aboard *Hebridean Princess*, cruising around Scotland and its islands.

Aboard the maiden voyage of P&O Cruises' *Britannia*.

added one ship for adults-only cruising (*Marella Explorer 2*), but all ships feature all-inclusive cruising.

MOPAS

Osaka Shosen Kaisha was founded in 1884 in Osaka, Japan. In 1964 it merged with Mitsui Steamship, to become Mitsui OSK Passenger Line (MOPAS). It is now one of the oldest and largest shipping companies in the world.

It entered cruise shipping in 1989 with *Fuji Maru*, the first cruise ship in the Japanese-speaking domestic market (now no longer in service). The company specialized in incentive meetings and groups at sea rather than cruising for individuals, but this steadily changed into more cruises for individuals. The firm operates a single ship, the very comfortable *Nippon Maru* (extensively refurbished in 2010), based in Japan for Japanese-speaking passengers. Gratuities are included.

NOBLE CALEDONIA

London-based Noble Caledonia, established in 1991, operates three boutique-size sister ships, *Caledonian Sky, Hebridean Sky,* and *Island Sky,* each carrying around 100 passengers. It also sells cruises aboard a wide range of small-ship and expedition cruise companies as well as river cruises. It markets to British passengers of mature years, and operates cruises, generally in sheltered water areas, with cultural-interest themes, and so is not recommended for children.

The company, whose financial partners include Sweden's Salen family, who have been very involved with expedition cruising in the past, has an excellent reputation for well-organized cruises and tours, accompanied by good lecturers. It specializes in itineraries that would be impossible to operate aboard larger ships. A Commodore Club gives repeat passengers advance information about new voyages and special offers. Gratuities are included.

OCEANIA CRUISES

The company's ships provide English-style charm in a country-club atmosphere ideal for middle-aged and older couples seeking relaxation. Cruises are usually 10–14 days. Its trademarks are comfortable (if small) cabins, attentive service, and decent-to-fine dining combining French culinary expertise and top-quality ingredients. Breads, pastries and other baked goods, are very good.

In 2006, Oceania Cruises was bought by Apollo Management, a private equity company that owns Regent Seven Seas Cruises and 50 percent of Norwegian Cruise Line (NCL), now under the umbrella of Prestige Cruise Holdings. There are six ships – *Insignia, Marina, Nautica, Regatta, Riviera,* and *Sirena* – catering to between 684 and 1,250 passengers. Two new 1,200-passenger ships (similar to *Marina* and *Riviera*) are on order, scheduled for delivery in 2023 and 2025.

With multiple-choice dining at no extra cost, these ships suit anyone who prefers small- and mid-sized ships to the large resort vessels. Bottled mineral water, soft drinks, and beer are included in the price, as is Wi-Fi (but only one device per cabin).

OCEANWIDE EXPEDITIONS

Founded in 1961 as the Dutch 'Plancius Foundation' to operate cruises around Spitzbergen (Norway), but became more focused on expedition cruises in 1993. The company changed its name in 1996 to Oceanwide Expeditions to offer adventures farther afield. It specializes in small group polar-expedition voyages and active shore visits rather than employing experienced lecturers. It operates the small (very basic) expedition ships, *Ortelius* and *Plancius*, and introduced newbuilds *Hondius* in 2019 and *Janssonius* in 2021.

P&O CRUISES

P&O's full name is the Peninsular and Oriental Steam Navigation Company, though none of its ships is powered by steam turbines. Based in Southampton, England, it was founded in 1837, just before Samuel Cunard established his company, and was awarded a UK government contract in 1840 to carry the mail from Gibraltar to Alexandria.

P&O Cruises acquired Princess Cruises in 1974, Swan Hellenic in 1982, and Sitmar Cruises in 1988. In 2000 it demerged from its parent and became P&O Princess plc. It was bought by the Carnival Corporation in 2003; its 175th anniversary was in 2012, when all seven ships (at the time) assembled in Southampton.

P&O Cruises has always been a traditional British cruise company, never quite matching the quality aboard the Cunard ships, which have more international passengers. With P&O having mainly British captains and navigation officers and Indian (Goanese) service staff, the British traditions of unobtrusive service are preserved. British food favorites provide down-home comfort factor in a single-language setting that provides home-from-home ships for families (*Azura, Iona, Britannia,* and *Ventura*), or on adults-only ships (*Arcadia* and *Aurora*).

The company attracts British passengers wanting to sail from a UK port – except for winter Caribbean cruises from Barbados, as well as for its adults-only ships, so the two products differ widely in their communal spaces. P&O also operates theme cruises – on antiques, art appreciation, classical music, comedy, cricket, gardening and horticulture, jazz, Scottish dancing, etc. The ships usually carry ballroom-dance instructors. Bed linen is changed twice a week – not as often as, for example, on MSC Cruises, where it is changed every two days. The decor is a mix of British traditional (think comfy, somewhat dated, non-glitzy armchairs, and wood panelling) and bland. British artists are featured aboard all ships – *Ventura,* for example, displays works by more than 40 of them. Its newest ship, *Iona,* is dual-fuel-powered (including LNG), debuted in 2021, while sister ship *Arvia* arrived in 2022.

P&O CRUISES AUSTRALIA

Founded in 1932, the Australian division of P&O Cruises provides fun entertainment for the beer-and-bikini brigade and their families, and specializes in cruises in the Pacific and to New Zealand. The cruise line is firmly established in region and is now a mainstream operator – with a renewed fleet of the latest ships, which are larger, more contemporary pre-owned vessels from P&O Cruises and Princess Cruises, The ships have open-seating dining and specialty restaurants, such as Australian celebrity chef Luke Mangan's 'Salt Grill.' Cruise pricing is in three levels, depending on what's included.

PAUL GAUGUIN CRUISE LINE

Created by the Boston-based tour operator Grand Circle Travel, Paul Gauguin Cruises (now named Paul Gauguin Cruise Line) took over the marketing and operation of *Paul Gauguin* in 2009 from Regent Seven Seas Cruises, which had operated the ship since its inception. In 2009, the ship was bought by the Tahiti-based investor Richard Bailey and his company Pacific Beachcomber, owner of Polynesian resort hotels (including four InterContinental Hotels), but was sold to French company Ponant in 2019, who then ordered two cruise ships for Paul Gauguin's Polynesian operations.

PEARL SEAS CRUISES

Founded in 2007 by Charles Robertson, Pearl Seas Cruises is a sister company to American Cruise Lines. It has a single ship, *Pearl Mist*, which was the subject of poor shipbuilding and contract arguments in its early days. *Pearl Mist* was rejected as not fit for purpose by the company, but the ship was finally completed and debuted in 2014.

Waterslides on the top deck of *Pacific Dawn*, **a P&O Australia ship.**

PHOENIX REISEN

Based in Bonn, Germany, the company for many years operated low-budget, tour-operator-style destination-intensive cruises for German speakers. It has a loyal, widespread audience, contemporary ships, with good food and service.

To keep costs down, Phoenix charters its ships for long periods. It is consistently praised for its extremely good itineraries, particularly on world cruises, its pre- and post-cruise programs, and its excellent value for money. The wonderfully comprehensive Phoenix brochure provides photographs of its captains and cruise director, as well as bar lists and drink prices – a refreshing change from the brochures provided by most cruise companies. Single-seating dining is standard, as are low drink prices, and there is no constant pushing for onboard revenue – again different from most rivals.

Phoenix acquired *Artania* (formerly *Artemis* but originally *Royal Princess*, named by Princess Diana) in 2011. Gratuities are included.

PLANTOURS CRUISES

This travel company, based in Bremen, Germany, provides low-budget cruises for German speakers aboard its single small, chartered cruise ship, *Hamburg*, which was formerly Hapag-Lloyd Cruises' mid-market *Columbus*. The company also sells cruises on the rivers of Europe, with riverships operated by various companies.

PONANT

The company was founded in 1988 by Philippe Videau and Jean-Emmanuel Sauvé, and started life as La Compagnie des Iles du Ponant, a subsidiary of the state-owned CMA CGM (Compagnie Maritime d'Affrètement/Compagnie Générale Maritime), until its acquisition by Bridgepoint Capital, a private equity company, in 2012. In 2015, Ponant was acquired by Groupe Artémis (which owns the art auction house Christies and Chateau Latour winery, among many other assets), the holding company of French billionaire François Pinault and his family.

Ponant's head office is in Marseille, France; it operates one boutique-size, high-tech sail-cruise ship, *Le Ponant*. In 2004, the company purchased the Paris-based tour operator Tapis Rouge International (specializing in premium travel). Ponant introduced four small ships starting in 2010; four more were delivered in 2018 and 2019. Ponant promotes French products and has partnerships with Veuve Clicquot, Hermès (bathroom products), Ladurée (macarons), and Alain Ducasse (Ducasse Conseil) – one of France's most highly decorated chefs.

Ponant increasingly markets cruises in both English and French to international passengers and onboard announcements are made in both languages, but the onboard product is decidedly French. Ponant purchased Paul Gauguin Cruise Line in 2019, and is building two ships for the company's Polynesian operations.

POSEIDON EXPEDITIONS

Poseidon Expeditions is an Arctic expedition cruise specialist (founded and owned by Nikolay Saveliev in 2003). Expeditions to the North Pole (90 degrees north) are operated at the height of the Arctic sum-

Paul Gauguin was built specifically to operate in French Polynesia.

mer, in June and July, aboard the Russian nuclear-powered *50 Years of Victory* (it can crush ice up to 10ft/3m thick). Only 10,741 people had ever been to the North Pole when I went in July 2016. The company operates under the strict guidelines of the Association of Arctic Expedition Cruise Operators (AECO), the body committed to minimizing the impact of visits to the Far North. Due to the ongoing conflict between Russia and Ukraine, these voyages are presently suspended.

The company also operates the smaller *Sea Spirit* on itineraries to the Antarctic Peninsula. Some activities (such as sea kayaking, stand-up paddle-boarding, and paddling excursions) are at extra cost. Gratuities are not included.

QUARK EXPEDITIONS

The company was founded in 1991 by Lars Wikander, Mike McDowell, and silent partners the Salen family (formerly of Salen-Lindblad Cruises). It specializes in providing up-close-and-personal Polar expedition cruises. Quark Expeditions is currently owned by New York-based KKR.

The company is an associate member of IAATO (International Association of Antarctica Tour Operators) and has specialized in chartering powerful Russian icebreakers to provide participants with memorable expedition experiences (adventure cruising for toughies). Quark Expeditions was the first company to operate a complete circumnavigation of Antarctica, in 1996–7, a voyage lasting just over two months. In 2021 the now Seattle-based company debuted its first newbuild, *Ultramarine* (the company had previously chartered specialist ships from several different owners). Some activities (such as sea kayaking, stand-up paddle-boarding, and paddling excursions) cost extra. Gratuities are not included.

REGENT SEVEN SEAS CRUISES

This company has a complicated history. It was born out of Seven Seas Cruises, which was originally based in San Francisco to market the cruise ship *Song of Flower* (belonging to 'K'-Line, a Japanese cargo ship operator with a base in New Jersey), and expedition cruises aboard the chartered *Hanseatic* (then operated by Hanseatic Tours). The lyre, logo of that ship, became RSSC's logo.

For many years, the company was part of the Carlson group, and operated as Radisson Seven Seas Cruises. Carlson Hospitality Worldwide ventured into cruising via its Radisson Hotels International division – hence, Radisson Diamond Cruises (when Radisson Diamond joined in 1992). In 1994 Radisson Diamond Cruises and Seven Seas Cruise Line merged to become Radisson Seven Seas Cruises, and in 2007 it became Regent Seven Seas Cruises.

In 2007 the company was bought by US-based investment group Apollo Management, and, together with Oceania Cruises, was placed under the umbrella

The softly lit Horizon Lounge Deck aboard *Seven Seas Voyager*.

of its Prestige Cruise Holdings. The company spent $40 million to refurbish its then fleet of three ships in 2009–10.

It operates worldwide itineraries and strives to pay close attention to detail and provide high-quality service aboard its small cruise ships, of which there are six: *Seven Seas Explorer*, *Seven Seas Grandeur*, *Seven Seas Mariner*, *Seven Seas Navigator*, *Seven Seas Splendor*, and *Seven Seas Voyager*.

The company provides drinks-inclusive cruising, which means that beverages and gratuities are included – even premium illy coffees, as are shore excursions. Passengers pay extra only for laundry services, beauty services, casino, and other personal items.

RESORTS WORLD CRUISES

Owned by Genting Cruise Lines, this brand is a former sister company to the now defunct Southeast Asia-based Star Cruises. *Genting Dream* started sailing in November 2016. The company is a more upscale and advanced version of Star Cruises, and is aimed specifically at the Asian (and particularly, mainland Chinese) market, with an abundance of bright decor and some very upbeat, colorful razzle-dazzle shows. Gratuities are included.

SAGA CRUISES

Saga, based in Folkestone, England, was created by Sidney De Haan as a company offering financial services and holidays to the over-60s. As the company's success grew, it reduced this limitation in 1995 to the over-50s and allowed companions older than 40. Its travel division flourished because it became known for providing personal attention from a caring staff. Instead of sending passengers to ships operated by other companies, it decided to buy its own ships and market its own product under the Saga Holidays brand.

Seabourn Odyssey's water-sports platform.

Saga Shipping (Saga Cruises), the cruising division of Saga Holidays, was set up in 1997 when it purchased *Saga Rose* (formerly *Sagafjord*), followed soon after by *Saga Ruby* (formerly *Vistafjord*), and, in 2010, *Saga Pearl II* (formerly *Astoria*). *Saga Sapphire* (ex-*Europa*) arrived in 2012.

Another brand, Spirit of Adventure, was added in 2006, and in 2007 Saga merged with Britain's Automobile Association. The 'Adventure' cruise brand ended in November 2013, when *Quest for Adventure* became *Saga Pearl II* again.

Saga emphasizes British seamanship and training, and its fleet manages to retain the feel of traditional, elegant, adults-only cruising. It offers open-seating dining, and attentive service from a mainly Filipino hotel service crew aboard ships with many solo-occupancy cabins. It takes care of some of the little details that other lines have long forgotten.

All gratuities, and door-to-door transfers, are included. The company operates two new ships: *Spirit of Discovery*, which debuted in 2019, and *Spirit of Adventure*, which followed in 2021.

SCENIC

This company was founded in Newcastle, Australia, in 1986 by Glen Moroney, under the brand name Scenic Tours, which began by operating coach tours throughout Australia. In 2008, it began river cruise operations in Europe (mainly for Australasian passengers). It now owns and operates several riverships in Europe under two brand names: Scenic, and Emerald Waterways. The company, which is still Australian owned, changed its name to Scenic in 2015, and operates two very upscale small 'discovery' ships, the first of which, *Scenic Eclipse*, debuted in 2019. A second ship, *Scenic Eclipse II*, debuted in 2023. Cruises are fully inclusive of gratuities and drinks, with a few select, cost-extra premium brands.

SEA CLOUD CRUISES

This company was founded in 1979 by a consortium of ship-owners and investors known as the Hansa Treuhand (headquartered in Hamburg, Germany). In 2022 it was acquired by The Yacht Portfolio (also involved in the start-up of The Ritz-Carlton Yacht Collection. It owns and operates two genuine tall ships (cruise-sail vessels), the legendary *Sea Cloud* (built in 1931 for the cereal heiress Marjorie Merriweather Post), and the 1990-built *Sea Cloud II*. A third sail-cruise ship, *Sea Cloud Spirit*, debuted in 2021.

The company has many corporate clients who charter the two sail-cruise ships, while a number of luxury cruise and travel specialist companies sell cruises to individuals. The onboard style and product delivery are something special, with elegant retro decor, and high-quality food and service.

SEABOURN

Originally founded in 1986 as Signet Cruise Line, the company, then owned by Norwegian industrialist Atle Brynestad, had to change its name in 1988 as a result of a lawsuit brought by a Texas ferry company that had already registered the name Signet Cruise Lines (no ships were ever built for cruising, however).

In 1998, a consortium, which included the Carnival Corporation and Norwegian investors, bought Seabourn Cruise Line and merged its operations into Cunard, which was acquired from Kvaerner. The fleet then included three ships plus *Seabourn Goddess I* and *Seabourn Goddess II* (bought by SeaDream Yacht Club in 2002 and named *SeaDream I* and *SeaDream II*) and *Seabourn Sun*. The Carnival Corporation acquired 100 percent of Seabourn Cruise Line in 1999.

Three new, larger ships joined the company between 2009 and 2011. All three have an aft watersports platform, as well as a wider number of dining and spa options, and a greater amount of space, for more passengers. Seabourn Cruise Line was briefly rebranded as The Yachts of Seabourn in 2009–10, but then became simply Seabourn. The company is managed from the headquarters of Carnival-owned Holland America Line in Seattle, USA.

In February 2013, the three original ships (*Seabourn Pride, Seabourn Legend, Seabourn Spirit*). were sold to Xanterra Parks & Resorts, parent company of Windstar Cruises, and transferred in 2014/15. Seabourn's new, larger ships were then ordered, and *Seabourn Encore* debuted in 2016, then *Seabourn Ovation* in 2018.

Quality has been noticeably reduced since the ships' management was taken over by Holland America Line, with various cutbacks reflecting the downgrade – examples include prosecco rather than champagne, poor canapés, and disappointing cheese and meat quality provided in place of the better offerings of yesteryear – and reduced dining hours and fixed disembarkation by 8am are now standard. Overall, it's less of an upmarket product than in the company's early years, for its mainly North American clientele. Gratuities are included.

Seabourn ventured into the soft expedition arena with *Seabourn Quest*, and then upped its game by ordering a ship more suited to expedition cruises, *Seabourn Venture*, which was delivered December 2021.

SEADREAM YACHT CLUB

Larry Pimentel, an American, and his Norwegian business partner Atle Brynestad, founder of Seabourn Cruise Line (now simply Seabourn), jointly created the company by buying the former Sea Goddess Cruises' ships. They introduced them in 2002 to an audience anxious for exclusivity, personal pampering, and cuisine prepared to order. Atle Brynestad is now the company's chairman and sole owner.

Its two ships, *SeaDream I* and *SeaDream II,* have been refreshed several times, and are often chartered by companies or private individuals who appreciate the refined, elegant, but casual atmosphere on board. The 112-passenger ships operate year-round in the Caribbean and Mediterranean, with all-inclusive beverages and open-seating dining, and a high degree of personalized service, all in a cosy, club-like atmosphere, with much attention to detail and personal idiosyncrasies. Gratuities are included.

SILVERSEA CRUISES

Silversea Cruises started as a mostly privately owned cruise line, founded in 1992 by the Lefebvre d'Ovidio family from Rome, based in Monaco. Antonio Lefeb-

vre d'Ovidio was a maritime lawyer and professor of maritime law before acquiring and operating cargo ships and ferries in the Adriatic. He took his family into partnership with Boris Vlasov's Vlasov Group (V-Ships) to co-own Sitmar Cruises, until that company merged with Princess Cruises in 1988.

Silversea Cruises has much loyalty from its frequent passengers, who view the ships as their own home from home. All Silversea ships have teak verandas, all-inclusive beverages, and open-seating dining. Silversea Cruises caters to a cosmopolitan passenger mix (compared to others like Seabourn and Regent, which typically have a greater percentage of North Americans).

The cruise line is known for its partnership with the hospitality organization Relais & Châteaux. *Silver Spirit* (2009) underwent a 'chop and stretch' operation in 2019 to make it more like *Silver Muse*, which debuted in 2017 (with more than a design nod to Hapag-Lloyd's *Europa 2*). In 2020 the company's remaining shares were purchased by the Royal Caribbean Group.

SILVERSEA EXPEDITION CRUISES

Silversea Expedition Cruises is a part of Silversea Cruises. based in Monaco. The company is now owned by the Royal Caribbean Group. It has two specialist ships: *Silver Explorer* and *Silver Origin* for year-round Galápagos cruises, plus the larger *Silver Cloud* and *Silver Wind*, adapted for 'soft' expedition-style cruises. Gratuities are included as part of the company's 'all-inclusive' culture.

STAR CLIPPERS

Swedish-born yachtsman Mikael Krafft founded Star Clippers in 1991 with *Star Flyer* and then *Star Clipper,*

Relaxed lifestyle aboard *SeaDream I.*

both true tall ships. The company went on to build the largest tall ship presently sailing, the five-mast *Royal Clipper,* a stunning ship when under full sail. Friendly service in an extremely laid-back setting, under the romance of sail (when there is enough wind) is what Star Clippers is all about, and the food variety, creativity, and quality are all extremely good. These real tall (sail-cruise) ships sail in the Caribbean, Baltic, Mediterranean, and Southeast Asia.

SWAN HELLENIC

Originally founded in 1954 By R.K. Swan, the company chartered small cruise ships for many years. It was purchased by P&O Cruises in 1982, but then changed hands when Carnival Corporation merged with P&O in April 2004. In 2007, the Carnival Corporation disbanded Swan Hellenic. Its single ship (*Minerva II*) was transferred to Princess Cruises as Royal Princess. Some months later, a semi-retired Lord Sterling purchased the brand from the Carnival Corporation, and he joined partners with the UK's Voyages of Discovery (now defunct).

The company's strengths are its program of highly academic lecturers and speakers, in a small ship setting that is unpretentious but comfortable, and includes gratuities, drinks (on Antarctic voyages), tailor-made shore excursions, and entrance fees to muse-

Mein Schiff 6's pool.

ums and places of interest. Its intellectual passengers are known as 'Swanners,'

TUI CRUISES

The Germany-based TUI Group has several divisions but started its own cruise line in 2009 with *Mein Schiff 1,* a mid-size ship (formerly *Celebrity Galaxy*) that underwent a huge reconstruction program. *Mein Schiff 2* (formerly *Celebrity Mercury*) was added in 2011. Further new ships followed: *Mein Schiff 3* debuted in 2014, *Mein Schiff 4* in 2015, *Mein Schiff 5* in 2016, and *Mein Schiff 6 in* 2017. Two more ships – the new *Mein Schiff 1* and *Mein Schiff 2* – joined the fleet in 2018 and 2019. In the summer of 2024, a new, larger *Mein Schiff 7* will debut.

Aboard all TUI Cruises ships, all cabins have an espresso machine, and a wide choice of dining venues and food styles, with an emphasis on healthy eating and high-quality ingredients. Much attention is placed on the extensive wellness facilities aboard the ships, which are geared extensively to family cruising. Gratuities are included, and the company provides many things that other cruise lines don't, making this a very good value-for-money, high-quality cruise line.

UNCRUISE ADVENTURES

This micro-cruise line was founded in 1997 as American Safari Cruises. It was bought in 2008 by InnerSea Discoveries, owned by the former chief executive officer of American Safari Cruises, Dan Blanchard. It purchased the website and database files of now-defunct Cruise West in order to expand its reach to small-ship enthusiasts, and has a fleet of very small motor yacht-type vessels for six to 86 passengers for expensive cruises in Alaska and the Pacific Northwest. While the vessels are decent, there are few facilities, and the one-seat dining experience is very casual. The advantage of these intimate vessels is that they can take you up close to fascinating parts of Alaska that larger ships can't reach. InnerSea Discoveries changed its name to UnCruise Adventures in 2013.

VIKING OCEAN CRUISES

A sister to the long-established Viking River Cruises, this company aims to provide both ocean-going and river cruises to the same passengers and market segment, which is a unique concept in the cruise industry. The product is aimed squarely at adults who want comfort and some elements of luxe, but no glitz, and at a price that includes many items other cruise lines charge extra for (such as ship-wide Wi-Fi). Their approach has proved to be a great success. Its chairman is Torstein Hagen, originally a major shareholder owner of the long-defunct but much-respected Royal Viking Line.

Staying away from large resort ships, the company ordered mid-size ships for 930 passengers. For the ships' size, they offer an impressive array of public

The main pool on *Viking Star* when the roof is closed.

rooms and dining options, and modern, uncluttered Scandinavian design. Itineraries are designed so that they stay longer in ports and include overnight stays at some ports, so that passengers can take in the night-life and cultural attractions of some destinations. Its first ship, *Viking Star*, debuted in spring 2015. The company has established a fine onboard product that is well placed for value.

VIRGIN VOYAGES

This new rock-star cruise line was established by Virgin Group founder Richard Branson, together with Bain Capital (the majority shareholder). The goal: to 'be different' to all other cruise lines. Virgin has put families to bed by creating adults-only party ships, with overflowing hip hype and marketing aimed at younger passengers.

The Florida-based company markets a twist on the classic Virgin brand – passengers are called 'sailors' and there are no dress codes or gratuities. The company's first ship is named, appropriately, *Scarlet Lady*, debuted in 2021, followed by *Valiant Lady* (2022) and *Resilient Lady* (2023). Jennifer Lopez (J.Lo) is an investor, and the company's 'lifestyle officer'.

VIVA EXPEDITION CRUISES

The parent company of VEC is Scylla AG, a Swiss company founded by the owning family Reitsma, who own a large fleet of riverships for European river cruises. The company purchased *Bremen* (built originally as *Frontier Spirit*), and renamed it *Seaventure*. Viva initially chartered the ship to Polar Latitudes, an adventure travel company based in Vermont, USA, for the winter 2021 Antarctic season.

WINDSTAR CRUISES

Founded by New York-based Karl Andren in 1984 as Windstar Sail Cruises, the company built high-class sail-cruise ships with computer-controlled sails, outfitting them in a contemporary decor designed by Marc Held. The first ship, *Wind Star*, debuted in 1986 to great acclaim, and was followed by *Wind Spirit* (1988) and *Wind Surf* (1990).

Windstar Cruises was sold to Holland America Line in 1988. The company, with headquarters in Seattle, US, was sold in 2007 to the Ambassadors Cruise Group, wholly owned by Ambassadors International. It was then sold again in 2011 to Xanterra Parks & Resorts.

In 2014, Windstar took delivery of the former *Seabourn Pride* (renamed *Star Pride*), and, in mid-2015, two more Seabourn ships – *Seabourn Legend* (now *Star Legend*), and *Seabourn Spirit* (now *Star Breeze*).

In 2019, the three ships underwent a 'chop-and-stretch' operation which added a mid-section of about 82ft (25m) and increased the passenger capacity from 212 to 312.

The style is casual and unregimented, but smart, with service by Indonesian and Filipino crew members. Itineraries include some off-the-beaten-track ports not frequented by large resort ships. The onboard product is decidedly American ultra-casual, with un-fussy bistro-style cuisine, and service that lacks the finesse and the small details that could make it a much better experience overall.

Luggage ready for pick-up.

WHAT TO DO IF ...

Here are 15 practical tips for a good cruise experience, and advice on what to do if you have a problem.

1. YOUR LUGGAGE DOES NOT ARRIVE AT THE SHIP

If you booked as part of the cruise line's air/sea package, the airline is responsible for locating your luggage and delivering it to the next port. Let the ship's reception desk staff know, and they'll initiate a search and trace procedure. If you arranged your own air transportation, it is wholly *your* problem. Always have easy-to-read name and address tags *inside* as well as *outside* your luggage. Keep track of claim documents, and give the airline an itinerary and list of port agents.

2. YOU MISS THE SHIP

If you miss the ship's departure at the port of embarkation, and you are traveling on an air/sea package, the airline will arrange to get you to the ship, possibly at the next port of call. If you are traveling 'cruise-only,' however, then you are responsible for flights, hotel stays, and transfers.

It is up to you to get back to the ship before the appointed sailing time. Miss the ship and you'll need to get to its next port at your own cost. *Always* take a copy of your passport with you, just in case.

Ships have also been known to leave port early because of impending inclement weather conditions or natural disasters. If this happens, the ship's port agent will be there to assist you. Always take the port agent's name and telephone contact details with you.

3. YOUR CABIN HAS NO AIR CONDITIONING, IT IS NOISY, OR THERE ARE PLUMBING PROBLEMS

If there is anything wrong in your cabin or bathroom, tell your cabin steward or go to the reception desk immediately.

Some cabins are located above the ship's laundry, generator, or galley; others may be above the disco. If the ship is full, it will be difficult to change.

4. YOU HAVE NOISY CABIN NEIGHBORS

First, politely tell your neighbors that you can hear them brushing their hair as the cabin walls are so thin, and would they please not slam the drawers shut at 2am! If that does not work, complain to the hotel manager (via the reception desk).

5. YOU HAVE A PROBLEM WITH A CREW MEMBER

Go to the reception desk and explain the problem. Insist on a full written report of the incident, which must be entered into the ship's daily log by the staff captain (deputy captain).

6. YOU DON'T LIKE YOUR DINING ROOM SEATING

Many ships operate two seatings for dinner. When you book your cruise, you choose whether you want the first or second seating. The line and the restaurant manager will make every attempt to please you, but there may be little the restaurant manager can do if the ship is full.

7. YOU CANNOT COMMUNICATE WITH YOUR WAITER

Dining room waiters might be of a nationality and language completely foreign to yours, with limited flu-

One answer to lack of storage space aboard *Queen Elizabeth*.

Larger restaurants, such as *Carnival Conquest*'s Renoir, seat hundreds of diners.

ency in your language. This could prove frustrating for a whole cruise. See the restaurant manager, and ask if there is a waiter with whom you can communicate.

8. THE FOOD IS NOT THE GOURMET CUISINE PORTRAYED IN THE BROCHURE

If the food is not as described (for example, whole lobster is shown in the brochure, but only cold lobster salad is provided once during the cruise, or the 'fresh squeezed' orange juice on the breakfast menu is anything but), inform the restaurant manager.

9. A LARGE GROUP HAS TAKEN OVER THE SHIP

Sometimes, large groups have pre-booked public rooms for meetings. Make your displeasure known to the hotel department immediately. If nothing is resolved, tell your booking agent, and write a follow-up letter to the line when you get home.

10. A PORT OF CALL IS DELETED FROM THE ITINERARY

Read the fine print in the brochure *before* you book. A cruise line is under no obligation to perform the stated itinerary. For whatever reason – political unrest, weather, mechanical problems, safety, etc. – the ship's captain has the ultimate say.

11. YOU LEAVE PERSONAL BELONGINGS ON A TOUR BUS

If you find you've left something on a tour bus, tell the

shore excursion staff. The tour operator will then be contacted to see whether any items have been handed in.

12. YOU ARE UNWELL ABOARD SHIP

There will be a qualified doctor (who generally operates as a concession). Medical facilities usually include a small pharmacy. Although there are charges for medical services, almost all cruise lines offer insurance packages that include medical coverage for most eventualities. It is wise to take out this insurance when you book.

13. THE LAUNDRY RUINS YOUR CLOTHES

If any of your clothing is ruined or discolored by the ship's laundry, tell your cabin steward(ess) and register a complaint at the reception desk. Obtain a copy of the complaint, so you can follow up. Unfortunately, you will probably find a disclaimer on the laundry list stating that liability is limited to about $1 per item.

14. YOU HAVE EXTRA CHARGES ON YOUR BILL

Check your itemized bill carefully, then go to the reception and ask to be shown the charge slips. Make sure you get a copy of your bill *after* any modifications have been made.

15. YOU ARE UNHAPPY WITH YOUR CRUISE EXPERIENCE

If your ship delivers less well than the brochure promises, then let your booking agent and the cruise line know immediately.

CRUISING AND THE ENVIRONMENT

Cruise companies are constantly striving to reduce pollution and air emissions, and to update older ships with more efficient equipment.

Although marine vessels are responsible for around three percent of the world's greenhouse gases, the world's fleet of oceangoing cruise ships produces around 0.2 percent of the total emissions.

ECO DILIGENCE

Today's newest ships are ultra-smart – engines and generators are the cleanest ever, and more fuel-efficient than even five years ago. The latest ships also have advanced waste water treatment and waste management systems, the latest in air quality systems, recycling and energy recovery, and shore power connection capabilities.

New ships benefit from improved hydrodynamic hull design, and advanced hull coatings also improve efficiency, while careful handling of solid and liquid waste helps lower fuel consumption and CO_2 emissions. Flue gas from shipboard incinerators is recycled and waste water is treated according to tough eco-friendly standards.

The result is a generous reduction in NOx – the term for a group of highly reactive gases containing nitrogen and oxygen in varying amounts. High-efficiency emissions-control technology such as selective catalytic converters further reduce NOx, and allows greater monitoring and computer control. *Europa 2* (2013) became the first cruise ship equipped with an SCR-catalytic converter, reducing nitrogen oxides (including nitrogen dioxide) by almost 95 percent.

SCRUBBER TECHNOLOGY

In a big effort to combat criticism, and be seen to care for the marine environment, some cruise companies have chosen to fit or retro-fit 'scrubber' technology to their ships. In 2013, *Norwegian Breakaway* became the first cruise ship to recover and re-use the heavy fuel oil (HFO) fraction of waste oil as fuel for its diesel engines. The waste separator system has only two moving parts and leaves only non-pumpable 'super-dry' solids for landing as dry waste. The separated water, with an oil content of less than 1,000ppm, is pumped to the bilge-water tank as part of its handling system.

Using scrubber technology allows ships to use cheaper HFO, because the sulfur content is removed by the scrubbers. However, 'open-loop' scrubbers don't quite

cut it, because the sulfurous waste goes straight into the sea, together with sulfuric acid, nitrates, and PAH (polycyclic aromatic hydrocarbons). These contaminants can build up in the aquatic food chain.

Cruise ships that *have* switched from heavy fuel oil to more expensive low-sulfur fuels have experienced greater fuel-pump wear, resulting in higher maintenance, operational, and replacement costs.

Some ship hulls are also treated with 'foul-release' paint containing fluoropolymers or glass-flake vinyl ester resins – non-toxic substances that help reduce CO_2 emissions by using less fuel.

OTHER MEASURES

Other eco-friendly measures include the use of LED lighting. Motion-activated cabin and closet lighting is now common, as is the replacement of single-use plastic cups by melamine and/or porcelain, the use of permanent dispensers instead of plastic single-use soap/shampoo bottles/packs, and the replacement of plastic laundry bags with washable cotton bags.

Solar panels aboard *Celebrity Solstice*.

Using darkness-activated sensors that switch on the ship's external lights at dusk and chilled river rocks that retain low temperatures for buffet items, rather than ice, also helps, as do heat-deflecting window coatings.

LNG (LIQUIFIED NATURAL GAS)

Until recently, most cruise ships have primarily been powered by HFO (heavy fuel oil) in diesel engines and MGO (marine gas oil) for gas turbine engines, but there has been a dramatic move towards LNG-powered ships. Liquified gas still comes mainly from a fossil fuel source, although it can also be made from the decomposition of waste products.

Several new cruise ships are now powered by LNG for propulsion: *AIDAnova* (AIDA Cruises), which debuted in 2018, became the first LNG-powered cruise ship. Using the same platform, *Costa Smeralda* (Costa Cruises), *Iona* (P&O Cruises), and *Carnival Mardi Gras* (Carnival Cruise Lines) followed. It is worth noting, however, that LNG storage tanks require 3.5 times the space of conventional fuel tanks, so retrofitting existing ships is impractical. If it were not liquified, it would take up all the space of a ship!

In its liquified state, LNG is odorless, colorless, non-toxic, and non-corrosive, therefore requiring less maintenance. It is also more cost effective in comparison to petroleum or gas. When it is burned in dual-fuel engines, it releases zero sulfur, 99 percent lower particulate emissions, 85 percent less NOx emissions, and 25 percent less greenhouse gas emissions. However, sourcing it is still not easy, and it's not entirely harmless, as it does produce some carbon dioxide.

The LNG-based power barges found in a handful of ports can generate and supply electricity while in port, although the LNG barge is itself powered by *diesel-*fueled tugs. As an example, a special barge (Q-LNG 4000) was built to provide the LNG fuel for *Carnival Mardi Gras* in Port Canaveral. This may be a better solution than 'bridge' (interim solution) technology 'cold

ironing,' where power is simply generated on land as normal and made available in port, so a cruise ship can turn off its generators to reduce emissions (although the land-based power may come from fossil fuels!)

Natural gas is extracted from the earth's core. It is then cooled to -260°F (-162°C) to turn in order to turn it into liquified gas. Although it is mostly methane, it becomes LNG *only* when it has been liquified. For ease of non-pressurised storage and transport, refrigeration is usually the chosen method, for safety. However, for reasons of space, the gas must be turned into a liquid, which requires 1/600th of the space compared to in its normal state.

The main advantages are:
• Lower cost
• Less wear and tear on an engine
• Cleaner emissions
• No need to install scrubber systems

It is, however, a finite fuel, and is estimated that with the present rate of consumption, supplies will last only another 50 years. Also, scientists report that LNG-fueled ships can leak significant amounts of gas into the atmosphere through unburned fuel.

BIOFUEL USE

In July 2022, *AIDAprima* (AIDA Cruises) became the first cruise ship to bunker with biofuel. The refueling took place in Rotterdam, and the biofuel was enough to power one dual-fuel 12-volt motor – sufficient for the ship in port. This really provided a blueprint for the gradual decarbonisation of cruise ships, including those already in service. Waste cooking oil, animal waste fats etc, can all be converted to biofuel.

MSC AND THE FUTURE OF CRUISING

MSC Cruises' sustainability programme is set to play a big part in future cruise choices for many.

Unquestionably, the sea is the driving force of MSC. I have been aware of the company's association with it ever since I sailed aboard *Achille Lauro, Melody,* and *Monterey* in the late 1980s (they first appeared in my *Berlitz Complete Guide to Cruising and Cruise Ships* in 1999). This was during the formative days of the company's cruise division following its purchase of Lauro Lines (later to become Star Lauro Line).

A former ship's captain himself and a lover of the sea (whose family has maritime connections dating back to 1675), Mr Gianluigi Aponte, and his wife Rafaella, together established MSC Cruises. Mrs Aponte has always been the brilliant interior designer of *all* the MSC Cruises ships.

Today MSC is investing heavily in the development of environmental technologies to make its objectives achievable. With the oceans covering over 70 percent of the earth's surface, and producing more than 50 percent of its oxygen, MSC rightly considers it vital that nature's delicate balance is maintained.

SUSTAINABILITY ACTION PLAN

Progress has been achieved in all areas of MSC Cruises' Sustainability Action Plan – here are the highlights.

PLANET

With a resolute determination, MSC Cruises is actively accelerating its efforts to achieve net zero emissions by 2050. Through close collaboration with renowned technology companies, shipyards, and fuel providers, it strives to push the limits of innovation and explore new possibilities. A momentous step in this crucial journey was the introduction of its inaugural LNG-powered ship in 2022, marking a significant milestone towards a more sustainable future. It remains steadfast in its commitment to creating a more environmentally responsible cruise industry.

LNG is the cleanest marine fuel currently available at scale, virtually eliminating local air pollutants and reducing greenhouse gas emissions significantly when compared with conventional marine fuels. This

MSC World Europa.

OCEAN CAY MSC MARINE RESERVE

In 2019, MSC purchased a 100-year lease of Ocean Cay, an island 20 miles southwest of Bimini, in the Bahamas. It was renamed Ocean Cay MSC Marine Reserve, and the island is founded on a commitment to protect and preserve the marine ecosystem.

is why MSC Crusies have invested around €3 billion in three LNG-powered cruise ships: the first, *MSC World Europa*, set sail in December 2022; the second, *MSC Euribia*, joined the fleet in June 2023; the third – *MSC World America* – is currently being built by Chantiers de l'Atlantique and will be launched in 2025.

PLACE

MSC Cruises allow people to visit some of the most beautiful and exciting destinations that the world has to offer. Investment in new sustainable cruise terminals is creating jobs and bringing new visitors to these places. It works collaboratively with Cruise Lines International Association (CLIA) to manage visitor numbers and support the sustainable tourism aspirations of the destinations its ships visit. As a member of both the CEO-led Sustainability Committee and the Sustainability Task Force of the World Travel & Tourism Council (WTTC), it works closely with industry partners to develop and implement sustainable solutions.

PEOPLE

The number one priority on any MSC cruise is keeping guests and crew safe and well. MSC offers excellent healthcare on its ships and, even though Covid-19 is no longer the threat it was, it continues to maintain exemplary hygiene practices. It has a comprehensive safety management system in place and aims to identify risks so it can act before incidents occur. The crew play a very important role in making the guest experience a success, and MSC provides all the training they need to do a good job.

PROCUREMENT

Every year, the cruise line needs to procure thousands of different items to run its operations, from engine parts to hand soap, crew uniforms to food and drink. Then it must get it on to its fleet of ships, which are constantly on the move. In 2022, MSC's Sustainable Procurement Committee initiated a comprehensive

MSC FOUNDATION

The MSC Foundation implements the MSC Group's marine conservation, humanitarian, and sustainable development commitments worldwide, utilising MSC's global reach and unique knowledge of the sea to protect and nurture the marine environment.

Coral and marine life is thriving in Ocean Cay.

review of its procurement processes and practices with the aim of identifying opportunities to improve its sustainability performance. Many products created for the MSC Cruises or Ocean Cay brands are made from natural materials – such as cotton, bamboo, and paper – and the company has removed all plastic from its packaging.

AN IMPROVED ENVIRONMENTAL FUTURE

MSC Cruises is on track to achieve the International Maritime Organization's 40 percent carbon intensity reduction for the maritime industry well ahead of the 2030 target. It continues to scrutinise every mile of its itineraries resulting in an average speed of 15.75 knots across the fleet in 2022, down from 17.55 in 2018 – a 10 percent reduction. In 2022, it completed the installation of Oceanly Performance on all ships in its fleet. This platform enables the continuous monitoring of thousands of raw data points on the position, speed, weather, engine load, flow meters, fuel consumption, torque meters, and all other on-board equipment which can be connected to a central data collector.

MSC is taking concrete steps to adopt and accelerate the use of shore power. Over half the fleet is now shore power compatible and, since early 2023, *MSC Virtuosa* is now consistently using shore power on her weekly visits to Southampton (UK).

Reminiscing about the early ships reminds me of just how far this family-owned company has come, and how speedily it can make any changes necessary. Even the shape of a ship enables more efficient use of the fuels presently available and solid oxide fuel could well become a reality, while fuel-efficient routing and other measures are already in place to ensure less environmental impact.

You can read more and keep up-to-date at www.msc cruises.com/sustainabilitytoday

CRUISING AND SAFETY

How likely is an accident at sea? What if there's a fire?
Can you fall overboard? How good are medical facilities
aboard? Here's a practical guide to onboard safety.

When Costa Cruises' 3,800-passenger *Costa Concordia* capsized off the coast of Tuscany in January 2012 with the loss of 32 lives, questions of safety at sea inevitably arose. But this tragedy was avoidable: if *Costa Concordia*'s captain hadn't deviated from his computer-set course to sail close to the island of Giglio, it could have been just another uneventful Mediterranean cruise. The company was so fortunate with its crew, who did a wonderful job of evacuating more than 3,000 passengers from the stricken ship, in what were rather chaotic circumstances.

Other losses over the past 25 years include *Jupiter* in 1988 and *Royal Pacific* in 1992, both following collisions; *Explorer*, which struck an iceberg near Antarctica in 2007; and *Sea Diamond*, which foundered on a reef off the Greek island of Santorini in 2007. Given that over 27 million people take a cruise every year, the number of serious incidents is extremely low. After more than 50 years of sea travel, during which I have experienced fires and groundings, I know that cruising remains one of the safest forms of transportation.

SAFETY MEASURES

All cruise ships built after 2010 with a length of 394ft (120m) or greater, or with three or more main vertical zones, must have two engine rooms, so that if one is flooded or rendered unusable, a ship can safely return to port without requiring evacuation. This requirement came about because of the increasing size of today's cruise ships, and the fact that several ship fires and loss of propulsion/steering have occurred.

Other safety measures include muster drills, bridge procedures, life-jacket availability and location, lifeboat loading drills, recording of passenger nationalities for on-shore emergency-services personnel, and the securing of heavy objects.

International regulations require all crew to undergo basic safety training *before* being allowed to work aboard any cruise ship (on-the-job training is no longer enough). All safety regulations are governed by the international SOLAS Convention, introduced in 1914 in the aftermath of *Titanic*'s sinking in 1912. A mandatory passenger muster drill prior to departure from the port of embarkation is part of the SOLAS Convention.

Passengers who don't attend may be disembarked prior to sailing.

All cruise ships built since 1986 must have either totally or partially enclosed lifeboats with diesel engines that can operate even if the lifeboat is inverted.

Since October 1997, cruise ships have had: all stairways enclosed as self-contained fire zones; smoke detectors and smoke alarms fitted in all passenger cabins and public spaces; low-level lighting showing routes of escape; all fire doors controllable from the ship's navigation bridge; all fire doors that can be opened from a remote location; and emergency alarms audible in all cabins.

Cabins are checked during a passenger emergency drill.

Since 2002, all ocean-going cruise ships on international voyages carry voyage data recorders (VDRs), similar to black boxes aboard aircraft, and, since October 2010, SOLAS regulations have prohibited the use of combustible materials in all new cruise ships.

Crew members attend frequent emergency drills, lifeboat equipment is regularly tested, and fire-detecting devices and alarm and fire-fighting systems are regularly checked. I have strongly recommended that all ships fit rechargeable flashlights under each passenger bed – advice that was forwarded to the IMO. In the meantime, take a small flashlight in case an emergency arises during a blackout or during the night.

WHAT TO DO IN ULTRA-ROUGH SEA CONDITIONS

Bring a hat and wear it in rough sea conditions, to avoid injuries from flying objects in any of the public rooms. Always carry medication with you so you're prepared in the event of a possible evacuation emergency, as happened in the case of *Viking Sky* in 2019, when the ship was drifting rather close to the shore due to loss of propulsion.

IS SECURITY GOOD ENOUGH?

Cruise lines are subject to stringent international security regulations. Passengers and crew can embark or disembark only by passing through a security checkpoint. Cruise ships maintain zero tolerance for crime or offenses against the person, and trained security professionals are employed aboard all cruise ships.

It is recommended that you keep your cabin locked at all times when you are not there. Cruise lines do not accept responsibility for any money or valuables left in cabins and suggest that you store them in your in-cabin safe.

You will be issued with a personal boarding pass when you embark. This includes your photo, muster or lifeboat station, restaurant seating, and other pertinent information, and must be shown at the gangway each time you board. You will be asked for a government-issued photo ID, such as a passport.

PASSENGER LIFEBOAT DRILL

A passenger lifeboat drill, announced publicly by the captain, must be held for embarking passengers *before* the ship departs the port of embarkation.

Attendance is compulsory. However, some cruise lines allow individuals to watch the safety drill from their smartphones or interactive cabin TV, before being checked off at the muster station – negating the need for mass attendance. Learn your boat station or assembly point and how to get there in an emergency. Note your exit and escape pathways and learn how to put on a lifejacket correctly. This drill is potentially

Fire drill aboard *Hanseatic*.

life-saving (the 600-passenger *Royal Pacific* took fewer than 20 minutes to sink after its collision in 1992).

CAN YOU ACCIDENTALLY FALL OVERBOARD?

All cruise ships have railings at least 3ft 7in (1.1m) high to protect you and your children, so rest assured that instances of passengers falling overboard are extremely rare. However, it does occasionally happen, as reports in the press testify – usually the tragic result of reckless behavior.

SHIPBOARD INJURY

Slipping, tripping, and falling are the major sources of shipboard injury. Here are some things you can do to minimize the chance of injury.

Aboard many ships, raised thresholds separate a cabin's bathroom from the sleeping area. Mind your step to avoid a stubbed toe or banged head.

Don't hang anything from the fire sprinkler heads on cabin ceilings.

Walk with caution when the outer decks are wet. This applies especially to solid steel decks – falling on them can be painful.

Don't throw a lit cigarette or cigar butt, or knock out a pipe, over the ship's side. These can easily be sucked into an opening in the ship's side, or fall onto an aft open deck area, and cause a fire.

SURVIVING A SHIPBOARD FIRE

Shipboard fires can generate an incredible amount of heat, smoke, and often panic. In the unlikely event that you are in one, try to remain calm and think logically and clearly.

When you first get to your cabin, check the way to the nearest emergency exits. Count the number of cabin doorways and other distinguishing features to the exits in case you have to escape without the benefit of lighting. All ships provide low location lighting systems.

Exit signs are normally located just above your head – this is virtually useless, as smoke and flames rise. Note the location of the nearest fire alarm and know how to use it in case of dense smoke.

If you are in your cabin, and there is fire in the passageway outside, put on your lifejacket. If the cabin's door handle is hot, soak a towel in water and use it to turn the handle. If a fire is raging in the passageway, cover yourself in wet towels or clothes if you decide to go through the flames.

Check the passageway. If there are no flames, walk to the nearest emergency exit or stairway. If there is smoke in the passageway, crawl to the nearest exit. If the exit is blocked, go to an alternate one. It may take considerable effort to open a heavy fire door to the exit. Don't use the elevators.

If there's a fire in your cabin or on the balcony, report it immediately by telephone. Then leave your cabin, close the door behind you, sound the alarm, and alert your neighbors.

Testing lifeboats on *Voyager of the Seas*.

SAFETY MEASURES

Fire control

If the fire alarm is sounded, an alarm is automatically set off on the bridge. A red panel light will be illuminated on a large plan, indicating the section of the ship that needs to be checked so the crew can take immediate action.

Ships are sectioned into various zones, each of which can be isolated. In addition, almost all ships have a water-fed sprinkler system that can be activated at the touch of a button, or automatically activated when sprinkler vials are broken by fire-generated heat.

Emergency ventilation control

This automatic fire-damper system also has a manual switch that is activated to stop or control the flow of air to all areas, reducing the fanning effect on flame and smoke via the air-conditioning and fan systems.

Watertight doors

Throughout the ship, watertight doors can be closed off to prevent or contain the movement of water through the vessel. A master switch activates all the doors in a matter of seconds, but they can also be operated manually, which means that nobody will be trapped in a watertight compartment.

Britannia Restaurant
aboard *Queen Elizabeth*.

HOW WE EVALUATE THE SHIPS

Ships and their facilities count, but just as important are the standards relating to food, service, staff training, and hospitality. This section explains how the points system works.

I have been evaluating and rating cruise ships and the onboard product professionally since 1980. I also receive reports from my small team of trained assessors. The ratings in this guide are conducted with *total objectivity*, from a set of predetermined criteria, using a modus operandi designed to work across the entire spectrum of oceangoing cruise ships, in all segments of the business.

There really is no 'best cruise line in the world' or 'best cruise ship' – only the ship and cruise that is right for you. After all, it's the overall enjoyment of a cruise as a vacation that's important. Therefore, different criteria are applied to ships of different sizes, styles, and market segments throughout the world (vacationers of different nationalities look for different things).

The evaluation and rating of cruise ships is about as contrary to soccer as you can get. In soccer, the goalposts are always in the same place. But with cruise ships, they keep changing, as the industry evolves.

This section includes over 300 oceangoing cruise ships in service (or due to enter service) and chosen by the author for inclusion when this book was completed. The ships have been carefully evaluated, taking into account up to 400 separate items based on personal cruises, visits, and revisits to ships. In the scoring room, these are channeled into 20 major areas, each with a possible 100 points. The maximum possible score for any ship is therefore 2,000 points.

For user-friendliness and reasons of space on the printed page, scores are further divided into five main sections: Ship, Accommodation, Food, Service, and Cruise Experience.

Cruise lines, ship owners, and operators should note that ratings may be adjusted annually as a result of increased competition, the introduction of newer ships with better facilities, and other market- or passenger-driven factors.

The ratings more reflect the standards of the cruise product (the software: the dining experience, the service, and the hospitality aspects of the cruise), and less the physical plant (the hardware). Thus, although a ship may be the latest, most stunning vessel in the world in terms of design and decor, if the 'software' and actual product delivery are not so good, the scores and ratings will reflect these aspects more clearly.

The stars beside the name of the ship at the top of each page indicate the 'Overall Rating.' The highest number of stars awarded is five stars (★★★★★), and the lowest is one star. This system has been universally recognized throughout the global hospitality industry for over 30 years. A plus (+) indicates that a ship deserves just that little bit more than the number of stars attained. However, it is the *number of points achieved* rather than the number of stars attained that perhaps is more meaningful when comparing ships.

THE STAR SYSTEM
★★★★★ 1,701–2,000 points
★★★★+ 1,551–1,700 points
★★★★ 1,401–1,550 points
★★★+ 1,251–1,400 points
★★★ 1,101–1,250 points
★★+ 951–1,100 points
★★ 801–950 points
★+ 651–800 points
★ 501–650 points

Douglas Ward at work.

Royal Caribbean International's *Harmony of the Seas*, *Allure of the Seas*, and *Oasis of the Seas* off Port Everglades, Florida.

WHAT THE RATINGS MEAN

1,701–2000 POINTS ★★★★★

You can expect a truly excellent, memorable cruise experience, with the finesse and attention to detail commensurate with the amount of money paid. The service and hospitality levels will be extremely high from all levels of officers and staff, with strong emphasis on fine hospitality training – all service personnel members must make you feel important.

The food will be at the high level expected from what is virtually the best possible at sea, with service that should be very attentive yet unobtrusive. The cuisine should be memorable, with ample taste. Special orders should never be a problem. There must be a varied selection of wines, which should be served in glasses of the correct size.

Entertainment is expected to be of prime quality and variety. Again, the word 'no' should not be in the vocabulary of any member of staff aboard a ship with this rating. Few things will cost extra on board, and brochures should be more 'truthful' than those for ships with a lower rating.

1,551–1,700 POINTS ★★★★+

You can expect to have a high-quality cruise experience that will be memorable, and just a little short of being excellent in all aspects. Perhaps the personal service and attention to detail could be slightly better, but, nonetheless, this should prove to be a fine all-round cruise experience, in a setting that is extremely clean and comfortable, with few lines (queues) anywhere, a caring attitude from service personnel, and a good standard of entertainment that appeals to a mainstream market.

The cuisine and service must be carefully balanced, with mostly fresh ingredients and varied menus that should appeal to almost anyone, all served on high-quality china.

This should prove to be an extremely well-rounded cruise experience, probably in a ship that is new or almost new. There will be fewer 'extra-cost' items than ships with a slightly lower rating.

1,401–1,550 POINTS ★★★★

You can expect to have a very good-quality all-round cruise experience, most probably aboard a modern, highly comfortable ship that will provide a good range of facilities and services. The food and service will be quite decent overall, although decidedly not as 'gourmet' and fanciful as the brochures with the always-smiling faces might have you believe.

The service on board will be well organized, if a little robotic and impersonal at times, and only as good as the cruise line's training program allows. You may notice a lot of things cost extra once you are on board, although the typically vague brochure tells you that these things are 'available' or are an 'option.' However, you should have a good time, and your bank account will be only moderately damaged.

1,251–1,400 POINTS ★★★+

You can expect to have a decent-quality cruise experience, aboard a ship where the service levels should be good, but perhaps without the finesse that could be expected from a more upscale environment. The crew aboard any ship achieving this score should reflect a positive attitude towards hospitality, and a willingness to accommodate your needs, up to a point. Staff training will probably be in need of more attention to detail and flexibility.

Food and service levels in the dining venues should be reasonably good, although special or unusual orders might prove more difficult to accommodate. There will probably be a number of extra-cost items you thought were included in the price of your cruise – although the brochure typically is vague and states that the things are 'available' or are an 'option.'

1,101–1,250 POINTS ★★★

You can expect a reasonably decent, middle-of-the-road cruise experience, with a moderate amount of space and quality in furnishings, fixtures, and fittings. The cabins are likely to be a little on the small side. The food and service levels will be quite acceptable, although not at all memorable, and somewhat inflexible with regard to special orders, as almost everything is standardized.

The level of hospitality will be moderate but little more, and the entertainment will probably be weak. This is a good option, however, for those looking for the reasonable comforts of home without pretentious attitudes, and comparatively little damage to their bank statement.

951–1,100 POINTS ★★+

You can expect an average cruise experience in terms of accommodation (typically with cabins that are dimensionally challenged), the quality of the ship's facilities, food, wine list, service, and hospitality levels, in surroundings that are unpretentious. In particular, the food and its service might be disappointing.

There will be little flexibility in the levels of service, hospitality, and staff training and supervision, which will be no better than poor in comparison with that of ships of a higher rating. Thus, the overall experience will be commensurate with the comparatively small amount of money you paid for the cruise.

801–950 POINTS ★★

You can expect to have a cruise experience of modest quality aboard a ship that is probably in need of more attention to maintenance and service levels, not to mention hospitality. The food may be quite lacking in taste, homogenized, and of low quality, and service is likely to be mediocre at best. Staff training is likely to be minimal, and staff turnover may be high. The 'end-of-pier' entertainment could well leave you wanting to read a good book.

651–800 POINTS ★+

You can expect to have only the most basic cruise experience, with little or no attention to detail, from a minimally trained staff that is probably paid low wages and to whom you are just another body. The ship will, in many cases, probably be in need of much maintenance and

upgrading, and will probably have few facilities. Dismal entertainment is also likely. On the other hand, the price of a cruise of this rating will probably be alluringly low.

501–650 POINTS ★

You can expect to have a cruise experience that is the bottom of the barrel, with little in terms of hospitality or finesse. Forget about attention to detail – there won't be any. This would equal a stay in the most basic motel on land, with few facilities, a poorly trained, seemingly uncaring staff, and a ship that needs better maintenance.

The low cost of a cruise aboard a ship with this rating should provide a strong clue to the complete absence of any quality, particularly for food, service, and entertainment. You might remember this cruise, but for all the wrong reasons.

DISTRIBUTION OF POINTS

These are the percentage of the total points available that are allocated to each of the main areas evaluated:
The ship: 25 percent
Accommodation: 10 percent
Food: 20 percent
Service: 20 percent
Entertainment: 5 percent
The cruise experience: 20 percent

The categories 'Entertainment' (including lecturers and expedition staff) and 'The cruise experience' may be combined for boutique ships, tall ships, and expedition ships, and adjusted accordingly.

A touch of real caviar aboard *SeaDream*.

CRITERIA

THE SHIP

Hardware/maintenance/safety. This score reflects the general profile and condition of the ship, its age, exterior paint, decking and caulking; swimming pool and surrounds; deck furniture; shore tenders; and lifeboats and other safety items. It also reflects interior cleanliness (public restrooms, elevators, floor and wall coverings, stairways, passageways, and doorways); food-preparation areas and refrigerators; and garbage handling, compacting, incineration, and waste-disposal facilities.

Outdoor facilities/space. This score reflects the overall open deck space; swimming pools/hot tubs and their surrounds; congestion; type of deck lounge chairs (with or without cushioned pads) and other deck furniture; sports facilities; shower enclosures; changing facilities; towels; and quiet areas.

Interior facilities/space/flow. This score reflects the use of public spaces; flow and congestion; ceiling height; lobby, stairways, and hallways; elevators; public restrooms and facilities; signage, lighting, air conditioning, and ventilation.

Decor/furnishings/artwork. This score reflects the overall interior decor and soft furnishings; carpeting (color, pattern, and practicality); chairs (comfort); ceilings and treatments; artwork (paintings, sculptures, and atrium centerpieces); and lighting.

Spa/fitness facilities. This score reflects the spa, wellness, and fitness facilities, including location, accessibility, lighting and flooring materials. Also: fitness machines and fitness programs; sports facilities and equipment; indoor pools; hot tubs; grand baths; hydrotherapy pools; saunas; steam rooms; treatment rooms; changing facilities; jogging and walking tracks; and open promenades.

ACCOMMODATION

Cabins: suites and cabins. This score reflects the design, layout, balconies and partitions (whether full floor-to-ceiling partition or part partitions), beds/berths, cabinetry, and other fittings; closet and drawer space, bedside tables and reading lights; vanity unit, bathroom facilities, cabinets and storage for toiletries; lighting, air conditioning, and ventilation; audio-visual facilities; artwork; insulation, noise, and vibration. Suites should not be so designated unless the bedroom is completely separated from the living area.

Also covers cabin service directory of services, interactive TV; paper and personalized stationery; telephone information; laundry lists; tea- and coffee-making equipment; flowers; fruit; bathroom personal amenities kits, bathrobes, slippers, and the size and quality of towels.

CUISINE

Cruise lines put maximum emphasis on how good their food is, often to the point of overstatement. There are, of course, at least as many different tastes as there are passengers. As in any good restaurant, you generally get what you pay for.

Dining venues/cuisine. This score reflects the physical structure of dining rooms, layout, seating, and waiter stations; lighting and ambience; table setups; linen, china, and cutlery quality and condition. Also: menus, food quality, creativity, appeal, taste, texture, presentation (garnishes and decorations); tableside cooking (if any); wine list; price range; and service. Alternative dining venues are also checked for menu variety, food and service, ambience, decor, seating, noise levels, china, cutlery, and glassware.

Casual eateries/buffets. This score reflects hot and cold display units and sneeze guards, 'active' stations, tongs and other serving utensils; food displays; temperatures; labeling; deck buffets; decorative elements; and staff communication.

Quality of ingredients. This score reflects taste, consistency, and portion size; grades of meat, fish, and fowl; and the price paid by the cruise line for food per passenger per day.

Tea/coffee/bar snacks. This score reflects the quality and variety of teas and coffees, including afternoon tea/coffee and presentation; whether mugs or cups and saucers are used; whether milk is served in the correct containers or in sealed packets; whether self-service or served. It also reflects the quality of cakes, scones, and pastries, bar/lounge snacks, hot and cold canapés, and hors d'oeuvres.

Balcony cabins at the aft (back) of *Costa Serena*.

SERVICE

Dining rooms. This score reflects staff professionalism: the maître d'hôtel (restaurant manager), section headwaiters, waiters and assistants (busboys), sommeliers and wine waiters; place settings, cutlery, and glasses; and proper service (serving, taking from the correct side), communication skills, attitude, flair, uniform, appearance, and finesse. Waiters should note whether passengers are right- or left-handed and, when tables are assigned, make sure that cutlery and glasses are placed on the side of preference.

Bars. This score reflects lighting and ambience; seating; noise levels; attitude and communication skills, personality, and service.

Cabins. This score reflects the cleaning and housekeeping staff, butlers (for suite occupants), supervisory staff, bedding/bathrobe changes, language and communication skills.

Open decks. This score reflects the service for beverages and food items; placement and replacement of towels on deck lounge chairs, and tidiness of any associated deck equipment.

ENTERTAINMENT

The score reflects the overall entertainment program and its appeal, showlounge (stage/bandstand); technical support, lighting, sound systems; production shows (story, plot, cohesion, costumes, quality, choreography, and vocal content); cabaret acts, bands and solo musicians.

Aboard specialist ships such as those offering expedition cruises, or sail-cruise ships such as *Sea Cloud*, where entertainment is not a feature, the score relates to the lecture program, library, movies on demand, videos, and use of water-sports items such as jet skis, windsurfers, kayaks, and snorkeling gear, etc.

THE CRUISE EXPERIENCE

Activities program. This score reflects social activities and events; cruise director and staff (visibility, professionalism, and communication); special-interest programs; port, shopping, and enrichment lecturers; water-sports equipment, instruction, marina or retractable water-sports platforms, and any enclosed swimming area.

Movies/television program. This score reflects movies picture and sound quality; in-cabin infotainment system and audio channels.

Hospitality factor. This score reflects the hospitality and professionalism of officers, middle management, cruise staff, and crew; appearance; and communication skills.

Overall product delivery. This score reflects the quality of the overall cruise as a vacation – what the brochure states and promises, and what is delivered.

NOTES ON THE RATING RESULTS

Ship evaluations and ratings have become ever more complex. Although a ship may be the newest, with all

Passenger space is an important factor in the enjoyment of a cruise.

the latest facilities, it is the food and service that often disappoint, plus security lines/checks and issues relating to signing up for activities.

Cruise companies state that food quality is a trade-off against lower prices, but this implies a downward spiral that affects quality and service.

Finally, it is the little things that add to points lost on the great scorecard.

WHAT THE DESCRIPTIONS MEAN

Each of the following ship reviews is preceded by a panel providing basic data on the ship's size and facilities. Here we explain how to interpret the categories.

SHIP SIZE (BASED ON LOWER BED CAPACITY)

Large resort ship: 2,501–6,500 passengers
Mid-size ship: 751–2,500 passengers
Small ship: 251–750 passengers
Boutique ship: 50–250 passengers

CRUISE LINE

The cruise and the operator may be different if the company that owns the ship does not routinely market and operate it. Tour operators often charter ships for their exclusive use (for example Thomson Cruises).

ENTERED SERVICE

Where two dates are given, the first is for the ship's maiden (paid) passenger voyage, and the second is the date it began service for the current operator.

PASSENGER CAPACITY

This is based on two lower beds per cabin, including cabins for solo occupancy.

THE STAR PERFORMERS

Having reviewed the following 300-plus cruise ships, Insight Guides names the top-rated ships in their size categories for 2024.

Despite constant claims by cruise companies that their ship has been named 'Best Cruise Line' or 'Best Cruise Ship' by this or that magazine or online readers' poll, there really is no such thing – there is only the ship that is right for you. Few operators can really deliver a ship, product, and crew worthy of the highest Insight Guide star rating – it's all about excellence and passion.

Here is a selection of best cruise ships (sister ships, in some cases, where they are close to identical) listed in order of points scored overall, with the highest-scoring ships first. Entries are listed according to their score, where applicable, or else in alphabetical order by cruise line or ship's name.

Crystal Symphony.

THE TOP 20 LARGE RESORT SHIPS
(2,501–6,500 PASSENGERS)

Queen Mary 2	1611/2000	★★★★+
Mein Schiff 1	1550/2000	★★★★
Mein Schiff 2	1550/2000	★★★★
Mein Schiff 6	1541/2000	★★★★
Mein Schiff 5	1540/2000	★★★★
Mein Schiff 3	1529/2000	★★★★
Mein Schiff 4	1528/2000	★★★★
MSC Euribia	1490/2000	★★★★
MSC World Europa	1490/2000	★★★★
MSC Grandiosa	1488/2000	★★★★
MSC Seaview	1481/2000	★★★★
MSC Seaside	1479/2000	★★★★
MSC Seashore	1476/2000	★★★★
MSC Meraviglia	1473/2000	★★★★
MSC Bellissima	1469/2000	★★★★
Genting Dream	1468/2000	★★★★
MSC Seascape	1463/2000	★★★★
MSC Divina	1462/2000	★★★★
MSC Virtuosa	1462/2000	★★★★
MSC Splendida	1451/2000	★★★★

THE TOP 20 MID-SIZE SHIPS
(751–2,500 PASSENGERS)

Viking Mars	1622/2000	★★★★+
Queen Victoria	1616/2000	★★★★+
Queen Elizabeth	1612/2000	★★★★+
Viking Orion	1606/2000	★★★★+
Viking Sky	1606/2000	★★★★+
Viking Sea	1605/2000	★★★★+
Viking Venus	1605/2000	★★★★+
Viking Star	1604/2000	★★★★+
Viking Neptune	1599/2000	★★★★+
Viking Jupiter	1596/2000	★★★★+
Crystal Serenity	1540/2000	★★★★
Riviera	1524/2000	★★★★
Marina	1519/2000	★★★★
Asuka II	1511/2000	★★★★
Crystal Symphony	1458/2000	★★★★
Spirit of Discovery	1458/2000	★★★★
Spirit of Adventure	1457/2000	★★★★
Disney Wish	1385/2000	★★★+
Bolette	1360/2000	★★★+
Artania	1356/2000	★★★+

Queen Mary 2.

THE TOP 20 SMALL SHIPS
(251–750 PASSENGERS)

Europa 2	1792/2000	★★★★★
Europa	1766/2000	★★★★★
Viking Polaris	1616/2000	★★★★+
Evrima	1611/2000	★★★★+
Silver Moon	1595/2000	★★★★+
Silver Dawn	1594/2000	★★★★+
Viking Octantis	1587/2000	★★★★+
Silver Muse	1585/2000	★★★★+
Silver Spirit	1558/2000	★★★★+
Seabourn Encore	1553/2000	★★★★+
Seabourn Ovation	1553/2000	★★★★+
Seabourn Odyssey	1549/2000	★★★★
Seven Seas Explorer	1543/2000	★★★★
Seabourn Sojourn	1533/2000	★★★★
Seven Seas Splendor	1532/2000	★★★★
Silver Shadow	1522/2000	★★★★
Silver Whisper	1522/2000	★★★★
Seabourn Pursuit	1500/2000	★★★★
Seabourn Venture	1498/2000	★★★★
Seven Seas Voyager	1493/2000	★★★★

Europa 2.

THE TOP 20 BOUTIQUE SHIPS
(50–250 PASSENGERS)

HANSEATIC spirit	1719/2000	★★★★★
HANSEATIC inspiration	1716/2000	★★★★★
HANSEATIC nature	1716/2000	★★★★★
Sea Cloud	1627/2000	★★★★+
Sea Cloud II	1626/2000	★★★★+
SeaDream II	1606/2000	★★★★+
SeaDream I	1605/2000	★★★★+
Silver Endeavor	1522/2000	★★★★
SH Diana	1497/2000	★★★★
Scenic Eclipse	1487/2000	★★★★
SH Vega	1459/2000	★★★★
SH Minerva	1458/2000	★★★★
Royal Clipper	1437/2000	★★★★
Le Bellot	1432/2000	★★★★
Le Jacques Cartier	1431/2000	★★★★
Le Bougainville	1430/2000	★★★★
National Geographic Endurance	1430/2000	★★★★
National Geographic Resolution	1430/2000	★★★★
Le Champlain	1429/2000	★★★★
Le Dumont d'Urville	1428/2000	★★★★

HANSEATIC nature.

ADVENTURE OF THE SEAS
★★★

Size	Large Resort Ship
Tonnage	138,100
Cruise Line	Royal Caribbean International
Former Names	None
Entered Service	2001
Total Crew	1,185
Passengers	3,319

This large resort ship has many family-friendly features, including outdoor decks with water parks and fun areas for children of all ages. Indoors, a Royal Promenade spanning four decks, lined with shops, extra-cost eateries and drinking venues, is the place to see and be seen. Accommodation ranges from small viewless interior cabins with little storage space to an expansive balconied Royal Suite designed for families; some 300-plus cabins have family-friendly connecting doors. Razzle-dazzle shows are presented in the large Lyric Theatre. The spa has several exercise and cost-extra body-pampering treatment rooms. Overall, the ship can deliver an orchestrated vacation, but with many cost-extra items and added service charges.

INSIGHT GUIDES' RATINGS

	Achieved	Possible
Ship	354	500
Accommodation	132	200
Food	220	400
Service	230	400
Entertainment	66	100
Cruise Experience	223	400
OVERALL SCORE	**1225**	**2000**

AIDABELLA
★★★

Size	Mid-size Ship
Tonnage	69,203
Cruise Line	AIDA Cruises
Former Names	None
Entered Service	2008
Total Crew	646
Passengers	2,050

This smart, sea-going urban theme park caters for youthful German-speaking families. All cabins have wood-trimmed cabinetry and the beds (no nightly turndown service) have a fabric canopy. Compact bathrooms are basic. Three large self-serve eateries, including Markt (Market) and Weite Welt (Wide World), have food islands and 'active' stations, tablecloth-less tables seating four to eight, and racked cutlery. Buffalo Steakhouse and Rossini (Italian) cost extra. The spa spans two decks, plus an 'FKK' (relaxation/nude sunbathing) deck. The two-decks-high Theater has bench seating, and lively, voluminous shows. Unfortunately, there is no walk-around outdoor deck.

INSIGHT GUIDES' RATINGS

	Achieved	Possible
Ship	360	500
Accommodation	130	200
Food	234	400
Service	209	400
Entertainment	72	100
Cruise Experience	237	400
OVERALL SCORE	**1242**	**2000**

AIDABLU
★★★

Size	Mid-size Ship
Tonnage	71,100
Cruise Line	AIDA Cruises
Former Names	None
Entered Service	2010
Total Crew	646
Passengers	2,194

You cannot miss the red lips and blue eyes of *Aida* (Verdi's 1871 opera) on the bows of AIDA's cruise ships. This family-friendly resort ship has dip pools, seating, splash and play areas on the pool deck. All cabins/suites have two beds (configurable to queen-size); some have extra beds/berths (no night-time turndown service). Three self-serve multiple-island eateries have cutlery racks on tablecloth-free, multi-seat tables, and acceptable food (better in the two extra-cost dinner only venues). Shows are in a glass domed Theatrium, with back-support seating on upper two (of three) levels. Limited open deck space, and no walk-around deck. Overall, this is a fun ship for laid-back urban families.

INSIGHT GUIDES' RATINGS		
	Achieved	Possible
Ship	358	500
Accommodation	129	200
Food	234	400
Service	212	400
Entertainment	72	100
Cruise Experience	238	400
OVERALL SCORE	**1243**	**2000**

AIDACOSMA
★★★+

Size	Large Resort Ship
Tonnage	183,900
Cruise Line	AIDA Cruises
Former Names	None
Entered Service	2022
Total Crew	1,500
Passengers	5,200

This lively, ultra-casual floating city/theme park has a large range of family-friendly facilities (and many programs and counselors for children and teens), plus a sports deck (something new for this company). There are several voluminous serve yourself and 'join a table' eateries plus a number of cost-extra eatery options. The mostly small cabins are disappointing, but that's because the company wants you out and about to spend money in the public rooms. There are numerous entertainment shows and options, all with high volume, while the spa facilities are really good but always crowded. Overall, this is a fun ship for all.

INSIGHT GUIDES' RATINGS		
	Achieved	Possible
Ship	365	500
Accommodation	134	200
Food	235	400
Service	213	400
Entertainment	73	100
Cruise Experience	235	400
OVERALL SCORE	**1255**	**2000**

AIDADIVA
★★★

Size	Mid-size Ship
Tonnage	69,203
Cruise Line	AIDA Cruises
Former Names	None
Entered Service	2007
Total Crew	646
Passengers	2,050

An ultra-casual, upbeat AIDA 'Club Ship' for cheerful family cruising, there is a wide range of public rooms, but no walk-around deck outdoors. There are several deluxe 'suites' through to interior, no-view cabins, but all have bright decor and round-edged, wood-trimmed cabinetry. The self-serve eateries (Markt, Bella Vista, and Weite Welt) have racked cutlery and push-button beer at large tables. Cost-extra venues Buffalo Steakhouse and Rossini may be worth it for à la carte cuisine. There are lively entertainment shows in the two-decks high Theater with bench seating, and good health spa facilities plus an 'FKK' relaxation area.

INSIGHT GUIDES' RATINGS		
	Achieved	Possible
Ship	351	500
Accommodation	129	200
Food	231	400
Service	211	400
Entertainment	70	100
Cruise Experience	237	400
OVERALL SCORE	**1229**	**2000**

AIDALUNA
★★★

Size	Mid-size Ship
Tonnage	69,203
Cruise Line	AIDA Cruises
Former Names	None
Entered Service	2009
Total Crew	646
Passengers	2,050

This lively, family-friendly 'club' ship offers a very casual cruising experience, with fairly basic food choices, and few staff. The range of public entertainment and drinking rooms is good. Cabins are small but bright, with a colorful canopy over the two beds (convertible to queen-size), although there is little storage space, and no nightly turn-down service. The windows have blackout blinds – useful in destinations with long daylight hours. Three large self-serve eateries have food islands and open seating at large, communal tables. Several extra-cost venues provide cooked-to-order items. The Body and Soul wellness facilities are extensive and good.

INSIGHT GUIDES' RATINGS		
	Achieved	Possible
Ship	351	500
Accommodation	129	200
Food	232	400
Service	212	400
Entertainment	72	100
Cruise Experience	238	400
OVERALL SCORE	**1234**	**2000**

AIDAMAR
★★★

Size	Mid-size Ship
Tonnage	71,304
Cruise Line	AIDA Cruises
Former Names	None
Entered Service	2012
Total Crew	646
Passengers	2,194

A ship for youthful German-speaking families, it is a veritable playground for the upbeat and active, with abundant play areas for youngsters. The cabins are small but bright, with colorful fabric canopies over the two beds (convertible to queen-size), but little storage space and no nightly turn-down service. The suites have more space, and a balcony. Three self-serve eateries (included) have food islands, four–eight person tables and racked cutlery. Smaller, reservations-required extra-cost eateries have cooked-to-order food and table service. The health spa facilities are extensive, and there is an 'FKK' (relaxation/nude sunbathing) area.

INSIGHT GUIDES' RATINGS

	Achieved	Possible
Ship	351	500
Accommodation	129	200
Food	232	400
Service	211	400
Entertainment	72	100
Cruise Experience	237	400
OVERALL SCORE	**1232**	**2000**

AIDANOVA
★★★+

Size	Large Resort Ship
Tonnage	183,900
Cruise Line	AIDA Cruises
Former Names	None
Entered Service	2018
Total Crew	1,500
Passengers	5,000

Super-large and bold, this ship for youthful German-speaking families has everything for active no-frills cruising, with multiple public room choices, abundant entertainment, and a large spa deck. The large self-serve, tablecloth-free Bella Donna, Markt, and Weite Welt eateries, with communal tables, have racked cutlery and push-button beer. Food islands provide selections of warm and cold food, although choice is limited. Family venues include East West, Fuego, and Sharfe Ecke (all are included in the cruise price). Pay extra to eat in one of several other venues. The spa and sports facilities are extensive.

INSIGHT GUIDES' RATINGS

	Achieved	Possible
Ship	405	500
Accommodation	144	200
Food	245	400
Service	222	400
Entertainment	77	100
Cruise Experience	260	400
OVERALL SCORE	**1353**	**2000**

AIDAPERLA
★★★+

Size	Large Resort Ship
Tonnage	125,572
Cruise Line	AIDA Cruises
Former Names	*None*
Entered Service	2017
Total Crew	900
Passengers	3,286

This colorful, ultra-casual 'Club' ship with stark, upright bows provides numerous choices for the whole family, with abundant play areas for kids and teens. There are several self-serve casual communal eateries, with large tables (shopping mall-style), and several cost-extra venues. The modern, cheerful and minimalist accommodation ranges from small interior (no-view) cabins to large two-bedroom suites (plus an owner's suite), but most have little drawer space. The included self-serve Markt and Weite Welt venues are large, but other (extra-cost, reservations required) venues have better cuisine and service. Body and Soul spa facilities are extensive, and good, as are the entertainment shows.

INSIGHT GUIDES' RATINGS

	Achieved	Possible
Ship	402	500
Accommodation	143	200
Food	241	400
Service	220	400
Entertainment	77	100
Cruise Experience	258	400
OVERALL SCORE	**1341**	**2000**

AIDAPRIMA
★★★+

Size	Large Resort Ship
Tonnage	125,572
Cruise Line	AIDA Cruises
Former Names	*None*
Entered Service	2016
Total Crew	900
Passengers	3,286

This bold, vibrant family-friendly 'Club' is good for a no-frills cruise, and was the first ship in the cruise industry fitted with a dual-fuel propulsion system. A fun waterslide starts at the funnel and courses through the colorful Beach Club area. There is also a private 'Patio-Bereich' adults-only retreat. Accommodation ranges from small interior (no-view) cabins with little storage space, to large suites with a balcony. There are numerous eateries (some have waiter service); the expansive self-serve Markt and Weite Welt venues have big tables, and armrest-less chairs. The Body and Soul spa facilities are extensive, and cost-extra body pampering treatments are available.

INSIGHT GUIDES' RATINGS

	Achieved	Possible
Ship	401	500
Accommodation	143	200
Food	241	400
Service	217	400
Entertainment	77	100
Cruise Experience	258	400
OVERALL SCORE	**1337**	**2000**

AIDASOL
★★★+

Size	Mid-size Ship
Tonnage	71,304
Cruise Line	AIDA Cruises
Former Names	None
Entered Service	2011
Total Crew	646
Passengers	2,194

This ultra-casual multi-choice playground in a beach-like environment could be good for youthful families. Dip pools, hot tubs and seating areas are in a tiered setting on the pool deck. Cabins are mostly small, but brightly decorated, with little storage space. The large self-serve, tablecloth-free Karibik and Markt eateries (tables seat four to eight), have racked cutlery and few staff, while food islands provide selections of warm and cold food items. Rossini and Buffalo Steakhouse are much smaller, cost-extra venues, with cooked-to-order food. Extremely good wellness facilities include an FKK deck. The 'rap'-rich music is everywhere, but, overall, it works.

INSIGHT GUIDES' RATINGS		
	Achieved	Possible
Ship	352	500
Accommodation	130	200
Food	237	400
Service	235	400
Entertainment	72	100
Cruise Experience	233	400
OVERALL SCORE	**1259**	**2000**

AIDASTELLA
★★★

Size	Mid-size Ship
Tonnage	71,304
Cruise Line	AIDA Cruises
Former Names	None
Entered Service	2013
Total Crew	646
Passengers	2,194

An upbeat, mid-size resort ship for German-speaking families, with a good range of facilities including dip pools, hot tubs, and seating areas in a tiered, beach-like setting on the pool deck. Indoors, the AIDA bar is the main gathering space. There are several accommodation grades, from 'deluxe suites' with balcony to interior, no-view cabins (no nightly turndown service) that have little storage space. All beds have a colorful fabric canopy overhead. There are three sizeable, casual eateries, with large tables, and cost-extra (better) specialist venues. The open-air health facilities (including an FKK deck) are good, and there is plenty of entertainment – in fact, there's no escape from constant 'music'.

INSIGHT GUIDES' RATINGS		
	Achieved	Possible
Ship	352	500
Accommodation	130	200
Food	232	400
Service	211	400
Entertainment	72	100
Cruise Experience	239	400
OVERALL SCORE	**1236**	**2000**

ALLURE OF THE SEAS
★★★+

Size	Large Resort Ship
Tonnage	225,282
Cruise Line	Royal Caribbean International
Former Names	*None*
Entered Service	2010
Total Crew	2,164
Passengers	5,408

This multi-choice ship is a moveable leisure resort for families. Much outdoor deck space is devoted to aqua parks and sports facilities, so sunbathing space is limited. Inside, public spaces are arranged as seven 'neighborhoods,' some including bars, cost-extra eateries and a fine carousel along 'The Boardwalk' outdoor deck. Accommodation ranges from small interior (no-view) cabins to balconied cabins, and lavish owner's suites. An expansive main dining room (Opus) spans three decks, but more intimate, cost-extra eateries may be an alternative. The Amber Theater's 'book' shows are excellent. It's really best to plan what you want to do to get the most out of your sea-going vacation, but it can be a really good experience.

INSIGHT GUIDES' RATINGS		
	Achieved	Possible
Ship	397	500
Accommodation	136	200
Food	225	400
Service	234	400
Entertainment	87	100
Cruise Experience	260	400
OVERALL SCORE	**1339**	**2000**

AMADEA
★★★★

Size	Small Ship
Tonnage	28,856
Cruise Line	Phoenix Reisen
Former Names	*Asuka*
Entered Service	1991, 2006
Total Crew	292
Passengers	594

This older but well-maintained and stylish small ship for German-speakers has a fine teakwood walk-around promenade deck, and there is an abundance of open-deck space. It features restrained interior decor, including some fascinating Japanese artwork. Most of the public rooms are aft, with cabins forward. There are just five types of suites and cabins, and all grades have ocean views, ample closet and drawer space, and refrigerator. Many bathrooms are small, however, with either a bathtub or shower. There are two main restaurants (both have the same very decent food), with open seating. There is also a spacious wellness center, with excellent facilities and spa treatments.

INSIGHT GUIDES' RATINGS		
	Achieved	Possible
Ship	363	500
Accommodation	156	200
Food	304	400
Service	253	400
Entertainment	74	100
Cruise Experience	261	400
OVERALL SCORE	**1411**	**2000**

AMBIANCE
★★★

Size	Mid-size Ship
Tonnage	70,285
Cruise Line	Ambassador Cruise Line
Former Names	*Pacific Dawn, Regal Princess*
Entered Service	1991, 2022
Total Crew	725
Passengers	1,596

Recognizable for its frontal dolphin head-like dome (designed by Renzo Piano), it is a modestly comfortable, but dated ship, and lacks a walk-around promenade deck. Inside is a three-deck high Centre Court lobby and grand staircase. Whether inside (no-view) or with outside view, the rather dated cabins have walk-in closets and decent storage space, and the bathrooms are quite large. Some 14 suites have a balcony and extensive storage space; bathrooms have a bathtub and separate shower. Buckingham Restaurant is the expansive main dining room (the food is average with limited choice), but four cost-extra venues are more intimate with better food choices.

INSIGHT GUIDES' RATINGS		
	Achieved	Possible
Ship	288	500
Accommodation	117	200
Food	239	400
Service	215	400
Entertainment	61	100
Cruise Experience	210	400
OVERALL SCORE	**1130**	**2000**

AMBITION
★★★

Size	Mid-size Ship
Tonnage	41,123
Cruise Line	Ambassador Cruise Line
Former Names	*AIDAmira, Costa neoRiviera, Mistral*
Entered Service	1999, 2023
Total Crew	600
Passengers	1,428

Chartered by the Scottish government to house Ukrainian refugees in 2022, *Ambition* made its maiden voyage in May 2023. It has limited outdoor space and no walk-around outdoor deck, but a wide range of public rooms; the tri-deck Centre Court is the place to see and be seen. From interior (no-view) cabins to more expansive private balconied suites with coffee machines, all have twin beds that convert to a queen-size bed, plenty of storage, and bright carpets. Internet access is costly. The Buckingham Restaurant (main dining room) is comfortable enough, but the food needs more attention. Cost-extra venues Sea and Grass (steaks and seafood) and Saffron (Indian-style cuisine) are better, but the Borough Market buffet is simply not good.

INSIGHT GUIDES' RATINGS		
	Achieved	Possible
Ship	303	500
Accommodation	120	200
Food	235	400
Service	229	400
Entertainment	60	100
Cruise Experience	241	400
OVERALL SCORE	**1188**	**2000**

AMERA
★★★+

Size	Mid-size Ship
Tonnage	38,848
Cruise Line	Phoenix Reisen
Former Names	*Royal Viking Sun*
Entered Service	1988, 2019
Total Crew	443
Passengers	835

Well-maintained, and with a delightfully shapely bow, this well-designed, former Royal Viking Line ship has the right ingredients for German-speakers, including a high degree of comfort and spacious public rooms. The swimming pool may be small, but open deck space is plentiful. There is ample space around dining room tables in the high-ceilinged Ocean Restaurant and the smaller Amera Restaurant (both have large ocean-view windows). The cuisine is decent enough, but the cost-extra 60-seat Pichler's Restaurant is really worth it. Cabins and bathrooms are well designed, with ample closet and storage space. Has self-serve launderettes – useful on longer voyages. This ship, with its very moderate pricing, offers excellent value.

INSIGHT GUIDES' RATINGS		
	Achieved	Possible
Ship	341	500
Accommodation	138	200
Food	268	400
Service	225	400
Entertainment	66	100
Cruise Experience	249	400
OVERALL SCORE	**1287**	**2000**

ANTHEM OF THE SEAS
★★★★

Size	Large Resort Ship
Tonnage	168,666
Cruise Line	Royal Caribbean International
Former Names	*None*
Entered Service	2015
Total Crew	1,300
Passengers	4,180

This ultra-modern, casual, family-friendly ship could be good if you have boundless energy. Try the North Star, a 14-person glass pod that lifts you above the pool deck for a bird's eye view, or RipCord by iFly for a simulated skydiving experience. There's almost round-the-clock entertainment and several cost-extra eatery and snacking choices (do try Wonderland – a small cost-extra venue based on Alice in Wonderland). The included, assigned restaurants – The Grande, Chic, American Icon Grill, and Silk – serve food that is standardized banquet catering, adequate rather than inspirational. The stunning Royal Theater hosts 'book' shows and large-scale production shows.

INSIGHT GUIDES' RATINGS		
	Achieved	Possible
Ship	407	500
Accommodation	135	200
Food	295	400
Service	229	400
Entertainment	88	100
Cruise Experience	265	400
OVERALL SCORE	**1419**	**2000**

ARCADIA
★★★

Size	Mid-size Ship
Tonnage	84,342
Cruise Line	P&O Cruises
Former Names	*None*
Entered Service	2005
Total Crew	886
Passengers	1,994

This is a comfortable ship for British mature-age adults. There is a walk-around outdoor deck, while a wide array of interior rooms, drinking places, and eateries provide ample choice. Unfortunately, there is no card room and the dance floor space is pitiful. The bi-level Meridian Restaurant (aft) is rather pleasant, and its two levels are connected by a spiral staircase. The cuisine is so-so mass catering (unless you pay extra for the reservations-required Ocean Grill by Marco Pierre White), but the accommodation is decent enough, and all cabins and suites have tea/coffee making sets. The Ocean Spa facilities are good, but body-pampering treatments cost extra. For shows, head to the Palladium Showlounge.

INSIGHT GUIDES' RATINGS		
	Achieved	Possible
Ship	340	500
Accommodation	131	200
Food	241	400
Service	214	400
Entertainment	68	100
Cruise Experience	233	400
OVERALL SCORE	**1227**	**2000**

ARTANIA
★★★+

Size	Mid-size Ship
Tonnage	44,348
Cruise Line	Phoenix Reisen
Former Names	*Artemis, Royal Princess*
Entered Service	1984, 2011
Total Crew	520
Passengers	1,176

This is a very comfortable mid-sized ship for German-speakers. It has a walk-around teak exterior deck, an extensive outdoor deck and sunbathing space, plus a neat Pacific Lounge set around the base of the funnel. All cabins have outside views (some 270 have balconies), although some on Apollo and Orion decks have lifeboat-obstructed views. The two principal restaurants (Artania and Four Seasons) offer good food choices, plus an indoor-outdoor casual eatery. Artania Spa has excellent facilities, including steam bath and ice fountain, plus a gym with muscle-toning equipment.

INSIGHT GUIDES' RATINGS		
	Achieved	Possible
Ship	343	500
Accommodation	133	200
Food	293	400
Service	253	400
Entertainment	74	100
Cruise Experience	260	400
OVERALL SCORE	**1356**	**2000**

ARVIA
★★★★

Size	Large Resort Ship
Tonnage	184,700
Cruise Line	P&O Cruises
Former Names	None
Entered Service	2022
Total Crew	1,762
Passengers	5,200

This super-large, family-friendly LNG-powered ship (named in Barbados, *Arvia* means 'from the seashore') features Altitude, an open-deck activity zone full of fun amusements for all (including a challenging high ropes course). New to the ship is a 12-seater aft swim-up bar for adults. Inside, the tri-deck atrium is the connection point for numerous public rooms, eateries, cafés, and shops, all with interior decor that is vibrant, yet restrained. The accommodation runs from interior (no-view) cabins to smart balconied suites, and all include tea/coffee making sets. The main (included) two-seating dining rooms are large, and there are also several cost-extra eateries, including Green & Co, a fish and plant-based venue.

INSIGHT GUIDES' RATINGS

	Achieved	Possible
Ship	396	500
Accommodation	163	200
Food	250	400
Service	257	400
Entertainment	77	100
Cruise Experience	302	400
OVERALL SCORE	**1445**	**2000**

ASTORIA GRANDE
★★★

Size	Mid-size Ship
Tonnage	38,557
Cruise Line	Miray Cruises
Former Names	AIDAcara, Das Clubschiff
Entered Service	1996, 2022
Total Crew	370
Passengers	1,180

Formerly *AIDAcara*, this ship (now Russian owned) is dedicated to cruising for Russian families, mainly in the Black Sea region, from its home port of Sochi. Outdoor deck space is limited, but dip pools, hot tubs and seating areas occupy a tiered setting. The public rooms (mostly unchanged from the original) and areas are extremely colorful, and there is plenty of space for sunbathing. Its large star-shaped bar is the main social gathering place. From viewless interior cabins to balconied suite-grade accommodation, all have a colorful over-bed canopy, but the bathrooms are compact. Two self-serve eateries have open seating at tables of four to eight. Spa facilities include large glass-walled saunas, ice walls, and body pampering rooms.

INSIGHT GUIDES' RATINGS

	Achieved	Possible
Ship	311	500
Accommodation	120	200
Food	216	400
Service	201	400
Entertainment	66	100
Cruise Experience	239	400
OVERALL SCORE	**1153**	**2000**

ASUKA II
★★★★

Size	Mid-size Ship
Tonnage	50,444
Cruise Line	Asuka Cruise
Former Names	*Crystal Harmony*
Entered Service	1990, 2006
Total Crew	490
Passengers	800

This ship has superbly shaped bows, a well-balanced profile, and wide exterior, real-teak decks. Its Japanese clientele enjoy the sense of space and calmness, with high-ceilinged, uncrowded public rooms. The Vista Lounge and Palm Court are outstanding and utter calmness prevails in the Chashitsu (tatami mat room). From the four very spacious Royal Suites to the smallest interior cabins, all are delightfully equipped, and all bathrooms have electric 'washlet' high-cleanse toilets. However, it is the food that excels, plus the service and attention to detail in the main dining room, while Umihiko is a delightful extra-cost venue for fresh sashimi. Another highlight is the Grand Spa, and grand bath, together with some other fine health facilities.

INSIGHT GUIDES' RATINGS

	Achieved	Possible
Ship	392	500
Accommodation	154	200
Food	336	400
Service	256	400
Entertainment	81	100
Cruise Experience	292	400
OVERALL SCORE	**1511**	**2000**

AURORA
★★★

Size	Mid-size Ship
Tonnage	76,152
Cruise Line	P&O Cruises
Former Names	*None*
Entered Service	2000
Total Crew	816
Passengers	1,864

This British-style adults-only ship has a nicely balanced profile. The interior focal point is a four-deck high atrium with a 35-ft (10.6-m) -tall fibreglass sculpture of two mythical figures behind a water wall. Notable lounges/bars include Anderson's, with fireplace and mahogany panelling, and the Crow's Nest, with a model of the P&O ship *Strathnavar* of 1931. There's a wide range of cabin sizes, from two penthouse suites to interior (no-view) cabins. All have a mini-fridge, but note that most cabin doorways are narrow. Alexandria and Medina (the main dining rooms), have no-nonsense British food. Cost-extra venues include Sindh, for Indian-fusion cuisine, and The Glasshouse (International). There is a good range of entertainment venues.

INSIGHT GUIDES' RATINGS

	Achieved	Possible
Ship	320	500
Accommodation	128	200
Food	244	400
Service	218	400
Entertainment	67	100
Cruise Experience	238	400
OVERALL SCORE	**1215**	**2000**

AZAMARA JOURNEY

★★★★

Size..Small Ship
Tonnage...30,277
Cruise Line...Azamara
Former Names ....*Blue Star, Blue Dream, R6*
Entered Service 2000, 2007
Total Crew...400
Passengers 680

This informal adults-only ship lacks a walk-around outdoor promenade deck, although the pool deck has plenty of space for sunbathers. Inside, the country-house style interior decor is in good taste, and public rooms are spread over three decks, so getting around is easy. The large Regency-style library is a standout. Cabins are compact, with little storage space, as are the shower-curtained bathrooms. Suites have better facilities, and more space. The main dining room has a low ceiling, and can be noisy. Meals are of decent quality, and are nicely presented. Cost-extra eateries Aqualina and Prime C (both have fine presentation) are good. Food in the casual, but compact self-serve buffet venue is average.

INSIGHT GUIDES' RATINGS		
	Achieved	Possible
Ship	380	500
Accommodation	134	200
Food	277	400
Service	285	400
Entertainment	73	100
Cruise Experience	272	400
OVERALL SCORE	**1421**	**2000**

AZAMARA ONWARD

★★★★

Size..Small Ship
Tonnage...30,277
Cruise Line...Azamara
Former Names ....*Pacific Princess, R3*
Entered Service 1998, 2022
Total Crew...373
Passengers 688

This is a smart-looking informal ship with uncrowded country-club-style decor for mature adults. Although there is no outdoor walk-around deck, the pool deck has ample space. Public rooms are mostly spread over three decks, including a delightful, expansive Regency-style library. Most cabins are really compact units, as are the shower-curtained bathrooms (one of the aft-facing 'suites' would be the best choice, as they are really quite spacious). The main dining room has a low ceiling, and can be noisy, but meals are of decent quality, and well presented. Cost-extra, reservations-required eateries Aqualina and Prime C (both have fine presentation) are good. Food in the compact and casual self-serve buffet venue is average.

INSIGHT GUIDES' RATINGS		
	Achieved	Possible
Ship	388	500
Accommodation	136	200
Food	280	400
Service	287	400
Entertainment	76	100
Cruise Experience	273	400
OVERALL SCORE	**1440**	**2000**

AZAMARA PURSUIT
★★★★

Size	Small Ship
Tonnage	30,277
Cruise Line	Azamara
Former Names	Adonia, Royal Princess, Minerva II, R8
Entered Service	2001, 2018
Total Crew	300
Passengers	710

The last in a series of eight almost identical ships built for long-defunct Renaissance Cruises, it is well proportioned and exudes the feeling of an uncrowded country club. The public rooms are spread over three decks. Nicest, perhaps, is the Regency-style library. The cabins are really very compact, as are the shower-curtained bathrooms. The aft-facing suites, however, are really rather pleasant. The large main dining room has a low ceiling and can be rather noisy. Meals are of a decent quality, and nicely presented. The smaller, cost-extra, reservations-required eateries Aqualina and Prime C, and the cooked-to-order food is nicely presented. However, food in the compact and casual self-serve buffet venue is average.

INSIGHT GUIDES' RATINGS

	Achieved	Possible
Ship	382	500
Accommodation	135	200
Food	279	400
Service	269	400
Entertainment	76	100
Cruise Experience	267	400
OVERALL SCORE	**1408**	**2000**

AZAMARA QUEST
★★★+

Size	Small Ship
Tonnage	30,277
Cruise Line	Azamara
Former Names	Blue Moon, Delphin Renaissance, R7
Entered Service	2000, 2007
Total Crew	306
Passengers	716

This smart-looking, but now dated floating country club is well-proportioned and quite comfortable. Although there is no outdoor walk-around deck, the pool deck has ample space. The public rooms are spread over three decks and, although all are quite pleasant and uncrowded, the Regency-style library really stands out. The cabins are disappointingly small, with little storage space; they also have shower-curtained bathrooms. However, the aft-facing suites are nice and spacious. The main dining room has a low ceiling, and can be rather noisy, but the meals themselves are of a decent quality, and come with good presentation. Food in the buffet venue is, however, unexciting.

INSIGHT GUIDES' RATINGS

	Achieved	Possible
Ship	380	500
Accommodation	134	200
Food	279	400
Service	262	400
Entertainment	76	100
Cruise Experience	265	400
OVERALL SCORE	**1396**	**2000**

AZURA
★★★+

Size	Large Resort Ship
Tonnage	115,055
Cruise Line	P&O Cruises
Former Names	None
Entered Service	2010
Total Crew	1,239
Passengers	3,094

Like sister ship *Ventura*, *Azura* is a large resort-style ship. Inside, a three-deck high atrium with dance floor is the focal point, with many connecting public rooms. There are six types of accommodation, from suites with balcony to interior (no-view) and solo traveler cabins, plus several wheelchair-accessible cabins. Peninsular, Oriental, and Meridian are main restaurants, with straight-forward, no nonsense British cuisine, well presented on Wedgewood china. Cost-extra (smaller) venues include Sindhu, Epicurian, and the Beach House. An 800-seat Playhouse Showlounge hosts colorful production shows and cabaret acts. Overall, this ship could be good for those with British tastes.

INSIGHT GUIDES' RATINGS

	Achieved	Possible
Ship	372	500
Accommodation	144	200
Food	246	400
Service	234	400
Entertainment	75	100
Cruise Experience	244	400
OVERALL SCORE	**1315**	**2000**

BALMORAL
★★★+

Size	Mid-size Ship
Tonnage	43,537
Cruise Line	Fred. Olsen Cruise Line
Former Names	*Norwegian Crown, Crown Odyssey*
Entered Service	1988, 2008
Total Crew	551
Passengers	1,325

This is a very comfortable older ship for travelers of a mature age, and it has an outdoor walk-around promenade deck. Inside, the lobby features a large gold sculpture in the shape of a world globe, by the Italian sculptor Arnaldo Pomodoro. Most cabins are of similar size and layout, and are well equipped. Some have an interconnecting door to make a two-room suite. The Avon, Ballindoch, and Spey restaurants all have two seatings, and are comfortable venues. Food is attractively presented, with abundant choice, including a decent selection of cheeses and vegetarian options. Overall, you should have a very pleasant cruise experience.

INSIGHT GUIDES' RATINGS

	Achieved	Possible
Ship	348	500
Accommodation	140	200
Food	258	400
Service	213	400
Entertainment	64	100
Cruise Experience	244	400
OVERALL SCORE	**1267**	**2000**

BOLETTE

★★★+

Size	Mid-size Ship
Tonnage	62,735
Cruise Line	Fred. Olsen Cruise Line
Former Names	*Amsterdam*
Entered Service	2000, 2022
Total Crew	645
Passengers	1,338

This smart-looking ship has nicely-raked bows, twin red funnels, a good amount of open deck space, and a domed (retractable roof) swimming pool. The interior decor retains much of the traditional ocean-liner look enjoyed by frequent passengers. A whimsical 'Astrolabe' (inclinometer) adorns a three-deck-high oval-shaped atrium lobby. Accommodation ranges from interior (no-view) cabins to balconied suites (with bathtub), in many price categories. A stained-glass ceiling adorns Bloomsbury, the large main dining room, with flexible dining times. Extra-cost venues include Colours and Tastes for Asian Fusion, and Goa for Goanese cuisine; both are small, comfortable venues. The fine spa includes a Turkish bath-style thermal suite.

INSIGHT GUIDES' RATINGS

	Achieved	Possible
Ship	395	500
Accommodation	165	200
Food	268	400
Service	216	400
Entertainment	66	100
Cruise Experience	250	400
OVERALL SCORE	**1360**	**2000**

BOREALIS

★★★+

Size	Mid-size Ship
Tonnage	61,849
Cruise Line	Fred. Olsen Cruise Line
Former Names	*Rotterdam*
Entered Service	1997, 2021
Total Crew	662
Passengers	1,360

This sister ship to *Bolette* also has really good amounts of open deck space, and a decent-sized pool with a retractable glass roof. The numerous public rooms, with traditional decor, include a pleasant observatory lounge and Morning Light pub – favorite meeting venues. The accommodation ranges from interior (no-view) cabins to balconied suites (with bathtub), in many price categories, but all have a decent amount of storage space. A stained-glass ceiling adorns the large Borealis main dining room, with flexible dining times, decent cuisine tailored to British tastes, and friendly service. Small, cost-extra eateries include the Canaletto Restaurant and Pinnacle Grill, where food is cooked to order. Overall, it's a rather comfortable ship.

INSIGHT GUIDES' RATINGS

	Achieved	Possible
Ship	392	500
Accommodation	165	200
Food	268	400
Service	215	400
Entertainment	66	100
Cruise Experience	250	400
OVERALL SCORE	**1356**	**2000**

BRILLIANCE OF THE SEAS
★★★

Size	Mid-size Ship
Tonnage	90,090
Cruise Line	Royal Caribbean International
Former Names	None
Entered Service	2002
Total Crew	869
Passengers	2,112

This mid-size resort-style ship has a well-balanced look and stylish decor for youthful, active families. The nine-deck-high lobby (Centrum) is the main area for socialising. Around the base of the funnel is a Viking Crown Lounge, with great views. Except for six large suites, almost all cabins have twin beds that convert to a queen-sized bed. All cabins have wood-style cabinetry, including a vanity desk with hairdryer. The large bi-level Minstrel dining room has so-so batch-cooked food with little taste. Try the extra-cost Chops Grille Steakhouse for cooked-to-order items. Upbeat entertainment shows are presented in the tri-deck Pacifica Showlounge. There are good spa facilities, with cost-extra treatments. Overall, it's a very pleasant ship.

INSIGHT GUIDES' RATINGS

	Achieved	Possible
Ship	336	500
Accommodation	134	200
Food	220	400
Service	228	400
Entertainment	70	100
Cruise Experience	225	400
OVERALL SCORE	**1213**	**2000**

BRITANNIA
★★★+

Size	Large Resort Ship
Tonnage	143,730
Cruise Line	P&O Cruises
Former Names	None
Entered Service	2015
Total Crew	1,400
Passengers	3,737

This large ship is a well-designed floating 'little Britain', for family-friendly cruising. Although it lacks an open walk-around deck (or a Deck 13), the main deck has two swimming pools, hot tubs, water splash areas and abundant deck chairs. A three-deck-high Atrium Lobby is the main gathering spot. There are over a dozen eateries, plus many bars (the Crow's Nest and Brodies are firm favorites). Accommodation ranges from single-occupancy cabins to suites; all have tea/coffee-making machines. Meridian, Oriental, and Peninsular are the main dining rooms, while cost-extra venues include Sindhu for British-Indian fusion cuisine. Features colorful production shows in Headliners Theatre, and decent (extra-cost) spa facilities.

INSIGHT GUIDES' RATINGS

	Achieved	Possible
Ship	400	500
Accommodation	151	200
Food	260	400
Service	236	400
Entertainment	73	100
Cruise Experience	253	400
OVERALL SCORE	**1373**	**2000**

CALEDONIAN SKY
★★★+

Size.. Boutique Ship
Tonnage..4,200
Cruise Line............................... Asian Pacific Touring
Former Names .... *Sunrise, Hebridean Spirit, Sun Viva 2, MegaStar Capricorn, Renaissance VI*
Entered Service 1991, 2023
Total Crew 74
Passengers 114

Here is a very small, modern, but ageing floating country inn to be enjoyed by well-seasoned travelers who don't need constant entertainment. There's ample open deck space with hardwood lounge chairs, while the interior design is reminiscent of a small country house hotel, with a traditional British drawing room look. Several support pillars obstruct some public areas, but the ambiance is warm and quiet. Cabins (for solo and double-occupancy) and suites have extensive facilities and are well designed. The restaurant has tables for two to eight, and the food is good. There is a good Asian-style spa aft. Overall, it is a very comfortable boutique (pocket-sized) ship experience.

INSIGHT GUIDES' RATINGS	Achieved	Possible
Ship	342	500
Accommodation	151	200
Food	317	400
Service	257	400
Entertainment	60	100
Cruise Experience	266	400
OVERALL SCORE	**1393**	**2000**

CARIBBEAN PRINCESS
★★★+

Size..Large Resort Ship
Tonnage...112,894
Cruise Line....................................Princess Cruises
Former Names ....*None*
Entered Service 2004
Total Crew 1,163
Passengers 3,114

This large, casual multi-choice, but ageing, family-friendly resort ship has an exterior promenade deck, and a bewildering choice of interior and outside-view cabins and prices. Some have interconnecting doors – good for families, while others have lifeboat-obstructed views. Drawer space is limited, and bathrooms are compact. Three main dining rooms each have multi-tier sections and a non-symmetrical design. The food is generally well presented, but is non-memorable. Try cost-extra Crown Grill or Sabatini's for a more personal experience. Colorful production shows are featured. Niggles include the user-unfriendly automated telephone system.

INSIGHT GUIDES' RATINGS	Achieved	Possible
Ship	347	500
Accommodation	122	200
Food	246	400
Service	232	400
Entertainment	74	100
Cruise Experience	243	400
OVERALL SCORE	**1264**	**2000**

CARNIVAL BREEZE
★★★

Size	Large Resort Ship
Tonnage	128,251
Cruise Line	Carnival Cruise Line
Former Names	*None*
Entered Service	2012
Total Crew	1,386
Passengers	3,690

This ultra-casual ship is a no-frills floating playground for the whole family. It has a WaterWorks pool deck full of amusements including a long, multi-deck Twister Slide and 'Power Drencher.' There's a poolside movie screen and laser light show, but little open deck space. The Caribbean-themed interior decor is bright, as is the 11-deck-high lobby. Numerous cabin price categories range from interior (no-view) cabins to (larger) suites. Two main dining rooms (each spanning two decks) feature lively service and ho-hum cuisine, but breakfast is good. Cost-extra Fahrenheit 555 Steakhouse has good steaks and seafood. The large Ovation Showlounge is the venue for colorful shows, while the large Cloud 9 Spa has cost-extra body treatments.

INSIGHT GUIDES' RATINGS

	Achieved	Possible
Ship	349	500
Accommodation	129	200
Food	210	400
Service	201	400
Entertainment	68	100
Cruise Experience	220	400
OVERALL SCORE	**1177**	**2000**

CARNIVAL CELEBRATION
★★★+

Size	Large Resort Ship
Tonnage	183,521
Cruise Line	Carnival Cruise Line
Former Names	*None*
Entered Service	2022
Total Crew	1,745
Passengers	5,374

This stunning, vibrant ship (sister to *Carnival Mardi Gras*) is packed with attractions for the whole family. Memorabilia from the original *Carnivale* and *Festivale* ships are displayed, including a bust of Carnival's founder Ted Arison. Accommodation ranges from small, viewless interior cabins to sizeable suites. Carnivale and Festivale are the large (included) dining venues, with banquet-catering food. Smaller, cost-extra venues include Fahrenheit 555 Steakhouse, Cucina del Capitano, and Bonsai Sushi, serving cooked-to-order food. Emeril's Bistro 1397 is the first at-sea dining venue by Emeril Lagasse, with down-home Southern cuisine. Grand Spectrum Theater has colorful, high-volume production shows and cabaret.

INSIGHT GUIDES' RATINGS

	Achieved	Possible
Ship	363	500
Accommodation	131	200
Food	235	400
Service	213	400
Entertainment	73	100
Cruise Experience	235	400
OVERALL SCORE	**1250**	**2000**

CARNIVAL CONQUEST
★★★

Size	Large Resort Ship
Tonnage	110,239
Cruise Line	Carnival Cruise Line
Former Names	None
Entered Service	2002
Total Crew	1,160
Passengers	2,974

This ultra-casual resort ship has a neat waterslide 200-ft (60-m) -long, tiered sunbathing decks positioned between two pools, and a poolside movie screen. The ship's interior decor focuses on impressionist painters like Degas, Cezanne, Gauguin, etc, and Murano glass flowers on antique brass stems are displayed in several public areas. Accommodation ranges from interior (no-view) cabins to suites with private balcony (some not so private, because they can be overlooked). Monet and Renoir are the two main dining rooms, both span two decks, and have two seatings. The food is carbo-heavy and non-memorable, with a few exceptions. Extra-cost dining is also available in The Point, a more intimate venue, with cooked-to-order food.

INSIGHT GUIDES' RATINGS		
	Achieved	Possible
Ship	335	500
Accommodation	125	200
Food	208	400
Service	197	400
Entertainment	68	100
Cruise Experience	212	400
OVERALL SCORE	**1145**	**2000**

CARNIVAL DREAM
★★★

Size	Large Resort Ship
Tonnage	128,251
Cruise Line	Carnival Cruise Line
Former Names	None
Entered Service	2009
Total Crew	1,367
Passengers	3,646

This is an ultra-casual ship with oodles of fun facilities for the whole family, including splashy waterslides and a 'Power Drencher' in the WaterWorks aqua park. There is a full walk-around promenade deck. Indoors, most public rooms, bars and lounges are on Dream Street or Upper Dream Street. Accommodation price depends on the grade and type you choose: from interior (no-view) cabins to large suites with balconies. Crimson and Scarlet are the large main restaurants, each with two levels, lively food service, and ho-hum cuisine (but good breakfasts). There are also smaller cost-extra venues, with food cooked to order (better). Shows are in the Encore Lounge. Overall, a cruise aboard this ship is a blast!

INSIGHT GUIDES' RATINGS		
	Achieved	Possible
Ship	344	500
Accommodation	129	200
Food	205	400
Service	201	400
Entertainment	68	100
Cruise Experience	214	400
OVERALL SCORE	**1161**	**2000**

CARNIVAL ELATION
★★+

Size	Mid-size Ship
Tonnage	70,390
Cruise Line	Carnival Cruise Line
Former Names	*Elation*
Entered Service	1998
Total Crew	920
Passengers	2,056

This really is a floating, but dated, fun palace, that could be good for an casual sea-going family vacation. The colorful interior design focuses on composers and their compositions, and mythical muses. An open atrium lobby (a good meeting place) spans six decks, and is topped by a glass dome. The accommodation is practical, although both suites and cabins are small. Two large main dining venues (Imagination and Inspiration) have ocean-view windows. The food is nothing special, and tends to be carbo-rich, although breakfasts are quite decent. Colorful, but volume-heavy production shows can be seen in the Mikado Showlounge.

INSIGHT GUIDES' RATINGS		
	Achieved	Possible
Ship	294	500
Accommodation	121	200
Food	202	400
Service	200	400
Entertainment	62	100
Cruise Experience	208	400
OVERALL SCORE	**1087**	**2000**

CARNIVAL FREEDOM
★★★

Size	Large Resort Ship
Tonnage	110,320
Cruise Line	Carnival Cruise Line
Former Names	*None*
Entered Service	2007
Total Crew	1,150
Passengers	2,974

This is a casual, vibrant, floating playground for the whole family, with glitz, glamor, and gaming galore. Outdoors a Seaside Theater hosts classic movies and sports events. Inside is a kaleidoscopic blend of colors to excite the senses, plus razzle-dazzle shows and late-night revelry. Accommodation ranges from interior (no-view) cabins to suites with private balcony, but the majority of standard cabins are modest. Chic and Posh are two main dining rooms. The cuisine is so-so, overly starchy, and lacks green vegetables. Shows are presented in the cavernous Victoriana Main Lounge, with seating on three levels and medieval decor. Overall, it's fun, fun, fun!

INSIGHT GUIDES' RATINGS		
	Achieved	Possible
Ship	344	500
Accommodation	125	200
Food	208	400
Service	200	400
Entertainment	66	100
Cruise Experience	212	400
OVERALL SCORE	**1155**	**2000**

CARNIVAL GLORY
★★★

Size	Large Resort Ship
Tonnage	110,239
Cruise Line	Carnival Cruise Line
Former Names	None
Entered Service	2003
Total Crew	1,160
Passengers	2,974

This is a multi-choice, floating playground for the whole family. Two additional decks were added in 2012, with additional cabins (but no additional elevators). The interior decor is a fantasyland of colors, in every hue of the rainbow, and most public rooms are located off Kaleidoscope Boulevard. Accommodation ranges from interior (no-view) cabins to suites with private balcony, but the majority of standard cabins are compact units with angular furniture. Golden and Platinum main dining rooms span two decks, with seating on both levels. The food is quite starchy, and green vegetables are lacking, but this is all about 'foodertainment'. The showy entertainment itself is in the large, multi-deck Amber Palace, because this is cruising Splash Vegas style.

INSIGHT GUIDES' RATINGS

	Achieved	Possible
Ship	340	500
Accommodation	125	200
Food	207	400
Service	197	400
Entertainment	64	100
Cruise Experience	209	400
OVERALL SCORE	**1142**	**2000**

CARNIVAL HORIZON
★★★

Size	Large Resort Ship
Tonnage	135,000
Cruise Line	Carnival Cruise Line
Former Names	None
Entered Service	2018
Total Crew	1,450
Passengers	3,954

This ship offers vibrant, no-frills cruising for the whole family in comfort-basic surroundings. Enjoy WaterWorks Aquapark, including its 445ft (136m) Kaleid-O-Slide (a twisting corkscrew-turning waterslide adventure), or pedal a bike on Sky Ride's suspended track. There is also a walk-around exterior deck. Inside, the Atrium is the ship's social center, while most public rooms, lounges, bars, and night spots are located on two main public room/entertainment decks. Reflections and Meridian are two large main dining venues, but there are several other eateries (some cost extra). Head to Liquid Lounge (showlounge) for Carnival's colorful Las Vegas-style shows and major cabaret acts. It's all a blast!

INSIGHT GUIDES' RATINGS

	Achieved	Possible
Ship	373	500
Accommodation	133	200
Food	211	400
Service	201	400
Entertainment	68	100
Cruise Experience	235	400
OVERALL SCORE	**1221**	**2000**

CARNIVAL INSPIRATION
★★+

Size	Mid-size Ship
Tonnage	70,367
Cruise Line	Carnival Cruise Line
Former Names	None
Entered Service	1996
Total Crew	920
Passengers	2,056

With its WaterWorks aqua park featuring a pool deck plus the Twister and Speedway Splash waterslides, this ship could suit families for a first cruise experience. With outdoor activities centered around the pool, the open deck and sunbathing space is limited. The interior focal point is a six-deck high atrium lobby. Most public rooms connect to a wide Inspiration Promenade deck. Cabins and the slightly larger 'suites' are adequate, but storage space is limited. The main dining rooms, Carnivale and Mardi Gras (the names of Carnival's first two ships) provide carbo-rich food with simple presentation. Deck food includes Guy's Burger Joint. Colorful, but volume-heavy production shows can be seen in the Paris Main Lounge.

INSIGHT GUIDES' RATINGS	Achieved	Possible
Ship	295	500
Accommodation	121	200
Food	202	400
Service	201	400
Entertainment	62	100
Cruise Experience	207	400
OVERALL SCORE	**1088**	**2000**

CARNIVAL JUBILEE
NYR

Size	Large Resort Ship
Tonnage	181,808
Cruise Line	Carnival Cruise Line
Former Names	None
Entered Service	2023
Total Crew	1,745
Passengers	5,282

This large, dual powered playground is packed with attractions for the whole family. Two whole decks include the large main restaurants, several smaller eateries, casino, plus numerous bars, lounges, and shops. Its Grand Central Atrium is the place to see and be seen. Accommodation ranges from viewless, interior cabins to the not-so-large Excel Presidential Suites. Banquet-catering-style food is served with entertaining flair in the large main dining rooms, but there are also several cost-extra venues including Emeril's Bistro 1397, Fahrenheit 555 Steakhouse, Cucina del Capitano, Bonsai Sushi, Guy's Pig & Anchor Smokehouse, and Seafood Shack for cooked-to-order food. For colorful production shows, head to the Jubilee Theater.

INSIGHT GUIDES' RATINGS	Achieved	Possible
Ship	NYR	500
Accommodation	NYR	200
Food	NYR	400
Service	NYR	400
Entertainment	NYR	100
Cruise Experience	NYR	400
OVERALL SCORE	**NYR**	**2000**

CARNIVAL LEGEND
★★★

Size	Mid-size Ship
Tonnage	85,942
Cruise Line	Carnival Cruise Line
Former Names	None
Entered Service	2002
Total Crew	1,030
Passengers	2,124

This is a contemporary ship with a pod propulsion system for almost noise-free cruising, and it's full of fun activities for the whole family. The open deck space is limited, but there are two swimming pools (one can be covered by a glass dome in inclement weather), and a whole Water Park full of features for kids. An adult-only (extra-cost) quiet area is available aft. There are numerous cabin categories, priced by category, size, and location. Truffles is the main, two-deck-high dining hall, offering either fixed time or flexible time dining. The food is so-so (breakfasts are good), but you can pay extra to eat in the intimate Golden Fleece Steakhouse. The ship has lively entertainment and a large spa (treatments cost extra).

INSIGHT GUIDES' RATINGS		
	Achieved	Possible
Ship	328	500
Accommodation	125	200
Food	207	400
Service	192	400
Entertainment	63	100
Cruise Experience	214	400
OVERALL SCORE	**1129**	**2000**

CARNIVAL LIBERTY
★★★

Size	Large Resort Ship
Tonnage	110,320
Cruise Line	Carnival Cruise Line
Former Names	None
Entered Service	2005
Total Crew	1,160
Passengers	2,974

This colorful floating playground has a fairly well-balanced look. A midship exterior pool deck features a large movie screen, plus waterslides and other play features for young-sters. The interior decor salutes the master trades: ironwork, masonry, plus painting and pottery. Accommodation includes many price categories, from balconied suites to windowless interior cabins. Golden Olympian (forward) and Silver Olympian (aft) are the two main dining rooms. Overall, the food is carbohydrate-rich and not memorable, except for breakfast. Features include large-scale production shows.

INSIGHT GUIDES' RATINGS		
	Achieved	Possible
Ship	330	500
Accommodation	126	200
Food	208	400
Service	191	400
Entertainment	64	100
Cruise Experience	209	400
OVERALL SCORE	**1128**	**2000**

CARNIVAL LUMINOSA
★★★

Size	Mid-size Ship
Tonnage	92,700
Cruise Line	Carnival Cruise Line
Former Names	*Costa Luminosa*
Entered Service	2009, 2022
Total Crew	1,050
Passengers	2,260

A vibrant, casual lifestyle awaits aboard this revitalized family-friendly ship, with its colorful, lively style. One of two outside deck pools can be covered by a glass dome. The interior decor is all about light and lighting, but you simply can't miss the huge bronze sculpture *Reclining Woman* by Fernando Botero in the lobby! There are many grades of cabin and (slightly larger) suites, but all have twin beds convertible to queen size, and include a vanity desk with built-in hairdryer. The large main restaurant (Taurus) is aft, with batch-cooked carbohydrate-rich food, although there are a few exceptions. Cost-extra eateries include favorites like Fahrenheit 555 Steakhouse, Chef's Table, and Bonsai Sushi Express.

INSIGHT GUIDES' RATINGS

	Achieved	Possible
Ship	370	500
Accommodation	134	200
Food	218	400
Service	197	400
Entertainment	60	100
Cruise Experience	212	400
OVERALL SCORE	**1191**	**2000**

CARNIVAL MAGIC
★★★

Size	Large Resort Ship
Tonnage	128,048
Cruise Line	Carnival Cruise Line
Former Names	*None*
Entered Service	2011
Total Crew	1,367
Passengers	3,646

The red, white, and blue wing-tipped funnel is instantly recognisable on this ultra-casual, floating fun palace for the whole family, sister to *Carnival Dream*. There's a full walk-around open walking deck, plus the WaterWorks pool deck has a great Twister waterslide. The interior decor is vivid, and an atrium lobby is the 'see-and-be-seen' meeting place. The Northern Lights (midships) and Southern Lights (aft) dining rooms both have two levels. Breakfasts are good, but other meals are starch-heavy and non-memorable. The Lido Marketplace self-serve buffet venue has something for everyone. As well as a good range of public rooms, bars, and lounges – with non-stop music everywhere – there are decent spa facilities (treatments cost extra).

INSIGHT GUIDES' RATINGS

	Achieved	Possible
Ship	332	500
Accommodation	128	200
Food	208	400
Service	194	400
Entertainment	64	100
Cruise Experience	213	400
OVERALL SCORE	**1139**	**2000**

CARNIVAL MARDI GRAS
★★★+

Size	Large Resort Ship
Tonnage	181,808
Cruise Line	Carnival Cruise Line
Former Names	None
Entered Service	2021
Total Crew	1,745
Passengers	5,282

New in 2021, this stunning, large, dual-powered floating playground is packed with features, attractions, and entertainment for the whole family. Two whole decks host the main restaurants, several smaller eateries, plus numerous lounges and bars, and a casino. Accommodation ranges from small, viewless interior cabins, to sizeable suites (those at the aft are desirable). Flamingo and Palm are the two large main (included) restaurants, with decent banquet-catering food. Several small cost-extra venues – including Emeril's Bistro 1397, Fahrenheit 555 Steakhouse, Cucina del Capitano, Bonsai Sushi, Seafood Shack, and Chef's Table – serve cooked-to-order food. For colorful, voluminous production shows, head to the large Mardi Gras Theater.

INSIGHT GUIDES' RATINGS

	Achieved	Possible
Ship	385	500
Accommodation	150	200
Food	256	400
Service	252	400
Entertainment	72	100
Cruise Experience	275	400
OVERALL SCORE	**1390**	**2000**

CARNIVAL MIRACLE
★★★

Size	Mid-size Ship
Tonnage	85,942
Cruise Line	Carnival Cruise Line
Former Names	None
Entered Service	2004
Total Crew	961
Passengers	2,124

This ultra-casual multi-choice floating playground could be a good choice for youthful cruisegoers. The open deck and sunbathing spaces aren't extensive, and the two swimming pools are small (one is coverable in inclement weather). Carnival's own beer is dispensed in the Thirsty Red Frog onboard brewery. Size, grade and location govern accommodation pricing – favorites are balcony cabins on the aft decks. Bacchus Dining Room is the voluminous main meal venue, while Horatio's Lido is for self-serve eats. For something more intimate and upscale, try Nick & Nora's (steaks and seafood). The Phantom Showlounge hosts large-scale volume-driven production shows. Overall, this is a fun ship.

INSIGHT GUIDES' RATINGS

	Achieved	Possible
Ship	331	500
Accommodation	126	200
Food	208	400
Service	191	400
Entertainment	63	100
Cruise Experience	211	400
OVERALL SCORE	**1130**	**2000**

CARNIVAL PANORAMA
★★★

Size	Large Resort Ship
Tonnage	135,000
Cruise Line	Carnival Cruise Line
Former Names	*None*
Entered Service	2019
Total Crew	1,450
Passengers	3,954

This is a large, high-energy ultra-casual resort ship with an abundance of family-friendly features. There are extensive aqua-park features with twisting waterslides, splash zones, and a challenging SkyCourse rope feature; it really is a bright and contemporary playground for the whole family. Inside, it's the Promenade Deck where all the action happens. Accommodation ranges from small interior (no-view) cabins to balconied suites. All are comfortable, but a little sparse in decoration. There are two main dining rooms (forward and aft), and both have two levels. The food choice is plentiful, although carbo-rich, while several other eateries (some cost extra) offer multiple choices. The entertainment is vibrant, loud, and colorful.

INSIGHT GUIDES' RATINGS

	Achieved	Possible
Ship	376	500
Accommodation	133	200
Food	211	400
Service	201	400
Entertainment	68	100
Cruise Experience	238	400
OVERALL SCORE	**1227**	**2000**

CARNIVAL PARADISE
★★+

Size	Mid-size Ship
Tonnage	70,390
Cruise Line	Carnival Cruise Line
Former Names	*Paradise*
Entered Service	1998
Total Crew	920
Passengers	2,052

Although over 20 years old, this colorful ship has a vibration-free ride thanks to its 'pod' propulsion system. Most outdoor activities are around the main pool and WaterWorks Aqua Park, but there's also Serenity – a cost-extra, adults-only quiet zone. The interior design is about yesteryear's ocean liners, and a wide indoor promenade (think 'Main Street') provides connection points for the many lounges, bars, shops, and entertainment spots. Accommodation varies from interior (no-view) cabins to balconied suites, but all are rather compact. Destiny (aft) and Elation (midship) main dining rooms are large and colorful, and the food is generally sound (breakfast is particularly good). Showy entertainment is in the multi-deck Amber Palace.

INSIGHT GUIDES' RATINGS

	Achieved	Possible
Ship	293	500
Accommodation	122	200
Food	203	400
Service	197	400
Entertainment	61	100
Cruise Experience	209	400
OVERALL SCORE	**1085**	**2000**

CARNIVAL PRIDE
★★★

Size	Mid-size Ship
Tonnage	85,920
Cruise Line	Carnival Cruise Line
Former Names	None
Entered Service	2002
Total Crew	1,029
Passengers	2,124

This smart-looking mid-size ship has an abundance of facilities to keep the whole family occupied and entertained. Its art-themed interior decor is from the Renaissance period – even the elevator doors feature grainy reproductions. Yellow Brick Road connects most public rooms, eateries, and entertainment venues, with a colorful atrium spanning eight decks. Cabins are priced by grade, location, and size (the best are aft-facing suites/cabins). The 1,300-seat, bi-level Normandie Restaurant has a choice of fixed or open dining times, with food that is carbohydrate-rich, but there is plenty of variety. For decent steaks, head to cost-extra David's Steakhouse. Shows can be seen in the glamorous 1,170-seat Taj Mahal Showlounge.

INSIGHT GUIDES' RATINGS

	Achieved	Possible
Ship	321	500
Accommodation	124	200
Food	207	400
Service	219	400
Entertainment	62	100
Cruise Experience	215	400
OVERALL SCORE	**1148**	**2000**

CARNIVAL RADIANCE
★★★

Size	Large Resort Ship
Tonnage	101,509
Cruise Line	Carnival Cruise Line
Former Names	Carnival Victory
Entered Service	2000
Total Crew	1,100
Passengers	2,758

This floating fun palace is for the whole family, and has upper decks filled with waterpark and sports attractions. The interior layout makes it easy to find your way around. Indoors, statues of Neptune stand at both ends of an indoor promenade, with lounges, bars, and casino. Atlantic (forward) and Pacific (aft) are the two main dining rooms (included); both have two meal seatings. While breakfasts are actually good, other meals are quite uninspiring. Cost-extra eateries include the popular 555 Fahrenheit Steakhouse, Cucina del Capitano, and Shaq's Big Chicken Eatery. From compact interior (no-view) cabins to exterior-view cabins (those at the stern are good) and large Captain's Suites, all are adequate, but lack storage space.

INSIGHT GUIDES' RATINGS

	Achieved	Possible
Ship	333	500
Accommodation	124	200
Food	207	400
Service	192	400
Entertainment	61	100
Cruise Experience	210	400
OVERALL SCORE	**1127**	**2000**

CARNIVAL SPIRIT
★★★

Size	Mid-size Ship
Tonnage	85,920
Cruise Line	Carnival Cruise Line
Former Names	None
Entered Service	2001
Total Crew	930
Passengers	2,124

Instantly recognisable because of its red, white, and blue wing-tipped funnel, this mid-sized ship is aimed at families. Its outdoor decks feature a water park with splash zones and a Green Thunder thrill ride that starts 100ft (30m) up, then plummets you in a near vertical drop. For some quiet 'me-time', adults can escape to The Sanctuary (extra cost). Accommodation ranges from small viewless interior cabins to pleasant aft-facing outdoor balconied suites. Meals are served in the cavernous Empire Restaurant, with mass-catering style food. For something different, try the more intimate cost-extra Nouveau Palace steakhouse, where food is cooked to order. Colorful shows and cabaret acts can be seen in the Pharaoh's Palace showlounge.

INSIGHT GUIDES' RATINGS

	Achieved	Possible
Ship	330	500
Accommodation	124	200
Food	207	400
Service	202	400
Entertainment	62	100
Cruise Experience	210	400
OVERALL SCORE	**1135**	**2000**

CARNIVAL SPLENDOR
★★★

Size	Large Resort Ship
Tonnage	113,323
Cruise Line	Carnival Cruise Line
Former Names	None
Entered Service	2008
Total Crew	1,150
Passengers	2,974

This family-friendly ship has high-energy and jazzy, voluminous entertainment. The deck layout is a little disjointed, but most public rooms sit above a main interior boulevard. Interior decor is basically 50 shades of pink. Accommodation ranges from suites and 'spa' suites with balcony, to interior (no-view) cabins. Black Pearl and the larger Gold Pearl are main dining rooms; both span two decks. Choose either fixed or flexible timings for dinner. Breakfast is quite decent, with ample choice, but dinners are so-so affairs. Pinnacle Steakhouse has cost-extra prime steaks and seafood. Cloud 9 Spa spans two decks and provides many body-pampering treatment options.

INSIGHT GUIDES' RATINGS

	Achieved	Possible
Ship	337	500
Accommodation	127	200
Food	208	400
Service	194	400
Entertainment	62	100
Cruise Experience	210	400
OVERALL SCORE	**1138**	**2000**

CARNIVAL SUNRISE
★★★

Size	Large Resort Ship
Tonnage	101,509
Cruise Line	Carnival Cruise Line
Former Names	*Carnival Triumph*
Entered Service	1999
Total Crew	1,100
Passengers	2,988

This 'fun' ship (updated in 2019) is a floating playground for ultra-casual family-friendly cruising. Inside, three decks are full of bars, lounges, and a nine-deck-high atrium lobby. As for accommodation, there are numerous price categories, but most have limited storage space. The London and Paris dining rooms each span two decks, with carbohydrate-rich food, plus an 'always available' selection. For something special and cooked to order, head to The Steakhouse, with its Scarlet O'Hara (*Gone with the Wind*) decor. For colorful production shows, there is the Rome Main Lounge. This is cruising Splash Vegas style, with high volume everything and everywhere.

INSIGHT GUIDES' RATINGS		
	Achieved	Possible
Ship	334	500
Accommodation	124	200
Food	206	400
Service	216	400
Entertainment	61	100
Cruise Experience	210	400
OVERALL SCORE	**1151**	**2000**

CARNIVAL SUNSHINE
★★★

Size	Large Resort Ship
Tonnage	102,853
Cruise Line	Carnival Cruise Line
Former Names	*Carnival Destiny*
Entered Service	1996
Total Crew	1,150
Passengers	3,006

Looking better following its 2018 revamp, this family-friendly ship was the first to exceed 100,000 gross tons when it originally debuted. Outdoor fun areas include a back-of-ship water park and Twister waterslide. Inside, the revamp result gives it a more upscale, quieter look, with muted colors. Sunrise and Sunset are the main dining rooms (the food is mass-catering so-so); they are noisy venues because of their low deck height. Pay extra for cooked-to-order food in one of several smaller venues such as Fahrenheit 555 Steakhouse, Cucina del Capitano, and Guy's Burger Joint, among others. High-energy shows, and smutty comedy are standard fare. Think full-time, rah-rah fun ship, and you will have a good time.

INSIGHT GUIDES' RATINGS		
	Achieved	Possible
Ship	327	500
Accommodation	123	200
Food	206	400
Service	197	400
Entertainment	62	100
Cruise Experience	215	400
OVERALL SCORE	**1130**	**2000**

CARNIVAL VALOR
★★★

Size	....	Large Resort Ship
Tonnage	....	110,239
Cruise Line	....	Carnival Cruise Line
Former Names	....	*None*
Entered Service	....	2004
Total Crew	....	1,160
Passengers	....	2,974

One of a series of look-alike ships, this casual, floating fun palace is a good all-rounder and suitable for all the family. Amidships on the open deck a 200-ft (60-m) -long waterslide spans two levels, while a cluttered pool area has a large movie screen. Indoors, a double-width promenade features public rooms with a famous personalities theme (eg. singer/dancer Josephine Baker and aviator Charles Lindbergh). Balcony cabins have glass balconies extending from the ship's side. Lincoln and Washington are the large main dining rooms, while extra-cost Scarlett's Steakhouse (think: *Gone With The Wind*'s Scarlett O'Hara) is small and good. The fine show-lounge has tri-level seating and volume-heavy shows.

INSIGHT GUIDES' RATINGS

	Achieved	Possible
Ship	329	500
Accommodation	124	200
Food	207	400
Service	191	400
Entertainment	61	100
Cruise Experience	211	400
OVERALL SCORE	**1123**	**2000**

CARNIVAL VENEZIA
★★★

Size	....	Large Resort Ship
Tonnage	....	135,500
Cruise Line	....	Carnival Cruise Line
Former Names	....	*Costa Venezia*
Entered Service	....	2019
Total Crew	....	1,278
Passengers	....	4,232

This lively Italian floating resort buzzes with activities for the whole family, with a design theme centered around Venice. Piazza San Marco (St Mark's Square – fortunately minus the pigeons) is its interior focal point. From the many interior (no-view) cabins to the largest suites (which are quite small), the decor is based on one of Italy's port cities. The Canal Grande (aft) and Marco Polo (forward) restaurants are large venues for all passengers, and feature cuisine that tends to be carbohydrate-rich and lacking in green vegetables. Smaller, cost-extra venues specialise in cooked-to-order food such as seafood, steaks, or Asian hot-pot dishes. Overall, it's fun, with volume to match.

INSIGHT GUIDES' RATINGS

	Achieved	Possible
Ship	372	500
Accommodation	141	200
Food	217	400
Service	208	400
Entertainment	70	100
Cruise Experience	232	400
OVERALL SCORE	**1240**	**2000**

CARNIVAL VISTA
★★★

Size	Large Resort Ship
Tonnage	135,000
Cruise Line	Carnival Cruise Line
Former Names	None
Entered Service	2016
Total Crew	1,450
Passengers	4,000

This is a floating palace for ultra-casual family-friendly cruising, with all the fun of the fair at sea. So, pedal the suspended track of SkyRide or go the WaterWorks route, featuring its 445ft (136m) Kaleid-O-Slide – a twisting waterslide adventure with kaleidoscopic effects – plus there's an outdoor walk-around deck and abundant sunlounges. Inside, facilities include an IMAX Theatre, plus a casino and many other public rooms, mostly located on two main entertainment decks, accessible via an 11-deck high central atrium. Accommodation includes family-friendly cabins that can sleep up to five. Horizons and Reflections are the two main voluminous dining rooms. The food is quite acceptable, but nothing special (breakfast has, perhaps, the best choices).

INSIGHT GUIDES' RATINGS

	Achieved	Possible
Ship	369	500
Accommodation	133	200
Food	210	400
Service	201	400
Entertainment	68	100
Cruise Experience	228	400
OVERALL SCORE	**1209**	**2000**

CELEBRITY APEX
★★★★

Size	Large Resort Ship
Tonnage	130,818
Cruise Line	Celebrity Cruises
Former Names	None
Entered Service	2021
Total Crew	1,320
Passengers	2,934

This smart-tech ship has a snub nose, tiered after decks, and a 25m swimming pool. Neat features include a novel exterior starboard side 'Magic Carpet' – a 90-seat bar/eatery on a 90-ton moveable, vertical platform. Inside is a range of lounges, bars, a casino, and several brand-name shops. The cabins are comfortable and all come with twin beds convertible to a double, but have little drawer space. There are also some delightful suites (occupants dine in Luminae – a smaller, dedicated restaurant). In addition to the main assigned dining room, there is a wide array of eateries with decent, sometimes 'edgy' cuisine. There are many public rooms and voluminous entertainment, but constant background music detracts from the overall experience.

INSIGHT GUIDES' RATINGS

	Achieved	Possible
Ship	408	500
Accommodation	158	200
Food	264	400
Service	243	400
Entertainment	80	100
Cruise Experience	275	400
OVERALL SCORE	**1428**	**2000**

CELEBRITY ASCENT
NYR

Size	Large Resort Ship
Tonnage	140,600
Cruise Line	Celebrity Cruises
Former Names	None
Entered Service	2023
Total Crew	1,320
Passengers	3,276

With similar features to *Celebrity Apex*, this 'edgy' ship also has the 'Magic Carpet' bar/eatery on a huge moveable platform. The interior design is light, open, and airy, and includes a whole host of bars and lounges, and a private enclave (Retreat) for those who pay more to get more. Four main dining rooms are included in the cruise fare (suite occupants eat in smaller venues, with cooked-to-order meals), with batch-cooked food that is generally decent. Extra-cost venues provide a change in smaller, more specialized eateries. This multi-choice sea-going resort has abundant entertainment, but constant background music is irritating.

INSIGHT GUIDES' RATINGS

	Achieved	Possible
Ship	NYR	500
Accommodation	NYR	200
Food	NYR	400
Service	NYR	400
Entertainment	NYR	100
Cruise Experience	NYR	400
OVERALL SCORE	**NYR**	**2000**

CELEBRITY BEYOND
★★★★

Size	Large Resort Ship
Tonnage	140,600
Cruise Line	Celebrity Cruises
Former Names	None
Entered Service	2022
Total Crew	1,400
Passengers	3,260

Another Celebrity ship with tiered aft decks and large (25m) swimming pool, and a decent amount of open deck space, its neat features include the gimmicky, exterior 'Magic Carpet' 90-seat bar/eatery on a moveable, platform. Inside, the design is light, open, and airy, and includes a wide range of bars and lounges, and a private enclave if you pay more to get more in The Retreat. The huge (included in the cruise fare) main dining room is divided into four sections, each with a different name. There are multiple smaller, more specialized eateries (many at extra cost) that may be good for a change of scenery and food cooked to order. Entertainment is edgy, and there is constant irritating 'background' music everywhere.

INSIGHT GUIDES' RATINGS

	Achieved	Possible
Ship	410	500
Accommodation	158	200
Food	264	400
Service	243	400
Entertainment	80	100
Cruise Experience	290	400
OVERALL SCORE	**1445**	**2000**

CELEBRITY CONSTELLATION
★★★+

Size... Mid-size Ship
Tonnage...90,940
Cruise Line.................................. Celebrity Cruises
Former Names .... *Constellation*
Entered Service 2002
Total Crew 999
Passengers 2,120

This comfortable, well-designed, mid-size ship has oodles of space and European style, but lacks a walk-around outdoor promenade deck. Inside, the decor is of understated elegance, and materials include marble, glass, and wood. Accommodation ranges from interior (no-view) cabins to large, balconied Penthouse suites, but all are comfortable and well designed, with ample storage space. The San Marco Restaurant spans two decks, has a huge aft-facing glass wall, and feeds over 2,000 in two dining times. The food is decent enough, but remember that this is high-volume catering. Qsine and Tuscan Grill, however, are small cost-extra venues, with better, cooked-to-order cuisine. Overall, it can be a pleasant vacation experience.

INSIGHT GUIDES' RATINGS		
	Achieved	Possible
Ship	354	500
Accommodation	148	200
Food	254	400
Service	228	400
Entertainment	71	100
Cruise Experience	238	400
OVERALL SCORE	**1293**	**2000**

CELEBRITY ECLIPSE
★★★+

Size..Large Resort Ship
Tonnage..121,878
Cruise Line.................................. Celebrity Cruises
Former Names .... *None*
Entered Service 2010
Total Crew 1,210
Passengers 2,852

Sister to *Celebrity Edge,* it also has the novel exterior starboard side 'Magic Carpet' with a 90-seat bar/eatery on a moveable platform. Inside, the design is light, open, and airy, and includes a wide range of bars and lounges, and a private enclave if you pay more to get more in The Retreat. The huge main dining room (included in the cruise fare) is divided into four sections, each with a different name. The food is generally sound, and nicely presented. As an alternative, you can eat in one of several (extra-cost) smaller venues for cooked-to-order meals. Suite occupants eat in a different venue, also with cooked-to-order cuisine. Overall, this is a contemporary multi-choice sea-going resort with constant entertainment and 'background music'.

INSIGHT GUIDES' RATINGS		
	Achieved	Possible
Ship	388	500
Accommodation	159	200
Food	259	400
Service	234	400
Entertainment	73	100
Cruise Experience	255	400
OVERALL SCORE	**1368**	**2000**

CELEBRITY EDGE
★★★★

Size	Large Resort Ship
Tonnage	129,500
Cruise Line	Celebrity Cruises
Former Names	None
Entered Service	2018
Total Crew	1,320
Passengers	2,918

This smart ship has the snub nose, tiered after decks, and 25m pool of its sister ships, and the novel exterior 'Magic Carpet' moveable bar/eatery. The interior design is light, open, and airy, and includes a whole host of bars and lounges, and a private enclave (Retreat) for those who pay more to get more. You dine in one of four main dining rooms (suite occupants eat in smaller venues, and cooked-to-order meals), with food that is generally decent. Has edgy, custom-designed shows, and throbbing nightclub venues. Overall, this multi-choice sea-going resort has constant entertainment and background 'music' everywhere.

INSIGHT GUIDES' RATINGS

	Achieved	Possible
Ship	407	500
Accommodation	158	200
Food	264	400
Service	243	400
Entertainment	80	100
Cruise Experience	273	400
OVERALL SCORE	**1425**	**2000**

CELEBRITY EQUINOX
★★★+

Size	Large Resort Ship
Tonnage	122,000
Cruise Line	Celebrity Cruises
Former Names	None
Entered Service	2009
Total Crew	1,210
Passengers	2,852

This resort ship has a contemporary profile, a steeply sloping stern, and two slim funnels. There are several pool and water play areas for the whole family, and a small pay-extra retreat area for adults. Inside, the decor is contemporary, even edgy, and there are numerous lounges, bars, a casino, and a range of shops. The accommodation is comfortable, and all cabins come with twin beds convertible to a double, although most have little drawer space. There are also some delightful suites and large cabins. Suite occupants dine in Luminae, while most eat in the large cruise-fare inclusive Silhouette. Extra-cost venues such as Tuscan Grille and QSine may also be worth a try.

INSIGHT GUIDES' RATINGS

	Achieved	Possible
Ship	387	500
Accommodation	159	200
Food	258	400
Service	237	400
Entertainment	73	100
Cruise Experience	255	400
OVERALL SCORE	**1369**	**2000**

CELEBRITY FLORA
★★★+

Size	Boutique Ship
Tonnage	5,739
Cruise Line	Celebrity Cruises
Former Names	None
Entered Service	2019
Total Crew	80
Passengers	100

Visit the Galápagos islands by using this stylish small-capacity ship – the first built specifically for the region – as your floating hotel, with a stern platform for Zodiac loading. It provides a base for feeding and resting after visiting the various islands to see and experience the unusual wildlife. From wood-trimmed suites to comfortable cabins, almost all have twin beds convertible to a queen-sized bed, and include a personal safe and USB ports. The comfortable dining room has open seating, with friendly but basic service. The meals are quite basic, but forget the hamburgers. Desserts are almost non-existent, as are between-meal snack items. Seeds are not permitted in the Galápagos, so fruit choice is limited.

INSIGHT GUIDES' RATINGS	Achieved	Possible
Ship	363	500
Accommodation	144	200
Food	242	400
Service	216	400
Entertainment	62	100
Cruise Experience	261	400
OVERALL SCORE	**1288**	**2000**

CELEBRITY INFINITY
★★★+

Size	Mid-size Ship
Tonnage	90,940
Cruise Line	Celebrity Cruises
Former Names	Infinity
Entered Service	2001
Total Crew	999
Passengers	2,170

This is a well-designed mid-size ship, with abundant space and European style, although it lacks a walk-around outdoor promenade deck. Inside, the decor is elegant without being overdone, with materials including marble, glass, and wood. The accommodation ranges from interior, no-view cabins to large balconied Penthouse suites, but all are comfortable and well designed, with abundant storage space. The Trellis main dining room seats 1,170, spans two decks at the back of the ship, and has two seating times for dinner. The cuisine is quite decent, well presented and served with some flair. For something different, it may be worth trying one of the extra-cost, small venues Tuscan Grille or QSine.

INSIGHT GUIDES' RATINGS	Achieved	Possible
Ship	355	500
Accommodation	148	200
Food	255	400
Service	229	400
Entertainment	71	100
Cruise Experience	237	400
OVERALL SCORE	**1295**	**2000**

CELEBRITY MILLENNIUM
★★★+

Size.. Mid-size Ship
Tonnage...90,940
Cruise Line... Celebrity Cruises
Former Names .... *Millennium*
Entered Service 2000
Total Crew 999
Passengers 2,158

This mid-sized ship has plenty of style and ample facilities for mature-age cruisegoers, although it lacks a walk-around outdoor promenade deck. The interior decor is quite elegant, and some areas have high ceilings. From viewless interior cabins to expansive balconied suites, the accommodation is well designed, with enough storage space. The large Metropolitan Restaurant (main dining room) seats 1,170, spans two decks at the back of the ship, and has two seating times for dinner. The cuisine is quite decent, well presented and served with flair. For something different, it could be worth trying one of the extra-cost, small venues QSine or Tuscan Grille.

INSIGHT GUIDES' RATINGS	Achieved	Possible
Ship	354	500
Accommodation	148	200
Food	255	400
Service	238	400
Entertainment	71	100
Cruise Experience	240	400
OVERALL SCORE	**1306**	**2000**

CELEBRITY REFLECTION
★★★★

Size..Large Resort Ship
Tonnage..126,366
Cruise Line.. Celebrity Cruises
Former Names .... *None*
Entered Service 2012
Total Crew 1,271
Passengers 3,046

This premium-quality ship oozes contemporary style and has a nicely balanced look. Behind its two funnels is a lawn club, with real grass for barefoot walking! Several pool and water play areas inhabit the Resort Deck. Interior spaces are well designed, and elevator call buttons are neatly housed in a floor-stand pod for easy use. Accommodation is both practical and comfortable, with numerous sizes and grades. Several restaurants feature creative cuisine that is slightly healthier than many ships (do try Qsine, with 80 seats, standing out as a quirky but fun eating experience). Spa facilities are extensive, but treatments are expensive. However, intrusive background music is played almost everywhere – even in the sauna.

INSIGHT GUIDES' RATINGS	Achieved	Possible
Ship	390	500
Accommodation	160	200
Food	260	400
Service	261	400
Entertainment	74	100
Cruise Experience	260	400
OVERALL SCORE	**1405**	**2000**

CELEBRITY SILHOUETTE
★★★+

Size	Large Resort Ship
Tonnage	122,210
Cruise Line	Celebrity Cruises
Former Names	None
Entered Service	2011
Total Crew	1,210
Passengers	2,886

This family-friendly, stylish resort ship has good facilities overall, but lacks a walk-around outdoor promenade deck. Several pools and water-play areas include one under a glass-roofed solarium. The interior spaces are well designed, with most public venues forward, and dining venues aft. One standout space is the open-ended library. There are numerous cabin grades, depending on size and location, but drawer and storage space is modest in most. Penthouse suites are the largest, with abundant space, larger balconies, and better personal care items. Suite occupants dine in Luminae, while most eat in the large cruise-fare inclusive Silhouette. Extra-cost venues such as Tuscan Grille and QSine may also be worth trying.

INSIGHT GUIDES' RATINGS		
	Achieved	Possible
Ship	387	500
Accommodation	159	200
Food	258	400
Service	236	400
Entertainment	73	100
Cruise Experience	255	400
OVERALL SCORE	**1368**	**2000**

CELEBRITY SOLSTICE
★★★+

Size	Large Resort Ship
Tonnage	121,878
Cruise Line	Celebrity Cruises
Former Names	None
Entered Service	2008
Total Crew	1,210
Passengers	2,852

This is a fairly sleek-looking, comfortable, family-friendly large resort ship, with reasonable open deck space, although much is taken up by swimming pools and water play areas. Inside, the decor is contemporary. There are numerous cabin grades, depending on size and location, but drawer and storage space is modest in most. Penthouse suites are the largest, with voluminous space, larger balconies, and better personal care items. Suite occupants eat in the more intimate Luminae. Meals in Grand Epernay (the expansive main dining room) are cruise-fare included, but better in the extra-cost alternative venues, such as in Tuscan Grille (reservations required) and the Lawn Club Grill. An expansive help-yourself Oceanview Café is for casual eats.

INSIGHT GUIDES' RATINGS		
	Achieved	Possible
Ship	386	500
Accommodation	161	200
Food	258	400
Service	243	400
Entertainment	73	100
Cruise Experience	258	400
OVERALL SCORE	**1379**	**2000**

CELEBRITY SUMMIT
★★★+

Size	Mid-size Ship
Tonnage	90,940
Cruise Line	Celebrity Cruises
Former Names	*Summit*
Entered Service	2001
Total Crew	999
Passengers	2,158

This well-designed mid-sized ship has a good amount of open deck space, but there is no walk-around outdoor promenade deck. The interior has understated decor, refreshed in 2019 to bring it more up to date and in line with the newer ships. From viewless interior cabins to expansive balconied suites, the accommodation is well designed, and has good storage space. The large aft Cosmopolitan Restaurant provides decent meals, but they're better in the extra-cost alternative venues, such as in Tuscan Grille (reservations required) and the Lawn Club Grill. The Spa by Canyon Ranch facilities are rather good, and include a 'health bar' for light breakfasts.

INSIGHT GUIDES' RATINGS

	Achieved	Possible
Ship	354	500
Accommodation	148	200
Food	253	400
Service	229	400
Entertainment	70	100
Cruise Experience	240	400
OVERALL SCORE	**1294**	**2000**

CELEBRITY XPEDITION
★★+

Size	Boutique Ship
Tonnage	2,842
Cruise Line	Celebrity Cruises
Former Names	*Sun Bay*
Entered Service	2001, 2022
Total Crew	64
Passengers	90

This contemporary boutique ship could be a really good base from which to explore the Galápagos and its stunning step-back-in-time nature and wildlife up close. The ship itself is comfortable, with mostly small cabins that are purpose-practical, with modest storage space (you won't need many clothes anyway), because most of the time, you will probably spend with nature, and being out and about on excursions. The food is nothing special, but it's quite acceptable. It's all about nature, so conversation and socializing are the evening entertainment. For many, it will prove a unique experience.

INSIGHT GUIDES' RATINGS

	Achieved	Possible
Ship	261	500
Accommodation	129	200
Food	221	400
Service	185	400
Entertainment	40	100
Cruise Experience	185	400
OVERALL SCORE	**1021**	**2000**

CELESTYAL CRYSTAL
★★+

Size	Mid-size Ship
Tonnage	25,611
Cruise Line	Celestyal Cruises
Former Names	*Louis Crystal, Silja Opera, SuperStar Taurus, Leeward, Sally Albatros, Viking Saga*
Entered Service	1980, 2007
Total Crew	400
Passengers	966

This former passenger ferry has a wedge-shaped profile, and a walk-around outdoor deck. It is a high-density ship, and lacks a forward-view lounge, but there are several public rooms, lounges, bars, a large duty-free shop, and a casino – all good for short-cruise itineraries for families with children. The suites have ample storage space and bathrooms with bathtub, but most other cabins are dimensionally-challenged. Olympus, the main dining room, has mostly two seatings. It features regional cuisine, and spa and vegetarian meals are available. There is also a buffet venue for casual meals. Overall, this is a good way to get to several islands in a short time, in a well-orchestrated cruise.

INSIGHT GUIDES' RATINGS

	Achieved	Possible
Ship	257	500
Accommodation	107	200
Food	202	400
Service	166	400
Entertainment	50	100
Cruise Experience	188	400
OVERALL SCORE	**970**	**2000**

CELESTYAL OLYMPIA
★★+

Size	Mid-size Ship
Tonnage	37,773
Cruise Line	Celestyal Cruises
Former Names	*Louis Olympia, Thomson Destiny, Sunbird, Song of America*
Entered Service	1982, 2012
Total Crew	540
Passengers	1450

Instantly recognisable for its wrap-around lounge around the ship's funnel, this dated ship (originally built for Royal Caribbean Cruises) is practical for Greek island cruises. There are two small swim pools on the open deck (one for adults, one for children), but sunbathing space is tight with a full ship. The interior decor is bright and breezy, and most public rooms have reasonably high ceilings. From viewless interior cabins to those designated as suites, all are ultra-compact, have little closet and drawer space (only suites have a refrigerator), and most have fixed beds. All have small, but manageable bathrooms (a small number have a bathtub). Mediterranean cuisine is provided in the Aegean Restaurant. Overall, it is a well-packaged cruise.

INSIGHT GUIDES' RATINGS

	Achieved	Possible
Ship	269	500
Accommodation	100	200
Food	204	400
Service	169	400
Entertainment	50	100
Cruise Experience	181	400
OVERALL SCORE	**973**	**2000**

CLUB MED 2
★★+

Size	Small Ship
Tonnage	14,983
Cruise Line	Club Med
Former Names	None
Entered Service	1992
Total Crew	214
Passengers	372

One of a pair of the world's largest high-tech sail-cruisers (the other is *Wind Surf*), with computer-controlled sails, while, an aft marina platform provides access to an array of water sports facilities. This is casual French style everywhere. Almost all cabins are of the same size and nicely outfitted, with blond wood decor and refrigerator (there are also five larger suites). The Le Magellan dining room has tables for two to eight, and open seating, so you sit with whom you wish. Le Mediterranee has a pleasant open terrace for informal meals. The food is quite decent, and wines and beers are complimentary. Spa facilities are minimal. Overall it is comfortable, but becoming dated.

INSIGHT GUIDES' RATINGS	Achieved	Possible
Ship	303	500
Accommodation	125	200
Food	218	400
Service	170	400
Entertainment	50	100
Cruise Experience	193	400
OVERALL SCORE	**1059**	**2000**

CORAL ADVENTURER
★★+

Size	Boutique Ship
Tonnage	5,599
Cruise Line	Coral Expeditions
Former Names	None
Entered Service	2019
Total Crew	48
Passengers	120

This very small Australian-owned ship debuted in 2019 and carries just 120 passengers, taking you up-close and personal to nature, but it is *not* an expedition ship as marketed. However, its size advantage means no queues. There is one comfortable lounge, and public areas feature Australian Indigenous art. The door-lock-less cabins are modestly comfortable. Two balconied 'suites' are sizeable, and bathrooms come with bathtubs. All cabins have a USB socket, and pre-paid Internet cards are available, although connection is unreliable. Meals are nicely presented in the compact dining room (with no assigned seating), and fresh seasonal produce is a key ingredient. Selected beers, wines, and spirits come with lunch and dinner.

INSIGHT GUIDES' RATINGS	Achieved	Possible
Ship	212	500
Accommodation	117	200
Food	259	400
Service	235	400
Entertainment	40	100
Cruise Experience	223	400
OVERALL SCORE	**1086**	**2000**

CORAL GEOGRAPHER
★★+

Size.. Boutique Ship
Tonnage...5,599
Cruise Line..Coral Expeditions
Former Names .... None
Entered Service 2021
Total Crew 48
Passengers 120

Sister ship to the *Coral Adventurer*, it was launched by Australian-based Coral Expeditions in 2021 for up-close and personal sailing to coastal areas and nature, but it is also *not* an expedition ship as marketed. It has one comfortable lounge, and public areas feature Australian Indigenous art. The door-lock-less cabins are modestly comfortable. Two balconied 'suites' are sizeable, and bathrooms come with bathtubs. All cabins have a USB socket, and pre-paid Internet cards are available, although connection is unreliable. Meals are nicely presented in the compact no assigned seating dining room, and fresh seasonal produce is a key ingredient. Selected beers, wines, and spirits come with lunch and dinner.

INSIGHT GUIDES' RATINGS		
	Achieved	Possible
Ship	216	500
Accommodation	117	200
Food	260	400
Service	237	400
Entertainment	40	100
Cruise Experience	225	400
OVERALL SCORE	**1095**	**2000**

CORAL PRINCESS
★★★

Size..Mid-Size Ship
Tonnage...91,627
Cruise Line..Princess Cruises
Former Names .... None
Entered Service 2002
Total Crew 900
Passengers 1,974

Sister to *Island Princess*, it is instantly recognisable for its two (mainly decorative) jet engine like pods sitting high up the ship's funnel. There are two whole decks full of lounges, bars, and other public rooms, but there are also several nooks and crannies – good for hiding away and reading a book. Forward, mid-ship, and aft stairways make access to anywhere fairly easy There are two main dining rooms, both with low ceilings. Food portions are generous, but this is banquet-style catering, with few green vegetables and an over-abundance of sauces. Colorful Hollywood-style shows are presented in the Princess Theater. Overall, it offers a well-packaged vacation in a comfortable environment, for mature-age cruisegoers.

INSIGHT GUIDES' RATINGS		
	Achieved	Possible
Ship	326	500
Accommodation	128	200
Food	243	400
Service	213	400
Entertainment	70	100
Cruise Experience	239	400
OVERALL SCORE	**1219**	**2000**

CORDELIA EMPRESS
★★+

Size	Mid-size Ship
Tonnage	48,563
Cruise Line	Cordelia Cruises
Former Names	Empress, Pullmantur Empress, Empress of the Seas, Nordic Empress
Entered Service	1990, 2021
Total Crew	671
Passengers	1,592

Although it has been well maintained by its several previous owners, this is a dated ship, with retro 1970s decor. Public rooms include lounges, bars, and shops. The cabins, many of which are the same size, are very small, with limited closet and drawer space. Located at the back of the ship, with large picture windows, the bi-level Starlight Restaurant is the main dining venue. Chopstix is an extra-cost venue featuring Chinese and other pan-Asian cuisines, while Windjammer Café is a casual, self-serve venue, for pan-Asian food items, tandoor specialities, and an international buffet. Vegetarian and Jain cuisine items are also available (but must be ordered in advance). One of the shows is at extra cost.

INSIGHT GUIDES' RATINGS

	Achieved	Possible
Ship	222	500
Accommodation	122	200
Food	230	400
Service	200	400
Entertainment	50	100
Cruise Experience	209	400
OVERALL SCORE	**1033**	**2000**

COSTA ATLANTICA
★★+

Size	Mid-size Ship
Tonnage	85,619
Cruise Line	Costa Cruises
Former Names	None
Entered Service	2000
Total Crew	902
Passengers	2,218

This lively family-friendly ship (sister to Costa Mediterranea) oozes Italian style. The interior design pays homage to Italy's great art and past masters. A winding shopping street has boutique stores, library, card room (with striking red/gold decor), and more, but several pillars obstruct passenger flow. About 80 percent of all cabins have an outside view; most have limited storage space and small bathrooms. Perhaps the best balcony suites are at the stern and face aft. Dining is in the large bi-level Tiziano Dining Room. The carbohydrate-rich food is mostly disappointing, with a few exceptions. There's a fine three-deck showlounge for production shows and cabaret acts. The Ischia Spa spans two decks and has body-pampering treatments.

INSIGHT GUIDES' RATINGS

	Achieved	Possible
Ship	325	500
Accommodation	124	200
Food	196	400
Service	185	400
Entertainment	55	100
Cruise Experience	197	400
OVERALL SCORE	**1082**	**2000**

COSTA DELIZIOSA
★★★

Size	Mid-size Ship
Tonnage	92,700
Cruise Line	Costa Cruises
Former Names	None
Entered Service	2010
Total Crew	1,050
Passengers	2,260

This family-friendly ship with a distinctive yellow and blue funnel was named in Dubai with date juice (not champagne), as the first new cruise ship naming ceremony in an Arab city. The marble/interior decor pays tribute to the senses – note that 'wallpaper' music is played 24/7. Although they are small, almost 70 percent of cabins and (the larger) suites have an outside view. All have twin beds convertible to queen size, and include a vanity desk with built-in hairdryer. The Albatros main dining room features carbohydrate-rich meals, including many different types of pasta made onboard. There are two smaller (cost-extra) venues – Club Deliziosa and Samsara. Overall, it promises to be a lively cruise experience in colorful surroundings.

INSIGHT GUIDES' RATINGS		
	Achieved	Possible
Ship	372	500
Accommodation	135	200
Food	219	400
Service	199	400
Entertainment	62	100
Cruise Experience	216	400
OVERALL SCORE	**1203**	**2000**

COSTA DIADEMA
★★★

Size	Large Resort Ship
Tonnage	132,500
Cruise Line	Costa Cruises
Former Names	None
Entered Service	2014
Total Crew	1,253
Passengers	3,708

This ship (its name means 'tiara') is really like a seaside Italian town, with all its attendant busy-ness and volume, but it really can be a lot of fun for Italian families with children. Easily identified by its bolt upright yellow funnel, the ship is equipped with 'cold-iron technology' that can access shoreside power. It has a 1,640ft (500m) walk-around outdoor promenade deck and the interior decor is rather bold and bright. There are multiple restaurants and eateries (some cost extra), but the main restaurant is the cavernous, aft-located Restaurant Sissi. The food is Continental European, including some regional dishes and multiple types of pasta. For entertainment, the 1,500-seat Emerald Theatre is spread over three decks.

INSIGHT GUIDES' RATINGS		
	Achieved	Possible
Ship	374	500
Accommodation	135	200
Food	219	400
Service	199	400
Entertainment	62	100
Cruise Experience	217	400
OVERALL SCORE	**1206**	**2000**

COSTA FASCINOSA
★★★

Size	Large Resort Ship
Tonnage	113,216
Cruise Line	Costa Cruises
Former Names	None
Entered Service	2012
Total Crew	1,100
Passengers	3,014

This family-friendly ship is full of life and Italian flair, although there are few Italian crew members. Inside is an atrium lobby spanning three decks, and a whole range of colorful public rooms. The Il Gattopardo and Otto e Mezzo main restaurants provide an abundance of carbohydrate-rich food, best described as low to adequate quality, with little variety (although the pasta dishes are decent enough), and very few green vegetables. Club Fascinosa is a cost-extra small restaurant, providing better food and service. Be aware of the many hidden costs (such as water with meals) when taking a cruise aboard this ship. The spa facilities are decent, but almost everything is at extra cost.

INSIGHT GUIDES' RATINGS

	Achieved	Possible
Ship	369	500
Accommodation	134	200
Food	219	400
Service	195	400
Entertainment	60	100
Cruise Experience	214	400
OVERALL SCORE	**1191**	**2000**

COSTA FAVOLOSA
★★★

Size	Large Resort Ship
Tonnage	113,216
Cruise Line	Costa Cruises
Former Names	None
Entered Service	2011
Total Crew	1,100
Passengers	3,014

A close sister to *Costa Serena*, this ship has a single, large funnel and a decent amount of open deck space. Outside, the pool areas can be covered by a glass dome, and there is a large movie screen. Three decks are full of bars, lounges, shops, and eateries. From two-bed viewless interior cabins to larger, outside-view cabins and spa suites, all are decent enough, although storage space is limited. Duke of Burgundy and Duke of Orleans are the main dining rooms. The cuisine is carbohydrate-rich, but includes some regional Italian dishes. The showlounge hosts high-energy production shows and cabaret. Families like Costa for its perceived 'Italian' style and facilities for kids, but there are many smokers and cost-extra items.

INSIGHT GUIDES' RATINGS

	Achieved	Possible
Ship	369	500
Accommodation	134	200
Food	229	400
Service	220	400
Entertainment	50	100
Cruise Experience	214	400
OVERALL SCORE	**1216**	**2000**

COSTA FIRENZE
★★★

Size	Large Resort Ship
Tonnage	136,156
Cruise Line	Costa Cruises
Former Names	None
Entered Service	2021
Total Crew	1,278
Passengers	4,232

Contemporary and stylishly loud (originally destined for the Asian cruise market, including a larger than normal casino), with upbeat surroundings and a decor design focus on Florence, and entertainment for the whole family. The accommodation varies from interior (no-view) cabins to grand suites with balcony. All have cubicle showers (two suites have a bathtub). The two large main dining rooms have ho-hum mass catering food with a big focus on pasta dishes. Pay extra and you can eat in one of the smaller, more specialized venues with cooked-to-order food. The Viareggio Lounge hosts the entertainment, with so-so shows. In 2024 this ship will become *Carnival Firenze*.

INSIGHT GUIDES' RATINGS

	Achieved	Possible
Ship	380	500
Accommodation	135	200
Food	220	400
Service	199	400
Entertainment	62	100
Cruise Experience	227	400
OVERALL SCORE	**1223**	**2000**

COSTA FORTUNA
★★★

Size	Large Resort Ship
Tonnage	102,587
Cruise Line	Costa Cruises
Former Names	None
Entered Service	2003
Total Crew	1,068
Passengers	2,716

This is a family-friendly floating resort, with interior decor focusing on Italian passenger ships of yesteryear. Three decks are full of lounges, eateries and bars, almost all of which have coffee machines. The accommodation ranges from two-bed interior (no-view) cabins to eight grand suites with private balconies. Some cabins have portholes instead of windows. Michelangelo and Raffaello are the two main dining rooms; both span two decks, with two meal seatings. The cuisine is Italian and rather carbohydrate-rich, with many pasta dishes. Has a stunning three-deck showlounge, and a large spa with decent facilities. Overall, it will be a lively sea-cation.

INSIGHT GUIDES' RATINGS

	Achieved	Possible
Ship	367	500
Accommodation	134	200
Food	219	400
Service	196	400
Entertainment	60	100
Cruise Experience	214	400
OVERALL SCORE	**1190**	**2000**

COSTA MEDITERRANEA
★★★

Size.. Mid-size Ship
Tonnage...85,700
Cruise Line.......................................Costa Cruises
Former Names .... *None*
Entered Service 2003
Total Crew 920
Passengers 2,112

This ship has a balanced exterior profile, with a large yellow Costa funnel. One of the two outdoor swimming pools has a retractable glass roof for use in inclement weather. Inside, the Italian decor is upbeat and vibrant for families, and there's a wide range of public rooms. The carbohydrate-rich food (think 50 ways of pasta) is so-so in the 1,320-seat Restaurante degli Argentieri (main dining room), but try the small extra-cost Club Medusa for a more upscale experience. An expansive Ischia Spa spans two decks and is good. Overall, this is vibrant cruising Italian style, and then some, but be aware of the many cost-extra items.

INSIGHT GUIDES' RATINGS

	Achieved	Possible
Ship	350	500
Accommodation	130	200
Food	212	400
Service	192	400
Entertainment	60	100
Cruise Experience	211	400
OVERALL SCORE	**1155**	**2000**

COSTA PACIFICA
★★★

Size...Large Resort Ship
Tonnage..114,500
Cruise Line.......................................Costa Cruises
Former Names .... *None*
Entered Service 2009
Total Crew 1,100
Passengers 3,012

This really is a lively family-friendly floating Italian resort, with two swimming pools – one coverable by retractable dome in inclement weather. Its atrium lobby spans nine decks, with 'greatest hits' music-themed decor. The accommodation ranges from small viewless interior cabins to eight balconied Grand Suites. New York and My Way are the two large (included in the cruise fare) restaurants. The pasta-rich cuisine is carbo-heavy, and vegetables are scarce. There are separate restaurants for suite occupants, with better cooked-to-order food. For a treat, it may be worthwhile to pay extra to eat in the small, elegant, reservations-required, Club Restaurant Blue Moon.

INSIGHT GUIDES' RATINGS

	Achieved	Possible
Ship	367	500
Accommodation	134	200
Food	219	400
Service	196	400
Entertainment	60	100
Cruise Experience	211	400
OVERALL SCORE	**1187**	**2000**

COSTA SERENA
★★★

Size	Large Resort Ship
Tonnage	114,147
Cruise Line	Costa Cruises
Former Names	*None*
Entered Service	2007
Total Crew	1090
Passengers	3,000

Upbeat and funky Italian decor abounds aboard this lively ship for families. Three decks of bars, lounges, and shops, and a nine-deck-high atrium lounge provide ample choice. Ceres and Vesta are the two expansive bi-deck main dining rooms, allocated by your cabin grade. The carbo-heavy pasta-rich cuisine lacks vegetables, and sauce-covered fish dishes are disappointing, so, overall, meals are mostly non-memorable (vegetarian dishes are available). Better, cooked-to-order cuisine is provided in the small cost-extra Bacco Club, while there are separate restaurants for suite occupants, with higher quality food. Overall, this is vibrant cruising Italian style, but be aware of the many cost-extra items.

INSIGHT GUIDES' RATINGS

	Achieved	Possible
Ship	367	500
Accommodation	134	200
Food	218	400
Service	196	400
Entertainment	60	100
Cruise Experience	210	400
OVERALL SCORE	**1185**	**2000**

COSTA SMERALDA
★★★+

Size	Large Resort Ship
Tonnage	185,010
Cruise Line	Costa Cruises
Former Names	*None*
Entered Service	2019
Total Crew	1,678
Passengers	5,224

One of the largest ships in the Costa Cruises fleet, this big, bold, casual, colorful, and extremely lively family-friendly floating Italian resort has hybrid dual-fuel technology. A super-large Splash AquaPark has multiple attractions for children, but there is little open sunbathing space for adults. The accommodation ranges from very small interior view-less cabins to larger aft-facing balconied suites. The two large, main dining rooms (La Columbina and il Meneghino) each has two seatings for dinner, but service is erratic and disjointed. The cuisine is carbohydrate-rich, with several types of pasta made aboard daily. There are also several small food venues and casual eateries (some cost extra, but are overpriced).

INSIGHT GUIDES' RATINGS

	Achieved	Possible
Ship	388	500
Accommodation	136	200
Food	220	400
Service	195	400
Entertainment	62	100
Cruise Experience	260	400
OVERALL SCORE	**1261**	**2000**

COSTA TOSCANA
★★★+

Size	Large Resort Ship
Tonnage	185,010
Cruise Line	Costa Cruises
Former Names	None
Entered Service	2022
Total Crew	1,678
Passengers	5,322

Big, bold, and colorful, this ship is one of largest in the Costa Cruises fleet, and has hybrid dual-fuel technology for emissions reduction. It is a casual, and lively ship for Italian family cruising, featuring a large Splash AquaPark with multiple attractions for youngsters. The accommodation ranges from small interior (no-view) cabins to larger balconied aft-facing suites. The two large main dining rooms (il Meneghino and il Rugantino) feature carbohydrate-rich meals, with multiple types of pasta made onboard, but service is mostly disjointed. There are numerous small eateries, but in almost all there is a distinct lack of green vegetables.

INSIGHT GUIDES' RATINGS	Achieved	Possible
Ship	390	500
Accommodation	136	200
Food	220	400
Service	195	400
Entertainment	62	100
Cruise Experience	262	400
OVERALL SCORE	**1265**	**2000**

CROWN PRINCESS
★★★+

Size	Large Resort Ship
Tonnage	116,000
Cruise Line	Princess Cruises
Former Names	None
Entered Service	2006
Total Crew	800
Passengers	3,114

This comfortable ship offers many lounges and open deck facilities, plus some cost-extra dining options. Outdoors, a sheltered walking deck almost wraps around the ship, with a walkway leading to the enclosed bows. The outdoor swimming pools have quasi-beach like surroundings, and include a Movies Under the Skies movie screen forward of the funnel. Inside, the decor is attractive, with abundant earthy tones. There are three main dining rooms, each divided into multi-tier sections. The meals are typical of production cooking, with few green vegetables and many things disguised by sauces. For something different, try Crown Grill or Sabatini's. The production shows in the Princess Theater are colorful and entertaining.

INSIGHT GUIDES' RATINGS	Achieved	Possible
Ship	357	500
Accommodation	139	200
Food	247	400
Service	239	400
Entertainment	74	100
Cruise Experience	243	400
OVERALL SCORE	**1299**	**2000**

CRYSTAL SERENITY
★★★★

Size	Mid-size Ship
Tonnage	68,870
Cruise Line	Crystal Cruises
Former Names	None
Entered Service	2003
Total Crew	650
Passengers	980

This close sister to *Crystal Symphony* is a well-built, spacious, extremely comfortable, and elegant ship. There is abundant open deck, sunning, and sports space. Inside, a range of elegant public rooms with high ceilings includes Palm Court, reminiscent of Colonial-style grand hotel lounges. From the smallest to the largest, all cabins and suites have plenty of closet and drawer space. More Penthouse Suites were added in a 2022 makeover. Waterside Restaurant is its comfortable main, open-seating dining room, with many tables for two, as well as larger tables. Smaller cost-extra venues are also available. It's a pleasant ship for the genteel cruisegoer.

INSIGHT GUIDES' RATINGS		
	Achieved	Possible
Ship	417	500
Accommodation	154	200
Food	309	400
Service	272	400
Entertainment	81	100
Cruise Experience	307	400
OVERALL SCORE	**1540**	**2000**

CRYSTAL SYMPHONY
★★★★

Size	Mid-size Ship
Tonnage	51,044
Cruise Line	Crystal Cruises
Former Names	None
Entered Service	1995
Total Crew	545
Passengers	848

This spacious older ship has nicely balanced lines, and a nicely-raked clipper bow. There is abundant open deck and sunbathing space, and a wide walk-around outdoor deck. Inside, high-ceilinged public rooms provide the intimate feeling of spaciousness found aboard small ships, with contemporary – and not brash – decor and surroundings. Its Palm Court observation lounge is a delightful, tranquil place for relaxation. From a range of large suites to the smallest cabin, all are extremely well designed and fitted out, with abundant closet and drawer space, and refined decor (more Penthouse Suites, with large bathrooms, were created in a 2022 makeover). With no sense of crowding anywhere, this ship has a high degree of comfort.

INSIGHT GUIDES' RATINGS		
	Achieved	Possible
Ship	376	500
Accommodation	132	200
Food	305	400
Service	268	400
Entertainment	80	100
Cruise Experience	297	400
OVERALL SCORE	**1458**	**2000**

DEUTSCHLAND
★★★+

Size	Small Ship
Tonnage	22,400
Cruise Line	Phoenix Reisen
Former Names	None
Entered Service	1998, 2022
Total Crew	270
Passengers	552

This dated small ship has a large squat, angular funnel and plenty of open deck space. The interior decor recreates the atmosphere of ocean liners of the 1920s. Favorite haunts include the Zum Alten Fritz Bar for its Belle Epoque ambiance, and the Lili Marleen Saloon, for its lovely mahogany channeled ceiling. Most cabins are disappointingly small, but closet and drawer space is generous, and the bathrooms are nicely appointed. The main 300-seat restaurant, Berlin, serves decent food. Restaurant Vierjahreszeiten (Four Seasons) is for suite occupants and à la carte diners. The pleasant spa on Deck 3 includes an indoor pool. For entertainment, Kaisersaal (Emperor's Saloon) is a galleried room with rich red seating.

INSIGHT GUIDES' RATINGS

	Achieved	Possible
Ship	380	500
Accommodation	122	200
Food	280	400
Service	220	400
Entertainment	56	100
Cruise Experience	221	400
OVERALL SCORE	**1279**	**2000**

DIAMOND PRINCESS
★★★+

Size	Large Resort Ship
Tonnage	115,875
Cruise Line	Princess Cruises
Former Names	None
Entered Service	2004
Total Crew	1,100
Passengers	2,670

This large sea-going resort was built in Japan, and could be good for all ages, with numerous public areas. The interior decor is quietly attractive, with abundant earthy tones. The focal point is a piazza-style atrium with numerous public rooms off it. The five main dining rooms are either assigned (according to your cabin grade) or 'anytime dining'. Cuisine is quite standardized (batch cooking), with few garnishes. Sterling Steakhouse and Kai Sushi are cost-extra venues to try for something different, and cooked to order. Glamorous production shows are featured in the Princess Theater. The Lotus Spa has Japanese-style decor, but I recommend that spa lovers go to Izumi, a separate Japanese onsen-style spa, which is delightful.

INSIGHT GUIDES' RATINGS

	Achieved	Possible
Ship	357	500
Accommodation	139	200
Food	253	400
Service	233	400
Entertainment	77	100
Cruise Experience	255	400
OVERALL SCORE	**1314**	**2000**

DISCOVERY PRINCESS
★★★+

Size	Large Resort Ship
Tonnage	141,000
Cruise Line	Princess Cruises
Former Names	None
Entered Service	2022
Total Crew	1,346
Passengers	3,560

This large, family-friendly multi-choice contemporary resort-style ship lacks a walk-around outdoor deck, but has 'The Sea-Walk' extending out over the water, and a decent amount of open deck space. The Sanctuary (an adults-only retreat) includes private cabanas, a swimming pool and relaxation zones. The multi-faceted social hub, the Piazza Atrium, has twin horse-shoe-shaped stairways. Five main accommodation types are in numerous price grades, but book suite-grade accommodation and you gain access to a private Concierge Lounge. The main restaurant features standardized meals, but pay extra and you can eat in the Crown Grill (for steaks), or Sabatini's (Italian). For colorful shows, the venue is the 1,000-seat Princess Theater.

INSIGHT GUIDES' RATINGS	Achieved	Possible
Ship	415	500
Accommodation	153	200
Food	220	400
Service	215	400
Entertainment	90	100
Cruise Experience	295	400
OVERALL SCORE	**1388**	**2000**

DISNEY DREAM
★★★+

Size	Mid-size Ship
Tonnage	129,690
Cruise Line	Disney Cruise Line
Former Names	None
Entered Service	2011
Total Crew	1,458
Passengers	2,500

Made of pieces of steel and pixie dust, plus Never-Never-land magic and story-telling fairy-tale mystique – delightful family-friendly cruising is what this ship is all about. Colorful characters and special animatronics are everywhere, themed to Disney films. Favorites include the Oceaneer Club and Star Wars: Cargo Bay area. Adult-only areas are good, too (with separate entertainment venues), and the accommodation, which consists of nine types of suites and cabins, is practical and well thought-out. There are three main dining rooms (you move to a different one each day), each with a different Disney-themed decor, plus Remy, an adults-only extra-cost venue. It really is a floating travel adventure for all.

INSIGHT GUIDES' RATINGS	Achieved	Possible
Ship	387	500
Accommodation	151	200
Food	212	400
Service	219	400
Entertainment	88	100
Cruise Experience	287	400
OVERALL SCORE	**1344**	**2000**

DISNEY FANTASY
★★★+

Size	Mid-size Ship
Tonnage	129,690
Cruise Line	Disney Cruise Line
Former Names	*None*
Entered Service	2012
Total Crew	1,458
Passengers	2,500

This family-friendly floating magical theme park has something for everyone, and is designed like the ocean liners of the 1930s. One wow factor is AquaDuck, a 765ft (233m) water coaster spanning four decks. Disney whimsy and Art Deco style are everywhere, and a bronze statue of Admiral Donald (Duck) himself stands in the main lobby. The suites and cabins are well designed. All bathrooms have round tubs with pull-down seat and hand-held shower hose for bathing little ones. Each day, you rotate through one of three main dining venues, each with identical seating, but different themed decor. Adults can also choose Remy, a cost-extra venue. Superb Disney shows are seen in the large Walt Disney Theater.

INSIGHT GUIDES' RATINGS	Achieved	Possible
Ship	387	500
Accommodation	151	200
Food	213	400
Service	219	400
Entertainment	88	100
Cruise Experience	290	400
OVERALL SCORE	**1348**	**2000**

DISNEY MAGIC
★★★+

Size	Mid-size Ship
Tonnage	83,338
Cruise Line	Disney Cruise Line
Former Names	*None*
Entered Service	1998
Total Crew	945
Passengers	1,750

This is the first cruise ship built with two funnels (one is a dummy, but includes a teen center) since the 1950s. An Aqua-Dunk waterslide is a real thrill ride. This delightful fairy-tale sea-going Never-Never Land has decor reminiscent of yesteryear's ocean liners. There is much Disney detailing on handrails in the three-deck-high main lobby, and a bronze 6ft (1.8m) Mickey Mouse helmsman. Accommodation is designed for families (the steamer trunk closets are neat), and many bathrooms have small bathtubs. Three main dining venues have daily rotational dining, with different themed decor. Adults can also choose Remy, a cost-extra venue. The large-scale shows in the showlounge are outstanding.

INSIGHT GUIDES' RATINGS	Achieved	Possible
Ship	368	500
Accommodation	143	200
Food	205	400
Service	215	400
Entertainment	86	100
Cruise Experience	280	400
OVERALL SCORE	**1297**	**2000**

DISNEY TREASURE
NYR

Size.. Mid-size Ship
Tonnage...145,281
Cruise Line..............................Disney Cruise Line
Former Names .... None
Entered Service 2024
Total Crew..1,555
Passengers...2,500

Disney Imagineers' LNG-powered floating theme park will weave its magic on the whole family, with Aladdin, Jasmine, and their Magic Carpet gracing the Grand Hall, and special Disney film themed animatronics and colorful characters everywhere. In separate areas for adults and youngsters, the decor is reminiscent of yesteryear's ocean liners. From viewless interior cabins to expansive balconied suites, all are designed for families; many have bathtubs. Three main dining venues have themed decor and identical seating. Adults can also choose Remy, a cost-extra reservations-required venue specializing in Italian-style meals. For Disney's family shows, head to the expansive Buena Vista Theater.

INSIGHT GUIDES' RATINGS		
	Achieved	Possible
Ship	NYR	500
Accommodation	NYR	200
Food	NYR	400
Service	NYR	400
Entertainment	NYR	100
Cruise Experience	NYR	400
OVERALL SCORE	**NYR**	**2000**

DISNEY WISH
★★★+

Size.. Mid-size Ship
Tonnage...144,000
Cruise Line..............................Disney Cruise Line
Former Names .... None
Entered Service 2022
Total Crew..1,555
Passengers...2,500

This LNG-powered sea-going theme park features yesteryear ocean liner design. It has separate areas for adults and children. Standouts include a dual-seat AquaMouse water coaster, and Star Wars Hyperspace Lounge, and look for Aladdin and his magic carpet in the main foyer. From viewless interior cabins to expansive balconied suites (plus a two-deck Wish Tower Suite in the second funnel), all are designed for families, and many have bathtubs for small children. Arendelle, Worlds of Marvel, and 1923 are the three main restaurants. Cost-extra eateries include Palo Steakhouse, for Wagyu beef steaks, and Chef Arnaud Lallement's Enchanté. Outstanding large-scale Disney shows are provided in the Walt Disney Theater.

INSIGHT GUIDES' RATINGS		
	Achieved	Possible
Ship	414	500
Accommodation	153	200
Food	220	400
Service	215	400
Entertainment	88	100
Cruise Experience	295	400
OVERALL SCORE	**1385**	**2000**

DISNEY WONDER
★★★+

Size	Mid-size Ship
Tonnage	85,000
Cruise Line	Disney Cruise Line
Former Names	None
Entered Service	1999
Total Crew	945
Passengers	1,750

This delightful fairy-tale sea-going Never-Never Land is designed in the tradition of real ocean liners of the past, and features story-telling to the 'nth degree, with facilities and entertainment for the whole family. Disney detailing is evident on the handrails in the tri-deck main lobby. Accommodation pricing depends on the type, size, and location chosen, but all are designed for families, with neat steamer trunk closets, and many have small bathtubs for small child washing. Each day, you rotate through one of three main dining venues, each with identical seating but different themed decor. Adults can also choose Remy, a cost-extra venue. The large-scale shows in the showlounge are outstanding.

INSIGHT GUIDES' RATINGS

	Achieved	Possible
Ship	369	500
Accommodation	143	200
Food	205	400
Service	215	400
Entertainment	86	100
Cruise Experience	283	400
OVERALL SCORE	**1301**	**2000**

EMERALD AZURRA
★★★+

Size	Boutique Ship
Tonnage	5,300
Cruise Line	Emerald Cruises
Former Names	None
Entered Service	2022
Total Crew	64
Passengers	96

Built to accommodate just 50 couples, this sleek-looking little ship with upright bows is designed for cruising along the Adriatic coast. It is a world away from large resort ships. There is abundant open deck space, a small aft 'infinity' pool, and an indoor/outdoor café. Most cabins have a simple layout, but include ample electrical outlets and charging points, plenty of storage space, and very comfortable beds. Suites with balconies are generously sized, and have large bathrooms. Amici Lounge includes a bar and coffee machine. La Cucina Restaurant provides decent, uncomplicated meals, although it cannot be called fine dining. Also, note that the drinks package is at an exorbitant extra cost!

INSIGHT GUIDES' RATINGS

	Achieved	Possible
Ship	418	500
Accommodation	153	200
Food	220	400
Service	215	400
Entertainment	90	100
Cruise Experience	298	400
OVERALL SCORE	**1394**	**2000**

EMERALD PRINCESS
★★★+

Size	Large Resort Ship
Tonnage	113,561
Cruise Line	Princess Cruises
Former Names	None
Entered Service	2007
Total Crew	1,200
Passengers	3,114

This family-oriented large ship has an (almost) wrap-around outdoor walking deck, a pool deck with Movies Under the Stars, and a relaxing adults-only cost extra Sanctuary – away from the more crowded spots. Ship lovers might enjoy the wood-panelled Wheelhouse Bar. There is a wide choice of accommodation, and around 100 cabins have family-friendly interconnecting doors. Three main dining rooms (Botticelli, Da Vinci, and Michelangelo) have split sections for a cosy ambiance. The food is standard banquet catering fare, with limited vegetable choices. For food cooked to order, try one of the cost-extra venues. Colorful production shows can be seen in the 800-seat Princess Theatre.

INSIGHT GUIDES' RATINGS

	Achieved	Possible
Ship	359	500
Accommodation	139	200
Food	248	400
Service	235	400
Entertainment	74	100
Cruise Experience	248	400
OVERALL SCORE	**1303**	**2000**

EMERALD SAKURA
NYR

Size	Boutique Ship
Tonnage	5,300
Cruise Line	Emerald Cruises
Former Names	None
Entered Service	2023
Total Crew	64
Passengers	96

Sister to *Emerald Azzurra*, this sleek-looking ship, with upright bows, looks more like a private yacht. It has abundant of open deck space, a small aft 'infinity' pool, and an indoor/outdoor café. Public rooms include a comfortable Horizon Lounge with integral bar (drink prices are high), and a small Observation Lounge. There are also two small elevators. The accommodation is well designed, and includes plenty of storage space, while the ensuite bathrooms have a shower, washbasin, bathrobes, and slippers. Its Reflections Restaurant seats all passengers in one sitting; meals are simple affairs, and soft drinks, beer, and wine are included with lunch and dinner.

INSIGHT GUIDES' RATINGS

	Achieved	Possible
Ship	NYR	500
Accommodation	NYR	200
Food	NYR	400
Service	NYR	400
Entertainment	NYR	100
Cruise Experience	NYR	400
OVERALL SCORE	**NYR**	**2000**

ENCHANTED PRINCESS
★★★+

Size	Large Resort Ship
Tonnage	145,281
Cruise Line	Princess Cruises
Former Names	None
Entered Service	2021
Total Crew	1,346
Passengers	3,660

This family-friendly, contemporary resort-style ship has two over the water 'SeaWalks' extending over the side by 30ft (9.1m), and an adults-only retreat called The Sanctuary, with private cabanas, pool, and relaxation areas. The ship's multi-faceted social hub is the Piazza Atrium, which has two horse-shoe-shaped stairways. There are five main accommodation types in numerous price grades. Booking suite-grade accommodation gains you access to a private Concierge Lounge. The three main restaurants (Amalfi, Capri, and Santorini) provide mostly non-memorable meals, while cost-extra venues include Crown Grill (for steaks) and Sabatini's (Italian). Colorful production shows can be seen in the large Princess Theater.

INSIGHT GUIDES' RATINGS	Achieved	Possible
Ship	412	500
Accommodation	153	200
Food	220	400
Service	214	400
Entertainment	89	100
Cruise Experience	293	400
OVERALL SCORE	**1381**	**2000**

ENCHANTMENT OF THE SEAS
★★★

Size	Mid-size Ship
Tonnage	81,500
Cruise Line	Royal Caribbean International
Former Names	None
Entered Service	1997
Total Crew	840
Passengers	2,252

This mid-size ship, with its aft funnel, had a 'chop and stretch' operation in 2005 that added a new 72.8ft (22.2m) mid-section, more public rooms, cabins, and an enhanced range of things for the whole family. Most cabins are of a similar size, and quite adequate, but certainly nothing special, and with little storage space. For dining, the My Fair Lady main dining room spans two decks. While the cuisine is mostly non-memorable banquet catering, but the presentation is quite decent. For cooked-to-order food, I recommend trying the extra-cost Chops Grille Steakhouse. There are also several other eateries, including an expansive Windjammer Marketplace self-serve buffet-style venue. Although dated, this is a comfortable ship,

INSIGHT GUIDES' RATINGS	Achieved	Possible
Ship	344	500
Accommodation	133	200
Food	220	400
Service	210	400
Entertainment	75	100
Cruise Experience	237	400
OVERALL SCORE	**1219**	**2000**

EURODAM
★★★+

Size	Mid-size Ship
Tonnage	86,273
Cruise Line	Holland America Line
Former Names	None
Entered Service	2008
Total Crew	929
Passengers	2,104

The company's Dutch heritage and style are evident aboard this mid-size ship, designed mainly for families. There are two working funnels (one behind the other) and two engine rooms. Although there is a teak promenade deck, it doesn't quite wrap around the forward section. Most public rooms occupy two decks (except for the four-deck-high showlounge). Accommodation ranges from small interior (no-view) cabins to balconied spa suites. The pleasant, aft-positioned Rembrandt Dining Room spans two decks and hosts most passengers for meals. The food is best described as quite acceptable, but nothing special, and green vegetables are lacking. Worth trying are the extra-cost Pinnacle Grill or Tamarind for pan-Asian cuisine.

INSIGHT GUIDES' RATINGS

	Achieved	Possible
Ship	388	500
Accommodation	144	200
Food	220	400
Service	216	400
Entertainment	72	100
Cruise Experience	259	400
OVERALL SCORE	**1299**	**2000**

EUROPA
★★★★★

Size	Small Ship
Tonnage	28,890
Cruise Line	Hapag-Lloyd Cruises
Former Names	None
Entered Service	1999
Total Crew	280
Passengers	408

This sophisticated and elegant small ship, carries Zodiac landing craft for close-up coastal shore excursions and 20 bicycles for passenger use when the ship is in port. A 2019 refurbishment saw the addition of two new dining venues – The Globe by Kevin Fehling, and Pearls, for seafood, including real caviar – plus the introduction of a more informal dress code and open seating dining, a refreshed atrium, and more contemporary artwork. Several high-ceilinged public rooms are located along a curved 'street' leading aft from the atrium. The Europa Restaurant is a beautiful high-ceilinged dining room, with fine table settings and proper waiter service. Venezia (Italian) and Pearls delight with quality food and service, at no extra cost.

INSIGHT GUIDES' RATINGS

	Achieved	Possible
Ship	463	500
Accommodation	182	200
Food	373	400
Service	309	400
Entertainment	90	100
Cruise Experience	349	400
OVERALL SCORE	**1766**	**2000**

EUROPA 2
★★★★★

Size	Small Ship
Tonnage	42,830
Cruise Line	Hapag-Lloyd Cruises
Former Names	*None*
Entered Service	2013
Total Crew	370
Passengers	516

This ship displays a sleek profile, with its nicely tiered aft decks, and Hapag-Lloyd's signature orange and blue funnel. There is a complete walk-around outdoor deck (unusual for a ship of this size), teak decking almost everywhere, plus nicely polished handrails, all exuding quality. The ship carries a fleet of 12 Zodiac landing craft, all named after Hamburg suburbs. A bi-level pool deck (the pool is heated) has a sliding glass roof to cover the area as needed; when closed it is like a cosy winter garden.

It is all about stylish, relaxed luxury and sophistication, including high-ceilinged public rooms, an outstanding array of artwork, food, and wellness. A specially commissioned grey Steinway piano graces the high-ceilinged atrium lobby.

Its eight accommodation price grades all feature an extra-wide balcony, an excellent amount of closet and drawer space, and large, well-designed bathrooms with high-class baths/showers. Two Owner's Suites, measuring 1,227 sq ft (34 sq m) plus balcony, feature butterfly artwork by Damien Hirst.

With its wide choice of fine dining venues all included, extremely high-quality food and presentation, this ship excels with its culinary fare, while a Miele Culinary School hosts sessions for foodies.

Also, the ship's expansive Ocean Spa is an excellent center for wellbeing. So, for sophisticated international travelers, discerning fine food devotees, and finely-tuned unobtrusive service from an attentive crew, it is, quite simply, the best.

INSIGHT GUIDES' RATINGS		
	Achieved	Possible
Ship	480	500
Accommodation	185	200
Food	373	400
Service	312	400
Entertainment	92	100
Cruise Experience	350	400
OVERALL SCORE	**1792**	**2000**

Daybeds on *Europa 2*'s deck.

EVRIMA
★★★★+

Size	Small Ship
Tonnage	25,401
Cruise Line	Ritz-Carlton Yacht Collection
Former Names	None
Entered Service	2022
Total Crew	246
Passengers	298

This contemporary Ritz-Carlton branded small ship has a well-balanced profile and a marina-style aft platform, but the faux teak decking is rather disappointing. The all-suite accommodation: 310 sq ft/29 sq m to 1,090 sq ft/101 sq m, plus balcony, has queen-sized beds, high-quality linen, and ample storage space. There are several eateries in addition to the main Evrima Room, including Aqua, by three Michelin star chef Sven Elverfeld (think: ultra-expensive wine-paired menu). In general, however, the hotel-style American cuisine is good, but not outstanding. Extra costs apply to faster Internet speeds, Ritz Kids Club, and the S.E.A 'gourmet' dining venue. Cruise fares earn Marriott Bonvoy points, but the redemption factor is poor.

INSIGHT GUIDES' RATINGS

	Achieved	Possible
Ship	428	500
Accommodation	174	200
Food	322	400
Service	280	400
Entertainment	77	100
Cruise Experience	330	400
OVERALL SCORE	**1611**	**2000**

EXPLORA 1
NYR

Size	Mid-size Ship
Tonnage	63,900
Cruise Line	Explora Journeys
Former Names	None
Entered Service	2023
Total Crew	700
Passengers	922

This ship has well-tiered aft decks and a nicely-balanced contemporary look. With four pools (one with a retractable roof), water is the focal point, and 64 bookable cabanas act as private retreats. Taking the best of MSC Yacht Club areas, this ship made them better, in a smaller, dedicated format. Dining is an important part of the journey, and there are several dining venues and eateries, including Sakura Grill (Japanese), Marble & Co. (steaks and grilled food), Fil Rouge (for French tasting cuisine), Med Yacht Club (Mediterranean cuisine), and EMPORIUM Marketplace (an all-day eatery).

INSIGHT GUIDES' RATINGS

	Achieved	Possible
Ship	NYR	500
Accommodation	NYR	200
Food	NYR	400
Service	NYR	400
Entertainment	NYR	100
Cruise Experience	NYR	400
OVERALL SCORE	**NYR**	**2000**

EXPLORER OF THE SEAS
★★★

Size	Large Resort Ship
Tonnage	137,308
Cruise Line	Royal Caribbean International
Former Names	None
Entered Service	2000
Total Crew	1,181
Passengers	3,114

This smart-looking resort ship has an abundance of family-friendly features, and outdoor decks busy with water parks. The interior decor is rainbow colorful. The place to see and be seen is the four-deck Royal Promenade, lined with shops, extra-cost eateries and drinking venues; it is also home to 138 cabins with promenade-view bay windows. Accommodation ranges from small interior (no-view) cabins, to an extra-large Royal Suite, and some 300-plus cabins have family-friendly connecting doors. Meals at the tri-deck Sapphire Dining Room are well prepared and presented, though nothing special. The 1,350-seat Palace Showlounge features colorful production shows, but the constant 'background' music around the ship is irritating.

INSIGHT GUIDES' RATINGS

	Achieved	Possible
Ship	353	500
Accommodation	131	200
Food	222	400
Service	216	400
Entertainment	74	100
Cruise Experience	232	400
OVERALL SCORE	**1228**	**2000**

FRAM
★★+

Size	Small Ship
Tonnage	11,647
Cruise Line	Hurtigruten Expeditions
Former Names	None
Entered Service	2007
Total Crew	75
Passengers	254

This modern, but minimalist ship focuses on discovery-style voyages, and is designed to operate in Polar waters. However, for Antarctica, it is simply oversized, and can still get stuck in heavy pack ice. After its 2019 refurbishment, it is modestly comfortable. Cabins are small, and have little storage space (there are many price categories), particularly for long voyages. They are also not very comfortable for expedition-style voyages (and many have pull-down berths); fortunately, no cabins have obstructed views. The food is modest, with little choice. However, this is all about discoveries, and expedition leaders are there to guide you.

INSIGHT GUIDES' RATINGS

	Achieved	Possible
Ship	338	500
Accommodation	112	200
Food	224	400
Service	162	400
Entertainment	60	100
Cruise Experience	199	400
OVERALL SCORE	**1095**	**2000**

FREEDOM OF THE SEAS
★★★

Size	Large Resort Ship
Tonnage	154,407
Cruise Line	Royal Caribbean International
Former Names	None
Entered Service	2006
Total Crew	1,360
Passengers	3,634

This big and bold, multiple-choice floating theme park (the length of 37 London double-decker buses) has a whole range of family-friendly features. Although the cabins are mostly compact units (note: outside-view cabins have even numbers, interior no-view cabins have odd numbers), the public areas are where the action takes place, although many popular facilities make you sign up (Flowrider surf area, rock-climbing wall, for example). Aside from the large (included) tri-level main dining room, most other (smaller) eateries cost extra. With multiple bars and eateries, and spa facilities, this ship is a veritable seagoing vacation playground, although there are extra costs for many items.

INSIGHT GUIDES' RATINGS

	Achieved	Possible
Ship	353	500
Accommodation	132	200
Food	222	400
Service	230	400
Entertainment	70	100
Cruise Experience	225	400
OVERALL SCORE	**1232**	**2000**

FRIDTJOF NANSEN
★★★

Size	Small Ship
Tonnage	20,889
Cruise Line	Hurtigruten Expeditions
Former Names	None
Entered Service	2020
Total Crew	150
Passengers	530

Named after the polar explorer and scientist Fridtjof Nansen, this ship may suit hardy outdoor types who do not mind a basic level of facilities and comfort. A half-ship walking deck encircles the front. Inside is Scandinavian minimalist decor, with artwork depicting the Arctic and Antarctic areas. Facilities include a lecture room, shop, Internet corner, lobby with reception desk, and video games room. While the suites are decent enough, most cabins are small and have little storage space. Most meals are buffet-style (some dinners have waiter service), and repetitious, but pay extra and you can eat cooked-to-order food in the Lindstrom Restaurant (free for suite occupants). Overall, it is simply a little too large, overhyped, and overpriced.

INSIGHT GUIDES' RATINGS

	Achieved	Possible
Ship	361	500
Accommodation	126	200
Food	232	400
Service	200	400
Entertainment	52	100
Cruise Experience	220	400
OVERALL SCORE	**1191**	**2000**

GENTING DREAM
★★★★

Size	Large Resort Ship
Tonnage	150,695
Cruise Line	Resorts World Cruises
Former Names	None
Entered Service	2016, 2022
Total Crew	2,030
Passengers	3,360

This high-tech ship has plenty of style and pizzazz for youthful Asian families. A 'Wet and Wild Water Park' includes six fun waterslides, and there's a compete walk-around exterior deck. Inside, is an ultra-colorful playground, with extensive casino/gaming facilities that include a private club. This large resort ship has abundant of facilities and extensive entertainment, and excellent health spa facilities and services. From the smallest viewless interior cabins to lavish Dream Suites, it is simply a question of 'pay more, get more.' The main bi-level dining room (Windows) is aft, but there are numerous pay-extra venue and food choices. Glamorous production shows are presented in the multi-deck Zodiac Theatre. It is Asian, through and through.

INSIGHT GUIDES' RATINGS		
	Achieved	Possible
Ship	412	500
Accommodation	153	200
Food	293	400
Service	240	400
Entertainment	84	100
Cruise Experience	286	400
OVERALL SCORE	**1468**	**2000**

GOLDEN HORIZON
NYR

Size	Small Ship
Tonnage	8,770
Cruise Line	DIV Group
Former Names	Flying Clipper
Entered Service	2021
Total Crew	159
Passengers	272

This steel-hulled, large, five mast barquentine tall ship (originally built as *Flying Clipper*) is completely different to 'normal' cruise ships, and features 35 sails, which means that ropes and rigging machinery inhabit the open deck. There is also a marina for watersports craft and equipment. The ship's interiors are stunning, but the stairways are steep. The cabins, and four suites (which feature a fireplace) all have outside views, ample space for luggage, and ensuite bathrooms (many of which have a bathtub). The multi-deck main dining room has a small eye-catching ceiling skylight, and features an open seating. While dinner is served, breakfast and lunch are buffet-style. A small spa includes a sauna, snow room, and hot tub.

INSIGHT GUIDES' RATINGS		
	Achieved	Possible
Ship	NYR	500
Accommodation	NYR	200
Food	NYR	400
Service	NYR	400
Entertainment	NYR	100
Cruise Experience	NYR	400
OVERALL SCORE	**NYR**	**2000**

GRANDEUR OF THE SEAS
★★★

Size	Mid-size Ship
Tonnage	73,817
Cruise Line	Royal Caribbean International
Former Names	*None*
Entered Service	1996
Total Crew	760
Passengers	1,950

This mid-size casual ship has a complete walk-around promenade deck. Inside, the Centrum lobby (main social hub) spans seven decks. Accommodation ranges from compact and dated interior (no view) cabins to a Royal Suite, with large balcony. All have pleasant, Scandinavian-style minimalist decor and twin beds convertible to a double bed (note: there are many interior no-view cabins). Also, the utilitarian bathrooms are small. The bi-level Great Gatsby dining room is included in the cruise fare, and has two seatings, but the food is mostly non-memorable banquet-style catering. There are several other (small) extra-cost eateries. Overall, this ship is better suited to couples, but the constant 'background' music around the ship is annoying.

INSIGHT GUIDES' RATINGS

	Achieved	Possible
Ship	333	500
Accommodation	129	200
Food	218	400
Service	184	400
Entertainment	70	100
Cruise Experience	225	400
OVERALL SCORE	**1159**	**2000**

GRAND PRINCESS
★★★

Size	Large Resort Ship
Tonnage	108,806
Cruise Line	Princess Cruises
Former Names	*None*
Entered Service	1998
Total Crew	1,100
Passengers	2,600

This is a pleasant, but seriously ageing floating resort for families has a flared dolphin-like bow and a galleon-like transom stern. Unfortunately, the outdoor space is rather limited. It has mostly high-ceilinged public rooms and entertainment areas. Wide range of cabins in a bewildering choice of price categories, and some Emerald Deck cabins have lifeboat-obstructed views. The three main dining rooms are included, with cost-extra venues available. Colorful Hollywood-style shows inhabit the two-deck high Princess Theater. Overall, it is pleasant enough, but the ship is approaching its sell-by date.

INSIGHT GUIDES' RATINGS

	Achieved	Possible
Ship	320	500
Accommodation	122	200
Food	240	400
Service	210	400
Entertainment	71	100
Cruise Experience	237	400
OVERALL SCORE	**1200**	**2000**

GREG MORTIMER
★★★

Size.. Boutique Ship
Tonnage..7,892
Cruise Line.. Aurora Expeditions
Former Names .... *None*
Entered Service 2019
Total Crew... 60
Passengers 160

With its novel 'X' bow design for smooth sea-keeping, this specialist expedition-style ship has good close-in expedition-style discovery capabilities. There is a small but decent boot-washing mudroom with storage. Two hot tubs on deck have great views. Non-balcony lower deck cabins have portholes, and cabins with balconies have floor-to-ceiling windows. Accommodation designated as suites are well equipped, with plenty of storage space. Bathrooms in all grades have heated floors. High ceilinged public rooms include a well-integrated lecture room and lounge, with comfortable seating. After dinner conversation is the entertainment.

INSIGHT GUIDES' RATINGS		
	Achieved	Possible
Ship	326	500
Accommodation	127	200
Food	221	400
Service	194	400
Entertainment	44	100
Cruise Experience	205	400
OVERALL SCORE	**1117**	**2000**

HAMBURG
★★+

Size..Small Ship
Tonnage...14,903
Cruise Line.. Plantours
Former Names ....*Columbus*
Entered Service 1997, 2012
Total Crew...120
Passengers 408

This is a pleasant small ship for German speakers with a nicely sloped stern, and an ice-strengthened hull – useful for cold-weather areas. It lacks an exterior walk-around promenade deck, but inside, the public areas are decent enough. Cabins are quite compact, all have a minibar/refrigerator. Few cabins have balconies, and 16 cabins on Deck 4 have lifeboat-obstructed views, but those overlooking the stern are very pleasant. The single-seating Alster Restaurant is comfortable and has large ocean-view windows on three sides. The food is non-memorable, and there is limited choice. The spa facilities are minimal, but, overall, this is a modestly comfortable ship, but is now dated.

INSIGHT GUIDES' RATINGS		
	Achieved	Possible
Ship	289	500
Accommodation	121	200
Food	203	400
Service	180	400
Entertainment	47	100
Cruise Experience	194	400
OVERALL SCORE	**1034**	**2000**

HANSEATIC INSPIRATION
★★★★★

Size .... Boutique Ship
Tonnage 16,100
Cruise Line .... Hapag-Lloyd Cruises
Former Names .... None
Entered Service 2019
Total Crew 170
Passengers 230

This is a superb expedition ship with a hardened hull, designed for up-close-and-personal experiences. The navigation bridge wings can fold inwards for navigation in the Great Lakes (its sister ships do not have them). There is abundant open deck space, and a forward observation deck for observation. Two suites have stunning over-the-sea glass balconies, but all accommodation is well designed, and all come with a heated wall for parkas and towels (thoughtful), coffee machine and stocked minibar. First rate cuisine and relaxed service are the hallmarks of Hapag-Lloyd Expedition Cruises, with a focus on seafood. Meanwhile, the spa has excellent facilities, including sea-view co-ed saunas.

INSIGHT GUIDES' RATINGS		
	Achieved	Possible
Ship	466	500
Accommodation	178	200
Food	353	400
Service	306	400
Entertainment	88	100
Cruise Experience	325	400
OVERALL SCORE	**1716**	**2000**

HANSEATIC NATURE
★★★★★

Size .... Boutique Ship
Tonnage 16,100
Cruise Line .... Hapag-Lloyd Cruises
Former Names .... None
Entered Service 2019
Total Crew 170
Passengers 230

This is probably the benchmark for specialist expedition ships, with an excellent, highly practical design, a very high comfort factor, ultra-fine food, service, and a relaxed environment. Has a dynamic positioning system – vital in polar ice conditions – where anchors cannot be used. You can almost touch the ice from the forward outdoor observation deck. The interior design is all about marine and animal life (a colorful penguin made of recycled plastics from Africa sits in a corner of an indoor-pool – neat! Has port and starboard 'over the sea' walks extending from the ship's sides. The cuisine is creative, with plenty of choice – the seafood is particularly good – and is nicely presented.

INSIGHT GUIDES' RATINGS		
	Achieved	Possible
Ship	466	500
Accommodation	178	200
Food	353	400
Service	306	400
Entertainment	88	100
Cruise Experience	325	400
OVERALL SCORE	**1716**	**2000**

HANSEATIC SPIRIT
★★★★★

Size	Boutique Ship
Tonnage	16,100
Cruise Line	Hapag-Lloyd Cruises
Former Names	*None*
Entered Service	2021
Total Crew	170
Passengers	230

This extremely well-designed expedition ship is of an ideal size for in-depth exploration. It has a dynamic positioning system (vital in polar ice conditions, where anchors cannot be used), and a boot storage room with specialized washing system. Its teak-covered pool deck can be covered in poor weather conditions. High-ceilinged public rooms and wide hallways provide a feeling of spaciousness. From the smallest to the largest (two Grand Suites) there is something to suit all wallets. All have a heated wall for parkas and towels (thoughtful), coffee machine and stocked minibar. First rate cuisine and relaxed service are the hallmarks of Hapag-Lloyd Expedition Cruises, with a focus on seafood.

INSIGHT GUIDES' RATINGS

	Achieved	Possible
Ship	468	500
Accommodation	178	200
Food	353	400
Service	305	400
Entertainment	88	100
Cruise Experience	327	400
OVERALL SCORE	**1719**	**2000**

HARMONY OF THE SEAS
★★★+

Size	Large Resort Ship
Tonnage	226,693
Cruise Line	Royal Caribbean International
Former Names	*None*
Entered Service	2016
Total Crew	2,394
Passengers	5,479

This super-large, vibrant seagoing resort is a stunning vacation center for the whole family, including kids of all ages. It is also more efficient than the first two ships in this series (*Allure of the Seas* and *Oasis of the Seas*). Inside, there's around three dozen bars and lounges to play in, with seven 'neighborhoods' to explore. From the smallest solo-occupancy cabins to the largest (Presidential Suite), there is something for all pockets. The cabin numbering system is confusing, however. The main restaurant is in three sections; food is clever, the production-cooking so-so, but cost-extra items (lobster or steaks) are cooked to order. Extra-cost venues offer more choice. Entertainment is constant. Overall, this is a stunning seagoing resort.

INSIGHT GUIDES' RATINGS

	Achieved	Possible
Ship	403	500
Accommodation	140	200
Food	226	400
Service	231	400
Entertainment	87	100
Cruise Experience	261	400
OVERALL SCORE	**1348**	**2000**

HEBRIDEAN PRINCESS
★★★+

Size	Boutique Ship
Tonnage	2,112
Cruise Line	Hebridean Island Cruises
Former Names	*Columba*
Entered Service	1964, 1989
Total Crew	38
Passengers	50

This charming floating Scottish inn has bucketloads of hospitality and down-home style. Although dated, it just oozes country-house comfort combined with stately home service. It is ideally suited to mature-age adult couples and solo travelers who don't like crowds, or much entertainment, or the noisy trappings of most cruise ships. All cabins have different names (no numbers, and no door keys – although cabins can be locked from the inside), and all have a private bathroom with bathtub or shower. Fresh ingredients are sourced for the Columba Dining Room, and the locally-sourced cuisine is excellent. Not to be missed is the traditional 'a tasting o' haggis wi' bashed neeps an champit tatties'! It is, quite simply, delightful.

INSIGHT GUIDES' RATINGS

	Achieved	Possible
Ship	346	500
Accommodation	151	200
Food	317	400
Service	257	400
Entertainment	60	100
Cruise Experience	266	400
OVERALL SCORE	**1397**	**2000**

HEBRIDEAN SKY
★★★+

Size	Boutique Ship
Tonnage	4,280
Cruise Line	Hebridean Island Cruises
Former Names	*Corinthian II, Island Sun, Sun, Renaissance VII, Regina Renaissance, Renaissance VII*
Entered Service	1991, 2016
Total Crew	66
Passengers	115

This is a very compact (but now quite dated) ship that has twin flared funnels and a narrow exterior walk-around deck. Its interior design is quite elegant, and features British-ness in its decor and style. It best suits mature-age adults who like to discover small ports in relaxed comfort. The cabins are quite spacious and feature, and combine imitation rosewood panelling, lots of mirrors and hand-crafted furniture, illuminated walk-in closets, and mini-refrigerator. The bathrooms are compact, but have teak wood floors and marble vanities, but all have showers. The open-seating dining room is very pleasant, with sit-down service for dinner. Food quality, choice and presentation are all good.

INSIGHT GUIDES' RATINGS

	Achieved	Possible
Ship	341	500
Accommodation	151	200
Food	303	400
Service	237	400
Entertainment	60	100
Cruise Experience	246	400
OVERALL SCORE	**1338**	**2000**

HERITAGE ADVENTURER
★★★+

Size.. Boutique Ship
Tonnage...8,378
Cruise Line... Heritage Expeditions
Former Names .... *None*
Entered Service 1993, 2022
Total Crew...100
Passengers 140

This well-cared-for expedition-style ship was purpose-built for discovery sailings, and has an impressive history of exploration firsts. Now dated, but still in excellent condition, it carries Zodiacs for up-close adventures, and there are several weather-protected areas for nature and wildlife viewing. On deck is a small heated salt-water pool. Cabins are well designed, and are very comfortable, outfitted in practical expedition style, with ample storage space. The dining room is spacious and can seat all participants in one seating, with cuisine tailored to the ship's lifestyle and cruise region.

INSIGHT GUIDES' RATINGS		
	Achieved	Possible
Ship	376	500
Accommodation	161	200
Food	268	400
Service	237	400
Entertainment	54	100
Cruise Experience	271	400
OVERALL SCORE	**1367**	**2000**

HONDIUS
★★★

Size.. Boutique Ship
Tonnage...6,603
Cruise Line..Oceanwide Expeditions
Former Names .... *None*
Entered Service 2019
Total Crew... 72
Passengers 170

With its good seakeeping characteristics, this very small specialist ship is designed for expedition-style voyages, and can take you far away from areas the big ships go. Note that several slim pillars obstruct sightlines in the few public rooms, the main one being the forward-view Observation Lounge. The accommodation is extremely compact and comfortable, although storage space is really at a premium (six cabins have a small balcony, and more space). The lowest deck of cabins has portholes instead of windows. All cabin bathrooms have heated floors. The restaurant is pleasant enough, and has big picture windows, but the choice of food is quite limited and essentially carbo-rich.

INSIGHT GUIDES' RATINGS		
	Achieved	Possible
Ship	313	500
Accommodation	130	200
Food	245	400
Service	200	400
Entertainment	70	100
Cruise Experience	236	400
OVERALL SCORE	**1194**	**2000**

INDEPENDENCE OF THE SEAS
★★★

Size	Large Resort Ship
Tonnage	154,407
Cruise Line	Royal Caribbean International
Former Names	None
Entered Service	2008
Total Crew	1,397
Passengers	3,634

This large resort ship has lots of pizzazz and facilities that the whole family can enjoy. Its connection with water is a 'wow' factor for children, with its 'Perfect Storm' dual waterslides. The four-deck-high Royal Promenade is the indoor mall-like connecting point for shops, several eateries, bars, and other venues. Accommodation ranges from two-bedroom balconied 'villas' to compact indoor no-view twins and bay window cabins with views into the Royal Promenade. Flexibility and choice are what dining is all about, with specially-cooked items at extra cost. For entertainment, head to the 1,350-seat Royal Theatre for colorful shows. Note: the constant 'background' music around the ship is annoying.

INSIGHT GUIDES' RATINGS		
	Achieved	Possible
Ship	352	500
Accommodation	132	200
Food	231	400
Service	234	400
Entertainment	71	100
Cruise Experience	225	400
OVERALL SCORE	**1245**	**2000**

INSIGNIA
★★★+

Size	Small Ship
Tonnage	30,277
Cruise Line	Regent Seven Seas Cruises
Former Names	Columbus 2, Insignia, R1
Entered Service	1998, 2014
Total Crew	386
Passengers	684

This compact ship has a good range of public rooms and open spaces. Interior decor is a comfortable stroll through the ocean liners of the 1920s, with both real (and faux) stairways. The reception area has a fine, scaled down version of *Titanic*'s (first-class) staircase. However, most cabins are extremely compact, and have small bathrooms. The suites – particularly the aft suites on decks 6, 7, and 8 – are much larger. Bathrooms have glazed in showers. The Grand Dining Room seats around 320, while extra-cost Toscana and Polo Grill are much smaller venues. With flexibility and choice, food is a big focus for this company. Overall, this is a comfortable, casual ship and cruise experience.

INSIGHT GUIDES' RATINGS		
	Achieved	Possible
Ship	354	500
Accommodation	126	200
Food	291	400
Service	232	400
Entertainment	67	100
Cruise Experience	237	400
OVERALL SCORE	**1307**	**2000**

IONA
★★★★

Size	Large Resort Ship
Tonnage	183,900
Cruise Line	P&O Cruises
Former Names	None
Entered Service	2020
Total Crew	1,800
Passengers	5,200

This family-friendly floating British playground mixes modern and classic interior decor styles. An outdoor promenade deck gives access to several indoor-outdoor eateries. Accommodation varies in size and price, but overall, is good. There is an abundance of public rooms and entertainment lounges and relaxation zones, but remember the ship carries over 5,000, so planning and scheduling are important, depending on the itinerary. Included main dining is in the two large rooms – Coral and Pearl – or in the smaller Aqua and Opal dining rooms; food is acceptable, not special. Pay extra eateries are worth it for better food enjoyment. Time-consuming tender ports can be frustrating, but overall, it all works.

INSIGHT GUIDES' RATINGS

	Achieved	Possible
Ship	390	500
Accommodation	160	200
Food	248	400
Service	256	400
Entertainment	74	100
Cruise Experience	322	400
OVERALL SCORE	**1450**	**2000**

ISLAND PRINCESS
★★★

Size	Mid-Size Ship
Tonnage	91,627
Cruise Line	Princess Cruises
Former Names	None
Entered Service	2003
Total Crew	900
Passengers	1,974

Instantly recognisable because of two (mainly decorative) jet engine-like pods sitting high up on the ship's funnel. With two decks full of public rooms and many nooks and crannies, it's possible to hide away and simply read a book. There's three sets of stairways and elevators (but the forward set is confusing). Two main dining rooms inhabit the lowest passenger decks forward, both with low ceilings. Food portions are generous, but it's really banquet-style catering, with few green vegetables. Princess Theater hosts excellent, colorful Hollywood-style shows. *Island Princess* delivers a consistently well-packaged vacation, with a good degree of style for mature-age cruisegoers.

INSIGHT GUIDES' RATINGS

	Achieved	Possible
Ship	326	500
Accommodation	128	200
Food	243	400
Service	213	400
Entertainment	70	100
Cruise Experience	239	400
OVERALL SCORE	**1219**	**2000**

ISLAND SKY
★★★+

Size	Boutique Ship
Tonnage	4,280
Cruise Line	Hebridean Island Cruises
Former Names	*Sky, Renai II, Renaissance VIII*
Entered Service	1991, 2004
Total Crew	66
Passengers	122

This charming, but dated little ship features up-close-and-personal cruises to areas devoid of large ships, and a fleet of Zodiac craft for shore landings. The interior design is quite elegant, with polished wood panelling. Cabins are spacious, well designed, have ample storage space, and include a mini-fridge; while the bathrooms are compact, they do feature real teak wood floors and marble vanities. The dining room has tables for two to eight, and open seating. It is buffet-style for breakfast and lunch, while dinners are served meals. The food quality, choice, and presentation are generally good, and, overall, it should suit travelers who like a relaxed lifestyle.

INSIGHT GUIDES' RATINGS

	Achieved	Possible
Ship	340	500
Accommodation	151	200
Food	317	400
Service	257	400
Entertainment	60	100
Cruise Experience	266	400
OVERALL SCORE	**1391**	**2000**

JANSSONIUS
★★★+

Size	Boutique Ship
Tonnage	5,537
Cruise Line	Oceanwide Expeditions
Former Names	*None*
Entered Service	2021
Total Crew	72
Passengers	178

This compact specialist expedition-style ship is as far away from big-ship cruising as you can get, with good sea-keeping capabilities, and it is quiet in operation. The main public rooms are a lecture room and an observation lounge, although several pillars obstruct the sightlines in both. The cabins are extremely compact, measuring 129–291 sq ft (12.0–27.0 sq m), and have limited storage space – six cabins have a small balcony. The dining room has large picture windows and is quite comfortable (but several pillars are intrusive). The limited-choice meals are mostly carbohydrate-rich, with few green vegetables in sight, but typical of most vessels of this type.

INSIGHT GUIDES' RATINGS

	Achieved	Possible
Ship	348	500
Accommodation	128	200
Food	230	400
Service	266	400
Entertainment	61	100
Cruise Experience	219	400
OVERALL SCORE	**1252**	**2000**

JEWEL OF THE SEAS
★★★

Size.. Mid-size Ship
Tonnage...90,090
Cruise Line................................Royal Caribbean International
Former Names .... *None*
Entered Service 2004
Total Crew...858
Passengers 2,110

This modern mid-size ship has a large two-deck-high Viking Crown Lounge in the funnel's forward section, with great views. Inside, the decor is modern, bright, and cheerful, with a nine-deck high atrium lobby. The accommodation ranges from interior (no-view) cabins to decent-sized suites. Some cabins have interconnecting doors – good for families with children. Tides (the main restaurant) spans two decks, and seats over 1,200, at tables of two to 10. The food is so-so, and there is a lack of green vegetables. Pay extra and you can have lobster and decent steaks cooked for you. There are also two cost-extra venues with cooked-to-order food. The entertainment is generally good, but the constant 'background' music around the ship is irritating.

INSIGHT GUIDES' RATINGS

	Achieved	Possible
Ship	343	500
Accommodation	132	200
Food	228	400
Service	228	400
Entertainment	71	100
Cruise Experience	225	400
OVERALL SCORE	**1227**	**2000**

KONINGSDAM
★★★+

Size..Large Resort Ship
Tonnage...99,500
Cruise Line...........................Holland America Line
Former Names .... *None*
Entered Service 2016
Total Crew...1,025
Passengers 2,650

This ship has contemporary features while maintaining a traditional Dutch heritage. The exterior is not exactly handsome, but its single large funnel somehow manages to make it appear balanced. Outside there is a pleasant walk-around teak promenade deck, while indoors a three-deck-high atrium is the main focal and meeting point, and there are several small public rooms. Accommodation ranges from small cabins for solo travelers to family-friendly cabins and the large Grand Pinnacle Suite with balcony. The main dining room is on two levels, each with two seating times; the cuisine is, with a few exceptions, rather unmemorable. The Greenhouse Spa is very pleasant and has multiple facilities, with cost-extra treatments available.

INSIGHT GUIDES' RATINGS

	Achieved	Possible
Ship	396	500
Accommodation	151	200
Food	225	400
Service	238	400
Entertainment	71	100
Cruise Experience	256	400
OVERALL SCORE	**1337**	**2000**

L'AUSTRAL
★★★★

Size .... Small Ship
Tonnage 10,944
Cruise Line .... Ponant Cruises
Former Names .... *None*
Entered Service 2011
Total Crew 160
Passengers 264

French-speakers should enjoy this small ship – one of several almost identical sisters (*L'Austral* means south wind). It has a dark grey hull and white upper structure, plus a smart 'sponson' stern for operational stability and for launching the fleet of Zodiac landing craft. Inside, the focal point is a two-deck main lobby. The decor is minimalist, but with an elegant 'feel', so it looks more like a private yacht. Almost all public rooms are aft, with the mostly compact but practical accommodation forward, all with good views. It has very decent food, including some French cheeses, and delightful desserts. Entertainment is so-so, and the spa facilities are minimal, but they're pleasant enough.

INSIGHT GUIDES' RATINGS

	Achieved	Possible
Ship	388	500
Accommodation	149	200
Food	288	400
Service	239	400
Entertainment	71	100
Cruise Experience	267	400
OVERALL SCORE	**1402**	**2000**

LA BELLE DES OCEANS
★★★

Size .... Boutique Ship
Tonnage 5,218
Cruise Line .... Ponant Cruises
Former Names .... *Silver Discoverer, Clipper Odyssey, Oceanic Odyssey, Oceanic Grace*
Entered Service 1989, 2019
Total Crew 70
Passengers 130

This now rather dated small, intimate ship (built as *Oceanic Grace* for Japan's Showa Line) has twin funnels, a fleet of Zodiac landing craft, and an abundance of open deck space for wildlife viewing. Inside, even with a low ceiling height, it is pleasant enough for intimate discovery-style voyages, although there are several obstructive pillars in the public rooms. The cabins may be compact, and only a few have narrow balconies, but they are quite well equipped, with decent facilities. The dining room has large ocean-view windows, and the food includes some well-known French brands, served with some flair.

INSIGHT GUIDES' RATINGS

	Achieved	Possible
Ship	254	500
Accommodation	114	200
Food	275	400
Service	238	400
Entertainment	50	100
Cruise Experience	249	400
OVERALL SCORE	**1180**	**2000**

LE BELLOT
★★★★

Size .... Boutique Ship
Tonnage 9,988
Cruise Line .... Ponant Cruises
Former Names .... None
Entered Service 2020
Total Crew 110
Passengers 184

Highlighting French style, this compact ship (named after the French explorer and naval officer Joseph René Bellot) has a good ambiance. It has a dark grey hull and white upper structure, plus a 'sponson' stern for operational stability, as well as for launching its fleet of Zodiac landing craft. There is no outside walking or jogging deck. Inside, its focal point is a two-deck main lobby. The decor is minimalist, but with an elegant 'feel' like you would find on a private yacht. From the smallest cabin to the largest suite, all are well designed and comfortable, and many have balconies. The aft-located dining room is chic, accommodates all passengers in one seating, and has decent cuisine choices.

INSIGHT GUIDES' RATINGS	Achieved	Possible
Ship	406	500
Accommodation	153	200
Food	289	400
Service	240	400
Entertainment	71	100
Cruise Experience	273	400
OVERALL SCORE	**1432**	**2000**

LE BOREAL
★★★+

Size .... Small Ship
Tonnage 10,944
Cruise Line .... Ponant Cruises
Former Names .... None
Entered Service 2010
Total Crew 135
Passengers 264

This very small, contemporary French ship is all about chic yacht-like style and discovery. Most public rooms are aft, with accommodation forward. Sadly, there is no outside walking or jogging deck. Decor is chic, with browns and creams, and a splash of red. The suites are of a decent size, but most cabins are compact, but comfortable. The bathrooms are small, but have a mini-bathtub and separate shower enclosure – some cabins can be combined into larger suites, so you get his and hers bathrooms. The unpretentious dining room is noisy, due to the adjacent galley doors. The food is very decent, and includes some well-known French brands. Entertainment is limited, as are the spa facilities.

INSIGHT GUIDES' RATINGS	Achieved	Possible
Ship	385	500
Accommodation	144	200
Food	288	400
Service	240	400
Entertainment	71	100
Cruise Experience	265	400
OVERALL SCORE	**1393**	**2000**

LE BOUGAINVILLE
★★★★

Size.. Boutique Ship
Tonnage...9,976
Cruise Line.................................... Ponant Cruises
Former Names ....*None*
Entered Service 2019
Total Crew 110
Passengers 180

This compact but stylish French ship (sister to *Le Champlain* and *Le Laperouse*) has some expedition-like features, including an open trawler-like stern that provides access to marine equipment and doubles as a platform for shore landings. It features a neat underwater lounge called the 'Blue Eye.' Most decks have a low ceiling height, and uncarpeted stairways. From the smallest cabin to the largest suite, all are well-designed and comfortable, and many have balconies. The aft-located dining room is chic and accommodates all passengers at one seating. The cuisine is good and includes many upmarket French brand items and excellent cheeses. Overall, this is a comfortable little ship.

INSIGHT GUIDES' RATINGS		
	Achieved	Possible
Ship	403	500
Accommodation	155	200
Food	289	400
Service	239	400
Entertainment	71	100
Cruise Experience	273	400
OVERALL SCORE	**1430**	**2000**

LE CHAMPLAIN
★★★★

Size.. Boutique Ship
Tonnage...9,976
Cruise Line.................................... Ponant Cruises
Former Names ....*None*
Entered Service 2018
Total Crew 110
Passengers 180

This small ship, named after the French explorer Samuel de Champlain, has French ambience in abundance, in a contemporary setting. Its open trawler stern provides access to the marine equipment and acts as a landing platform. It features a neat underwater 'Blue Eye' lounge. Generally, however, the feeling is of being a little closed in due to the low ceiling heights, and the main stairways are uncarpeted. From the smallest viewless interior cabin to the largest balconied suite, all are quite comfortable. The Restaurant, aft, is noisy but comfortable; the cuisine is generally sound, and there is always a good cheese selection. Due to its size, the disjointed spa facilities are minimal.

INSIGHT GUIDES' RATINGS		
	Achieved	Possible
Ship	403	500
Accommodation	155	200
Food	289	400
Service	239	400
Entertainment	71	100
Cruise Experience	272	400
OVERALL SCORE	**1429**	**2000**

LE COMMONDANT CHARCOT
★★★★

Size..Small Ship
Tonnage..31,757
Cruise Line................................ Ponant Cruises
Former Names .... None
Entered Service 2021
Total Crew...187
Passengers 270

This sleek French expedition ship , named after the famed polar scientist, has Polar Class 2 ice-breaking capabilities and eco-friendly propulsion for exploring more remote regions. An outdoor promenade deck encircles the ship, while public areas include an indoor resistance pool and wellness area. The cabins are chic and have good beds, lighting, storage, refrigerator, bathrobe, US and European power outlets, and small but practical bathrooms. The aft Gastronomique Restaurant seats all participants. Haute Couture meals are by world-famous French chef Alain Ducasse (of Le Louis XV in Monaco), while a detox bar has fresh vegetable/fruit juices made to order. The ship exudes understated elegance, inclusive pricing and fine cuisine.

INSIGHT GUIDES' RATINGS

	Achieved	Possible
Ship	424	500
Accommodation	160	200
Food	295	400
Service	240	400
Entertainment	71	100
Cruise Experience	302	400
OVERALL SCORE	**1492**	**2000**

LE DUMONT D'URVILLE
★★★★

Size................................... Boutique Ship
Tonnage..9,976
Cruise Line................................ Ponant Cruises
Former Names .... None
Entered Service 2019
Total Crew...110
Passengers 180

This stylish French ship (named after the French explorer and naval officer Sebastien Cesar Dumont d'Urville) has an underwater lounge called the 'Blue Eye', that's reached by a dedicated elevator. There are some expedition-like features, including an open trawler-like stern that provides marine equipment access and doubles as a platform for shore landings. From the smallest cabin to the largest suite, all are well designed and comfortable, and many have narrow balconies. The aft-located dining room is chic and accommodates everyone at one sitting. The cuisine is good and includes many upmarket French brand items. Some Alain Ducasse-designed special menu items add sparkle, including some excellent cheeses.

INSIGHT GUIDES' RATINGS

	Achieved	Possible
Ship	401	500
Accommodation	155	200
Food	289	400
Service	239	400
Entertainment	71	100
Cruise Experience	273	400
OVERALL SCORE	**1428**	**2000**

LE JACQUES CARTIER
★★★★

Size	Boutique Ship
Tonnage	9,976
Cruise Line	Ponant Cruises
Former Names	Le Surville
Entered Service	2020
Total Crew	112
Passengers	184

Contemporary French styling and quirkiness await aboard this discovery-style ship, which has an aft marina platform for launching its Zodiac craft for up-close landings, plus a hardened hull for ice, and small swimming pool. Most public rooms are aft, except for the forward Panoramic Lounge, with accommodation forward, but the ship lacks an outside walking/jogging deck. From the smallest cabin to the largest suite, all are well designed and comfortable (a good number have small balconies. The Restaurant has single-seating, with tablecloths for dinner only. It is comfortable, but noisy due to the constant opening and closing of galley doors.

INSIGHT GUIDES' RATINGS		
	Achieved	Possible
Ship	404	500
Accommodation	155	200
Food	289	400
Service	239	400
Entertainment	71	100
Cruise Experience	273	400
OVERALL SCORE	**1431**	**2000**

LE LAPÉROUSE
★★★★

Size	Boutique Ship
Tonnage	9,976
Cruise Line	Ponant Cruises
Former Names	None
Entered Service	2018
Total Crew	112
Passengers	180

French chic and stylish comfort can be found aboard this boutique-sized ship designed to take you comfortably to more remote areas. Its hydraulic stern platform for marine equipment acts as a landing stage for its Zodiac landing craft. Do try the impressive underwater 'Blue Eye' lounge. From interior (no-view) cabins to the largest suite, all are quite comfortable, with wood-look decor and white cabinetry. Bathrooms are compact, but have decent showers. The restaurant is comfortable (with tablecloths for dinner only), but rather noisy, with the constant opening and closing of galley doors. The cuisine is good (particularly the cheese selection). Note: the main stairways are uncarpeted and spa facilities are minimal.

INSIGHT GUIDES' RATINGS		
	Achieved	Possible
Ship	402	500
Accommodation	155	200
Food	289	400
Service	239	400
Entertainment	71	100
Cruise Experience	272	400
OVERALL SCORE	**1428**	**2000**

LE LYRIAL
★★★★

Size.. Boutique Ship
Tonnage..10,992
Cruise Line.................................... Ponant Cruises
Former Names ....*None*
Entered Service 2015
Total Crew 140
Passengers 244

This boutique ship – whose name refers to the Lyra constellation in the northern hemisphere – has a fleet of 12 Zodiac rubber craft for up-close landings in soft expedition areas. It has trendy, uncluttered super-yacht style interior decor, and most public rooms are aft, with accommodation forward. There are 122 suites/cabins – all with outside views, cabinetry featuring elegant wood, and a personal safe, refrigerator, and French bathroom products. Dining is in the Restaurant Gastronomique; it is chic, but not overly pretentious, and accommodates all passengers in one sitting. The service crew is English- and French-speaking. French ambiance and good style are this ship's hallmarks.

INSIGHT GUIDES' RATINGS		
	Achieved	Possible
Ship	396	500
Accommodation	153	200
Food	288	400
Service	246	400
Entertainment	72	100
Cruise Experience	268	400
OVERALL SCORE	**1423**	**2000**

LE PONANT
★★★

Size.. Boutique Ship
Tonnage..1,489
Cruise Line.................................... Ponant Cruises
Former Names ....*None*
Entered Service 2009
Total Crew 32
Passengers 64

This rather sleek, contemporary yacht with three masts could be an antidote to cruising aboard large cruise ships for anyone wanting a quieter pace of life. Electric winches assist in furling and unfurling the sails. There are few facilities, so the experience of yachting is all about being laid back. Cabins have portholes, blond wood trim, a refrigerator, and twin beds convertible to a double, but the bathrooms are extremely small. The Karukera dining room is delightful and features French cuisine. There is also an outdoor café under a sailcloth awning. The yacht has an aft marina platform and a boat for water-skiing. Overall, it should be a pleasant experience.

INSIGHT GUIDES' RATINGS		
	Achieved	Possible
Ship	340	500
Accommodation	148	200
Food	267	400
Service	232	400
Entertainment	70	100
Cruise Experience	192	400
OVERALL SCORE	**1249**	**2000**

LE SOLEAL
★★★+

Size	Small Ship
Tonnage	10,992
Cruise Line	Ponant Cruises
Former Names	None
Entered Service	2013
Total Crew	140
Passengers	264

This compact but stylish French ship, with its dark grey hull, has French ambiance, premium style, and very decent food. The main stairways are uncarpeted and noisy and the spa facilities are minimal. However, while the cabins are quite small, they are nicely outfitted, though there is little storage space. Some cabins can be combined to provide larger units (with two bathrooms). Note that bed frame corners are square, making leg bruising possible. Also, there is little storage space in the bathrooms. The Restaurant Gastronomique is chic but unpretentious, with open seating. Meals feature French cuisine, with decent mains and delightful desserts.

INSIGHT GUIDES' RATINGS		
	Achieved	Possible
Ship	388	500
Accommodation	151	200
Food	278	400
Service	243	400
Entertainment	72	100
Cruise Experience	266	400
OVERALL SCORE	**1398**	**2000**

LIBERTY OF THE SEAS
★★★

Size	Large Resort Ship
Tonnage	154,407
Cruise Line	Royal Caribbean International
Former Names	None
Entered Service	2007
Total Crew	1,397
Passengers	3,630

This large resort ship provides a great playground for the whole family, with outdoor decks full of water-themed play areas. The Royal Promenade hosts a range of shops, eateries, bars, and lounges. Except for the multi-bed premium suites, the cabins are small, with little storage space, but they are practical. Botticelli, Michelangelo, and Rembrandt are the three main dining rooms. The food is standardized and adequately presented, but lacks green vegetables. Vegetarian and children's menus are available too. For better food, pay extra to eat in one of the small specialty venues, such as diner-style Johnny Rocket's. Outstanding Ice Follies shows can be seen in the Studio B ice rink. The spa facilities are good; body treatments are at an extra cost.

INSIGHT GUIDES' RATINGS		
	Achieved	Possible
Ship	354	500
Accommodation	132	200
Food	218	400
Service	233	400
Entertainment	71	100
Cruise Experience	225	400
OVERALL SCORE	**1233**	**2000**

MAGELLAN EXPLORER
★★★

Size	Boutique Ship
Tonnage	4,900
Cruise Line	Antarctica 21
Former Names	None
Entered Service	2019
Total Crew	60
Passengers	73

This very small ship has been custom-built to the latest Polar Code specifications for Antarctic air cruises, with a maximum of 73 passengers. It is built specifically to get you up close and personal with a fleet of 10 Zodiac landing craft, and you can go right up to the ship's bow. Inside is a glass-enclosed Antarctica Lounge with integral bar, a library, meeting room, and a small, but nicely equipped spa. Accommodation ranges from 210–480 sq ft (19–44 sq m), and includes dedicated solo traveler cabins. The cosy restaurant has large picture windows, attractive table settings, and well-presented food.

INSIGHT GUIDES' RATINGS

	Achieved	Possible
Ship	286	500
Accommodation	128	200
Food	288	400
Service	252	400
Entertainment	50	100
Cruise Experience	183	400
OVERALL SCORE	**1187**	**2000**

MAJESTIC PRINCESS
★★★+

Size	Large Resort Ship
Tonnage	144,216
Cruise Line	Princess Cruises
Former Names	None
Entered Service	2017
Total Crew	1,346
Passengers	3,560

This family-oriented multi-choice ship has a walk-around outdoor deck, and an over-the-water SeaWalk as part of a lounge-bar area. Piazza Atrium is the ship's multi-faceted, multi-level social and dining hub, complete with a flowing, horseshoe-shaped stairway. With six accommodation types and numerous price grades, pricing depends on size and location (some of the most sought-after suites are located aft). Allegro, Concerto, and Symphony are the three main dining rooms, assigned according to your accommodation grade. Cost-extra venues include the Crown Grill for steaks and seafood. Princess loves entertainment and prides itself on its colorful production shows, presented in its two-deck high Princess Theater.

INSIGHT GUIDES' RATINGS

	Achieved	Possible
Ship	394	500
Accommodation	139	200
Food	268	400
Service	244	400
Entertainment	82	100
Cruise Experience	273	400
OVERALL SCORE	**1400**	**2000**

MARELLA DISCOVERY
★★★

Size.. Mid-size Ship
Tonnage..69,472
Cruise Line... Marella Cruises
Former Names .... *TUI Discovery, Splendour of the Seas*
Entered Service 1996, 2016
Total Crew...720
Passengers 1,830

Although dated, this is a comfortable older ship with many public rooms, decent open deck space, and cost-extra dining options. Two decks host a range of lounges, bars, and shops. Most cabins are rather small and have little storage space, but all have twin beds that convert to a double; bathrooms are extremely small. Cabin 8500, however, is a large, well-designed living space, and includes a grand piano. The main dining room spans two decks, and is very comfortable. Food is decent enough, and is well presented. Reservations required, cost-extra venues include Surf 'n' Turf (steaks and seafood) and Kora La (pan-Asian style cuisine). For shows, head to the large Broadway Show Lounge, which has good sightlines from most seats.

INSIGHT GUIDES' RATINGS		
	Achieved	Possible
Ship	324	500
Accommodation	123	200
Food	242	400
Service	204	400
Entertainment	64	100
Cruise Experience	229	400
OVERALL SCORE	**1186**	**2000**

MARELLA DISCOVERY 2
★★★

Size.. Mid-size Ship
Tonnage..69,472
Cruise Line... Marella Cruises
Former Names ....*Legend of the Seas*
Entered Service 1995, 2022
Total Crew...726
Passengers 1,804

British cruisegoers should feel comfortable aboard this nicely refurbished older ship. It has a seven-deck-high atrium lobby – *the* social meeting point – and a good range of public rooms, including lounges and bars. Except for accommodation designated as suites, most cabins are rather small, with limited storage space, and compact bathrooms with showers. The large main restaurant (featuring standard British cuisine) spans two decks, linked by a grand stairway, while part of the upper level has a separate Italian restaurant. Reservations required, cost-extra venues include the smaller Surf 'n' Turf (steaks and seafood) and Kora La (pan-Asian style cuisine, including curries).

INSIGHT GUIDES' RATINGS		
	Achieved	Possible
Ship	335	500
Accommodation	128	200
Food	238	400
Service	209	400
Entertainment	70	100
Cruise Experience	236	400
OVERALL SCORE	**1216**	**2000**

MARELLA EXPLORER
★★★

Size	Mid-size Ship
Tonnage	76,998
Cruise Line	Marella Cruises
Former Names	*Galaxy*
Entered Service	1996, 2022
Total Crew	726
Passengers	1,804

This now dated ship has modern styling, for British family-friendly cruises in comfortable surroundings. There is a decent amount of open deck space, but it can be cramped when the ship is full. Inside is a four-deck-high main foyer, and an abundance of public rooms and lounges. Cabins are generously sized and nicely outfitted, with ample storage space. Restaurants and bistros range from full service to self-serve buffets. Atlantik Restaurant is the main bi-level dining hall with a grand stairway, and tables for two to ten. Cost-extra, reservations required venues include The Dining Club, Surf 'n' Turf Steakhouse, and Kora-La (Asian-style curries and noodle dishes). The spa facilities are good, and private cost-extra spa suites are available.

INSIGHT GUIDES' RATINGS

	Achieved	Possible
Ship	326	500
Accommodation	124	200
Food	244	400
Service	212	400
Entertainment	64	100
Cruise Experience	230	400
OVERALL SCORE	**1200**	**2000**

MARELLA EXPLORER 2
★★★

Size	Mid-size Ship
Tonnage	72,458
Cruise Line	Marella Cruises
Former Names	*Century*
Entered Service	1995, 2022
Total Crew	780
Passengers	1,924

This is basically a comfortable (ex-Celebrity Cruises) adults-only ship with British-style surroundings and a good range of public rooms, some of which have high ceilings, and a good amount of open deck space. There are several extra-cost items, such as sparkling wine at embarkation, Verandah cabanas, and accommodation upgrades when available. The range of cabins is good, and all have detailed wood cabinetry and a good amount of storage space. Latitude 53 is the main (included) dining room; it has expansive windows and modestly decent cuisine. There are also several smaller extra-cost eateries, and a Market Place buffet with a very limited food selection.

INSIGHT GUIDES' RATINGS

	Achieved	Possible
Ship	334	500
Accommodation	126	200
Food	245	400
Service	207	400
Entertainment	66	100
Cruise Experience	235	400
OVERALL SCORE	**1213**	**2000**

MARELLA VOYAGER
★★★

Size.. Mid-size Ship
Tonnage...77,302
Cruise Line.................................... Marella Cruises
Former Names ....*Mein Schiff Herz, Celebrity Mercury, Mercury*
Entered Service 1995, 2023
Total Crew...780
Passengers 1,904

The pointed bows really help make it look like a well-balanced cruise ship. Inside, it is quite spacious, with a pleasant main lobby foyer and a wide range of public rooms, most with elegant, understated decor, wood panelling and pleasant artwork. Cabins are well designed and appointed, and have ample storage space, while suites have abundant space and large bathrooms. The spacious bi-level Manhattan Restaurant, located aft, has huge picture windows and is very comfortable. The food is well presented and decent enough, but not outstanding, because this is mass catering. Smaller venues include Abuela's (for Mexican-style bites), and Nonna's (Italian). For shows, head to the 1,000-seat Broadway Showlounge, with its excellent sightlines.

INSIGHT GUIDES' RATINGS		
	Achieved	Possible
Ship	335	500
Accommodation	125	200
Food	244	400
Service	208	400
Entertainment	65	100
Cruise Experience	237	400
OVERALL SCORE	**1214**	**2000**

MARINA
★★★★

Size... Mid-size Ship
Tonnage...66,084
Cruise Line....................................Oceania Cruises
Former Names .... *None*
Entered Service 2011
Total Crew..800
Passengers 1,250

The ship's exterior has a nicely rounded front. Inside, the straightforward layout and country house-like style decor are good: the main lobby features a stunning wrought iron and Lalique (French) glass horseshoe-shaped staircase. After a 2012 drydocking, the lighting is better and there is more storage space in the suites/cabins, which range from about 282 sq ft (26 sq m) to around 2,000 sq ft (16 sq m) and teak decking. Bathrooms have bathtubs and good storage space. There are several open-seating dining venues (some have banquette seating – individual seating is better), with a focus on food choice, quality, and presentation. Along with cabaret-style entertainment, the spa itself is good, but treatments are overpriced.

INSIGHT GUIDES' RATINGS		
	Achieved	Possible
Ship	420	500
Accommodation	169	200
Food	309	400
Service	257	400
Entertainment	77	100
Cruise Experience	287	400
OVERALL SCORE	**1519**	**2000**

MARINER OF THE SEAS
★★★

Size	Large Resort Ship
Tonnage	137,276
Cruise Line	Royal Caribbean International
Former Names	None
Entered Service	2004
Total Crew	1,185
Passengers	3,114

This ultra-casual resort ship is great for families, with its many water-themed play areas. A regulation ice skating rink (Studio B) is a standout, as is its four-deck-high Royal Promenade. Accommodation ranges from interior (no-view) cabins to huge premium suites with balconies, but most cabins lack storage. The main dining room seats around 1,900, on three levels. Menu descriptions sound enticing, but the batch-cooked food is simply average, although some items can be cooked to order (if you pay extra). Vegetarian and children's menus are also available. Cost-extra venues like Chop's Grille and Jamie's are worth trying. Colorful shows are performed in the stunning Savoy Lounge. The constant 'background' music on the ship can be annoying.

INSIGHT GUIDES' RATINGS

	Achieved	Possible
Ship	343	500
Accommodation	132	200
Food	221	400
Service	228	400
Entertainment	71	100
Cruise Experience	225	400
OVERALL SCORE	**1220**	**2000**

MAUD
★★+

Size	Small Ship
Tonnage	16,053
Cruise Line	Hurtigruten Expeditions
Former Names	Midnatsol
Entered Service	2003
Total Crew	75
Passengers	532

Maud pretends to be an 'expedition' ship, but was originally built for Norwegian coastal sailings. It was updated with more environmentally friendly engines and technical equipment. There is little open deck space, and no walkaround deck, although there is a hot tub. The interiors feature Norwegian modern art pieces, and a two-deck observation lounge is the main public room. The compact cabins (several have interconnecting doors) have little drawer space for clothing items, a few have narrow balconies, but all have underfloor heating. The bathrooms are tiny, but organised. Suites have a little more space. The food in Aune (main restaurant) is basic, with little choice, and mostly buffet-style meals.

INSIGHT GUIDES' RATINGS

	Achieved	Possible
Ship	337	500
Accommodation	112	200
Food	224	400
Service	162	400
Entertainment	60	100
Cruise Experience	199	400
OVERALL SCORE	**1094**	**2000**

MEIN SCHIFF 1
★★★★

Size	Large Resort Ship
Tonnage	111,900
Cruise Line	TUI Cruises
Former Names	None
Entered Service	2018
Total Crew	1,000
Passengers	2,534

This stylish multi-choice seagoing resort for German-speaking families has an ultra-quiet propulsion system, a half-Olympic-sized swimming pool (82ft/25m), and a bucketful of European style. There is wide range of lounges, bars, and shops (including a Klanghaus concert hall/movie theater, with excellent acoustic properties). The cabins and suites are well outfitted, but there are too many categories. However, all include a personal safe and Nespresso coffee machines. Atlantik (the main included dining room) has three sections, each with a different menu. Other smaller eateries include Gosch Sylt for fresh seafood, including oysters from the island of Sylt, and Surf 'n' Turf Steakhouse.

INSIGHT GUIDES' RATINGS

	Achieved	Possible
Ship	425	500
Accommodation	162	200
Food	316	400
Service	278	400
Entertainment	83	100
Cruise Experience	286	400
OVERALL SCORE	**1550**	**2000**

MEIN SCHIFF 2
★★★★

Size	Large Resort Ship
Tonnage	111,900
Cruise Line	TUI Cruises
Former Names	None
Entered Service	2019
Total Crew	1,000
Passengers	2,534

This large multi-choice ship exudes European style and makes a good choice for youthful German-speaking families. It has a half Olympic-sized pool, at 82ft (25m). The cabins and suites are well designed, and include Nespresso coffee machines. There is a wide range of lounges, bars, restaurants, and specialized eateries like Gosch Sylt (for fresh oysters and seafood), and the Surf 'n' Turf Steakhouse (with meat in cold-store display cabinets). In fact, the food is the star of the show, and the freshly baked bread selection is outstanding. There are also reservations-required, cost-extra venues, worth it for their high-quality food. The Spa and Meer wellness facilities are extensive, and body pampering treatments are good.

INSIGHT GUIDES' RATINGS

	Achieved	Possible
Ship	425	500
Accommodation	162	200
Food	316	400
Service	278	400
Entertainment	83	100
Cruise Experience	286	400
OVERALL SCORE	**1550**	**2000**

MEIN SCHIFF 3
★★★★

Size	Large Resort Ship
Tonnage	99,300
Cruise Line	TUI Cruises
Former Names	None
Entered Service	2014
Total Crew	1,000
Passengers	2,506

This contemporary ship features excellent facilities for German-speaking families, including a half-Olympic-size swimming pool. Inside is an extensive array of lounges (including a Klanghaus concert hall/movie theater with excellent acoustics), bars, shops, and eateries. The cabins and suites are well designed and include Nespresso coffee machines, good storage, and bathrooms with space for toiletries. Atlantik Restaurant is the main dining room; its three sections each focuses on different cuisines. Gosch Sylt (oysters and seafood), Surf 'n' Turf Steakhouse (with cold-store meat display cabinets), and Hanami are three cost-extra venues. The Spa and Meer wellness facilities are extensive, and body pampering treatments are high quality.

INSIGHT GUIDES' RATINGS

	Achieved	Possible
Ship	417	500
Accommodation	160	200
Food	313	400
Service	276	400
Entertainment	82	100
Cruise Experience	281	400
OVERALL SCORE	**1529**	**2000**

MEIN SCHIFF 4
★★★★

Size	Large Resort Ship
Tonnage	99,300
Cruise Line	TUI Cruises
Former Names	None
Entered Service	2015
Total Crew	1,000
Passengers	2,506

This ship has excellent facilities that are totally geared to German-speaking families. It includes an 82ft (25m) swimming pool, while inside is a wide array public rooms (including a Klanghaus concert hall/movie theater, with superb acoustics), lounges, bars, eateries, and shops. The accommodation is well designed, and all include a Nespresso coffee machine, and ample closet and drawer space. There are numerous restaurants and eateries (some cost extra), but the choice and quality of food is quite outstanding. The Spa and Meer wellness facilities are also extensive, and body pampering treatments are worth the cost.

INSIGHT GUIDES' RATINGS

	Achieved	Possible
Ship	417	500
Accommodation	160	200
Food	313	400
Service	276	400
Entertainment	82	100
Cruise Experience	280	400
OVERALL SCORE	**1528**	**2000**

MEIN SCHIFF 5
★★★★

Size	Large Resort Ship
Tonnage	99,800
Cruise Line	TUI Cruises
Former Names	None
Entered Service	2016
Total Crew	1,000
Passengers	2,552

This colorful, stylish, multi-choice ship exudes European flair and should be a good choice for youthful German-speaking families. Look for the 'Blue Balcony' glass floor extending over the sea from the ship's side. There is an extensive array of lounges (including a Klanghaus concert hall/movie theater, with fine acoustic properties) bars, and shops. The cabins and suites are well designed, and include Nespresso coffee machines and a personal safe. There are numerous restaurants and eateries (some cost extra), but food choice and quality are outstanding for the price. The Spa and Meer wellness facilities are extensive, and body pampering treatments are good. Overall, this is a very comfortable ship for a laid-back vacation.

INSIGHT GUIDES' RATINGS

	Achieved	Possible
Ship	422	500
Accommodation	161	200
Food	314	400
Service	277	400
Entertainment	82	100
Cruise Experience	284	400
OVERALL SCORE	**1540**	**2000**

MEIN SCHIFF 6
★★★★

Size	Large Resort Ship
Tonnage	99,800
Cruise Line	TUI Cruises
Former Names	None
Entered Service	2017
Total Crew	1,000
Passengers	2,552

This contemporary ship has fine facilities for youthful, German-speaking families, including a large 82ft (25m) swimming pool (half Olympic-sized). Inside is an extensive array of lounges, including an acoustically excellent Klanghaus concert hall/movie theater, bars, shops, and eateries. In addition to the (included) main dining rooms Classic, Broccoli, and Mediterranean, smaller, cost-extra eateries include Schmankerl, for authentic Austrian regional specialities in an Austrian tavern setting; Hanami, for Japanese-style cuisine; Gosch Sylt, for oysters and seafood; and Surf 'n' Turf Steakhouse, with meat in cold-store display cabinets. Its Spa and Meer wellness facilities are extensive, with excellent body pampering treatments.

INSIGHT GUIDES' RATINGS

	Achieved	Possible
Ship	422	500
Accommodation	161	200
Food	314	400
Service	277	400
Entertainment	82	100
Cruise Experience	285	400
OVERALL SCORE	**1541**	**2000**

MSC ARMONIA
★★★+

Size	Mid-size Ship
Tonnage	65,542
Cruise Line	MSC Cruises
Former Names	*European Vision*
Entered Service	2001, 2004
Total Crew	721
Passengers	1,952

This is a busy but comfortable mid-sized ship for pan-European cruisegoers, with tasteful decor, although there's a slightly disjointed layout after the ship had an expansive mid-section added in 2014. Size, grade, and location determine the price you pay. The 610-seat Marco Polo dining room has two sittings for dinner, with generally sound meals, including regional Italian specialities, and pasta made freshly each day. Vegetarian dishes are also available. Occupants of suite-grade accommodation eat in the separate La Pergola. Teatro La Fenice is the place for colorful entertainment shows and cabaret, and the Atlantica Spa offers body-pampering treatments.

INSIGHT GUIDES' RATINGS

	Achieved	Possible
Ship	362	500
Accommodation	148	200
Food	238	400
Service	253	400
Entertainment	60	100
Cruise Experience	252	400
OVERALL SCORE	**1313**	**2000**

MSC BELLISSIMA
★★★★

Size	Large Resort Ship
Tonnage	171,598
Cruise Line	MSC Cruises
Former Names	*None*
Entered Service	2019
Total Crew	1,536
Passengers	4,488

Designed for family-immersive cruising, this contemporary ship has an aft Aqua Park play area full of spray cannons, water jets, tipping buckets, three waterslides, and more. Galleria Bellissima is its extensive indoor promenade (and good meeting point) full of shops, bars, eateries, with a 260-ft (80-m) -long LED dome displaying a constant stream of digital scenes and themes. The standard or more exclusive Yacht Club accommodation is well designed and comfortable. Black Crab and Villa Rosssa are the main dining rooms – suite occupants dine in Le Muse, a separate venue. The cuisine includes regional Italian specialities, and pasta freshly made daily onboard.

INSIGHT GUIDES' RATINGS

	Achieved	Possible
Ship	421	500
Accommodation	161	200
Food	275	400
Service	258	400
Entertainment	78	100
Cruise Experience	276	400
OVERALL SCORE	**1469**	**2000**

MSC DIVINA
★★★★

Size	Large Resort Ship
Tonnage	137,936
Cruise Line	MSC Cruises
Former Names	None
Entered Service	2012
Total Crew	1,370
Passengers	3,274

Sister to *MSC Preziosa*, this ship has green-technology engines. Its interior decor is vibrantly colorful, with a gorgeous three-deck-high lobby that has shimmering Swarovski crystal stairways. Multiple lounges flow into each other (so does the music). Accommodation ranges from two Royal Suites (in an exclusive Yacht Club area – 16007 is the Sophia Loren Suite) and a mix of outside-view (with or without balconies) and interior (no-view) cabins. Black Crab (bi-level) and Villa Rosa are the main eateries (all pizza dough and fresh pasta is made daily), while Yacht Club occupants eat in the small Le Muse. Highly visual shows are in the bi-level Pantheon Theater, while the Aurea Spa has excellent facilities and body pampering treatments.

INSIGHT GUIDES' RATINGS

	Achieved	Possible
Ship	418	500
Accommodation	160	200
Food	273	400
Service	258	400
Entertainment	78	100
Cruise Experience	275	400
OVERALL SCORE	**1462**	**2000**

MSC EURIBIA
★★★★

Size	Large Resort Ship
Tonnage	184,541
Cruise Line	MSC Cruises
Former Names	None
Entered Service	2023
Total Crew	1,388
Passengers	3,502

Named after the ancient goddess Euribia, this family-friendly ship is LNG-powered and has a visually stunning hull. Multiple play areas include a Coral Reef Aquapark for youngsters, and one of two swimming pools can be covered by a glass dome in inclement weather. Indoors, Galleria Euribia's double deck promenade has a domed digital projection ceiling, eateries, bars, boutiques, a chocolate café, and more. Accommodation ranges from viewless interior cabins to interconnecting cabins for families, and Yacht Club suites. The main dining rooms include regional Italian specialities, and pasta made fresh daily. For something different, Kaito Sushi Bar's revolving sushi counter is neat, while Teppanyaki Grill is entertaining.

INSIGHT GUIDES' RATINGS

	Achieved	Possible
Ship	426	500
Accommodation	162	200
Food	277	400
Service	260	400
Entertainment	78	100
Cruise Experience	287	400
OVERALL SCORE	**1490**	**2000**

MSC FANTASIA
★★★★

Size	Large Resort Ship
Tonnage	137,936
Cruise Line	MSC Cruises
Former Names	None
Entered Service	2008
Total Crew	1,370
Passengers	3,274

Measuring about 33ft (10m) longer than the Eiffel Tower is high, this is a colorful and stylish family-oriented ship. It has a multitude of public rooms (many with have high ceilings) and some very bold Italian decorative styles. There is an exclusive area called the MSC Yacht Club for occupants of the 99 suites. There are several eateries (some cost extra), apart from the voluminous, two-deck-high Red Velvet dining room, with assigned seating. Regional Italian cuisine is featured, and, overall, the meals are decent enough. The L'Avanguardia showlounge seats over 1,600 for its colorful, mainly visual shows, while a large Aurea Spa has a fine array of treatment rooms and facilities. Overall, this is a fine seagoing resort.

INSIGHT GUIDES' RATINGS

	Achieved	Possible
Ship	403	500
Accommodation	160	200
Food	271	400
Service	256	400
Entertainment	77	100
Cruise Experience	278	400
OVERALL SCORE	**1445**	**2000**

MSC GRANDIOSA
★★★★

Size	Large Resort Ship
Tonnage	181,000
Cruise Line	MSC Cruises
Former Names	None
Entered Service	2019
Total Crew	1,703
Passengers	4,842

A close sister to *MSC Bellissima* and *MSC Meraviglia*, this stunning, stylish, multi-choice ship has European flair and should appeal to the young at heart. Inside, there are serious wow factors in public spaces, with the two-deck-high Grandiosa Promenade featuring an impressive 98.5m-long domed LED projection ceiling that streams thematic digital scenes. Suite-grade 'ship within a ship' cabins offer exclusivity, otherwise, cabin price depends on size, grade, and location. MSC Cruises highlights regional Italian cuisine, featuring food from various areas. The Aurea Spa has excellent facilities with hands-on body treatments. Overall, it is a stunning, family-oriented ship.

INSIGHT GUIDES' RATINGS

	Achieved	Possible
Ship	425	500
Accommodation	162	200
Food	276	400
Service	260	400
Entertainment	78	100
Cruise Experience	287	400
OVERALL SCORE	**1488**	**2000**

MSC LIRICA
★★★+

Size	Mid-size Ship
Tonnage	65,875
Cruise Line	MSC Cruises
Former Names	*None*
Entered Service	2003
Total Crew	721
Passengers	1,976

This sister ship to *MSC Opera* is the first newly built ship for MSC Cruises, and was lengthened in 2014, with a new midsection to provide more public rooms, cabins, and facilities. The pan-European family-oriented ship has stylish, jazzy interiors, including the use of real wood and marble, reflecting the company's commitment to high quality. From suites with private balcony to interior (no-view) cabins, all are well designed and outfitted. La Bussola and L'Ippocampo are the included main dining rooms, and both highlight regional Italian cuisine. Risotto is a daily signature item, and all pizza dough is made on board. Shanghai (for Asian dishes) is a popular cost-extra venue. Spa lovers should enjoy the excellent Aurea Spa.

INSIGHT GUIDES' RATINGS		
	Achieved	Possible
Ship	373	500
Accommodation	150	200
Food	237	400
Service	249	400
Entertainment	60	100
Cruise Experience	245	400
OVERALL SCORE	**1314**	**2000**

MSC MAGNIFICA
★★★+

Size	Large Resort Ship
Tonnage	95,128
Cruise Line	MSC Cruises
Former Names	*None*
Entered Service	2010
Total Crew	1,038
Passengers	2,518

One of a quartet of similar size and facilities (the others are *MSC Musica, MSC Poesia,* and *MSC Orchestra*), this large, family-friendly ship exudes pan-European style. The layout and passenger flow are both decent enough, with a range of public rooms including a three-deck-high lobby with a water feature backdrop. A standout is the big-game-themed Tiger Lounge and Bar. Cabins have high-quality bed linen, mini-bar, safe, and decent closet space. L'Edera and Quattro Venti are the two main dining rooms (allocated according to your cabin grade). Pasta from different Italian regions is made fresh daily. For variety, Shanghai is a small extra-cost venue, for excellent wok-cooked cuisine.

INSIGHT GUIDES' RATINGS		
	Achieved	Possible
Ship	402	500
Accommodation	151	200
Food	242	400
Service	248	400
Entertainment	62	100
Cruise Experience	266	400
OVERALL SCORE	**1371**	**2000**

MSC MERAVIGLIA
★★★★

Size	Large Resort Ship
Tonnage	167,900
Cruise Line	MSC Cruises
Former Names	None
Entered Service	2017
Total Crew	1,540
Passengers	4,488

A close sister to *MSC Bellissima* and *MSC Grandiosa*, this stylish, multi-choice ship exudes European flair and should appeal to the young at heart. It features a two-deck-high Grandiosa Promenade with an impressive 32-ft (98.5-m) -long domed LED projection ceiling with constantly changing digital thematic scenes. It features Yacht Club 'ship within a ship' suite-grade cabins for exclusivity; otherwise cabin price depends on size, grade, and location, but all are well designed. The ship highlights Italian cuisine, featuring food from various regions such as Calabria, Piedmont, Lazio, Puglia, and Sicily. An excellent Aurea Spa has multiple facilities and hands-on body treatments. Overall, this is a stunning family-oriented ship.

INSIGHT GUIDES' RATINGS	Achieved	Possible
Ship	415	500
Accommodation	161	200
Food	276	400
Service	258	400
Entertainment	78	100
Cruise Experience	285	400
OVERALL SCORE	**1473**	**2000**

MSC MUSICA
★★★+

Size	Large Resort Ship
Tonnage	92,409
Cruise Line	MSC Cruises
Former Names	None
Entered Service	2006
Total Crew	1,014
Passengers	2,550

This smart-looking ship exudes European style for family-friendly cruising. Interior decor is colorful, fittings and furnishings are high quality, and the main lobby spanning three decks has a water-feature backdrop. From balconies suites to interior (no-view) cabins, all have a minibar and personal safe. Outside, unfortunately, there is no walk-around outdoor deck. The main restaurants, Le Maxim's and L'Oleandro, are located aft, and have tables for two to eight. The food includes some regional Italian classics, with multiple pasta varieties made fresh each day. Il Giardino (Italian) and Kaito (a Japanese sushi bar) are fine extra-cost venues. The spa facilities are quite extensive, with high quality body treatments in a pleasing environment.

INSIGHT GUIDES' RATINGS	Achieved	Possible
Ship	396	500
Accommodation	150	200
Food	242	400
Service	248	400
Entertainment	61	100
Cruise Experience	264	400
OVERALL SCORE	**1361**	**2000**

MSC OPERA
★★★+

Size	Mid-size Ship
Tonnage	65,875
Cruise Line	MSC Cruises
Former Names	*None*
Entered Service	2004
Total Crew	721
Passengers	2,142

This smart-looking, chopped-and-stretched ship has an abundance of family-friendly features, and some colorful public room decor to suit those with a European lifestyle. From interior (no-view) cabins to 'suites' with outside balconies, all are well out-fitted and comfortable, and have a minibar and personal safe. The La Caravella main dining room is large, and dining is at tables for two to eight. Regional Italian cuisine is featured, and, overall, the meals are decent enough. L'Approdo Restaurant, for 'suite' occupants, is rather more intimate, and has better food. The showlounge has tiered, plush seating and good sightlines from most seats. The spa has fine facilities and body-pampering treatments. Overall, a very comfortable cruise experience.

INSIGHT GUIDES' RATINGS		
	Achieved	Possible
Ship	378	500
Accommodation	151	200
Food	239	400
Service	245	400
Entertainment	60	100
Cruise Experience	251	400
OVERALL SCORE	**1324**	**2000**

MSC ORCHESTRA
★★★+

Size	Large Resort Ship
Tonnage	92,409
Cruise Line	MSC Cruises
Former Names	*None*
Entered Service	2007
Total Crew	1,054
Passengers	2,550

This colorful and lively sea-going resort can be enjoyed by the whole family. A focal point is the three-deck-high lobby with water feature backdrop and crystal piano. Accommodation prices depend on size and location, but all are comfortable and have a mini-bar and high-quality bed linen. Among the various lounges and bars, the Out of Africa Savannah Lounge really stands out. There are two large main dining rooms (Villa Borghese and L'Ibiscus), and both feature two seating times for dinner. The food includes regional Italian classics, with multiple pasta varieties freshly made each day. Smaller, cost-extra venues include Four Seasons and Shanghai. Visually entertaining shows can be seen in the stunning Covent Garden showlounge.

INSIGHT GUIDES' RATINGS		
	Achieved	Possible
Ship	396	500
Accommodation	151	200
Food	241	400
Service	248	400
Entertainment	62	100
Cruise Experience	266	400
OVERALL SCORE	**1364**	**2000**

MSC POESIA
★★★+

Size	Large Resort Ship
Tonnage	92,627
Cruise Line	MSC Cruises
Former Names	*None*
Entered Service	2008
Total Crew	1,039
Passengers	2,550

Designed for family-friendly cruising with European style, the interior decor is colorful, fittings and furnishings are high quality, and the main lobby spanning three decks has a water-feature backdrop. The hull has circular (rather than square) windows, and there is no walk-around outdoor deck. From balconies suites to interior (no-view) cabins, all have a minibar and personal safe. Main restaurants Le Fontane and Il Palladio are aft, with tables for two to eight. The food includes several regional Italian classics, with multiple pasta varieties made fresh daily. Small extra-cost venues include Kaito, a Japanese sushi bar. For high-quality (extra-cost) body pampering treatments, head to the Poesia Health Centre.

INSIGHT GUIDES' RATINGS		
	Achieved	Possible
Ship	395	500
Accommodation	151	200
Food	241	400
Service	248	400
Entertainment	62	100
Cruise Experience	266	400
OVERALL SCORE	**1363**	**2000**

MSC PREZIOSA
★★★★

Size	Large Resort Ship
Tonnage	139,400
Cruise Line	MSC Cruises
Former Names	*None*
Entered Service	2013
Total Crew	1,370
Passengers	3,502

This family-friendly resort ship has an Aqua Park with multiple water features, swimming pools, and play areas. Inside, there is an array of public rooms, lounges, and bars with high-quality, colorful furnishings. From the smallest cabins to the largest suites, the accommodation is well designed with ample storage. An exclusive MSC Yacht Club area has facilities for occupants of 'suite-grade' accommodation. Golden Lobster and L'Arabesque are the two main dining rooms, and feature fine table settings. The food is decent and varied (all pizza dough and fresh pasta is made on board). The Platinum Theatre (three-deck-high show-lounge) features highly visual shows, while the Aurea Spa has excellent facilities and body pampering treatments.

INSIGHT GUIDES' RATINGS		
	Achieved	Possible
Ship	402	500
Accommodation	157	200
Food	273	400
Service	258	400
Entertainment	76	100
Cruise Experience	276	400
OVERALL SCORE	**1442**	**2000**

MSC SEASCAPE
★★★★

Size	Large Resort Ship
Tonnage	169,380
Cruise Line	MSC Cruises
Former Names	None
Entered Service	2022
Total Crew	1,413
Passengers	4,540

This really is an immersive family-resort ship and features many American touches (there is even a Statue of Liberty in the casino), mixed with European decor and fabrics. It also has a wide range of facilities, restaurants, eateries, and bars, a 360-degree walk-around outdoor deck, a stunning upper-deck Robotron ride, and Aqua-Park play areas aft for youngsters. Indoors, its double-deck promenade has an LED-screen domed ceiling, and a multi-deck atrium lined with bars, eateries, and shops. Size, location, and grade determine cabin pricing, with more exclusivity in Yacht Club accommodation. Main dining is in the voluminous Seascape Restaurant, with Mediterranean cuisine and fresh pasta daily. The vast Chora Theatre puts on colorful shows.

INSIGHT GUIDES' RATINGS		
	Achieved	Possible
Ship	413	500
Accommodation	157	200
Food	275	400
Service	258	400
Entertainment	77	100
Cruise Experience	283	400
OVERALL SCORE	**1463**	**2000**

MSC SEASHORE
★★★★

Size	Large Resort Ship
Tonnage	170,412
Cruise Line	MSC Cruises
Former Names	None
Entered Service	2021
Total Crew	1,648
Passengers	4,810

This stunning multi-choice seagoing resort really has everything for the whole family, with water parks, several swimming pools, multiple play areas, and wide walk-around promenade deck. The interior decor is bold, and the furnishings are of high quality to complement the range of lounges, bars, and eateries. For a more exclusive experience, book Yacht Club accommodation, which includes private dining, pools and relaxation zones. Central Park, Tribeca, and 5th Avenue are the main (included) restaurants, with meals that include regional Italian classics, and pasta varieties freshly made daily. Cost-extra (high quality) food venues include Kaito Sushi Bar, Ocean Cay, and Butcher's Cut. Finally, head to the spa for some body-pampering.

INSIGHT GUIDES' RATINGS		
	Achieved	Possible
Ship	421	500
Accommodation	162	200
Food	277	400
Service	257	400
Entertainment	77	100
Cruise Experience	282	400
OVERALL SCORE	**1476**	**2000**

MSC SEASIDE

★★★★

Size	Large Resort Ship
Tonnage	153,516
Cruise Line	MSC Cruises
Former Names	*None*
Entered Service	2017
Total Crew	1,413
Passengers	4,134

This colorful and lively floating resort has an abundance of things for the whole family to enjoy. Its European interior decor features high-quality fittings and fixtures throughout. Finding your way around is easy because most public rooms 'flow' into each other. Accommodation price grades depend on size and location. All are well-designed, with ample closet and drawer space. Pay more to upgrade to the more exclusive Yacht Club accommodation, lounge, sunbathing, deck and private dining venue. Seaside and Ipanema are the main dining rooms, with tables seating two to eight. The food includes regional Italian classics and fresh pasta varieties made daily. There are also cost-extra (high quality) food venues. Overall, an excellent choice.

INSIGHT GUIDES' RATINGS

	Achieved	Possible
Ship	422	500
Accommodation	162	200
Food	277	400
Service	258	400
Entertainment	78	100
Cruise Experience	282	400
OVERALL SCORE	**1479**	**2000**

MSC SEAVIEW

★★★★

Size	Large Resort Ship
Tonnage	153,519
Cruise Line	MSC Cruises
Former Names	*None*
Entered Service	2018
Total Crew	1,413
Passengers	4,134

This good-looking, immersive family-resort ship oozes style and has a wide range of facilities, eateries, and entertainment. It has a 360-degree walk-around outdoor deck, and an Aqua-Park deck full of play areas. The interior layout is mostly user-friendly; MSC Yacht Club is an exclusive area for occupants of 'suite-grade' accommodation. Most other cabins are well de-signed, with ample closet and storage space. The Golden Sand and Silver Dolphin main dining rooms are comfortable, and food is well presented. Some regional Italian classics, and all the pasta, is made on board. Cost-extra venues include a Mediter-ranean Steakhouse, an Asian Fusion venue, and a teppanyaki grill. Spa facilities are extensive and body treatments are good.

INSIGHT GUIDES' RATINGS

	Achieved	Possible
Ship	421	500
Accommodation	162	200
Food	277	400
Service	258	400
Entertainment	78	100
Cruise Experience	285	400
OVERALL SCORE	**1481**	**2000**

MSC SINFONIA
★★★+

Size	Mid-size Ship
Tonnage	65,542
Cruise Line	MSC Cruises
Former Names	*European Stars*
Entered Service	2002, 2005
Total Crew	721
Passengers	1,952

Sister to *MSC Armonia*, this ship had a 'chop and stretch' operation, which added an 82ft (25m) mid-section, some 200 cabins, plus more public rooms, entertainment venues, and a large waterpark for children. There is abundant European style and color throughout the decor aboard this lively family-oriented ship. From interior no-view cabins to suites with outside balconies, the accommodation is practical. Two large main dining rooms (Il Galeone and Il Covo) feature regional Italian cuisine, and good pasta dishes (fresh pasta is made on board daily). Light 'always available' and vegetarian dishes are available daily. The spa facilities (including a thermal suite) are extensive.

INSIGHT GUIDES' RATINGS

	Achieved	Possible
Ship	366	500
Accommodation	148	200
Food	238	400
Service	239	400
Entertainment	55	100
Cruise Experience	242	400
OVERALL SCORE	**1288**	**2000**

MSC SPLENDIDA
★★★★

Size	Large Resort Ship
Tonnage	137,936
Cruise Line	MSC Cruises
Former Names	*None*
Entered Service	2009
Total Crew	1,370
Passengers	3,274

This colorful, stylish family-oriented ship has a multitude of public rooms, lounges, and bars (many of which have high ceilings), and bold Italian decor. An exclusive area called the MSC Yacht Club, for suite-category occupants, includes a dedicated restaurant and relaxation areas. Apart from the voluminous, two-deck-high La Reggia restaurant, with assigned seating, there are several other eateries (some cost extra). Regional Italian cuisine features and, overall, the meals are decent enough, but for something special, try the cost-extra L'Olivo, with food cooked to order. The showlounge seats over 1,600 and hosts colorful, mainly visual shows, while the Aurea Spa has an array of treatment rooms, facilities, and body pampering treatments.

INSIGHT GUIDES' RATINGS

	Achieved	Possible
Ship	410	500
Accommodation	156	200
Food	275	400
Service	257	400
Entertainment	77	100
Cruise Experience	276	400
OVERALL SCORE	**1451**	**2000**

MSC VIRTUOSA
★★★★

Size	Large Resort Ship
Tonnage	181,519
Cruise Line	MSC Cruises
Former Names	None
Entered Service	2021
Total Crew	1,536
Passengers	5,282

This family-friendly resort ship has an Aqua Park with multiple water features, swimming pools, and play areas. Inside, the ship has bold, colorful European styling and an outstanding central double-height connected area lined with shops, eateries, and more, with constantly-changing thematic ceiling displays – a charming robotic bartender makes and shakes drinks in the Starship Club. Accommodation price depends on size and location, with a separate area for Yacht Club suite occupants (and a dedicated restaurant and relaxation areas). The main restaurant, Blue Danube, has very decent food. Spa facilities and treatments are extensive.

INSIGHT GUIDES' RATINGS

	Achieved	Possible
Ship	412	500
Accommodation	157	200
Food	275	400
Service	258	400
Entertainment	77	100
Cruise Experience	238	400
OVERALL SCORE	**1462**	**2000**

MSC WORLD EUROPA
★★★★

Size	Large Resort Ship
Tonnage	215,863
Cruise Line	MSC Cruises
Former Names	None
Entered Service	2022
Total Crew	2,138
Passengers	5,400

Simply stunning! With its wavy sand dune-like exterior and upright bows this ultra-large, LNG-powered ship has numerous 'wow' factors for families, including a thrilling 11-deck 'indoor' waterslide (The Spiral). Its central double-height connected area includes high-quality eateries, bars, brand-name shops, constantly-changing thematic ceiling displays, and a casino. Accommodation ranges from interior viewless cabins to exclusive balconied Yacht Club suites. Hexagon and La Foglia – the expansive main dining rooms – feature regional Italian classics, with different pasta varieties made daily. Cost-extra venues include some delightful grown-aboard microgreens in Niklas Ekstedt's Chef's Garden Kitchen.

INSIGHT GUIDES' RATINGS

	Achieved	Possible
Ship	426	500
Accommodation	162	200
Food	277	400
Service	260	400
Entertainment	78	100
Cruise Experience	287	400
OVERALL SCORE	**1490**	**2000**

NATIONAL GEOGRAPHIC ENDEAVOUR II
★★★

Size	Boutique Ship
Tonnage	2,695
Cruise Line	National Geographic Cruises
Former Names	*Via Australis*
Entered Service	2005, 2022
Total Crew	63
Passengers	96

This ship underwent a major refurbishment in 2016 in order to equip it for service in the Galápagos islands. It has a glass-bottomed boat and several kayaks, and there is a good amount of outdoor deck space. Public rooms include a lounge at the front of the ship (under the navigation bridge), a library/lounge, and a small gym and spa. The cabins are compact, ranging from 130–270 sq ft (12–25 sq m), and are reasonably comfortable, but the bathrooms really are tight, and have a high step. The restaurant seats everyone, but the food is simple and mostly local. There are no dedicated facilities for children.

INSIGHT GUIDES' RATINGS		
	Achieved	Possible
Ship	306	500
Accommodation	116	200
Food	244	400
Service	214	400
Entertainment	50	100
Cruise Experience	251	400
OVERALL SCORE	**1181**	**2000**

NATIONAL GEOGRAPHIC ENDURANCE
★★★★

Size	Boutique Ship
Tonnage	12,786
Cruise Line	National Geographic Cruises
Former Names	*None*
Entered Service	2020
Total Crew	112
Passengers	126

This polar expedition-style small ship has inverted bows to enhance its seakeeping abilities. It is stylish and has some decent public rooms, although some have wide view-obstructing pillars. The two aft-located enclosed geodesic glass igloo pods on deck are novel, and are bookable for use at night (although there is no adjacent toilet). The cabins are mostly compact, and moderately comfortable (all have twin beds convertible to doubles), with window or porthole, reading lamp, and bathrooms with showers, but little storage space. There are also some well-equipped suites (some with bathtub). The main dining room is comfortable, but the food is carbohydrate-rich and green vegetables are rather scarce. There are two saunas and a yoga studio.

INSIGHT GUIDES' RATINGS		
	Achieved	Possible
Ship	377	500
Accommodation	152	200
Food	235	400
Service	278	400
Entertainment	66	100
Cruise Experience	322	400
OVERALL SCORE	**1430**	**2000**

NATIONAL GEOGRAPHIC EXPLORER
★★+

Size	Boutique Ship
Tonnage	6,471
Cruise Line	National Geographic Cruises
Former Names	*Lyngen, Midnatsol II, Midnatsol*
Entered Service	1982, 2008
Total Crew	70
Passengers	152

This sturdy little ship was originally built for northern Europe coastal sailings with a strengthened hull for ice, and stabilizers, so movement is minimised. It is best suited to adventurous types who don't really mind the most basic facilities and minimal comfort. There are several cabins for solo occupancy, while most are for two or more; some have fixed beds that cannot be moved, and others have beds that can be joined together. The main dining room is quite practical, with spartan decor. Meals are acceptable, but quite basic, and rather carbohydrate-rich with few green vegetables. Lectures, briefings, and after-dinner recaps provide the entertainment.

INSIGHT GUIDES' RATINGS

	Achieved	Possible
Ship	257	500
Accommodation	109	200
Food	198	400
Service	182	400
Entertainment	60	100
Cruise Experience	205	400
OVERALL SCORE	**1011**	**2000**

NATIONAL GEOGRAPHIC ISLANDER II
★★★

Size	Boutique Ship
Tonnage	3,370
Cruise Line	National Geographic Cruises
Former Names	*Crystal Esprit, MegaStar Taurus, Lady D, Lady Diana, Aurora I*
Entered Service	1989, 2022
Total Crew	91
Passengers	104

This dated pocket-sized ship was originally built in 1982 for the long-defunct British company Windsor Line. It has a modicum of style and is quite comfortable, with a limited number of public rooms, although they are not really needed for the Galápagos discovery-style voyages. Note that there is no elevator. The well-designed cabins are small, comfortable, and practical, and all have bathrooms with showers and ample storage space – not even the owner's suite has a bathtub. The restaurant itself is comfortable (although it has a low ceiling) and the food is appropriate for this very special region. A cruise onboard this ship is really all about personal discovery and nature.

INSIGHT GUIDES' RATINGS

	Achieved	Possible
Ship	284	500
Accommodation	106	200
Food	236	400
Service	194	400
Entertainment	60	100
Cruise Experience	263	400
OVERALL SCORE	**1143**	**2000**

NATIONAL GEOGRAPHIC ORION
★★★+

Size	Boutique Ship
Tonnage	4,050
Cruise Line	National Geographic Cruises
Former Names	*Orion*
Entered Service	2003, 2014
Total Crew	75
Passengers	102

Nature travelers might well enjoy this pocket-sized, 'soft' expedition-style ship. It carries 14 heavy-duty Zodiac inflatable landing craft, and has a 'mud room' adjacent to the aft loading area. The interior decor is modern and comfortable. Public rooms include an observation lounge and library, a main lounge, and a dedicated surround-sound theater. The suites and cabins are comfortable (all cabinetry is hand-made), and all have twin beds convertible to queen-size doubles, a mini-fridge, and decent closet space. Meals provided in The Restaurant – whose artwork is based on the astrological signs – are generally decent enough. There is also a small outdoor café for continental breakfasts.

INSIGHT GUIDES' RATINGS		
	Achieved	Possible
Ship	364	500
Accommodation	151	200
Food	226	400
Service	269	400
Entertainment	71	100
Cruise Experience	267	400
OVERALL SCORE	**1348**	**2000**

NATIONAL GEOGRAPHIC RESOLUTION
★★★★

Size	Boutique Ship
Tonnage	12,786
Cruise Line	National Geographic Cruises
Former Names	*None*
Entered Service	2021
Total Crew	112
Passengers	126

This polar expedition-style small ship has inverted bows for enhanced seakeeping abilities. It is stylish and has some decent public rooms, although some have several thick view-obstructing pillars. The two aft-located enclosed geodesic glass igloo pods on deck are novel, and are bookable for use at night (but there is no adjacent toilet). Cabins are mostly compact, and moderately comfortable (all have twin beds convertible to doubles), with a window or porthole, reading lamp, and bathrooms with showers, but little storage space. There are also well-equipped suites (some with bathtub). The main dining room is comfortable, but the food is carbohydrate-rich, and green vegetables are rather scarce. There are two saunas and a yoga studio.

INSIGHT GUIDES' RATINGS		
	Achieved	Possible
Ship	377	500
Accommodation	152	200
Food	235	400
Service	278	400
Entertainment	66	100
Cruise Experience	322	400
OVERALL SCORE	**1430**	**2000**

NATIONAL GEOGRAPHIC SEA LION
★+

Size	Boutique Ship
Tonnage	630
Cruise Line	National Geographic Cruises
Former Names	*Great Rivers Explorer*
Entered Service	1982, 2009
Total Crew	25
Passengers	62

Looking well-worn and tired, this very small, dated ship has only most basic facilities. It is in its element navigating small coastal inlets that larger ships cannot possibly reach. The cabins have only the most basic facilities; all have twin narrow beds that cannot be moved (except for four cabins that can be made into double beds), and little storage space, while bathrooms have only basic camping-style facilities. There is one small lounge/bar, and the dining room has one seating, with limited food choices. Passengers wear name tags for easy recognition, and early morning wake-up calls are part of the adventure. Itineraries are nature immersive.

INSIGHT GUIDES' RATINGS

	Achieved	Possible
Ship	174	500
Accommodation	68	200
Food	166	400
Service	150	400
Entertainment	41	100
Cruise Experience	173	400
OVERALL SCORE	**772**	**2000**

NAUTICA
★★★+

Size	Small Ship
Tonnage	30,277
Cruise Line	Oceania Cruises
Former Names	*R5*
Entered Service	1998, 2005
Total Crew	386
Passengers	684

This pleasant ship has a wide array of public rooms and decent food, although the cabins are rather small, as are the bathrooms, unless you opt for one of the suites (the aft-facing suites are particularly good). Teak overlaid decking and quality lounge chairs provide high comfort on the Lido and Pool deck. The interior decor is a comfortable stroll through the ocean liners of the 1920s, with both real, and faux, stairways and fireplaces. The Grand Dining Room (main restaurant), which can seat over 350, is located aft, with open seating, but the noise level can be high due to its low ceiling height. Other smaller venues include Toscana and Polo Grill. Both require reservations, but the cooked-to-order food experience is excellent.

INSIGHT GUIDES' RATINGS

	Achieved	Possible
Ship	356	500
Accommodation	126	200
Food	291	400
Service	232	400
Entertainment	67	100
Cruise Experience	237	400
OVERALL SCORE	**1309**	**2000**

NAVIGATOR OF THE SEAS
★★★

Size	Large Resort Ship
Tonnage	137,276
Cruise Line	Royal Caribbean International
Former Names	None
Entered Service	2002
Total Crew	1,185
Passengers	3,286

This is a large, family-oriented floating leisure resort, including an adrenaline-pumping two-person raft and 'The Blaster' – a 800-ft (243-m) -long Aquacoaster – among other rides. Inside is a four-deck-high Royal Promenade: a fun street full of places to hang out, shop, eat, and drink. Plan wisely, because you need to sign up for many things. From interior (virtual-view) and solo-occupancy cabins to large suites (with balcony), the price depends on the grade you choose. Meals are in the cavernous tri-level Sapphire Dining Room (seats over 1,800). Food is mass catering so-so, but you can pay extra to have steak or lobster cooked to order, or eat in one of several smaller venues. There is almost continuous entertainment and 'background' music.

INSIGHT GUIDES' RATINGS		
	Achieved	Possible
Ship	354	500
Accommodation	137	200
Food	220	400
Service	207	400
Entertainment	73	100
Cruise Experience	238	400
OVERALL SCORE	**1229**	**2000**

NIEUW AMSTERDAM
★★★+

Size	Mid-size Ship
Tonnage	86,700
Cruise Line	Holland America Line
Former Names	None
Entered Service	2010
Total Crew	929
Passengers	2,106

Named after the Dutch moniker for New York City, this ship's interior decor also reflects the great metropolis. It has a delightful walk-around promenade deck with steamer-style sun loungers. One of the two outdoor pools can be covered by a retractable glass roof. There are abundant public rooms and entertainment venues, but many pillars obstruct passenger flow almost everywhere. Accommodation is comfortable, from small solo traveler cabins to the expansive Grand Pinnacle suites. The Manhattan Dining Room spans two decks, and both open and assigned seating are available. HAL can provide Kosher meals (if requested when you book). Most food is so-so, but pay extra and you can dine in the Pinnacle Grill. Overall, this is a very pleasant ship.

INSIGHT GUIDES' RATINGS		
	Achieved	Possible
Ship	366	500
Accommodation	142	200
Food	220	400
Service	224	400
Entertainment	70	100
Cruise Experience	251	400
OVERALL SCORE	**1273**	**2000**

NIEUW STATENDAM
★★★+

Size	Mid-size Ship
Tonnage	86,700
Cruise Line	Holland America Line
Former Names	None
Entered Service	2018
Total Crew	929
Passengers	2,106

Dutch influences feature throughout this pleasant Pinnacle class ship, which has a complete walk-around exterior deck. One of the two outside pools has a retractable glass roof – good for inclement weather conditions. Most public rooms are on two decks, plus there's a Crow's Nest observations lounge. Holland America Line is known for its relaxed pace, so there are no climbing walls, rope walks, or other distractions. From small cabins for solo travelers to grand suites, the accommodation is well designed. The dual-level Americana-themed dining room is dressed in white and cream. Meals are generally underwhelming, but there are exceptions. For cooked-to-order steaks and seafood, the cost-extra Pinnacle Grill is recommended.

INSIGHT GUIDES' RATINGS

	Achieved	Possible
Ship	396	500
Accommodation	151	200
Food	225	400
Service	238	400
Entertainment	75	100
Cruise Experience	256	400
OVERALL SCORE	**1341**	**2000**

NIPPON MARU
★★★+

Size	Small Ship
Tonnage	22,472
Cruise Line	Mitsui OSK Line
Former Names	None
Entered Service	1990
Total Crew	230
Passengers	408

For Japanese-speaking travelers, this now rather outdated ship has comfortable styling, and its interior focal point is an atrium lobby that spans six decks. There are several public lounges and bars: the Neptune Bar probably has the most extensive assortment of Scotch whiskies (including some very rare single malts) at sea. Accommodation ranges from very small indoor (no-view) cabins to some newer suites with separate living and sleeping areas. All standard cabins have blond wood cabinetry. The ship is praised for its high food quality and the Mizuho dining room serves both traditional Japanese cuisine as well as some western dishes. Features include traditional Japanese baths (one for women, one for men) and associated washrooms.

INSIGHT GUIDES' RATINGS

	Achieved	Possible
Ship	342	500
Accommodation	144	200
Food	307	400
Service	250	400
Entertainment	73	100
Cruise Experience	256	400
OVERALL SCORE	**1372**	**2000**

NOORDAM
★★★+

Size	Mid-size Ship
Tonnage	82,318
Cruise Line	Holland America Line
Former Names	None
Entered Service	2006
Total Crew	820
Passengers	1,924

This ship combines the company's traditional Dutch heritage with European style. The twin working funnels are the result of the ship's slightly unusual machinery configuration. Features include a complete exterior walk-around deck, with teak steamer-style sunloungers. Inside, a three-deck lobby features a Waterford crystal world globe and there are two whole decks of public rooms, lounges, bars, and a showlounge that spans four decks. From the small viewless interior solo traveler cabins to Grand Pinnacle suites with balconies, almost all have good storage and comfortable bathrooms. The Vista Dining Room spans two decks. The cuisine is standard catering fare, so for something more, try the extra-cost Pinnacle Grill.

INSIGHT GUIDES' RATINGS		
	Achieved	Possible
Ship	368	500
Accommodation	142	200
Food	220	400
Service	223	400
Entertainment	69	100
Cruise Experience	251	400
OVERALL SCORE	**1273**	**2000**

NORWEGIAN BLISS
★★★+

Size	Large Resort Ship
Tonnage	168,028
Cruise Line	Norwegian Cruise Line
Former Names	None
Entered Service	2018
Total Crew	1,730
Passengers	4,004

This ship has colorful, splashy artwork on its white hull by marine artist Robert Wyland. It's an uber-casual, floating playground for active families, and kids will love its extensive outdoor AquaPark and all its play areas. Most public rooms are on an indoor-outdoor complex called 678 Ocean Place. Accommodation ranges from interior (no-view) cabins and small solo-occupancy cabins to spacious suites in a more private area called The Haven. Three main dining rooms are cruise fare-inclusive (the food is standard banquet catering), but extra-cost venues such as Cagney's Steakhouse, Moderna Churrascaria, Le Bistro, and others, are available – these are smaller reservations-required venues with food cooked to order – as well as other casual spots.

INSIGHT GUIDES' RATINGS		
	Achieved	Possible
Ship	400	500
Accommodation	143	200
Food	244	400
Service	227	400
Entertainment	78	100
Cruise Experience	270	400
OVERALL SCORE	**1362**	**2000**

NORWEGIAN BREAKAWAY
★★★+

Size .... Large Resort Ship
Tonnage 144,017
Cruise Line .... Norwegian Cruise Line
Former Names .... None
Entered Service 2013
Total Crew 1,657
Passengers 3,963

This is a multiple-choice seagoing resort for casual, lively, family-friendly cruising. The hull was decorated with a New York design by the America-based illustrator Peter Max. The pool deck and Aqua Park offer five thrilling waterslides, rope courses, plus a rock climbing and rappelling wall. Open space for sunbathing is limited. Inside, the jazzy decor is upbeat, with many public rooms, bars, lounges, and casino area thronging a three-deck-high promenade called 678 Ocean Place. Accommodation ranges from viewless interior cabins to balconied suites in a private enclave. There are numerous restaurants and eateries (the largest being Savor and Taste), and some cost extra.

INSIGHT GUIDES' RATINGS		
	Achieved	Possible
Ship	395	500
Accommodation	144	200
Food	245	400
Service	225	400
Entertainment	86	100
Cruise Experience	259	400
OVERALL SCORE	**1354**	**2000**

NORWEGIAN DAWN
★★★+

Size .... Mid-size Ship
Tonnage 92,250
Cruise Line .... Norwegian Cruise Line
Former Names .... SuperStar Scorpio
Entered Service 2002
Total Crew 1,032
Passengers 2,340

A fun vacation awaits aboard this family-oriented mid-size ship, sister to Norwegian Star. Although the suites and junior suites are quite spacious – including the Horizon and Vista garden villas, which overlook the main pool deck – most standard viewless interior and outside view cabins are compact. Many cabins have 3rd and 4th berths, useful for families with children, although storage space is limited. With Freestyle Dining, you can choose which dining venue to eat in, at what time, and with whom. There are three principal dining rooms, plus several themed eateries, some of which (such as Cagney's Steakhouse) cost extra. In general, meals may not be so memorable, but there are some exceptions. For colorful shows, head to the Stardust Theater.

INSIGHT GUIDES' RATINGS		
	Achieved	Possible
Ship	356	500
Accommodation	138	200
Food	235	400
Service	218	400
Entertainment	67	100
Cruise Experience	245	400
OVERALL SCORE	**1259**	**2000**

NORWEGIAN ENCORE
★★★+

Size .... Large Resort Ship
Tonnage 167,600
Cruise Line .... Norwegian Cruise Line
Former Names .... None
Entered Service 2019
Total Crew 1,730
Passengers 4,004

A close sister to *Norwegian Bliss*, this ship has colorful, splashy artwork on its white hull. It really is a floating playground for active families, and kids will love its extensive outdoor Aqua-Park facilities. A triple-deck indoor promenade complex houses shops, bars, entertainment spots, themed eateries, and a large casino. Accommodation varies from small interior (no-view) cabins to expansive two-bedroom suites. For exclusivity, book Haven area accommodation. With many choices of dining and eating venues, Freestyle Dining means you choose which venue you want to eat in (some eateries cost extra), but there is a wide choice. Entertainment is almost non-stop, and includes colorful razzle-dazzle Vegas-style shows for the whole family.

INSIGHT GUIDES' RATINGS

	Achieved	Possible
Ship	390	500
Accommodation	136	200
Food	245	400
Service	232	400
Entertainment	86	100
Cruise Experience	257	400
OVERALL SCORE	**1346**	**2000**

NORWEGIAN EPIC
★★★+

Size .... Large Resort Ship
Tonnage 155,873
Cruise Line .... Norwegian Cruise Line
Former Names .... None
Entered Service 2010
Total Crew 1,724
Passengers 4,100

This epic-sized floating resort could be ideal for its unabashed, playful, family-friendly features and South Beach nightlife. Accommodation ranges from interior (no-view) cabins to Courtyard Villas positioned in a private enclave, with an expansive balcony. 'Freestyle Dining' means you can try many different types of food in an assortment of venues, although making reservations can be frustrating. Favorite small venue eateries include Cagney's Steakhouse, Churrascaria (for skewered meats served by Gauchos), and Le Bistro (for French-style cuisine). Excellent full-on storybook production shows can be seen in the Epic Theater, while The Cavern Club is a hotspot for rock 'n' roll lovers.

INSIGHT GUIDES' RATINGS

	Achieved	Possible
Ship	378	500
Accommodation	141	200
Food	240	400
Service	223	400
Entertainment	85	100
Cruise Experience	253	400
OVERALL SCORE	**1320**	**2000**

NORWEGIAN ESCAPE
★★★+

Size .... Large Resort Ship
Tonnage 165,157
Cruise Line .... Norwegian Cruise Line
Former Names .... *None*
Entered Service 2015
Total Crew 1,733
Passengers 4,266

With a less boxy look than larger sibling *Norwegian Epic*, this ship is a large, bold, multiple-choice floating theme park, with a wide range of family-friendly features for trendy urbanites. The ambiance is South Beach in heat, with all its hype and volume. A three-deck indoor/outdoor complex (678 Ocean Place) has themed eateries, bars, lounges, and a large casino. Freestyle Dining means no assigned dining rooms, so you eat when and where you want. There is abundant entertainment and music everywhere. The two-deck spa is always busy, plus there's an Aqua Park with multiple waterslides, neat multi-elevated rope course, a climbing cage, and more. Overall, this is a lively ship, and time spent planning will help you make good decisions.

INSIGHT GUIDES' RATINGS		
	Achieved	Possible
Ship	396	500
Accommodation	144	200
Food	245	400
Service	232	400
Entertainment	86	100
Cruise Experience	264	400
OVERALL SCORE	**1367**	**2000**

NORWEGIAN GEM
★★★+

Size .... Mid-size Ship
Tonnage 93,530
Cruise Line .... Norwegian Cruise Line
Former Names .... *None*
Entered Service 2007
Total Crew 1,070
Passengers 2,394

This floating leisure center has abundant outdoor space, while inside there is a good range of public areas, lounges, and bars. A multitude of themed dining spots and eatery choices helps make it highly suitable for families with children. Accommodation ranges from small interior (no-view) cabins to lavish suites in a private courtyard setting. Magenta and Pacific are the main (included) dining rooms, but there are other more intimate cost-extra venues with food cooked to order. Favorites include Cagney's Steak House, Moderno Churrascaria (Argentinian-style grilled meats), and Le Bistro (classic French cuisine).

INSIGHT GUIDES' RATINGS		
	Achieved	Possible
Ship	350	500
Accommodation	141	200
Food	234	400
Service	219	400
Entertainment	66	100
Cruise Experience	243	400
OVERALL SCORE	**1253**	**2000**

NORWEGIAN GETAWAY
★★★+

Size	Large Resort Ship
Tonnage	145,655
Cruise Line	Norwegian Cruise Line
Former Names	*None*
Entered Service	2014
Total Crew	1,646
Passengers	3,929

Sister to *Norwegian Breakaway*, this family-friendly resort ship has multiple eateries and good entertainment shows. The ambiance is South Beach in heat, with all the hype and volume to prove it. Families can enjoy the extensive Aqua Park facilities, with waterslides, rope walks, and a climbing wall. For accommodation, it is, quite simply pay more, get more, from windowless cabins for solo occupancy to exclusive large suites in The Haven. Freestyle Dining means no assigned dining rooms, or tables, or seats, so you choose where and when you want to eat. Pay extra and you can eat in one of the smaller, specialist venues like Cagney's Steakhouse, Moderna Churrascaria, and Le Bistro (reservations-required venues with cooked-to-order food).

INSIGHT GUIDES' RATINGS

	Achieved	Possible
Ship	397	500
Accommodation	144	200
Food	244	400
Service	222	400
Entertainment	86	100
Cruise Experience	263	400
OVERALL SCORE	**1356**	**2000**

NORWEGIAN JADE
★★★+

Size	Mid-size Ship
Tonnage	93,558
Cruise Line	Norwegian Cruise Line
Former Names	*Pride of Hawaii*
Entered Service	2006, 2008
Total Crew	1,037
Passengers	2,402

This comfortable mid-size ship has a wide range of facilities, and the dress code is ultra-casual. Accommodation comes in multiple price grades, with sizes varying from very small interior cabins to lavish multi-room villas. However, even the smallest cabins have decent storage space. The 37-ft (11-m) lap pool (part of the Yin and Yang spa complex) is good, and there is an abundance of facilities and body pampering treatment rooms. The interior focal gathering point is Bar Central, and there are numerous bars and lounges, and plenty of live music. The Stardust Theater – with over 1,000 seats – hosts colorful Las Vegas-style production shows. Overall, it's lively, with multiple choices (many at extra cost).

INSIGHT GUIDES' RATINGS

	Achieved	Possible
Ship	349	500
Accommodation	141	200
Food	234	400
Service	219	400
Entertainment	66	100
Cruise Experience	242	400
OVERALL SCORE	**1251**	**2000**

NORWEGIAN JEWEL
★★★+

Size.. Mid-size Ship
Tonnage...93,502
Cruise Line.........................Norwegian Cruise Line
Former Names .... None
Entered Service 2005
Total Crew 1,069
Passengers 2,376

This ship is a floating leisure center for families with children due to its wide range of public areas, lounges and bars, themed dining spots, and eatery choices. Accommodation ranges from small interior (no-view) cabins to lavish suites in a private courtyard setting. Tsar's Palace (reminiscent of the interior of Catherine the Great's St Petersburg Palace) and Azura are the main (large) included dining rooms, with standard banquet catering. There are other smaller (more intimate) cost-extra venues with food cooked to order. These include Cagney's Steak House, Moderno Churrascaria (Argentinian-style grilled meats), and Le Bistro (classic French cuisine). For colorful production shows, head to the large Stardust Theater.

INSIGHT GUIDES' RATINGS		
	Achieved	Possible
Ship	347	500
Accommodation	141	200
Food	234	400
Service	244	400
Entertainment	66	100
Cruise Experience	242	400
OVERALL SCORE	**1274**	**2000**

NORWEGIAN JOY
★★★+

Size..Large Resort Ship
Tonnage...167,725
Cruise Line.........................Norwegian Cruise Line
Former Names .... None
Entered Service 2017
Total Crew 1,821
Passengers 3,883

This uber casual and lively seagoing resort has outdoor decks full of entertaining features, play and rest areas for the whole family. Its colorful bows feature the mythical phoenix bird by renowned Chinese artist Tan Ping. An activity-driven Aquapark with thrilling waterslides and rope course keeps youngsters occupied, but the big thrill is the go-kart track, where speeds of up to 20mph (32kph) can be reached! Inside, most public rooms, including eateries, shops and casino, are found on a three-deck indoor-outdoor complex. Accommodation ranges from viewless interior cabins to balconied enclave suites. Freestyle Dining provides multiple complimentary eateries, plus several premium cost-extra venues for choice.

INSIGHT GUIDES' RATINGS		
	Achieved	Possible
Ship	386	500
Accommodation	143	200
Food	258	400
Service	252	400
Entertainment	77	100
Cruise Experience	269	400
OVERALL SCORE	**1385**	**2000**

NORWEGIAN PEARL
★★★

Size	Mid-size Ship
Tonnage	93,530
Cruise Line	Norwegian Cruise Line
Former Names	None
Entered Service	2006
Total Crew	1,072
Passengers	2,394

Sparkling jewel artwork adorns the hull of this mid-size, family-friendly ship. Inside is an eclectic mix of colors and decor, numerous bars, and lounges. One standout for ship lovers is Magnum's Champagne and Wine Bar, with decor that recalls 1920s Paris and the ocean liner *Normandie*. From small, viewless interior cabins to lavish Penthouse Suites in a private courtyard setting (part of 'The Haven' complex), there is ample choice. Freestyle Dining means no assigned restaurants, tables, or seats, so you choose where and when to eat, but note that some smaller venues (such as the popular Cagney's Steakhouse and Le Bistro) cost extra. The largest – Indigo and Summer Palace – are included in the fare and feature acceptable batch-cooked meals.

INSIGHT GUIDES' RATINGS	Achieved	Possible
Ship	347	500
Accommodation	138	200
Food	235	400
Service	219	400
Entertainment	66	100
Cruise Experience	244	400
OVERALL SCORE	**1249**	**2000**

NORWEGIAN PRIMA
★★★+

Size	Large Resort Ship
Tonnage	143,535
Cruise Line	Norwegian Cruise Line
Former Names	None
Entered Service	2022
Total Crew	1,388
Passengers	3,215

With its short, slightly inverted bows and jazzy contemporary looks, this is a floating fun palace with all the trimmings and fast-paced lifestyle for multi-generational fun, and numerous facilities for children. There is a decent amount of open deck space, and a whole host of features, including a Prima Speedway tri-level race track. A converted Airstream food truck in the Indulge Food Hall is also a big hit. The accommodation range is wide, well designed, and comfortable. Suite accommodation, with a separate dining venue, lounge and other facilities, are in a designated area. There is a wide array of entertainment, including lavish and colorful production shows, plus music at every turn.

INSIGHT GUIDES' RATINGS	Achieved	Possible
Ship	345	500
Accommodation	137	200
Food	233	400
Service	217	400
Entertainment	71	100
Cruise Experience	261	400
OVERALL SCORE	**1264**	**2000**

NORWEGIAN SKY
★★★+

Size .... Mid-size Ship
Tonnage 77,104
Cruise Line ....Norwegian Cruise Line
Former Names ....*Pride of Aloha*
Entered Service 1999, 2008
Total Crew 899
Passengers 2,004

This comfortable, mid-size casual ship for families has many bars and lounges and multiple dining and snacking options. From interior (no-view) cabins to a large Owner's Suites, all are quite compact, but have ample closet space. With Freestyle Dining, you choose where, when and with whom you want to eat. The largest venues are the Crossings and Palace restaurants (both included, and each with around 500 seats), but there are also several other cost-extra, reservation-required venues; favorites include Cagney's Steakhouse and the elegant French Bistro. For entertainment, head to the 1,000-seat Stardust Theater for colorful and voluminous large-scale shows.

INSIGHT GUIDES' RATINGS

	Achieved	Possible
Ship	347	500
Accommodation	138	200
Food	234	400
Service	215	400
Entertainment	74	100
Cruise Experience	242	400
OVERALL SCORE	**1250**	**2000**

NORWEGIAN SPIRIT
★★★

Size .... Mid-size Ship
Tonnage 75,904
Cruise Line ....Norwegian Cruise Line
Former Names ....*SuperStar Leo*
Entered Service 1998, 2004
Total Crew 912
Passengers 2,018

This casual family-friendly, mid-sized, multi-choice ship (originally built for short cruises) has an outdoor promenade deck, and good facilities for children. Indoors is a two-deck boulevard and a large central atrium lobby, with cafés, shops, and three glass-walled elevators. The accommodation ranges from very small interior viewless cabins to large, lavishly decorated suites. With Freestyle Dining and eight places to eat, including some that cost extra, you will need to plan and book accordingly. The complimentary Windows dining room is the largest, with over 600 seats. High energy, razzle-dazzle shows are presented in the Stardust Theater. The ship also has a spa, and separate gymnasium.

INSIGHT GUIDES' RATINGS

	Achieved	Possible
Ship	348	500
Accommodation	138	200
Food	234	400
Service	219	400
Entertainment	66	100
Cruise Experience	242	400
OVERALL SCORE	**1247**	**2000**

NORWEGIAN STAR
★★★+

Size	Mid-size Ship
Tonnage	91,740
Cruise Line	Norwegian Cruise Line
Former Names	*SuperStar Libra*
Entered Service	2001
Total Crew	1,031
Passengers	2,348

This mid-size ship is a lively playground for the whole family, and has all the trimmings for an enjoyable seagoing vacation. Its main lobby is quite a stunning area. From small viewless interior cabin to two huge Garden Villas, it is simply a question of pay more, get more. With Freestyle Dining, you can try different types of cuisine, in different settings, and eat when you want, although reservations are needed. Although, in general, the food is not memorable, there are some exceptions. Aqua and Versailles are the largest venues, but Versailles (for classic French cuisine) and Cagney's Steakhouse are popular cost-extra small venue alternatives, with cooked-to-order food. All the big shows can be seen in the Stardust Theater.

INSIGHT GUIDES' RATINGS		
	Achieved	Possible
Ship	356	500
Accommodation	138	200
Food	235	400
Service	216	400
Entertainment	67	100
Cruise Experience	243	400
OVERALL SCORE	**1255**	**2000**

NORWEGIAN SUN
★★★+

Size	Mid-size Ship
Tonnage	78,309
Cruise Line	Norwegian Cruise Line
Former Names	*None*
Entered Service	2001
Total Crew	906
Passengers	1,936

This mid-size ship has a reasonable amount of deck space, particularly with its extra wide pool decks. The accommodation has many different price categories, depending on size and location, but most are small. Freestyle Dining means eat where and when you like, but advance planning and reservations are advised. The Four Seasons and Seven Seas are the largest, both with tables for two to eight. For better quality food, it might be worth paying extra to eat in one of the smaller, specialized venues such as Le Bistro (classic French cuisine), or Moderno Churrascaria (Brazilian-style steakhouse). For colorful production shows head to the bi-level Stardust Theater.

INSIGHT GUIDES' RATINGS		
	Achieved	Possible
Ship	355	500
Accommodation	138	200
Food	234	400
Service	215	400
Entertainment	74	100
Cruise Experience	243	400
OVERALL SCORE	**1259**	**2000**

NORWEGIAN VIVA
NYR

Size	Large Resort Ship
Tonnage	142,500
Cruise Line	Norwegian Cruise Line
Former Names	None
Entered Service	2023
Total Crew	1,388
Passengers	3,219

With its jazzy contemporary looks, fast-paced lifestyle and extra features, this ship really is a floating fun palace for multi-generational fun. There is a decent amount of open deck space, and many facilities for children, including a Speedway (think: dodgem cars). The accommodation range is wide and includes many small cabins, well designed, and comfortable. Suite accommodation with a designated dining venue, lounge and other facilities are in a separate area. Palomar (seafood speciality venue) and Hsuki (Japanese-style cuisine) are extra-cost eateries. A wide entertainment mix includes lavish production shows, and music at every turn.

INSIGHT GUIDES' RATINGS

	Achieved	Possible
Ship	NYR	500
Accommodation	NYR	200
Food	NYR	400
Service	NYR	400
Entertainment	NYR	100
Cruise Experience	NYR	400
OVERALL SCORE	**NYR**	**2000**

OASIS OF THE SEAS
★★★+

Size	Large Resort Ship
Tonnage	225,282
Cruise Line	Royal Caribbean International
Former Names	None
Entered Service	2009
Total Crew	2,164
Passengers	5,400

A super family-friendly experience awaits aboard this stunning, ultra-large ship (the world's first measuring over 200,000 gross tons). It has a host of play and entertainment areas for the whole family. Numerous accommodation and price grades reflect the size and location choice. There are many bars and places to eat or snack, in public places arranged in seven 'neighborhoods', with an extensive Royal Promenade the main social point. The cavernous main dining room spans three decks. The cuisine is standardized, but pay extra and you can get some items cooked to order. The 1,380-seat Opal Theatre hosts colorful shows and the ice rink has superb ice-skating productions. There are many cost-extra items (and added service charges), so choose wisely.

INSIGHT GUIDES' RATINGS

	Achieved	Possible
Ship	397	500
Accommodation	140	200
Food	220	400
Service	231	400
Entertainment	87	100
Cruise Experience	259	400
OVERALL SCORE	**1334**	**2000**

OCEAN ALBATROS
NYR

Size	Boutique Ship
Tonnage	8,035
Cruise Line	American Queen Voyages
Former Names	None
Entered Service	2023
Total Crew	74
Passengers	160

Joining sister ship *Ocean Victory* in 2023, this small discovery-style vessel also has an 'X-Bow' design, providing good seakeeping capabilities. There is a mudroom for pre/post shipside Zodiac landings, an aft platform for water sports and associated equipment, and a small but well-equipped boot-washing area. The main public rooms include a lecture room, an observation lounge (both have high ceilings), and a library, but note that several slim pillars obstruct sightlines; there is also a small gym, and sauna. The (mostly) compact cabins are quite comfortable, although there is little storage space for any long voyages, and about 90 percent have a small balcony, The aft-facing dining room has windows on three sides.

INSIGHT GUIDES' RATINGS		
	Achieved	Possible
Ship	NYR	500
Accommodation	NYR	200
Food	NYR	400
Service	NYR	400
Entertainment	NYR	100
Cruise Experience	NYR	400
OVERALL SCORE	**NYR**	**2000**

OCEAN DISCOVERER
NYR

Size	Boutique Ship
Tonnage	8,035
Cruise Line	American Queen Voyages
Former Names	None
Entered Service	2023
Total Crew	74
Passengers	186

This very small discovery and expedition-style ship can take you up-close-and-personal, and away from areas where big-ship cruises go, and there is a small but practical mudroom/boot-washing area, with storage cupboards. Lecturers from the California State Polytechnic University accompany the voyages. The cabins (not suites) are compact but comfortable, with adequate storage space. Its limited public rooms include an observation lounge, lecture room (both have relatively high ceilings), and small library, but many slim pillars obstruct sightlines. The main, aft-facing restaurant is comfortable.

INSIGHT GUIDES' RATINGS		
	Achieved	Possible
Ship	NYR	500
Accommodation	NYR	200
Food	NYR	400
Service	NYR	400
Entertainment	NYR	100
Cruise Experience	NYR	400
OVERALL SCORE	**NYR**	**2000**

OCEAN VICTORY
★★★

Size	Boutique Ship
Tonnage	8,181
Cruise Line	Albatros Expeditions
Former Names	*None*
Entered Service	2021
Total Crew	100
Passengers	181

This very small expedition-style ship has good seakeeping capabilities due to its novel 'X-Bow' design. Designed to get you up-close-and-personal, and away from areas where big-ship cruises go, it has a small but practical mudroom/boot-washing area, and storage cupboards for boots. Its high-ceilinged public rooms include a well-integrated lecture room/lounge with comfortable seating, but note that several pillars obstruct sightlines. Cabins on the lowest accommodation deck have portholes and all others have windows or slide-door balconies, but most are compact. The bathrooms have showers and heated floors. Note that some activities are at an extra cost.

INSIGHT GUIDES' RATINGS

	Achieved	Possible
Ship	348	500
Accommodation	126	200
Food	228	400
Service	240	400
Entertainment	60	100
Cruise Experience	218	400
OVERALL SCORE	**1220**	**2000**

OCEANA
★★★

Size	Mid-size Ship
Tonnage	77,499
Cruise Line	P&O Cruises
Former Names	*None*
Entered Service	2000, 2002
Total Crew	850
Passengers	1,950

This smart-looking mid-size ship is all about British-ness, for families with children wanting to travel and take their home comforts with them, There is decent open deck space and a complete walkaround deck. along with numerous cabin grades from suite with private balcony to compact interior (no-view) cabins. Adriatic and Ligurian are the two asymmetrically designed dining rooms, each with around 500 seats. The cuisine is decidedly British, mostly unadventurous, and includes many 'comfort food' items. The aft-located spa has a decent range of facilities and body pampering treatments. There are many cost-extra items, but the ship does provide a comfortable environment for a family-friendly seagoing vacation.

INSIGHT GUIDES' RATINGS

	Achieved	Possible
Ship	330	500
Accommodation	127	200
Food	235	400
Service	220	400
Entertainment	68	100
Cruise Experience	218	400
OVERALL SCORE	**1198**	**2000**

ODYSSEY OF THE SEAS
★★★+

Size	Large Resort Ship
Tonnage	169,379
Cruise Line	Royal Caribbean International
Former Names	None
Entered Service	2021
Total Crew	1,550
Passengers	4,198

This large resort ship has just about everything for an entertaining vacation for the whole family, with multiple play areas. For a neat bird's eye view of the ship, try North Star ride, while sportier types might enjoy Seaplex facilities. Inside, the Royal Esplanade has bars, lounges, entertainment venues, and brand-name shops. Accommodation ranges from space-limited interior (no-view) cabins to opulent balconied suites, but the numbering system is confusing. The included food venues are mediocre and carbohydrate-rich. For better food cooked to order, try smaller, cost-extra venues such as Giovanni's Italian Kitchen, Izumi, or Chops Grill. There are many cost-extra items and added service charges, and the constant 'background' music is irritating.

INSIGHT GUIDES' RATINGS

	Achieved	Possible
Ship	405	500
Accommodation	137	200
Food	290	400
Service	222	400
Entertainment	88	100
Cruise Experience	252	400
OVERALL SCORE	**1394**	**2000**

OOSTERDAM
★★★

Size	Mid-size Ship
Tonnage	82,305
Cruise Line	Holland America Line
Former Names	None
Entered Service	2003
Total Crew	800
Passengers	1,918

With its twin funnels, this is one of a series of ships designed for multi-generational cruisegoers, and has a pleasant exterior walk-around teak deck with comfortable lounge chairs. One of two outside pools can be covered in inclement weather conditions. Public rooms are comfortable, and the three-deck-high lobby has a rotating Waterford crystal world globe. From solo-occupancy cabins to Grand Pinnacle suites, all are well outfitted, but the air-conditioning is noisy and cannot be turned off. There's a stunning two-deck dining room aft, although the cuisine itself is mostly unmemorable and lacks green vegetables (note that lighter options are always available). Perhaps the best food experience is in the extra-cost Pinnacle Grill.

INSIGHT GUIDES' RATINGS

	Achieved	Possible
Ship	356	500
Accommodation	144	200
Food	220	400
Service	204	400
Entertainment	67	100
Cruise Experience	236	400
OVERALL SCORE	**1227**	**2000**

OTTO SVERDRUP
★★+

Size	Small Ship
Tonnage	15,690
Cruise Line	Hurtigruten Expeditions
Former Names	*Finnmarken*
Entered Service	2002
Total Crew	150
Passengers	526

Named after one of Norway's Arctic heroes, this ship (now over 20 years old) was revitalised in 2021 and is biofuel-powered as part of the company's expedition-style voyages. The interiors are modestly comfortable, but there are few public rooms, and many pillars obstruct sightlines. Cabins range from a miniscule 53 sq ft (8 sq m) with almost no storage space, to so-called suites with a healthier 400 sq ft (37 sq m). Most fittings are basic, as is the decor, and the air-conditioning is noisy. Aune, the main restaurant, provides very modest but hearty meals, but the 'service' needs help. Lindstrom is a cost-extra venue for cooked-to-order food. There are some basic spa-like facilities.

INSIGHT GUIDES' RATINGS

	Achieved	Possible
Ship	336	500
Accommodation	112	200
Food	224	400
Service	160	400
Entertainment	60	100
Cruise Experience	203	400
OVERALL SCORE	**1095**	**2000**

OVATION OF THE SEAS
★★★+

Size	Large Resort Ship
Tonnage	168,666
Cruise Line	Royal Caribbean International
Former Names	*None*
Entered Service	2016
Total Crew	1,300
Passengers	4,180

This high-energy, multi-faceted, bling-filled resort ship could be a fine choice for families with children, with multiple play areas and constant entertainment. North Star is a glass pod that lifts you off the ship's uppermost deck for a neat bird's eye view. Inside, the Royal Esplanade has bars (including a 'bionic bar'), entertainment venues, lounges, and brand-name shops to enjoy. Cabins range from interior (no-view) units to large balconied suites (and solo-occupancy cabins); all have well-designed bathrooms. There are multiple restaurants and eateries, but no main dining room as such. Food is acceptable, but spending more to eat in one of the speciality venues may be worthwhile. For colorful production shows, head to the showlounge.

INSIGHT GUIDES' RATINGS

	Achieved	Possible
Ship	404	500
Accommodation	137	200
Food	289	400
Service	222	400
Entertainment	88	100
Cruise Experience	252	400
OVERALL SCORE	**1392**	**2000**

PACIFIC ADVENTURE
★★★

Size	Large Resort Ship
Tonnage	108,865
Cruise Line	P&O Australia
Former Names	*Golden Princess*
Entered Service	2001, 2022
Total Crew	1,100
Passengers	2,636

This large ship for Aussie-style cruising has decent outdoor space, and a movie theater adjacent to one of two main swimming pools (the other can be covered by a sliding glass dome in case of inclement weather). There is a wide array of public rooms, but the main lobby is the place to see and be seen. Accommodation varies from small viewless interior cabins to balconied family suites. Waterfront (for Aussie cuisine), Angelo's (Italian) are the main eateries, but for something different, try the cost-extra Dragon Lady (with its shared tables and origami-fold menu) or the small Salt Grill (for steaks and seafood). For entertainment, head to the Marquee Theatre.

INSIGHT GUIDES' RATINGS		
	Achieved	Possible
Ship	332	500
Accommodation	133	200
Food	245	400
Service	212	400
Entertainment	72	100
Cruise Experience	241	400
OVERALL SCORE	**1235**	**2000**

PACIFIC ENCOUNTER
★★★

Size	Large Resort Ship
Tonnage	108,977
Cruise Line	P&O Australia
Former Names	*Star Princess*
Entered Service	200, 2022
Total Crew	1,100
Passengers	2,600

Following a 2021 refit, this large, multiple-choice ship is tailored to Australasian passengers. There is a good range of colorful public rooms, lounges, bars (try the Bonded Store for special cocktails and beers), and entertainment venues, including a three-deck-high atrium lobby, which is a good meeting place. The accommodation is mostly so-so. Food choice and the range of eateries are good. In addition to The Waterfront, the (included) main dining room, cost-extra speciality venues include Angelo's (Italian), Dragon Lady (Asian Fusion, with a cute origami-fold menu), Luke's Bar & Grill (seafood), and 400 Gradi (a Johnny DeFrancesco venue). Family shows are seen in the Marquee Theatre.

INSIGHT GUIDES' RATINGS		
	Achieved	Possible
Ship	333	500
Accommodation	133	200
Food	245	400
Service	213	400
Entertainment	72	100
Cruise Experience	242	400
OVERALL SCORE	**1238**	**2000**

PACIFIC EXPLORER
★★★+

Size	Mid-size Ship
Tonnage	77,441
Cruise Line	P&O Australia
Former Names	*Dawn Princess*
Entered Service	1997, 2017
Total Crew	924
Passengers	1,998

This smart-looking mid-size ship oozes friendly Australian style, and has a decent walk-around outdoor deck. There are a couple of neat waterslides and good play areas for children of all ages. The interior features a four-deck-high atrium lobby with two winding stairways. The accommodation is comfortable, with numerous price categories. The main Waterfront Restaurant is aft, with comfortable seating at mostly large tables, and the Aussie-based cuisine is well presented. Dragon Lady (for Asian cuisine, with a cute origami-fold menu) and Angelo's (Italian) are two reservations-required alternative eateries, but there is no extra cost.

INSIGHT GUIDES' RATINGS		
	Achieved	Possible
Ship	351	500
Accommodation	145	200
Food	239	400
Service	250	400
Entertainment	68	100
Cruise Experience	243	400
OVERALL SCORE	**1296**	**2000**

PAUL GAUGUIN
★★★+

Size	Small Ship
Tonnage	19,200
Cruise Line	Paul Gauguin Cruise Line
Former Names	*None*
Entered Service	1998
Total Crew	215
Passengers	332

Pleasant, almost elegant little ship, though now becoming a bit outdated. It operates warm-weather cruises in Tahiti and her islands, and was specially built to operate in the area's shallow waters. It could carry more, but is not allowed to do so by French law. It is well suited to couples and solo travelers seeking out-of-the-ordinary itineraries. The interiors focus on French Polynesia, and, naturally, Paul Gauguin. The relaxed atmosphere is delightful, becoming a little dressier at night. The suites/cabins are well outfitted, and all have wood-accented cabinetry. L'Etoile (main dining room) is open just for dinner, with Le Verandah and Le Grill open for other meals. Local Polynesian shows take place in Le Grand Salon. All in all, it is pleasant and relaxing.

INSIGHT GUIDES' RATINGS		
	Achieved	Possible
Ship	351	500
Accommodation	139	200
Food	270	400
Service	237	400
Entertainment	60	100
Cruise Experience	227	400
OVERALL SCORE	**1284**	**2000**

PEARL MIST
★★★+

Size	Boutique Ship
Tonnage	5,600
Cruise Line	Pearl Seas Cruises
Former Names	None
Entered Service	2014
Total Crew	60
Passengers	206

This very small ship specializes in coastal cruising, far away from the hunting grounds of the large resort-style ships. It is best suited to couples and solo travelers of mature years who want to cruise in an all-American environment. It typically cruises in the east coast waters of the US and Canada during the summer, and in the Caribbean during the winter. Cabins are rather small, but all have outside views, and a narrow balcony. There is open seating dining in its aft restaurant, with American cuisine. The Main Lounge hosts evening entertainment and lectures. Overall, this is quite a comfortable little ship.

INSIGHT GUIDES' RATINGS

	Achieved	Possible
Ship	361	500
Accommodation	140	200
Food	264	400
Service	224	400
Entertainment	57	100
Cruise Experience	226	400
OVERALL SCORE	**1272**	**2000**

PRIDE OF AMERICA
★★★

Size	Mid-size Ship
Tonnage	80,439
Cruise Line	Norwegian Cruise Line
Former Names	None
Entered Service	2005
Total Crew	927
Passengers	2,186

This family-friendly ship features Hawaiian inter-island cruises in a comfortable environment. There are expansive open deck areas. Indoors, the design theme is 'Best of America' with public rooms named after famous Americans. The eight-deck-high main lobby is said to be inspired by the Capitol Building and the White House. About 75 percent of all accommodation has outside views; there are also some family-friendly inter-connecting cabins (which can sleep up to six). There are two principal dining rooms, and several cost-extra smaller venues for better food cooked to order. Production shows and local Hawaiian entertainment is in the Hollywood Theater. Note that Hawaii's sales tax is added to *anything* purchased on board.

INSIGHT GUIDES' RATINGS

	Achieved	Possible
Ship	346	500
Accommodation	139	200
Food	211	400
Service	159	400
Entertainment	68	100
Cruise Experience	217	400
OVERALL SCORE	**1140**	**2000**

QUANTUM OF THE SEAS
★★★★

Size	Large Resort Ship
Tonnage	168,666
Cruise Line	Royal Caribbean International
Former Names	None
Entered Service	2014
Total Crew	1,300
Passengers	4,180

This ultra-colorful, lively family-friendly large floating resort (with low emissions) has numerous 'wow' factors. Check out Felicia, a magenta-colored bear outside on the starboard side aft on Deck 15. The accommodation ranges from view-less interior cabins to balconied family suites, plus several solo-occupancy cabins. Quite simply: pay more, get more. Grand, Chic, Silk, and American Icon Grille (each with over 400 seats) are included, as is the large self-serve buffet venue Windjammer Marketplace, with other dining haunts at extra cost. There are abundant entertainment choices and production shows. Overall, it could be a good choice for families, but the constant 'background' music around the ship is annoying.

INSIGHT GUIDES' RATINGS

	Achieved	Possible
Ship	408	500
Accommodation	136	200
Food	292	400
Service	223	400
Entertainment	85	100
Cruise Experience	257	400
OVERALL SCORE	**1401**	**2000**

QUEEN ANNE
NYR

Size	Large Resort Ship
Tonnage	113,000
Cruise Line	Cunard
Former Names	None
Entered Service	2024
Total Crew	1,245
Passengers	3,000

This newest addition to the Cunard fleet has an instantly recognisable profile, with its dark hull, white superstructure, and red funnel. The decor includes a range of contemporary artwork by UK- and US-based artists. A Royal Arcade houses shops, bars, and eateries; favorites include a Golden Lion Pub and a Commodore Club (observation lounge with adjacent cigar lounge). Accommodation ranges from small and basic to large and opulent, and includes solo-occupancy cabins. There are four main dining venues: Queens Grill, Princess Grill (both on an upper deck), Britannia Club, and Britannia Restaurant (the largest). Cunard is respected for its well-prepared and presented food. For shows, it's the Royal Court Theatre.

INSIGHT GUIDES' RATINGS

	Achieved	Possible
Ship	NYR	500
Accommodation	NYR	200
Food	NYR	400
Service	NYR	400
Entertainment	NYR	100
Cruise Experience	NYR	400
OVERALL SCORE	**NYR**	**2000**

QUEEN ELIZABETH
★★★★+

Size	Mid-size Ship
Tonnage	90,900
Cruise Line	Cunard
Former Names	*None*
Entered Service	2010
Total Crew	1,005
Passengers	2,101

This contemporary cruise ship has an iconic red funnel, white upper structure, and black hull. Inside, the British heritage and tasteful interior styling replicates ocean liners of yesteryear. The Royal Arcade houses shops, bars, and eateries; favorite haunts include a Golden Lion Pub and a Commodore Club. Four Grand Suites (Bisset, Charles, Illingworth, and Rostron) are named after former Cunard captains. Whichever accommodation grade you choose is matched to one of four restaurants: Queens Grill, Princess Grill (both have open dining times and cooked-to-order cuisine); the intimate Britannia Grill and the larger two-deck Britannia Restaurant. The Royal Court Theatre, designed like a classic opera house, has 20 reservable private boxes.

INSIGHT GUIDES' RATINGS

	Achieved	Possible
Ship	424	500
Accommodation	144	200
Food	301	400
Service	314	400
Entertainment	81	100
Cruise Experience	348	400
OVERALL SCORE	**1612**	**2000**

QUEEN MARY 2
★★★★+

Size	Large Resort Ship
Tonnage	151,400
Cruise Line	Cunard
Former Names	None
Entered Service	2004
Total Crew	1,250
Passengers	2,705

A ship of superlatives, this is a real ocean liner, built for tough regularly scheduled Transatlantic crossings in comfortable British style. It is the largest ocean liner ever built, and its powerful propulsion system means it can go backwards faster than many ships can go forward. On deck there is a wide walk-around outdoor promenade. Inside, the wide range of public rooms includes an outstanding library, with over 100 bookcases (it takes around 20 minutes to unlock them all) and around 8,000 books in several languages. From interior (no-view) cabins, and specially-built solo traveler cabins, to superb suites (with extensive private balconies) overlooking the ship's bows, the accommodation is matched to the appropriate restaurant – either Grill Class (Queens Grill and Princess Grill) or Britannia Class. All restaurants and eateries have ocean views. The largest is the two-deck Britannia Restaurant, which spans the entire beam of the ship (there are many tables for two, as well as larger tables). Pub lovers will find traditional British fare in the popular Golden Lion pub, while comfort food is available in the vast King's Court, and at night, decorated screens transform sections into cost-extra eateries. Colorful production shows are presented in the Royal Court Theatre, with well-tiered seating for over

INSIGHT GUIDES' RATINGS

	Achieved	Possible
Ship	435	500
Accommodation	174	200
Food	319	400
Service	285	400
Entertainment	86	100
Cruise Experience	312	400
OVERALL SCORE	**1611**	**2000**

1,000. Adjacent is Illuminations, which incorporates the only planetarium at sea and its outstanding, out-of-this-world astronomical presentations narrated by stars of stage and screen. The ship also has kennels for use on transatlantic crossings (overseen by a kennel master), plus a real New York fire hydrant and a British lamppost. Overall, this really is a fine way to cross the North Atlantic.

Queen Mary 2 Q2 Stateroom.

QUEEN VICTORIA
★★★★+

Size	Mid-size Ship
Tonnage	90,049
Cruise Line	Cunard
Former Names	*None*
Entered Service	2007
Total Crew	1,001
Passengers	2,083

With traditional decor, style and Britishness, this pretend ocean liner (it does have a strengthened hull) should appeal to any Anglophile. Edwardian/Victorian style decor prevails in the public areas; the Royal Arcade houses shops, bars, and eateries; and favorite haunts include a Golden Lion Pub and a Commodore Club. Accommodation ranges from small and basic (including solo-occupancy cabins) to large and opulent. Cunard is respected for its cuisine, with well-prepared and presented food. There are three venues: Queens Grill, Princess Grill, and Britannia Restaurant (the largest). Entertaining production shows are presented in the opera-style Royal Court Theatre. It's all rather delightful.

INSIGHT GUIDES' RATINGS

	Achieved	Possible
Ship	428	500
Accommodation	144	200
Food	301	400
Service	311	400
Entertainment	82	100
Cruise Experience	350	400
OVERALL SCORE	**1616**	**2000**

RADIANCE OF THE SEAS
★★★

Size	Mid-size Ship
Tonnage	90,090
Cruise Line	Royal Caribbean International
Former Names	*None*
Entered Service	2001
Total Crew	858
Passengers	2,146

Modern design brings abundant light to many areas, while one of two swimming pools can be covered by a glass dome for use in inclement weather. The Centrum (lobby) spans nine decks and is the ship's social hub. Modestly comfortable cabins may be size-challenged (except for suites), bathrooms are compact, and storage space is limited. Cascades, spanning two decks, is the main dining room, but meals are mostly carbo-rich and disappointing, with few green vegetables. For something different, Crown Grill has cost-extra cooked-to-order steaks and seafood. For colorful production shows, head to the large Aurora Theater.

INSIGHT GUIDES' RATINGS

	Achieved	Possible
Ship	335	500
Accommodation	134	200
Food	230	400
Service	228	400
Entertainment	70	100
Cruise Experience	225	400
OVERALL SCORE	**1222**	**2000**

REGAL PRINCESS
★★★+

Size..Large Resort Ship
Tonnage...142,229
Cruise Line...Princess Cruises
Former Names .... *None*
Entered Service 2014
Total Crew 1,346
Passengers 3,560

This multi-choice ship has a nicely balanced exterior look. Inside, Piazza Atrium acts as its multi-faceted social hub, and includes eateries, bars, entertainment, and shopping areas, plus guest services. Accommodation comes in six main categories, and many variations, from grand suites to interior (no-view) cabins. Allegro, Concerto, and Symphony are the main dining rooms, with the included food that is, well, 'production cuisine,' but you can pay more for better eats in one of several other smaller eateries. Features colorful 'production' shows in the large bi-level Princess Theater. Spa and fitness facilities are nothing special. Overall, this is a consistently decent, well-packaged cruise vacation.

INSIGHT GUIDES' RATINGS	Achieved	Possible
Ship	393	500
Accommodation	139	200
Food	267	400
Service	244	400
Entertainment	82	100
Cruise Experience	271	400
OVERALL SCORE	**1396**	**2000**

REGATTA
★★★+

Size...Small Ship
Tonnage...30,277
Cruise Line...Oceania Cruises
Former Names *R2*
Entered Service 1998, 2003
Total Crew 386
Passengers 684

For mature-age cruisegoers, this older but well-kept ship provides a country-club-like ambiance. Teak overlaid decking and quality lounge chairs provide high comfort Lido and Pool decks. The interior decor is elegant and a throwback to the ocean liners of an earlier age. From very tight interior (no-view) cabins to the aft-located Owner's Suites, it is simply 'pay more, get more.' Dining and the food experience is what Oceania Cruises does well (it is provided by a respected maritime catering company), and there are no cost-extra venues. The main dining room seats over 300, but with the low ceilings, it can be quite noisy. For entertainment, the Regatta Lounge features small 'production' shows and cabaret acts.

INSIGHT GUIDES' RATINGS	Achieved	Possible
Ship	360	500
Accommodation	132	200
Food	291	400
Service	232	400
Entertainment	67	100
Cruise Experience	237	400
OVERALL SCORE	**1319**	**2000**

RESILIENT LADY
★★★+

Size	Large Resort Ship
Tonnage	110,000
Cruise Line	Virgin Voyages
Former Names	*None*
Entered Service	2023
Total Crew	1,100
Passengers	2,860

Red, white, and pizzazz all over, with a Virgin mermaid logo on its upright bows – this is a vibrant, colorful, and loud playground for youthful urban adults. The accommodation ranges from interior (no-view) cabins to balconied rock star suites (plus two 'Massive Suites'). Several restaurants and eateries (all are included in the cruise price) provide predictably edgy food that naturally includes vegetarian and vegan items. The Wake is the most glam venue; it is based on London classic The Wolseley (which is nothing special), while The Galley is the closest thing to a buffet with its food court-like setting. Wellness enthusiasts should delight in the Redemption Spa. Overall, this is all a bit of a lively, quirky experience, and then some!

INSIGHT GUIDES' RATINGS

	Achieved	Possible
Ship	400	500
Accommodation	136	200
Food	236	400
Service	248	400
Entertainment	76	100
Cruise Experience	261	400
OVERALL SCORE	**1357**	**2000**

RESORTS WORLD ONE
★★★

Size	Mid-size Ship
Tonnage	75,338
Cruise Line	Resorts World Cruises
Former Names	*Explorer Dream, SuperStar Virgo*
Entered Service	1999, 2023
Total Crew	1,225
Passengers	1,870

This is a pleasant mid-size resort ship for the whole family. Outside there's a walk-around promenade deck, good for strolling. Inside are two boulevards and a fine two-deck-high atrium with three glass-walled elevators. Aside from shops, bars, and casual eateries, is a large well-lit casino and smaller members-only VIP gaming room. There are also private Mahjong and karaoke rooms. While most cabins are small, each has a personal safe and bathrooms are generously sized; there are also spacious balconied suites. There is a wide choice of restaurants and eateries, including Chinese, Italian, and Japanese. Completing the picture is a large showlounge with main and balcony levels, and a spa with body-treatment rooms.

INSIGHT GUIDES' RATINGS

	Achieved	Possible
Ship	328	500
Accommodation	126	200
Food	242	400
Service	213	400
Entertainment	66	100
Cruise Experience	250	400
OVERALL SCORE	**1225**	**2000**

RHAPSODY OF THE SEAS
★★★

Size	Mid-size Ship
Tonnage	78,491
Cruise Line	Royal Caribbean International
Former Names	None
Entered Service	1997, 2017
Total Crew	765
Passengers	2,000

This decent, but ageing family-friendly, multi-choice, mid-size ship has a pleasant domed Viking Crown lounge above the seven-deck-high atrium lobby (The Centrum), the ship's interior focal hub, with access to bars, lounges, service counters etc. There are many accommodation grades, and most have quite decent closet and drawer space, but small bathrooms. The two-level Edelweiss Dining Room is attractive and works well as a large venue, with standard batch cooking and few green vegetables, but there are also smaller cost-extra eateries, with food cooked to order. Head to the large Broadway Melodies Theater for its lively and colorful shows.

INSIGHT GUIDES' RATINGS		
	Achieved	Possible
Ship	337	500
Accommodation	126	200
Food	220	400
Service	210	400
Entertainment	63	100
Cruise Experience	233	400
OVERALL SCORE	**1189**	**2000**

RIVIERA
★★★★

Size	Mid-size Ship
Tonnage	66,084
Cruise Line	Oceania Cruises
Former Names	None
Entered Service	2012
Total Crew	800
Passengers	1,258

A country-club atmosphere prevails aboard this ship for mature-age cruisegoers who appreciate plenty of space and comfort, and a high level of cuisine and service. Inside, the focal point is a stunning wrought-iron and Lalique-glass horseshoe-shaped staircase. With several suite and cabin grades, but all have good-sized bathrooms with separate tub and shower enclosure. There are a number of dining venues, the largest being the Grand Dining Room, set with fine chinaware. Breads and croissants are particularly good – made with fine French flour and d'Isigny butter. Other eateries provide a wide choice, including steaks, seafood, and Italian cuisine. The fitness center is good, but body treatments are outrageously expensive.

INSIGHT GUIDES' RATINGS		
	Achieved	Possible
Ship	423	500
Accommodation	170	200
Food	309	400
Service	257	400
Entertainment	77	100
Cruise Experience	288	400
OVERALL SCORE	**1524**	**2000**

ROALD AMUNDSEN
★★★

Size	Small Ship
Tonnage	20,889
Cruise Line	Hurtigruten Expeditions
Former Names	*None*
Entered Service	2019
Total Crew	120
Passengers	528

For hardy outdoor types who don't mind fairly basic facilities, this expedition-style ship has Scandinavian minimalist decor, with some artwork depicting Arctic and Antarctic regions. A half-ship walking deck encircles the front, while inside there's a lecture room, shop, Internet corner, lobby with reception and shore excursion counter, and video games room. Accommodation pricing varies, in three grades, and depending on the size and location. Most meals are buffet-style (some dinners have waiter service), and repetitious, but pay extra and you can eat cooked-to-order food in the Lindstrom Restaurant. Overall, it's a little large, overhyped, and overpriced.

INSIGHT GUIDES' RATINGS		
	Achieved	Possible
Ship	361	500
Accommodation	126	200
Food	232	400
Service	204	400
Entertainment	52	100
Cruise Experience	219	400
OVERALL SCORE	**1194**	**2000**

ROTTERDAM
★★★+

Size	Mid-size Ship
Tonnage	59,855
Cruise Line	Holland America Line
Former Names	*None*
Entered Service	1997, 2021
Total Crew	620
Passengers	1,404

This ship has many traditional Dutch features and restrained interior decor, with pleasant ocean liner detailing. There are three main stairways, so accessing anywhere is easy. The three-deck-high atrium lobby's focal point is a huge custom-made clock based on an antique Flemish original; it includes an astrolabe, an astrological clock, and 14 other clocks. Accommodation is priced by grade, size, and location, but all have good closet space, though small bathrooms. Assigned or open seating are available in the La Fontaine dining room. With a few exceptions, the food is mostly unmemorable. Overall, it's a comfortable ship, and has decent spa facilities, with body-pampering treatments at extra cost.

INSIGHT GUIDES' RATINGS		
	Achieved	Possible
Ship	374	500
Accommodation	142	200
Food	220	400
Service	218	400
Entertainment	73	100
Cruise Experience	251	400
OVERALL SCORE	**1278**	**2000**

ROYAL CLIPPER
★★★★

Size	Boutique Ship
Tonnage	5,061
Cruise Line	Star Clippers
Former Names	None
Entered Service	2000
Total Crew	106
Passengers	228

This large five-mast sail-cruise ship oozes character and old-world style, and is a stunning sight under full sail. Its masts reach 197ft (60m) above the waterline, and the top 19ft (5.8m) can be hinged over 90 degrees to clear bridges. There is ample open deck space, three small dip pools, and also has water sports equipment. Inside is a small three-deck-high atrium, a forward observation lounge (sitting under one of the pools) and a lovely Edwardian library. There are several accommodation types, all with polished wood-trimmed cabinetry, twin/double beds, and personal safe. The dining room is on several connecting levels (stairs are steep), and is noisy (waiters must reach over to serve at some tables for six).

INSIGHT GUIDES' RATINGS		
	Achieved	Possible
Ship	401	500
Accommodation	138	200
Food	288	400
Service	246	400
Entertainment	80	100
Cruise Experience	284	400
OVERALL SCORE	**1437**	**2000**

ROYAL PRINCESS
★★★+

Size	Large Resort Ship
Tonnage	142,229
Cruise Line	Princess Cruises
Former Names	None
Entered Service	2013
Total Crew	1,346
Passengers	3,560

This is a large, family-friendly, resort-style ship. It lacks a walk-around outdoor deck, but it does have two over the water 'Sea-Walks' extending over the side by 30ft (9.1m). An adults-only retreat (The Sanctuary) includes private cabanas and retreat pool and relaxation areas. The ship's multi-faceted social hub is the Piazza Atrium, with its twin horseshoe-shaped stairways. There are five main types of accommodation, in numerous price grades. Anyone booking suite-grade accommodation gains access to a private Concierge Lounge. Allegro, Concerto, and Symphony are the three main restaurants, but cost-extra venues include Crown Grill (for steaks) and Sabatini's (Italian). For colorful shows, head to the 1,000-seat Princess Theater.

INSIGHT GUIDES' RATINGS		
	Achieved	Possible
Ship	393	500
Accommodation	139	200
Food	268	400
Service	243	400
Entertainment	82	100
Cruise Experience	270	400
OVERALL SCORE	**1395**	**2000**

RUBY PRINCESS
★★★+

Size...Large Resort Ship
Tonnage...113,561
Cruise Line....................................Princess Cruises
Former Names ....None
Entered Service 2008
Total Crew...1,200
Passengers 3,114

This is a family-friendly resort-style ship with pleasant decor and dining options. It accommodates around 500 more passengers than its half-sisters, such as *Diamond Princess*, but with the same amount of outdoor deck space and elevator numbers. The main public bars and lounges are located off a double-wide promenade deck. The Plaza is the central meeting point. Accommodation ranges from suites to interior (no-view) cabins. Three large dining rooms are included; the cuisine is acceptable but nothing special. There are some cost-extra venues. The Princess Theater has colorful production shows with a live band. Spa facilities are good, but treatments costly. Overall, it's a comfortable experience, but beware of the many cost-extra options.

INSIGHT GUIDES' RATINGS	Achieved	Possible
Ship	348	500
Accommodation	122	200
Food	247	400
Service	257	400
Entertainment	74	100
Cruise Experience	243	400
OVERALL SCORE	**1291**	**2000**

SAPPHIRE PRINCESS
★★★+

Size...Large Resort Ship
Tonnage...115,875
Cruise Line....................................Princess Cruises
Former Names ....None
Entered Service 2004
Total Crew...1,348
Passengers 2,674

This large multi-choice, resort-style ship has two jet-engine-like pods adorning the funnel. Several outdoor areas focus on swimming pools and family activity centers, while the interior focal point is a piazza-style atrium lobby with numerous venues and a casino – one favorite room is the wood-panelled Wheelhouse Bar, with its ship models. The main dining rooms are assigned according to your cabin grade. Cuisine is acceptable but non-memorable, and there are few garnishes. Head to Sterling Steakhouse and Kai Sushi for cost-extra, cooked-to-order food. The Princess Theater presents colorful production shows. Also, Americans can be legally married by the ship's captain (with arrangements made in advance).

INSIGHT GUIDES' RATINGS	Achieved	Possible
Ship	348	500
Accommodation	139	200
Food	247	400
Service	239	400
Entertainment	76	100
Cruise Experience	257	400
OVERALL SCORE	**1306**	**2000**

SCARLET LADY
★★★+

Size .... Large Resort Ship
Tonnage 110,000
Cruise Line .... Virgin Voyages
Former Names .... *None*
Entered Service 2020
Total Crew 1,150
Passengers 2,860

This floating adult playground has a streamlined look reminiscent of Japanese Shinkansen 'bullet' trains, with Virgin's scarlet red logo on the bows. There's bling everywhere for youthful urban adults, and the interiors sport an edgy, urgent feel. Its several 'neighborhoods' are utterly casual, and fun. Accommodation goes from interior (no-view) cabins to rock star suites, plus two 'Massive Suites.' All eateries are price-inclusive; food is predictably edgy, and naturally includes vegetarian and vegan items. The closest thing to a buffet is The Galley, with its food court-like setting. Upbeat acts and razzle-dazzle drag shows provide the entertainment. Overall, there is a lot of hype for the hyperactive in this floating playground.

INSIGHT GUIDES' RATINGS		
	Achieved	Possible
Ship	398	500
Accommodation	136	200
Food	236	400
Service	248	400
Entertainment	76	100
Cruise Experience	255	400
OVERALL SCORE	**1349**	**2000**

SCENIC ECLIPSE
★★★★

Size .... Boutique Ship
Tonnage 17,545
Cruise Line .... Scenic Cruises
Former Names .... *None*
Entered Service 2019
Total Crew 176
Passengers 228

Designed specifically for in-depth soft expedition adventures, this ultra-smart ship was aimed to operate in the polar regions from the beginning, and has Azipod marine propulsion units for operational flexibility. It has a six-person semi-submarine and six-person helicopter. Public rooms include an observation lounge, a library, and lecture theater. From an expansive Owner's Suite to the smallest suite, all are comfortable, well designed, with ample storage space, and balconies. Several eateries (all included in the price) provide ample choice, while Epicure is a fully equipped culinary studio for cost-extra classes. Overall, this is a fine ship and cruise experience.

INSIGHT GUIDES' RATINGS		
	Achieved	Possible
Ship	413	500
Accommodation	144	200
Food	306	400
Service	240	400
Entertainment	77	100
Cruise Experience	307	400
OVERALL SCORE	**1487**	**2000**

SCENIC ECLIPSE II
NYR

Size	Boutique Ship
Tonnage	17,545
Cruise Line	Scenic Cruises
Former Names	*None*
Entered Service	2023
Total Crew	176
Passengers	228

Joining the Scenic fleet in 2023, this is another ship designed to operate in the polar regions, with Azipod marine propulsion units for the best in operational flexibility. An eight-person submarine, and six-person helicopter provide added possibilities. Public rooms include an observation lounge, a library, and lecture theater, while the accommodation is well-designed and appointed, from the smallest cabin to lavishly appointed penthouse suites, all with balconies of various sizes. Several eateries (all included in the price) provide ample choice – some venues have menus that change daily, others change less often. The spa area is larger than on *Scenic Eclipse*, and includes a steam room and a salt therapy lounge with beds.

INSIGHT GUIDES' RATINGS		
	Achieved	Possible
Ship	NYR	500
Accommodation	NYR	200
Food	NYR	400
Service	NYR	400
Entertainment	NYR	100
Cruise Experience	NYR	400
OVERALL SCORE	**NYR**	**2000**

SEA CLOUD
★★★★+

Size	Boutique Ship
Tonnage	2,532
Cruise Line	Sea Cloud Cruises
Former Names	*Sea Cloud of Grand Cayman, IX-99, Antama, Patria, Angelita, Sea Cloud, Hussar*
Entered Service	1931, 1979
Total Crew	60
Passengers	64

This is, quite simply, the most beautiful sail-cruise ship in the world, and it celebrated its 90th birthday in 2021. This was the largest private yacht ever built when completed in 1931 by Edward F. Hutton for his wife, Marjorie Merriweather Post, the American cereal heiress. It is both stunning and exhilarating under its 30 sails, and everything is done by hand. There is lots of open space on the decks – which are solid oak and mahogany – although ropes are everywhere, and the 'Blue Lagoon' is at the stern for star gazing. The handcrafted interiors include ornate ceilings, oodles of brass, and a great feeling of warmth throughout. The food and service are extremely good. The experience is like being on a floating stately home, and utterly relaxing.

INSIGHT GUIDES' RATINGS		
	Achieved	Possible
Ship	432	500
Accommodation	174	200
Food	336	400
Service	286	400
Entertainment	91	100
Cruise Experience	308	400
OVERALL SCORE	**1627**	**2000**

SEA CLOUD II
★★★★+

Size	Boutique Ship
Tonnage	3,849
Cruise Line	Sea Cloud Cruises
Former Names	None
Entered Service	2001
Total Crew	60
Passengers	94

This wind-in-your-sails ship provides a truly relaxing sea-going holiday in style. This three-mast tall ship (called a barque) is a modern interpretation of the original *Sea Cloud*, and has the look and feel of a 1930s sailing vessel. Its elegant main lounge is extremely comfortable, and features a beautiful ornate ceiling. Cabins have a 1920s retro look, with birds-eye maple wood panelling and brass accents, while two suites have a separate bedroom with four-poster bed, and bathrooms with a bathtub. Dining in the open-seating dining room can be a pleasant experience, with fine table settings and well-prepared and presented food. Overall, this should prove to be a memorable sailing experience.

INSIGHT GUIDES' RATINGS	Achieved	Possible
Ship	432	500
Accommodation	173	200
Food	339	400
Service	285	400
Entertainment	90	100
Cruise Experience	307	400
OVERALL SCORE	**1626**	**2000**

SEA CLOUD SPIRIT
★★+

Size	Boutique Ship
Tonnage	5,431
Cruise Line	Sea Cloud Cruises
Former Names	None
Entered Service	2021
Total Crew	85
Passengers	138

Experience the sheer power of the wind in its 32 traditionally-rigged sails as they propel this majestic three-mast barquentine, the world's largest sailing ship currently in service. Interiors have the look and feel of a sailing ship from another era, but with modern conveniences including an elevator. Some 25 cabins (out of a total of 69) feature a balcony, but all are well designed and outfitted in retro style. The restaurant, with tables for two to eight, is well designed and comfortable; food is well prepared and presented, and an open-deck bistro provides snack items. There is also an extensive spa, with sauna, steam room, relaxation area, and hairdresser. This is an excellent, highly comfortable way to connect with yesteryear.

INSIGHT GUIDES' RATINGS	Achieved	Possible
Ship	433	500
Accommodation	173	200
Food	312	400
Service	X	400
Entertainment	88	100
Cruise Experience	X	400
OVERALL SCORE	**1006**	**2000**

SEA SPIRIT

★★★

Size	Boutique Ship
Tonnage	4,200
Cruise Line	Poseidon Expeditions
Former Names	*Spirit of Oceanus, Megastar Sagittarius, Sun Viva, Renaissance V*
Entered Service	1991
Total Crew	72
Passengers	114

This dated, but comfortable boutique-sized ship undertakes soft expedition-style cruises. It has moderately comfortable public rooms, including a good library, although some areas are showing their age. The comfortable accommodation is well designed, and has highly polished imitation rosewood panelling and trim, with ample storage space, and marble-clad bathrooms with showers and teak wood floors. There is also one Owner's Suite, which has abundant space. The dining room is cosy and quite pleasant. Breakfast and lunch are self-serve style, with waiter service for dinner. The food is basically sound, although it does tend to be carbo-rich, with few green vegetables.

INSIGHT GUIDES' RATINGS

	Achieved	Possible
Ship	300	500
Accommodation	164	200
Food	268	400
Service	210	400
Entertainment	60	100
Cruise Experience	179	400
OVERALL SCORE	**1181**	**2000**

SEA VENTURE

★★★+

Size	Boutique Ship
Tonnage	6,752
Cruise Line	Viva Expeditions
Former Names	*Bremen, SeaQuest, Frontier Spirit*
Entered Service	1990, 2022
Total Crew	94
Passengers	144

This is a well-designed, rugged little ship built specifically for expedition voyages. It has stabilisers, a fleet of Zodiac inflatable landing craft, and there is even a walk-around exterior deck (although there are a few steps at the front). The well-appointed public rooms are aft, with accommodation forward. Cabins have portholes on the lowest accommodation deck, and windows on other decks; some have a narrow balcony. Note that public address announcements cannot be turned off. Some 12 pillars obstruct sightlines in the open seating dining room, which is otherwise comfortable. The food is expedition basic, carbohydrate-rich and hearty.

INSIGHT GUIDES' RATINGS

	Achieved	Possible
Ship	302	500
Accommodation	161	200
Food	278	400
Service	253	400
Entertainment	60	100
Cruise Experience	203	400
OVERALL SCORE	**1257**	**2000**

SEABOURN ENCORE
★★★★+

Size	Small Ship
Tonnage	40,350
Cruise Line	Seabourn
Former Names	None
Entered Service	2016
Total Crew	450
Passengers	604

Quite elegant, this small, contemporary ship offers many creature comforts, including two outdoor pools, and a neat hot tub on the open deck near the front – delightful for evening star gazing. Seabourn Square is its social gathering point, and includes a library, shops, Internet-connected computers, an outdoor terrace, concierge services, and a coffee shop. The front section of the ship houses the accommodation, with public rooms aft, in a vertical stacking that is not so user-friendly. There are six accommodation grades (pay more, get more space), all with a 'private' balcony and unimaginative decor, but all have ample closet and storage. The white-dressed dining room is charming, and the cuisine is decent enough.

INSIGHT GUIDES' RATINGS	Achieved	Possible
Ship	428	500
Accommodation	178	200
Food	310	400
Service	278	400
Entertainment	76	100
Cruise Experience	283	400
OVERALL SCORE	**1553**	**2000**

SEABOURN ODYSSEY
★★★★

Size	Small Ship
Tonnage	32,000
Cruise Line	Seabourn
Former Names	None
Entered Service	2009
Total Crew	330
Passengers	450

This is quite an elegant small ship that could suit well-traveled high comfort seekers. Most of the public rooms are located aft in a vertical stacking that is not particularly user-friendly. Seabourn Square acts as the town center and meeting place; it is a relaxed area, with library, computer terminals, concierge, coffee bar, and an outdoor terrace. Accommodation is in a range of sizes (about 90 percent have a balcony), but in the smaller units there is little space between the bed and the wall. The Restaurant has open seating, with food that is less than outstanding. A smaller Grill by Thomas Keller offers cost-extra steaks and seafood choices. The spa facilities are good, but treatments are expensive. Note: this ship will leave the fleet in August 2024.

INSIGHT GUIDES' RATINGS	Achieved	Possible
Ship	426	500
Accommodation	178	200
Food	309	400
Service	278	400
Entertainment	76	100
Cruise Experience	282	400
OVERALL SCORE	**1549**	**2000**

SEABOURN OVATION
★★★★+

Size ....Small Ship
Tonnage 40,350
Cruise Line ....Seabourn
Former Names .... None
Entered Service 2018
Total Crew 330
Passengers 604

Stylish and elegant, this nicely appointed small ship is quite spacious, and has a warm, country-club like ambiance. Most public rooms are located aft in a vertical stacking that is not particularly user-friendly, with accommodation forward. Seabourn Square acts as its town center and meeting place; it is a relaxed area, with library, computer terminals, concierge, coffee bar, and an outdoor terrace. The accommodation is marketed as 'all suites' but really, many are simply large cabins, although almost all have a small private balcony. The white-dressed Restaurant has open seating, and is a comfortable venue, but the food is less than outstanding. An extra-cost Thomas Keller Grill features cooked-to-order food, but is nothing special.

INSIGHT GUIDES' RATINGS		
	Achieved	Possible
Ship	428	500
Accommodation	178	200
Food	309	400
Service	278	400
Entertainment	76	100
Cruise Experience	284	400
OVERALL SCORE	**1553**	**2000**

SEABOURN PURSUIT
★★★★

Size ....Small Ship
Tonnage 23,000
Cruise Line ....Seabourn Expeditions
Former Names .... None
Entered Service 2023
Total Crew 120
Passengers 264

This ship was specifically designed for discovery-style voyages, with upright bows and some features found on real expedition ships, including 24 rigid-rubber Zodiacs (stored in an unusual top deck area) for shore visits. Two custom-built submersibles can also be used at certain destinations, at a rather large extra cost. The accommodation is practical and spread over several decks. Public areas include a Bow Lounge and a Constellation Lounge at the front of the ship, with Seabourn Square being the 'town center' gathering spot, with reception and concierge service desks. Most dining takes place in the Main Restaurant, but cost-extra specialities are available in The Colonnade (for items by celebrity chef Thomas Keller), with sushi bites in The Club.

INSIGHT GUIDES' RATINGS		
	Achieved	Possible
Ship	400	500
Accommodation	176	200
Food	305	400
Service	272	400
Entertainment	60	100
Cruise Experience	287	400
OVERALL SCORE	**1500**	**2000**

SEABOURN QUEST
★★★★

Size	Small Ship
Tonnage	32,346
Cruise Line	Seabourn
Former Names	None
Entered Service	2011
Total Crew	330
Passengers	450

There is a very comfortable, upscale country club feeling aboard this handy-size ship, with no sense of crowding anywhere. Accommodation is in the forward section, with most public rooms aft. Seabourn Square is the relaxed 'town center' and gathering spot, with library, computer terminals, concierge, coffee bar, and a small outdoor terrace. The accommodation is in a range of sizes (about 90 percent have a balcony), but in the smaller units there is little space between bed and wall; all have a separate bathtub and shower. The white-dressed Restaurant has open seating, and is a comfortable venue, but the food is less than outstanding. The small, worth the extra cost, Thomas Keller Grill features cooked-to-order steaks and seafood.

INSIGHT GUIDES' RATINGS

	Achieved	Possible
Ship	412	500
Accommodation	169	200
Food	292	400
Service	258	400
Entertainment	61	100
Cruise Experience	262	400
OVERALL SCORE	**1454**	**2000**

SEABOURN SOJOURN
★★★★

Size	Small Ship
Tonnage	32,344
Cruise Line	Seabourn
Former Names	None
Entered Service	2010
Total Crew	330
Passengers	450

This is a comfortable ship with contemporary facilities for the well-traveled; its hot tub on the foredeck is a delightful and peaceful spot at night. Most public rooms are aft, with accommodation forward, and the Seabourn Square acts as the town center and meeting place; it is a relaxed area, with library, computer terminals, concierge, coffee bar, and outdoor space. Accommodation is in a range of sizes (about 90 percent have a balcony). In the smaller units there is little space between bed and wall, but plenty of closet and drawer space. The white decor in the main dining room is delightful, but the food is rather underwhelming. The Grill by Thomas Keller may be worth the extra cost for cooked-to-order steaks and seafood.

INSIGHT GUIDES' RATINGS

	Achieved	Possible
Ship	414	500
Accommodation	178	200
Food	306	400
Service	278	400
Entertainment	76	100
Cruise Experience	281	400
OVERALL SCORE	**1533**	**2000**

SEABOURN VENTURE
★★★★

Size	Small Ship
Tonnage	23,000
Cruise Line	Seabourn Expeditions
Former Names	None
Entered Service	2022
Total Crew	120
Passengers	264

Designed specifically for discovery-style voyages, this ship features some of the things found on a real expedition ship, including 24 rigid-rubber Zodiacs for shore visits. The accommodation is practical, and spread over several decks. Public areas include a Bow Lounge and Constellation Lounge. both at the front of the ship, with the familiar Seabourn Square as the 'town center' and gathering spot (it includes reception and concierge service desks). Most dining takes place in the Main Restaurant, but cost-extra specialities are available in The Colonnade (for items by celebrity chef Thomas Keller), with sushi bites in The Club. Two custom-built submersibles can be used in certain destinations, but are little more than an expensive gimmick.

INSIGHT GUIDES' RATINGS

	Achieved	Possible
Ship	400	500
Accommodation	176	200
Food	305	400
Service	272	400
Entertainment	60	100
Cruise Experience	285	400
OVERALL SCORE	**1498**	**2000**

SEADREAM I
★★★★+

Size	Boutique Ship
Tonnage	4,254
Cruise Line	Seadream Yacht Cruises
Former Names	Seabourn Goddess I, Sea Goddess I
Entered Service	1984, 2002
Total Crew	95
Passengers	112

For stylish, relaxed cruising in a pocket-sized ship, this is rather like having your own personal yacht. Its fully-stocked library is a delightful room. While cabins are compact, they are well-designed and laid out, and have ample storage space, and the small bathrooms come with a comfortable glazed-in shower. There are no balconies, as the accommodation is too close to the waterline. A favorite meeting place is the open-air Top of the Yacht Bar, with its wooden bar stools and other comfortable seating areas. The Restaurant is elegant and inviting, with candlelit dinners, and all meals prepared individually to order, using high quality ingredients. Entertainment is minimal, because this is all about relaxation.

INSIGHT GUIDES' RATINGS

	Achieved	Possible
Ship	415	500
Accommodation	162	200
Food	336	400
Service	307	400
Entertainment	80	100
Cruise Experience	305	400
OVERALL SCORE	**1605**	**2000**

SEADREAM II
★★★★+

Size	Boutique Ship
Tonnage	4,253
Cruise Line	Seadream Yacht Cruises
Former Names	*Seabourn Goddess II, Sea Goddess II*
Entered Service	1985, 2002
Total Crew	95
Passengers	112

Sister to *SeaDream I*, this pocket-sized ship has contemporary style and a little pizzazz thrown in, and it is rather like having your own private yacht. Inside, there is unabashed but discreet sophistication. The main social gathering places are the lounge, a delightful library/living room with about 1,000 books, a piano bar, and a small casino with blackjack tables and several slot machines. The Restaurant is a delightfully elegant room, with candlelit dinners, and all meals prepared individually to order, using high-quality ingredients. A Topside Restaurant acts as a casual open-air eatery, open for breakfast, lunch, and, occasionally, dinner. Entertainment is minimal, because this is all about indulgent relaxation.

INSIGHT GUIDES' RATINGS		
	Achieved	Possible
Ship	416	500
Accommodation	162	200
Food	336	400
Service	307	400
Entertainment	80	100
Cruise Experience	305	400
OVERALL SCORE	**1606**	**2000**

SERENADE OF THE SEAS
★★★

Size	Mid-size Ship
Tonnage	90,090
Cruise Line	Royal Caribbean International
Former Names	*None*
Entered Service	2003
Total Crew	858
Passengers	2,092

This casual multi-choice, family-friendly resort ship has a nicely rounded stern, and one of two swimming pools can be covered by a glass dome in inclement weather. A good photo opportunity exists at the front of the ship (think of that *Titanic* pose). The interior focal point is the Centrum, a nine-deck-high atrium lobby. Except for six Owner's Suites, the cabins are mostly small; some have ceiling-recessed pull-down berths for 3rd and 4th guests. Reflections – the main dining room – is cavernous, but eight thick pillars obstruct views. Extra-cost, reservation-required eateries include Chops Grille Steakhouse, Portofino, or Giovanni's Table – worth it for cooked-to-order food. There is abundant entertainment, but also constant 'background' music.

INSIGHT GUIDES' RATINGS		
	Achieved	Possible
Ship	362	500
Accommodation	131	200
Food	222	400
Service	209	400
Entertainment	75	100
Cruise Experience	232	400
OVERALL SCORE	**1231**	**2000**

SEVEN SEAS EXPLORER
★★★★

Size	Small Ship
Tonnage	56,000
Cruise Line	Regent Seven Seas Cruises
Former Names	None
Entered Service	2016
Total Crew	552
Passengers	750

This all-suite, all-balcony ship has the right ingredients for a highly comfortable cruise experience, wrapped up in a welcoming country-club-like environment, with artwork personally chosen by the company president. Note that there is no walk-around outdoor promenade deck. Inside, a lovely two-deck lobby has a fine horseshoe-shaped stairway. From the smallest suite to the largest – the opulent Regent Suite – all have plenty of drawers and other storage space. Main dining is in the Compass Rose Restaurant, or you could choose Restaurant Chartreuse for opulent French cuisine, Prime 7 for good steaks and other meat dishes individually cooked to order, or Pacific Rim for Asian-style cuisine.

INSIGHT GUIDES' RATINGS		
	Achieved	Possible
Ship	427	500
Accommodation	171	200
Food	299	400
Service	273	400
Entertainment	78	100
Cruise Experience	295	400
OVERALL SCORE	**1543**	**2000**

SEVEN SEAS MARINER
★★★★

Size	Small Ship
Tonnage	48,075
Cruise Line	Regent Seven Seas Cruises
Former Names	None
Entered Service	2001
Total Crew	445
Passengers	709

Mature-age cruisegoers should enjoy the space, comfort levels, and food, and do not mind the busy itineraries. The ship has forward, aft and central stairways, making it easy to find your way around. All suites and cabins have a balcony, and most grades have a bathtub. The Compass Rose restaurant is the main dining venue, with open-seating. The company focuses on its cuisine, which is generally very good and varied (Kosher meals can also be provided). Prime 7 and Chartreuse are two cost-extra, reservation-required venues, but the low ceiling height makes them feel confined. Overall, however, you should have a fine experience.

INSIGHT GUIDES' RATINGS		
	Achieved	Possible
Ship	397	500
Accommodation	164	200
Food	296	400
Service	258	400
Entertainment	77	100
Cruise Experience	278	400
OVERALL SCORE	**1470**	**2000**

SEVEN SEAS NAVIGATOR
★★★+

Size	Small Ship
Tonnage	28,550
Cruise Line	Regent Seven Seas Cruises
Former Names	None
Entered Service	1999
Total Crew	325
Passengers	490

With a hull from a former Russian ship, the ship was built in Italy. After a 2016 makeover, the interiors exude a modern Italian style. About 90 percent of accommodation has a balcony, and suites and cabins are generously sized, well outfitted, comfortable, and have walk-in closets. Compass Rose (the main restaurant) is noisy, due to its low ceiling height. The food is generally sound and well presented, but green vegetables are rather scarce. Cost-extra Prime 7 steakhouse is more intimate, and may be worth the extra cost. The spa has decent facilities, but body-pampering treatments are expensive. Overall, this almost-inclusive smaller ship provides a comfortable experience for mature-age cruisegoers.

INSIGHT GUIDES' RATINGS		
	Achieved	Possible
Ship	328	500
Accommodation	155	200
Food	275	400
Service	227	400
Entertainment	68	100
Cruise Experience	259	400
OVERALL SCORE	**1312**	**2000**

SEVEN SEAS SPLENDOR
★★★★

Size	Small Ship
Tonnage	56,182
Cruise Line	Regent Seven Seas Cruises
Former Names	None
Entered Service	2021
Total Crew	551
Passengers	750

This is a good-looking, contemporary-style ship with a wide range of facilities and ample space for passenger comfort. It also has a complete walk-around outdoor promenade deck. The accommodation is well designed and comfortable, with a range of sizes, all with walk-in closets and marble-clad bathrooms. For meals, the Compass Rose restaurant is the main dining venue. The company focuses on food and the dining experience, and Kosher meals can be booked with advance pre-cruise notice. The cuisine is generally sound and well presented, with some highlights, although green vegetables are rather scarce. Cost-extra Prime 7 steakhouse is more intimate, and may be worth it for steak lovers.

INSIGHT GUIDES' RATINGS		
	Achieved	Possible
Ship	417	500
Accommodation	171	200
Food	299	400
Service	273	400
Entertainment	77	100
Cruise Experience	295	400
OVERALL SCORE	**1532**	**2000**

SEVEN SEAS VOYAGER
★★★★

Size	Small Ship
Tonnage	42,363
Cruise Line	Regent Seven Seas Cruises
Former Names	None
Entered Service	2003
Total Crew	445
Passengers	708

This small, but spacious ship has oodles of space and style, and a good walk-around outdoor wooden promenade deck. All accommodation grades have marble-clad bathrooms and walk-in closets, and the largest suites are simply opulent spaces. The ship's central hallway design allows for cabins that are larger than on close sister *Seven Seas Mariner.* The 570-seat Compass Rose restaurant is the main dining venue, with tables seating from two to 10. The food is generally sound, with a few highlights, and is nicely presented. For more intimate experiences, try Prime 7 or Signatures (both are cost-extra venues, but the food is better). There is a spa, but body pampering treatments are very expensive.

INSIGHT GUIDES' RATINGS

	Achieved	Possible
Ship	403	500
Accommodation	169	200
Food	298	400
Service	262	400
Entertainment	77	100
Cruise Experience	284	400
OVERALL SCORE	**1493**	**2000**

SH DIANA
★★★★

Size	Boutique Ship
Tonnage	12,100
Cruise Line	Swan Hellenic
Former Names	None
Entered Service	2023
Total Crew	141
Passengers	192

This well-designed, small, soft expedition-style ship has a good Basecamp preparation area for Zodiac landings and adventure outings. The Scandinavian style multi-purpose Observation Lounge is well designed, but be aware that legs stick out from some chairs. Cabins (and eleven suites) have flame-effect holographic fireplaces, plenty of well-designed storage space, but the water soakaway in the showers is poor, and cabin thermostats lack temperature displays and settings. The Swan Restaurant is buffet-style for breakfast and lunch, with served dinners at well-dressed tables on most days. There is a good range of food, and the overall cuisine of the cuisine is a very decent standard.

INSIGHT GUIDES' RATINGS

	Achieved	Possible
Ship	410	500
Accommodation	156	200
Food	302	400
Service	286	400
Entertainment	68	100
Cruise Experience	275	400
OVERALL SCORE	**1497**	**2000**

SH MINERVA
★★★★

Size	Boutique Ship
Tonnage	10,600
Cruise Line	Swan Hellenic
Former Names	None
Entered Service	2021
Total Crew	120
Passengers	140

This small, well-designed, soft expedition-style ship has abundant space per passenger, a good comfort level, and the Basecamp preparation area for Zodiac landings and outings. The Scandinavian style multi-purpose Observation Lounge is well designed, although some chairs have legs that protrude. All rooms and suites have a holographic fireplace and plenty of well-designed storage space, but the water soakaway in the showers is poor, and cabin thermostats lack temperature display and settings. The Swan Restaurant is typically buffet-style for breakfast and lunch, with served dinners at well-dressed tables on most days. Overall, the cuisine is very good.

INSIGHT GUIDES' RATINGS		
	Achieved	Possible
Ship	393	500
Accommodation	151	200
Food	298	400
Service	283	400
Entertainment	66	100
Cruise Experience	267	400
OVERALL SCORE	**1458**	**2000**

SH VEGA
★★★★

Size	Boutique Ship
Tonnage	10,600
Cruise Line	Swan Hellenic
Former Names	None
Entered Service	2022
Total Crew	120
Passengers	140

Designed for cruising to off-the-beaten-path regions, this soft expedition-style ship has a strengthened hull, stabilisers, and a Basecamp preparation area for Zodiac outings. Inside is a well-designed, practical Scandinavian-style multi-purpose Observation Lounge. The cabins, and six larger suites, have abundant, well-designed storage space and holographic fireplaces, but in the showers, the water soakaway is not good, and cabin thermostats lack a temperature display. The Swan Restaurant is buffet-style for breakfast and lunch, with served dinners at well-dressed tables on most days, and a decent range of food. Overall, the cuisine is very good.

INSIGHT GUIDES' RATINGS		
	Achieved	Possible
Ship	393	500
Accommodation	151	200
Food	298	400
Service	283	400
Entertainment	66	100
Cruise Experience	268	400
OVERALL SCORE	**1459**	**2000**

SILVER CLOUD
★★★+

Size	Small Ship
Tonnage	16,927
Cruise Line	Silversea Cruises
Former Names	None
Entered Service	1994, 2014
Total Crew	200
Passengers	260

This dated, but comfortable small ship could be good for discovery-style cruises, for which it has been adapted. There is good outdoor deck space, with deck lounge chairs. From the smallest Vista Suites (no balcony) to the large Owner's and Royal suites, all have good closet and drawer space, and double-vanity bathrooms. The Restaurant (main dining room) features open seating with decent table spacing in somewhat elegant surroundings, with decent, nicely presented meals. For something special, try a meal in the smaller, intimate, extra-cost Le Saletta, while casual eats can be found in self-serve La Terrazza. Spa facilities are modest.

INSIGHT GUIDES' RATINGS

	Achieved	Possible
Ship	326	500
Accommodation	140	200
Food	283	400
Service	228	400
Entertainment	66	100
Cruise Experience	248	400
OVERALL SCORE	**1291**	**2000**

SILVER DAWN
★★★★+

Size	Small Ship
Tonnage	40,844
Cruise Line	Silversea Cruises
Former Names	None
Entered Service	2022
Total Crew	411
Passengers	596

This ship has a decent amount of open deck space, and comfortable deck lounge chairs. Most of the public rooms are aft (except for an Observation Lounge), in a cake-layer stacking, with accommodation forward. From the smallest balcony-less Vista Suites to the large, well-designed Owner's and Royal suites, all have a good amount of closet and drawer space, and double-vanity bathrooms. Atlantide and Indochine are the open-seating (included) dining rooms, with fine table settings and decent cuisine, while La Dame and Kabuki are cost-extra, more specialized eateries. Hot Rocks Café is on the pool deck outdoors (for lava-grilled steaks, plus seafood), while the Arts Café features good coffee and snacks.

INSIGHT GUIDES' RATINGS

	Achieved	Possible
Ship	423	500
Accommodation	179	200
Food	321	400
Service	288	400
Entertainment	84	100
Cruise Experience	299	400
OVERALL SCORE	**1594**	**2000**

SILVER ENDEAVOR
★★★★

Size	Boutique Ship
Tonnage	20,449
Cruise Line	Silversea Expeditions
Former Names	*Crystal Endeavor*
Entered Service	2021, 2022
Total Crew	200
Passengers	200

This smart, highly specialized expedition-style ship is designed for sailing in the polar ice regions, with good facilities including two mud rooms. There is a generous amount of open deck space plus a good range of public lounges, bars, and other areas (some with double-height ceilings). The accommodation ranges from super-large suites to good sized cabins: all are very well equipped, although they lack proper hanging space for parkas. The main dining room has a high ceiling and large windows, and seats all participants. La Dame (French gourmet-style meals) and Il Terrazzino (Italian) are smaller, additional-cost restaurants. With Silversea's decent food and service, this could be a good, if expensive choice for long voyages of discovery.

INSIGHT GUIDES' RATINGS	Achieved	Possible
Ship	410	500
Accommodation	168	200
Food	298	400
Service	274	400
Entertainment	75	100
Cruise Experience	297	400
OVERALL SCORE	**1522**	**2000**

SILVER MOON
★★★★+

Size	Small Ship
Tonnage	40,844
Cruise Line	Silversea Cruises
Former Names	None
Entered Service	2022
Total Crew	411
Passengers	596

This small ship has a good amount of open deck space, and comfortable deck lounge chairs. Most of the public rooms are aft (except for an Observation Lounge), in a cake-layer stacking, with accommodation forward. From the smallest balcony-less Vista Suites to the large, well-designed Owner's and Royal suites, all have a good amount of closet and drawer space, and double-vanity bathrooms. Atlantide and Indochine are the main (included) open-seating dining rooms, with fine table settings and decent cuisine, while La Dame and Kabuki are cost-extra venues. Outside on the pool deck is Hot Rocks Café, for lava-grilled steaks and seafood, with the Arts Café featuring good coffee and snacks. Overall, this is a very comfortable ship.

INSIGHT GUIDES' RATINGS	Achieved	Possible
Ship	424	500
Accommodation	179	200
Food	321	400
Service	288	400
Entertainment	84	100
Cruise Experience	299	400
OVERALL SCORE	**1595**	**2000**

SILVER MUSE
★★★★+

Size	Small Ship
Tonnage	40,844
Cruise Line	Silversea Cruises
Former Names	*None*
Entered Service	2017
Total Crew	411
Passengers	596

This ship exudes comfort and style, including a little 'Italian flair' for the well-traveled, and there is a good amount of open deck space, with comfortable deck lounge chairs. Most of the public rooms are aft, in a cake-layer stacking, with accommodation forward. Accommodation comes in several sizes, locations, and price grades (including four Owner's Suites), but all balconies have faux teak decking. There is open seating in several dining venues (some of which cost extra), the two largest are Atlantide (for seafood) and Indochine (for Indian, Vietnamese cuisine). Service is quite well polished and largely unobtrusive, and tables have tablecloths. Zagara Spa facilities are quite decent, with personal treatments costing extra.

INSIGHT GUIDES' RATINGS	Achieved	Possible
Ship	417	500
Accommodation	179	200
Food	320	400
Service	288	400
Entertainment	84	100
Cruise Experience	297	400
OVERALL SCORE	**1585**	**2000**

SILVER NOVA
NYR

Size	Small Ship
Tonnage	54,700
Cruise Line	Silversea Cruises
Former Names	*None*
Entered Service	2023
Total Crew	556
Passengers	728

Launching in 2023 as sister to *Silver Origin*, this is larger than most Silversea ships, with more space per person, and uses advanced technology and LNG fuel for a lower environmental impact. It has a little Italian flair and a good amount of outdoor deck and sunbathing space, including a large pool with underwater seats at the shallow end. There are over a dozen accommodation grades, and all have balconies. Atlantide and S.A.L.T. (Sea and Land Taste) are the main dining rooms. Other eateries include La Dame, a reservation-only, extra-cost dinner venue for classic French cuisine; Kaiseki, a Japanese-style food bar for typical sushi dishes; and The Marquee, a 200-seat alfresco eatery (above the bridge), for pizzas and barbecued food.

INSIGHT GUIDES' RATINGS	Achieved	Possible
Ship	NYR	500
Accommodation	NYR	200
Food	NYR	400
Service	NYR	400
Entertainment	NYR	100
Cruise Experience	NYR	400
OVERALL SCORE	**NYR**	**2000**

SILVER ORIGIN
★★★+

Size	Boutique Ship
Tonnage	6,365
Cruise Line	Silversea Cruises
Former Names	*None*
Entered Service	2021
Total Crew	90
Passengers	100

Built specifically for operations in the ecology hotspot of the Galápagos islands, this compact, contemporary ship has a Basecamp storage and preparation and area for Zodiac landings. The ship operates back-to-back eastern and western journeys (good if you want to spend more time with the wildlife). The main public rooms include a rather small, forward-view Observation Lounge, plus a much larger Explorer Lounge aft which has both indoor and outdoor seating areas. The Restaurant and The Grill (under a deck canopy for shade) both seat all guests. Most seafood and vegetables are sourced from the area; meat is from the Ecuadorian mainland.

INSIGHT GUIDES' RATINGS

	Achieved	Possible
Ship	402	500
Accommodation	160	200
Food	285	400
Service	250	400
Entertainment	75	100
Cruise Experience	200	400
OVERALL SCORE	**1372**	**2000**

SILVER RAY
NYR

Size	Small Ship
Tonnage	54,700
Cruise Line	Silversea Cruises
Former Names	*None*
Entered Service	2024
Total Crew	556
Passengers	728

Sister to *Silver Nova* and planned for launch in 2024, it will also be larger than most Silversea ships, with more space per person, and uses advanced technology and LNG fuel for a lower environmental impact. It has a little Italian flair and a good amount of outdoor deck and sunbathing space, including a large swimming pool. There are over a dozen accommodation grades, all have balconies and good-sized bathrooms. Atlantide and S.A.L.T. are the main dining rooms. Other eateries include La Dame, a reservation-only extra-cost venue for classic French cuisine; Kaiseki, a Japanese-style food bar for typical sushi dishes; and The Marquee, a 200-seat alfresco eatery (pizza and barbecue), while light bites are provided in the Silver Note jazz bar.

INSIGHT GUIDES' RATINGS

	Achieved	Possible
Ship	NYR	500
Accommodation	NYR	200
Food	NYR	400
Service	NYR	400
Entertainment	NYR	100
Cruise Experience	NYR	400
OVERALL SCORE	**NYR**	**2000**

SILVER SHADOW
★★★★

Size	Small Ship
Tonnage	28,258
Cruise Line	Silversea Cruises
Former Names	*None*
Entered Service	2000
Total Crew	302
Passengers	388

Spacious but dated, this small ship for mature-age travelers is quite comfortable for longer voyages, and the many international passengers blend well. There is a generous amount of outdoor deck space, with decent deck lounge furniture. From the smallest Vista Suites (without balcony) to the large Owner's and Royal suites, all have good closet, drawer and storage space, and double-vanity bathrooms. There is open seating in The Restaurant (main dining room) with decent table spacing, cuisine and service. For something more special, try booking a meal in the more intimate (extra-cost) Le Champagne. Casual eats can be found in La Terrazza. Spa facilities are modest.

INSIGHT GUIDES' RATINGS		
	Achieved	Possible
Ship	400	500
Accommodation	177	200
Food	311	400
Service	268	400
Entertainment	78	100
Cruise Experience	288	400
OVERALL SCORE	**1522**	**2000**

SILVER SPIRIT
★★★★+

Size	Small Ship
Tonnage	39,519
Cruise Line	Silversea Cruises
Former Names	*None*
Entered Service	2009
Total Crew	412
Passengers	608

This stylish ship for the well-traveled underwent a 49ft (15m) mid-section stretch in 2018, which added more cabins and public space. Most public rooms are aft, in a cake-layer stacking, with accommodation forward (for noise reduction). The interior decor is understated and quite elegant. Accommodation is according to size, location, and price grade, including four Owner's Suites, but all balconies have faux teak decking. Open seating prevails in several dining venues, some of which cost extra: Atlantide (seafood), Indochine (Indian, Vietnamese) and a smaller Seishin (Japanese). Casual eats can be found in La Terrazza. The Zagara Spa facilities are reasonable – body pampering treatments cost extra.

INSIGHT GUIDES' RATINGS		
	Achieved	Possible
Ship	413	500
Accommodation	177	200
Food	316	400
Service	278	400
Entertainment	83	100
Cruise Experience	291	400
OVERALL SCORE	**1558**	**2000**

SILVER WHISPER
★★★★

Size	Small Ship
Tonnage	28,258
Cruise Line	Silversea Cruises
Former Names	*None*
Entered Service	2001
Total Crew	302
Passengers	388

This small ship has a good amount of open deck space, but the swimming pool is small. The accommodation is according to size, location, and price grades. All have decent storage space and spacious bathrooms, but balconies have faux teak decking. The Restaurant, with its white decor, is very comfortable, but the cuisine itself is underwhelming. Cost-extra eatery Le Champagne is a smaller, reservation-required, intimate venue with degustation menus and food individually cooked to order. Casual meals are available in La Terrazza. Body-pampering treatments are available in The Spa at Silversea. Overall, this is a comfortable ship with unhurried style.

INSIGHT GUIDES' RATINGS

	Achieved	Possible
Ship	399	500
Accommodation	178	200
Food	311	400
Service	268	400
Entertainment	78	100
Cruise Experience	288	400
OVERALL SCORE	**1522**	**2000**

SILVER WIND
★★★+

Size	Small Ship
Tonnage	17,400
Cruise Line	Silversea Cruises
Former Names	*None*
Entered Service	1995
Total Crew	222
Passengers	302

For soft exploration-style cruising, this dated ship offers a comfortable basecamp, for which it has been adapted. There is a good amount of outdoor deck space. Most public rooms are aft, and accommodation forward. From the smallest balcony-less Vista Suites to the large balconied Owner's and Royal suites, all have decent amount of closet and drawer space, and double-vanity bathrooms. The Restaurant (main dining room) features open seating with good table spacing in somewhat elegant surroundings and decent meals. For something special, try a meal in the small, intimate (extra-cost) Le Saletta. Casual eats can be found in self-serve La Terrazza. Spa facilities are modest.

INSIGHT GUIDES' RATINGS

	Achieved	Possible
Ship	343	500
Accommodation	158	200
Food	293	400
Service	251	400
Entertainment	67	100
Cruise Experience	282	400
OVERALL SCORE	**1394**	**2000**

SIRENA
★★★+

Size	Small Ship
Tonnage	30,277
Cruise Line	Oceania Cruises
Former Names	*Tahitian Princess, R Four*
Entered Service	1998, 2016
Total Crew	373
Passengers	688

This well-designed, but older ship has been nicely refitted for comfortable adult cruising, although it lacks an exterior walk-around deck. It has easy-on-the-eye decor, traditional touches of a grand hotel, and throwbacks to ocean liners of yesteryear, including real and faux wrought-iron staircase railings. Public rooms are spread over three decks, with plenty of bars and lounges to choose from. From very small interior (no-view) cabins with little storage space, to the aft-located Owner's Suites, it is simply 'pay more, get more.' Its aft-located, open seating dining room has windows on three sides, and decent cuisine. Smaller, alternative eateries include Red Ginger and Tuscan Grille. Spa facilities are small; treatments are expensive.

INSIGHT GUIDES' RATINGS		
	Achieved	Possible
Ship	360	500
Accommodation	127	200
Food	291	400
Service	232	400
Entertainment	67	100
Cruise Experience	237	400
OVERALL SCORE	**1314**	**2000**

SKY PRINCESS
★★★★

Size	Large Resort Ship
Tonnage	145,281
Cruise Line	Princess Cruises
Former Names	*None*
Entered Service	2019
Total Crew	1,346
Passengers	3,660

This family-friendly, multi-choice ship has many public rooms and wholesome entertainment. Inside are two principal stair towers and elevator banks, while the central connection point is a multi-faceted, multi-level Piazza Atrium. Accommodation ranges from small viewless interior cabins to balconied aft suites. Allegro, Concerto, and Symphony are the main included dining rooms – choose either fixed or Anytime Dining – providing standardized (but decent enough) cuisine, though with few green vegetable choices. For cost-extra, cooked-to-order cuisine, try the more intimate Crown Grill or Sabatini's (Italian). Colorful shows are presented in the Princess Theater, while for body-pampering treatments, the Lotus Spa is the place.

INSIGHT GUIDES' RATINGS		
	Achieved	Possible
Ship	400	500
Accommodation	139	200
Food	268	400
Service	243	400
Entertainment	82	100
Cruise Experience	270	400
OVERALL SCORE	**1402**	**2000**

SPECTRUM OF THE SEAS
★★★+

Size	Large Resort Ship
Tonnage	168,800
Cruise Line	Royal Caribbean International
Former Names	None
Entered Service	2019
Total Crew	1,300
Passengers	4,180

This energetic large family-oriented ship incorporates the latest tech-intensive bling and has nicely sloping, tiered aft decks. Interior decor is rainbow colorful, and high-vibe jazzy. Numerous accommodation categories and price grades range from interior (no-view) and solo occupancy cabins to large family suites, but even the smallest cabin bathroom is well designed, and has a night light. The cavernous main dining room (included in the price) spans two decks. The food is ho-hum, but paying extra to eat in one of several other venues may be worth it. This stunning ship delivers a well-orchestrated seagoing vacation, but there are many cost-extra items and added service charges, so choose wisely.

INSIGHT GUIDES' RATINGS

	Achieved	Possible
Ship	402	500
Accommodation	137	200
Food	289	400
Service	222	400
Entertainment	88	100
Cruise Experience	252	400
OVERALL SCORE	**1390**	**2000**

SPIRIT OF ADVENTURE
★★★★

Size	Mid-size Ship
Tonnage	58,250
Cruise Line	Saga Cruises
Former Names	None
Entered Service	2021
Total Crew	540
Passengers	987

British cruisers of a mature age should enjoy this spacious, premium quality ship. Notable public rooms include the Living Room (a cosy multi-purpose lounge) and the two-deck-high Britannia Lounge (observation lounge), but there are several other delightful lounges and bars. From the smallest cabins to the four largest balconied suites, all are comfortable and feature balconies (over 100 cabins are for solo travelers). The single-seating, high-ceilinged Grand Dining Room is an elegant venue, with good food and service with a smile. Coast to Coast (seafood) and East to West (Pan-Asian) are smaller alternatives. The Spa has an indoor pool (an unusual, but much liked feature), fitness center, saunas, steam rooms, and treatment rooms.

INSIGHT GUIDES' RATINGS

	Achieved	Possible
Ship	412	500
Accommodation	152	200
Food	280	400
Service	252	400
Entertainment	83	100
Cruise Experience	278	400
OVERALL SCORE	**1457**	**2000**

SPIRIT OF DISCOVERY
★★★★

Size	Mid-size Ship
Tonnage	58,250
Cruise Line	Saga Cruises
Former Names	*None*
Entered Service	2019
Total Crew	540
Passengers	987

This ship has a quintessentially Britishness feel, and stylish surroundings with elegant decor to match. The public rooms are well designed and comfortable, and favorites include the Living Room and the two-deck-high Britannia Lounge (observation lounge). From the smallest cabin to the largest balconied suites, all are comfortable and have balconies. The single-seating Grand Dining Room – split over two floors – is an elegant restaurant, with good food and service with a smile. Other venues (none cost extra) include The Grill (grilled meats, and seafood), Coast to Coast (seafood), and East to West (Pan-Asian). The Spa has an indoor pool (an unusual, but very welcome feature), fitness center, saunas, steam rooms, and treatment rooms.

INSIGHT GUIDES' RATINGS

	Achieved	Possible
Ship	412	500
Accommodation	152	200
Food	281	400
Service	252	400
Entertainment	83	100
Cruise Experience	278	400
OVERALL SCORE	**1458**	**2000**

STAR BREEZE
★★★+

Size	Small Ship
Tonnage	12,995
Cruise Line	Windstar Cruises
Former Names	*Seabourn Spirit*
Entered Service	1989, 2015
Total Crew	164
Passengers	312

In 2020, this ship underwent a 'chop and stretch' operation, with a new mid-section, 50 additional cabins and new public areas all added. It has an aft water-sports platform useable in suitably calm weather areas. The public rooms are mostly aft (the ship has elevators), with accommodation forward. Cabins are well designed and outfitted, have a decent amount of storage space, electric window blinds, and marble-clad bathrooms. The Amphora Restaurant has portholes rather than windows, restful decor, and spacious table seating; cuisine is contemporary, but casual, and includes many Mexican-style dishes. Cuadro 44 is new to the ship and features Spanish-style food.

INSIGHT GUIDES' RATINGS

	Achieved	Possible
Ship	368	500
Accommodation	167	200
Food	270	400
Service	242	400
Entertainment	71	100
Cruise Experience	270	400
OVERALL SCORE	**1388**	**2000**

STAR CLIPPER
★★★

Size .... Boutique Ship
Tonnage 2,298
Cruise Line ....Star Clippers
Former Names .... *None*
Entered Service 1992
Total Crew 72
Passengers 170

Sister to *Star Flyer*, this is a real 'wind-in-your-sails' experience, in a very casual but comfortable setting, and a completely different experience to 'normal' cruise ships. The sailing rig consists of 16 manually furled sails, measuring a billowing 36,221 sq ft (3,365 sq m), and you'll need to be aware of the many ropes on the open deck. The interiors have classic Edwardian-style nautical decor. Cabins are quite well equipped, and have fine rosewood-trimmed cabinetry; bathrooms are compact, but practical. The open seating dining room is quite attractive, and meals are casual affairs, though breakfasts are repetitious. Overall, this sail-cruise ship can provide a fine background for relaxation.

INSIGHT GUIDES' RATINGS		
	Achieved	Possible
Ship	346	500
Accommodation	131	200
Food	233	400
Service	214	400
Entertainment	65	100
Cruise Experience	231	400
OVERALL SCORE	**1220**	**2000**

STAR FLYER
★★★

Size .... Boutique Ship
Tonnage 2,298
Cruise Line ....Star Clippers
Former Names .... *None*
Entered Service 1991
Total Crew 72
Passengers 170

This real sailing ship is a four-mast, barquentine-rigged schooner, and could provide an ideal antidote to 'normal' cruise ships. It is the first clipper sailing ship to be built for 140 years – sister to *Star Clipper* – and it's simply breathtaking when under full sail rigging, and that's what this experience is all about. The interiors have classic Edwardian nautical decor throughout. There are six price grades of accommodation, plus the Owner's Suite. Cabins are quite well equipped, with rosewood-trimmed cabinetry, but the bathrooms are best described as compact. The open seating dining room is quite attractive, and meals are casual affairs, though breakfasts can be repetitious. Overall, the ship can provide a delightful, relaxing experience.

INSIGHT GUIDES' RATINGS		
	Achieved	Possible
Ship	347	500
Accommodation	131	200
Food	233	400
Service	213	400
Entertainment	65	100
Cruise Experience	233	400
OVERALL SCORE	**1222**	**2000**

STAR LEGEND
★★★+

Size	Small Ship
Tonnage	12,995
Cruise Line	Windstar Cruises
Former Names	*Royal Viking Queen*
Entered Service	1992, 2015
Total Crew	164
Passengers	312

This handy-sized, modern-ish cruise ship underwent a 'chop and stretch' operation in 2021, which added a new mid-section, more public rooms and 50 extra cabins. It has an aft water-sports platform that can be used in suitable calm weather areas. The public rooms are aft (the ship has elevators), with accommodation forward. Cabins are spread over three decks, all with outside views (many have French balconies). All are well designed and outfitted, with abundant storage space, and electric window blinds. The AmphorA Restaurant is comfortable, and there are many tables for two to four. The cuisine is contemporary, but casual. Overall, this could be a good ship for mature travelers.

INSIGHT GUIDES' RATINGS

	Achieved	Possible
Ship	374	500
Accommodation	169	200
Food	270	400
Service	242	400
Entertainment	71	100
Cruise Experience	272	400
OVERALL SCORE	**1398**	**2000**

STAR PRIDE
★★★+

Size	Small Ship
Tonnage	12,995
Cruise Line	Windstar Cruises
Former Names	*Seabourn Pride*
Entered Service	1988, 2014
Total Crew	164
Passengers	312

In 2021, this ship underwent a 'chop and stretch' operation, which added a new mid-section, 50 new cabins, and extra public areas, providing more choice without the ship feeling crowded anywhere. Although now dated, it still has a contemporary look and feel. An aft watersports platform and 'marina' can be used in suitably calm weather areas. The accommodation is both well-designed and practical, with blond wood cabinetry, walk-in closets and abundant storage space. AmphorA is the main dining room, and the ship caters well to a range of dietary needs. Other venues include Candles, a small dining venue, and Quadro 44 by Anthony Sasso (Spanish). The re-imagined spa is extremely pleasant.

INSIGHT GUIDES' RATINGS

	Achieved	Possible
Ship	369	500
Accommodation	167	200
Food	270	400
Service	242	400
Entertainment	71	100
Cruise Experience	270	400
OVERALL SCORE	**1389**	**2000**

SUN PRINCESS
NYR

Size	Large Resort Ship
Tonnage	175,500
Cruise Line	Princess Cruises
Former Names	None
Entered Service	2024
Total Crew	1550
Passengers	4,320

This stunning LNG-powered floating resort is the largest in the Princess fleet, and has a South Beach vibe. Highlights include a three-deck Piazza atrium with adjacent coffee shop (Coffee Currents) and Alfredo's Pizzeria, while The Dome is a stunning glass-enclosed multi-level covered deck. Horizons dining room features different food on each of its three decks. Cost-extra venues include Crown Grill (steaks and seafood) and Sabatini's (Italian). Its wide accommodation choice features a new range of suites, including a Signature Collection with its own restaurant and private area of The Sanctuary. Colorful shows take place in the immersive Princess Arena showlounge in the round. Note: there is no Deck 13.

INSIGHT GUIDES' RATINGS

	Achieved	Possible
Ship	NYR	500
Accommodation	NYR	200
Food	NYR	400
Service	NYR	400
Entertainment	NYR	100
Cruise Experience	NYR	400
OVERALL SCORE	**NYR**	**2000**

SYLVIA EARLE
★★★

Size	Boutique Ship
Tonnage	7,892
Cruise Line	Aurora Expeditions
Former Names	None
Entered Service	2021
Total Crew	74
Passengers	140

This is a decent, but compact expedition-style ship, with its novel 'X-Bow' design and good seakeeping capabilities. Facilities include a practical mudroom, several outdoor viewing areas, a small heated swimming pool, and two jacuzzis on deck, which have great views. Inside, the high-ceilinged public rooms include an integrated lecture room, and a library lounge. Non-balcony, lower-deck cabins have portholes, and cabins with balconies have floor-to-ceiling windows. Accommodation designated as suites are well equipped, and include ample storage space. The bathrooms in all grades have heated floors. Entertainment is not on the menu, but after-dinner conversation is.

INSIGHT GUIDES' RATINGS

	Achieved	Possible
Ship	348	500
Accommodation	126	200
Food	230	400
Service	240	400
Entertainment	60	100
Cruise Experience	219	400
OVERALL SCORE	**1223**	**2000**

SYMPHONY OF THE SEAS
★★★+

Size	Large Resort Ship
Tonnage	228,081
Cruise Line	Royal Caribbean International
Former Names	None
Entered Service	2018
Total Crew	2,200
Passengers	5,503

This large resort ship really is a bold, colorful, and ultra-lively sea-going resort with an abundance of family-friendly features, including an extensive water park with the mind-numbing 'Perfect Storm' waterslides. Accommodation ranges from interior (no-view) units to large suites. The Chic, The Grande, and American Icon are separate sections within the cavernous three-deck dining room. Most meals are carbohydrate-rich, so choosing one of the many smaller, specialized pay-extra eateries may be worth it for cooked-to-order food. For entertainment, the special production of *Hair* (the musical) in the reservations-required Royal Theater is excellent. Also good are the ice-skating shows, and the aquatic/acrobatic show at the aft aquatic pool.

INSIGHT GUIDES' RATINGS	Achieved	Possible
Ship	404	500
Accommodation	140	200
Food	226	400
Service	231	400
Entertainment	87	100
Cruise Experience	262	400
OVERALL SCORE	**1350**	**2000**

VALIANT LADY
★★★+

Size	Large Resort Ship
Tonnage	110,000
Cruise Line	Virgin Voyages
Former Names	None
Entered Service	2022
Total Crew	1,150
Passengers	2,860

This ship is red, white, and pizzazz all over, with a Virgin mermaid logo on its upright bows. This vibrant, colorful, and loud playground is for youthful urban adults. Bright and cheerful accommodation ranges from interior (no-view) cabins to balconied rock star suites, plus two 'Massive Suites'. Numerous restaurants and eateries (all included in the price), provide predictably edgy food that naturally includes vegetarian and vegan items. The Wake is the most glam venue, and is based on London classic The Wolseley (it's nothing special), while The Galley is the closest thing to a buffet with its food court-like setting. Wellness enthusiasts should delight in the Redemption Spa. This is all a bit of a lively, quirky experience, and then some!

INSIGHT GUIDES' RATINGS	Achieved	Possible
Ship	400	500
Accommodation	136	200
Food	236	400
Service	248	400
Entertainment	76	100
Cruise Experience	255	400
OVERALL SCORE	**1351**	**2000**

VASCO DA GAMA
★★★

Size... Mid-size Ship
Tonnage...55,819
Cruise Line..Nicko Cruises
Former Names .... *Pacific Eden, Statendam*
Entered Service 1994, 2022
Total Crew...560
Passengers 1,260

Now operated by Germany's Nicko Cruises, this could be a decent ship for budget-minded, mature travelers. When it was acquired (by Portuguese owner Mystic Cruises), it underwent a refurbishment program that included technical equipment and the interiors. It has a complete walk-around teak outdoor deck – good for strolling – and one of the two outdoor pools can be covered by a glass dome. Some public rooms have high ceilings, giving a sense of spaciousness. One favorite hangout is the Observation Lounge, above the navigation bridge. Accommodation ranges from viewless interior cabins to large balconied suites, but most have limited closet space (the upper grades have bathrooms with small bathtubs).

INSIGHT GUIDES' RATINGS		
	Achieved	Possible
Ship	308	500
Accommodation	125	200
Food	222	400
Service	182	400
Entertainment	67	100
Cruise Experience	217	400
OVERALL SCORE	**1121**	**2000**

VENTURA
★★★+

Size..Large Resort Ship
Tonnage..116,017
Cruise Line.. P&O Cruises
Former Names .... *None*
Entered Service 2008
Total Crew...1,239
Passengers 3,074

This is a comfortable large ship that exudes Britishness in decor, style, and food. Inside, a three-deck atrium lobby is the focal meeting point – rather like a town center, and the place to see and be seen. From modest interior (no-view) cabins to balconied suites, plus a few solo-occupancy cabins, most have open (no door) closets. Bay Tree, Cinnamon, and Saffron are the three main dining rooms, with straight forward (uninspiring) food. Pay extra to eat in the smaller, reservation-required venues Epicurian (Fine Dining) and Sindhu (Indian). The Arena Theatre is the main 785-seat showlounge, featuring colorful production shows and cabaret, with live music in several lounges. Overall, this is a pleasant, enjoyable ship.

INSIGHT GUIDES' RATINGS		
	Achieved	Possible
Ship	337	500
Accommodation	142	200
Food	246	400
Service	268	400
Entertainment	68	100
Cruise Experience	256	400
OVERALL SCORE	**1317**	**2000**

VIKING JUPITER
★★★★+

Size	Mid-size Ship
Tonnage	47,800
Cruise Line	Viking
Former Names	*None*
Entered Service	2022
Total Crew	545
Passengers	928

This good-looking, well-balanced ship for mature travelers seeking to explore destinations in comfort, has Nordic design features that make you feel at home. It is powered by energy-efficient hybrid engines, and has a walk-around outside promenade deck. Inside, its three-deck, open atrium lobby has light wood and abundant glass that lets in plenty of natural light, while an expansive Explorer's Lounge incorporates a library and a deli-counter along with displays of exploration and discovery. The accommodation is very practical, with abundant storage, and bathrooms have heated floors. There are several restaurants and eateries, all with open seating. The well-designed Nordic spa includes a salt-water pool, ice-room, and saunas.

INSIGHT GUIDES' RATINGS		
	Achieved	Possible
Ship	452	500
Accommodation	162	200
Food	338	400
Service	271	400
Entertainment	76	100
Cruise Experience	297	400
OVERALL SCORE	**1596**	**2000**

VIKING MARS
★★★★+

Size	Mid-size Ship
Tonnage	47,800
Cruise Line	Viking
Former Names	*None*
Entered Service	2022
Total Crew	545
Passengers	928

This smart-looking ship is one of a series of eight, and has a design reminiscent of the former Royal Viking Line ships, including a walk-around exterior promenade deck. The interior feature a three-deck-high atrium lobby with seating on all levels, and decor that includes light woods, large glass windows, a large screen, and a grand piano on the lowest floor. Main public rooms include an Explorer's Lounge, which combines an observation lounge with an integral library and a Viking Café. Cabins and suites are well designed and equipped, with abundant drawer and storage space, plus real or French balconies. A well-designed Nordic spa includes a salt-water pool, ice-room, saunas, and well-trained staff.

INSIGHT GUIDES' RATINGS		
	Achieved	Possible
Ship	453	500
Accommodation	162	200
Food	338	400
Service	295	400
Entertainment	76	100
Cruise Experience	298	400
OVERALL SCORE	**1622**	**2000**

VIKING NEPTUNE

★★★★+

Size	Mid-size Ship
Tonnage	47,800
Cruise Line	Viking
Former Names	None
Entered Service	2022
Total Crew	545
Passengers	928

This smart mid-size ship has a complete walk-around exterior deck. Inside, its chic design features make you feel at home, and is comfortable for anyone who likes style without glitz, with its uncluttered Scandinavian design and decor. Its focal point is a three-deck-high atrium lobby, while a two-floor, forward-view Explorer's Lounge includes a homely library and Viking Café deli counter for snacks. There are several restaurants and eateries to choose from (all included). International cuisine is featured, and comfort food items are always available. The Spa is expansive, well-designed, and practical. This ship could be a good choice for anyone seeking some elements of luxe without any hint of glitz.

INSIGHT GUIDES' RATINGS

	Achieved	Possible
Ship	453	500
Accommodation	162	200
Food	338	400
Service	270	400
Entertainment	76	100
Cruise Experience	300	400
OVERALL SCORE	**1599**	**2000**

VIKING OCTANTIS

★★★★+

Size	Mid-size Ship
Tonnage	30,500
Cruise Line	Viking Expedition Cruises
Former Names	None
Entered Service	2022
Total Crew	256
Passengers	378

Specially designed and built for exploration-style voyages, its stunning design has been creatively adapted from the sister company's oceangoing cruise ships (including a full walk-around promenade deck). Its Nordic design features provide a warm, comfortable environment. The Aula Auditorium and a two-deck Explorer's Lounge (forward) and library are the main public rooms. Accommodation is well designed, with abundant storage space, and real or French balconies, plus bathrooms with large shower enclosures. Aula is its main, bi-level, open seating restaurant, featuring a range of well-prepared meals. Two smaller, reservation-required venues include Mamsen's (Scandinavian cuisine) and Manfredi's (Italian).

INSIGHT GUIDES' RATINGS

	Achieved	Possible
Ship	455	500
Accommodation	162	200
Food	335	400
Service	273	400
Entertainment	70	100
Cruise Experience	292	400
OVERALL SCORE	**1587**	**2000**

VIKING ORION
★★★★+

Size	Mid-size Ship
Tonnage	47,800
Cruise Line	Viking
Former Names	None
Entered Service	2018
Total Crew	545
Passengers	928

This smart mid-size ship has a complete walk-around exterior deck. Inside, its chic design features make you feel at home, and is comfortable for anyone who likes style without glitz, with uncluttered Scandinavian design and decor. Its focal point is a three-deck-high atrium lobby, while a two-floor, forward-view Explorer's Lounge includes a homely library and Viking Café deli counter for snacks. The cabins and suites are well designed and equipped, with abundant drawer and storage space and real or French balconies. There are several restaurants and eateries (all included). International cuisine is featured, and comfort food items are always available. The Nordic spa is simply delightful.

INSIGHT GUIDES' RATINGS

	Achieved	Possible
Ship	458	500
Accommodation	162	200
Food	338	400
Service	275	400
Entertainment	76	100
Cruise Experience	297	400
OVERALL SCORE	**1606**	**2000**

VIKING POLARIS
★★★★+

Size	Small Ship
Tonnage	30,500
Cruise Line	Viking Expedition Cruises
Former Names	None
Entered Service	2022
Total Crew	256
Passengers	378

Sister ship to *Viking Octantis*, this vessel has been specifically designed for exploration-style voyages, with a design creatively adapted from the sister company's series of oceangoing cruise ships, including a full walk-around promenade deck. Nordic design features provide a warm, comfortable environment. The Aula Auditorium (aft) and a two-deck Explorer's Lounge (forward) and library are the main public rooms. The well-designed accommodation has abundant storage space, and real or French balconies. Bathrooms have large shower enclosures and space for toiletries. Aula is the main, open-seating restaurant, with a range of well-prepared meals. Reservation-required venues include Mamsen's (Scandinavian cuisine) and Manfredi's (Italian).

INSIGHT GUIDES' RATINGS

	Achieved	Possible
Ship	455	500
Accommodation	162	200
Food	336	400
Service	298	400
Entertainment	70	100
Cruise Experience	295	400
OVERALL SCORE	**1616**	**2000**

VIKING SEA
★★★★+

Size... Mid-size Ship
Tonnage...47,800
Cruise Line... Viking
Former Names ....None
Entered Service 2016
Total Crew...545
Passengers..928

This smart-looking mid-size ship has a complete walk-around exterior deck. It is comfortable for mature travelers who like style without glitz, with its uncluttered Scandinavian design elements. The interior focal point is a three-deck-high atrium lobby, while the two-floor Explorer's Lounge includes a library and Viking Café. Just five accommodation types make choice easy, and all feature a balcony and king-size bed. Choose one of the Explorer's Suites at the front or aft if you like a bathroom with bathtub (most other cabins have showers). There are several restaurants and eateries, all with open seating. The well-designed Nordic spa includes a salt-water pool, ice-room, saunas, and well-trained staff. Delightful!

INSIGHT GUIDES' RATINGS

	Achieved	Possible
Ship	457	500
Accommodation	162	200
Food	338	400
Service	275	400
Entertainment	76	100
Cruise Experience	297	400
OVERALL SCORE	**1605**	**2000**

VIKING SKY
★★★★+

Size... Mid-size Ship
Tonnage...47,800
Cruise Line... Viking
Former Names ....None
Entered Service 2017
Total Crew...545
Passengers..928

One of a series of eight identical smart-looking ships, it has a walk-around exterior deck, and features contemporary, Scandinavian decor. Abundant glass windows create a feeling that you are cruising in a floating residence. Its interior focal point is a three-deck-high atrium lobby (called the Living Room), while the two-floor Explorer's Lounge includes a very comfortable library and Viking Café. There are just five accommodation categories, with well-designed, practical cabins and suites, all with private balconies, and king-size bed. Choose an Explorer Suites at the front or aft if you like a bathroom with a bathtub (most cabins have showers). There are several restaurants and eateries, all with open seating, and a good range of well-prepared food.

INSIGHT GUIDES' RATINGS

	Achieved	Possible
Ship	457	500
Accommodation	162	200
Food	338	400
Service	275	400
Entertainment	76	100
Cruise Experience	298	400
OVERALL SCORE	**1606**	**2000**

VIKING STAR

★★★★+

Size	Mid-size Ship
Tonnage	47,800
Cruise Line	Viking
Former Names	None
Entered Service	2015
Total Crew	545
Passengers	928

Mature travelers should enjoy this handsome-looking ship, which is reminiscent of former Royal Viking Line vessels. There are many public areas and dining options for its size, and the sleek, uncluttered Scandinavian design plus an abundance of glass throughout makes it feel like you are cruising in a floating residence. It also has a walk-around open promenade deck. With just five accommodation categories and minimalist design, the cabins feature a king-size bed. All dining rooms have an open seating policy, and well-orchestrated cuisine. The ship's beautifully designed Nordic spa has many facilities, including a large salt-water pool, ice-room, saunas, and well-trained staff.

INSIGHT GUIDES' RATINGS		
	Achieved	Possible
Ship	457	500
Accommodation	162	200
Food	338	400
Service	275	400
Entertainment	76	100
Cruise Experience	296	400
OVERALL SCORE	**1604**	**2000**

VIKING VENUS

★★★★+

Size	Mid-size Ship
Tonnage	47,800
Cruise Line	Viking
Former Names	None
Entered Service	2021
Total Crew	545
Passengers	928

This well-proportioned ship (one of a series of identical ships) has an abundance of glass walls that help connect you with the sea on many levels, and there is a walk-around open deck for strolling. Also outside is an infinity pool and terrace seating area for alfresco meals. The interior focal point is a tri-deck atrium, while the two-floor Explorer's Lounge includes a library and Viking Café. Just five accommodation types make choosing easy; all feature balconies and a king-size bed. Choose an Explorer's Suite at the front or aft if you like a bathroom with bathtub (most cabins have showers). There are several restaurants and eateries, all with open seating. The well-designed Nordic spa includes a salt-water pool, ice-room, and saunas.

INSIGHT GUIDES' RATINGS		
	Achieved	Possible
Ship	456	500
Accommodation	162	200
Food	338	400
Service	275	400
Entertainment	76	100
Cruise Experience	298	400
OVERALL SCORE	**1605**	**2000**

VISION OF THE SEAS
★★★

Size	Mid-size Ship
Tonnage	78,491
Cruise Line	Royal Caribbean International
Former Names	None
Entered Service	1998
Total Crew	735
Passengers	2,000

Instantly recognisable with its aft funnel and nicely-rounded stern, this well-designed ship has an array of public rooms. Its focal point is the Centrum, a place to see and be seen – as is the nautically-themed Schooner Bar. Cabins are comfortable, and have enough closet and drawer space, while suites, naturally, are larger, but nothing special. Aquarius is the large two-level main dining room, with food that is pleasant enough. However, paying extra to eat in a smaller venue – such as Chops Grille – may be worth it for a change, with food cooked to order. The Masquerade Theater, with main and balcony levels and good seating, features colorful production shows. Overall, it is a pleasant experience and a good alternative to large resort ships.

INSIGHT GUIDES' RATINGS

	Achieved	Possible
Ship	348	500
Accommodation	137	200
Food	222	400
Service	208	400
Entertainment	73	100
Cruise Experience	231	400
OVERALL SCORE	**1219**	**2000**

VOLENDAM
★★★

Size	Mid-size Ship
Tonnage	61,214
Cruise Line	Holland America Line
Former Names	None
Entered Service	1999
Total Crew	650
Passengers	1,432

This dated ship (its name is taken from a fishing village north of Amsterdam) features comfortable decor with many Dutch influences. The interior focal point is a huge crystal sculpture, *Caleido* by Luciano Vistosi, in the three-deck-high atrium. From interior (no-view) cabins to a Penthouse Suite (with baby grand piano, and a balcony), the accommodation is all tastefully furnished. The two-level Rotterdam Dining Room is comfortable, but with a few exceptions, the meals are mainly unmemorable, though nicely presented on Rosenthal china. For something more special, try the extra-cost Pinnacle Grill, which features Pacific Northwest cuisine. For casual eats, head to the Lido Market. Overall, this is a comfortable ship, but nothing special.

INSIGHT GUIDES' RATINGS

	Achieved	Possible
Ship	297	500
Accommodation	125	200
Food	218	400
Service	201	400
Entertainment	60	100
Cruise Experience	212	400
OVERALL SCORE	**1113**	**2000**

VOYAGER OF THE SEAS
★★★

Size	Large Resort Ship
Tonnage	137,280
Cruise Line	Royal Caribbean International
Former Names	None
Entered Service	1999
Total Crew	1,176
Passengers	3,114

This resort ship is full of family-friendly features, including outdoor decks with water parks and fun areas for children (and adults), leaving little room for simply sitting and relaxing. Inside there are many lounges, bars, shops, casual eateries, and a casino. Accommodation ranges from small interior (no-view) cabins to large family suites with balconies. The main dining room is on three levels, but wide pillars obstruct sightlines from many seats. The cuisine is standard banquet catering, but some cooked-to-order options are available at extra cost. Several cost-extra venues provide better food, including the popular Chops Grille Steakhouse and diner-style Johnny Rockets. For casual eating, head to the cavernous Windjammer Marketplace.

INSIGHT GUIDES' RATINGS		
	Achieved	Possible
Ship	342	500
Accommodation	131	200
Food	220	400
Service	208	400
Entertainment	73	100
Cruise Experience	228	400
OVERALL SCORE	**1202**	**2000**

WESTERDAM
★★★

Size	Mid-size Ship
Tonnage	82,348
Cruise Line	Holland America Line
Former Names	None
Entered Service	2004
Total Crew	817
Passengers	1,916

This comfortable, mid-size ship is designed to appeal to younger, active vacationers. One likeable feature is its complete walk-around exterior deck. Inside, the decor includes many examples of the company's Dutch heritage. The main lobby spans three decks, and is topped by a stunning rotating Waterford crystal globe of the world. Accommodation ranges from viewless interior cabins to large balconied suites (pay more, get more space). Spanning two decks, the 1,045-seat Vista Dining Room has both open and assigned seating. With a few exceptions, the cuisine is mostly non-memorable banquet cuisine. For something more special, try the Pinnacle Grill, which features Pacific Northwest cuisine (premium-quality steaks and seafood).

INSIGHT GUIDES' RATINGS		
	Achieved	Possible
Ship	358	500
Accommodation	142	200
Food	234	400
Service	204	400
Entertainment	67	100
Cruise Experience	237	400
OVERALL SCORE	**1242**	**2000**

WIND SPIRIT
★★★

Size	Boutique Ship
Tonnage	5,350
Cruise Line	Windstar Cruises
Former Names	None
Entered Service	1988
Total Crew	88
Passengers	148

This modern sail-cruise ship (the sails are computer controlled) is comfortable, and has a low-key vibe. Sister to *Wind Star*, it has four masts that tower 170ft (52m) above the deck. Because of the complex machinery, there is little open deck space. The vessel's nicely crafted interiors have blond woods, and soft complementary colors. The cabins are nicely equipped, including a minibar/refrigerator, and outside-view portholes, while bathrooms have a wall-mounted hairdryer and showers. The open-seating restaurant is delightful, with large picture windows and wood-panelled walls. Overall, it's a very pleasant experience.

INSIGHT GUIDES' RATINGS	Achieved	Possible
Ship	324	500
Accommodation	139	200
Food	240	400
Service	210	400
Entertainment	67	100
Cruise Experience	231	400
OVERALL SCORE	**1211**	**2000**

WIND STAR
★★★

Size	Boutique Ship
Tonnage	5,350
Cruise Line	Windstar Cruises
Former Names	None
Entered Service	1986
Total Crew	88
Passengers	148

This stylish-looking contemporary sail-cruise vessel is part yacht, part cruise ship, with four masts towering 170ft (52m) above the deck, and computer-controlled sails. The interiors are nicely crafted, with blond woods, and chic, cool decor. It's a very comfortable, low-key experience, with nicely-equipped cabins, each with two portholes, ample storage space, a TV that swivels so it can be viewed from the bed, and bathrooms with a wall-mounted hairdryer. The open-seating main restaurant, AmphorA, has wood-panelled walls and picture windows but is open only for dinner. The food is generally sound, but casual, and geared toward American tastes. Grilled seafood and steaks are sometimes available under the stars.

INSIGHT GUIDES' RATINGS	Achieved	Possible
Ship	324	500
Accommodation	139	200
Food	240	400
Service	210	400
Entertainment	66	100
Cruise Experience	231	400
OVERALL SCORE	**1210**	**2000**

WIND SURF
★★★+

Size	Small Ship
Tonnage	14,745
Cruise Line	Windstar Cruises
Former Names	None
Entered Service	1990, 1998
Total Crew	163
Passengers	312

With contemporary style and yachting-like chic, this five-masted sail-cruise ship exudes relaxation and is good for anyone not wanting the inconvenience associated with a real tall ship. This is a larger sister to the other Windstar sail-cruise ships, and carries seven triangular self-furling computer-controlled sails. Cabins are nicely outfitted and include a minibar. Bathrooms are compact, designed in a figure of eight, and have good storage space for toiletries. AmphorA, the main restaurant, has open-seating, but is open for dinner only. Other venues provide alternatives for other meals. The food is generally good, and geared toward American tastes. Spa facilities are split over three decks, making them a little disjointed.

INSIGHT GUIDES' RATINGS		
	Achieved	Possible
Ship	343	500
Accommodation	144	200
Food	259	400
Service	218	400
Entertainment	68	100
Cruise Experience	257	400
OVERALL SCORE	**1289**	**2000**

WONDER OF THE SEAS
★★★+

Size	Large Resort Ship
Tonnage	236,857
Cruise Line	Royal Caribbean International
Former Names	None
Entered Service	2022
Total Crew	2,300
Passengers	5,734

This really is a stunning, high-energy, family-oriented ship, with a huge range of amusements, activities, and entertainment venues. By gross tonnage, it is the world's largest floating resort, and accommodation ranges from small viewless interior cabins to an expansive balconied Royal Suite designed for families. Its cavernous main dining room spans three decks, with high-volume batch-cooked catering meals, but if you pay extra some items can be cooked to order. As an alternative, try one of the extra-cost venues (booking in advance is recommended), where the dining experience is more personal. Overall, this floating resort ship can provide a well-orchestrated vacation, but be aware of the many cost-extra items and added service charges.

INSIGHT GUIDES' RATINGS		
	Achieved	Possible
Ship	448	500
Accommodation	133	200
Food	224	400
Service	195	400
Entertainment	82	100
Cruise Experience	249	400
OVERALL SCORE	**1331**	**2000**

WORLD ADVENTURER
NYR

Size .... Boutique Ship
Tonnage 9,934
Cruise Line .... Atlas Ocean Voyages
Former Names .... None
Entered Service 2023
Total Crew 125
Passengers 176

This specialized niche market ship (one of a series) is designed for polar region adventures, in comfort. There are 12 Zodiac rigid craft for close-in exploration and landings, and a small 'mud' room for boot washing. Public rooms include a glass-domed Observation Lounge, an Explorer's Lounge, and a lecture theater. There are several cabin grades, from 183 sq ft (17 sq m) to 466 sq ft (46 sq m). Window-only cabins occupy the lowest cabin deck; all others include a step-out balcony. The (aft) dining room is comfortable, and seats everyone for served dinners; breakfasts and lunches are self-serve. Cuisine includes uncomplicated Portuguese specialities. A small L'Occitane spa with sauna and changing rooms is located around the funnel.

INSIGHT GUIDES' RATINGS		
	Achieved	Possible
Ship	NYR	500
Accommodation	NYR	200
Food	NYR	400
Service	NYR	400
Entertainment	NYR	100
Cruise Experience	NYR	400
OVERALL SCORE	**NYR**	**2000**

WORLD DISCOVERER
NYR

Size .... Boutique Ship
Tonnage 9,934
Cruise Line .... Atlas Ocean Voyages
Former Names .... None
Entered Service 2023
Total Crew 125
Passengers 176

This small, well-designed, explorer-style ship has a hardened hull and nicely-raked bows. It has 12 Zodiac rigid craft for shore landings and close-in exploration, and a small 'mud' room for boot washing (rubber boots are supplied). The comfortable, homely public rooms include a glass-domed Observation Lounge, the Explorer's Lounge, and a lecture theater. Cabin sizes range from 183 sq ft (17 sq m) to 466 sq ft (46 sq m). Window-only cabins occupy the lowest cabin deck; all others include a step-out balcony. The dining room (aft) is comfortable, and seats everyone in one seating, and the unfussy cuisine includes some Portuguese specialties. A small L'Occitane spa with sauna and changing rooms sits around the funnel.

INSIGHT GUIDES' RATINGS		
	Achieved	Possible
Ship	NYR	500
Accommodation	NYR	200
Food	NYR	400
Service	NYR	400
Entertainment	NYR	100
Cruise Experience	NYR	400
OVERALL SCORE	**NYR**	**2000**

WORLD EXPLORER
★★★+

Size	Boutique Ship
Tonnage	9,934
Cruise Line	Atlas Ocean Voyages
Former Names	None
Entered Service	2019, 2024
Total Crew	125
Passengers	176

This specialized ship carries 12 Zodiac rigid craft for shore landings and close-in exploration, and has a small 'mud' room for boot washing. A retro-chic main lounge is comfortable, and has a pleasant vibe. There are several cabin grades: the smallest window-only cabins are on the lowest accommodation deck, all others (including suite grades) have a small step-out balcony. Sizes range from 183 sq ft (17 sq m) to 466 sq ft (46 sq m). For meals, the dining room (aft) is comfortable, and seats everyone for served dinners. The food is quite decent, with a nod to uncomplicated Portuguese cuisine. Breakfasts and lunches are self-serve. A small L'Occitane spa with sauna and changing rooms is located around the funnel.

INSIGHT GUIDES' RATINGS		
	Achieved	Possible
Ship	347	500
Accommodation	135	200
Food	255	400
Service	252	400
Entertainment	68	100
Cruise Experience	280	400
OVERALL SCORE	**1337**	**2000**

WORLD NAVIGATOR
★★★+

Size	Boutique Ship
Tonnage	9,934
Cruise Line	Atlas Ocean Voyages
Former Names	None
Entered Service	2021
Total Crew	125
Passengers	176

With its hardened hull for ice and nicely-raked bows, this stylish, well-designed ship carries 12 Zodiac rigid craft for shore landings and exploration, and has a small 'mud' room for boot washing (rubber boots are supplied). Public rooms include a pleasant glass-domed Observation Lounge, an Explorer's Lounge, and a lecture theater. There are several cabin grades, with sizes range from 183 sq ft (17 sq m) to 466 sq ft (46 sq m). The smallest window-only cabins are on the lowest cabin deck; all others have a step-out balcony. The aft-located dining room is comfortable, and seats everyone in one seating. The food is quite unfussy, and always includes some Portuguese specialties. A small spa area with changing rooms and sauna is set around the funnel.

INSIGHT GUIDES' RATINGS		
	Achieved	Possible
Ship	345	500
Accommodation	135	200
Food	255	400
Service	276	400
Entertainment	67	100
Cruise Experience	303	400
OVERALL SCORE	**1381**	**2000**

WORLD SEEKER
NYR

Size .... Boutique Ship
Tonnage 9,934
Cruise Line ....Atlas Ocean Voyages
Former Names .... *None*
Entered Service 2024
Total Crew 125
Passengers 176

This small, well-designed, specialized ship has a hardened hull, nicely raked bows, carries 12 Zodiac rigid craft for close-in exploration and shore landings, and has a 'mud' room with a boot washing area (rubber boots are supplied). The public rooms include a very pleasant glass-domed Observation Lounge, an Explorer's Lounge, and a lecture theater. All passengers can be seated in the main dining room (located aft). The meals are unfussy, and include several Portuguese specialities. Dinner is served by waiters, while breakfasts and lunches are self-serve. A small spa area with changing rooms and sauna is set around the funnel.

INSIGHT GUIDES' RATINGS		
	Achieved	Possible
Ship	NYR	500
Accommodation	NYR	200
Food	NYR	400
Service	NYR	400
Entertainment	NYR	100
Cruise Experience	NYR	400
OVERALL SCORE	**NYR**	**2000**

WORLD TRAVELER
★★★+

Size .... Boutique Ship
Tonnage 9,934
Cruise Line ....Atlas Ocean Voyages
Former Names .... *None*
Entered Service 2022
Total Crew 125
Passengers 176

With its well-raked bows and hardened hull, this intimate, stylish and well-balanced ship carries 12 Zodiac rigid craft for shore landings and exploration, and there is a small 'mud' room for boot washing (rubber boots are supplied). Public rooms include a pleasant observation lounge, a main lounge, and a small spa area with changing rooms and sauna is set around the funnel. Cabins and suites range from 183 sq ft (17 sq m) to 466 sq ft (46 sq m), but storage space in the smaller cabins is limited. For meals, the (aft) dining room is comfortable, and seats everyone – dinner is by waiter service, while breakfasts and lunches are self-serve. The food is decent and unfussy, and always includes Portuguese specialties. Overall, a comfortable, cosy little ship.

INSIGHT GUIDES' RATINGS		
	Achieved	Possible
Ship	347	500
Accommodation	135	200
Food	255	400
Service	251	400
Entertainment	68	100
Cruise Experience	281	400
OVERALL SCORE	**1337**	**2000**

WORLD VOYAGER
★★★+

Size	Boutique Ship
Tonnage	9,934
Cruise Line	Atlas Ocean Voyages
Former Names	*None*
Entered Service	2021
Total Crew	125
Passengers	176

Germany's Nicko Cruises operates this small ship for intimate expedition- and discovery-style cruises. With well-raked bows and a hardened hull, it carries 12 Zodiac rigid craft for shore landings and exploration, and has a small 'mud' room for boot washing (rubber boots are supplied). Public rooms include a pleasant glass-domed observation lounge, and a large main lounge. Cabins and suites range from 183 sq ft (17 sq m) to 466 sq ft (46 sq m), but storage space in the smaller cabins is limited. All have outside views, however. For meals, the aft-located dining room is comfortable, and seats everyone in one seating. A small spa area with changing rooms and sauna is set around the ship's funnel.

INSIGHT GUIDES' RATINGS		
Achieved	Possible	
Ship	345	500
Accommodation	135	200
Food	255	400
Service	276	400
Entertainment	67	100
Cruise Experience	303	400
OVERALL SCORE	**1381**	**2000**

ZAANDAM
★★★

Size	Mid-size Ship
Tonnage	61,396
Cruise Line	Holland America Line
Former Names	*None*
Entered Service	2000
Total Crew	650
Passengers	1,432

With its dark blue hull and white superstructure, this pleasant midsize ship has a well-balanced look. Inside, three main stairways provide easy access to almost any area, while the decor and abundant wood accenting maintains the traditional look the company is known for. An auction at Christies, London, provided guitars once owned by the Rolling Stones and other rock stars, plus a Conn saxophone mouthpiece signed by Bill Clinton. The interior focal point is a three-deck-high atrium. Accommodation ranges from a balconied Penthouse Suite to viewless interior cabins; all have disappointingly small bathrooms. There's open or assigned seating in the bi-level dining room, with food that is decent enough, but mostly unmemorable.

INSIGHT GUIDES' RATINGS		
	Achieved	Possible
Ship	308	500
Accommodation	127	200
Food	218	400
Service	217	400
Entertainment	63	100
Cruise Experience	221	400
OVERALL SCORE	**1154**	**2000**

SHIPS RATED BY SCORE

Ship name	Rating	Score	Ship name	Rating	Score
Europa 2	★★★★★	1792	MSC World Europa	★★★★	1490
Europa	★★★★★	1766	MSC Grandiosa	★★★★	1488
HANSEATIC spirit	★★★★★	1719	Scenic Eclipse	★★★★	1487
HANSEATIC inspiration	★★★★★	1716	MSC Seaview	★★★★	1481
HANSEATIC nature	★★★★★	1716	MSC Seaside	★★★★	1479
Sea Cloud	★★★★+	1627	MSC Seashore	★★★★	1476
Sea Cloud II	★★★★+	1626	MSC Meraviglia	★★★★	1473
Viking Mars	★★★★+	1622	Seven Seas Mariner	★★★★	1470
Queen Victoria	★★★★+	1616	MSC Bellissima	★★★★	1469
Viking Polaris	★★★★+	1616	Genting Dream	★★★★	1468
Queen Elizabeth	★★★★+	1612	MSC Seascape	★★★★	1463
Evrima	★★★★+	1611	MSC Divina	★★★★	1462
Queen Mary 2	★★★★+	1611	MSC Virtuosa	★★★★	1462
SeaDream II	★★★★+	1606	SH Vega	★★★★	1459
Viking Orion	★★★★+	1606	Crystal Symphony	★★★★	1458
Viking Sky	★★★★+	1606	SH Minerva	★★★★	1458
SeaDream I	★★★★+	1605	Spirit of Discovery	★★★★	1458
Viking Sea	★★★★+	1605	Spirit of Adventure	★★★★	1457
Viking Venus	★★★★+	1605	Seabourn Quest	★★★★	1454
Viking Star	★★★★+	1604	MSC Splendida	★★★★	1451
Viking Neptune	★★★★+	1599	Iona	★★★★	1450
Viking Jupiter	★★★★+	1596	Arvia	★★★★	1445
Silver Moon	★★★★+	1595	Celebrity Beyond	★★★★	1445
Silver Dawn	★★★★+	1594	MSC Fantasia	★★★★	1445
Viking Octantis	★★★★+	1587	MSC Preziosa	★★★★	1442
Silver Muse	★★★★+	1585	Azamara Onward	★★★★	1440
Silver Spirit	★★★★+	1558	Royal Clipper	★★★★	1437
Seabourn Encore	★★★★+	1553	Le Bellot	★★★★	1432
Seabourn Ovation	★★★★+	1553	Le Jacques Cartier	★★★★	1431
Mein Schiff 1	★★★★	1550	Le Bougainville	★★★★	1430
Mein Schiff 2	★★★★	1550	National Geographic Endurance	★★★★	1430
Seabourn Odyssey	★★★★	1549	National Geographic Resolution	★★★★	1430
Seven Seas Explorer	★★★★	1543	Le Champlain	★★★★	1429
Mein Schiff 6	★★★★	1541	Celebrity Apex	★★★★	1428
Crystal Serenity	★★★★	1540	Le Dumont d'Urville	★★★★	1428
Mein Schiff 5	★★★★	1540	Le Lapérouse	★★★★	1428
Seabourn Sojourn	★★★★	1533	Celebrity Edge	★★★★	1425
Seven Seas Splendor	★★★★	1532	Le Lyrial	★★★★	1423
Mein Schiff 3	★★★★	1529	Azamara Journey	★★★★	1421
Mein Schiff 4	★★★★	1528	Anthem of the Seas	★★★★	1419
Riviera	★★★★	1524	Amadea	★★★★	1411
Silver Endeavor	★★★★	1522	Azamara Pursuit	★★★★	1408
Silver Shadow	★★★★	1522	Celebrity Reflection	★★★★	1405
Silver Whisper	★★★★	1522	L'Austral	★★★★	1402
Marina	★★★★	1519	Sky Princess	★★★★	1402
Asuka II	★★★★	1511	Quantum of the Seas	★★★★	1401
Seabourn Pursuit	★★★★	1500	Majestic Princess	★★★+	1400
Seabourn Venture	★★★★	1498	Le Soleal	★★★+	1398
SH Diana	★★★★	1497	Star Legend	★★★+	1398
Seven Seas Voyager	★★★★	1493	Hebridean Princess	★★★+	1397
Le Commondant Charcot	★★★★	1492	Azamara Quest	★★★+	1396
MSC Euribia	★★★★	1490	Regal Princess	★★★+	1396

Ship name	Rating	Score	Ship name	Rating	Score
Royal Princess	★★★+	1395	Wonder of the Seas	★★★+	1331
Emerald Azzurra	★★★+	1394	MSC Opera	★★★+	1324
Odyssey of the Seas	★★★+	1394	Norwegian Epic	★★★+	1320
Silver Wind	★★★+	1394	Regatta	★★★+	1319
Caledonian Sky	★★★+	1393	Ventura	★★★+	1317
Le Boreal	★★★+	1393	Azura	★★★+	1315
Ovation of the Seas	★★★+	1392	Diamond Princess	★★★+	1314
Island Sky	★★★+	1391	MSC Lirica	★★★+	1314
Carnival Mardi Gras	★★★+	1390	Sirena	★★★+	1314
Spectrum of the Seas	★★★+	1390	MSC Armonia	★★★+	1313
Star Pride	★★★+	1389	Seven Seas Navigator	★★★+	1312
Discovery Princess	★★★+	1388	Nautica	★★★+	1309
Star Breeze	★★★+	1388	Insignia	★★★+	1307
Disney Wish	★★★+	1385	Celebrity Millennium	★★★+	1306
Norwegian Joy	★★★+	1385	Sapphire Princess	★★★+	1306
Enchanted Princess	★★★+	1381	Emerald Princess	★★★+	1303
World Navigator	★★★+	1381	Disney Wonder	★★★+	1301
World Voyager	★★★+	1381	Crown Princess	★★★+	1299
Celebrity Solstice	★★★+	1379	Eurodam	★★★+	1299
Britannia	★★★+	1373	Disney Magic	★★★+	1297
Nippon Maru	★★★+	1372	Pacific Explorer	★★★+	1296
Silver Origin	★★★+	1372	Celebrity Infinity	★★★+	1295
MSC Magnifica	★★★+	1371	Celebrity Summit	★★★+	1294
Celebrity Equinox	★★★+	1369	Celebrity Constellation	★★★+	1293
Celebrity Eclipse	★★★+	1368	Ruby Princess	★★★+	1291
Celebrity Silhouette	★★★+	1368	Silver Cloud	★★★+	1291
Heritage Adventurer	★★★+	1367	Wind Surf	★★★+	1289
Norwegian Escape	★★★+	1367	Celebrity Flora	★★★+	1288
MSC Orchestra	★★★+	1364	MSC Sinfonia	★★★+	1288
MSC Poesia	★★★+	1363	Amera	★★★+	1287
Norwegian Bliss	★★★+	1362	Paul Gauguin	★★★+	1284
MSC Musica	★★★+	1361	Deutschland	★★★+	1279
Bolette	★★★+	1360	Rotterdam	★★★+	1278
Resilient Lady	★★★+	1357	Norwegian Jewel	★★★+	1274
Artania	★★★+	1356	Nieuw Amsterdam	★★★+	1273
Borealis	★★★+	1356	Noordam	★★★+	1273
Norwegian Getaway	★★★+	1356	Pearl Mist	★★★+	1272
Norwegian Breakaway	★★★+	1354	Balmoral	★★★+	1267
AIDAnova	★★★+	1353	Costa Toscana	★★★+	1265
Valiant Lady	★★★+	1351	Caribbean Princess	★★★+	1264
Symphony of the Seas	★★★+	1350	Norwegian Prima	★★★+	1264
Scarlet Lady	★★★+	1349	Costa Smeralda	★★★+	1261
Disney Fantasy	★★★+	1348	AIDAsol	★★★+	1259
Harmony of the Seas	★★★+	1348	Norwegian Dawn	★★★+	1259
National Geographic Orion	★★★+	1348	Norwegian Sun	★★★+	1259
Norwegian Encore	★★★+	1346	Sea Venture	★★★+	1257
Disney Dream	★★★+	1344	AIDAcosma	★★★+	1255
AIDAperla	★★★+	1341	Norwegian Star	★★★+	1255
Nieuw Statendam	★★★+	1341	Norwegian Gem	★★★+	1253
Allure of the Seas	★★★+	1339	Janssonius	★★★+	1252
Hebridean Sky	★★★+	1338	Norwegian Jade	★★★+	1251
AIDAprima	★★★+	1337	Carnival Celebration	★★★+	1250
Koningsdam	★★★+	1337	Norwegian Sky	★★★+	1250
World Explorer	★★★+	1337	Le Ponant	★★★	1249
World Traveler	★★★+	1337	Norwegian Pearl	★★★	1249
Oasis of the Seas	★★★+	1334	Norwegian Spirit	★★★	1247

Ship name	Rating	Score	Ship name	Rating	Score
Independence of the Seas	★★★	1245	Costa Fortuna	★★★	1190
AIDAblu	★★★	1243	Rhapsody of the Seas	★★★	1189
AIDAbella	★★★	1242	Ambition	★★★	1188
Westerdam	★★★	1242	Costa Pacifica	★★★	1187
Carnival Venezia	★★★	1240	Magellan Explorer	★★★	1187
Pacific Encounter	★★★	1238	Marella Discovery	★★★	1186
AIDAstella	★★★	1236	Costa Serena	★★★	1185
Pacific Adventure	★★★	1235	National Geographic Endeavour II	★★★	1181
AIDAluna	★★★	1234	Sea Spirit	★★★	1181
Liberty of the Seas	★★★	1233	La Belle des Oceans	★★★	1180
AIDAmar	★★★	1232	Carnival Breeze	★★★	1177
Freedom of the Seas	★★★	1232	Carnival Dream	★★★	1161
Serenade of the Seas	★★★	1231	Grandeur of the Seas	★★★	1159
AIDAdiva	★★★	1229	Carnival Freedom	★★★	1155
Navigator of the Seas	★★★	1229	Costa Mediterranea	★★★	1155
Explorer of the Seas	★★★	1228	Zaandam	★★★	1154
Arcadia	★★★	1227	Astoria Grande	★★★	1153
Carnival Panorama	★★★	1227	Carnival Sunrise	★★★	1151
Jewel of the Seas	★★★	1227	Carnival Pride	★★★	1148
Oosterdam	★★★	1227	Carnival Conquest	★★★	1145
Adventure of the Seas	★★★	1225	National Geographic Islander II	★★★	1143
Resorts World One	★★★	1225	Carnival Glory	★★★	1142
Costa Firenze	★★★	1223	Pride of America	★★★	1140
Sylvia Earle	★★★	1223	Carnival Magic	★★★	1139
Radiance of the Seas	★★★	1222	Carnival Splendor	★★★	1138
Star Flyer	★★★	1222	Carnival Spirit	★★★	1135
Carnival Horizon	★★★	1221	Ambiance	★★★	1130
Mariner of the Seas	★★★	1220	Carnival Miracle	★★★	1130
Ocean Victory	★★★	1220	Carnival Sunshine	★★★	1130
Star Clipper	★★★	1220	Carnival Legend	★★★	1129
Coral Princess	★★★	1219	Carnival Liberty	★★★	1128
Enchantment of the Seas	★★★	1219	Carnival Radiance	★★★	1127
Island Princess	★★★	1219	Carnival Valor	★★★	1123
Vision of the Seas	★★★	1219	Vasco da Gama	★★★	1121
Costa Favolosa	★★★	1216	Greg Mortimer	★★★	1117
Marella Discovery 2	★★★	1216	Volendam	★★★	1113
Aurora	★★★	1215	Coral Geographer	★★+	1095
Marella Voyager	★★★	1214	Fram	★★+	1095
Brilliance of the Seas	★★★	1213	Otto Sverdrup	★★+	1095
Marella Explorer 2	★★★	1213	Maud	★★+	1094
Wind Spirit	★★★	1211	Carnival Inspiration	★★+	1088
Wind Star	★★★	1210	Carnival Elation	★★+	1087
Carnival Vista	★★★	1209	Coral Adventurer	★★+	1086
Costa Diadema	★★★	1206	Carnival Paradise	★★+	1085
Costa Deliziosa	★★★	1203	Costa Atlantica	★★+	1082
Voyager of the Seas	★★★	1202	Club Med 2	★★+	1059
Grand Princess	★★★	1200	Hamburg	★★+	1034
Marella Explorer	★★★	1200	Cordelia Empress	★★+	1033
Oceana	★★★	1198	Celebrity Xpedition	★★+	1021
Hondius	★★★	1194	National Geographic Explorer	★★+	1011
Roald Amundsen	★★★	1194	Sea Cloud Spirit	★★+	1006
Carnival Luminosa	★★★	1191	Celestyal Olympia	★★+	973
Costa Fascinosa	★★★	1191	Celestyal Crystal	★★+	970
Fridtjof Nansen	★★★	1191	National Geographic Sea Lion	★+	772

Ship name	Rating	Score
Carnival Jubilee	NYR	NYR
Celebrity Ascent	NYR	NYR
Disney Treasure	NYR	NYR
Emerald Sakura	NYR	NYR
Explora 1	NYR	NYR
Golden Horizon	NYR	NYR
Norwegian Viva	NYR	NYR
Ocean Albatros	NYR	NYR
Ocean Discoverer	NYR	NYR
Queen Anne	NYR	NYR
Scenic Eclipse II	NYR	NYR
Silver Nova	NYR	NYR
Silver Ray	NYR	NYR
Sun Princess	NYR	NYR
World Adventurer	NYR	NYR
World Discoverer	NYR	NYR
World Seeker	NYR	NYR

CREDITS

PHOTO CREDITS

Aaron Spelling/Love Boat/Kobal/Shutterstock 32
AIDA 151, 197B, 198B, 198T, 199T, 199B, 200B, 201T, 200T
Albatros Expeditions 311T
All Leisure Holidays 103, 167
Ambassador Cruise Line 160, 203T, 203B
American Queen Voyages 311B, 312T
Amy Harris/Shutterstock 91
Antarctica 21 276T
Atlas Ocean Voyages 365B, 366B, 367T
Aurora Expeditions 352B
Ayako Ward 9, 86, 177, 189, 191
Azamara Club Cruises 161, 208T, 208B, 209T
Carnival Cruises 15, 23, 153, 169, 214T, 214B, 215T, 215B, 216T, 216B, 217T, 217B, 218T, 218B, 219T, 219B, 220B, 221T, 221B, 222T, 222B, 223T, 223B, 224T, 224B, 225T, 225B, 226B, 226T, 227T
Carnival/Andy Newman 18
Celebrity Cruises 8, 55, 125, 179, 227B, 228T, 228/229B, 230T, 231T
Celebrity/Michel Verdure 155
Celebrity/Quentin Bacon 143
Celestyal Cruises 120, 235T, 235B
Coral Expeditions 104, 236B, 237T
Cordelia Cruises 238T
Costa Cruises 238B, 239T, 239B, 240T, 240B, 241T, 241B, 242T, 242B, 243T, 243B, 244T, 245B
CroisiEurope Cruises 269B
Cruise & Maritime Voyages 354T
Crystal Cruises 162
Cunard 40, 80, 107, 108, 109, 110, 112, 163, 318B, 319T, 319B, 320T, 320B, 321T
Cunard/Indusfoto 188
Daily Mail/Shutterstock 36
Dennis Jarvis 317T
Disney Cruise Line 41, 73, 92, 131, 144, 164, 247B, 248T, 248B, 249T, 249B, 250T
Douglas Ward 7, 10, 16, 24, 25, 26, 31, 35, 61, 65, 88, 89, 93, 95, 99, 105, 115, 122, 129, 137, 146, 173, 176, 184, 185, 186, 192, 196B, 197T, 201B, 207T, 245T, 253T, 260B, 263T, 284T, 288B, 299B, 300B, 301T, 322B, 334B, 335B, 336B, 345T, 346B, 361T
Dream Cruises 258T
Emerald Cruises 250B, 251B
Ester Kokmeijer 256B

Explora Journeys 255B
Fincantieri 355B
Fred. Olsen Cruise Lines 165, 210B, 211T, 211B
Getty Images 12, 20, 82, 141
Granger/Shutterstock 27
Hapag-Lloyd Cruises 19, 68, 94, 145, 166, 195BL, 195BR, 254T, 254B, 261T, 261B, 262T
Hege Abrahamsen/Hurtigruten 114
Heritage Expeditions 264T
Holland America Line 157, 253T, 268B, 300T, 313B, 325B, 360B, 361B, 367B
Hurtigruten 257B, 314T, 325T
Hurtigruten/Ørjan Bertelsen 101
iStock 121
James D Morgan/Getty Images/Carnival 220T
James Marsh/Shutterstock 43
Joseph Thompson Photography 258B
Lindblad Expeditions 63, 295B, 296B, 296T, 297T, 297B, 299T
Meike Sjoer/Oceanwide Expeditions 267B
Michael S. Nolan/Linblad 97
Michel Verdure/Royal Caribbean 190
Ming Tang-Evans/Apa Publications 116
Miray Cruises 206B
MSC Cruises 1, 4/5, 6, 28, 45, 70, 78, 81, 83, 150, 182, 183, 284B, 285T, 285B, 286T, 286B, 287T, 287B, 288T, 289T, 289B, 290T, 290B, 291T, 291B, 292T, 292B, 293T, 293B, 294T, 294B
NCL 52, 57, 79, 90, 133, 136, 139, 142, 156, 301B, 302T, 302B, 303T, 303B, 304T, 304B, 305T, 305B, 306T, 306B, 307T, 307B, 308T, 308B, 309T, 309B, 310T, 317B
NCL/Susan Seubert 138
Nick Rogers/Shutterstock 33
nicko cruises 365T
Noble Caledonia 213T, 263B, 267T
Oceania Cruises 265B, 279B, 298B, 324B, 347T
Oscar Farrera Gonzalez/Hurtigruten 280B
P&O Cruises Australia 315T, 315B, 316T
P&O Cruises 111, 205T, 206B, 207B, 210T, 212B, 266T, 312B, 354B
Paul Gauguin Cruises 170, 316B
Phoenix Reisen 202B, 204T, 205B, 246T
Pjotr Mahhonin 236T
Ponant 269T, 270T, 271T, 271B, 272T, 272B,

273T, 273B, 274T, 274B, 275T
Poseidon Expeditions 331T
Princess Cruises 47, 48,50, 76, 213B, 237B, 244B, 246B, 247T, 251T, 252T, 259B, 266B, 276B, 322T, 326B, 327T, 327B, 347B, 352T
Public domain 338B
Ralph Lee Hopkins/Lindblad Expeditions 98, 295T
Regent Seven Sea Cruises 67, 148, 171, 337T, 337B, 338T, 339T
Regent Seven Seas Cruises/Michel Verdure 14
René Supper/TUI Cruises 2/3, 174
Resorts World Cruises 323B
Ritz-Carlton 255T
Royal Caribbean 11, 39, 46, 49, 56, 59, 60, 62, 71, 74, 84, 124, 127, 132, 159, 196T, 202T, 204B, 209B, 212T, 229T, 229B, 230B, 231B, 232T, 232B, 233T, 233B, 234T, 234B, 252B, 256T, 257T, 259T, 262B, 265T, 268T, 275B, 280T, 299T, 310B, 313T, 314B, 318T, 321B, 324T, 348T, 353T, 360T, 363B
Saga Group Limited 348B, 349T
Sara Jenner/Oceanwide Expeditions 264B
Scenic 328B, 329T
Sea Cloud Cruises 106, 329B, 330B
Sea Cloud 330T
Sea Dream Yacht Club 140
Seabourn 172, 332T, 332B, 333T, 333B, 334T, 335T
SeaDream Yacht Club 134, 336T
Shiphistory62 356B
Shutterstock 22, 119, 178, 181, 187, 193, 194, 195T, 356T, 357B, 358T
Silversea Cruises 341T, 341B, 342T, 342B, 343B, 343T, 344T, 344B, 345B, 346T
Star Clippers 326T, 350T, 350B
Steve Dunlop Photographer/P&O Cruises 168
Swan Hellenic 339B, 340T, 340B
TUI Group 277T, 277B, 278T, 278B, 279T, 281T, 281B, 282T, 282B, 283T, 283B
Viking Cruises 51, 175, 355T, 357T, 358B, 359T, 359B
Virgin Voyages 323T, 328T, 353B
Viva Cruises 331B
Windstar Cruises 349B, 351T, 351B, 362T, 362B, 363T
Wolfgang Fricke 260T, 270B

COVER CREDITS

Front cover: Cruiseship docked in Alanya harbour, Turkey **Shutterstock**
Back cover: MSC World Europa **MSC Cruises;** Daybeds on the deck of the MS EUROPA 2

Hapag-Lloyd Cruises; Queen Mary 2 arriving in New York **Cunard;** Douglas Ward **Christin Rodemann**

The Heart

of *Kaviar.*

Unsere neue Clean-Label-Linie.
Kaviar, Meersalz, viel Erfahrung.

Pure

INSIGHT GUIDE CREDITS

Distribution
UK, Ireland and Europe
Apa Publications (UK) Ltd
sales@insightguides.com

United States and Canada
Ingram Publisher Services
ips@ingramcontent.com

Australia and New Zealand
Woodslane
info@woodslane.com.au

Southeast Asia
Apa Publications (SN) Pte
singaporeoffice@insightguides.com

Worldwide
Apa Publications (UK) Ltd
sales@insightguides.com

Special Sales, Content Licensing and CoPublishing
Insight Guides can be purchased in bulk quantities at discounted prices. We can create special editions, personalised jackets and corporate imprints tailored to your needs. sales@insightguides.com; www.insightguides.biz

Printed in China

This book was produced using **Typefi** automated publishing software.

First Edition 1985
Twenty-Ninth Edition 2023

www.insightguides.com

Author
Douglas Ward

Managing Editor
Rachel Lawrence

Copyeditor
Tim Binks

Picture Editor
Tom Smyth

Head of DTP and Pre-Press
Rebeka Davies

Head of Publishing
Sarah Clark

TELL US YOUR THOUGHTS

Dear Cruiser,

I hope you have found this edition of Insight Guides Cruising and Cruise Ships both enjoyable and useful. If you have any comments or queries, or experiences of cruising that you would like to pass on, or perhaps some ideas for subjects that could be included in the future, I would be delighted to read them. With your help, I can improve and expand the guide in future editions.

The world of cruising is evolving fast and certain facts and figures may have changed since this guide went to print, so if you have found any outdated information in these pages, please do let me know and I will make sure it is corrected as soon as possible.

You can write to me by email at:
hello@insightguides.com

Thank you,
Douglas Ward

INDEX